# Oxford Beginner's Japanese Dictionary

*Edited by*
Jonathan Bunt
Gillian Hall

OXFORD
UNIVERSITY PRESS

# OXFORD
UNIVERSITY PRESS

Great Clarendon Street, Oxford OX2 6DP

Oxford University Press is a department of the University of Oxford.
It furthers the University's objective of excellence in research, scholarship,
and education by publishing worldwide in

Oxford New York

Auckland Cape Town Dar es Salaam Hong Kong Karachi Kuala Lumpur
Madrid Melbourne Mexico City Nairobi New Delhi Shanghai Taipei Toronto

With offices in

Argentina Austria Brazil Chile Czech Republic France Greece Guatemala
Hungary Italy Japan Poland Portugal Singapore South Korea Switzerland
Thailand Turkey Ukraine Vietnam

Oxford is a registered trade mark of Oxford University Press
in the UK and in certain other countries

Published in the United States
by Oxford University Press Inc., New York

© Jonathan Bunt 2000

The moral rights of the author have been asserted

Database rights Oxford University Press (makers)

First published as The Oxford Starter Japanese Dictionary 2000

Republished as Oxford Beginner's Japanese Dictionary 2006

British Library Cataloguing Publication Data

Data available

Library of Congress Cataloging in Publication Data

Data available

ISBN 978-0-19-929852-5


Typeset by Graphicraft Limited, Hong Kong
Printed and bound in Italy by L.E.G.O. S.p.A. Lavis (TN)

# Contents

# Oxford Beginner's Japanese Dictionary

**Contributors and acknowledgements**

**Chief editors**
Jonathan Bunt
with
Gillian Hall
Japan Centre North West – University of Manchester

**Editors and Contributors**
Miyoko Yamashita
Ayako Somers
Yukiko Shaw
Motoi Kitamura
Yumi Tozuka
Nobumi Kitamura

**Appendices**
Lynne Strugnell
Michiko Sugino

and many other family, friends and visitors to the Japan Centre who the editors
would like to thank for their patience and their valiant attempts to answer
impossible questions.

Special thanks to Suzuko Anai.

Thanks also to colleagues from the BATJ (British Association for the Teaching of
Japanese) for their interest and support.

## Proprietary terms

This dictionary includes some words which are, or are asserted to be, proprietary
names or trade marks. Their inclusion does not imply that they have acquired for
legal purposes a non-proprietary or general significance, nor is any other judgement
implied concerning their legal status. In cases where the editor has some evidence
that a word is used as a proprietary name or trade mark, this is indicated by the
symbol ®, but no judgement concerning the legal status of such words is made or
implied thereby.

# About this dictionary

To get the most out of the information contained in this dictionary please see **How to use this Dictionary**.

This book is designed to help English-speaking students of all ages who are studying Japanese in schools, colleges, universities, evening classes and in a business context. It is also aimed at people living in Japan.

In the Japanese to English section, we have given a wide range of Japanese words with English equivalents and suggestions as to how to understand and translate them. We have tried to be simple and straightforward and have therefore not included all possible meanings. Our guide for selection was usefulness not only to students but also to those visiting or working in Japan who will encounter a wide range of vocabulary, including culturally specific items needing explanation rather than just a translation.

In the English to Japanese section, the English words are followed by either translations or a suggested method of conveying English uses in Japanese. This section is mostly aimed at those studying the language formally. Such people often have to write short essays and diaries or make short presentations as part of their course and need to supplement their textbooks with other sources of Japanese. We have not tried to give all possible ways of expressing the English and our guideline for inclusion or exclusion was whether it seemed likely that students could use the word or expression in the contexts in which we as teachers at school and university think that they are likely to need it. This will not produce perfect solutions to the problem of moving between two very different languages but it is better to try something and then find out why it is not right in a particular case than to not try at all. We expect that qualified teachers will be seeing and responding to most of the material generated from our explanations. This interaction of learner and teacher will fine-tune the use of the information in this dictionary. We have (after much consideration) been consistent in giving examples in the forms to which most learners are first exposed 〜です・〜ます forms.

We have tried to give some indication of the various styles of Japanese speech and guidance on how to find a Japanese word that does not at first seem to be included by breaking it down into meaningful elements or by changing its form – see **How to use this Dictionary**.

One important feature of the Japanese-English section is that we have given the most common verbs used by beginners in their 〜ます and 〜て forms. These entries are cross-referenced and will provide support in learning the relations between forms which are vital for understanding the grammar of Japanese and making progress with the language. This information is further supported by the notes on verbs.

Another unusual feature of this dictionary is that it avoids romanized Japanese. It is not usually the practice to teach Japanese seriously using roman script so we have given the translations and examples in syllabic scripts and an alternative using Chinese characters where this is appropriate. This helps learners to master the scripts quickly, learn Japanese word-order patterns, and avoid reliance on romanized forms which can lead to errors – especially in pronunciation. The syllabic scripts are easily learned and we have given a reference chart to help during early stages of script learning. We have kept to the government list of approved characters in the English to Japanese section examples. In the Japanese to English section we have kept some non-standard forms as they are likely to be encountered by people in Japan. Remember that kanji are not compulsory in many situations. Space prevents this dictionary including Chinese character look-up information but as many students will also be studying the use of Chinese characters, we have given some information relating to them throughout the main entries and notes. In particular, we have given as main entries in the Japanese to English section a very wide range of suffixes and prefixes which will allow careful users to find the meanings of a vastly greater number of words than are here as headword entries. For information on how to do this see **How to use this Dictionary**.

We hope that in addition to being a supplementary reference for learners working with a textbook this dictionary will prove *interesting*! The value of browsing and curiosity as part of language learning is all too often forgotten and teachers and learners tend to stick to self-contained textbooks. We would like to think that any learner who is interested in Japanese can find something of interest and value by dipping into this book. Japanese is a fascinating language and it is the interest and enjoyment of our students that has led us to want to produce a much-needed resource for them.

## To teachers

We hope that you can find something of value to your students and humbly suggest that the best way to get your students to use this dictionary to improve their Japanese is for you to show them how. Helping a student to make the most of a dictionary should be an essential element of any language course as it gives the learner a chance to fly (even if they may be unsteady for a while!). We would greatly welcome your comments and suggestions for improvements.

先生方へ

　この辞書が学生に効果的に活用されるために、先生方のご指導が必要です。先生方の協力によって、この辞書が学生に有意義に使用され、また、日本語への新たな興味をわかせる貴重な一冊になることを望んでやみません。

# Japanese Script

Japanese is usually written using a combination of scripts. It can be written horizontally from left to right よこがき・横書き or, more traditionally, in vertical columns from right to left たてがき・縦書き. Vertical writing tends to be used for books, newspapers, formal letters and essays.

There are two series of phonetic symbols or かな of 46 sounds each which can be combined to write the sounds of the language, and Chinese characters or かんじ・漢字 which carry meaning and may have more than one way of being pronounced depending on the context. See the entries on おんよみ and くんよみ for more about the use of Chinese characters. The characters used in books and newspapers are largely limited to those in the official list produced for schools and those which can be used for personal names. The characters for schoolchildren to be taught are called じょうようかんじ・常用漢字 which means 'characters for everyday use'. There are 1945 of them.

In a sentence such as 'I am going to London tomorrow' the Japanese will feature かたかな・片仮名 for the place name, ひらがな・平仮名 for the grammatical particles and the ending on the verb and かんじ・漢字 for the words 'tomorrow' and 'I' as well as the stem of the verb 'to go'. わたしは あした ロンドンへ いきます。・私は明日ロンドンへ行きます。

The main use of かたかな is to write words of foreign origin and it is used for the names of non-Japanese people and places. By convention the names of Chinese and Korean people and places are often left in characters and a pronunciation indicated in ふりがな・振り仮名 (see below). かたかな is also used for onomatopoeia, some adverbs and as a kind of italic script for emphasis. It is common for the pronunciation of (possibly) unfamiliar characters to be indicated by small script above or to the side. This is called ふりがな, ルビ or よみがな and can be in either ひらがな or かたかな. This also appears in textbooks to help learners with new かんじ readings.

This dictionary uses either ひらがな or かたかな for the headwords in the Japanese to English section and the translations in the English to Japanese section as appropriate. Where かんじ would normally be employed we have given a 'standard' script form immediately after the かな version. There is some flexibility about whether or not to use かんじ for a particular word or just ひらがな. We have tried to give something approximating standard usage and so we have some characters not in the government lists where we judge them to be in common use and we have left some words without characters even though the characters are common if it felt stylistically better in a given case.

We advise beginners not to attempt to copy out the more complicated kanji until they are more confident with Japanese writing. A word written in legible hiragana is much better than a badly copied kanji which will be difficult for the intended reader to understand.

# Structure of Japanese-English entries

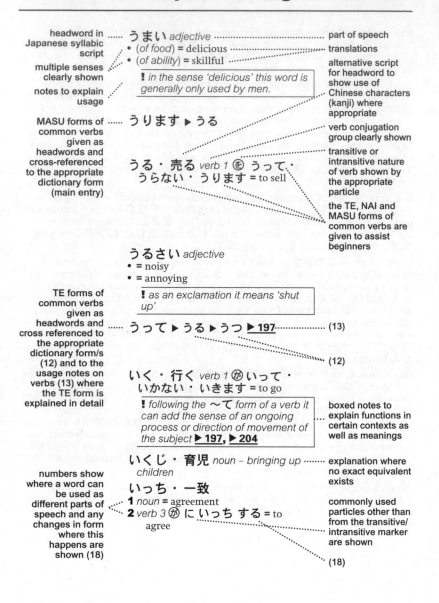

headword in Japanese syllabic script

multiple senses clearly shown

notes to explain usage

MASU forms of common verbs given as headwords and cross-referenced to the appropriate dictionary form (main entry)

TE forms of common verbs given as headwords and cross referenced to the appropriate dictionary form/s (12) and to the usage notes on verbs (13) where the TE form is explained in detail

numbers show where a word can be used as different parts of speech and any changes in form where this happens are shown (18)

うまい *adjective*
• *(of food)* = delicious
• *(of ability)* = skillful

**!** *in the sense 'delicious' this word is generally only used by men.*

うります ▶ うる

うる・売る *verb 1* ㊫ うって・うらない・うります = to sell

うるさい *adjective*
• = noisy
• = annoying

**!** *as an exclamation it means 'shut up'*

うって ▶ うる ▶ うつ ▶ **197** ........... (13)

.......... (12)

いく・行く *verb 1* ㋕ いって・いかない・いきます = to go

**!** *following the 〜て form of a verb it can add the sense of an ongoing process or direction of movement of the subject* ▶ **197,** ▶ **204**

いくじ・育児 *noun* – bringing up children

いっち・一致
**1** *noun* = agreement
**2** *verb 3* ㋕ に いっち する = to agree

part of speech

translations

alternative script for headword to show use of Chinese characters (kanji) where appropriate

verb conjugation group clearly shown

transitive or intransitive nature of verb shown by the appropriate particle

the TE, NAI and MASU forms of common verbs are given to assist beginners

boxed notes to explain functions in certain contexts as well as meanings

explanation where no exact equivalent exists

commonly used particles other than from the transitive/ intransitive marker are shown

.......... (18)

# Structure of English-Japanese entries

headword ····· **able** *adjective* ················· part of speech

cross reference to information associated with the entry ···· to be able to... = use the potential ········· information on how to translate into Japanese
form of the verb or the dictionary form of the verb + こと が できる ▶191

example of usage ····· to be able to swim = および げる・ 泳げる ················ translations of example in kana only and then repeated in standard Japanese script (kanjikana-majiri)

I am able to read hiragana = ひらが なを よむ こと が できます。・ ひ らがなを 読む こと が できます。

**ambitious** *adjective*
= やしんてき(な)・ 野心的(な) ············ associated elements which are present in some circumstances appear in brackets

**American** ▶172
**1** *adjective*
different parts of speech with the same form clarified by use of numbers = アメリカの
**2** *noun*
American person = アメリカじん・ アメリカ人

**brother** ····· issues associated with word use are highlighted

> **!** *Remember there are two sets of words for family members* ▶177

*noun*
(*your own older brother*) = あに・ 兄 ···· potentially misleading translations are clarified and suggestions made
sub-divisions of meaning clearly indicated and separately translated
(*your own younger brother*) = おとう と・ 弟
(*someone else's older brother*) = おに いさん・ お兄さん
(*someone else's younger brother*) = おとうとさん・ 弟さん ···· translations written in Japanese syllabic script

**feel** *verb*
• = かんじる・ 感じる ···· alternative script version of the translations to show use of Chinese characters (kanji) where appropriate

> **!** *Japanese is very different to English when describing feelings, it is often best to translate with an adjective +* です *when referring to yourself* ▶178

different senses clearly marked
(*referring to an emotion, an impression or a physical feeling*)
multiple examples to clarify usage
I feel lonely = さびしいです。・ 寂し いです。
it feels cold = さむい です。
I feel tired = つかれた・ 疲れる
it feels nice = きもち いいです。・ 気持ち いいです。 ···· information on how to translate into Japanese
• (*to touch*) = さわる・ 触る
• to feel like... = use the pre ます form of the verb + たい for yourself and the pre ます form of the verb + たがる for others ▶191 ···· cross references to detailed usage notes section

# How to use this dictionary

## Japanese into English side

*There are a lot more words in this dictionary than it may at first appear!*

The following section gives advice on what to do if the word you want does not seem to be present.

Japanese verbs and certain adjectives can have a variety of endings. If the form of a word in front of you does not seem to be in the dictionary try and identify what kind of word it is. Verbs are often at the end of sentences and will have some hiragana characters after the Chinese characters (if they are used) i.e. いきます・行きます. Adjectives may also be detectable by their 'tail' of hiragana characters after the Chinese character/s i.e. あたらしい・新しい. The notes on verbs and adjectives give tables showing possible endings which can help you identify an unknown word. For convenience a table is given below with some of the most common inflectional endings and ideas on how to convert them back to a form that can be looked up.

Also note that it is common practice in Japanese textbooks for beginners where words are spaced, any particles are added to words without a space separating them. The same is true of です・でした and する and related forms して・した etc. Make sure you are not trying to look up a form of a word that is the word itself plus a particle or one of these words! There is a list of particles in the note on ▶ 205

If the word you want to look up has one of the following endings try to change it as indicated in the table below and look up the new form and the ending as separate items. This is not guaranteed but should give you a very good chance of finding the word you want. If the word does not seem to have one of these endings see the note on prefixes and suffixes below.

| ending | how to change it back to a form you can look up | Example from | Example to |
|---|---|---|---|
| 〜かった | remove ending and add い | さむかった | さむい |
| 〜くない | remove ending and add い | おおきくない | おおきい |
| 〜くなかった | remove ending and add い | おいしくなかった | おいしい |
| 〜た 〜て | remove ending and add る | たべた・たべて | たべる |
| 〜った 〜った | remove ending and add る or う | あった・あって | ある・あう |
| 〜んだ 〜んで | remove ending and add む or ぶ or ぬ there is only one verb with the latter ending | よんだ・あそんだ・あそんで・しんで | よむ・あそぶ・しぬ |
| 〜いた 〜いて | remove ending and add く | きいた・きいて | きく |

| ending | how to change it back to a form you can look up | Example from | Example to |
|---|---|---|---|
| 〜いだ<br>〜いだ | remove ending and add ぐ | およいだ・<br>およいで | およぐ |
| 〜した<br>〜して | remove ending and add す | はなした・<br>はなして | はなす |
| 〜たい | remove ending and add る or change the last syllable before the ending from '-i' to '-u' i.e. り to る or き to く etc. | みたい・<br>やりたい<br>あいたい・<br>ききたい | みる・<br>やる・<br>あう・<br>きく |
| 〜たくない | as above | みたくない | みる |
| 〜ます | remove ending and add る or change the last syllable before the ending from '-i' to '-u' i.e. り to る or き to く etc. | たべます・<br>おきます・<br>とります・<br>ว ききます | たべる・<br>おきる・<br>とる・<br>きく |
| 〜ません | as above | とりません | とる |
| 〜ました | as above | ききました | きく |
| 〜ましょう | as above | いきましょう | いく |
| 〜ない | remove ending and add る or change the last syllable before the ending from '-a' to '-u' i.e. ら to る or か to く etc. | たべない・<br>おわらない・<br>いかない | たべる・<br>おわる・<br>いく |
| 〜なかった | as above | とらなかった<br>みなかった | とる<br>みる |
| 〜ら | always follows either 〜た or 〜だ so find the appropriate form of that ending in the chart | きいたら | きく |
| initial word followed by する、しない、した、したい、します、しません、しましょう、したら、すれば | look up the initial word and then the relevant part of する in the verb note. Note that the elements in front of these forms are usually nouns written with Chinese characters | べんきょうすれば<br>けんきゅうした | べんきょう<br>けんきゅう |
| 〜なければ<br>なりません | as for 〜ない or 〜く ない | かかなければ<br>なりません | かく |

| ending | how to change it back to a form you can look up | Example from | Example to |
|---|---|---|---|
| 〜なければな らなかった | as for 〜ない or 〜くな い | いかなければ ならなかった | いく |
| 〜ければ | remove ending and add い | たかければ | たかい |
| 〜えば or other endings with -eba such as 〜せば or 〜てば | remove the ば and add る or remove the ば and change the preceding '-e' to '-u' i.e. せ to す | とれれば・ みせれば・ はなせば | とる・ みせる・ はなす |
| 〜くて | remove ending and add い | あたらしくて | あたらしい |

Exercise

Try to find the basic forms of the following and their meaning from the chart above using only the main entries. Use the notes on verbs or adjectives only to check!

あつかった　おいしくない　みた　よまない
いきたい　けんぶつしました　かえらなければならなかった

**Prefixes and Suffixes**

If a word is not in the dictionary try separating the first one or two symbols and looking it/them up to see if it/they is/are a common prefix element. You can also try looking at the final few syllables and trying the same thing to check for suffixes.

Exercise

Try to find the following words' meanings and the elements of which they are composed

*prefix*

ふてきとう　ごあいさつ　おしろ

*suffix*

がくせいむき　せんせいらしい　えきちょう

**A Note on Verb Forms**

There are two common styles of Japanese verbs and textbooks for beginners tend to use the polite (as opposed to plain) style as this is the normal way of talking to people other than friends and family. The plain style tends to be introduced at a later stage but is important for the learning of grammar and in a wide range of constructions. Because the polite style of a verb is not a basic 'word' but a form of the plain or dictionary 'word' we have followed usual dictionary practice and given verb entries in what is often called the dictionary form. The same applies in the English to Japanese section. However, as beginners tend to use the polite style we have kept examples in that form. We have also selected some of the most common verbs in beginners' textbooks and given them as main entries in their so-called ～ます form and conjunctive or ～て form in the Japanese-English section. This will allow you to look up a verb in these forms so even if you have not yet studied the relation of plain and polite style verbs or learned the formation of conjunctives you can find a cross-reference to the dictionary form where a translation and conjugation information will be found. The verb entries have numbers referring to the conjugation patterns and symbols to show if they are transitive or intransitive and reference can be made to the notes and tables situated between the Japanese-English and English-Japanese sections. The table above will also assist you to find a dictionary form of a verb.

Try to find the dictionary form and meaning of the following polite style verbs

### たべます　みます　おきます　おわります

Try to find the dictionary form and meaning of the verbs from the following conjunctive forms

### のんで　いって　まって　およいで

For further information see the notes on **plain and polite style** and **verbs**

## English into Japanese side

The English into Japanese side of the dictionary attempts to give full guidance on how to write and speak correctly in Japanese. Plenty of examples are given to demonstrate not only the translation of words into Japanese but also their usage in Japanese sentences. You will find additional information on grammatical points, such as the use of words in certain contexts, in the grammatical notes that occur within the entries on certain words. These notes are designed to help you produce correct Japanese in areas where mistakes are frequently made due to Japanese usage being different from English.

If you are unable to translate an English word into Japanese because you cannot find it in the wordlist, try to use another word with the same or a similar meaning, or choose another form of wording which will enable you to find what you're looking for. For instance, if you want to translate the adjective *complex* but cannot find it in the dictionary, you could try *complicated* as an alternative, which gives ふくざつ（な）・複雑（な）as the Japanese equivalent.

A very useful feature of this dictionary are the usage notes which cover sets of related words based on topics such as *family, dates,* and *nationalities etc.* You will find these in the centre of the dictionary.

# Glossary of grammatical terms

This section explains the basic terms that are used in this dictionary to help you to find the information that you need. This list does not provide a full analysis of the Japanese parts of speech.

**Adjective** An adjective is used to add extra information to or describe a noun – *a difficult* job, *a beautiful* girl, *a fat cat*. In Japanese: むずかしい しごと・難しい 仕事 きれいな おんなの ひと・きれい な 女の人 ふとっている ねこ・太って いる猫

There are 2 main types of Japanese adjectives described in a note ▶ **201**

**Adverb** An adverb is used to add extra information to or describe a verb, an adjective, or another adverb – *to walk slowly*, *extremely difficult*, *come quickly*. ゆっくり あるきます・ゆっくり歩きま す ひじょうに むずかしい・非常に 難 しい はやく くる・早く来る. Nouns and な adjectives can be made into adverbs by addition of the particle に. い adjectives can become adverbs by changing the final い to く as in あたらしい ⇒ あたらしく 'new' and 'newly'. See the note on adjectives ▶ **201**

**Auxiliary verb** An auxiliary verb is a verb, such as *be, do, have*, which is used to form a particular tense or grammatical function of another verb, or to form an interrogative, negative, or imperative sentence. Here are some English examples: *it **is** raining; **did** you see him?; she **didn't** come; he **has** left; **don't** go!*. Japanese does not use auxiliary verbs in this way.

**Comparative** The comparative, as its name indicates, is the form of the adjective or adverb which enables us to compare two or more nouns or pronouns. In English, this is usually done by putting *more, less*, or *as* before the appropriate adjective or adverb, or by changing the base form to the comparative form ending in *-er*. Japanese adjectives and adverbs do not have different comparative forms. The comparison is often indicated by the particle より the Japanese equivalent of *than*.

**Conditional** A conditional sentence is one in which the statement contained in the main clause can only be fulfilled if the condition stated in the subordinate clause is also fulfilled. In the first example below going to the seaside and in the second example going to Japan are the main clauses. This condition is usually introduced by *if* in English. Japanese has a variety of structures with similar functions. See the note on verbs ▶ **191**

*If it is fine tomorrow, we'll go to the seaside* = あした いい てんき だったら かいが んへ いきます・明日、いい天気だ ったら、海岸へ 行きます

*I would go to Japan if I had lots of money* = おかねが たくさん あったら、にほ んへ いきます・お金がたくさんあ ったら、日本へ 行きます

**Conjunction** A conjunction can be either (i) a word like *and* or *but* which is used to join words or simple sentences together, or (ii) a word like *when, although, if, where*, which is used to form a complex sentence. Japanese conjunctions are often combinations of particles or words plus particles.

**Determiner** A determiner is used before a noun in order to identify more precisely what is being referred to. Here are some examples:

*the book* = ほん・本
*a book* = ほん・本
*that book* = そのほん・その本 or あのほん・あの本
*these books* = このほん・この本
*some books* = ほん・本

Note that the English *a* and *the* have no equivalent in Japanese and
For other determiners look up the English word in the English to Japanese section.

**Exclamation** An exclamation is a word or phrase conveying a reaction such as surprise, shock, disapproval, indignation, amusement, etc. In English it is usually followed by an exclamation mark.

*Excellent! What nice weather!*

**Imperative** An imperative sentence is used to indicate an order, command, prohibition, suggestion, etc. Japanese has imperative forms of verbs but usually uses request structures as imperatives are considered rude. See the note on verbs for further information.

**Counter** Japanese numbers and the counting system are different from English and counters are words which attach to numbers to show the type of thing being counted ▶ **181**

**Noun** A noun is used to identify a person, an animal, an object, an idea, or an emotion. It can also be the name of an individual, a company, or an institution.

*student* = がくせい・学生
*dog* = いぬ・犬
*table* = テーブル
*plan* = けいかく・計画
*happiness* = しあわせ・幸せ
*Peter* = ピーター
*America* = アメリカ

Japanese nouns do not have plural forms and so the nouns above can mean 'students', 'dogs', tables' etc.

**Object** The object of a sentence is the word or group of words which is immediately affected by the action indicated by the verb. In the following English sentence, the word *child* is the subject, *broke* is the verb and *the toy* is the object. Similarly, in the Japanese translation こども is the subject, こわしました is the verb and おもちゃ is the object.

> the child broke the toy = こどもが おもちゃを こわしました・こどもが おもちゃを 壊しました

There may be two kinds of object in a sentence, a direct object and an indirect object. In the example above, *the toy* and おもちゃ are strictly direct objects. However, in the following English sentence, *he* is the subject, *gave* is the verb, *the child* is the indirect object and *a toy* is the direct object. Similarly, in the Japanese translation, かれ is the subject, あげました is the verb, こども is the indirect object and おもちゃ is the direct object. In general terms, the indirect object indicates the person or thing which 'benefits' from the action of the verb upon the direct object.

> he gave the child a toy = かれは こどもに おもちゃを あげました・彼は子供に おもちゃを 上げました

Note that unlike English the objects and subject in Japanese sentences are marked with particles and that word order is less important. See the notes on particles ▶ 205

**Phrasal verb** A phrasal verb is a verb combined with a preposition or an adverb and having a particular meaning. For example, *to **run** away*, meaning to flee, and *to **see** to* something, meaning to ensure that something is done, are phrasal verbs. If you look up *to run away* for example, you will see that the phrasal verbs beginning with the word *run* are listed after all the other meanings of the word *run*, in alphabetical order of the following adverb or preposition. Japanese does not have phrasal verbs as English does.

**Preposition** A preposition is a word, such as *under, beside, across, in*, which is usually followed by a noun in English. In Japanese there is no part of speech equivalent to them. Japanese has particles which are placed after the noun which often act in a similar ways. See the note on particles for more information ▶ 205

**Pronoun** A pronoun is used instead of a noun in order to avoid repeating it unnecessarily. There are the personal pronouns *I, you, he, she, it, we, you* (plural), *they*; the possessive pronouns *mine, yours, his, hers, its, ours, yours* (plural), *theirs;* the interrogative pronouns used in questions *who, which, what;* the demonstrative pronouns *this, that, these, those;* the relative pronouns used in relative clauses *who, which, whose;* and the reflexive pronouns *myself, yourself, himself, herself, itself, ourselves, yourselves, themselves*. Japanese does not use pronouns in the same way as English. People's names are preferred to words like 'he' and 'she' and there are no reflexive pronouns as in English. To find the Japanese equivalents of sentences using these pronouns, please look them up in the English-Japanese side of the dictionary.

**Particle** These are placed after elements in a Japanese sentence to show the grammatical relationships and can be thought of as similar in function to English prepositions such as 'to', 'at', 'from' and 'by' etc.

There is also a group of particles which come at the end of sentences and which give an element of emphasis or emotional tone and distinguish male and female speech.

The functions of particles are such that it is not always possible to give a translation under the headword although we have tried to assist with possible equivalents. ▶ 205

**Subject** The subject of a sentence is the word or group of words which performs the action indicated by the verb. In the sentence *John laughed, John* is the subject of the verb *laughed*. Of course, the verb doesn't necessarily express an action as such. Japanese uses particles は, も and が to mark subjects. ▶ 205

**Superlative** The superlative is the form of the adjective or adverb which is used to express the highest or lowest degree. In English, the adjective or adverb is usually preceded by *most* or *least*. Some adjectives and adverbs (usually of one syllable) have their own form: *best, worst, biggest, smallest, fastest, slowest*, etc. In Japanese, the superlative is most commonly expressed by putting いちばん・一番 before the adjective or adverb.

**Tense** The tense of a verb expresses whether the action takes place in the past, present, or future. Japanese verbs have only a past and a non-past tense. The tense of a sentence is determined by the *final* verb. Continuous states or activities are shown with the ～て form of a verb and the addition of います but this is not a 'tense' although sometimes it is introduced as the 'present continuous tense'. See the note on verbs ▶ 191 Japanese adjectives also show tense. See the note on adjectives ▶ 201

**Verb** The verb propels the sentence along, telling us what is happening. Sometimes, of course, the verb doesn't describe an action, but rather a state of affairs. The verb is at the end of basic sentences and expresses politeness as well as tense. Japanese verbs do not change form for 'I', 'you', 'he' etc. and the translation is very heavily dependent on the context. See the note on verbs ▶ **191**

**Attributive** A part of speech that is used in Japanese without an exact parallel in English.

**Ordinal number** The sequence of numbers $1^{st}$, $2^{nd}$, $3^{rd}$ etc.

**Cardinal Number** The sequence of numbers 1,2,3, etc.

# あア

**ああ** *adverb*
- = such
- = that

**ああいう** *attributive*
- = that kind
- = like that

**ああして** *adverb*
- = like that
- = in that way

**あい・愛**
**1** *noun* = love
**2** *verb 3* ㊥ あいする = to love

**あいかわらず・相変わらず**
*adverb* = the same as ever

**あいさつ・挨拶**
**1** *noun*
- = greetings
- = a brief speech
**2** *verb 3* ㊥ に あいさつする
= to greet

**あいじょう・愛情** *noun*
= affection

**あいず・合図**
**1** *noun* = signal
**2** *verb 3* ㊥ に あいず (を)する
= to signal

**アイスクリーム** *noun* = ice cream

**あいだ・間** *noun*
- = a space
- = a while
- = between
- = during

**あいだがら・間柄** *noun*
= relationship

**あいづち・相づち** *noun* – noises
and words used to show someone
that you are listening to what is being
said (rather like 'uh-huh' etc. in
English)

**あいて・相手** *noun*
- = the other person
- = opponent
- = partner

**あいて ▶ あく ▶ 197**

**アイデア** *noun* = idea

**あいにく** *adverb* = unfortunately

**あいまい(な)** *adjective* = vague

**あいます ▶ あう ▶ 191**

**アイロン** *noun* = iron
**アイロンを かける** = to iron

**あう・会う・遭う** *verb 1* ㊥ に
と あって・あわない・あいます
- = to meet
- = to encounter

**あう・合う** *verb 1* ㊥ と に あって
・あわない・あいます
- = to fit
- = to be right
- = to be correct

**あお・青** *noun* = blue

**あおい・青い** *adjective* = blue

> ! refers to both the blue of the sky
> and the green of vegetation and
> traffic lights

**あおぐ・仰ぐ** *verb 1* ㊦ = to look
up (at)

**あおぐ・扇ぐ** *verb 1* ㊦ = to fan

**あおじろい・青白い** *adjective*
= pale

**あおぞら・青空** *noun* = blue skies

**あか・垢** *noun*
- = scum
- = dirt

**あか・赤** *noun* = red

**あかい・赤い** *adjective* = red

**あかちゃん・赤ちゃん** *noun*
= baby

**あかり・明かり** *noun* = light

**あがり・上がり** *noun* = rise
▶ おあがり

**あがる・上がる** *verb 1* ㊥ あがっ
て・あがらない・あがります
- = to rise
- = to stop (rain)
- = to become nervous
- = to enter (a house)

あかるい・明るい *adjective*
- = bright
- = cheerful

あかんぼう・赤ん坊 *noun* = baby

あき・秋 *noun* = autumn, fall

あき・空き *prefix* = empty

あきち・空き地 *noun* = disused plot of land

あきあき(する)・
飽き飽き(する) *verb 3* ⓚ に
= to be fed up

あきます ▶あく

あきらか・明らか
**1** *adjective* あきらか(な) = clear
**2** *adverb* あきらかに = clearly

あきらめる・諦める *verb 2* ⓔ
= to abandon

あきる・飽きる *verb 2* = to be tired of

あきれる・呆れる *verb 2* ⓚ に
- = to be astonished
- = to be appalled

あく・開く *verb 1* ⓚ あいて・
あかない・あきます
- = to open
- = to be open

あく・空く *verb 1* ⓚ あいて・
あかない・あきます = to be empty

あくしゅ・握手
**1** *noun* = handshake
**2** *verb 3* ⓚ あくしゅ する = to shake hands

アクセサリー *noun – fashion accessories and especially jewellery*

アクセント *noun* = accent (emphasis)

あくび・欠伸
**1** *noun* = yawn
**2** *verb 3* ⓚ あくびをする = to yawn

あくま・悪魔 *noun* = the devil

あくまでも *adverb* = persistently

あくるひ・明くる日 *noun* = the next day

あけがた・明け方 *noun*
= daybreak

あけて ▶あける ▶ **197**

あげて ▶あげる ▶ **197**

あけまして おめでとう ござい
ます *phrase* = Happy New Year!

あけます ▶あける

あげます ▶あげる

あけて ▶あける ▶ **197**

あげて ▶あげる ▶ **197**

あける・開ける *verb 2* ⓔ あけて
・あけない・あけます = to open

あける・明ける *verb 2* ⓜ
= to dawn

あげる・上げる *verb 2* ⓔ あげて
・あげない・あげます
- = to give
- = to raise

> **!** *when following the 〜て form of a verb it indicates that the action of that verb is being done for someone else and is to their benefit* ▶ **179,** ▶ **197**

みせて あげます = I will show you
みて あげる = I'll look at it for you

あこがれ・憧れ *noun* = yearning

あこがれる・憧れる *verb 2* ⓔ
に = to yearn for

あさ・朝 *noun* = morning

あざ *noun*
- = bruise
- = birthmark

あさい・浅い *adjective* = shallow

あさごはん・朝ご飯 *noun* =
breakfast

あさって・明後日 *noun* = the day after tomorrow

あさねぼう・朝寝坊
**1** *noun* = oversleeping
**2** *verb 3* ⓚ あさねぼうする = to sleep late

あざやか(な)・鮮やか(な)
*adjective*
- = vivid
- = fresh

あし・足 *noun*
- = leg
- = foot

あじ・味 *noun* = flavour
〜の あじがする = to taste of ...

アジア *noun* = Asia

あしあと・足跡 *noun* = footprint

あしおと・足音 *noun* = footsteps

あした・明日 *noun* = tomorrow

あしもと・足元 *noun* – *literally 'the area around the feet' it can be translated as 'footing' or 'around you' depending on the context*

あじわう・味わう *verb 1* 圏
• = to taste
• = to experience

あずかる・預かる *verb 1* 圏
= to take charge of

❗ *used when something of someone else's is taken to be looked after in some way such as by a cloakroom or a bank* ▶ おあずかり

あずける・預ける *verb 2* 圏
• = to entrust
• = to leave

❗ *used when something is given to be looked after in some way such as a jacket to a cloakroom or children to a nursery*

あせ・汗 *noun* = sweat
あせを かく = to sweat

あせる・焦る *verb 1* 圏 = to be in a hurry

あそこ *noun*
• = there
• = over there
• = that place

あそび・遊び *noun*
• = play
• = game

あそびに いく・遊びに行く *verb 1* 圏 に = to (go and) visit

あそびに くる・遊びに来る *verb 3* 圏 に = to (come and) visit

あそびます ▶ あそぶ

あそぶ・遊ぶ *verb 1* 圏 と あそんで・あそばない・あそびます
• = to play
• = to be with (friends)

あたえる・与える *verb 2* 圏
• = to give
• = to cause
• = to provide

あたし *noun* – *a version of* わたし *used by some girls and young women*

あたたか(な) ▶ あたたかい

あたたかい・暖かい・温かい *adjective*
• = warm

❗ *the first Chinese character is used when referring to the weather and air temperature while the second is used for warm to the touch*

あたたまる・暖まる・温まる *verb 1* 圏
• = to get warm
• = to get hot – *see the note to* あたたかい

あたためる・温める・暖める *verb 2* 圏
• = to warm
• = to heat – *see the note to* あたたかい

あたま・頭 *noun* = head

あたらしい・新しい *adjective*
= new

あたり・辺り *noun*
• = area
• = surroundings

あたり・当たり *noun* = a hit – *literally 'being on target' it is used of someone's answer to a question to mean 'you're right'*

あたりまえ(な・の)・当たり前(な・の) *adjective*
• = as you would expect
• = natural
• = reasonable

あたる・当たる *verb 1* 圏 に
• = to hit
• = to be right
• = to win

あちこち ▶ あちらこちら

あちら *noun*
• = that place
• = over there
• = in that direction

❗ *not near either the speaker or listener*

あちらこちら *noun* = here and there

あつい・暑い・熱い *adjective*
= hot

**!** *the first Chinese character is used for weather and air temperature while the second is used for things hot to the touch*

**あつい・厚い** *adjective* = thick

**あつかい・扱い** *noun* = handling

**あつかう・扱う** *verb 1* ㊾ と
• = to handle
• = to deal with

**あつかましい・厚かましい** *adjective* = cheeky

**あっち ▶ あちら**

**あって ▶ あう ▶ ある ▶ 197**

**あっとうてき(な)・圧倒的(な)** *adjective* = overwhelming

**あつまり・集まり** *noun*
• = collection
• = meeting

**あつまる・集まる** *verb 1* ㊾ に
• = to be gathered

**あつめる・集める** *verb 2* ㊾
• = to gather
• = to attract

**あて・宛・宛て** *suffix* = addressed to

**あてじ・当て字** *noun* – *Chinese characters borrowed to write a Japanese word and whose usual pronunciations (in Japanese use) or original meanings are disregarded or altered*

**あてな・宛名** *noun* = address

**あてはまる・当てはまる** *verb 1* ㊾ に
• = to apply to
• = to fulfil

**あてはめる・当てはめる** *verb 2* ㊾
• = to adapt
• = to apply

**あてる・当てる** *verb 2* ㊾
• = to hit
• = to win
• = to guess

**あと・後** *noun*
• = back
• = after
• = remainder

**あと・跡** *noun* = remains

**あな・穴** *noun*
• = a hole
• = a cave

**アナウンサー** *noun* = TV or radio presenter

**あなた** *noun* = you

**!** *the word is not equivalent to 'you' in English as Japanese people prefer to use a person's name or title (when necessary) and it can be rude to use あなた. Also used by women to call their husbands*

**あに・兄** *noun* = one's own older brother ▶ 177

**あね・姉** *noun* = one's own older sister ▶ 177

**あの** *attributive*
• = that
• = the

**!** *refers to a person, place or thing distant from speaker and listener or which is previously known to both of them. It must be followed by a noun.*

**あのね** *interjection* = I say

**あのう** *interjection* – *indicates hesitation in speaking and so can be used as 'excuse me' or just 'er... er ... er .... um ...'*

**アパート** *noun*
• = apartment
• = (small) block of apartments

**あばれる・暴れる** *verb 2* ㊾
• = to behave violently
• = to run riot

**あびる・浴びる** *verb 2* ㊾
= to bathe
シャワーを あびる = to have a shower

**あぶない・危ない** *adjective* = dangerous

**あぶら・油** *noun* = oil

**あぶら・脂** *noun* = fat

**あぶらっぽい・油っぽい** *adjective* = oily

**アフリカ** *noun* = Africa

**あふれる・溢れる** *verb 2* ⓚ
= to overflow

**あまい・甘い** *adjective*
- = sweet
- = lenient

**あまえる・甘える** *verb 2* ⓚ に
– to rely on someone's being nice or to play up to someone

**あまぐ・雨具** *noun* = rainwear

**アマチュア** *noun* = amateur

**あまど・雨戸** *noun* = shutters

**あまやかす・甘やかす** *verb 1* ⓦ
= to spoil (a child)

**あまり・余り**
**1** *noun* = remainder
**2** *adverb*
- = too
- = very
- (*with negative*) = not very
- = not much
- = not often
**3** *suffix* = more than

**あまる・余る** *verb 1* ⓚ
- = to be left
- = to be more than required

**あみもの・編み物** *noun*
- = knitwear
- = knitting

**あむ・編む** *verb 1* ⓦ = to knit

**あめ・雨** *noun* = rain

**あめ・飴** *noun* = candy

**アメリカ** *noun* = America

**あやしい・怪しい** *adjective*
= suspicious

**あやまり・誤り** *noun*
- = mistake
- = misunderstanding

**あやまる・謝る** *verb 1* ⓦ に
= to apologise

**あら** *interjection* – used by women to express surprise

**あらい・粗い・荒い** *adjective*
= rough

**あらいます** ▶ あらう

**あらう・洗う** *verb 1* ⓦ あらって・あらわない・あらいます = to wash

**あらし・嵐** *noun* = storm

**あらすじ・粗筋** *noun* = plot (of a story)

**あらそう・争う** *verb 1* ⓦ と
- = to dispute
- = to compete

**あらた(な)・新た(な)**
**1** *adjective* = new
**2** *adverb* あらたに
- = anew
- = once again

**あらためて・改めて** *adverb*
- = again
- = anew

**あらためる・改める** *verb 2* ⓦ
- = to change
- = to renew
- = to correct

**あらって** ▶ あらう ▶ **197**

**あらっぽい・粗っぽい・荒っぽい** *adjective* = rough

**あらゆる** *attributive* = every

**あらわす・現す** *verb 1* ⓦ
= to appear

**あらわす・表す** *verb 1* ⓦ
- = to show
- = to express

**あらわす・著す** *verb 1* ⓦ
= to write

**あらわれ・現れ** *noun*
- = sign
- = expression

**あらわれる・現れる** *verb 2* ⓚ
- = to appear
- = to show up

**ありがたい** *adjective*
- = grateful
- = thankful

**ありがとう・有り難う** *phrase*

❗ used in a variety of forms of the full phrase どうも ありがとう ございます to mean 'thank you (very much)'

**あります** ▶ ある

**ある・或** *attributive*
- = a certain
- = a

**ある・在る・有る** *verb 1* ㊥ に
あって・ない・あります
- = to be
- = to have
- = to happen

**あるいて** ▶あるく

**あるいは** *conjunction*
- = or
- = either

**あるきます** ▶あるく

**あるく・歩く** *verb 1* ㊥ あるいて・
あるかない・あるきます = to walk

**アルバイト**
**1** *noun* = part time job
**2** *verb 3* ㊥ アルバイト(を)する
= to do a part time job – *and refers
to a job which is not permanent but
which can be full time such as a
student holiday job*

**アルバム** *noun* = photo album

**あれ** *interjection – used to express
surprise*

**あれ** *noun*
- = that
- = that thing
- = it

> ❗ *used to refer to something distant
> from both speaker and listener or
> something that is previously known
> to both of them*

**あれこれ** *adverb* = this and that

**あれる・荒れる** *verb 2* ㊥
- = to be rough

**アレルギー** *noun* = allergy

**あわ・泡** *noun*
- = bubble
- = foam

**あわい・淡い** *adjeective*
- = pale
- = faint

**あわせる・合わせる** *verb 2* ㊦
- = to join together
- = to fit in with
- = to adjust
- = to mix

**あわただしい・慌ただしい**
*adjective*

- = hurried
- = flustered

**あわてる・慌てる** *verb 2* ㊥
- = to hurry
- = to be flustered

**あわれ・哀れ** *noun* = pity

**あん・案** *noun* = plan

**あんい(な)・安易(な)** *adjective*
= relaxed

**あんがい・案外**
**1** *adverb* あんがい = unexpectedly
**2** *adjective* あんがい ... (な)
= unexpected

**あんき・暗記**
**1** *noun* = rote learning
**2** *verb 3* ㊦ あんきする = to
memorise

**アンケート** *noun*
- = questionnaire
- = survey

**あんしん・安心**
**1** *noun* = peace of mind
**2** *verb 3* ㊥ あんしんする
- = to feel relieved
- = to feel safe
**3** *adjective* あんしん(な)
- = reassuring
- = safe

**あんぜん・安全**
**1** *noun* = safety
**2** *adjective* あんぜん(な) = safe

**あんてい・安定**
**1** *noun* = stability
**2** *verb 3* ㊥ あんていする = to be
stable

**あんな** *adjective*
- = that
- = like that

**あんない・案内**
**1** *noun* = information
**2** *verb 3* ㊦ あんないする
- = to guide
- = to show around
- = to show the way

**あんなに** *adverb*
- = like that
- = in that way

**あんまり** ▶あまり

# いイ

い・胃 *noun* = stomach

い・位 *suffix* = position

いい・良い *adjective* = good

> ❗ *the past and negative forms are made from the alternative form* よい ▶ 201

いいえ *interjection* = no

いいかげん(な)・いい加減(な) *adjective* – the literal meaning is that the quantity of something is just right but it is more common as an idiom meaning that something is 'inadequate' in some way and when applied to people's actions and behaviour the translation and meaning will vary greatly depending on the context and the expectation of the person judging
　このしごとは けっこう いいかげんです = this job has not been done properly
　いいかげんに しなさい = That's Enough!

いいだす・言い出す *verb 1* 㐀 = to propose

いいつける・言いつける *verb 2* 㐀 = to tell someone (to do something)

いいます ▶ いう

いいわけ・言い訳 *noun* = excuse

いいん・委員 *noun* = committee member

いう・言う *verb 1* 㐀 と いって・いわない・いいます = to say
　これは にほんごで なんといいますか = what do you call this in Japanese?
　かれが「ぼく やめる」と いいました = He said "I quit!"
　かれは やめると いいました = he said that he would quit
　▶ という

いえ・家 *noun* = house

いか・以下 *suffix*
• = less than
• = under

いがい・以外 *suffix* = apart from

いがい(な)・意外(な) *adjective* = unexpected

いかが *adverb*
• = how
• = how about
　えいがを みるのは いかがですか = how about seeing a film?
　しごとは いかがですか = how is work?

いがく・医学 *noun* = medical science

いかす・活かす *verb 1* 㐀 = to make active use of

いかり・怒り *noun* = anger

いき・行き *noun* = outward journey

いき・息 *noun* = breath

いぎ・意義 *noun* = significance

いぎ・異議 *noun* = objection

いきいき(と) *adverb* = vividly

いきおい・勢い *noun* = vigour

いきなり *adverb* = unexpectedly

いきます ▶ いく

いきもの・生き物 *noun* = living creatures

イギリス *noun* = Britain, UK, England

いきる・生きる *verb 2* 㐀 = to live

いく・行く *verb 1* 㐀 いって・いかない・いきます = to go

> ❗ *following the* 〜て *form of a verb it can add the sense of an ongoing process or direction of movement of the subject* ▶ 197, ▶ 204

いくじ・育児 *noun* – bringing up children

いくつ *adverb* = how many
　(お)いくつですか = how old are you?

いくつか *noun* = some

いくぶん・幾分 *adverb* = a little

いくら *adverb* = how much
　いくら べんきょうしても なかな
　か むずかしいです = no matter
　how much I study it's still difficult
　いくらですか = how much is it?

いけ・池 *noun* = pond

いけない *adjective* = bad

> ! *following the ～て form of a verb
> and は it means something should
> not be done* ▶ **197**

いけばな・生け花 *noun* = flower
arrangement

いけません *a politer version of*
いけない

いけん・意見 *noun* = opinion

いご・以後 *noun and suffix* = since

いこう・以降 *noun and suffix*
= since

イコール *noun* = equals

いさましい・勇ましい *adjective*
= brave

いし・石 *noun* = stone

いし・医師 *noun* = doctor

いし・意志 *noun* = will

いし・意思 *noun* = intention

いじ・維持
**1** *noun* = maintenance
**2** *verb 3* ㊣ いじする = to maintain

いしき・意識 *noun* = consciousness

いじめ *noun* = bullying

いじめる *verb 2* ㊣ = to bully

いしゃ・医者 *noun* = doctor

いじょう・以上 *noun* = the
foreground

> ! *often used in the form* いじょう
> です *to end an announcement*

いじょう・異常
**1** *noun* = abnormality
**2** *adjective* いじょう(な)
　= exceptional
**3** *adverb* いじょうに = exceptionally

いじわる・意地悪
**1** *noun* = malice
**2** *adjective* いじわる(な) = malicious

いす・椅子 *noun* = chair

いずみ・泉 *noun* = (natural) spring

いずれ *adverb* = one day
　いずれに しても = in any event

いせき・遺跡 *noun* = remains

いぜん・以前 *noun*
• = before
• = once

いぜん・依然 *noun* = as it was before

いそいで ▶ いそぐ ▶ **197**

いそがしい・忙しい *adjective*
= busy

いそぎます ▶ いそぐ

いそぐ・急ぐ *verb 1* ㋕ いそいで
・いそがない・いそぎます = to
hurry

いた・板 *noun*
• = board
• = skis

いたい・痛い *adjective* = painful

いだい(な)・偉大(な) *adjective*
= grand

いだく・抱く *verb 1* ㊣ = to hold

いたす・致す *verb 1* ㊣ – a
humble equivalent of する ▶ **189**

いたずら
**1** *noun*
• = pranks
• = vandalism
**2** *verb 3* ㋕ いたずら(を)する
• = to play pranks
• = to deliberately behave badly

いただいて ▶ いただく ▶ **197**

いただきます *phrase – used before
eating it is somewhat similar to the
Christian grace 'for what we are about
to receive may the Lord make us truly
thankful' but literally a form of the
humble verb 'to receive' without any
religious meaning* ▶ いただく

いただく・頂く *verb 1* ㊣ いただ
いて・いただかない・いただき
ます
• = to take
• = to receive
• = to eat
• = to drink

いたみ・痛み *noun* = pain

いたむ・痛む *verb 1* ㋕ いたんで
・いたまない・いたみます = to
hurt

いち・一 *noun* = one ▶ **181**

いち・市 *noun* = market

いち・位置 *noun* = position

いちいち・一々 *adverb*
- = in detail
- = one by one

いちおう・一応 *adverb*
- = for the time being
- = just in case

いちご・苺 *noun* = strawberry

いちじ・一時 *adverb*
- = for a while
- = once
- = one o'clock ▶ **186**

いちど・一度 *noun* = once

いちどに・一度に *adverb* = at one time

いちば・市場 *noun* = market

いちばん・一番 *noun*
- = the first, number one
- = the most/best

いちぶ・一部
1 *noun* = part
2 *adverb* = partly

いちりゅう・一流 *noun* = first class

いつ *adverb* = when

いつか・五日 ・ 5日 *noun*
- = the fifth day of the month
- = five days ▶ **174**

いつか *noun* = someday

いっか・一家 *noun* = family

いっさくじつ・一昨日 *noun*
= the day before yesterday

いっさくねん・一昨年 *noun*
= the year before last

いっしゅ・一種 *noun* = kind (of)

いっしゅうかん・一週間 *noun*
= one week ▶ **174**

いっしゅん・一瞬 *noun*
- = an instant
- = for a moment

いっしょ・一緒 *noun*
- = together
- = with

いっしょう・一生 *noun* = life

いっしょうけんめい・一生懸命
1 *adjective* いっしょうけんめい(な)
= hard working

2 *adverb* いっしょうけんめい（に）
- = as hard as possible
- = to the best of one's ability

いっしょに・一緒に *adverb*
- = together
- = at the same time

いっせいに・一斉に *adverb*
= simultaneously

いっそう・一層 *adverb* = all the more

いったい・一体 *adverb* – *literally meaning '(as) one body' it is most common with questions indicating surprise or threat as in English 'what on earth ...?.*

いったん・一旦 *adverb* = once

いっち・一致
1 *noun* = agreement
2 *verb* 3 ㊧ に いっち する = to agree

いつつ・五つ *noun* = five ▶ **181**

いって ▶ いく ▶ いう ▶ **197**

いってい(の)・一定 (の)
*adjective* = fixed

いっていらっしゃい *phrase* – *literally meaning 'go and come back' this phrase is used to people leaving the home (or other place if they are expected to return there)* ▶ いってきます

いってきます *phrase* – *literally '(I will) go and come back' this phrase is used by people leaving the home (or other place if they expect to return there)*

いってまいります *phrase* – *a more polite version of* いってきます

いつでも *adverb*
- = always
- = anytime

いつのまにか・いつの間にか
*adverb* = before (I) really noticed

いっぱい
1 *adjective* いっぱい(の・な)
- = full
2 *adverb*
- = lots of
- = until the end of

いっぱい・一杯 *counter*
- = a cup of
- = a glass of
- = a bowl of ▶ **181**
  いっぱいする = to have a drink

いっぱん(に)・一般(に) *adverb*
= generally

いっぽう・一方
**1** *noun*
- = one side
- = one end
- = more and more
**2** *conjunction* = on the other hand
しけんが むずかしく なる いっ
ぽう です = the exams get more
and more difficult

いつまでも *adverb* = always

いつも *adverb*
- = always
- = as usual

いて ▶ いる ▶ **197**

いてん・移転
**1** *noun* = transfer
**2** *verb 3* ㋕ に いてんする = to move
(to)

いでんし・遺伝子 *noun* = gene

いと・糸 *noun* = thread

いど・井戸 *noun* = a well

いどう・移動
**1** *noun* = movement
**2** *verb 3* ㋕ に いどう する = to move

いとこ *noun* = cousin ▶ **177**

いない・以内 *suffix* = within

いなか・田舎 *noun* – *the basic
meaning is 'country' as opposed to
'urban' but it can carry connotations
of backwardness and a lack of
sophistication. Sometimes used of
urban areas smaller than Tokyo and
Osaka. Can be used to mean 'home
town' especially in the phrase*
いなかに かえる = go home

いぬ・犬 *noun* = dog

いね・稲 *noun* = rice plant

いねむり・居眠り
**1** *noun* = doze
**2** *verb 3* ㋕ いねむり(を)する
= to doze off

いのち・命 *noun* = life

いのり・祈り *noun* = prayer

いのる・祈る *verb 1* ㋕ を
= to pray

いばる・威張る *verb 1* ㋕
- = to boast
- = to be proud

いはん・違反
**1** *noun* = violation
**2** *verb 3* ㋕ いはん する = to break
(a rule)

いふく・衣服 *noun* = clothing

いま・今
**1** *noun*
- = now
- = at the moment
**2** *adverb* = right away

いま・居間 *noun* = living room

います ▶ いる

いまに・今に *adverb* = soon

いまにも・今にも *adverb* = at any
moment

いみ・意味
**1** *noun*
- = meaning
- = sense
**2** *verb 3* ㋕ いみ する = to mean

イメージ *noun* = image

いもうと・妹 *noun* = one's own
younger sister ▶ **177**

いもうとさん・妹さん *noun*
= someone else's younger sister ▶ **177**

いや(な)・嫌(な) *adjective*
- = unpleasant
- = annoying
- = disgusting

いや *interjection – contradicts a
previous statement and so can be
translated as either 'yes' or 'no'
depending on whether it refers to a
positive or a negative statement*

いやがる・嫌がる *verb 1* ㋕
- = to dislike (doing something)
- = to be unwilling (to do something)

いよいよ *adverb*
- = even more
- = at last

いらい・以来 *suffix* = since

いらい・依頼
**1** *noun* = request
**2** *verb 3* ㉜ いらいする = to request

いらいら(する) *verb 3* ㉜ = to get annoyed

いらっしゃい *phrase* – used to mean 'welcome' or 'come in' and carries a nuance of 'thank you for coming'

いらっしゃいませ *phrase* – used to welcome customers and meaning 'welcome' or 'may I help you?' depending on the context

いらっしゃる *verb 1* ㉜ いらっしって・いらっしゃらない・いらっしゃいます
• = to go
• = to come
• = to be

> ❗ *honorific equivalent of* いく, くる *and* いる ▶ **204**

いりぐち・入り口 *noun*
= entrance

いりょう・医療 *noun* = medical treatment

いる・居る *verb 2* ㉜ いて・いない・います
• (*of people or animals*) = to be
• = to exist
• (*of a place*) = to live
• = to be
• (*of a family member*) = to have
　いもうとと あにが います = I have a younger sister and an elder brother

> ❗ *after the* 〜て *form of a verb it indicates continuous action or continuing or completed states.*
> ▶ **197**

いる・要る *verb 1* ㉜ いって・いらない・いります
• = to be necessary
• = to want

いる・炒る・煎る *verb 1* ㉜
= to roast

いれて ▶ いれる ▶ 〜て ▶ **197**

いれます ▶ いれる

いれもの・入れ物 *noun*
= container

いれる・入れる *verb 2* ㉜ いれて・いれない・いれます
• = to put in
• = to let in
• = to turn on (a switch)

いろ・色 *noun* = colour

いろいろ(な)・色々(な) *adjective*
• = various
• = all sorts of

いわ・岩 *noun* = rock

いわい・祝い *noun*
• = celebration
• = a present

いわう・祝う *verb 1* ㉜ = to celebrate

いわば・言わば *adverb* = so to speak

いわゆる・ *attributive* = so-called

いん・員 *suffix* = member

いんかん・印鑑 *noun* – an official name stamp that functions as a signature on documents

インク *noun* = ink

いんさつ・印刷
**1** *noun* = printing
**2** *verb 3* ㉜ いんさつ する = to print

いんしょう・印象 *noun*
= impression
　いんしょうを あたえる = to give an impression

いんたいする・引退する *verb 3* ㉜ ㉜ = to retire

インタビュー *noun* = interview

インテリ *noun* = intellectual

いんよう・引用 *noun* = quotation

いんりょく・引力 *noun* = gravity

# うウ

**ウイスキー** *noun*
- = whiskey
- = whisky

**ウール** *noun* = wool

**ううん** *interjection* = no

> ! *informal equivalent of* いいえ

**うえ・上** *noun*
- = on
- = over
- = above
- = top
- = older

**ウェートレス** *noun* = waitress

**うえき・植木** *noun* – trees, plants and pots in a garden

**うえきや・植木屋** *noun* – a person or business growing trees and plants for gardens

**うえる・植える** *verb 2* 㐂
= to plant

**うえる・飢える** *verb 2* 㐂
= to starve

**うお・魚** *noun* = fish

**うがい**
**1** *noun* = gargling
**2** *verb 3* 㐂 **うがいする** = to gargle

**うかがう・伺う** *verb 1* 㐂 **うかがって・うかがわない・うかがいます**
- = to visit
- = to ask
- = to be told

> ! *this is a humble equivalent of the verbs* たずねる *and* いう ▶ **191**

**うかぶ・浮かぶ** *verb 1* 㐂
- = to float
- = to show

**うかべる・浮かべる** *verb 2* 㐂
- = to float
- = to occur

**うかる・受かる** *verb 1* 㐂 に
= to pass (an exam)

**うく・浮く** *verb 1* 㐂 = to float up

**うけいれる・受け入れる**
*verb 2* 㐂 = to accept

**うけたまわる・承る** *verb 1* 㐂
- = to hear
- = to know
- = to be told
- = to take an order

**うけつけ・受け付け** *noun*
= reception

**うけつける・受け付ける**
*verb 2* 㐂 = to accept

**うけて ▶ うける ▶ 197**

**うけとめる・受け止める**
*verb 2* 㐂
- = to catch
- = to react

**うけとり・受け取り** *noun*
- = receipt
- = receiving

**うけとる・受け取る** *verb 1* 㐂
= to receive

**うけます ▶ うける**

**うけもつ・受け持つ** *verb 1* 㐂
= to be in charge of

**うける・受ける** *verb 2* 㐂 **うけて・うけない・うけます**
- = to receive
- (*of an exam*) = to take
- (*of harmful effects*) = to suffer

**うごかす・動かす** *verb 1* 㐂
= to move

**うごく・動く** *verb 1* 㐂 = to move

**うごき・動き** *noun* = movement

**うさぎ・兎** *noun* = rabbit

**うし・牛** *noun* = cow

**うしなう・失う** *verb 1* 㐂 = to lose

**うしろ・後ろ** *noun*
- = behind
- = back
- = rear

**うすい・薄い** *adjective*
- = thin
- (*of drinks*) = weak
- (*of colours*) = pale

**うすぐらい・薄暗い** *adjective*
= dim

うすめる・薄める *verb 2* 🅰
= to dilute

うそ・嘘 *noun* = lie
　うそを つく = to (tell a) lie

> ❗ as an exclamation it indicates
> surprise and is similar to 'you must
> be joking!'

うそつき *noun* = liar

うた・歌 *noun* = song

うたいます ▶ うたう

うたう・歌う *verb 1* 🅰 うたって
・うたわない・うたいます = to
sing

うたがい・疑い *noun* = suspicion

うたがう・疑う *verb 1* 🅰
• = to suspect
• = to doubt

うたって ▶ うたう ▶ **197**

うち・家 *noun*
• = house
• = home
• = family

> ❗ sometimes translatable 'we' or 'us'
> when talking about a company or a
> family etc.

　うちの いぬ = our dog

うち・内 *noun*
• = while
• = during
• = in
• (of a number of items) = from

> ❗ following the 〜ない form of a verb
> it conveys the meaning of 'before'

　あめが ふらない うちに かえり
　ましょう・雨が 降らない うち
　に 帰りましょう = let's go home
　before it rains ▶ **191**

うちあわせ・打ち合わせ *noun*
= arrangement

うちあわせる・打ち合わせる
*verb 2* 🅰 = to arrange

うちけす・打ち消す *verb 1* 🅰
= to deny

うちゅう・宇宙 *noun*
• = the universe
• = space

うちわ・団扇 *noun* = hand-held fan

うつ・打つ *verb 1* 🅰
• = to hit
• = to type

うつ・撃つ *verb 1* 🅰 = to shoot

うっかり(と) *adverb* = carelessly

うつくしい・美しい *adjective*
= beautiful

うつす・移す *verb 1* 🅰 = to
transfer

うつす・写す *verb 1* 🅰 = to copy

うつす・映す *verb 1* 🅰 = to reflect

うったえる・訴える *verb 2* 🅰
• = to sue
• = to complain

うって ▶ うる ▶ うつ ▶ **197**

うつる・移る *verb 1* 🅱
• = to move
• (of a cold etc.) = to be contagious

うつる・写る *verb 1* 🅱
• (of a photograph) = to come out (well)
• (of something in a photograph) = to be
　in

うつる・映る *verb 1* 🅱 = to be
reflected

うつわ・器 *noun* = container

うで・腕 *noun* = arm
　うでを みがく = to practise

うでどけい・腕時計 *noun*
= (wrist) watch

うてん・雨天 *noun* = rainy weather

うどん *noun* – a kind of thick, white
noodle

うながす・促す *verb 1* 🅰 に
= to urge

うなぎ・鰻 *noun* = eel

うなずく *verb 1* 🅱 = to nod

うなる・唸る *verb 1* 🅱 = to groan

うばう・奪う *verb 1* 🅰 = to steal

うま・馬 *noun* = horse

うまい *adjective*
• (of food) = delicious
• (of ability) = skillful

> ❗ in the sense 'delicious' this word is
> generally only used by men.

うまれ・生まれ *noun* = birth

うまれつき(の)・
生まれつき(の) *adjective*
(*of talent etc.*) = natural

うまれて ▶ うまれる

うまれます ▶ うまれる

うまれる・生まれる *verb 2* ㋕
うまれて・うまれない・うまれ
ます = to be born

うみ・海 *noun* = sea

うむ・産む・生む *verb 1* ㋾
• = to give birth to
• = to produce

うめ・梅 *noun* = plum

うめぼし・梅干し *noun* – salty
pickled plum

うめる・埋める *verb 2* ㋾
• = to bury
• = to make up (for)
• = to fill in (the gaps)

うやまう・敬う *verb 1* ㋾ = to
respect

うら・裏 *noun*
• = back
• = behind

うらがえし・裏返し *noun*
= inside out

うらがえす・裏返す *verb 1* ㋾
= to turn inside out

うらぎる・裏切る *verb 1* ㋾
= to betray

うらない・占い *noun* = fortune
telling

うらないし・占い師 *noun*
= fortune-teller

うらなう・占う *verb 1* ㋾ = to tell
someone's fortune

うらみ・恨み *noun*
• = ill will
• = grudge

うらむ・恨む *verb 1* ㋾ = to resent

うらやましい・羨ましい
*adjective*
• = envious
• = enviable

うらやむ・羨む *verb 1* ㋾ = to
envy

うりあげ・売り上げ *noun* = sales

うりきれ・売り切れ *noun* = sold
out

うりきれる・売り切れる
*verb 2* ㋕ = to be sold out

うりだし・売り出し *noun* = sale

うりだす・売り出す *verb 1* ㋾
= to put on sale

うりば・売り場 *noun and suffix*
= department

うります ▶ うる

うる・売る *verb 1* ㋾ うって・
うらない・うります = to sell

うるさい・煩い・五月蠅い
*adjective*
• = noisy
• = annoying

! *as an exclamation it means 'shut
up'*

うれしい・嬉しい *adjective*
• = glad
• = happy

うれゆき・売れ行き *noun* = sales

うれる・売れる *verb 2* ㋕ = to be
sold

うろうろ(する) *verb 3* ㋕ = to loiter

うわき・浮気
**1** *noun* = affair
**2** *verb 3* ㋕ うわきする = to have an
affair

うわぎ・上着 *noun* – clothing for
the upper body, especially in the
sense of a coat or jacket

うわさ・噂 *noun* = rumour

うわまわる・上回る *verb 1* ㋾
= to exceed

うん *interjection*
• = yes
• = ok

! *informal equivalent of* はい

うん・運 *noun*
• = fate
うんが いい = lucky
うんが わるい = unlucky

うんえい・運営
**1** *noun* = management
**2** *verb 3* ㋾ うんえいする = to
manage

うんが・運河 *noun* = canal

うんざり(する) *verb 3 ㊙ に*
= to be fed up

うんちん・運賃 *noun* = fare

うんてん・運転
**1** *noun* = driving
**2** *verb 3 ㊎ ㊙* うんてんする = to
drive

うんてんしゅ・運転手 *noun*
= driver

うんてんめんきょ・運転免許
*noun* = driving licence

うんと *adverb*
• = very
• = hard

うんどう・運動
**1** *noun*
• = exercise
• = movement
**2** *verb 3 ㊙* うんどうする
• = to exercise
• = to move

うんどうかい・運動会 *noun* –
*a sports competition*

うんどうじょう・運動場 *noun*
• = playground
• = playing field
• = sports ground

# えエ

え・絵 *noun* = picture

えいえん・永遠 *noun* = eternity

えいが・映画 *noun*
• = movie
• = film

えいきゅう・永久
**1** *adjective* えいきゅう(の) = eternal
**2** *adverb* えいきゅうに = for ever

えいきょう・影響
**1** *noun* = influence
**2** *verb 3 ㊙ に* えいきょうする
= to have an influence

えいぎょう・営業
**1** *noun* = business

**2** *verb 3 ㊙* えいぎょうする = to do
business

えいご・英語 *noun* = English
(language)

えいこく・英国 *noun* = the United
Kingdom ▶ 172

えいせい・衛生 *noun* = hygiene

えいせい・衛星 *noun* = satellite

えいぶん・英文 *noun* – written in
English

えいよう・栄養 *noun* = nutrition

えいわ・英和 *noun and suffix*
= English and Japanese language

えいわじてん・英和辞典 *noun*
= English-Japanese dictionary

ええ *interjection* = yes

! *a less formal equivalent of* はい

ええと *interjection* – *a noise indicating
hesitation or consideration*

えがお・笑顔 *noun* = smiling face

えがく・描く *verb 1 ㊦*
• = to draw
• = to paint

えき・駅 *noun* = station

えき・液 *suffix* = liquid

えきたい・液体 *noun* = liquid

えさ・餌 *noun* = feed (for animals)

エスカレーター *noun* = escalator

えだ・枝 *noun* = branch (of a tree)

エネルギー *noun* = energy

エプロン *noun* = apron

えほん・絵本 *noun* – *an illustrated
book for children*

えらい・偉い *adjective*
• = wonderful
• = praiseworthy
• = important

えらぶ・選ぶ *verb 1 ㊦* = to choose

えり・襟 *noun* = collar

える・得る *verb 2 ㊦*
• = to get
• = to obtain

エレベーター *noun* = elevator

えん・円 *noun and suffix* = yen

えん・縁 *noun* = relationship

えんかい・宴会 *noun – a formal party where food and drink are served*

えんき・延期
**1** *noun* = postponement
**2** *verb 3* ㉠ えんきする = to postpone

えんぎ・演技 *noun* = performance

えんぎ・縁起 *noun* = omen

えんげい・園芸 *noun*
- = gardening
- = horticulture

えんげき・演劇 *noun*
- = drama
- = play

えんしゅう・円周 *noun*
= circumference

えんしゅう・演習 *noun* = practice

えんじょ・援助
**1** *noun* = assistance
**2** *verb 3* ㉠ えんじょする = to assist

エンジニア *noun* = engineer

エンジン *noun* = engine

えんぜつ・演説
**1** *noun* = speech
**2** *verb 3* ㉠ えんぜつする = to deliver a speech

えんそう・演奏
**1** *noun* = performance
**2** *verb 3* ㉠ えんそうする = to perform

えんそく・遠足 *noun*
- = outing
- = trip

えんちょう・延長
**1** *noun* = extension
**2** *verb 3* ㉠ えんちょうする = to extend

えんとつ・煙突 *noun* = chimney

えんぴつ・鉛筆 *noun* = pencil

えんりょ・遠慮
**1** *noun* = restraint
**2** *verb 3* ㉠ ㋕ えんりょする = to refrain from

> ! *often used with the sense of taking other people's feelings or situations into consideration and acting accordingly rather than just doing what you yourself feel like*

# おオ

O

> ! *note that the direct object particle is written with the ひらがな character を or (very occasionally) the かたかな character ヲ ▶ を ▶ 205*

お *prefix*

> ! *when put in front of certain nouns it makes them polite. It can also used to refer to items which are connected with a person to whom respect should be shown ▶ 189*

おあがり（ください）・お上がり（ください）*phrase – literally meaning 'please step up' it means 'please come in' and is said to someone entering a house by stepping up from ground level or* げんかん *Also used to mean 'please eat'*

おあずかりします・お預かりします *phrase – meaning 'I|we will take charge of" it is used when receiving something of someone else's to be looked after in some way such as at a cloakroom or in a bank*

おい・甥 *noun* = nephew ▶ 177

おいかける・追いかける *verb 2* ㉠ = to chase

おいこす・追い越す *verb 1* ㉠ = to overtake

おいしい *adjective* = delicious

おいつく・追い付く *verb 1* ㉠ に = to catch up

おいて ▶ おく ▶ 197

おいで・お出で
- = to come
- = to go
- = to be
（ちょっと）おいで = come here!

**！** *a noun which forms an honorific equivalent of the verbs* いく、くる *and* いる *when used with* に なる *or* です ▶ **189**

**オイル** *noun* = oil

**おう・王** *noun* = king

**おう・追う** *verb 1* を = to follow

**おうえん・応援**
**1** *noun*
• = support
• = cheering
**2** *verb 3* を おうえんする
• = to support
• = to cheer

**おうじる・応じる** *verb 2* か に
= to respond

**おうせつ・応接**
**1** *noun* = entertaining guests
**2** *verb 3* を おうせつする = to entertain guests

**おうたい・応対**
**1** *noun* = attending to (guests)
**2** *verb 3* を おうたいする = to deal with (guests etc.)

**おうだん・横断**
**1** *noun* = crossing
**2** *verb 3* を おうだんする = to go across

**おうふく・往復**
**1** *noun* = return (ticket)
**2** *verb 3* か おうふくする = to make a return journey

**おうべい・欧米** *noun* = Europe and America

**おうよう・応用**
**1** *noun* = application
**2** *verb 3* を おうようする = to put to use

**おえる・終える** *verb 2* を = to finish

**おお・大** *prefix* – *used to add the meaning of 'great' to a following noun such as* あめ ▶ おおあめ

**おおあめ・大雨** *noun* = heavy rain

**おおい・多い** *adjective* = numerous

**おおいに** *adverb* = greatly

**おおう・覆う** *verb 1* を = to cover

**おおき(な)** *adjective* = big

**おおきい・大きい** *adjective*
= large

**オーエル** *noun* – female clerical worker

**！** *usually written with the capital roman letters OL which stand for 'office lady'*

**オーケストラ** *noun* = orchestra

**おおげさ・大袈裟**
**1** *noun* = exaggeration
**2** *adjective* おおげさ(な)
= exaggerated
**3** *adverb* おおげさに = exaggeratedly

**おおざっぱ**
**1** *adjective* おおざっぱ(な)
= approximate
**2** *adverb* おおざっぱに = roughly

**おおぜい・大勢** *adverb* = in great numbers

**おおどおり・大通り** *noun* = main street

**オートバイ** *noun* = motor bike

**オートマチック(な)** *adjective*
= automatic

**オープン**
**1** *noun* = opening
**2** *verb 3* か を オープン する = to open

**オーバー** *noun* = overcoat

**おおや・大家** *noun* – *the owner of a rental property and so often translatable as either 'landlord' or 'landlady' as appropriate*

**おおやけに・公に** *noun* = in public

**おおやさん・大家さん** ▶ おおや

**おおよそ・大凡** *adverb*
= approximately

**おか・丘** *noun* = hill

**おかあさん・お母さん** *noun*
= mother ▶ **177**

**おかえり(なさい)** *phrase*
• = welcome home
• = welcome back

**おかげ** *noun* – *used in the form* の おかげ で *to mean 'thanks to ...' usually in a positive sense*

おォ

おかげさまで・お蔭様で *phrase*
– means 'Yes, thanks to you, all is
well' as a polite response to enquiries
about health etc. and so often
translatable as 'fine, thank you'

おかし・お菓子 *noun*
• = confectionery

おかしい *adjective*
• = funny
• = peculiar

おかず *noun* – dishes eaten with rice
as part of a meal

おかね・お金 *noun* = money

おかまいなく・お構いなく
*phrase* – a polite phrase used in
response to an offer etc. meaning
'please don't trouble yourself on my
behalf'

おがむ・拝む *verb 1* 🅰 = to
worship

おかわり・お代わり *noun*
= second helping of food

おき・沖 *noun* = open sea

おき・置き *suffix*
• = every other ....
• = at intervals of ....
　いちにちおき = every other day

おきて ▶ おきる

おぎなう・補う *verb 1* 🅰 = to
make up for

おきのどく・お気の毒 *phrase* –
used in response to bad news
affecting others with the sense of
'I'm very sorry to hear that'

おきます ▶ おきる ▶ おく

おきる・起きる *verb 2* 🅺 おきて
・おきない・おきます = to get up

おく・置く *verb 1* 🅰 において・
おかない・おきます = to put

! when attached to the 〜て form of
a verb it adds the meaning that the
action of that verb has been done in
preparation for some future need or
left 'as it as' ▶ 197

おく・億 *counter* = unit
▶ unit of 100,000,000 ▶ 181

おく・奥 *noun* = the inner part

おくがい・屋外 *noun* = outdoors

おくさま・奥様 *noun* = someone
else's wife ▶ 177

! a very polite term also used to
address a female customer

おくさん・奥さん *noun*
= someone else's wife ▶ 177

! a polite term also used to address
a female customer

おくじょう・屋上 *noun* = rooftop

おくりがな・送り仮名 *noun* –
the part of a Japanese word written
in hiragana following a Chinese
character stem. The word おおきい
'big' is normally written 大きい and
the き and い are okurigana ▶ vii

おくりもの・贈り物 *noun*
= present

おくる・送る *verb 1* 🅰
• = to send
• = to see off

おくる・贈る *verb 1* 🅰 = to give a
(present etc.)

おくれて ▶ おくれる

おくれます ▶ おくれる

おくれる・遅れる *verb 2* 🅺
おくれて・おくれない・おくれ
ます = to be late

おげんきですか・お元気です
か *phrase* = how are you?

おこさま・お子様 *noun* = child

! a very polite way of referring to
someone else's child ▶ 177

おこさん・お子さん *noun* = child

! a polite way of referring to
someone else's child ▶ 177

おこして ▶ おこす

おこします ▶ おこす

おこす・起こす *verb 1* 🅰 おこし
て・おこさない・おこします
= to wake someone up

おこたる・怠る *verb 1* 🅰 = to
neglect

おこなう・行う *verb 1* 🅰
• = to do
• = to hold (an exam etc.)

おこる・起こる *verb 1* ⓚ = to take place

おこる・怒る *verb 1* ⓚ に = to lose one's temper

おごる・奢る *verb 1* ⓦ = to treat someone (to food or drinks)

おさえる・押さえる・抑える *verb 2* ⓦ
• = to hold down
• = to suppress

おさきに・お先に *phrase – used when leaving work etc. before other people and translatable as 'see you' or 'goodbye'*

おさけ・お酒 *noun*
• = Japanese sake (rice wine)
• = alcoholic drink in general

おさない・幼い *adjective* = very young

おさまる・治まる *verb 1* ⓚ = to calm down

おさまる・納まる *verb 1* ⓚ = to be paid

おさまる・収まる *verb 1* ⓚ
• = to fit
• = to be kept in

おさめる・治める *verb 2* ⓦ = to rule

おさめる・納める *verb 2* ⓦ
• = to pay
• = to put back

おさめる・収める *verb 2* ⓦ = to put away

おじ・叔父・伯父 おじさん ▶177

おしい・惜しい *adjective*
• = precious
• = regrettable

❗ *as an exclamation it means 'good try!' or 'nearly right'*

おじいさん・お祖父さん *noun* = grandfather ▶177

おじいさん・お爺さん *noun – general term of address and reference for older men*

おしいれ・押し入れ *noun – a built-in storage closet used to store things like futons and bedding and to hang clothes*

おしえて ▶おしえる ▶197

おしえます ▶おしえる

おしえる・教える *verb 2* ⓦ に おしえて・おしえない・おしえます
• = to teach
• = to tell (the way etc.)

おじぎ・お辞儀
**1** *noun* = bow
**2** *verb 3* ⓚ おじぎ（を）する = to bow

おじさん・小父さん *noun – general term of address and reference for middle aged men*

おじさん・叔父さん・伯父さん *noun* = uncle

❗ *if the brother is older than your father or mother* 伯父さん*, is used, if younger* 叔父さん ▶177

おしまい・お終い *noun* = the end

おしゃれ・お洒落 *noun*
• = smartly dressed person

おしゃべり・お喋り
**1** *noun* = a talkative person
**2** *verb 3* ⓚ おしゃべりする = to chatter

おじゃまします *phrase – a polite phrase derived from a verb 'to interrupt', 'to visit' and used when entering a room or someone's house* ▶じゃま

おじょうさん・お嬢さん *noun – a polite term for someone else's daughter or a young girl in general* ▶177

おす・押す *verb 1* ⓦ = to push

おすまい・お住まい・お住い *noun* = (your) house
おすまい は どこですか = where do you live?

おせわになりました・お世話になりました *phrase – said to someone to show the feeling that they have been of assistance, especially in the context of work. It's direct translation would be 'you have looked after me, (thank you)' but often left untranslated as there is no real English equivalent in many situations*

おせん・汚染 *noun* = pollution

おそい・遅い *adjective* = late

おそらく・恐らく *adverb*
- = probably
- = possibly

おそれいりますが・
恐れ入りますが *phrase* –
*used when excusing yourself for
interrupting or when asking questions
and so translatable as 'excuse me but
...'. More polite than* すみません

おそれる・恐れる *verb 2* か
- = to be frightened

おそろしい・恐ろしい *adjective*
= frightening

おそわる・教わる *verb 1* か に
= to be taught

おだいじに・お大事に *phrase* –
*used to people who are ill or appear
tired it means 'please take care of
your health'*

おたがいさま・お互い様 *phrase*
= in the same circumstances

おだやか・穏やか
**1** *adjective* おだやか (な) = calm
**2** *adverb* おだやか に = calmly

おちつく・落ち着く *verb 1* か
= to calm down

おちゃ・お茶 *noun* = tea
おちゃを いれる = to make tea

> ! *used for Japanese tea and
> especially green tea as opposed to*
> こうちゃ

おちる・落ちる *verb 2* か = to fall
しけんに おちました・試験
に落ちました = (I) have failed the
exam

おっしゃる *verb 1* を = to say

> ! *this is an honorific equivalent of*
> いう ▶ **189**

おっと・夫 *noun* = one's own
husband – ▶ **177**

おつまみ *noun* – side dishes and
snacks eaten with alcoholic drinks

おてあらい・お手洗い *noun*
= toilet

おでかけ・お出掛け *noun* = going
out
おでかけ ですか・お出掛け
ですか = are you going out?

おてすう・お手数 *noun* = trouble
おてすうですが = I'm sorry to
trouble you but would you mind
(doing something for me)?

おてつだいさん・お手伝いさん
*noun* = maid

おと・音 *noun*
- = sound
- = noise
おとが した・音がした = there
was a noise

おとうさん・お父さん *noun*
= father ▶ **177**

おとうと・弟 *noun* = younger
brother ▶ **177**

おとうとさん・弟さん *noun*
= someone else's younger brother
▶ **177**

おどかす・脅かす *verb 1* を
= to threaten

おとこ・男 *noun* = man

おとこのこ・男の子 *noun* = boy

おとこのひと・男の人 *noun*
= man

おとしもの・落とし物 *noun*
= lost property

おとす・落とす *verb 1* を = to drop

おとずれる・訪れる *verb 2* か
= to visit

おととい・一昨日 *noun* = the day
before yesterday

おととし・一昨年 *noun* = the year
before last

おとな・大人 *noun* = adult

おとなしい *adjective* = quiet

おどり・踊り *noun* = dance

> ! *usually refers to Japanese
> traditional dancing*

おとる・劣る *verb 1* か = to be
inferior

おどる・踊る *verb 1* か おどって
・おどらない・おどります = to
dance

おとろえる・衰える *verb 2* か
= to weaken

おどろかす・驚かす *verb 1* を
= to startle

おどろく・驚く *verb 1* か に
= to be startled

おなか *noun* = stomach

おなじ・同じ *adjective* = same

> **!** *note that there is no change in form when used in front of a noun*

おなじく・同じく *adverb*
= similarly

おに・鬼 *noun* – *the giant monster of Japanese folk tales which is often translated as 'ogre'*

おにいさん・お兄さん *noun*
= older brother ▶ **177**

> **!** *also used as a general term for a young man*

おねえさん・お姉さん *noun*
= older sister ▶ **177**

> **!** *also used as a general term for a young woman*

おねがい・お願い
**1** *noun* = a request
**1** *verb 3* を に おねがい する
= to ask

> **!** *usually used as a set phrase in the form* おねがいします *meaning 'please' and indicating that a favour has been asked*

おのおの・各々 *noun* = each

おば・叔母・伯母 *noun* = aunt
▶ **177**

> **!** *if an older sibling of the parent* 伯母 *is used, if a younger* 叔母

おばあさん・お祖母さん *noun*
= grandmother ▶ **177**

おばあさん・お婆さん *noun* – *a general term for an older woman*

おばさん・叔母さん・伯母さん
*noun* = aunt ▶ **177**

> **!** *if an older sibling of the parent* 伯母さん *is used, if a younger* 叔母さん

おばさん・小母さん *noun* – *a general term for a mature woman*

おはよう *phrase* = good morning

> **!** *usually as a set expression*
> おはようございます

おび・帯 *noun* – *the wrap around "belt" on a Japanese* きもの

おひる・お昼 *noun* = lunch (time)

オフィス *noun* = office

おふくろ *noun* – *a man's way of referring to his mother*

おぼえる・覚える *verb 2* を
• = to learn
• = to memorise

おぼれる・溺れる *verb 2* か
= to drown

おまいり・お参り
**1** *noun* – *a visit to a temple or shrine for prayer, especially at the family graves*
**2** *verb 3* か に おまいり する
= to visit a shrine

おまえ・お前 *noun* = you

> **!** *this is a term used by superior males to inferior status individuals. While common in the workplace hierarchy it is best avoided by non-Japanese.*

おまたせ(しました)・
お待たせ(しました) *phrase*
= sorry to have kept you waiting

おまちください・お待ちください *phrase* = please wait

おまちどおさま *phrase* = sorry to have kept you waiting

おまわりさん・お巡りさん
*noun* = police officer

おみあい・お見合い *noun* – *an arranged introduction to a potential marriage partner*

おみあいけっこん・お見合い結婚 *noun* = arranged marriage

おむつ *noun*
• = nappy
• = diaper

おめでたい *adjective* = joyous

おめでとう *phrase*
= congratulations!

> ! usually in the form おめでとうございます

**おめにかかる・お目に掛かる**
verb 1 を に = to meet with

> ! humble equivalent of あう ▶ **189**

**おもい・重い** adjective = heavy

**おもいがけない・思い掛けない**
adjective = unexpected

**おもいきって・思い切って**
adverb = resolutely

**おもいきり・思い切り**
**1** noun = decisiveness
**2** adverb – gives the idea that something is done with energy, to the best of one's ability or as much as possible

**おもいこむ・思い込む** verb 1 か
と = to assume

**おもいだす・思い出す** verb 1 を
= to remember

**おもいつく・思い付く** verb 1 を
= to think of (an idea etc.)

**おもいで・思い出** noun
= recollection

**おもいます** ▶ おもう

**おもう・思う** verb 1 を と おもって・おもわない・おもいます
• = to think
• = to hope
• = to intend

**おもしろい・面白い** adjective
• = interesting
• = amusing

**おもたい・重たい** adjective = heavy

**おもちゃ・玩具** noun = toy

**おもって** ▶ おもう ▶ **197**

**おもて・表** noun
• = surface
• = front

**おもな・主な** adjective = main

**おもに・主に** adverb = mainly

**おもむき・趣** noun
• = intention
• = appearance

**おもむく・赴く** verb 1 か に –
used to mean to go いく especially in the sense of being sent on a posting from work

**おもわず・思わず** adverb
= inadvertently

**おや・親** noun = parent ▶ **177**

**おやじ・親父** noun = father

> ! a rough term used by men to refer to their own father

**おやすみ・お休み** noun = good night

> ! usually as a fixed phrase おやすみなさい ▶ やすみ

**おやつ** noun = snack

**おやゆび・親指** noun = thumb

**およいで** ▶ およぐ ▶ **197**

**およぎます** ▶ およぐ

**およぐ・泳ぐ** verb 1 か に およいで・およがない・およぎます
= to swim

**およそ** adverb = about

**および・及び** conjunction = and

**およぼす・及ぼす** verb 1 を
• = to exercise
• = to exert

**おり・折り** noun = occasion

**おり・檻** noun = cage

**おりがみ・折り紙** noun – the traditional Japanese craft of folding paper to create models

**おりて** ▶ おりる ▶ **197**

**おります** ▶ おりる ▶ おる

**おりもの・織物** noun = fabric

**おりる・降りる・下りる**
verb 2 か おりて・おりない・おります
• = to get off (a vehicle)
• = to go down (stairs etc.)

**おる・折る** verb 1 を = to fold
ほねを おる = to break a bone

**おる・居る** verb 1 か に = to be

> ! humble equivalent of いる ▶ **189**

**おる・織る** verb 1 を = to weave

**おれ・俺** noun = I

> ! an informal word used by men

**おれい・お礼** noun
• = thanks

- = reward
- = fee
  **おれいを いう** = to say thank you

**おれる・折れる** *verb 2* ㋥ = to break

**オレンジ** *noun* = orange

**オレンジいろ・オレンジ色** *noun* = orange

**おろす・降ろす・下ろす** *verb 1* ㋗
- = to drop
- = to set down (a passenger)
- = to lower
- = to withdraw (money from the bank)

**おろす・卸す** *verb 1* ㋗ = to sell (wholesale)

**おわって** ▶ おわる ▶ **197**

**おわり・終わり** *noun* = end

**おわります** ▶ おわる

**おわる・終わる** *verb 1* ㋥ おわって・おわらない・おわります = to finish

**おん・恩** *noun*
- = obligation
  **おんを かえす・恩を返す** = to repay a favour

**おん・音** *noun* = sound

**おんがく・音楽** *noun* = music

**おんけい・恩恵** *noun* = favour

**おんしつ・温室** *noun* = greenhouse

**おんしらず・恩知らず** *phrase* = ungrateful

**おんせん・温泉** *noun* – a hot mineral spring used for bathing for health benefits or a resort based on such a spring

**おんだん・温暖** *noun* = mild (climate)

**おんちゅう・御中** *noun* – a formal title used after the name of a company when addressing a letter without using an individual's name

**おんど・温度** *noun* = temperature

**おんな・女** *noun* = woman

  **!** Impolite. Use **おんなのひと**

**おんなの・女の** *adjective* = female

**おんなのこ・女の子** *noun* = girl

**おんなのひと・女の人** *noun* = woman

**おんよみ・音読み** *noun* – the pronunciation assigned to a Chinese character **かんじ** which is predominantly used when 2 or more characters are combined to form a word ▶ **vii**

**オンライン** *adjectival noun* = on line (computer network)

# か カ

**か** *particle*

  **!** the main functions of the particle **か** are to mark questions and to show uncertainties or alternatives ▶ **205**

**か・蚊** *noun* = mosquito

**か・課** *suffix* = section

**か・日** *suffix* = day ▶ **174**

**カー** *noun* = car

**カーテン** *noun* = curtain

**カード** *noun* = card

**カーブ** *noun* = curve

**カーペット** *noun*
- = carpet
- = rug

**かい・会** *noun and suffix* = meeting

**かい** *particle* (**!** an informal version of **か** used by men)

**かい・貝** *noun* = shellfish

**かい・回** *counter* = times ▶ **181**

**かい・階** *counter* = floor ▶ **181**

**がい・害** *noun* = damage

**がい・外** *suffix* = outside

**かいいん・会員** *noun* = member

**かいが・絵画** *noun* = painting

## かいかい・開会
**1** *noun* = opening
**2** *verb 3* ㊫ ㋕ かいかいする = to open

## かいかいしき・開会式 *noun*
= opening ceremony

## かいがい・海外 *noun* = overseas

## かいかく・改革
**1** *noun* = reorganisation
**2** *verb 3* ㊫ かいかくする = to reform

## かいかん・会館 *noun*
▶ a public building for meetings and functions

## かいがん・海岸 *noun*
• = coast
• = beach

## かいぎ・会議 *noun* = meeting

## かいけい・会計 *noun* = accounting

## かいけいし・会計士 *noun*
= accountant

## かいけつ・解決
**1** *noun* = solution
**2** *verb 3* ㊫ かいけつする = to solve

## かいけん・会見
**1** *noun*
• = meeting
• = interview
**2** *verb 3* ㋕ と かいけんする = to have an interview

## かいご・介護
**1** *noun* = nursing
**2** *verb 3* ㊫ かいごする = to nurse

## かいごう・会合
**1** *noun* = assembly
**2** *verb 3* ㋕ かいごうする = to assemble

## がいこう・外交 *noun* = diplomacy

## がいこく・外国 *noun* = abroad

## がいこくじん・外国人 *noun*
= foreigner

## かいさつ・改札 *noun* = ticket inspection

## かいさつぐち・改札口 *noun* –
the ticket barrier forming the entrance and exit points to stations

## かいさん・解散
**1** *noun* = dissolution
**2** *verb 3* ㋕ ㊫ かいさんする = to break up

## かいし・開始
**1** *noun* = start
**2** *verb 3* ㊫ かいしする = to start

## かいしゃ・会社 *noun* = company

> **!** *often used in the sense of (place of) 'work'*

## かいしゃく・解釈
**1** *noun* = interpretation
**2** *verb 3* ㊫ かいしゃくする = to interpret

## かいじゅう・怪獣 *noun* = monster

## がいしゅつ する・外出する
*verb 3* ㋕ = to go out

## かいしょ・楷書 *noun* – printed style Japanese characters as opposed to the handwritten forms. Often used in the sense of 'please write in block capitals''

## かいじょう・会場 *noun* = meeting place

## かいすいよく・海水浴 *noun*
= bathing in the sea

## かいすう・回数 *noun* = number of times

## かいすうけん・回数券 *noun* –
book of tickets for several journeys on public transport

## かいせい・改正
**1** *noun* = revision
**2** *verb 3* ㊫ かいせいする = to amend

## かいせい・快晴 *noun* = fine weather

## かいせつ・解説
**1** *noun* = commentary
**2** *verb 3* ㋕ ㊫ かいせつする = to analyse

## かいぜん・改善
**1** *noun* = improvement
**2** *verb 3* ㋕ かいぜんする = to improve

## かいだん・階段 *noun*
• = stairs
• = steps

## かいだん・会談
**1** *noun* = conference
**2** *verb 3* ㋕ かいだんする = to have discussions

## かいて ▶ かく ▶ **197**

**かいてき（な）・快適（な）**
*adjective* = pleasant

**かいてん・回転**
1 *noun* = rotation
2 *verb 3* 🐾 かいてんする = to revolve

**ガイド** *noun* = guide

**かいとう・回答** *noun* = response

**かいとう・解答**
1 *noun* = answer
2 *verb 3* 🐾 かいとうする = to solve

**がいとう・街頭** *noun* = streets

**がいとう・街灯** *noun* = street light

**かいとうようし・解答用紙**
*noun* = answer paper (for an exam)

**かいはつ・開発**
1 *noun* = development
2 *verb 3* 🐾 かいはつする = to develop

**がいぶ・外部** *noun* = exterior

**かいふく・回復**
1 *noun* = recovery
2 *verb 3* 🐾 かいふくする = to recover

**かいほう・開放**
1 *noun* = opening
2 *verb 3* 🐾 かいほうする = to open

**かいほう・解放**
1 *noun* = liberation
2 *verb 3* 🐾 かいほうする = to release

**かいます** ▶ かう

**かいもの・買物**
1 *noun* = shopping
2 *verb 3* 🐾 かいもの（を）する
• = to go shopping
• = to shop

**かいよう・海洋** *noun* = the seas

**がいらいご・外来語** *noun* –
words of foreign origin used in
Japanese and specifically those
words predominantly from western
languages and written in the かた
かな script ▶ **vii**

**がいろん・概論** *noun* = outline

**かいわ・会話**
1 *noun* = conversation
2 *verb 3* 🐾 かいわする = to talk with

**かう・買う** *verb 1* 🐾 かって・
かわない・かいます = to buy

**かう・飼う** *verb 1* 🐾 = to keep
(an animal)

**かえす・返す** *verb 1* 🐾 = to return

**かえす・帰す** *verb 1* 🐾 = to send
home

**かえって・却って** *adverb* = on
the contrary

**かえって** ▶ かえる ▶ **197**

**かえて** ▶ かえる ▶ **197**

**かえり・帰り** *noun*
• = journey back
• = homecoming

**かえります** ▶ かえる

**かえる・変える・代える・
換える・替える** *verb 2* 🐾 🐾
かえて・かえない・かえます
= to change

**かえる・帰る** *verb 1* 🐾 に かえっ
て・かえらない・かえります
• = to return
• = to go home
• = to come home

**かえる・返る** *verb 1* 🐾 に かえっ
て・かえらない・かえります
= to be returned

**かお・顔** *noun* = face

**かおく・家屋** *noun* = house

**かおり・香り** *noun* = scent

**がか・画家** *noun* = artist

**かかえる・抱える** *verb 2* 🐾
= to hold (in one's arms)

**かかく・価格** *noun* = cost

**かがく・科学** *noun* = science

**かがく・化学** *noun* = chemistry

**かかって** ▶ かかる ▶ **197**

**かがみ・鏡** *noun* = mirror

**かがやく・輝く** *verb 1* 🐾
• = to shine
• = to sparkle

**かかり・係り** *suffix* = in charge of

**かかりのひと・係りの人** *noun*
= the person in charge (of ...)

**かかります** ▶ かかる

**かかる・掛かる** *verb 1* 🐾 かかっ
て・かからない・かかります
• = to take (time or money)
• = to be telephoned

• = to hang
• = to be locked

かかわる・係わる *verb 1* に ⓐ
= to have to do with

かぎ・鍵 *noun*
• = key
• = lock
　かぎを かける = to lock
　かぎが かかる = to be locked

かきとめ・書留 *noun* = registered
post

かきとり・書き取り *noun*
= dictation

かきね・垣根 *noun* = fence

かきます ▶かく

かぎり・限り *suffix – sometimes
used as a noun meaning 'limits' but
often attached to verbs to give the
meaning of 'as far as' or 'as long as'.
With a negative verb it can often be
translated 'unless'*

かぎる・限る *verb 1* ⓐ に = to be
limited

かく・核 *prefix* = nuclear

かく・書く *verb 1* ⓐ かいて・
　かかない・かきます = to write

かく・描く *verb 1* ⓐ かいて・
　かかない・かきます
• = to draw
• = to paint

かく・欠く *verb 1* ⓐ = to lack

かく・掻く *verb 1* = to scratch

かく・格 *noun* = rank

かく・各 *prefix* = each

かぐ・家具 *noun* = furniture

かぐ・嗅ぐ *verb 1* ⓐ
• = to smell
• = to sniff

がく・学 *noun* = learning

かくう(の)・架空(の) *adjective*
= fictional

かくご・覚悟
**1** *noun*
• = readiness
• = resolution
**2** *verb 3* ⓐ かくごする
• = to be resigned to
• = to be ready for

かくじ・各自 *noun* = each person

かくじつ(な)・確実な *adjective*
• = definite
• = reliable

がくしゃ・学者 *noun* = academic

がくしゅう・学習
**1** *noun* = studying
**2** *verb 3* ⓐ がくしゅうする = to
study

かくす・隠す *verb 1* ⓐ = to hide
something

がくせい・学生 *noun* = student

かくだい・拡大
**1** *noun* = magnification
**2** *verb 3* ⓐ かくだいする = to
enlarge

かくち・各地 *noun* = each place

かくちょう・拡張
**1** *noun* = extension
**2** *verb 3* ⓐ かくちょうする = to
widen

かくど・角度 *noun* = angle

かくにん・確認
**1** *noun* = confirmation
**2** *verb 3* ⓐ かくにんする = to
confirm

がくねん・学年 *noun* = school
year

がくぶ・学部 *noun* = faculty

かくべつ・格別
**1** *adjective* かくべつの = exceptional
**2** *adverb* かくべつに = particularly

かくめい・革命 *noun* = revolution

かくりつ・確率 *noun* = probability

がくりょく・学力 *noun*
= academic ability

かくれる・隠れる *verb 2* ⓐ = to
be hidden

かげ・影 *noun* = shadow

かげ・陰 *noun* = shade

かけざん・掛け算
**1** *noun* = multiplication
**2** *verb 3* ⓐ かけざんを する = to
multiply

かけつ(する)・可決(する)
　*verb 3* ⓐ = to approve (a motion)

かけて ▶かける ▶**197**

かけます ▶かける

かける・掛ける・懸ける *verb 2*
⦿ かけて・かけない・かけます
- = to take (time, money)
- = to put over
- = to hang
- = to lock
- = to telephone
- = to multiply by
- = to be wearing (glasses)

かける・駆ける *verb 2* ⦿ = to run

かける・欠ける *verb 2* ⦿
- = to be lacking
- = to be chipped

かげん・加減 *noun* = condition

かこ・過去 *noun* = past

かご・籠 *noun* = basket

かこう・火口 *noun* = crater

かこう・下降
**1** *noun* = descent
**2** *verb 3* ⦿ ⦿ かこうする = to go down

かこう・加工
**1** *noun* = process
**2** *verb 3* ⦿ かこうする = to process

かこけい・過去形 *noun* – the past tense of verbs, in this dictionary we have usually referred to the 〜た form
▶ **191**

かこむ・囲む *verb 1* ⦿ = to surround

かさ・傘 *noun* = umbrella

かさい・火災 *noun* = fire

かさなる・重なる *verb 1* ⦿ かさなって・かさならない・かさなります
- = to be piled up
- = to happen at the same time

かさねる・重ねる *verb 2* ⦿ = to pile up

かざりもの・飾り物 *noun*
- = decoration
- = ornament

かざる・飾る *verb 1* ⦿
- = to decorate
- = to display

かざん・火山 *noun* = volcano

かし・菓子 *noun*
- = confectionery
- = snacks

かじ・火事 *noun* = fire

かじ・家事 *noun* = housework

かしこい・賢い *adjective* = clever

かしこまりました・畏まりました *phrase*
▶ used in the sense of 'certainly' to show not only understanding but that an order or request will be acted upon

かしだす・貸し出す *verb 1* ⦿
- = to lend
- = to rent out

かしつ・過失 *noun* = a blunder

かして ▶ かす ▶ **197**

かします ▶ かす

かしや・貸し家 *noun* = house for rent

かしゅ・歌手 *noun* = singer

かしょ・個所 *suffix* = place ▶ **181**

かじょう(の)・過剰(の) *adjective* = excessive

かじる *verb 1* ⦿ = to chew

かす・貸す *verb 1* ⦿ かして・かさない・かします
- = to lend
- = to rent

かず・数 *noun*
- = number
- = quantity

ガス *noun* = gas

かぜ・風 *noun* = wind

かぜ・風邪 *noun* = a cold
かぜを ひく = to catch a cold

かぜい・課税 *noun* = taxation

かせん・下線 *noun* = underline

かせぐ・稼ぐ *verb 1* ⦿ = to earn money

カセット *noun* = cassette

かぞえて ▶ かぞえる ▶ **197**

かぞえます ▶ かぞえる

かぞえる・数える *verb 2* ⦿ かぞえて・かぞえない・かぞえます
= to count

かそく・加速
**1** *noun* = acceleration
**2** *verb 3* ⦿ かそくする = to accelerate

かぞく・家族 *noun* = family ▶ **177**

かそくど・加速度 *noun*
= acceleration

ガソリン *noun*
• = petrol
• = gasoline

ガソリンスタンド *noun*
• = petrol station
• = gasoline station

かた・方 *noun* = person

かた・肩 *noun* = shoulder

かた・型 *noun*
• = style
• = mould

かた・方 *suffix – when added to the pre ～ます form of a verb it means 'way of ...ing'* ▶ **191**

かたい・固い・堅い・硬い *adjective*
• = hard
• = stiff

がたい・難い *suffix – when added to the pre ～ます form of a verb it means 'difficult to ...'* ▶ **191**

かたがた・方々 *noun* = people

かたかな・片仮名 *noun – the script primarily used to write words of foreign origin and which functions as a kind of italic* ▶ **vii**

かたち・形 *noun*
• = form
• = shape

かたづく・片付く *verb 1 ⑰* かたづいて・かたづかない・かたづきます *(of a room)* = to be tidy

かたづけて ▶ かたづける ▶ **197**

かたづけます ▶ かたづける

かたづける・片付ける *verb 2 ⑳* かたづけて・かたづけない・かたづけます = to tidy up

かたまり・塊 *noun – bits which are stuck together, a lump*

かたまる・固まる *verb 1 ⑰* = to harden

かたみち・片道 *noun* = one-way (ticket)

かたむく・傾く *verb 1 ⑰* = to incline

かたよる・片寄る・偏る *verb 1 ⑰* = to be prejudiced (in favour of)

かたる・語る *verb 1 ⑳* = to tell

かち・価値 *noun* = value

かち・勝ち *noun* = victory

がち *suffix*

> ! *added to the pre* ます *form of a verb it adds the meaning of 'tends to ...'* ▶ **191**

かつ・勝つ *verb 1 に ⑰* かって・かたない・かちます = to win

がつ・月 *suffix* = month ▶ **174**

がっか・学科 *noun* = university or school department

がっかい・学会 *noun* = academic conference

がっかり(する) *verb 3 ⑰ に* = to be disappointed

かっき・活気 *noun* = vigour

がっき・楽器 *noun* = (musical) instrument

がっき・学期 *noun*
• = semester
• = term

かつぐ・担ぐ *verb 1 ⑳* = to carry (on the shoulders)

かっこ・括弧 *noun* = brackets

かっこう・格好 *noun*
= appearance
かっこういい = of nice appearance
• = stylish
かっこうわるい = not stylish
• = not attractive

がっこう・学校 *noun* = school

かつじ・活字 *noun* = print

がっしょうだん・合唱団 *noun*
= choir

かって・勝手 *noun* = kitchen

かって ▶ かう ▶ かつ ▶ **197**

かってに・勝手に *adverb*
• = without asking permission
• = selfishly

かつどう・活動
**1** *noun* = activity

**2** *verb 3* ㊟ に かつどうする = to work actively

## かつやく・活躍
**1** *noun* = activity
**2** *verb 3* ㊟ に かつやくする = to play an active role

## かつよう・活用
**1** *noun*
• = utilisation
• = conjugation
**2** *verb 3* ㊞ ㊟ かつようする
• = to make use of
• = to conjugate (verbs)

## かつりょく・活力 *noun* = vitality

## かてい・仮定
**1** *noun* = assumption
**2** *verb 3* ㊞ かていする = to assume

## かてい・家庭 *noun* = household

## かてい・過程 *noun* = process

## かてい・課程 *noun* = curriculum

## かど・角 *noun* = corner

## かな・仮名 *noun*

> **!** the Japanese syllabic scripts ひらがな and かたかな as opposed to Chinese characters or かんじ ▶vii

## かない・家内 *noun* = one's own wife ▶**177**

## かなしい・悲しい *adjective* = sad

## かなしむ・悲しむ *verb 1* ㊞ = to be sad about

## かなづかい・仮名遣い *noun* – the way of using かな in the writing of Japanese ▶vii

## かなづち・金槌 *noun* = hammer

## かならず・必ず *adverb* = definitely

## かならずしも・必ずしも *adverb* (preceding a negative) = not necessarily

## かなり *adverb* = considerably

## かね・金 *noun* = money ▶ おかね

## かね・鐘 *noun* = bell

## かねない ▶ かねる

## かねつ(する)・加熱(する) *verb 3* ㊞ = to heat

## かねもち・金持ち *noun* = a rich person

## かねる・兼ねる *verb 2* ㊞ = to serve as (both of) two things at the same time

## かねる *suffix* – attached to the pre ～ます form of a verb it adds the meaning of being unable to do to a preceding verb and is thus often translated as 'cannot' and indicates a refusal of a request. Although the meaning is negative the form is positive and even native-speakers can get it wrong! The negative form かねない it is used for the meaning 'I wouldn't put it past (somebody) to do that'. ▶191

## かのう (な)・可能 (な) *adjective* = possible

## かのうせい・可能性 *noun* = possibility
> かのうせいが こい = it is very likely

## カバー
**1** *noun* = cover
**2** *verb 3* ㊞ カバーする = to cover

## かばん・鞄 *noun* = bag

## かはんすう・過半数 *noun* = majority

## かび *noun* = mould

## かびん・花瓶 *noun* = vase

## かぶ・株 *noun* = stocks

## かぶしき・株式 *noun* = shares

## かぶしきがいしゃ・株式会社 *noun* = corporation

## かぶせる・被せる *verb 2* ㊞ = to cover

## かぶる・被る *verb 1* ㊞
• = to put on
• = to be wearing (a hat)

## かべ・壁 *noun* = wall

## かま・釜 *noun*
▶ large pot for cooking rice

## かまいません *phrase* – deriving from かまう this phrase is used to mean 'it doesn't matter' and in the question form かまいませんか to mean 'would you mind if ...?'

かまう・構う *verb 1* ㉒ = to mind

がまん・我慢
**1** *noun* = endurance
**2** *verb 3* ㉒ がまんする = to endure

がまんづよい・我慢強い
　*adjective* = patient

かみ・髪 *noun* = hair (on head)

かみ・紙 *noun* = paper

かみ・神 *noun* = god

かみ・上 *prefix*
• = upper (part)
• = first (part)

かみくず・紙屑 *noun* = waste paper

かみさま・神様 *noun* = God

かみそり・剃刀 *noun*
• = shaver
• = razor

かみなり・雷 *noun* = thunder

かみのけ・髪の毛 *noun* = hair (on the head)

かむ・噛む *verb 1* ㉒
• = to bite
• = to chew

ガム *noun* = chewing gum

ガムテープ *noun* = sticky tape

カメラ *noun* = camera

かもく・科目・課目 *noun* = objective

かもしれません ▶ かもしれない

かもしれない *phrase*
• = probably
• = perhaps

かもつ・貨物 *noun* = freight

かゆい・痒い *adjective* = itchy

かよう・通う *verb 1* ㉕ に
• = to commute
• = to travel
• = to attend

かよう・歌謡 *noun* = song

かようび・火曜日 *noun* = Tuesday

から・殻 *noun* = shell

から *particle*
• = because
• = from ▶ **205**

がら・柄 *noun*
• = pattern
• = design
• = nature

から(の)・空(の) *adjective* = empty

カラー *noun* = colour

からい・辛い *adjective* = spicy

カラオケ *noun* – singing to the accompaniment of a backing tape especially at bars

からかう *verb 1* ㉒ = to tease

ガラス *noun* = glass

からだ・体 *noun* = body

からっぽ *adjective* = empty

かりて ▶ かりる ▶ **197**

かりに・仮に *adverb*
• = temporarily
• = supposing

かります ▶ かりる

かりる・借りる *verb 2* ㉒ に
かりて・かりない・かります
• = to borrow
• = to rent
• = to hire

かる・刈る *verb 1* ㉒ = to cut

がる *suffix* – when added to the stem of adjectives of emotion or sensation it indicates that the state is not that of the speaker or writer but refers to some other person. ▶ **201**

かるい・軽い *adjective* = light

かるた・カルタ *noun* – traditional Japanese playing cards featuring poems or proverbs

カルテ *noun* = medical record

かれ・彼 *noun* = he

カレー *noun* = curry

かれし・彼氏 *noun* = boyfriend

かれら・彼ら *noun* = they

かれる・枯れる *verb 2* ㉕ = to wither

カレンダー *noun* = calendar

かろう・過労 *noun* = overwork

かろうじて・辛うじて *adverb* = only just

カロリー *noun* = calorie

かわ・川・河 *noun* = river

かわ・皮 *noun* = skin

かわ・革 *noun* = leather

がわ・側 *suffix* = side

かわいい・可愛い *adjective* = cute

かわいがる・可愛がる *verb 1* 倒
= to love (grandchildren or pets etc.)

かわいそう・可哀相
**1** *adjective* かわいそう(な) = pitiful
**2** *adverb* かわいそうに = sadly

> ❗ *often used in the sense 'oh that's terrible (news)!' or 'what a pity!'*

かわいらしい ▶ かわいい

かわかす・乾かす *verb 1* 倒 = to dry

かわく・渇く *verb 1* 倒
のどが かわく = to be thirsty

かわく・乾く *verb 1* 倒 = to get dry

かわす・交わす *verb 1* 倒 = to exchange

かわせ・為替 *noun* = exchange (rate)

かわって ▶ かわる ▶ 197

かわり(に)・代わり(に) *noun*
= instead of

かわり・変わり・替わり *noun*
= change

かわります ▶ かわる

かわる・変わる *verb 1* 倒 かわって・かわらない・かわります
= to change

かわる・代わる *verb 1* 倒 かわって・かわらない・かわります
= to replace

かわるがわる(に) *adverb* = in turn

かん・缶 *noun*
• = can (of ...)
• = tin (of ...)

かん・間 *suffix* – adds the sense of duration to time words ▶ 186

かん・巻 *counter* = volume

かん・勘 *noun* = intuition

がん・癌 *noun* = cancer

かんえい(じてん)・漢英(辞典) *noun*

> ❗ *a dictionary of* かんじ *characters with explanations in English*
> ▶ かんわ

かんがえ・考え *noun*
• = idea
• = way of thinking

かんがえて ▶ かんがえる ▶ 197

かんがえます ▶ かんがえる

かんがえる・考える *verb 2* 倒 かんがえて・かんがえない・かんがえます
• = to think about
• = to expect

がんか・眼科 *noun*
= opthalmologist

かんかく・感覚 *noun* = sense(s)

かんかく・間隔 *noun* = interval
かんかくを おく = leave space (between)

かんき・換気
**1** *noun* = ventilation
**2** *verb 3* 倒 かんきする = to ventilate

かんきせん・換気扇 *noun*
= extractor fan

かんきゃく・観客 *noun*
= spectators

かんきょう・環境 *noun*
• = environment
• = surroundings

かんきょうおせん・環境汚染
*noun* = pollution

かんけい・関係 *noun*
• = relationship
• = connection

かんげい・歓迎
**1** *noun* = welcome
**2** *verb 3* 倒 かんげいする = to welcome

かんげいかい・歓迎会 *noun* –
*a formal welcome party*

かんけいない・関係ない
*adjective*
• = unconnected

> ❗ *as a phrase it can mean 'that's nothing to do with it' or 'it's none of your business'*

かんげき・感激
**1** *noun* = deep emotion

かカ

**2** *verb 3* ㉑ に かんげきする = to moved

かんご・看護 *noun* = nursing

かんご・漢語 *noun* – words written with Chinese characters ▶ **vii**

がんこ(な)・頑固な *adjective* = stubborn

かんこう・観光
**1** *noun* = sightseeing
**2** *verb 3* ㉑ かんこうする = to sightsee

かんこうきゃく・観光客 *noun* = tourist

かんこく・勧告 *noun* = advice

かんこく・韓国 *noun* = South Korea ▶ **172**

かんごふ・看護婦 *noun* = nurse

かんさい・関西 *noun* – the region of Japan around Osaka, Kyoto and Kobe

かんさつ・観察
**1** *noun* = observation
**2** *verb 3* ㉑ かんさつする = to observe

かんじ・漢字 *noun* = Chinese characters ▶ **vii**

かんじ・感じ *noun* = feeling

がんじつ・元日 *noun* = new year's day

かんしゃ・感謝
**1** *noun* = gratitude
**2** *verb 3* ㉑ に かんしゃする
• = to be grateful
• = to thank

かんじゃ・患者 *noun* = patient (at a hospital etc.)

かんしゅう・観衆 *noun*
• = audience
• = spectators

かんしょう・干渉
**1** *noun* = interference
**2** *verb 3* ㉑ に かんしょうする = to interfere

かんしょう・鑑賞
**1** *noun* = appreciation
**2** *verb 3* ㉑ かんしょうする = to enjoy

かんじょう・感情 *noun* = emotions

かんじょう・勘定 *noun* = the bill

かんじる・感じる *verb 2* ㉑
• = to feel
• = to sense

かんしん・感心
**1** *noun* = admiration
**2** *adjective* かんしん(な) = admirable
**3** *verb 3* に かんしんする = to be impressed

かんしん・関心 *noun* = concern

かん(する)・関(する) *verb 3* ㉑ に = to be concerned (with)

かんずる・感ずる *verb 3* ㉑ = to feel

かんせい・完成
**1** *noun* = completion
**2** *verb 3* ㉑ かんせいする = to complete

かんせつ・間接
**1** *adjective* かんせつ(の) = indirect
**2** *adverb* かんせつに = indirectly

かんぜん・完全
**1** *adjective* かんぜん(な) = complete
**2** *adverb* かんぜんに = fully

かんそう・乾燥
**1** *noun* = drying
**2** *verb 3* ㉑ かんそうする = to dry

かんそう・感想 *noun* = impression

かんそく・観測
**1** *noun* = observation
**2** *verb 3* ㉑ かんそくする
• = to observe
• = to predict

かんたん・簡単
**1** *adjective* かんたん(な) = easy
**2** *adverb* かんたんに = easily

かんちょう・官庁 *noun* = government agency

かんちがい・勘違い *noun* = misunderstanding

かんづめ・缶詰 *noun*
• = tinned goods
• = canned goods

かんでんち・乾電池 *noun* = battery

かんとう・関東 *noun* (**!** the area around Tokyo)

かんどう・感動
**1** *noun* = deep emotion

**2** *verb 3* ㋕ に かんどうする = to be moved

**かんとく・監督**
**1** *noun*
- = directing
- = director
**2** *verb 3* ㋔ かんとくする = to direct (a film)

**カンニング**
**1** *noun* = cheating
**2** *verb 3* ㋕ カンニングする = to cheat

**かんねん・観念**
**1** *noun*
- = idea
- = sense
**2** *verb 3* ㋕ かんねんする = to be resigned (to one's fate)

**かんぱい・乾杯**
**1** *noun* = toast
**2** *verb 3* ㋕ かんぱいする = to drink a toast

> **!** *as a phrase it is used like English 'cheers' before drinking*

**がんばって** ▶ がんばる ▶ **197** – *on its own or in the form* がんばってください *it is an expression meaning 'do your best'*

**がんばります** ▶ がんばる – *an expression meaning 'I'll try' or 'I'll do my best'*

**がんばる・頑張る** *verb 1* ㋕ がんばって・がんばらない・がんばります = to do one's best

**かんばん・看板** *noun* = sign

**かんぺき・完璧**
**1** *adjective* かんぺき(な) = perfect
**2** *adverb* かんぺきに = perfectly

**かんべん・勘弁**
**1** *noun* = pardon
**2** *verb 3* ㋔ かんべんする = to pardon

**かんむり・冠** *noun*
- = crown
- = the top part of a Chinese character

**かんり・管理**
**1** *noun* = management
**2** *verb 3* ㋔ かんりする
- = to control
- = to manage

**かんりょう・完了**
**1** *noun* = completion
**2** *verb 3* ㋔ かんりょうする = to complete

**かんりょう・官僚** *noun*
= bureaucracy

**かんれん(する)・関連(する)**
*verb 3* ㋕ = to be connected

**かんわ(じてん)・漢和(辞典)**
*noun* – a dictionary of かんじ characters with their meanings and readings (designed for the use of native-speakers of Japanese)
▶ かんえい

# きキ

**き・木** *noun* = tree

**き・気** *noun*
▶ *variously translatable as 'mood', 'mind', 'spirits'*
きに いる = to like
きを つける = to be careful
きを つけてください = please be careful!
きに する = to worry
きに なる = to feel bothered by
きが つく = to notice

**き・機** *suffix* = machine

**きあつ・気圧** *noun* = air pressure

**きいろ・黄色** *noun* = yellow

**きいろい・黄色い** *adjective*
= yellow

**ぎいん・議員** *noun*
- = assembly member
- = member of parliament
- = member of congress

**きえる・消える** *verb 2* ㋕ きえて・きえない・きえます
- (of a light) = to go out
- = to disappear

**きおく・記憶** *noun* = memory

**きおん・気温** *noun* = (air) temperature

きかい・機会 *noun* = opportunity

きかい・機械 *noun* = machine

ぎかい・議会 *noun*
• = assembly
• = parliament
• = congress

きがえ・着替え
**1** *noun* = change of clothes
**2** *verb 3* ㋕ に きがえ(を)する = to change clothes

きがえる・着替える *verb 2* ㋾ に きがえて・きがえない・きがえます = to change (clothes)

きかん・期間 *noun* = period of time

きかん・機関 *noun* = institution

きき・危機 *noun* = crisis

ききとり・聞き取り *noun* = listening

ききます ▶ きく

きぎょう・企業 *noun* = business

ききん・飢饉 *noun* = famine

きく・聞く・聴く *verb 1* ㋾ に きいて・きかない・ききます
• = to hear
• = to ask
• = to listen

きく・効く *verb 1* ㋕ に きいて・きかない・ききます = to work (to have an effect)

きぐ・器具 *noun* = appliance

きけん・危険
**1** *noun* = danger
**2** *adjective* きけん(な) = dangerous

きげん・期限 *noun* = time limit

きげん・機嫌 *noun* = mood

きこう・気候 *noun* = climate

きごう・記号 *noun* = symbol

きこえる・聞こえる *verb 2* ㋕ きこえて・きこえない・きこえます = (to be able) to hear

きざむ・刻む *verb 1* ㋾ = to carve

きし・岸 *noun*
• = coast
• = shore
• = (river) bank

きじ・記事 *noun* = article (in the press)

きじ・生地 *noun*
• = cloth
• = material

ぎし・技師 *noun* = engineer

ぎしき・儀式 *noun* = ceremony

きしゃ・貴社 *noun* – polite way of referring to someone's company

きしゃ・記者 *noun* = journalist

きしゃ・汽車 *noun* = steam locomotive

ぎじゅつ・技術 *noun* = technique

きじゅん・基準 *noun* = standard

きしょうする・起床する *verb 3* ㋕ = to get up

きず・傷・疵 *noun*
• = injury
• = damage
　きずを つける = to injure = to damage

きすう・奇数 *noun* = odd number

既製 *as prefixing element* = ready made

きせつ・季節 *noun* = season

きせる・着せる *verb 2* ㋾ きせて・きせない・きせます = to dress (somebody)

きそ・基礎 *noun* = foundation

きそく・規則 *noun* = regulation

きた・北 *noun* = north

ギター *noun* = guitar

きたい・期待
**1** *noun* = expectation
**2** *verb 3* ㋾ きたいする = to expect

きたい・気体 *noun* = gas

きたく(する)・帰宅(する) *verb 3* ㋕ = to go home

きたない・汚い *adjective*
• = dirty
• = untidy

きち・基地 *noun* = base

きちょう(な)・貴重な *adjective* = valuable

きちょうひん・貴重品 *noun* = valuables

**きちんと** *adverb*
- = neatly
- = properly

**きつい** *adjective*
- = severe
- (*shoes, clothes*) = tight

**きっかけ** *noun* = chance

**きづく・気付く** *verb 1* ⑳ に きづいて・きづかない・きづきます
= to notice

**きっさてん・喫茶店** *noun*
= coffee shop

**ぎっしり** *adverb* = tightly

**きって・切手** *noun* = stamp

**きって ▶ きる ▶ 197**

**きっと** *adverb* = definitely

**きっぷ・切符** *noun* = ticket

**きて ▶ きる ▶ くる ▶ 197**

**きにゅう・記入**
**1** *noun* = (text) entry
**2** *verb 3* ⑳ きにゅうする = to fill in

**きぬ・絹** *noun* = silk

**きねん・記念**
**1** *noun* = anniversary
**2** *verb 3* ⑳ きねんする = to
    commemorate

**きねんび・記念日** *noun*
= anniversary

**きのう・昨日** *noun* = yesterday

**きのう・機能** *noun* = function

**きのどく・気の毒** *phrase* – used
in the sense of 'I'm very sorry to hear
it'!' when expressing sympathy or
condolences

**きばん・基盤** *noun* = base

**きびしい・厳しい** *adjective*
= strict

**きふ・寄付** *noun* = donation

**きぶん・気分** *noun* = mood

**きぼう・希望**
**1** *noun* = hope
**2** *verb 3* ⑳ きぼうする = to hope for

**きほん・基本** *noun* = basis

**きほんてき・基本的**
**1** *adjective* きほんてき(な)
    = fundamental

**2** *adverb* きほんてきに
    = fundamentally

**きます ▶ くる ▶ きる**

**きまり・決まり** *noun* = rule

**きまる・決まる** *verb 1* ⑳ きまって・きまらない・きまります
= to be decided

**きみ・君** *noun* = you

**きみ・気味** *noun* = feeling
きみが わるい = eerie

**ぎみ・気味** *suffix* – added to nouns
like かぜ meaning 'a cold' to give
compounds like かぜぎみ 'having a
touch of cold'

**きみょう・奇妙**
**1** *adjective* きみょうな = strange
**2** *adverb* きみょうに = strangely

**ぎむ・義務** *noun* = duty

**きめる・決める** *verb 2* ⑳ きめて
・きめない・きめます = to decide

**きもち・気持ち** *noun* = feeling
きもちいい = pleasant
きもちわるい = unpleasant

**きもの・着物** *noun* – used to mean
clothes in general and the traditional
Japanese women's kimono in
particular

**ぎもん・疑問** *noun* = doubt

**きゃく・客** *noun* = customer

**ぎゃく・逆**
**1** *noun* = opposite
**2** *adjective* ぎゃくの = opposite
**3** *adverb* ぎゃくに
- = on the contrary
- = in reverse

**きゃくせき・客席** *noun*
- = seat
- = passenger seat

**きゃくま・客間** *noun* = drawing
room

> **!** the room in a Japanese house
> which is used for entertaining
> guests

**キャッチ**
**1** *noun* = catch
**2** *verb 3* ⑳ キャッチする = to hear

**ギャング** *noun* = gang

きキ

**キャンプ**
1 *noun* = camp
2 *verb 3 ㉚* **キャンプする** = to camp

**きゅう・九** *noun* = nine

**きゅう・急**
1 *adjective* **きゅう(な)** = sudden
2 *adverb* **きゅうに** = suddenly

**きゅう・旧** *prefix* = former (state)

**きゅうか・休暇** *noun*
• = holiday
• = break

**きゅうがく・休学**
1 *noun* = absence (from school or university)
2 *verb 3 ㊦* **きゅうがくする** = to take a year off (from school or university)

**きゅうきゅうしゃ・救急車**
*noun* = ambulance

**きゅうぎょう・休業** *noun*
= holiday (for a business or shop)

**きゅうけい・休憩**
1 *noun* = break
2 *verb 3 ㊦* **きゅうけいする** = to take a break

**きゅうげき・急激**
1 *adjective* **きゅうげきな** = drastic
2 *adverb* **きゅうげきに** = suddenly

**きゅうこう・急行** *noun* = express (train)

**きゅうこう・休講** *noun*
= cancellation of lecture/s

**きゅうじつ・休日** *noun* = holiday (for a business or restaurant)

**きゅうしゅう・吸収**
1 *noun* = absorption
2 *verb 3 ㊦* **きゅうしゅうする**
= to absorb

**きゅうじょ・救助**
1 *noun* = rescue
2 *verb 3 ㊦* **きゅうじょする**
= to rescue

**きゅうしょく・給食** *noun*
= school meals

**きゅうそく・休息**
1 *noun* = rest
2 *verb 3 ㉚* **きゅうそくする** = to rest

**きゅうそく(な)・急速な**
*adjective* = rapid

**きゅうに・急に** ▶ きゅう

**ぎゅうにゅう・牛乳** *noun* = milk

**きゅうよ・給与** *noun* = wage

**きゅうよう・休養** *noun* = rest

**きゅうよう・急用** *noun* = urgent business

**きゅうりょう・給料** *noun*
= salary

**きよい・清い** *adjective* = pure

**きよう・器用**
1 *adverb* **きように** = skillfully
2 *adjective* **きような** = adroit

**きょう・今日** *noun* = today

**ぎょう・行** *noun* = line

**きょういく・教育**
1 *noun* = education
2 *verb 3 ㊦* **きょういくする** = to educate

**きょういん・教員** *noun* = teacher

**きょうかする・強化する**
*verb 3 ㊦* = to strengthen

**きょうかい・境界** *noun*
= boundary

**きょうかい・教会** *noun* = church

**きょうかしょ・教科書** *noun*
= textbook

**きょうぎ・競技** *noun* = contest

**ぎょうぎ・行儀** *noun* = manners

**きょうきゅう・供給**
1 *noun* = supply
2 *verb 3 ㊦* **きょうきゅうする**
= to supply

**きょうさんしゅぎ・共産主義**
*noun* = communism

**きょうし・教師** *noun* = teacher

**ぎょうじ・行事** *noun* = event

**きょうしつ・教室** *noun*
= classroom

**きょうじゅ・教授** *noun*
= professor

**きょうしゅく・恐縮** – *in the expressions* **きょうしゅくですが** *and* **きょうしゅくしますが** *it means 'sorry to trouble you' or 'I'm sorry to interupt but ...'*

きょうせい(する)・強制(する)
verb 3 ⓦ = to compel

きょうせいてき(な)・
強制的(な) adjective = compulsory

ぎょうせい・行政 noun
= administration

きょうそう・競争
1 noun = competition
2 verb 3 ⓚ と きょうそうする = to
compete

きょうだい・兄弟 noun
= brothers

> ! often meaning 'brothers and
sisters' ▶ 177

きょうちょう・強調
1 noun = emphasis
2 verb 3 ⓦ きょうちょうする = to
emphasise

きょうつう(の)・共通(の)
adjective = (in) common

きょうどう・共同
1 noun = collaboration
2 verb 3 ⓦ きょうどうする = to
share

きょうふ・恐怖 noun = fear

きょうみ・興味 noun = interest

きょうよう・教養 noun
= education

きょうりょく・協力
1 noun = cooperation
2 verb 3 ⓚ きょうりょくする = to
cooperate

きょうりょく(な)・強力(な)
adjective = powerful

ぎょうれつ・行列 noun
= procession

きょか・許可 noun = pemission

ぎょぎょう・漁業 noun = fishing
industry

きょく・曲 noun
• = tune
• = song

きょく・局 suffix
• = office
• = store

きょくせん・曲線 noun = curve

きょだい(な)・巨大(な)
adjective) = enormous

きょねん・去年 noun = last year

きょひ・拒否
1 noun = refusal
2 verb 3 ⓦ きょひする = to refuse

きょり・距離 noun = distance

きらい(な)・嫌い(な) adjective
• = hated
• = disliked

きらう・嫌う verb 1 ⓦ ⓚ
• = to dislike
• = to hate

きらく・気楽
1 adjective きらく(な) = comfortable
and relaxed
2 adverb きらくに = freely

きり・霧 noun
• = fog
• = mist

ぎり・義理 noun = obligation

> ! Used with the sense of a
favour|favor being owed. Also
used with family words in the form
ぎりの〜 to mean '- in law'.

きり suffix = only

きります ▶ きる

きりつ(する)・起立 (する)
verb 3 ⓚ = to stand up

きりつ・規律 noun = rules

きる・切る verb 1 ⓦ きって・
きらない・きります = to cut

きる・着る verb 2 ⓦ きて・
きない・きます
• = to put on
• = to be wearing

きれい・奇麗
1 adjective きれい(な)
• = pretty
• = clean
• = tidy
2 adverb きれいに = tidily

きれる・切れる verb 2 ⓚ = to be
cut

き+

キロ *noun*
- = kilogram
- = kilometre

きろく・記録 *noun* = record

キログラム *noun* = kilogram

キロメートル *noun* = kilometre

ぎろん・議論
**1** *noun* = argument
**2** *verb 3* ㊧ ぎろんする = to argue

きん・金 *noun* = gold

きん・菌 ▶ばいきん

ぎん・銀 *noun* = silver

きんえん・禁煙 *noun* = no smoking

きんがく・金額 *noun* = amount (of money)

きんきゅう(の)・緊急(の) *adjective* = urgent

きんぎょ・金魚 *noun* = goldfish

きんこう・近郊 *noun* = suburbs

ぎんこう・銀行 *noun* = bank

きんし・禁止
**1** *noun* = prohibition
**2** *verb 3* ㊧ きんしする = to forbid

きんじょ・近所 *noun* = neighbourhood

きんせん・金銭 *noun* = money

きんぞく・金属 *noun* = metal

きんだい・近代
**1** *noun* = the modern age
**2** *adjective* きんだいの = modern

きんだいてき(な)・近代的な *adjective* = modern

きんちょう・緊張
**1** *noun* = tension
**2** *verb 3* ㊧ きんちょうする = to feel nervous

きんにく・筋肉 *noun* = muscle

きんべん(な)・勤勉(な) *adjective* = diligent

きんゆう・金融 *noun* = finance

きんようび・金曜日 *noun* = Friday

きんろうかんしゃのひ・勤労感謝の日 *noun* – Labor Thanksgiving Day (November 23) – a Japanese public holiday

# くク

く・九 *noun* = nine ▶ **181**

ぐあい・具合 *noun* = condition

くいき・区域 *noun* = zone

くう・食う *verb 1* ㊧ = to eat

くうき・空気 *noun* = air

くうこう・空港 *noun* = airport

ぐうすう・偶数 *noun* = even number

ぐうぜん・偶然
**1** *adjective* ぐうぜん(の) = (by) chance
**2** *adverb* ぐうぜんに
- = by chance
- = by coincidence

くうそう・空想
**1** *noun* = fantasy
**1** *verb 3* ㊧ くうそうする = to imagine

くうちゅう(の)・空中(の) *adjective* = mid-air

クーラー *noun* = air conditioning

くかん・区間 *noun* = section

くぎ・釘 *noun* = nail

くぎる・区切る *verb 1* ㊧ = to divide (off)

くさ・草 *noun* = grass

くさい・臭い *adjective* = bad smelling

くさり・鎖 *noun* = chain

くさる・腐る *verb 1* ㊦ = to rot

くし *noun* = comb

くしゃみ
**1** *noun* = sneeze
**1** *verb 3* ㊦ くしゃみを する = to sneeze

くじょう・苦情 *noun* = complaint

くしん・苦心
**1** *noun* = effort
**1** *verb 3* ㊦ くしんする = to take pains (over)

くず・屑 *noun* = waste

くすぐったい *adjective*
• = ticklish
• = it tickles!

くすぐる *verb 1* を = to tickle

くずす・崩す *verb 1* を = to break down

くすり・薬 *noun*
• = medicine
• = chemicals

くずれる・崩れる *verb 2* か = to break down

くせ・癖 *noun* = habit
　くせに = in spite of

くだ・管 *noun* = pipe

ぐたいてき・具体的
**1** *adjective* ぐたいてき（な）
　= concrete
**2** *adverb* ぐたいてきに = concretely

くだく・砕く *verb 1* を = to pulverise

くだける・砕ける *verb 2* か = to be crushed

ください・下さい – *added to the* ～て *form of a verb it means 'please (do)' and when following an object marked with* を *it means 'please give me'. Following the ending* ～ないで *it means 'please don't (do)'* ▶ **197**

くださる・下さる *verb 1* を = to give

**!** *honorific verb which often follows the* ～て *form of another verb to show that an action has been done for the benefit of speaker by someone of higher status.* ▶ **vii,** ▶ **vii**

くたびれる *verb 2* か = to become tired

くだもの・果物 *noun* = fruit

くだらない *adjective* = worthless

くだり・下り *noun* = descent

くだりざか・下り坂 *noun* = downward slope

くだる・下る *verb 1* か = to descend

くち・口 *noun* = mouth

ぐち・愚痴 *noun* = complaint

くちびる・唇 *noun* = lip

くちべに・口紅 *noun* = lipstick

くつ・靴 *noun* = shoes

くつう・苦痛 *noun* = pain

くつした・靴下 *noun* = socks

くっつく *verb 1* か に = to be stuck

くっつける *verb 2* を = to stick

ぐっすり *adverb* = deeply (asleep)

くどい *adjective*
• = insistent
• = tedious

くとうてん・句読点 *noun –*
*Japanese punctuation marks.*
　▶ くてん ▶ とうてん

くに・国 *noun* = country

**!** *used not only in the sense of 'nation' but of also of the place where your family home is situated. Japanese people talk of* くに *in the sense of 'home country' when referring to non-Japanese and in the sense of 'home region' when referring to other Japanese*

くばる・配る *verb 1* を = to distribute

くび・首 *noun* = neck
（くびに なる）= to be fired

くふう・工夫
**1** *noun*
• = trick
• = method
**2** *verb 3* を くふうする = to devise

くべつ・区別
**1** *noun* = distinction
**2** *verb 3* を くべつする = to distinguish (between)

くみ・組み *noun*
• = group

**!** *as a suffix it can mean (school) class*

くみあい・組合 *noun*
• = trade union
• = labor union

くみあわせ・組み合わせ *noun*
= combination

くみたてる・組み立てる
*verb 2* を = to assemble

くむ・組む verb 1 ⍏ = to cross (arms or legs)

くむ・汲む・酌む verb 1 ⍏ = to scoop

くも・雲 noun = cloud

くも・蜘蛛 noun = spider

くもり・曇り noun = cloudy weather

くもる・曇る verb 1 ⍏ = to cloud over

くやしい・悔しい adjective
• = mortifying
• = regrettable

くやむ・悔やむ verb 1 ⍏ = to feel vexed by

くらい・暗い adjective = dark

くらい・位 ▶ ぐらい

ぐらい noun = approximately

くらし・暮らし noun = way of life

クラシック noun = classical music

くらす・暮らす verb 1 ⍏ = to live

クラス noun = class (at school)

グラス noun = glass (for drinking)

クラブ noun = club

グラフ noun = graph

くらべる・比べる verb 2 ⍏ = to compare

グラム noun = gram(me)

クリーニング noun = dry cleaning

クリーニングや・クリーニング屋 noun = dry cleaner

クリーム noun = cream

くりかえす・繰り返す verb 1 ⍏ = to repeat

クリスマス noun = Christmas

クリック verb = to click (a mouse)

くる・来る verb 3 ⍏ きて・こない・きます = to come ▶ **191**, ▶ **204**

くるう・狂う verb 1 ⍏ = to go mad

グループ noun = group

くるしい・苦しい adjective = painful

くるしむ・苦しむ verb 1 ⍏ = to suffer

くるしめる・苦しめる verb 2 ⍏ = to cause suffering

くるま・車 noun
• = car
• = vehicle

くるまいす・車椅子 noun = wheelchair

くるむ・包む verb 1 ⍏ = to wrap

くれ・暮れ noun = end of the year

グレー
**1** noun = grey
**2** adjective グレー(の) = grey

くれぐれも adverb
• = please
• = sincerely

> ! used to indicate sincerity in formal requests

クレジットカード noun = credit card

くれます ▶ くれる

くれる verb 2 ⍏ くれて・くれない・くれます
• = to give
• = to be given

> ! meaning 'given to the speaker' it is often added to the 〜て form of a preceding verb to indicate that the action was done for the speaker's benefit by somebody else ▶ あげる ▶ **179**, ▶ **197**

くれる・暮れる verb 2 ⍏ = to draw to a close

くろ・黒 noun = black

くろい・黒い adjective = black

くろう・苦労
**1** noun = difficulty
**2** verb 3 ⍏ くろうする = to work hard

くろうと・玄人 noun = specialist

くわえる・加える verb 2 ⍏ = to add

くわえる・咥える verb 2 ⍏ = to hold (in the mouth)

くわしい・詳しい adjective
• = detailed
• = knowledgeable

くわわる・加わる verb 1 ⍏ に = to join

くん・訓 ▶くんよみ

くん・君 *suffix* – added to family names of males to form a title. Commonly used in schools by a teacher as a way of addressing boys or in companies by bosses to address junior staff. It is sometimes used with women's names in large companies. Also used between male friends.

ぐん・群 *noun* = county

ぐん・軍 *noun* = army

ぐんたい・軍隊 *noun* = troops

くんよみ・訓読み *noun* – the reading assigned to a かんじ character in Japanese usage (typically as a noun or root of a word) ▶おんよみ ▶vii

くんれん・訓練
1 *noun* = training
2 *verb 3* ㊙ くんれんする = to practise

# けケ

け・毛 *noun*
• = hair
• = wool

け・家 *suffix* = family

げ・下 *noun* = lowest grade

げ・気 *suffix* – added to adjective stems it means 'seemingly ...'

ケアラ *noun* = carer

けい・計 *noun*
• = total
• = plan

げい・芸 *noun* = skill

けいい・敬意 *noun* = respect

けいい・経緯 *noun* = circumstances

けいえい・経営
1 *noun* = management
2 *verb 3* ㊙ けいえいする = to manage

けいえいしゃ・経営者 *noun* = manager

けいかく・計画
1 *noun* = plan
2 *verb 3* ㊙ けいかくする = to plan

けいかん・警官 *noun* = police officer

けいき・景気 *noun* – the climate for doing business or the 'general economic situation'.

けいぐ・敬具 *noun* – used to end a formal letter and so roughly equivalent to 'yours sincerely' ▶はいけい

けいけん・経験
1 *noun* = experience
2 *verb 3* ㊙ けいけんする = to experience

けいこ・稽古
1 *noun* = practice
2 *verb 3* ㊙ けいこする = to practice

けいご・敬語 *noun* – polite forms of language used to indicate respect ▶189

けいこう・傾向 *noun* = tendency

けいこう・蛍光 *prefix* = florescent

けいこく・警告
1 *noun* = warning
2 *verb 3* ㊙ けいこくする = to warn

けいざい・経済 *noun* = (the) economy

けいざいがく・経済学 *noun* = economics (academic subject)

けいさつ・警察 *noun* = police

けいさつかん・警察官 *noun* = police officer

けいさん・計算
1 *noun* = calculation
2 *verb 3* ㊙ けいさんする = to calculate

けいさんき・計算機 *noun* = calculator

けいじ・刑事 *noun* = detective

けいじ(する)・掲示する(する) *verb 3* ㊙ = to put up a notice

けいじばん・掲示板 *noun* = notice board

けいしき・形式 *noun* = formality

**けいしきてき・形式的**
**1** *adjective* けいしきてき(な)
= superficial
**2** *adverb* けいしきてきに = as a formality

**げいじゅつ・芸術** *noun* = the arts

**けいぞく・継続**
**1** *noun* = continuation
**2** *verb 3* ⓐ ⓟ けいぞくする = to continue

**けいたい(する)・携帯(する)**
*verb 3* ⓐ = to carry around

**けいたいでんわ・携帯電話**
*noun* = mobile phone

**けいと・毛糸** *noun* = wool

**けいとう・系統** *noun*
• = system
• = lineage

**けいとうてき・系統的**
**1** *adjective* けいとうてき(な)
= systematic
**2** *adverb* けいとうてきに
= systematically

**げいのうかい・芸能界** *noun*
= show business world

**げいのうじん・芸能人** *noun*
= show business personality

**けいば・競馬** *noun* = horse racing

**けいばじょう・競馬場** *noun*
= horse race track

**けいひ・経費** *noun* = expenses

**けいび・警備**
**1** *noun* = defence
**2** *verb 3* ⓐ けいびする = to guard

**けいべつ・軽蔑**
**1** *noun* = contempt
**2** *verb 3* ⓐ けいべつする = to look down on (somebody)

**けいやく・契約** *noun* = contract

**けいゆ・経由** *suffix* = via

**けいようし・形容詞** *noun*
= adjective

**けいようどうし・形容動詞**
*noun*
▶ *a part of speech often called* な *adjectives*

**けいれき・経歴** *noun* = career history

**けいろうのひ・敬老の日** *noun* –
*Respect for the Aged Day (September 15) – a Japanese public holiday*

**ケーキ** *noun* = (western style) cake

**ケーキや・ケーキ屋** *noun*
= (western style) cake shop

**ケース** *noun* = case

**ゲーム** *noun* = game

**けが・怪我**
**1** *noun* = injury
**2** *verb 3* ⓟ に けが(を)する = to be injured

**げか・外科** *noun* = surgery

**けがわ・毛皮** *noun* = fur

**げき・劇** *noun* = drama

**げきじょう・劇場** *noun* = theatre

**げこう・下校**
**1** *noun* = leaving school
**2** *verb 3* ⓟ げこうする = to go home from school

**けさ・今朝** *noun* = this morning

**けしき・景色** *noun* = scenery

**けしゴム・消しゴム** *noun* = eraser

**げしゃ(する)・下車(する)**
*verb 3* ⓟ
• = to get off (a train or bus)
• = to get out of (a vehicle)

**げじゅん・下旬** *noun* – *the last ten days of the month which can often be translated as 'towards the end of the month'*

**けしょう・化粧**
**1** *noun* = makeup
**2** *verb 3* ⓟ けしょう(を)する = to put on makeup

**けしょうひん・化粧品** *noun*
= cosmetics

**けす・消す** *verb 1* ⓐ
• = to put out
• = to turn off

**げすい・下水** *noun* = sewage

**けずる・削る** *verb 1* ⓐ
• = to shave bits off
• = to sharpen

**けた・桁** *suffix* – *when attached to a number it indicates how many digits there are*

**げた・下駄** *noun – Japanese traditional wooden shoes*

**けち(な)** *adjective* = mean

**けつあつ・血圧** *noun* = blood pressure

**けつえき・血液** *noun* = blood

**けっか・結果** *noun* = result

**けっかん・欠陥** *noun* = defect

**げっきゅう・月給** *noun* = monthly salary

**けっきょく・結局** *adverb* = in the end

**けっこう(な)・結構(な)** *adjectival noun* = good

> **!** *sometimes used to express 'quite/very' with adjectives. When used in the expression* けっこうです *it shows refusal of an invitation or (when accompanied by appropriate gesture or context) acceptance. The phrase* (いいえ) もうけっこうです *means 'I have had sufficient'.*

**けっこん・結婚**
1 *noun* = marriage
2 *verb 3* と けっこんする = to marry

**けっこんしき・結婚式** *noun* = wedding ceremony

**けっさく・傑作** *noun* = masterpiece

**けっして・決して** *adverb* (*with negative*) = utterly (not)

**けっしん・決心**
1 *noun* = decision
2 *verb 3* を けっしんする = to resolve (to do)

**けっせき・欠席**
1 *noun* = absence
2 *verb 3* を けっせきする = to be absent (from school etc.)

**けってい・決定**
1 *noun* = decision
2 *verb 3* が を に けっていする = to decide

**けってん・欠点** *noun*
• = weak point
• = minus point

**げつまつ・月末** *noun* = the end of the month

**げつようび・月曜日** *noun* = Monday

**けつろん・結論** *noun* = conclusion

**けはい・気配** *noun* = indication

**げひん(な)・下品(な)** *adjective* = vulgar

**けむい・煙い** *adjective* = smoky

**けむり・煙** *noun* = smoke

**げり・下痢** *noun* = diarrhoea

**ける・蹴る** *verb 1* を = to kick

**けれど(も)** *conjunction* = however
• = but

**けわしい・険しい** *adjective* = steep

**けん・件** *noun* = incident

**けん・県** *noun – Japan is divided into administrative regions which are called 'prefectures' in English and are similar to 'states' or 'counties'*

**けん・券** *noun* = ticket

**けん・軒** *counter* = houses ▶ **181**

**げん・現** *prefix* = current

**げんいん・原因** *noun* = cause

**けんお・嫌悪** *noun* = hatred

**けんか・喧嘩**
1 *noun*
• = quarrel
• = fight
2 *verb 3* と けんかする
• = to argue
• = to fight

**けんかい・見解** *noun* = opinion

**げんかい・限界** *noun* = limit

**けんがく・見学**
1 *noun* = educational visit
2 *verb 3* を けんがくする = to visit (for the purpose of learning about)

**げんかん・玄関** *noun – the entrance to a Japanese house which is a small hallway where shoes are left before stepping up into the house itself. The word is also used in the sense of 'front door'*

**げんき・元気**
1 *noun* = energy

**2** *adjective* **げんき(な)**
- = energetic
- = healthy

**3** *adverb* **げんきに** = spiritedly
（お）げんきですか = How are you?
げんきです = I'm fine

**けんきゅう・研究**
**1** *noun* = research
**2** *verb 3* 🈡 の けんきゅう(を)する
= to research

**けんきゅうしゃ・研究者** *noun*
= researcher

**けんきゅうせい・研究生** *noun*
= research student

**けんきょ・謙虚**
**1** *noun* = modesty
**2** *adjective* **けんきょ(な)** = modest

**げんきん・現金** *noun* = cash

**げんご・言語** *noun* = language/s

**げんごがく・言語学** *noun*
= linguistics

**けんこう・健康** *noun* = health

**けんこうてき・健康的**
**1** *adjective* **けんこうてき(な)**
= healthy
**2** *adverb* **けんこうてきに**
= healthily

**げんこうようし・原稿用紙**
*noun – squared writing paper used for
writing Japanese vertically*

**けんこくきねんび・建国記念日**
*noun – National Foundation Day
(February 11) – a Japanese public
holiday*

**けんさ・検査**
**1** *noun* = inspection
**2** *verb 3* 🈡 けんさする = to test

**げんざい・現在**
**1** *noun* = (at the) present time
**2** *adjective* **げんざいの** = present

**けんさく・検索**
**1** *noun* = reference, retrieval
**2** *verb 3* 🈡 = retrieve, search (*generally
and on Internet*)

**げんし・原子** *noun* = atom

**げんしばくだん・原子爆弾**
*noun* = atomic bomb

**げんしてき(な)・原始的(な)**
*adjective* = primitive

**けんじつ・堅実**
**1** *adjective* **けんじつ(な)** = steady
**2** *adverb* **けんじつに** = steadily

**げんじつ・現実**
**1** *noun* = reality
**2** *adjective* **げんじつの** = real

**げんじつてき・げんじつてき**
**1** *adjective* **げんじつてき(な)**
= realistic
**2** *adverb* **げんじつてきに**
= realistically

**けんしゅう・研修**
**1** *noun* = training
**2** *verb 3* 🈡 の けんしゅうをする
= to study

**けんしゅうせい・研修生** *noun*
= trainee

**げんじゅう・厳重**
**1** *adjective* **げんじゅう(な)** = strict
**2** *adverb* **げんじゅうに** = strictly

**げんしょう・現象** *noun*
= phenomenon

**げんじょう・現状** *noun* = current
situation

**げんしりょく・原子力** *noun*
= nuclear power

**げんしろ・原子炉** *noun* = nuclear
reactor

**けんせつ・建設**
**1** *noun* = construction
**2** *verb 3* 🈡 けんせつする = to build

**げんぞう・現像**
**1** *noun* = developing (of pictures)
**2** *verb 3* 🈡 げんぞうする = to
develop (photographs)

**げんそく・原則** *noun* = principle
（げんそくとして）= generally

**けんそん・謙遜**
**1** *noun* = humility
**2** *adjective* **けんそん(な)** = modest
**3** *verb 3* 🈬 に けんそんする = to
behave humbly towards

**げんだい・現代**
**1** *noun* = the present day
**2** *adjective* **げんだいの**
= contemporary

**けんちく・建築**
**1** *noun*

• = construction
• = architecture
**2** *verb 3* ㊰ けんちくする = to construct

けんちくし・建築士 *noun*
= architect

けんちょう・県庁 *noun* – the office of Japanese prefectural government and figuratively 'local government' ▶ けん

げんど・限度 *noun* = limit

けんとう・見当 *noun* = estimate
けんとうを つける = to guess
けんとうが つかない = I have no idea

けんとう・検討
**1** *noun* = investigation
**2** *verb 3* ㊰ けんとうする = to investigate

げんに・現に *adverb* = actually

げんば・現場 *noun* = scene (of an event)

げんばく・原爆 *noun* = nuclear explosion

けんびきょう・顕微鏡 *noun* = microscope

けんぶつ・見物
**1** *noun* = sightseeing
**2** *verb 3* ㊰ けんぶつする = to sightsee

けんぽう・憲法 *noun* = constitution

けんぽうきねんび・憲法記念日 *noun* – Constitution Memorial Day (March 3$^{rd}$) – a Japanese public holiday

けんめい・懸命
**1** *adjective* けんめい(な) = diligent
**2** *adverb* けんめいに = hard

けんり・権利 *noun* = right/s

げんり・原理 *noun* = principle

けんりつ・県立 *prefix* – established by the prefectural government ▶ けん

げんりょう・原料 *noun* = natural resources

# こコ

こ・子 *noun* = child

こ・小 *prefix* = small

こ・個 *counter* – used for counting small, rounded things such as pieces of fruit ▶ 181

こ・粉 *noun*
• = flour
• = powder

ご・五 *noun* = five ▶ 181

ご・語 *noun* = word

ご・語 *suffix* – added to the name of a country to indicate the language spoken there or attached to the names of languages ▶ 172

ご・後 *suffix* = after

ご・碁 *noun* – a Japanese board game

ご・御 *prefix* – added to certain words made up of Chinese characters (sometimes those with some connection to a respected person) it shows politeness ▶ 189

こい・濃い *adjective*
• = thick
• (of colours) = dark
• (of drinks) = strong

こい・恋
**1** *noun* = love
**1** *verb 3* ㊰ に こい(を)する = to be in love with

こい・鯉 *noun* = carp

ごい・語彙 *noun* = vocabulary

こいしい・恋しい *adjective* = dear

こいびと・恋人 *noun*
• = boyfriend
• = girlfriend

こう *adverb*
• = this way
• = like this
こうすると = if this is done then ...
こうして = in this way ▶ こういう

こう・高 *prefix* = high

こう・校 *suffix* = school

こう・港 *suffix* = harbour

ごう・号 *suffix* – added to numbers to mean 'issue number ...' of a magazine

こうい・行為 *noun* = behaviour

ごうい・合意
**1** *noun* = agreement
**2** *verb 3* ⓝ に ごういする = to agree

こういう *attributive* = this kind of

こういん・工員 *noun* = factory worker

ごういん・強引
**1** *adjective* ごういん(な) = pushy
**2** *adverb* ごういんに = forcibly

こううん・幸運 *noun* = good luck

こうえん・公園 *noun*
• = park
• = playground

こうえん・講演 *noun*
• = lecture
• = performance

こうか・効果 *noun* = effect

こうか・硬貨 *noun* = coin

こうか (な)・高価 (な) *adjective* = expensive

ごうか(な)・豪華(な) *adjective* = magnificent

こうかい・後悔
**1** *noun* = regret
**2** *verb 3* ⓦ こうかいする = to regret

こうがい・郊外 *noun* = suburbs

こうがい・公害 *noun*
• = pollution
• = environmental damage

こうがく・工学 *noun* = engineering

ごうかく・合格
**1** *noun* = pass (in an exam)
**2** *verb 3* ⓝ に ごうかくする = to pass an exam

こうかてき・効果的
**1** *adjective* こうかてき(な) = effective
**2** *adverb* こうかてきに = effectively

こうかん・交換
**1** *noun* = exchange
**2** *verb 3* ⓦ こうかんする = to exchange

こうき・後期 *noun*
• = second half of the year
• = second semester

こうぎ・講義 *noun* = lecture

こうぎ・抗議
**1** *noun* = protest
**2** *verb 3* ⓝ こうぎする = to protest

こうきゅう(な)・高級 (な) *adjective* = high-quality

こうきょう・公共 *noun* = (the) public

こうぎょう・工業 *noun* = industry

こうくうがいしゃ・航空会社 *noun* = airline

こうくうけん・航空券 *noun* = plane ticket

こうくうびん・航空便 *noun* = airmail

こうけい・光景 *noun* = scene

こうげい・工芸 *noun* = craft

ごうけい・合計 *noun* = total

こうげき・攻撃
**1** *noun* = attack
**2** *verb 3* ⓦ こうげきする = to attack

こうけん・貢献
**1** *noun*
• = contribution
• = donation
**1** *verb 3* ⓦ に こうけんする = to contribute
• = to donate

こうこう・高校 *noun* = senior high school ▶ **185**

こうこう・孝行 *noun and adjective* (な) – being obedient to one's parents and behaving in a dutiful manner towards them

こうこがく・考古学 *noun* = archaeology

こうこく・広告
**1** *noun*
• = advertisement (in newspaper etc.)
• = advertising
**2** *verb 3* ⓦ こうこくする = to advertise

こうさ・交差
**1** *noun* = intersection

**2** *verb 3* ⓐ と こうさする = to intersect

**こうさい・交際**
**1** *noun* = acquaintance (with)
**2** *verb 3* ⓐ と こうさいする = to associate with

**こうさてん・交差点** *noun* = crossroads

**こうし・講師** *noun* = lecturer

**こうじ・工事**
**1** *noun* = construction work
**1** *verb 3* ⓐ こうじする = to be worked on

**こうしき・公式**
**1** *adjective* こうしきの
• = formal
• = official
**2** *adverb* こうしきに
• = officially
• = formally

**こうしきてき・公式的**
**1** *adjective* こうしきてき(な)
= official
**2** *adverb* こうしきてき(に)
= officially

**こうじちゅう・工事中** *noun*
• = under construction
• = under repair

**こうじつ・口実** *noun* = excuse

**こうして** *adverb*
• = like this
• = in this way

**こうしゃ・後者** *noun* = the latter

**こうしゃ・校舎** *noun* = school building

**こうしゅう・公衆**
**1** *noun* = the public
**2** *adjective* こうしゅうの = public

**こうしゅうでんわ・公衆電話** *noun* = public telephone

**こうしゅうべんじょ・公衆便所** *noun* = public toilet

**こうじょう・工場** *noun* = factory

**こうすい・香水** *noun* = perfume

**こうずい・洪水** *noun* = flood

**こうせい・公正**
**1** *noun* = justice
**2** *adjective* こうせいの = fair
**3** *adverb* こうせいに = fairly

**こうせい・構成**
**1** *noun* = structure
**2** *verb 3* ⓐ こうせいする = to make up

**こうせき・功績** *noun* = achievement

**こうせん・光線** *noun* = beam of light

**こうそうビル・高層ビル** *noun* = high rise building

**こうぞう・構造** *noun*
• = structure
• = construction

**こうそくどうろ・高速道路** *noun* = expressway

**こうたい・交代・交替**
**1** *noun*
• = alternation
• = (factory) shift
**2** *verb 3* ⓐ こうたいする
• = to take turns
• = to swap

**こうち・耕地** *noun* = arable land

**こうちゃ・紅茶** *noun* = tea

> ❗ *this refers to black tea (with or without milk) in contrast to Japanese teas such as green tea* ▶ おちゃ

**こうつう・交通** *noun*
• = transport
• = traffic

**こうつうあんぜん・交通安全** *noun* = road safety

**こうつういはん・交通違反** *noun* = traffic offence

**こうつうきかん・交通機関** *noun* = transportation system

**こうつうじゅうたい・交通渋滞** *noun* = traffic jam

**こうつうひ・交通費** *noun* = travel expenses

**こうてい・校庭** *noun* = school grounds

**こうてい・肯定**
**1** *noun* = affirmation
**2** *verb 3* ⓔ こうていする = to affirm

**こうど・高度**
**1** *noun* = altitude
**2** *adjective* こうど(な) = high level

**こうとう(な)・高等(な)**
adjective = advanced

**こうどう・行動**
1 noun = behaviour
2 verb 3 ㊍ こうどうする = to behave

**こうどう・講堂** noun
= auditorium

**ごうとう・強盗** noun
• = robbery
• = robber

**こうとうがっこう・高等学校**
noun = senior high school

**こうどく・購読**
1 noun = subscription
2 verb 3 ㊥ に こうどくする = to subscribe

**こうにゅう・購入**
1 noun = purchase
2 verb 3 ㊥ こうにゅうする = to purchase

**こうはい・後輩** noun – a junior person (in comparison to a specific senior) in either an educational establishment or the workplace
▶ せんぱい

**こうはん・後半** noun = second half (of a match etc.)

**こうばん・交番** noun – a 'police box' (substation) where police officers are stationed

**こうひょう・公表**
1 noun = (official) announcement
2 verb 3 ㊥ こうひょうする = to announce

**こうふく・幸福** noun = happiness

**こうぶつ・鉱物** noun = mineral

**こうふん・興奮**
1 noun = excitement
2 verb 3 ㊍ こうふんする = to be excited

**こうへい・公平**
1 noun = fairness
2 adjective こうへい(な) = fair
3 adverb こうへいに = fairly

**こうほしゃ・候補者** noun
= candidate

**こうむいん・公務員** noun – this term refers to people working for national or local government

**こうもく・項目** noun = item

**こうよう・紅葉** noun – the period or phenomenon of the leaves changing colour in autumn|fall. One of the tourist season highlights in Japan.

**こうりつ(の)・公立 (の)**
adjectival noun = public

**こうりつ・効率** noun = efficiency

**ごうりてき・合理的**
1 adjective ごうりてき(な) = reasonable
2 adverb ごうりてきに = rationally

**こうりゅう・交流** noun
= interchange (between countries)

**ごうりゅう(する)・合流(する)**
verb 3 ㊍ = to merge

**こうりょ・考慮**
1 noun = consideration
2 verb 3 ㊥ こうりょする = to consider

**こうりょく・効力** noun
こうりょくの ある = valid
こうりょくの ない = invalid

**こえ・声** noun
• (people) = voice
• (birds and animals) = cry

**こえる・超える** verb 2 ㊍
• = to exceed

**こえる・越える** verb 2 ㊍
• = to go over

**ごえんりょなく・ご遠慮なく**
phrase – used to urge people to accept something or do something and meaning something like 'please feel free to ...'

**コース** noun = course

**コーチ** noun = coach

**コート** noun = coat

**コード** noun = electrical wire

**コーヒー** noun = coffee

**こおり・氷** noun = ice

**こおる・凍る** verb 1 ㊍ = to freeze

**ゴール** noun = goal

**コールセンター** noun = call centre

**ごかい・誤解**
1 noun = misunderstanding
2 verb 3 ㊥ ごかいする = to misinterpret

ごがく・語学 *noun* = (the study of) languages

こがす・焦がす *verb 1* 㪍 = to burn

こがた (の)・小型 (の) *adjectival noun* = small sized

こぎって・小切手 *noun* = cheque

こきゅう・呼吸
**1** *noun* = breathing
**2** *verb 3* 㪍 㪎 こきゅうする = to breathe

こきょう・故郷 *noun* = home (town)

こぐ・漕ぐ *verb 1* 㪍
• = to pedal
• = to row

ごく・極 *adverb* = extremely

こくご・国語 *noun*
• = the Japanese language
• = Japanese classes in Japanese school

こくごじてん・国語辞典 *noun* = Japanese-Japanese dictionary

こくさい・国際 *prefix* = international

こくさいか・国際化 *noun* = internationalisation

こくさいこうりゅう・国際交流 *noun* = international relations

こくさいてき・国際的
**1** *adjective* こくさいてき(な) = international
**2** *adverb* こくさいてきに = internationally

こくせき・国籍 *noun* = nationality

こくばん・黒板 *noun* = blackboard

こくふく(する)・克服(する) *verb 3* 㪍 = to conquer

こくみん・国民 *noun* = citizens of a country

こくみんのきゅうじつ・国民の休日 *noun* – Nation's day (May 4) – a Japanese public holiday

こくもつ・穀物 *noun* = cereal (crops)

こくりつ・国立 *prefix* = national

こくりつこうえん・国立公園 *noun* = national park

こくれん・国連 *noun* = the United Nations

ごくろうさま (でした)・ご苦労様(でした) *phrase* – used to thank someone for their work and used to someone who is leaving the workplace in place of 'thank you' and 'goodbye'. Not used to superiors

こげる・焦げる *verb 2* 㪎 = to be burnt

ここ *noun* = here

ごご・午後 *noun*
• = afternoon
• = p.m.

ここのか・九日 *noun*
• = the ninth day of the month
• = nine days ▶ **174**

ここのつ・九つ *noun* = nine ▶ **181**

こころ・心 *noun*
• = heart
• = mind

こころあたり・心当たり *noun*
こころあたりが ある = to have an idea of
こころあたりが ない = to have no idea of

こころえる・心得る *verb 2* 㪍 = to be aware of

こころみる・試みる *verb 1* 㪍 と = to attempt

こころよい・快い *adjective* = pleasant

ございます・御座います *phrase* – following the particle で it is used as an honorific equivalent of です and it is used on its own as an equivalent of ある and いる as well as in certain everyday expressions. ▶ **189**

ござる・御座る *verb 1* 㪎 ございます・ございません – an honorific substitute for です, ある and いる ▶ ございます note that there is no 〜て form and no plain negative for this verb ▶ **189**

こし・腰 *noun*
• = lower back
• = hips

こしが いたい = (to have) backache

こしを かけてください = please sit down

こしかけ・腰掛け *noun* = seat

こしかける・腰掛ける *verb 2* ㋕ に = to sit down

ごじゅうおん・五十音 *noun* – the chart of the かな syllabic scripts which is used as the Japanese equivalent of 'alphabetic' order in lists and dictionaries (such as this one) etc.

こしょう・故障
**1** *noun* = breakdown
**2** *verb 3* ㋕ こしょうする = to be not working

こしょう・胡椒 *noun* = pepper

こしらえる・拵える *verb 2* ㋔ = to make

こじん・個人 *noun* = individual

こじんてき・個人的
**1** *adjective* こじんてき(な) = personal
**2** *adverb* こじんてきに = personally

こす・越す *verb 1* ㋔ = to go over

こす・超す *verb 1* ㋔ = to exceed

こする・擦る *verb 1* ㋔ = to rub

こせき・戸籍 *noun* – the family register kept by local government which records births, marriages and deaths. A certified copy of the family register is used to prove identity.

こぜに・小銭 *noun* = small change

ごぜん・午前 *noun* = (in the) morning

ごぜんちゅう・午前中 *noun*
= morning
• = during the morning

ごぞんじ・ご存知 *phrase* – usually in the form ごぞんじですか this is a polite equivalent of しる and means 'do you know?' ▶ **189**

こたい・固体
**1** *noun* = solid
**2** *adjective* こたいの = solid

こたえ・答え *noun* = answer

こたえる・答える *verb 2* ㋕ に こたえて・こたえない・こたえます = to answer

ごちそう・ご馳走
**1** *noun* = treat
**2** *verb 3* ㋔ に ごちそうする = to treat

! *usually used for meals and other entertainments*

ごちそうさま・ご馳走様 *phrase* – most commonly in the form ごちそうさまでした which is the phrase said at the conclusion of a meal and as a way of thanking someone for entertainment or a treat

こちら *noun*
• = here
• = this direction
• = this person
• = this thing

こちらこそ *phrase* – used to respond to expressions of thanks with the sense of 'not at all' and meaning that on the contrary it is you who should be expressing thanks

こっか・国家 *noun* = nation

こっかい・国会 *noun* = the (Japanese) parliament

こづかい・小遣い *noun* = pocket money

こっきょう・国境 *noun* = (international) border

コック *noun* = chef

こっせつ・骨折
**1** *noun*
• = break
• = fracture
**2** *verb 3* ㋔ こっせつする = to break (a bone)

こっそり(と) *adverb* = secretly

こっち *noun* – a less formal version of こちら

こづつみ・小包 *noun*
• = parcel
• = package

コップ *noun* = glass (for drinking)

こてん・古典 *noun* – *while meaning 'classics' in a general sense it often refers to the major works of classical Japanese literature*

こてんてき(な)・古典的(な) *adjective* = classical

こと・事 *noun*
• = thing
• = matter
• = incident
　　～ことが ある = have done ...
　　～ことが できる = can ...
　　～ことに なる = to be scheduled to ...
　　～ことに する = decide to ...

> ! *when it occurs as a modifying phrase in the forms listed above it is attached to a verb which will determine the translation.*

こと・琴 *noun* – *a traditional Japanese stringed musical instrument*

ごと *suffix* = every other

ことし・今年 *noun* = this year

ことづけ・言付け *noun* = message left in someone's absence

ことづて・言づて・言伝 *noun* = message

ことなる・異なる *verb 1* ⓚ = to be different

ことに・殊に *adverb* = especially

ことば・言葉 *noun*
• = word/s
• = language

ことばづかい・言葉づかい *noun* = choice of words

こども・子ども・子供 *noun*
• = child
• = children

こどもたち・子供たち・子供達 *noun* = children

こどものひ・子供の日 *noun* – *Children's Day (May 5) – a Japanese public holiday*

ことわざ・諺 *noun* = proverb

ことわる・断る *verb 1* ⓚ
• = to refuse

> ! *in the form* ことわっておく *it means 'get permission in advance'.*

こな・粉 *noun*
• = flour
• = powder

こない・来ない ▶ くる

この *attributive* = this

このあいだ *phrase*
• = recently
• = the other day
• = last time

このごろ *phrase* = recently

このたび・この度 *phrase*
• = this time
• = last time

このつぎ・この次 *phrase* = next (time)

このまえ・この前 *phrase* = previously

このましい・好ましい *adjective* = desirable

このまま *phrase* = as it is (now)

このみ・好み *noun* = taste

このむ・好む *verb 1* ⓚ = to like

ごはん・ご飯・御飯 *noun*
• = (cooked) rice
• = meal

コピー
**1** *noun* = (photo)copy
**2** *verb 3* ⓚ コピーする = to (photo)copy

コピーき・コピー機 *noun* = photocopier

ごぶさた・ご無沙汰 *noun* – *used in the form* ごぶさた しています *which means '(sorry) I have not written/been in contact for a long time'*

こぼす・零す *verb 1* ⓚ = to spill

こぼれる・零れる *verb 2* ⓚ = to be spilled

こまかい・細かい *adjective*
• = very small
• (*of money*) = small change
• = detailed

こまる・困る *verb 1* ⓚ こまって・こまらない・こまります = to be in an awkward situation

> ! *in the form* こまったね *it means either 'that's terrible, what are you going to do?' or 'what shall I do?'*

**ごみ・ゴミ** *noun*
- = rubbish
- = garbage

**ごみばこ・ごみ箱** *noun*
- = rubbish bin
- = garbage can

**コミュニケーション** *noun*
= communication

**こむ・込む・混む** *verb 1* 㕥
  こんで・こまない・こみます
= to be crowded
  **みちが こんでいる** = the traffic is
  heavy

**ゴム** *noun* = rubber

**こむぎ・小麦** *noun* = wheat

**こむぎこ・小麦粉** *noun* = flour

**こめ・米** *noun* = (uncooked) rice

**ごめん・御免** *phrase – informal*
*equivalent of* ごめんなさい

**ごめんください・御免下さい**
*phrase – used on entry to the* げんか
ん *of a house and equivalent to*
*'excuse me is there anyone at home?'.*
*Also used to attract the attention of a*
*clerk in a shop if nobody seems to be*
*around.*

**ごめんなさい・御免なさい**
*phrase – meaning 'sorry' it is used as*
*both an apology and as a refusal of a*
*request*

**こや・小屋** *noun*
- = hut
- = shed

**こゆび・小指** *noun* = little finger

**こよう・雇用**
**1** *noun* = employment
**1** *verb 3* 㕥 **こようする** = to employ

**こらえる・堪える** *verb 2* 㕥
= to endure

**ごらく・娯楽** *noun*
= entertainment

**ごらん・ご覧・御覧** *phrase – in*
*the form* ごらんに なる *this is an*
*honorific equivalent of* みる. *Note*
*that* ごらん *can substitute for* みる
*following a* 〜て *form with the*
*meaning 'try'. Following* ちょっと *or*
*followed by* ください *or* なさい *it*
*means 'please look' or 'look'*

**これ** *noun*
- = this
- = it

**これから** *phrase* = (from) now

**これで** *phrase* = with this

**これでいい** *phrase* = this/that will
do

**コレクション** *noun* = collection

**ころ** *noun* = time

> **!** *often attached to words and*
> *phrases about time to mean 'the*
> *time when ...', 'about' or ' time*
> *to|for ...'*

**ころがす・転がす** *verb 1* 㕥
= to roll (something)

**ころがる・転がる** *verb 1* 㕥
= to roll

**ころす・殺す** *verb 1* 㕥 = to kill

**ころぶ・転ぶ** *verb 1* 㕥 = to fall

**こわい・恐い・怖い** *adjective*
- = frightened
- = frightening

**こわす・壊す** *verb 1* 㕥 = to
break

**こわれる・壊れる** *verb 2* 㕥
  こわれて・こわれない・こわれ
ます = to be broken

**こん・紺** *noun* = navy blue

**こん・今** *prefix* = this

**こんかい・今回** *noun*
- = this time
- = next time

**コンクール** *noun* = contest

**コンクリート** *noun* = concrete

**こんげつ・今月** *noun* = this
month

**こんご・今後** *noun and adverb*
= from now on

**こんごう・混合**
**1** *noun* = mixture
**2** *verb 3* 㕥 **こんごうする** = to mix

**コンサート** *noun* = concert

**こんざつ・混雑**
**1** *noun* = congestion
**2** *verb 3* 㕥 **こんざつする** = to be
crowded

こんしゅう・今週 _noun_ = this week

コンタクト _noun_
- = contact
- = contact lens
  コンタクトを つける = to put in contact lenses
  コンタクトを する = to wear contact lenses

こんだて・献立 _noun_ = menu

こんど・今度 _noun_
- = this time
- = next time

こんな _attributive_
- = this
- = like this

こんなに _adverb_
- = like this
- = to this extent

こんなん・困難
**1** _noun_ = difficulty
**2** _adjective_ こんなん(な) = difficult

こんにち・今日 _noun_
- = today
- = the present

こんにちは・今日は _phrase_
= hello

こんばんは・今晩は _phrase_
= good evening

コンピューター _noun_ = computer

こんぽんてき(な)・根本的(な)
**1** _adjective_ = basic
**2** _adverb_ こんぽんてきに = fundamentally

こんやく・婚約
**1** _noun_ = engagement
**2** _verb 3_ ⑰ と こんやくする = to get engaged

こんやくゆびわ・婚約指輪
_noun_ = engagement

こんらん・混乱
**1** _noun_ = confusion
**2** _verb 3_ ⑰ こんらんする = to be in confusion

# さ サ

さ・差 _noun_ = difference

さ _suffix_ – added to adjective stems to produce a noun i.e. ながい 'long' and ながさ 'length' ▶ **201**

さ _particle_ – used at the end of sentences or phrases in colloquial speech to add emphasis ▶ **205**

さあ _interjection_ – used when commencing something and translatable as 'well' or 'now'

サークル _noun_ = club

サービス
**1** _noun_
- = service
- = service
- = given as a free gift
**2** _verb 3_ ⑧ ⑰ サービスする
- = to give away for free
- = to serve

さい・際 _noun_ = occasion

さい・再 _prefix_ = again

さい・最 _prefix_ = most

さい・才・歳 _counter_ = years old ▶ **171**

さい・祭 _suffix_ = festival

さいかい・再開
**1** _noun_ = reopening
**2** _verb 3_ ⑧ さいかいする = to reopen

ざいがく・在学
**1** _noun_ = attending school/college
**2** _verb 3_ ⑰ に ざいがくする = to attend school

さいきん・最近
**1** _noun_ = recently
**2** _adverb_ = recently
**3** _adjective_ さいきんの = recent

さいきん・細菌 _noun_
= microscopic organisms

さいご・最後
**1** _noun_ = (the) last
**2** _adjective_ さいごの = last
**3** _adverb_ さいごに = finally

さサ

**ざいこ・在庫**
1 *noun* = (in) stock
2 *verb 3* ㉑ ざいこする = to be in
stock

**さいこう・最高** *noun* = (the) best
さいこうです = brilliant!

**さいさん・再三** *adverb* = again
and again

**ざいさん・財産** *noun*
• = property
• = fortune

**さいじつ・祭日** *noun* = national
holiday (celebrating something)

**さいしゅう・最終** *noun* = final

**さいしょ・最初**
1 *noun* = (the) first
2 *adjective* さいしょ(の) = first
3 *adverb* さいしょに = firstly

**さいしょう・最小** *noun*
= minimum

**さいしょくしゅぎ・菜食主義**
*noun – another way of saying*
*'vegetarian'* ベジタリアン

**さいしょくしゅぎしゃ・**
**菜食主義者** *noun* = (a) vegetarian
▶ さいしょくしゅぎ

**サイズ** *noun* = size

**さいそく・催促**
1 *noun* = reminder (bill)
2 *verb 3* ㉑ さいそくする = to
demand (repayment)

**さいだい・最大** *noun* = maximum

**さいちゅう・最中** *noun* = in the
middle of

**さいて** ▶ さく ▶ 197

**さいてい・最低** *noun* = (the)
lowest
さいていだ = that's horrible!

**さいてん・採点**
1 *noun* = marking
2 *verb 3* ㉑ さいてんする = to mark

**さいなん・災難** *noun* = disaster

**さいのう・才能** *noun* = talent

**さいばん・裁判** *noun*
• = trial
• = court

**さいばんかん・裁判官** *noun*
= judge

**さいばんしょ・裁判所** *noun*
• = court
• = courthouse

**さいふ・財布** *noun*
• = wallet
• = purse

**さいほう・裁縫** *noun*
= needlework

**さいぼう・細胞** *noun* = cell

**ざいもく・材木** *noun* = timber

**さいよう・採用**
1 *noun*
• = adoption
• = employment
2 *verb 3* ㉑ さいようする
• = to adopt
• = to employ

**ざいりょう・材料** *noun*
• = materials
• = ingredients

**さいわい・幸い**
1 *adjective* さいわい(な) = happy
2 *adverb* さいわい(に) = fortunately

**サイン**
1 *noun*
• = signature
• = autograph
• = sign
2 *verb 3* ㉑ ㉑ に サインする = to
sign

**さお・竿** *noun* = pole

**さか・坂** *noun* = slope

**さかい・境** *noun* = boundary

**さかさ・逆さ** *noun etc. – an*
*alternative form of* さかさま

**さかさま・逆さま**
1 *noun* = disorder
2 *adjective* さかさま(の)
• = upside down
• = reversed
3 *adverb* さかさまに = wrong way up

**さがす・探す・捜す** *verb 1* ㉑
• = to look for
• = to search

**さかな・魚** *noun* = fish

さかな・肴 *noun* – small dishes of food to accompany drinks
▶おつまみ

さかなや・魚屋 *noun* = fishmonger

さかのぼる・遡る *verb 1 ⑩* に
= to date back to

さかば・酒場 *noun* = bar

さからう・逆らう *verb 1 ⑩* に
= to go against

さがる・下がる *verb 1 ⑩*
• = to go down
• = to step back

さかり・盛り *noun* = the height (of)

さがります ▶さがる

さき・先 *noun*
• = tip (of something)
• = future
• = ahead

さぎ・詐欺 *noun* = fraud

さきに *adverb*
• = in advance
• = ahead ▶おさきに

さきほど・先ほど *noun* = just now

さきます ▶さく

さぎょう・作業
**1** *noun* = work
**2** *verb 3 ⑩* さぎょうする = to work

さく・柵 *noun* = fence

さく・咲く *verb 1 ⑩* さいて・さかない・さきます = to bloom

さく・裂く *verb 1 ⑧* = to tear

さく・昨 *prefix* = last

さくいん・索引 *noun* = index

さくじつ・昨日 *noun* = yesterday

さくしゃ・作者 *noun*
• = author

さくじょ(する)・削除(する)
*verb 3 ⑧* = to delete

さくせい・作成
**1** *noun* = production (of a document)
**2** *verb 3 ⑧* さくせいする = to put together (a document)

さくひん・作品 *noun*
• = work (of art)
• = piece (of work)

さくぶん・作文 *noun*
• = (piece of) writing
• = essay

さくもつ・作物 *noun* = crops

さくら・桜 *noun*
• = cherry tree
• = cherry blossom

さぐる・探る *verb 1 ⑧*
• = to search for
• = to sound out

さけ・酒 *noun*
• = sake (rice wine)
• = alcoholic drink

さけ・鮭 *noun* = salmon

さげて ▶さげる ▶ **197**

さけぶ・叫ぶ *verb 1 ⑩ ⑧* と
• = to shout
• = to cry out

さける・裂ける *verb 2 ⑩* = to rip

さける・避ける *verb 2 ⑧* = to avoid

さげる・下げる *verb 2 ⑧* さげて・さげない・さげます
• = to lower
• = to wear (hanging items)
• = to clear away (dishes and plates)

ささえる・支える *verb 2 ⑧*
= to support

ささやく *verb 1 ⑩* に = to whisper

さしあげる・差し上げる
*verb 2 ⑧* = to give

> **!** respectful equivalent of **あげる**
> ▶ **189**

ざしき・座敷 *noun* – a traditional Japanese style room usually used for entertaining and floored with **たたみ** mats

さしず・指図 *noun* = orders

さしだす・差し出す *verb 1 ⑧*
• = to hold out
• = to present

さしつかえ・差し支え *noun* – it often means 'interference' or 'difficulty' but can also be translated as 'bland' or 'inoffensive' in negatives and refers to not causing difficulty or trouble

さしひく・差し引く *verb 1* ㉔
= to deduct

さしみ・刺し身・刺身 *noun* –
*thin slices of raw fish and meat*

さす・指す *verb 1* ㉔
• = to point (to)

さす・刺す *verb 1* ㉔
• = to stab
• = to sting

さす *verb 1* ㉔
• = to put up (an umbrella)

さす *suffix* – *a spoken equivalent of
the* させる *suffix used for forming the
causative of a verb*
▶ 191

さすが (に) *adverb* – *indicates
that something has happened as
expected and often translatable as
'truly' or 'indeed'*

ざせき・座席 *noun* = seat

させる *verb 2* ㉔ させて・させな
い・させます – *this is the causative
form of* する *and a suffix for verbs
indicating causation* ▶ 191

さそう・誘う *verb 1* ㉔ = to invite

さつ・札 *noun* = (bank) note

さつ・冊 *counter* = book

> ! *used for counting books and
> magazines* ▶ 181

さつえい・撮影
**1** *noun*
• = filming
• = taking photographs
**2** *verb 3* ㉔ さつえいする
• = to photograph
• = to film

ざつおん・雑音 *noun*
= interference (static noise)

さっか・作家 *noun*
• = writer

サッカー *noun* = football

さっき *adverb*
• = a little while ago
• = some time ago

さっきょく・作曲
**1** *noun* = noun
**2** *verb 3* ㉔ さっきょくする = to
compose

さっきょくか・作曲家 *noun*
= composer

さっさと *adverb* = quickly

ざっし・雑誌 *noun* = magazine

さつじん・殺人 *noun*
• = murder
• = murderer

さっする・察する *verb 3* ㉔
= to guess

さっそく・早速 *adverb* = straight
away

ざっと *adverb*
• = briefly
• = roughly

さっぱり *adverb* (with negatives)
= (not) at all

さっぱり(する) *verb 3* ㉓
• = to feel refreshed

さて *interjection* – *used to mark a
change of topic and translatable as
'well' or 'next'*

さとう・砂糖 *noun* = sugar

さばく・砂漠 *noun* = desert

さび・錆 *noun* = rust

さびしい・寂しい *adjective*
• = lonely
• = sad

さびる・錆びる *verb 2* ㉓ = to rust

ざぶとん・座布団 *noun* – *a large
flat cushion used for sitting on and
placed on the floor of rooms with*
たたみ *mats*

さべつ・差別
**1** *noun* = discrimination
**2** *verb 3* ㉓ さべつする = to
discriminate

さほう・作法 *noun* = manners

さま・様 *suffix* – *a more polite
equivalent for* さん *and attached to
names of clients to show politeness;
used after a person's name when
addressing a letter, and in certain
idioms with the original meaning of
'seeming to be ...' or 'appearance'*

さまざま・様々
**1** *adjective* さまざま(な) = various
**2** *adjective* さまざまに = variously

さます・冷ます *verb 1* ⓦ = to cool (something)

さます・覚ます *verb 1* ⓦ めを さます = to wake up

さまたげる・妨げる *verb 2* ⓦ = to obstruct

さむい・寒い *adjective* = cold

さめる・冷める *verb 2* ⓘ – い cool

さめる・覚める *verb 2* ⓘ めが さめる = to wake up

さゆう・左右
**1** *noun* = right and left
**2** *verb 3* ⓦ さゆうする = to influence

さようなら *phrase* = goodbye

さら・皿 *noun*
• = dish
• = plate

さらいげつ・再来月 *noun* = the month after next

さらいしゅう・再来週 *noun* = the week after next

さらいねん・再来年 *noun* = the year after next

さらう *verb 1* ⓦ = to kidnap

サラダ *noun* = salad

さらに・更に *adverb*
• = further
• = even more

サラリーマン *noun* – an employee of one of the large Japanese corporations (or a white collar worker in general)

される *verb 2* ⓘ されて・されない・されます – this is the passive form of する ▶ 191

さる・去る *verb 1* ⓘ ⓦ = to leave

さる・猿 *noun* = monkey

さわがしい・騒がしい *adjective* = noisy

さわぎ・騒ぎ *noun* = uproar

さわぐ・騒ぐ *verb 1* ⓘ = to make a noise

さわやか(な)・爽やか(な) *adjective* = refreshing

さわる・触る *verb 1* ⓘ に = to touch

さん・三 *noun* = three ▶ 181

さん・山 *suffix* = mountain

さん・産 *suffix* = made in

さん *suffix* – added to surnames it is an equivalent of English titles such as 'Mr', 'Mrs' and 'Ms'' but is used far more extensively. It can sometimes be added to given names and job titles.

さんか・参加
**1** *noun* = participation
**2** *verb 3* ⓘ に さんかする = to participate

さんかく・三角 *noun* = triangle

さんぎょう・産業 *noun* = industry

さんこう・参考 *noun* = reference

ざんこく・残酷 *adverb* ざんこくに = cruelly

さんしょう(する)・参照 (する) *verb 3* ⓦ = to refer to

ざんねん(な)・残念(な) *adjective* = regretable

# しシ

し *particle* = and (when giving a list of reasons)

し・四 *noun* = four ▶ 181

し・市 *suffix* = city

し・死 *noun* = death

し・詩 *noun* = poem

し・氏 *suffix* = Mr

し・史 *suffix* = history

じ・字 *noun* – this can be either a letter (of the alphabet), a character of Japanese or other script or someone's 'handwriting'

じ・時 *suffix*
• = o'clock
• = time ▶ 186

じ・寺 *suffix* = temple

しあい・試合
1 _noun_ = match
2 _verb 3_ ㊥ しあい(を)する = to play (against)

しあげる・仕上げる _verb 2_ ㊦
= to finish something

しあさって _noun_ = in three days time

しあわせ・幸せ
1 _noun_ = happiness
2 _adjective_ しあわせ(な) = happy
3 _adverb_ しあわせに = happily

シーズン _noun_ = season

シーツ _noun_ = sheet

シートベルト _noun_ = seatbelt

ジーパン _noun_ = jeans

じえいぎょう・自営業 _noun_
= self employment

じえいたい・自衛隊 _noun_ = the Japanese self defence forces

ジェット _prefix_ = jet

しえん・支援
1 _noun_ = support
2 _verb 3_ ㊦ しえんする = to support

しお・塩 _noun_ = salt

しお・潮 _noun_ = tide

しおからい・塩辛い _adjective_
= salty

しか・鹿 _noun_ = deer

しか・歯科 _noun_ = dentistry

しか _particle_
• = only
• = nothing to do but ...

! _requires a negative_

わたしは にせんえんしか ない
= I have only two thousand yen

しかい・視界 _noun_ = (field of) vision

しがい・市街 _noun_ = streets

しかいしゃ・司会者 _noun_
= master of ceremonies

しかく・四角
1 _noun_ = square
2 _adjective_ しかく(な) = square
▶ しかくい

しかく・資格 _noun_ = qualification

しかくい・四角い _adjective_
= square

しかし _conjunction_
• = however
• = but

しかしながら _conjunction_
= however

しかた・仕方 _noun_ = way of doing (it)

しかた(が)ない・仕方がない
_phrase_
• = it can't be helped
• = there's nothing to be done (about it)
• = there's no point (doing it)

! _following the ～て form of a verb it adds the meaning 'be dying to (do)'_ ▶ **191**

しかたなく _adverb_ = reluctantly

じかに・直に _adverb_ = directly

しかも _conjunction_
• = besides
• = never the less

しかる・叱る _verb 1_ ㊦ = to tell off

じかん・時間
1 _noun_ = time
2 _counter_ = hours ▶ **186**

じかんめ・時間目 _suffix_ = period (of the school timetable) ▶ **185**

じかんわり・時間割 _noun_
= timetable

しき・式 _noun_ = ceremony

! _as a suffix it can also mean 'style'_ ▶ わしき ▶ ようしき

しき・四季 _noun_ = the four seasons

じき・時期 _noun_ = period

しきち・敷地 _noun_ = site

じきに・直に _adverb_
• = soon
• = readily

しきゅう・至急
1 _adverb_ = urgently
2 _adjective_ しきゅうの = urgent

しきゅう・支給
1 _noun_ = provision
2 _verb 3_ ㊦ に しきゅうする = to provide

しきゅう・子宮 *noun* = womb

じきゅう・時給 *noun* = hourly payment

しきりに *adverb*
- = frequently
- = constantly

しきる・仕切る *verb 1* 㐂 = to partition

しきん・資金 *noun* = fund

しく・敷く *verb 1* 㐂
- = to spread
- = to lay

> ! *used of futons in the sense of 'prepare the bed'*

しげき・刺激
**1** *noun* = stimulus
**2** *verb 3* 㐂 しげきする = to stimulate

しける・湿気る *verb 1* 㐂 = to be damp

しけん・試験 *noun*
- = examination
- = test

しげん・資源 *noun* = resources

じけん・事件 *noun*
- = incident
- = case
- = matter

じこ・事故 *noun* = accident

じこ・自己 *prefix* = self

しこうさくご・試行錯誤 *noun*
= trial and error

じごうじとく・自業自得 *noun*
= one's just desserts

じこしょうかい・自己紹介
*noun* = self introduction

じこくひょう・時刻表 *noun*
= (transport) timetable

じごく・地獄 *noun* = hell

しごと・仕事 *noun*
- = work
- = job

しごと・仕事
**1** *noun*
- = work
- = job
**2** *verb 3* 㐂 しごとをする = to work

じさ・時差 *noun* = time zone difference

じさつ・自殺
**1** *noun* = suicide
**2** *verb 3* 㐂 じさつする = to commit suicide

しじ・支持
**1** *noun* = support
**2** *verb 3* 㐂 しじする = to support

しじ・指示
**1** *noun* = instructions
**2** *verb 3* 㐂 しじする = to give instructions (that ..)

じじつ・事実 *noun*
- = the facts
- = reality

じしゃく・磁石 *noun* = magnet

じしゅ・自主 *prefix*
- = voluntary
- = independent

ししゅう・刺繍 *noun*
= embroidery

しじゅう・始終 *adverb*
- = often
- = frequently

じしゅう・自習
**1** *noun* = self-study
**2** *verb 3* 㐂 じしゅうする = to study unsupervised

ししゅつ・支出 *noun*
= expenditure

じしょ・辞書 *noun* = dictionary
▶ **dictionary**

しじょう・市場 *noun* = market

じじょう・事情 *noun*
- = situation
- = circumstances

じしょく・辞職
**1** *noun* = resignation
**2** *verb 3* 㐂 じしょくする = to resign from a job

じじょでん・自叙伝 *noun*
= autobiography

ししん・指針 *noun* = guidelines

しじん・詩人 *noun* = poet

じしん・自信 *noun* = self confidence

じしん・地震 *noun* = earthquake

**じしん・自身** *noun – used as a suffix to the preceding noun to add the sense of 'self' and so variously translatable as 'himself', 'herself', 'myself', 'themselves' etc.*

**しずか・静か**
1 *adjective* しずか（な）= quiet
2 *adverb* しずかに = quietly

**システム** *noun* = system

**しずまる・静まる・鎮まる** *verb 1 ㋑*
• = to grow quiet
• = to subside

**しずむ・沈む** *verb 1 ㋑* = to sink

**しせつ・施設** *noun* = facilities

**しぜん・自然**
1 *noun* = nature
2 *adjective* しぜん（な）= natural
3 *adverb* しぜんに = naturally

**じぜんに・事前に** *adverb* = in advance

**じぜん・慈善** *noun* = charity

**しそう・思想** *noun* = thought

**じぞう・地蔵** *noun – a Buddhist guardian of children and travellers or statues of him. Usually in the form じぞうさま. These statues are found in temples and all over Japan at the roadside and on paths*

**じそく・時速** *noun* = speed (per hour)

**しそん・子孫** *noun* = descendents

**した・下** *noun*
• = under
• = below
• = down
• = lower
• = younger

**した・舌** *noun* = tongue

**した** ▶ する

**したい・死体** *noun* = dead body

**しだい・次第**
1 *suffix* = it depends on
かれしだい です = it's up to him
2 *adverb* しだいに = gradually

**じたい・事態** *noun* = situation

**じだい・時代** *noun and suffix*
• = age
• = period

**じだいげき・時代劇** *noun* = historical dramas

**したう・慕う** *verb 1 を*
• = to adore
• = to miss

**したうけ・下請け** *noun*
• = subcontract
• = subcontractor

**したがう・従う** *verb 1 に* = to obey

**したがえる・従える** *verb 2 を* = to be accompanied by

**したがき・下書き** *noun* = draft (of a piece of writing)

**したがって** *adverb*
• = therefore
～にしたがって = in accordance with

**したぎ・下着** *noun* = underwear

**したく・支度**
1 *noun* = preparation
2 *verb 3 ㋑* したく（を）する = to prepare

**じたく・自宅** *noun*
• = (one's own) home
• = house

**したごころ・下心** *noun* = hidden motive

**したしい・親しい** *adjective*
• = intimate
• = close

**したまち・下町** *noun – the older residential parts of a city or 'downtown'*

**しち・七** *noun* = seven ▶ **181**

**しちがつ・7月・七月** *noun* = July ▶ **174**

**しつ・質** *noun* = quality

**しつ・室** *noun and suffix* = room

**じつ・実** *noun* = the truth ▶ じつは

**じつ・日** *suffix* = day

**しっかり（と）** *adverb* = firmly
しっかり している = reliable

**じっかん・実感**
**1** *noun* = realisation
**2** *verb 3* ㊎ じっかんする = to realise

**しっき・湿気** ▶ しっけ

**しつぎょう・失業**
**1** *noun* = unemployment
**2** *verb 3* ㊑ しつぎょうする = to become unemployed

**しつぎょうしゃ・失業者** *noun*
= unemployed person/people

**しつぎょうてあて・失業手当**
*noun* = unemployment benefit

**じつぎょうか・実業家** *noun*
• = businessman
• = businesswoman

**じっくり(と)** *adverb*
• = carefully
• = thoroughly

**しつけ・躾**
**1** *noun* = discipline
**2** *verb 3* ㊎ に しつけ(を)する
= to teach discipline (to)

**しっけ・湿気** *noun*
• = dampness
• = humidity

**じっけん・実験**
**1** *noun* = experiment
**2** *verb 3* ㊎ じっけんする = to experiment

**じつげん・実現**
**1** *noun* = realization
**2** *verb 3* ㊎㊑ じつげんする
• = to realize
• = to come true

**じっけんだい・実験台** *noun*
= (experimental) guinea pig

**しつこい** *adjective* = persistent

**じっこう・実行**
**1** *noun* = execution
**2** *verb 3* ㊎ じっこうする = to carry out

**じっさい・実際**
**1** *noun* = fact
**2** *adjective* じっさいの = actual
**1** *adverb* じっさい(に) = actually
じっさいは = actually

**じっさいてき(な)** *adjective*
= practical

**じっし・実施**
**1** *noun* = carrying out
**2** *verb 3* ㊎ じっしする = to implement

**じっしゅう・実習**
**1** *noun*
• = practice
• = practical element of a course
**2** *verb 3* ㊎ じっしゅうする = to practise

**しっしん・湿疹** *noun* = (a) rash

**じっせき・実績** *noun* = results

**しって** ▶ しる ▶ **197**

**しっと・嫉妬**
**1** *noun* = jealousy
**2** *verb 3* ㊎ に しっとする = to be jealous

**しつど・湿度** *noun* = humidity

**じっと**
**1** *adverb* = intently
**2** *verb 3* ㊑ じっとする = to remain still

**じつに・実に** *adverb* = very

**じつは・実は** *adverb* = actually

**しっぱい・失敗**
**1** *noun* = failure
**2** *verb 3* ㊑ に しっぱいする = to fail

**しっぴつ・執筆**
**1** *noun* = writing
**2** *verb 3* ㊎ しっぴつする = to write

**しっぴつしゃ・執筆者** *noun*
= writer

**じつぶつ・実物** *noun* = the real thing

**しっぽ・尻尾** *noun* = tail

**しつぼう・失望**
**1** *noun* = disappointment
**2** *verb 3* ㊑ に しつぼうする = to be disappointed

**しつもん・質問**
**1** *noun* = question
**2** *verb 3* ㊎ に しつもんする = to ask questions

**じつよう・実用** *noun* = practical use

**じつようてき(な)・実用的(な)**
*adjective* = practical

**じつりょく・実力** *noun* = capability

**しつれい・失礼**
**1** *noun* = impoliteness
**2** *adjective* しつれい(な) = rude

しシ

**3** *verb 3* ㉟ しつれいする
- = to be rude
- = to leave

> ! there are idiomatic uses of this word given under the next two entries

**しつれいします・失礼します** *phrase*
- = (I'm) leaving
- = excuse me (for interrupting)

> ! used when entering a room or interrupting a conversation and when about to leave as a polite way of saying 'goodbye'

**しつれいしました・失礼しました** *phrase*
- = excuse me (I'm sorry)

> ! used to apologise and also when leaving a room as a polite way of saying 'goodbye'

**して** ▶ **する** ▶ **197**

**してい・指定**
**1** *noun* = designation
**2** *verb 3* ㉠ していする = to designate

**していけん・指定券** *noun*
= reservation ticket

**していせき・指定席** *noun*
= reserved seat

**してきする・指摘する** *verb 3* ㉠
= to point out

**してん・支店** *noun and suffix*
= branch (of a bank or store)

**じてん・辞典** *noun* = dictionary

**じてんしゃ・自転車** *noun*
= bicycle

**しどう・指導**
**1** *noun* = guidance
**2** *verb 3* ㉠ しどうする = to instruct

**じどう・児童** *prefix* = child

**じどうし・自動詞** *noun* – *verbs which do not have a direct object. For explanations of this important concept in Japanese grammar* ▶ **191** *In this dictionary a* じどうし *is marked with the symbol* ㉟ *in the entry and the opposite type of verb (transitive)* たどうし *is marked with the symbol* ㉠

**しどうしゃ・指導者** *noun*
= leader

**じどうしゃ・自動車** *noun* = car

**しな・品** *noun*
- = article
- = goods

**しない** ▶ **する**

**しなもの・品物** *noun* = goods

**しぬ・死ぬ** *verb 1* ㉟ = to die

**しはい・支配**
**1** *noun* = rule
**2** *verb 3* ㉠ しはいする = to rule

**しばい・芝居** *noun* = (a) play

**しはいにん・支配人** *noun*
= manager

**しばしば** *adverb* = often

**しばふ・芝生** *noun* = lawn

**しはらい・支払い** *noun*
= payment

**しはらう・支払う** *verb 1* ㉠
= to pay

**しばらく・暫く** *adverb*
- = for a while
  しばらくですね = I haven't seen you for a while! ▶ ひさしぶり

**しばる・縛る** *verb 1* ㉠ = to bind

**じばん・地盤** *noun* = ground

**じびいんこうか・耳鼻咽喉科** *noun* = ear, nose and throat doctor

**じびか・耳鼻科** ▶ じびいんこうか

**しびれる** *verb 2* ㉟
- = to be numb
- = to have pins and needles

**しぶき** *noun* = splash

**しぶしぶ** *adverb* = unwillingly

**じぶん・自分** *noun* = oneself

**しへい・紙幣** *noun* = paper money

**しぼう・死亡**
**1** *noun* = death
**2** *verb 3* ㉟ しぼうする = to die

**しぼう・脂肪** *noun*
- = fat

**しぼう・志望**
**1** *noun* = desire
**2** *verb 3* ㉠ しぼうする = to want

しぼむ・萎む *verb 1* ⓐ = to wither

しぼる・絞る *verb 1* ⓑ
- = to wring out
- = to squeeze

しほん・資本 *noun* = capital (sum of money)

しほんしゅぎ・資本主義 *noun* = capitalism

しま・島 *noun* = island

しま・縞
1 *noun* = stripe
2 *adjective* しまの(ある) = striped

しまい・終い *noun* = (the) end

! *often found in the form* おしまい

しまい・姉妹 *noun* = sisters

! *often used for 'twinning' as in* しまいとし・姉妹都市 *'sister city'/'twin town' and* しまいこう・姉妹校 *'sister school'*

しまう *verb 1* ⓑ = to put away

! *following the* 〜て *form of a verb it adds the meaning of something being completely finished or being regretable in some way.* ▶ 191

しまう *verb 1* ⓐ
- = to shut
- = to close

じまく・字幕 *noun* = subtitles

しましょう ▶ する

します ▶ する

しません ▶ する

しませんか ▶ する

しまって ▶ しまる

しまった *exclamation* = oh no!

しまります ▶ しまる

しまる・閉まる *verb 1* ⓐ しまって・しまらない・しまります
= to be shut

じまん・自慢
1 *noun* = boasting
2 *verb 3* ⓑ じまんする = to boast

じみ(な)・地味(な) *adjective* = plain

しみじみ(と) *adverb* = deeply

しみん・市民 *noun*
- = citizen
- = inhabitant (of a city)

じむ・事務 *noun* = office work

じむいん・事務員 *noun* = clerk

じむきょく・事務局 *noun* = secretariat

じむしつ・事務室 *noun* = office (room)

じむしょ・事務所 *noun* = office

しめい・氏名 *noun* = full name

しめきり・締め切り *noun* = deadline

しめす・示す *verb 1* ⓑ = to indicate

しめて ▶ しめる ▶ 197

しめます ▶ しめる

しめる・閉める *verb 2* ⓑ しめて・しめない・しめます = to shut

しめる・締める *verb 2* ⓑ = to fasten

しめる・占める *verb 2* ⓑ = to occupy

しめる・湿る *verb 1* ⓐ = to get damp

じめん・地面 *noun* = ground

しも・霜 *noun* = frost

しも・下 *prefix*
- = lower
- = second

しも *particle* = (not) necessarily

しゃ・者 *suffix* = person

しゃ・車 *suffix* = vehicle

しゃ・社 *suffix* = company

じゃ – reduced form of では *used in the formation of some negative sentences. See the entries for* じゃ ありません *and* じゃ ない *below.*

じゃあ *conjunction*
- = well (then)

! *used as an informal way of saying 'goodbye', especially in the form* じゃあ、またね *or simply* じゃあ

しシ

じゃありません – *negative form of* です *and variously translatable as* 'am not', 'is not', *or* 'are not'

じゃありませんでした – *past form of* じゃありません *and translatable as* 'was not' *or* 'were not'

ジャーナリスト *noun* = journalist

しゃかい・社会 *noun* = society

しゃかいかがく・社会科学 *noun* = social science

しゃかいしゅぎ・社会主義 *noun* = socialism

しゃがむ *verb 1* ⓝ = to squat

じゃく・弱 *suffix* = less than

じゃぐち・蛇口 *noun* = tap, faucet

じゃくてん・弱点 *noun* = weak point

しゃこ・車庫 *noun* = garage (for storing car)

しゃしょう・車掌 *noun* = ticket collector (buses and trains)

しゃしん・写真 *noun* = photograph

ジャズ *noun* = jazz

しゃせい・写生
1 *noun* = sketch
2 *verb 3* を しゃせいする = to sketch

しゃせつ・社説 *noun* = (newspaper) editorial

しゃたく・社宅 *noun* – *housing provided by a company for workers*

しゃちょう・社長 *noun* = president (of a company)

シャツ *noun* = shirt

じゃっかん・若干 *noun* = a few

しゃっきん・借金
1 *noun* = loan
2 *verb 3* ⓝ しゃっきんする = to take out a loan

しゃっくり
1 *noun* = hiccup
2 *verb 3* ⓝ しゃっくりする = to hiccup

しゃない・社内 *noun* = within the company

しゃない・車内 *noun* = inside (of a vehicle)

じゃない – *plain equivalent of* じゃありません ▶ 187

じゃなかった – *past form of* じゃない ▶ 187

しゃぶる *verb 1* を = to suck

しゃべる・喋る *verb 1* ⓝ
• = to chat
• = to speak

じゃま・邪魔
1 *noun*
• = hindrance
• = obstruction
2 *adjective* じゃま(な) = obstructive
3 *verb 3* ⓝ じゃま(を)する
• = to hinder
• = to visit

じゃまもの・邪魔物 *noun* = nuisance

しゃみせん・三味線 *noun* – *a traditional Japanese stringed musical instrument*

しゃめん・斜面 *noun* = slope

じゃり・砂利 *noun* = gravel

しゃりん・車輪 *noun* = wheel

しゃれ・洒落 *noun* = joke

ジャム *noun* = jam

シャワー *noun* = shower
シャワーを あびる = to take a shower

シャンプー *noun* = shampoo

しゅ・手 *suffix* = person

しゅ・酒 *suffix* = alcoholic drink

しゅう・週 *noun and suffix* = week

しゅう・州 *noun and suffix* = state

! *often used to translate the English words* 'state', 'province' *or* 'county'

しゅう・集 *suffix* = collection

じゆう・自由
1 *noun* = freedom
2 *adjective* じゆう(な) = free
3 *adverb* じゆうに = freely

じゅう・十 *noun* = ten ▶ 181

じゅう・銃 *noun* = gun

じゅう・中 *suffix* = throughout

じゅう・重 *suffix* = fold

しゅうい・周囲 *noun*
= circumference

しゅうかい・集会 *noun*
= gathering

しゅうかく・収穫
**1** *noun* = harvest
**2** *verb 3* Ⓐ しゅうかくする = to
　harvest

しゅうかん・週間 *counter* = week
▶ **186**

しゅうかん・習慣 *noun* = custom

しゅうぎいん・衆議院 *noun*
= house of representatives

しゅうぎいんぎいん・
衆議院議員 *noun* = member of the
house of representatives

じゅうきょ・住居 *noun*
= residence

しゅうきょう・宗教 *noun*
= religion

じゅうぎょういん・従業員
*noun* = employee

しゅうきん・集金
**1** *noun* = collecting money
**2** *verb 3* Ⓐ しゅうきんする = to
　collect money

しゅうげき・襲撃
**1** *noun* = assault
**2** *verb 3* Ⓐ しゅうげきする = to
　attack

しゅうごう・集合
**1** *noun* = gathering
**2** *verb 3* Ⓚ しゅうごうする = to
　gather

しゅうし・収支 *noun* = income
and expenditure

しゅうし・終始 *adverb* = from
beginning to end

しゅうし・修士 *noun* = Master's
degree

しゅうじ・習字 *noun* = (Japanese)
calligraphy

じゅうし (する)・重視(する)
*verb 3* Ⓐ = to consider important

じゅうじつ・充実
**1** *noun* = fulfillment
**2** *verb 3* Ⓚ じゅうじつする = to be
　fulfilling

しゅうしゅう・収集
**1** *noun* = collection
**2** *verb 3* Ⓐ しゅうしゅうする = to
　collect

じゅうしょ・住所 *noun* = address

しゅうしょく・就職
**1** *noun* = finding a job
**2** *verb 3* Ⓚ に しゅうしょくする
　= to get a job

しゅうしょくかつどう・
就職活動 *noun* = looking for a job

じゅうじろ・十字路 *noun*
= crossroads

ジュース *noun* = soft drink(s)

しゅうせい・修正
**1** *noun* = modification
**2** *verb 3* Ⓐ しゅうせいする = to
　amend

しゅうぜん・修繕
**1** *noun* = repair
**2** *verb 3* Ⓐ しゅうぜんする = to
　repair

じゅうたい・渋滞
**1** *noun* = traffic jam
**2** *verb 3* Ⓚ じゅうたいする = to be
　congested

じゅうたい・重態・重体 *noun*
= in a serious condition

じゅうだい(な)・重大(な)
*adjective* = serious

じゅうたく・住宅 *noun*
• = house
• = housing

しゅうだん・集団 *noun* = group

じゅうたん・絨毯 *noun*
• = carpet
• = rug

しゅうちゅう・集中
**1** *noun* = concentration
**2** *verb 3* Ⓚ に しゅうちゅうする
　= to concentrate

しゅうてん・終点 *noun*
= terminus

じゅうなんせい・柔軟性 *noun*
= flexibility

しシ

しゅうにゅう・収入 *noun*
= income

しゅうにん・就任
**1** *noun* = taking up a post
**2** *verb 3* ㉝ しゅうにんする = to take office

しゅうのう・収納 *noun* = storage

じゅうびょう・重病 *noun*
= serious illness

しゅうぶんのひ・秋分の日
*noun – Autumnal Equinox Day – a Japanese public holiday*

じゅうぶん・十分
**1** *noun* = enough
**2** *adverb* = thoroughly
**3** *adjective* じゅうぶん(な)
= adequate

しゅうへん・周辺 *noun* = vicinity

しゅうまつ・週末 *noun*
= weekend

じゅうみん・住民 *noun* = resident

じゅうみんぜい・住民税 *note*
*– tax paid to local government by all residents of a town, village or city*

じゅうやく・重役 *noun*
= executive

しゅうよう・収容
**1** *noun* = capacity
**2** *verb 3* ㉗ しゅうようする = to accommodate

じゅうよう(な)・重要(な)
*adjective* = important

じゅうらい・従来 *noun* = until now

しゅうり・修理
**1** *noun* = repair
**2** *verb 3* ㉗ しゅうりする = to repair

しゅうりょう・終了
**1** *noun* = close
**2** *verb 3* ㉝ ㉗ しゅうりょうする
= to finish

じゅうりょう・重量 *noun*
= weight

しゅうりょうしょう・修了証
*noun* = certificate (of completing a course)

しゅうりょうしょうしょ・
修了証書 *noun – alternative form of*
しゅうりょうしょう

じゅうりょく・重力 *noun*
= gravity

しゅかんてき・主観的
**1** *adjective* しゅかんてき(な)
= subjective
**2** *adverb* しゅかんてきに
= subjectively

しゅぎ・主義 *suffix – similar to the English suffix '-ism' as in 'patriotism' etc.*

じゅぎょう・授業 *noun* = class

じゅく・塾 *noun – a supplementary 'cram' school attended by children after (or even before!) normal school hours. Usually providing supplementary teaching towards school or university entrance examinations but some* じゅく *provide special subjects not covered at school such as abacus or calligraphy or just 'top up' teaching of the same materials as the ordinary school syllabus.*

じゅくご・熟語 *noun – words or idiomatic phrases made up several elements, especially in the sense of compound use of Chinese characters and translatable as 'kanji compounds'*
▶ vii

しゅくじつ・祝日 *noun – a national holiday celebrating something*

しゅくしょう・縮小
**1** *noun* = reduction
**2** *verb 3* ㉗ ㉝ しゅくしょうする
= to reduce

しゅくだい・宿題
**1** *noun* = homework
**2** *verb 3* ㉝ しゅくだい(を)する
= to do homework

じゅけん・受験
**1** *noun* = (entrance) examination
**2** *verb 3* ㉗ じゅけんする = to take an examination

じゅけんしゃ・受験者 *noun*
= examination candidate

じゅけんせい・受験生 *noun*
= examination candidate (student)

じゅけんべんきょう・受験勉強
*noun* = studying in preparation for an exam

**じゅけんりょう・受験料** *noun*
= examination fee

**しゅざい・取材**
**1** *noun* = gathering materials
**2** *verb 3* ㊗ **しゅざいする**
• = to research (a story)
• = to cover (an event)

**しゅざいきしゃ・取材記者**
*noun* = reporter

**しゅし・趣旨** *noun*
• = gist
• = purpose

**しゅじゅつ・手術** *noun*
= operation

**しゅしょう・首相** *noun and suffix*
= Prime Minister

**しゅじん・主人** *noun* = (one's own)
husband ▶ **177**

> ❗ *also used about the 'owner' of a
> shop, restaurant or bar and
> translatable as 'proprietor'*

**しゅじんこう・主人公** *noun*
= the leading role

**しゅだん・手段** *noun* = means

**しゅちょう・主張**
**1** *noun* = insistence
**2** *verb 3* ㊗ **しゅちょうする** = to
insist

**しゅっきん・出勤**
**1** *noun* = coming/going to work
**2** *verb 3* ㊗ に **しゅっきんする** = to
go/come to work

**しゅっけつ・出血**
**1** *noun* = bleeding
**2** *verb 3* ㊗ **しゅっけつする** = to
bleed

**しゅっさん・出産** *noun*
= childbirth

**しゅつじょう・出場**
**1** *noun* = participation
**2** *verb 3* ㊗ **しゅつじょうする** = to
take part

**しゅっしん・出身** *noun and suffix*
• = place of birth
• = graduate of

**しゅっせ・出世**
**1** *noun* = success (in life)
**2** *verb 3* ㊗ **しゅっせする** = to be
successful (in life)

**しゅっせき・出席**
**1** *noun* = attendance
**2** *verb 3* ㊗ に **しゅっせきする** = to
attend

**しゅっちょう・出張**
**1** *noun* = business trip
**2** *verb 3* ㊗ **しゅっちょうする** = to go
on a business trip

**しゅっぱつ・出発**
**1** *noun* = departure
**2** *verb 3* ㊗ **しゅっぱつする** = to
depart

**しゅっぱん・出版**
**1** *noun* = publishing
**2** *verb 3* ㊗ **しゅっぱんする** = to
publish

**しゅっぱんしゃ・出版社** *noun*
= publisher (company)

**しゅっぴ・出費** *noun*
= expenditure

**しゅっぴん(する)・出品(する)**
*verb 3* ㊗ = to exhibit

**しゅと・首都** *noun* = capital (city)

**しゅのう・首脳** *noun* = leader/s

**しゅび・守備**
**1** *noun* = defence
**2** *verb 3* ㊗ **しゅびする** = to defend

**しゅふ・主婦** *noun* = housewife

> ❗ *used to refer to married women
> generally even if they work*

**しゅみ・趣味** *noun*
• = hobby
• = taste

**じゅみょう・寿命** *noun* = life
expectany

**じゅもく・樹木** *noun* = trees

**しゅやく・主役** *noun* = leading
role

**しゅよう(な)・主要(な)**
*adjective* = main

**しゅよう・腫瘍** *noun* = tumour

**じゅよう・需要** *noun* = demand

**しゅるい・種類** *noun* = kind (of)

**じゅわき・受話器** *noun*
= (telephone) receiver

**じゅん・順** *suffix* = (in) order

**しゅんかん・瞬間** *noun* = moment

**じゅんかん・循環** *noun*
= circulation

**じゅんさ・巡査** *noun* = police officer

**じゅんじょ・順序** *noun* = order
　じゅんじょのある = orderly
　じゅんじょがたたない
　　= disorderly

**じゅんじょう（な）・純情（な）**
*adjective* = naive

**じゅんすい（な）・純粋（な）**
*adjective* = pure

**じゅんちょう・順調**
1 *adjective* じゅんちょう（な）= going well
2 *adverb* じゅんちょうに = smoothly

**じゅんばん・順番** *noun* = turn
　じゅんばんに = in turn

**じゅんび・準備**
1 *noun* = preparation
2 *verb 3* ⓦ じゅんび（を）する = to prepare

**しゅんぶんのひ・春分の日**
*noun* – Vernal Equinaox Day – a Japanese public holiday

**しょ・初** *prefix* = first

**しょ・諸** *prefix* = various

**しょ・書** *suffix* = written item

**しょ・所** *suffix* = place

**じょ・所** *suffix* = place

**じょ・女** *prefix and suffix* = woman

**しよう・使用**
1 *noun* = use
2 *verb 3* ⓦ しようする = to use

**しよう・仕様** ▶ しょうがない

**しよう** ▶ する

**しょう・小** *prefix* = small

**しょう・賞** *noun and suffix* = prize

**しょう・章** *noun and suffix*
= chapter

**しょう・省** *suffix* = ministry

**じょう・上** *noun* = the best

**じょう・上** *prefix* = upper

**じょう・上** *suffix* = concerning

**じょう・情** *noun* = emotion

**じょう・場** *suffix* = place

**じょう・畳** *suffix* – the counter for たたみ mats when used as an indication of the floor area of a house or apartment. Each piece of matting is approximately 90 x 180 cm ▶ 181

**じょう・状** *suffix* = letter

**しょうか・消火**
1 *noun* = fire fighting
2 *verb 3* ⓦ しょうかする = to extinguish

**しょうか・消化**
1 *noun* = digestion
2 *verb 3* ⓦ しょうかする = to digest

**しょうかい・紹介**
1 *noun* = introduction
2 *verb 3* ⓦ しょうかいする = to introduce

**しょうかき・消化器** *noun* = fire extinguisher

**しょうがい・障害** *noun* = obstacle

**しょうがい・生涯** *noun*
= throughout one's life

**しょうがいじ・障害児** *noun*
= disabled child

**しょうがいしゃ・障害者** *noun*
= disabled person

**しょうがいがくしゅう・生涯学習** *noun* = continuing education

**しょうがくきん・奨学金** *noun*
= scholarship

**しょうがくせい・小学生** *noun*
= elementary school student ▶ 185

**しょうがつ・正月** *noun* = new year

**しょうがっこう・小学校** *noun*
= elementary school ▶ 185

**しょうがない** *phrase*
• = there's no choice
• = it can't be helped
• = it's hopeless

**しょうぎ・将棋** *noun* – a Japanese board game with some similarities to chess

**じょうき・蒸気** *noun* = steam

**じょうき（の）・上記（の）**
*adjective* = the above

**!** *formal phrase for letters similar to 'the aforesaid' and 'the above-mentioned'*

# じょうぎ・定規 *noun* = (a) ruler

## じょうきゃく・乗客 *noun*
= passenger

## じょうきゅう・上級 *noun and prefix* = advanced (level)

## しょうぎょう・商業
**1** *noun* = commerce
**2** *adjective* しょうぎょうの
= commercial

## じょうきょう・上京
**1** *noun* = going/coming to Tokyo
**2** *verb 3* ⑰ じょうきょうする = to go/come to Tokyo

## じょうきょう・状況 *noun*
= situation

## しょうきょくてき・消極的
**1** *adjective* しょうきょくてき(な)
= negative
**2** *adverb* しょうきょくてきに
= unenthusiastically

## しょうきん・賞金 *noun* = prize money

## じょうげ・上下
**1** *noun*
• = top and bottom
• = upper and lower
**2** *verb 3* じょうげする
• = to fluctuate
• = to vary

## じょうけん・条件 *noun*
= condition

## しょうこ・証拠 *noun* = proof

## しょうご・正午 *noun* = noon

## しょうこうかいぎしょ・商工会議所 *noun* = chamber of commerce

## しょうさい・詳細 *noun* = the details

## しょうじ・障子 *noun* – sliding paper screen doors

## じょうし・上司 *noun* – someone who is higher in authority than you at work so translatable as 'boss', 'management' or 'my superiors' etc. depending on the situation

## しょうじき・正直
**1** *adjective* しょうじき(な) = honest
**2** *adverb* しょうじきに = honestly

## じょうしき・常識 *noun*
= common sense

## しょうしゃ・商社 *noun* = trading company

## じょうしゃ・乗車
**1** *noun* = boarding (a vehicle)
**2** *verb 3* ⑰ に じょうしゃする
= to get on/into (a vehicle)

## じょうしゃけん・乗車券 *noun*
= ticket (bus or train)

## じょうじゅん・上旬 *noun* = the first ten days of the month ▶ 174

## しょうじょ・少女 *noun* = girl

## しょうしょう・少々 *adverb*
= a little

## しょうしょう(お)まち (ください)・少々(お)待ち (ください) *phrase* = please wait a moment

## しょうじる・生じる *verb 3* ⑰
• = to occur
• = to come about

## しょうしん・昇進
**1** *noun* = promotion
**2** *verb 3* ⑰ しょうしんする = to be promoted

## じょうず・上手
**1** *adjective* じょうず(な) = skillful
• = good at ...
**2** *adverb* じょうずに
• = skillfully
• = well

## しょうすう・少数 *noun*
• = small number
• = minority

## しょうすうみんぞく・少数民族 *noun* = ethnic minority

## しょうせつ・小説 *noun* = novel

## しょうたい・招待
**1** *noun* = invitation
**2** *verb 3* ㊅ しょうたいする = to invite

## じょうたい・状態 *noun*
• = condition
• = state

## しょうたいじょう・招待状 *noun* = (letter of) invitation

じょうたつ・上達
1 *noun* = improvement
2 *verb 3 ㋑* じょうたつする = to make progress

じょうだん・冗談 *noun* = joke
じょうだんを いう = to tell a joke

しょうち(する)・承知(する)
*verb 3 ㋑*
• = to be aware
• = to consent
（ご）しょうちの ように = as you know
しょうちの とおり = as you know

じょうちょ・情緒 *noun*
= emotions

じょうちょてき・情緒的
1 *adjective* じょうちょてき(な)
= emotional
2 *adverb* じょうちょてきに
= emotionally

しょうちょう・象徴 *noun*
= symbol

しょうてん・商店 *noun* = store

しょうてん・焦点 *noun* = focus
しょうてんを あわせる = to focus

しょうてんがい・商店街 *noun*
= shopping area/centre

じょうとう(な)・上等(な)
*adjective* = high quality

しょうどく・消毒
1 *noun* = sterilisation
2 *verb 3 ㋔* しょうどくする
= to sterilize

しょうとつ・衝突
1 *noun* = collision
2 *verb 3 ㋑* に しょうとつする
= to collide

しょうにん・商人 *noun* = person in business

しょうにん・承認
1 *noun* = approval
2 *verb 3 ㋔* しょうにんする
= to approve

じょうねつ・情熱 *noun* = passion

じょうねつてき・情熱的
1 *adjective* じょうねつてき(な)
= enthusiastic
2 *adverb* じょうねつてきに
= enthusiastically

しょうねん・少年 *noun* = boy

しょうはい・勝敗 *noun* = victory and defeat

しょうばい・商売
1 *noun* = trade
2 *verb 3 ㋑* しょうばい(を)する
= to do business

じょうはつ・蒸発
1 *noun* = evaporation
2 *verb 3 ㋑* じょうはつする = to evaporate

しょうひ・消費
1 *noun* = consumption
2 *verb 3 ㋔* しょうひする = to consume

しょうひしゃ・消費者 *noun*
= consumer

しょうひぜい・消費税
1 *noun* = 'consumption tax' – *a tax levied on goods and services by central government*

しょうひん・商品 *noun* = goods

じょうひん(な)・上品(な)
*adjective*
• = elegant
• = refined

しょうぶ・勝負
1 *noun* = match
2 *verb 3 ㋑* しょうぶする = have a game

じょうぶ(な)・丈夫(な)
*adjective*
• = sturdy
• = strong

しょうべん・小便
1 *noun* = urine
2 *verb 3 ㋑* しょうべんする = to urinate

しょうぼうしゃ・消防車 *noun*
= fire engine

しょうぼうしょ・消防署 *noun*
= fire station

じょうほう・情報 *noun*
= information

じょうほうこうがく・情報工学
*noun* = information technology

しょうみ・正味
1 *adverb*
• = fully
• = nett

**しょうめい・証明**
1 *noun* = proof
2 *verb 3* 圏 しょうめいする = to prove

**しょうめい・照明** *noun* = lighting

**しょうめん・正面** *noun* = front

**しょうめんしょうとつ・正面衝突** *noun* = head on collision

**しょうもう・消耗**
1 *noun* = using up
2 *verb 3* 圏 しょうもうする = to exhaust

**じょうやく・条約** *noun* = treaty

**しょうゆ・醤油** *noun* = soy sauce

**しょうらい・将来** *noun* = (the) future

**じょうりく・上陸**
1 *noun* = landing (from a boat)
2 *verb 3* 圏 じょうりくする = to land

**しょうりゃく・省略**
1 *noun* = shortening
2 *verb 3* 圏 しょうりゃくする = to abridge

**しょうわ・昭和** *noun* – era name for 1926 to 1989 and used for dates during that period ▶ 174

**じょおう・女王** *noun* = queen

**しょきゅう・初級** *noun and prefix* = beginners (level)

**ジョギング**
1 *noun* = jogging
2 *verb 3* 圏 ジョギングする = to jog

**しょく・職** *noun* = occupation

**しょくいん・職員** *noun* = staff

**しょくいんかいぎ・職員会議** *noun*
• = staff meeting
• = teachers' meeting

**しょくいんしつ・職員室** *noun*
• = staff room
• = teachers' room

**しょくぎょう・職業** *noun* = occupation

**しょくじ・食事**
1 *noun* = meal
2 *verb 3* 圏 しょくじ する = to have a meal

**しょくたく・食卓** *noun* = dining table

**しょくどう・食堂** *noun*
• = canteen
• = dining room

**しょくにん・職人** *noun* = craftsman

**しょくば・職場** *noun* = workplace

**しょくパン・食パン** *noun* = loaf of bread

**しょくひん・食品** *noun* = foods

**しょくぶつ・植物** *noun* = plants

**しょくもつ・食物** *noun* = food

**しょくよく・食欲** *noun* = appetite

**しょくりょう・食糧** *noun* = foodstuffs

**しょくりょうひん・食料品** *noun* = groceries

**しょさい・書斎** *noun* = study (room)

**しょじ・所持**
1 *noun* = possession
2 *verb 3* 圏 しょじする = to have

**じょし・女子** *noun*
• = woman
• = female

> ! *often occurs as a prefix to add the meaning 'women's' or girls' especially in the names of schools, colleges and universities*

**じょし・助詞** *noun* – part of speech usually called particle or postposition which expresses grammatical relations. Also sometimes called てにをは. For further information on these words and their uses ▶ 205

**じょしゅ・助手** *noun* = assistant

**しょじゅん・初旬** *noun* – the first ten days of the month and translatable as 'at the beginning of the month'

**じょじょに・徐々に** *adverb* = gradually

**じょせい・女性** *noun*
• = woman
• = women

**しょせき・書籍** *noun* = books

## しょち・処置
**1** *noun* = measures
**2** *verb 3* 🈯 しょちする = to deal with

## しょっき・食器 *noun* – plates, bowls and utensils for eating
しょっきを あらう = to wash the dishes

## ショック *noun* = shock

## しょっちゅう *adverb*
• = constantly
• = often

## ショップ *noun* = shop

## しょてん・書店 *noun* = bookstore

## しょどう・書道 *noun* = traditional Japanese calligraphy

## しょとく・所得 *noun* = income

## しょとくぜい・所得税 *noun* = income tax

## しょうひぜい・消費税 *noun* = VAT

## しょぶん・処分
**1** *noun*
• = disposal
• = punishment
**2** *verb 3* 🈯 しょぶんする
• = to dispose of
• = to punish

## しょめい・署名
**1** *noun* = signature
**2** *verb 3* 🈯 にしょめいする = to sign

## しょもつ・書物 *noun* = books

## しょゆう・所有
**1** *noun* = possession
**2** *verb 3* 🈯 しょゆうする = to own

## じょゆう・女優 *noun* = actress

## しょゆうしゃ・所有者 *noun* = owner

## しょり・処理
**1** *noun* = treatment
**2** *verb 3* 🈯 しょりする = to deal with

## しょるい・書類 *noun* = documents

## しらが・白髪 *noun* = white hairs

## しらせ・知らせ *noun*
• = notification
• = news

## しらせる・知らせる *verb 2* 🈯 = to inform

## しらべ・調べ *noun* = investigation

## しらべる・調べる *verb 2* 🈯
• = to investigate
• = to look up

## しり・尻 *noun* = (person's) bottom

## しりあい・知り合い *noun* = acquaintance

## シリーズ *noun* = series

## しりつ・私立 *prefix* – established privately (as opposed to by prefectural or national government)

## しりょう・資料 *noun*
• = data
• = materials

## しります ▶ しる

## しる・知る *verb 1* 🈯 = to know

## しる・汁 *noun*
• = soup
• = juice

## しるし・印 *noun* = sign

## しろ・白 *noun* = white

## しろ・城 *noun* = castle

## しろい・白い *adjective* = white

## しろうと・素人 *noun* = (an) amateur

## しろくろ・白黒 *noun* = black and white

## しわ・皺 *noun*
• = wrinkles
• = creases

## しん・芯 *noun*
• = core
• = (pencil) lead

## しん・新 *prefix* = new

## じん・人 *suffix* – added to country names it means person from that country ▶ 172

## しんがく・進学
**1** *noun* = advancing to the next level of education
**2** *verb 3* 🈯 しんがくする = to advance to the next educational level

## しんかんせん・新幹線 *noun* – the high speed 'bullet train' express linking many of Japan's cities

## しんくう・真空 *noun* = vacuum

## しんけい・神経 *noun* = nerve

**しんけいしつ(な)・神経質(な)**
*adjective* = nervous

**しんけん・真剣**
**1** *adjective* しんけん(な) = serious
**2** *adverb* しんけんに = seriously

**しんこう・進行**
**1** *noun* = advance
**2** *verb 3* ⓖ しんこうする = to advance

**しんこう・信仰**
**1** *noun* = (religious) faith
**2** *verb 3* ⓞ しんこうする = to believe (in)

**しんごう・信号** *noun*
- = traffic lights
- = traffic signals

**じんこう・人口** *noun* = population

**じんこう・人工** *prefix*
- = artificial
- = man-made

**しんこく・深刻**
**1** *adjective* しんこく(な) = serious
**2** *adverb* しんこくに = seriously

**しんさつ・診察**
**1** *noun* = medical examination
**2** *verb 3* ⓞ しんさつする = to examine

**じんじ・人事** *prefix* = personnel

**しんじゃ・信者** *noun* = (religious) believer

**じんじゃ・神社** *noun* = a Shinto shrine

**しんじゅ・真珠** *noun* = pearl

**じんしゅ・人種** *noun* = race

**じんしゅさべつ・人種差別**
*noun* = racial discrimination

**しんじる・信じる** *verb 2* ⓞ = to believe

**しんせい・申請**
**1** *noun* = application
**2** *verb 3* ⓞ しんせいする = to apply (for)

**じんせい・人生** *noun* = (a person's) life

**しんせき・親戚** *noun* = relatives

**しんせつ・親切**
**1** *adjective* しんせつ(な) = kind
**2** *adverb* しんせつに = kindly

**しんせん(な)・新鮮(な)**
*adjective* = fresh

**しんぞう・心臓** *noun* = heart

**じんぞう・人造** *prefix* = artificial

**しんたい・身体** *noun* = the body

**しんだい・寝台** *noun* = bed

**しんだん・診断**
**1** *noun* = diagnosis
**2** *verb 3* ⓞ しんだんする = to diagnose

**しんちょう・身長** *noun* = (person's) height

**しんちょう・慎重**
**1** *adjective* しんちょう(な) = careful
**2** *adverb* しんちょうに = carefully

**しんど・震度** *noun* – *indicates the scale of an earthquake on the Japanese scale (not the Richter scale) and is therefore followed by a number from 1 (weakest) to 8*

**しんとう・神道** *noun* – *a Japanese religion*

**しんどう・振動**
**1** *noun* = vibration
**2** *verb 3* ⓖ しんどうする = to shake

**しんどう・震動** *noun* = earth tremor

**しんにゅう・侵入**
**1** *noun* = raid
**2** *verb 3* ⓖ しんにゅうする = to invade

**しんねん・新年** *noun* = new year
しんねん あけまして おめでとう ございます = Happy New Year!

**しんぱい・心配**
**1** *noun* = worry
**2** *verb 3* ⓞ しんぱいする = to worry

**しんぱん・審判** *noun* = referee

**しんぴてき(な)・神秘的(な)**
*adjective* = mysterious

**しんぷ・新婦** *noun* = bride

**しんぷ・神父** *noun and suffix* – *used to mean 'father' for Catholic priests*

**じんぶつ・人物** *noun* = person

**しんぶん・新聞** *noun* = newspaper

**じんぶんかがく・人文科学**
*noun* = the humanities

しシ

しんぽ・進歩
1 *noun* = progress
2 *verb 3* ㊙ しんぽする = to make progress

しんぼう・辛抱 *noun* = patience

じんめい・人命 *noun* = (human) life

しんや・深夜 *prefix* = in the middle of the night

しんゆう・親友 *noun* = close friend

しんよう・信用
1 *noun* = trust
2 *verb 3* ㊗ しんようする = to rely on

しんらい・信頼
1 *noun* = trust
2 *verb 3* ㊗ しんらいする = to trust

しんり・心理 *noun* = state of mind

しんり・真理 *noun* = truth

しんりがく・心理学 *noun* = psychology

しんりゃく・侵略
1 *noun* = (military) aggression
2 *verb 3* ㊗ しんりゃくする = to invade

しんりん・森林 *noun* = forest(s)

しんるい・親類 *noun* = relative

じんるい・人類 *noun* = humanity

しんろ・進路 *noun* = course

しんろう・新郎 *noun* = bridegroom

しんわ・神話 *noun* = myth

# すス

す・巣 *noun* = nest

す・酢 *noun* = vinegar

すいえい・水泳
1 *noun* = swimming

すいか・西瓜 *noun* = water melon

すいさん・水産 *prefix* = fisheries

すいじ・炊事
1 *noun* = cooking
2 *verb 3* ㊙ すいじする = to cook

すいじゅん・水準 *noun* = standard

すいせん・推薦
1 *noun* = recommendation
2 *verb 3* ㊗ すいせんする = to recommend

すいせんじょう・推薦状 *noun* = a reference (for a job etc.)

すいそ・水素 *noun* = hydrogen

すいそく・推測
1 *noun* = guess
2 *verb 3* ㊗ すいそくする = to guess

すいちょく・垂直
1 *adjective* すいちょく(な) = vertical
2 *adverb* すいちょくに = vertically

スイッチ *noun* = switch
スイッチを いれる = to turn on

すいて ▶すく ▶ **197**

すいてい・推定
1 *noun* = estimate
2 *verb 3* ㊗ すいていする = to estimate

すいてき・水滴 *noun* = drop of water

すいでん・水田 *noun* = paddy field

すいとう・水筒 *noun* = water bottle

すいどう・水道 *noun* = water supply

ずいひつ・随筆 *noun* = essay (article)

すいぶん・水分 *noun* = water

ずいぶん・随分 *adverb* = very

すいへい(な)・水平(な)
*adjective* = level

すいへいせん・水平線 *noun* = horizon

すいます ▶すう

すいみん・睡眠 *noun* = sleep

すいみんぶそく・睡眠不足
*noun* = lack of sleep

すいめん・水面 *noun* = surface (of the water)

すいようび・水曜日 *noun* = Wednesday

すう・吸う *verb 1* ㊗ すって・すわない・すいます
• = to smoke
• = to take in (air or liquid)

すう・数 *prefix* = several

すうがく・**数学** *noun*
= mathematics

すうじ・**数字** *noun* = numbers

ずうずうしい・**図々しい**
*adjective* = cheeky

スーツ *noun* = suit

スーツケース *noun* = suitcase

ずうっと *adverb* = continuously

スーパー *noun* = supermarket

スープ *noun* = soup

すえ・**末** *noun* = end

すえっこ・**末っ子** *noun*
= youngest child

すえる・**据える** *verb 2* 㐂 = to place

すがた・**姿** *noun*
• = shape
• = figure (of)

スカート *noun* = skirt

スカーフ *noun* = scarf

ずかん・**図鑑** *noun*
• = illustrated book
• = reference work

すき(な)・**好き(な)**
**1** *adjective* = favourite/favorite
　すきなようにする = do as one pleases

> ! *although an adjective in Japanese it is often best translated using a verb such as 'to like'*

　テニスが すきです = (I) like tennis

すぎ・**杉** *noun* = cedar

すぎ・**過ぎ** *suffix* – *adds the meaning of 'after' or 'more than' to nouns and (following the pre* 〜ます *form) it adds the meaning of 'done to excess' to verbs* ▶ **186**
　ろくじすぎ = after six o'clock
　たべすぎ = overeating

スキー
**1** *noun*
• = skis
• = skiing
**2** *verb 3* 㐂 スキーをする = to ski

すききらい・**好き嫌い** *noun*
= likes and dislikes
　すききらいが ある = to be fussy

すきずき・**好き好き** *noun*
= personal taste

すきとおる・**透き通る** *verb 1* 㐂
= to be transparent

すきま・**隙間** *noun* = a gap

すきまかぜ・**隙間風** *noun* = a draft

すぎる・**過ぎる** *verb 2* 㐂
• = to be more than
• = to pass through

> ! *added to verbs and adjectives to make compounds with the meaning '... too much'*

すく・**空く** *verb 1* 㐂 すいて
すかない すきます
• = to not be crowded
• = to be empty
　おなかが すいている = to be hungry

すぐ・**直ぐ** *adverb*
• = immediately
• = soon
• = as soon as

すくう・**救う** *verb 1* 㐂 = to save

すくない・**少ない** *adjective*
= few

すくなくとも・**少なくとも**
*adverb* = at least

すぐれる・**優れる** *verb 2* 㐂
= to excel

スケート
**1** *noun* = ice skating
**2** *verb 3* 㐂 スケートをする = to ice skate

スケートぐつ・**スケート靴**
*noun* = ice skates

スケジュール *noun*
• = schedule
• = plans

すごい・**凄い** *adjective*
• = tremendous
• = brilliant

すこし・**少し** *adverb*
• = a few
• = some
• = a short time
• = a little bit of

すこしも・**少しも** *adverb* (with negative) = (not) at all

すス

すごす・過ごす　verb 1 を
• = to pass
• (of time) = to spend

すじ・筋　noun
• = muscle
• = stripe
• = logic
• = reason
　すじが とおった = logical

すずしい・涼しい　adjective
= (pleasantly) cool

すすむ・進む　verb 1 か
• = to make progress
• = to advance

すすめる・進める　verb 2 を
= to proceed with

すすめる・勧める・薦める
　verb 2 を
• = to advise
• = to recommend

スター　noun = star

スタート　noun = start

スタイル　noun = style

スタジアム　noun = stadium

スタジオ　noun = studio

スタンド　noun
• = desk light
• = stands

ずつ　suffix = each

ずつう・頭痛　noun = headache

すっかり　adverb
• = completely
• = perfectly

すっきり(した)　adjectival phrase
• = refreshing
• = clear

すっきり(する)　verb 3 か = to feel
　refreshed

すって ▶ すう ▶ 197

すっと　adverb
• = gently
• = quietly

ずっと　adverb
• = directly
• = for a long time

すっぱい・酸っぱい　adjective
= sour

ステージ　noun = stage
(for performances)

すてき(な)　adjective = lovely

すでに・既に　adverb = already

すてる・捨てる・棄てる
　verb 2 を = to throw away

ストーブ　noun – a free-standing
room heater

ストッキング　noun = stockings
• = tights

ストップ
1 noun = stop
2 verb 3 を ストップする = to stop

ストレス　noun = stress

すな・砂　noun = sand

すなお・素直
1 adjective = obedient
2 adverb すなおに = obediently

すなわち・即ち　conjunction = that
is to say

ずのう・頭脳　suffix = brain

すばやい・素早い　adjective = very
quick

すばらしい・素晴らしい
　adjective = wonderful

スピーカー　noun = speaker/s

スピーチ
1 noun = speech
2 verb 3 か スピーチ(を)する
　= to make a speech

スピード　noun = speed

スピードカメラ　noun = speed camera

ずひょう・図表　noun = chart

スプーン　noun = spoon

スペース　noun = space

すべて・全て　noun = all (of them)

すべる・滑る　verb 1 か
• = to slip
• = to ski

スポーツ
1 noun = sport
2 verb 3 か スポーツ(を)する = to do
sport

ズボン　noun = trousers

スマート(な)　adjective = slim

すまい・住まい　noun = home

**すませる・済ませる** *verb 2* ㊟
• = to finish
• = to manage

**すまない・済まない** *adjective*
= unpardonable

> **!** *used as an informal apology for causing trouble to somebody*
> ▶ すみません

**すみ・墨** *noun* = ink
**すみ・炭** *noun* = charcoal
**すみ・隅** *noun* = corner
**すみます** ▶ すむ
**すみません** *phrase*
• = excuse me
• = sorry

**すむ・住む** *verb 1* ㊚ に すんで
すまない すみます = to live (in)
**すむ・済む** *verb 1* ㊚
• = to be finished
• = to get through
**すむ・澄む** *verb 1* ㊚ = to become clear

**すもう・相撲** *noun* = sumo wrestling
**ずらり(と)** *adverb* = in a line
**すり** *noun* = pickpocket
**スリッパ** *noun* = slippers
**する** *verb 3* ㊟ して・しない・します

> **!** *although the principle meaning of this verb is 'to do' it has many uses and can be translated as 'to play', "to put on", 'to cost', 'to decide to' and 'to be' as well as appearing in various constructions where it will not be translated as a verb. It is used to transform nouns into verbs. Try looking up the word|s with which it occurs. For more on する* ▶ **191**

**ずるい** *adjective*
• = unfair
• = sly
**すると** *conjunction*
• = in that case
• = just at that moment
**するどい・鋭い** *adjective*
• = sharp
**ずれ** *noun*
• = discrepancy
• = lag

**すれちがう・擦れ違う** *verb 1* ㊚
= to pass someone or something coming from the opposite direction
**すれる・擦れる** *verb 2* ㊚ = to rub
**ずれる** *verb 2* ㊚ = to be out of place/position
**すわって** ▶ すわる ▶ **197**
**すわります** ▶ すわる
**すわる・座る** *verb 1* ㊚ すわって・すわらない・すわります = to sit
**すんで** ▶ すむ ▶ **197**
**すんぽう・寸法** *noun*
= measurements

せセ

# せセ

**せ・背** *noun* = back
せが たかい = tall
**せい・背** *noun* = (person's) height
**せい・性** *noun and prefix* = gender
**せい・性** *suffix*
• = character
• = nature
**せい・姓** *noun* = surname
**せい・所為** *noun* = (somebody's) fault
**せい・製** *suffix*
• = made in ...
• = made of ...
• = made from ...
**ぜい・税** *prefix and suffix element*
= tax
**せいかく・性格** *noun* = character
**せいかく・正確**
**1** *adjective* せいかく(な) = accurate
**2** *adverb* せいかくに = accurately
**せいかつ・生活** *noun* = life (style)
**ぜいかん・税関** *noun* = customs
**せいき・世紀** *noun and suffix*
= century
**せいきゅう・請求**
**1** *noun*
• = demand
• = claim

**2** *verb 3* 圏 せいきゅうする
- = to demand
- = to claim

せいきゅうしょ・請求書 *noun*
= bill

ぜいきん・税金 *noun* = tax

せいけつ(な)・清潔(な)
*adjective* = clean

せいげん・制限
**1** *noun* = restriction
**2** *verb 3* 圏 せいげんする = to restrict

せいこう・成功
**1** *noun* = success
**2** *verb 3* 困 せいこうする = to succeed

せいさく・製作
**1** *noun* = manufacturing
**2** *verb 3* 圏 せいさくする = to manufacture

せいさく・制作
**1** *noun* = production
**2** *verb 3* 圏 せいさくする = to produce

せいさく・政策 *noun* = policy

せいさん・生産
**1** *noun* = output
**2** *verb 3* 圏 せいさんする = to produce

せいじ・政治 *noun* = politics

せいじか・政治家 *noun*
= politician

せいしき・正式
**1** *adjective* せいしき(な) = official
**2** *adverb* せいしきに = formally

せいしつ・性質 *noun*
- = nature
- = character

せいしょ・聖書 *noun* = (the) bible

せいしょうねん・青少年 *noun*
- = youth
- = young people

せいしん・精神 *noun*
- = spirit
- = mind

せいじん・成人 *noun* = adult

❗ *adulthood begins at 20 in Japan*

せいじんしき・成人式 *noun* –
*ceremony marking coming of age at 20*

せいしんてき・精神的
**1** *adjective* せいしんてき(な)
= mental
**2** *adverb* せいしんてきに = mentally

せいじんのひ・成人の日 *noun* –
*Coming of Age Day (January 15) – a Japanese public holiday*

せいぜい・精々 *adverb*
- = at most
- = as much as possible

せいせき・成績 *noun* = (school or exam) results

せいせきひょう・成績表 *noun* –
*school report*

せいそう(する)・清掃 (する)
*verb 3* 圏 = to clean

せいそうしゃ・清掃車 *noun*
= garbage truck

せいぞう・製造
**1** *noun* = manufacture
**2** *verb 3* 圏 せいぞうする = to manufacture

せいぞん・生存
**1** *noun* = survival
**2** *verb 3* 困 せいぞんする = to exist

せいぞんしゃ・生存者 *noun*
= survivor

ぜいたく・贅沢
**1** *noun* = luxury
**2** *adjective* ぜいたく(な) = luxurious
**3** *adverb* ぜいたくに = luxuriously

せいちょう・成長
**1** *noun* = growth
**2** *verb 3* 困 せいちょうする = to grow

せいてん・晴天 *noun* = fine weather

せいと・生徒 *noun* = school student

せいど・制度 *noun* = system

せいとう・政党 *noun* = political party

せいねん・青年 *noun*
- = young man
- = youth

せいねんがっぴ・生年月日
*noun* = date of birth

せいのう・性能 *noun*
= performance

せいび・整備
**1** *noun* = maintenance

**2** *verb 3* 圏 せいびする
- = to maintain
- = to repair

**せいひん・製品** *noun* = article

**せいふ・政府** *noun* = government

**せいふく・制服** *noun* = uniform

**せいぶつ・生物** *noun* = living thing

**せいぶつがく・生物学** *noun* = biology (as a subject)

**せいぶん・成分** *noun* = ingredients

**せいべつ・性別** *noun* = distinction by gender

**せいぼ・歳暮** ▶ おせいぼ

**せいめい・生命** *noun* = life

**せいめい・姓名** *noun* = full name

**せいもん・正門** *noun* = main entrance

**せいよう・西洋** *prefix* = Western (style)

**せいり・整理**
**1** *noun* = putting in order
**2** *verb 3* 圏 せいりする = to put in order

**せいり・生理** *noun*
- = physiology
- = (menstrual) period

**せいりつ・成立**
**1** *noun* = formation
**2** *verb 3* 圀 せいりつする = to come into existence

**せいれき・西暦** *noun* = (western calendar) date

❗ *although the western calendar is also in widespread use, Japan still uses its own calendar system based on the ruling emperor and the number of years of his reign* ▶ 174

**セーター** *noun* = jumper/sweater

**セール** *noun* = sale

**せおう・背負う** *verb 1* 圏 = to carry (on the back)

**せかい・世界** *noun* = world

**せき・席** *noun* = seat

**せき・咳** *noun* = cough
　せきが でる = to cough

**せき・隻** *counter* = ships ▶ 181

**せきたん・石炭** *noun* = coal

**せきどう・赤道** *noun* = equator

**せきにん・責任** *noun* = responsibility

**せきゆ・石油** *noun* = oil

**せけん・世間** *noun* = the world

**せけんばなし・世間話** *noun* = small talk

**せじ・世辞** ▶ おせじ

**せたい・世帯** *noun* = household

**せだい・世代** *noun* = generation

**せつ・説** *suffix* = explanation

**せっかく・折角**
**1** *adverb* = specially
**2** *adjective* せっかくの = valuable

**せっきょくてき・積極的**
**1** *adjective* せっきょくてき(な) = positive
**2** *adverb* せっきょくてきに = positively

**せっきん・接近**
**1** *noun* = approach
**2** *verb 3* 圀 せっきんする = to approach

**セックス**
**1** *noun* = sex
**2** *verb 3* 圀 と セックス(を)する = to have sex

**せっけい・設計**
**1** *noun* = plan
**2** *verb 3* 圏 せっけいする = to design

**せっけん・石鹸** *noun* = soap

**せっしょく・接触**
**1** *noun* = contact
**2** *verb 3* 圀 と せっしょくする = to touch

**せっする・接する** *verb 3* 圀 と
- = to touch
- = to be in contact

**せっせと** *adverb* = hard

**せつぞく・接続**
**1** *noun* = connection
**2** *verb 3* 圀 圏 せつぞくする = to connect

**ぜったい(に)・絶対(に)** *adverb*
- = definitely
- (*with negative*) = absolutely (not)

**セット** *noun* = set

せせ

**せっとく・説得**
1 *noun* = persuasion
2 *verb 3* Ⓥ せっとくする = to persuade

**せつび・設備** *noun*
• = equipment
• = facilities

**せつめい・説明**
1 *noun* = explanation
2 *verb 3* Ⓥ せつめいする = to explain

**せつめいしょ・説明書** *noun*
= instruction manual

**ぜつめつ・絶滅**
1 *noun* = extinction
2 *verb 3* Ⓘ ぜつめつする = to be extinct

**せつやく・節約**
1 *noun* = economisation
2 *verb 3* Ⓥ せつやくする = to economise

**せつりつ・設立**
1 *noun* = foundation
2 *verb 3* Ⓥ せつりつする = to found

**せともの・瀬戸物** *noun*
• = porcelain
• = china

**せなか・背中** *noun* = (person's) back

**ぜひ・是非**
1 *noun* = the rights and wrongs
2 *adverb*
• = without fail
• = definitely
• = no matter what

**せびろ・背広** *noun* = suit (clothing)

**せまい・狭い** *adjective*
• = narrow
• = cramped

> ❗ used to mean 'small' when describing a room|house

**せまる・迫る** *verb 1* Ⓘ = to draw near

> ❗ often used with a sense of 'time pressing' and in the passive form it can mean 'to be under pressure'

**せみ** *noun* = cicada

**ゼミ** *noun* = seminar

**せめて** *adverb* = at least

**せめる・責める** *verb 2* Ⓥ = to blame

**せめる・攻める** *verb 2* Ⓥ = to attack

**セメント** *noun* = cement

**ゼリー** *noun* = jelly

**せりふ・台詞** *noun* = lines (of a script)

**ゼロ** *noun* = zero ▶ **181**

**せろん・世論** *noun* = public opinion

**せわ・世話**
1 *noun* = care
2 *verb 3* Ⓥ せわする = to look after
▶ おせわに なりました

**せん・千** *noun, prefix and suffix* = thousand ▶ **181**

**せん・線** *noun and suffix*
• = line
• = railway line

**せん・栓** *noun*
• = stopper
• = plug
• = cork

**せん・戦** *suffix* = war

**ぜん・善** *noun* = good

**ぜん・全** *prefix* = all

**ぜん・前** *prefix* = former

**ぜん・前** *suffix* = before

**ぜんいん・全員** *noun*
• = all (the members)
• = everyone

**せんきょ・選挙**
1 *noun* = election
2 *verb 3* Ⓥ せんきょ(を)する = to elect

**ぜんご・前後** *noun*
• = before and after
• = front and rear

**ぜんご・前後** *suffix* = about

**せんこう・専攻**
1 *noun* = subject (of study)
2 *verb 3* Ⓥ せんこうする = to major (in)

**ぜんこく・全国** *noun and prefix* = nationwide

**せんざい・洗剤** *noun* = detergent

せんじつ・先日 *noun*
- = the other day
- = a few days ago

せんしゃ・戦車 *noun* = tank

ぜんしゃ・前者 *noun* = the former

せんしゅ・選手 *noun* – *this word can be used on its own to mean a sportsman or sportswoman and is thus translated as 'player' or 'athlete' or other terms depending on the sport. Since it can also be plural in meaning another possible translation is 'team'. Also added as a suffix to individual family names as a title to address and refer to sportsmen and sportswomen.*

せんしゅう・先週 *noun* = last week

ぜんしん・前進
**1** *noun* = advance
**2** *verb 3* ㋕ ぜんしんする = to advance

ぜんしん・全身 *noun*
- = the whole body
- = all over (the body)

せんす・扇子 *noun* = (folding) fan

センス *noun*
- = sense (of fashion etc.)
- = (good) taste (in)

せんすい・潜水 *noun and prefix* = underwater

せんすいかん・潜水艦 *noun* = submarine

せんせい・先生 *noun and suffix* – *on its own the word is used to mean 'teacher' and 'doctor' and it is used as a way of addressing and referring to teachers, professors, doctors, politicians and lawyers either directly or as a title attached to a family name.*

ぜんぜん・全然 *adverb*
- (*with negative*) = not at all
- (*with positive*) = completely

せんぞ・先祖 *noun* = ancestors

せんそう・戦争 *noun* = war

センター *noun and suffix* = centre (as an institutional name)

ぜんたい・全体 *noun* = (the) whole

せんたく・洗濯
**1** *noun* = (the) washing
**2** *verb 3* ㋕ せんたくする = to wash (clothes)

せんたく・選択
**1** *noun* = selection
**2** *verb 3* ㋕ せんたくする = to choose

せんたくき・洗濯機 *noun* = washing machine

せんたくもの・洗濯物 *noun* = (the) washing
　せんたくものを ほす = to hang the washing to dry

センチ *noun* = centimetre/s

センチメートル ▶ センチ

せんでん・宣伝
**1** *noun*
- = advertisement
- = publicity
**2** *verb 3* ㋕ せんでんする = to advertise

せんてんてき・先天的
**1** *adjective* せんてんてき(な) = innate
**2** *adverb* せんてんてきに = naturally

せんとう・先頭 *noun*
- = head
- = lead

せんとう・銭湯 *noun* – *a public bath house often found in older residential areas of Japanese towns*

せんぬき・栓抜き・栓抜 *noun*
- = bottle opener
- = corkscrew

せんぱい・先輩 *noun* – *a junior person in relation to a senior in either an educational establishment or the workplace. It is used alone to address people or can be attached to names as a title of address and reference* ▶ こうはい

ぜんはん・前半 *noun* = first half (of a match etc.)

ぜんぱんてき・全般的
**1** *adjective* ぜんぱんてき(な) = overall
**2** *adverb* ぜんぱんてきに = generally

ぜんぶ・全部 *noun*
- = all
- = everything

**せんぷうき・扇風機** *noun*
= electric fan

**せんめん・洗面**
**1** *noun* = washing (the face)
**2** *verb 3* ㋕ せんめん(を)する = to wash the face

**せんめんじょ・洗面所** *noun*
• = washroom

> ❗ a place where there is a sink for washing the face and hands

**せんもん・専門** *noun*
• = academic subject
• = major

**せんもんか・専門家** *noun*
= specialist

**ぜんりゃく・前略** *phrase* – used to open an informal letter and meaning something like 'this is just a quick note to say ...'

**せんりょう・占領**
**1** *noun* = occupation
**2** *verb 3* ㋷ せんりょうする = to occupy

**せんりょく・戦力** *noun* = military power

**ぜんりょく・全力** *noun* = all one's strength
ぜんりょくをつくす = to try as hard as possible

**せんろ・線路** *noun* = railway (track)

---

# そソ

---

**そ ▶ そう**

**ぞ** *particle* – used to add emphasis to a statement, especially one expressing intention. Used by males

**ぞい・沿い** *suffix* – means 'running parallel to' some kind of line of things such as a street or a river and translatable as ' along the ...' or 'running along the ...'

**そう** *adverb*
• = that way
• = like that ▶ そういう

> ❗ very common in the form そうです or informally just as そう (sometimes repeated for emphasis) which is used to show agreement with a question and translatable as 'that's right'. In the form そうですね it indicates a hesitation in answering and can be translated as 'well' or 'let me see'. Take care to distinguish this from the noun phrase そうです which is mentioned two entries below. In the form そうですか or そうか it is used to indicate that new information has been received by the listener and can be thought of as roughly similar to 'really?', 'is that so?' or 'is that right?'

**そう・総** *prefix*
• = all
• = general

**そう** *noun* – used in the form そうです or そうだ at the end of a statement|sentence it means 'apparently' or 'it's said that ...' or 'I heard that ...'
かいぎは あした だ そうです
= apparently the meeting is tomorrow

**ぞう・象** *noun* = elephant

**そうい・相違**
**1** *noun* = difference
**2** *verb 3* ㋕ そういする = to differ

**そういえば・そう言えば** *phrase*
• = by the way
• = speaking of which

**そうおん・騒音** *noun* = (unpleasant) loud noise

**ぞうか・増加**
**1** *noun* = increase
**2** *verb 3* ㋕ ㋷ ぞうかする = to increase

**そうきん・送金**
**1** *noun* = money transfer
**2** *verb 3* ㋷ そうきんする = to send money

**ぞうきん・雑巾** *noun* = cloth (for cleaning)

**ぞうげん・増減**
**1** *noun* = fluctuation
**2** *verb 3* ㋕ ぞうげんする = to fluctuate

そうこ・倉庫 *noun*
- = warehouse
- = store room

そうご(の)・相互(の) *noun*
(*used as adjective*) = mutual

そうさ・操作
**1** *noun* = operation (of a machine etc.)
**2** *verb 3* Ⓐ そうさする = to operate

そうさ・捜査
**1** *noun* = (criminal) investigation
**2** *verb 3* Ⓐ そうさする = to investigate

そうさく・創作
**1** *noun* = creation (of something)
**2** *verb 3* Ⓐ そうさくする = to create

そうじ・掃除
**1** *noun* = cleaning
**2** *verb 3* Ⓐ そうじする = to clean

そうじき・掃除機 *noun* = vacuum cleaner
　そうじきを かける = to vacuum

そうしき・葬式 *noun* = funeral

そうして
**1** *conjunction* = and then
**2** *adverb*
- = that way
- = like that

そうじゅう・操縦
**1** *noun* = operation of controls (of plane or ship)
**2** *verb 3* Ⓐ そうじゅうする
- = to pilot
- = to fly

そうじゅうし・操縦士 *noun* = pilot

そうすると ▶ そう

そうぞう・想像
**1** *noun* = imagination
**2** *verb 3* Ⓐ そうぞうする = to imagine

そうぞう・創造
**1** *noun* = creation
**2** *verb 3* Ⓐ そうぞうする = to create

そうぞうりょく・想像力 *noun* = imagination

そうぞうりょく・創造力 *noun* = creativity

そうぞうしい・騒々しい
*adjective* = noisy

ぞうだい・増大
**1** *noun* = increase
**2** *verb 3* Ⓝ ぞうだいする = to increase

そうだん・相談
**1** *noun* = discussion
**2** *verb 3* Ⓐ そうだんする
- = to consult
- = to discuss

そうち・装置 *noun*
- = equipment
- = device

そうとう・相当
**1** *adverb*
- = considerably
- = quite
**2** *adjective* そうとう(な)・そうとう(の) = considerable

そうとう・相当 *suffix*
- = worth
- = equivalent to

そうば・相場 *noun* = exchange rate

そうべつかい・送別会 *noun* – a formal farewell party

ぞうり・草履 *noun* – flat sandals worn with きもの or for nipping out of a house (*which means putting on and removing footwear of some kind*)

そうりだいじん・総理大臣
*noun* = Prime Minister

そうりょう・送料 *noun* = postage (cost)

そく・足 *counter* = pairs of (shoes or socks) ▶ **181**

ぞく(する)・属(する) *verb 3* Ⓝ
- = to belong to
- = to be attached to

ぞくぞく(と)・続々(と) *adverb* = one after another

そくたつ・速達 *noun* = express delivery (post)

そくてい・測定
**1** *noun* = measurement
**2** *verb 3* Ⓐ そくていする = to measure

そくど・速度 *noun* = speed

そくばく・束縛
**1** *noun* = restriction
**2** *verb 3* Ⓐ そくばくする = to restrict

そ/ソ

**そくりょう・測量**
1 *noun* = survey
2 *verb 3* 🅰 そくりょうする = to survey

**そくりょうぎし・測量技師**
*noun* = surveyor

**そくりょく・速力** *noun* = speed

**そこ** *noun*
• = there
• = that

**そこ・底** *noun* = bottom (of the sea etc.)

**そこで** *conjunction*
• = so
• = therefore

**そこなう・損なう** *verb 1* 🅰 – *on it's own the verb means 'to impair' and it is common as a suffix element in the pre 〜ます form of verbs to add the meaning 'fail to (do)'* ▶ **191**

**そしき・組織** *noun*
• = organisation
• = system

**そしきてき・組織的**
1 *adjective* そしきてき(な) = systematic
2 *adverb* そしきてきに = methodically

**そしつ・素質** *noun* = qualities

**そして** *conjunction*
• = and
• = and then

**そせん・祖先** *noun* = ancestors

**そそぐ・注ぐ** *verb 1* 🅰 = to pour

**そそっかしい** *adjective* = careless

**そだち・育ち** *suffix* = brought up in

**そだつ・育つ** *verb 1* 🅘
• = to grow up
• = to be brought up

**そだって・育って** ▶ そだつ ▶ **197**

**そだてる・育てる** *verb 2* 🅰
• = to bring up (children)
• = to grow (vegetables)

**そちら** *noun*
• = over there
• = that one
• = that way
• = you

**そっち** *noun* – *informal version of* そちら

**そつぎょう・卒業**
1 *noun* = graduation
2 *verb 3* 🅰 そつぎょうする = to graduate

**そっくり**
1 *adjective* そっくり(な)・ そっくり(の) = exactly like
2 *adverb* = entirely

**そっちょく・率直**
1 *adjective* そっちょく(な) = frank
2 *adverb* そっちょくに = candidly

**そっと** *adverb*
• = quietly
• = gently

**そで・袖** *noun* = sleeve

**そと・外** *noun*
• = outside
• = outdoors

**そなえる・備える** *verb 2* 🅰 に
• = to prepare
• = to install

**その** *attributive*
• = that
• = it

> ❗ *meaning 'close to the listener' it is also often used to refer to something previously mentioned*

**そのうえ・その上** *conjunction* = moreover

**そのうち(に)・その内(に)** *adverb*
• = soon
• = before long

**そのころ** *noun* = (about) then

**そのとおり・その通り** *phrase* = you are right!

**そのほか・その外・その他** *noun* = the rest

**そのまえ(に)・その前(に)** *adverb*
• = before that
• = in front of (it)

**そのまま** *phrase*
• = as it is
• = straightaway

**そば** *noun*
• = side

- = beside
- = near

そば *noun* – thin buckwheat noodles

そふ・祖父 *noun* = grandfather
▶ **177**

ソファー *noun*
- = sofa
- = armchair

ソフト *noun and adjectival noun*
- = software
- = soft

そぼ・祖母 *noun* = grandmother
▶ **177**

そまつ・粗末
**1** *adjective* そまつ(な) = poor (quality)
- = simple
**2** *adverb* そまつに = roughly

そむく・背く *verb 1* ⓗ
- = to disobey
- = to disregard

そら・空 *noun* = sky

そる・剃る *verb 1* ⓦ = to shave

それ *noun*
- = that
- = it

  **!** *meaning 'close to the listener' it is
  also often used to refer to something
  previously mentioned*

それから *conjunction*
- = after that
- = since then

それぞれ *adverb*
- = each
- = respectively

それで *adverb*
- = and then
- = therefore

それでは *conjunction*
- = in that case
- = well

  **!** *sometimes used informally to say
  'I'm leaving', 'that's all' or 'let's go'*

それでも *conjunction*
- = but
- = even so

それと *conjunction*
- = and
- = plus

それとも *conjunction* = or

それなのに *conjunction* = even so

それなら *conjunction* = in that case

それに *conjunction*
- = and
- = what's more

それほど *noun*
- = that many/much
- = so many/much

そろう・揃う *verb 1* ⓗ
- = to be gathered
- = to be complete (as a group or set)

そろえる・揃える *verb 2* ⓦ
- = to put in order
- = to arrange

そろそろ *adverb*
- = soon
- = almost

  **!** *often used as an abbreviated form
  of* そろそろ しつれい します
  *meaning 'I must be going'*

そろばん・算盤 *noun* = abacus

そん・損 *noun*
- = disadvantage
- = loss

そん・損
**1** *noun* = loss
- = disadvantage
**2** *verb 3* ⓦ そんする = to lose

そんがい・損害 *noun* = damage

そんけい・尊敬
**1** *noun* = respect
**2** *verb 3* ⓦ そんけいする = to respect

そんけいご・尊敬語 *noun* –
*respect language used towards
older people and to be polite and
deferential in general* ▶ **189**

そんざい・存在
**1** *noun* = existence
**2** *verb 3* ⓗ そんざいする = to exist

ぞんざい
**1** *adjective* ぞんざい(な) = rough
**2** *adverb* ぞんざいに = roughly

ぞんじる・存じる *verb 3* ⓦ –
*humble equivalent of verbs* しる
*and* わかる *and thus translatable
as 'to know' or 'to think'* ▶ **189**
▶ ごぞんじ

そソ

## そんちょう・尊重
**1** *noun* = respect
**2** *verb 3* ⓐ そんちょうする = to respect

## そんな *attributive*
- = such
- = like that

## そんなに *adverb*
- = such
- = so much
- = (not all) that

---

# た タ

---

た・田 *noun* = paddy field

た・他 *noun* = (the) other/s

だ – *plain form of* です *and translatable as 'am', 'is' or 'are'* ▶ **187**

たい・対 *suffix and prefix – placed between two two sets of numbers or two people/teams it means 'versus' or '(as opposed) to'. As a prefix it means 'concerning ...' or 'towards ...'*

たい *suffix – added to the pre* ～ます *form of a verb it adds the meaning 'want to'* ▶ **191**

だい・大 *noun* = (a) large (one)

だい・台 *noun* = stand

だい・台 *counter – used for large items such as vehicles, machines and (large) electrical goods* ▶ **181**

だい・題 *noun* = title

だい・第 *prefix – indicates ordinal numbers such as* だいいち・第一 *'the first' or* だいさん・第三 *'the third'*

だい・代 *suffix – a bill (for gas, electricity, water or telephone)*

たいいく・体育 *noun – this term covers physical education and sports as school and college subjects and sports and training more generally*

たいいくかん・体育館 *noun*
- = sports hall
- = gymnasium

たいいくのひ・体育の日 *noun – Health and Sports Day (October 10) – a Japanese public holiday*

## だいいち・第一
**1** *noun*
- = the first
- = the most important
**2** *adverb* だいいち(に) = first of all

だいいちじせかいたいせん・第一次世界大戦 *noun* = the first world war

## たいいん・退院
**1** *noun* = coming out of hospital
**2** *verb 3* ⓝ たいいんする = to leave hospital

たいおん・体温 *noun* = (body) temperature

たいおんけい・体温計 *noun* = thermometer (for the body)

たいかい・大会 *noun*
- = contest
- = convention

## たいがく・退学
**1** *noun* = withdrawing from school/college
**2** *verb 3* ⓝ たいがくする = to withdraw from school or college

だいがく・大学 *noun* = university

だいがくいん・大学院 *noun – this word is used in place of* だいがく *'university' when referring to post-graduate work and study*

たいがくしょぶん・退学処分 *noun* = expulsion from school/college

たいき・大気 *noun* = (the) atmosphere

だいきん・代金 *noun*
- = payment
- = amount

だいく・大工 *noun* = carpenter

## たいくつ・退屈
**1** *adjective* たいくつ(な) = boring
**2** *verb 3* ⓝ たいくつする = to be bored

たいけい・体系 *noun* = system

**たいけいてき・体系的**
**1** adjective たいけいてき(な)
= systematic
**2** adverb たいけいてきに
= systematically

**たいこ・太鼓** noun – a traditional Japanese drum and the playing of Japanese drums as a style of music

**たいざい・滞在**
**1** noun = stay
**2** verb 3 ㊙ に たいざいする = to stay

**たいざいきかん・滞在期間**
noun = length of stay

**たいさく・対策** noun
• = measures
• = countermeasures

**たいし・大使** noun = ambassador

**たいしかん・大使館** noun
= embassy

**だいじ・大事**
**1** adjective だいじ(な) = important
**2** verb 3 ㊙ だいじにする
• = to treat well
• = to treat carefully

**たいした・大した** phrase
(as adjective)
• (with positive) = quite a ...
• (with negative) = not much of a ...

**たいして・大して** adverb
• = not very
• = not much

**たいして・対して** phrase – in the form ～にたいして this is used to express ideas like 'towards', 'regarding' and 'about'. It can also be used to mean 'as opposed to' and 'in contrast to' when a contrast is stated

**たいじゅう・体重** noun = body weight

**たいじゅうけい・体重計** noun – scales for measuring body weight

**たいしょう・対象** noun
• = object
• = subject

**たいしょう・対照**
**1** noun = contrast
**2** verb 3 ㊙ と たいしょうする
= to compare
• = to contrast

**だいしょう・大小** noun
• = large and small
• = size

**だいじょうぶ(な)・大丈夫(な)**
adjective
• = OK
• = all right
• = safe

**たいしょく・退職**
**1** noun
• = retirement
• = resignation
**2** verb 3 ㊙ たいしょくする
• = to retire
• = to resign

**だいじん・大臣** noun and suffix
= (government) minister

**たいする・対する** verb 3 ㊙ に
= to be against ▶ たいして

**たいせい・体制** noun = system

**たいせき・体積** noun = volume

**たいせつ・大切**
**1** adjective たいせつ(な) = important
**2** adverb たいせつに = carefully

**たいせん・大戦** noun – used to mean a great war and especially to refer to the first and second world wars ▶ だいいちじせかいたいせん ▶ だいにじせかいたいせん

**たいそう・体操** noun = gymnastics

**たいそう・大層** adverb = greatly

**だいたい・大体**
**1** noun = general idea (of)
**2** adverb
• = approximately
• = generally

**たいてい・大抵**
**1** noun = most (of)
**2** adverb = generally

**たいど・態度** noun = attitude

**だいとうりょう・大統領** noun
= President

**だいどころ・台所** noun = kitchen

**だいにじせかいたいせん・第二次世界大戦** noun = the second world war

**たいはん・大半** noun = the greater part (of)

**だいひょう・代表** *noun* = (a) representative

**タイプ** *noun* = type (of person)

**タイプ**
1 *noun* = typing
2 *verb 3* 炙 タイプする = to type

**だいぶ・大分** *adverb*
• = considerably
• = mostly

**たいふう・台風** *noun* = typhoon

**だいぶぶん・大部分**
1 *noun* = most (of )
2 *adverb* = mostly

**たいへん・大変**
1 *adjective* たいへん(な)
• = hard
• = awful
2 *adverb*
• = very
• = extremely
　たいへんです = 'oh no!'

> ❗ often used to describe something which might be translated as 'serious' or 'difficult'. Also used to show sympathy as in 'oh no, how awful!'

**たいほ・逮捕**
1 *noun* = arrest
2 *verb 3* 炙 たいほする = to arrest

**タイマー** *noun* = timer

**タイミング** *noun* = timing

**だいめい・題名** *noun* = title

**ダイヤ** *noun*
• = timetable (for public transport)
• = diamond

**ダイヤル**
1 *noun* = dial
2 *verb 3* 炙 に ダイヤルする = to dial

**たいよう・太陽** *noun* = the sun

**たいら(な)・平ら(な)** *adjective*
• = flat
• = level

**だいり・代理** *noun*
• = representative
• = agent

**だいりてん・代理店** *noun* = agency

**たいりく・大陸** *noun* = continent

**たいりつ・対立**
1 *noun* = conflict
2 *verb 3* 炙 に たいりつする = to be opposed

**たいりょく・体力** *noun* = strength

**たえず・絶えず** *adverb* = continually

**たえる・耐える** *verb 2* 炙 に = to endure

**だえんけい・楕円形** *noun* = oval

**たおす・倒す** *verb 1* 炙 = to knock down

**タオル** *noun* = towel

**たおれる・倒れる** *verb 2* 炙 = to fall down

**だが** *conjunction* = however

**たかい・高い** *adjective*
• = high
• = expensive

**たがい・互い** *noun* = each other
▶ おたがいに

**たかめる・高める** *verb 2* 炙 = to raise

**たがやす・耕す** *verb 1* 炙 = to plough

**たから・宝** *noun* = treasure

**たからくじ・宝くじ** *noun* = lottery

**だから** *conjunction*
• = therefore
• = so

**だからこそ** *phrase* = therefore

**たがる** *suffix* – added to the pre ～ます of a verb to give the meaning 'wants to' when referring to people other than oneself ▶ たい ▶ がる
▶ **191**

**たき・滝** *noun* = waterfall

**たきます** ▶ たく

**だきょう・妥協**
1 *noun* = compromise
2 *verb 3* 炙 だきょうする = to compromise

**たく・炊く** *verb 1* 炙 = to cook (rice)

だく・抱く *verb 1* ㋫
- = to hug

だくおんふ・濁音符 *noun –*
*the two marks placed beside* かな
*characters which change the*
*pronunciation from 'ka'* か *to 'ga'*
が *etc.* ▶ vii

たくさん・沢山 *adverb*
- = a lot of

タクシー *noun* = taxi

たけ・竹 *noun* = bamboo

だけ *suffix*
- = only
- = just
  できるだけ = as much as possible

だげき・打撃 *noun* = (a) blow

だけど *conjunction* = however

だけれども ▶ だけど

たしか・確か
**1** *adverb* = perhaps
**2** *adjective* たしか(な) = definite
**3** *adverb* たしかに = definitely

たしかめる・確かめる *verb 2* ㋫
= to confirm

だして ▶ だす ▶ **197**

だします ▶ だす

たしょう・多少
**1** *noun* = large and small
**2** *adverb*
- = some
- = a bit

たす・足す *verb 1* ㋫ = to add

だす・出す *verb 1* ㋫
- = to hold out
- = to take out (of)
- = to hand in
- = to put out
- = to send
- = to give out
- = to publish

> ! *commonly added to the pre*
> ～ます *form of verbs to add the*
> *meaning 'start to' or to indicating the*
> *direction of action as outwards* ▶ **191**

たすう・多数 *noun*
- = a large number
- = majority

たすうけつ・多数決 *noun*
= majority decision

たすかる・助かる *verb 1* ㋑
- = to be helped
- = to be rescued

たすける・助ける *verb 2* ㋫
- = to help
- = to rescue

たずねる・訪ねる *verb 2* ㋫
= to visit

たずねる・尋ねる *verb 2* ㋫
= to ask

ただ
**1** *noun* = free of charge
**2** *adverb* = only
**3** *adjective* ただの
- = the only
- = merely
**3** *conjunction* = however

ただいま *adverb* = just now

> ! *also as a greeting phrase used*
> *when returning to the home or*
> *workplace having been away for a*
> *while. It is usually met with the*
> *response* おかえりなさい *and is*
> *translatable as either 'I'm home!' or*
> *'I'm back!' depending on the*
> *context*

たたかい・戦い *noun*
- = battle
- = struggle

たたかう・戦う *verb 1* ㋑ と
- = to fight
- = to struggle (against)

たたく・叩く *verb 1* ㋫
- = to hit
- = to beat

ただし・但し *conjunction* = however

ただしい・正しい *adjective*
- = correct

ただちに・直ちに *adverb* = at once

たたみ・畳 *noun –* *flooring mats that*
*are used inside Japanese homes and*
*made from straw and rushes woven*
*together*

たたむ・畳む *verb 1* ㋫ = to fold

たち・達 *suffix –* *added to words*
*referring to people to make them*
*specifically plural i.e.* こども *means*
*'child' or 'children' but* こどもたち
*means 'children'*

たタ

たちあがる・立ち上がる
verb 1 ㋒
• = to stand up

たちどまる・立ち止まる
verb 1 ㋒ = to stop (and stand still)

たちば・立場 noun
• = standpoint
• = position

たちます ▶ たつ

たちまち adverb = swiftly

たちよる・立ち寄る verb 1 ㋒
= to drop in (at/on)

たつ・立つ verb 1 ㋒ たって・
たたない・たちます
• = to stand
• = to rise

たつ・経つ verb 1 ㋒ = to pass

たつ・発つ verb 1 ㋒ = to depart

たつ・絶つ verb 1 ㋒ = to cut off

たっする・達する verb 3 ㋒ に
= to reach (achieve)

たった adverb = only

だった – the past of だ which is a
plain equivalent of です. Translatable
as 'was' or 'were'. ▶ 187

だったら conjunction = if that's the
case

❗ added to nouns and な adjectives
to form a conditional ▶ 201

たって ▶ たつ ▶ 197

だって phrase – an informal version
of でも which is used to mean 'even'
or give a sense of 'every' when giving
examples and to emphasise
negatives. Also used to mean 'but' or
'because' when explaining and
making excuses.

たっぷり adverb
• = fully
• = lots of

❗ added to nouns to give the
meaning 'plenty of'

たて・縦 noun – the word means
'vertical plane' as opposed to よこ
'horizontal plane' and is used both to

mean 'vertical' and to give length
when talking of measurements and
thus translatable as 'long'

たて suffix – adds the meaning of
just (having been done) to a
preceding verb in the pre 〜ます
form ▶ 191

たてがき・縦書き noun – vertical
writing (of Japanese) as used in
(formal) letters, books and
newspapers ▶ vii

たてまえ・建前 noun – what is
said and done to be superficially
polite and agreeable as opposed to
what is really thought and felt.
▶ ほんね

たてもの・建物 noun = (a) building

たてる・立てる・建てる
verb 2 ㋾
• = to build
• = to put up
• = to raise

だとう(な)・妥当(な) adjective
= appropriate

たとえ adverb = even if

たとえ・例え noun
• = example
• = analogy

たとえば・例えば adverb = for
example

たとえる verb 2 ㋾ に = to compare

たな・棚 noun = shelf

たに・谷 noun = valley

たにん・他人 noun = other people

たね・種 noun = seed

たのしい・楽しい adjective
= enjoyable

たのしみ・楽しみ noun
• = pleasure
たのしみに している = to be
looking forward to ...

たのしみます ▶ たのしむ

たのしむ・楽しむ verb 1 ㋾
たのしんで・たのしまない・
たのしみます = to look forward to

たのしんで・楽しんで
▶ たのしむ ▶ 197

たのみ・頼み *noun* = (a) request

たのみます ▶ たのむ

たのむ・頼む *verb 1* 愛 たのんで
・たのまない・たのみます
• = to ask (something as a favour)
• = to order

たのもしい・頼もしい *adjective*
= reliable

たば・束 *counter* = bunch (of) ▶ 181

たばこ・煙草 *noun*
• = cigarette
• = tobacco

たび・旅 *noun*
• = journey
• = travel

たび・度 *noun*
• = every time (something happens)
• = occasion

たび・足袋 *noun* – a kind of
traditional Japanese footwear
something like a sock with a sole

たびたび・度々 *adverb*
• = many times
• = repeatedly

ダブる *verb 1* 自
• = to overlap
• = to be double

> ❗ often used in the sense of
> something being done twice and
> thus unnecessarily

たぶん・多分 *adverb*
• = perhaps
• = possibly
• = probably

たべて ▶ たべる ▶ 197

たべます ▶ たべる

たべもの・食べ物 *noun* = food

たべる・食べる *verb 2* 愛 たべて
・たべない・たべます = to eat

たま・球 *noun* = ball

> ❗ used in the sense of 'globe' or
> 'globular' it is also written 玉

たま・弾 *noun* = bullet

たま(に・の) ▶ たまに

たまご・卵 *noun* = egg

だます *verb 1* 愛
• = to trick
• = to deceive

たまたま *adverb* = by chance

たまに *adverb* = occasionally

たまりません ▶ たまらない

たまらない *adjective* = unbearable

> ❗ as an auxiliary following the 〜て
> form of the verb it adds the meaning
> 'unbearably' or 'unrestrainedly' and
> can suggest eagerness to do
> something. It is translatable as 'be
> dying to (do something)' ▶ 197

たまる・溜まる *verb 1* 自 = to be
accumulated

たまる・貯まる *verb 1* 自 = to be
saved up

だまる・黙る *verb 1* 自 = to say
nothing

ダム *noun* = dam

ため・為 *noun*
• = for the sake of
• = for the purpose of
• = because of

だめ(な)・駄目(な) *adjective*
• = useless
• = forbidden
• = broken
　だめに なる = to be ruined

> ❗ だめ(だ) can mean 'No!' or that
> something is forbidden or otherwise
> 'wrong' or not as it should be

ためいき・溜め息 *noun* = sigh

ためし・試し
**1** *noun* = trial
**2** *adverb* ためしに = experimentally

ためす・試す *verb 1* 愛 = to try out

ために ▶ ため

ためらう *verb 1* 自 愛 = to hesitate

ためる・貯める *verb 2* 愛 = to
amass (money)

ためる・溜める *verb 2* 愛 = to
store up

たもつ・保つ *verb 1* 愛
• = to maintain
• = to preserve

たタ

**たより・便り** *noun – means news of/from someone and is often translatable as 'letter'*

**たより・頼り** *noun* = dependability
たよりに なる = reliable
たよりに ならない = unreliable

**たよる・頼る** *verb 1* を に = to rely (on)

**たら** *suffix – created by adding* ら *to the past form of verb or adjective it can indicate meanings 'if' and 'when' and is used in a number of expressions such as* 〜たら どうですか *meaning 'how about (doing ...)?' or 'why don't you ...'.* ▶ 191, ▶ 201

**だらけ** *suffix – adds the sense of 'being covered with' or 'being full of' with a negative nuance*

**だらしない** *adjective*
• = untidy
• = slovenly

**たり** *suffix – usually appearing as an ending on the pre* 〜ます *stem of a pair of verbs (or more) and followed by* する *it indicates that the actions were simultaneous, in succession or just part of all those that took place and translatable as 'and so on' or 'and things like that'. These forms can also express opposites.*

**たりる・足りる** *verb 2* が = to be sufficient

**だるい** *adjective*
• = dull
• = listless

**たれる・垂れる** *verb 2* が
• = to be dangling
• = to hang down

**だれ・誰** *noun* = who

**だれか・誰か** *noun*
• = someone
• = anyone

**だれも・誰も** *phrase (with a negative)* = no one

**タレント** *noun* = star (entertainer)

**だろう** – *plain form of* でしょう *often translatable as 'I suppose' and also used to get confirmation from the*

listener that what is being said is correct so translatable as 'isn't it?', 'aren't they?', 'haven't they?', 'didn't he?' etc. ▶ 187

**だん・段** *step* = step

**だん・団** *suffix* = group

**たんい・単位** *noun*
• = unit
• = credit unit at university or college

**だんかい・段階** *noun* = stage

**たんき(な)・短気(な)** *adjective* = short tempered

**たんき・短期** *noun* = a short period of time

**たんきかん・短期間** *noun* = a short period of time

**たんきだいがく・短期大学** ▶ たんだい

**たんご・単語** *noun* = word

**だんし・男子** *noun*
• = boy
• = male

**たんじゅん・単純**
**1** *adjective* たんじゅん(な) = simple
**2** *adverb* たんじゅんに = simply

**たんしょ・短所** *noun* = weak point

**たんじょう・誕生** *noun* = birth

**たんじょうび・誕生日** *noun* = birthday
たんじょうび おめでとう = Happy Birthday!

**たんしんふにん・単身赴任** *noun – a posting to a workplace in another city or country which entails living away from the family*

**たんす** *noun*
• = chest of drawers
• = wardrobe

**ダンス**
**1** *noun*
• = dancing
• = dance
**2** *verb 3* が ダンス(を)する = to dance

**たんすい・淡水** *noun* = fresh water

だんせい・男性 *noun*
- = man
- = male

だんせいてき(な)・男性的(な)
*adjective* = male

たんそ・炭素 *noun* = carbon

たんだい・短大 *noun* – an abbreviation of たんきだいがく a junior college where the courses last for 2 years ▶ 185

だんたい・団体 *noun* = group

だんたいりょこう・団体旅行 *noun*
- = a group tour
- = package holiday

だんだん・段々 *adverb* = gradually

だんち・団地 *noun* – an estate of apartment housing in public ownership

たんちょう(な)・単調(な) *adjective* = monotonous

だんてい・断定
**1** *noun* = decision
**2** *verb 3* 釜 だんていする = to decide

たんとう・担当
**1** *noun*
- = (person) in charge
- = responsibility (for)
**2** *verb 3* 釜 たんとうする = to be in charge of

たんとうしゃ・担当者 *noun* = person in charge

だんな・旦那 *noun* = (one's own) husband ▶ 177

だんなさん・旦那さん *noun* = (someone else's) husband ▶ 177

たんなる・単なる *phrase* = nothing more than

たんに・単に *adverb* = simply

たんぱくしつ・蛋白質 *noun* = protein

たんぺん・短編 *noun* = short story

たんぺんしゅう・短編集 *noun* = collection (book) of short stories

たんぼ・田んぼ・田圃 *noun* = rice paddy

だんぼう・暖房 *noun* = heater

だんりょく(せい)・弾力(性) *noun* = elasticity

# ちチ

ち・血 *noun* = blood

ち・地 *noun* = (the) ground

ちあん・治安 *noun* – this word means 'safety' with reference to issues of law and order and crime
ちあんが いい = safe
ちあんが わるい = unsafe

ちい・地位 *noun*
- = position
- = standing

ちいき・地域 *noun* = area

ちいさい・小さい *adjective* = small

ちいさな・小さな *adjective* = small

チーズ *noun* = cheese

チーム *noun* = team

チームワーク *noun* = teamwork

ちえ・知恵 *noun*
- = intelligence
- = sense

ちか・地下 *noun* = underground

ちかい・近い *adjective* = close

ちがい・違い *noun* = difference

ちがいない・違いない *adjective*
- = certain
- = definite

! usually in the form 〜に ちがい ない

ちがいます・違います *phrase* – means 'No!' or 'Wrong!' ▶ ちがう

ちかう・誓う *verb 1* 釜 = to swear (promise)

ちがう・違う *verb 1* 釜
- = to be different
- = to be wrong

ちかく・近く
**1** *noun* = neighbourhood
**2** *adverb*
- = almost
- = soon

ちチ

! *the translation will vary depending on the context but 'around', 'local' and 'close to' are possible renderings and if no reference point is supplied it means 'around here'.*

ちかごろ(の) ・ 近頃(の) *noun*
= recently

ちかづく ・ 近づく *verb 1* 㐧
• = to approach
• = to draw near

ちかづける ・ 近づける *verb 2* 㢟
= to bring nearer

ちがって ▶ ちがう ▶ **197**

ちかてつ ・ 地下鉄 *noun* – *an underground railway so variously translatable as 'subway', 'metro', 'underground' etc.*

ちかよる ・ 近寄る *verb 1* 㐧 = to get near (to)

ちから ・ 力 *noun*
• = power
• = strength
• = ability
　ちからを いれる = to make an effort

ちからづよい ・ 力強い *adjective*
= powerful

ちきゅう ・ 地球 *noun* = the earth (world)

ちきゅうおんだんか ・ 地球温暖化 *noun* = global warming

ちぎる ・ 契る *verb 1* 㢟 = to swear (promise)

ちぎる ・ 千切る *verb 1* 㢟 = to tear into pieces

ちく ・ 地区 *noun* = area

ちくいち ・ 逐一 *adverb* = in detail

ちくさん ・ 畜産 *noun* = farming (animals)

ちくしょう ・ 畜生 *noun* – *a (somewhat) vulgar expression of annoyance and disappointment used in situations where many English speakers would probably swear*

ちこく(する) ・ 遅刻(する)
*verb 3* 㐧 = to be late

ちこくしゃ ・ 遅刻者 *noun*
= latecomer

ちじ ・ 知事 *noun* = governor (of a state or prefecture)

ちしき ・ 知識 *noun* = knowledge

ちしつ ・ 地質 *noun* = geology (of )

ちしつがく ・ 地質学 *noun*
= geology (subject)

ちじん ・ 知人 *noun* = acquaintance

ちず ・ 地図 *noun* = map

ちせい ・ 知性 *noun* = intelligence

ちせいてき(な) ・ 知性的(な) *adjective* = intelligent

ちたい ・ 地帯 *noun* = zone

ちち ・ 父 *noun* = (one's own) father ▶ **177**

ちちおや ・ 父親 *noun* = (one's own) father ▶ **177**

ちぢむ ・ 縮む *verb 1* 㐧 = to shrink

ちぢめる ・ 縮める *verb 2* 㢟 = to shrink (something)

ちぢれる ・ 縮れる *verb 2* 㐧 = to become curled (hair)

ちつじょ ・ 秩序 *noun* = order

ちっそ ・ 窒素 *noun* = nitrogen

ちっとも *adverb* (*with negative*)
= utterly (not)

チップ *noun*
• = tip
• = gratuity

ちてき(な) ・ 知的(な) *adjective*
= intellectual

ちてん ・ 地点 *noun*
• = place
• = spot

ちのう ・ 知能 *noun* = intelligence

ちへいせん ・ 地平線 *noun*
= horizon

ちほう ・ 地方 *noun*
• = district
• = region

! *often used with a sense of 'rural' or 'local' to describe areas both geographically distant from a centre and for 'local' government or businesses and organisations having a regional focus.*

**ちめい・地名** *noun* = (place) name

**ちめいてき(な)・致命的(な)**
*adjective* = fatal

**ちゃ・茶** *noun* = tea

**ちゃいろ・茶色**
**1** *noun* = brown
**2** *adjective* ちゃいろの = brown

**ちゃいろい・茶色い** *adjective*
= brown

**ちゃく・着** *suffix* = arrival

**ちゃく・着** *counter*
• = suits
• = dresses ▶ **181**

**ちゃくじつ・着実**
**1** *adjective* ちゃくじつ(な) = steady
**2** *adverb* ちゃくじつに = steadily

**ちゃくしゅ・着手**
**1** *noun* = commencement
**2** *verb 3* ㋕ ちゃくしゅする = to
  commence

**ちゃくせき(する)・着席(する)**
*verb 3* ㋕ = to sit down

**ちゃくちゃく(と)・着々(と)**
*adverb* = steadily

**ちゃくばらい・着払い** *noun*
= payment on delivery

**ちゃくメロ・着メロ** *noun*
= ringtone

**ちゃくりく・着陸**
**1** *noun* = (of a plane) landing
**2** *verb 3* ㋕ ちゃくりくする = (of a
  plane) to land

**チャット** *verb* = to chat (online)

**ちゃのま・茶の間** *noun* = living
room

**ちゃのゆ・茶の湯** *noun* = tea
ceremony ▶ さどう

**ちゃぶだい・卓袱台** *noun* – a
*small low table used for traditional
Japanese dining*

**チャレンジ**
**1** *noun*
• = (a) challenge
• = try
**2** *verb 3* ㋕ に チャレンジする = to
  attempt

**ちゃわん・茶碗** *noun*
• = bowl for rice
• = (tea) cup

**ちゃん** *suffix* – *attached especially to
children's and girls' names as an
informal or affectionate tag.*

**ちゃんと** *adverb*
• = properly

**ちゃんとした** *adjective* = proper

**チャンネル** *noun* = TV channel

**ちゅう・中** *noun* = medium

**ちゅう・中** *suffix* = in the middle
(of)

**ちゅうい・注意**
**1** *noun*
• = warning
• = care
**2** *verb 3* ちゅういする
• = to take care
• = to warn
• = to tell off

**ちゅういぶかい・注意深い**
*adjective* = cautious

**ちゅうおう・中央** *noun* = (the)
centre

**ちゅうがく・中学** ▶ ちゅうがっ
こう ▶ **185**

**ちゅうがくせい・中学生** *noun* –
*middle school student* ▶ **185**

**ちゅうがっこう・中学校** *noun* –
*a middle school or junior high school
(ages 12 to 15)* ▶ **185**

**ちゅうかん・中間** *noun* = midway

**ちゅうこ・中古** *adjective* = second-
hand

**ちゅうこしゃ・中古車** *noun*
= second-hand car

**ちゅうこひん・中古品** *noun*
= second-hand item

**ちゅうこく・忠告**
**1** *noun* = advice
**2** *verb 3* ㋐ に ちゅうこくする = to
  advise

**ちゅうごく・中国** *noun* = China
▶ **172**

> **!** *beware of confusion with an area
> of Japan called* **ちゅうごくちほ
> う** *and sometimes referred to by
> this name*

ちチ

**ちゅうごくご・中国語** *noun*
= Chinese (language) ▶ **172**

**ちゅうし・中止**
ちゅうしに なる = to be called off
2 *verb 3* ㊥ ちゅうしする = to call off

**ちゅうしゃ・注射**
1 *noun* = injection
2 *verb 3* ㊥ ちゅうしゃする = to inject

**ちゅうしゃ・駐車**
1 *noun* = parking
2 *verb 3* ㉿ ちゅうしゃする = to park

**ちゅうしゃじょう・駐車場**
*noun* = car-park

**ちゅうじゅん・中旬** *noun* = the
middle ten days of the month ▶ **174**

**ちゅうしょうてき(な)・
抽象的(な)** *adjective* = abstract

**ちゅうしょく・昼食** *noun* = lunch

**ちゅうしん・中心** *noun* = centre

**ちゅうだん・中断**
1 *noun* = interruption
2 *verb 3* ㉿ ㊥ ちゅうだんする
• = to be interrupted
• = to interrupt

**ちゅうと・中途** *noun* = midway

**ちゅうとう・中東** *noun* = the
Middle East

**ちゅうねん・中年** *noun* = middle
age

**ちゅうもく・注目**
1 *noun* = attention
2 *verb 3* ㉿ ㊥ に ちゅうもくする
= to pay attention (to)

**ちゅうもん・注文**
1 *noun* = order (goods or food)
2 *verb 3* ㊥ ちゅうもんする = to
order (goods or food)

**ちょう・蝶** *noun* = butterfly

**ちょう・長** *suffix* – added to other
nouns describing work to denote
someone in charge and so
translatable as 'head ...'.or 'chief ...'

**ちょう・兆** *noun* – 'trillion' (U.S) or
'billion' (U.K) ▶ **181**

**ちょう・町** *suffix* – used with place
names it denotes either a town or an
area of a city

**ちょう・庁** *suffix* – government
agency

**ちょうか・超過**
1 *noun* = excess
2 *verb 3* ㊥ ちょうかする = to exceed

**ちょうかん・長官** *noun* = director

**ちょうき・長期** *noun and prefix* –
used alone to mean 'a long period of
time' and translatable as 'long term ...'
in compounds

**ちょうこく・彫刻** *noun*
• = sculpture
• = carving

**ちょうさ・調査**
1 *noun* = survey
2 *verb3* ㊥ ちょうさする = to carry
out a survey

**ちょうし・調子** *noun*
• = condition
• = manner
• = health
ちょうしが いい = in good
condition = working well
ちょうしが わるい = in poor
condition = not working properly

**ちょうしょ・長所** *noun*
• = strong point
• = merit

**ちょうじょ・長女** *noun* = eldest
daughter ▶ **177**

> **!** *can be used even if there is only
> one daughter*

**ちょうじょう・頂上** *noun*
= summit

**ちょうせい・調整**
1 *noun* = adjustment
2 *verb 3* ㊥ ちょうせいする = to adjust

**ちょうせつ・調節**
1 *noun*
• = adjustment
• = control
2 *verb 3* ㊥ ちょうせつする
• = to control
• = to adjust

**ちょうだい・頂戴** – *used as
an informal version of* ください
*meaning* '(please) give me' or
'(please) do ... for me'. *Also used as
a humble verb in the form* ちょうだ
いする *which means* 'to receive' or
'to have (food and drink)'

**ちょうてん・頂点** *noun* = peak

**ちょうど** *adverb*
- = exactly
- = just

**ちょうなん・長男** *noun* = the eldest son ▶ **177**

> **!** *can be used even if there is only one son*

**ちょうみりょう・調味料** *noun* = seasoning

**ちょうめ・丁目** *suffix – a numbered area of a Japanese town used as a subdivision in addresses*

**ちょうり・調理** *noun* = cooking

**ちょうりし・調理師** *noun* = chef

**ちょうりほう・調理法** *noun* = cooking instructions

**チョーク** *noun* = chalk

**ちょきん・貯金**
**1** *noun* = savings
**2** *verb 3* 釒 **ちょきんする** = to save

**ちょくご・直後** *noun* = immediately after

**ちょくせつ・直接**
**1** *adverb*
- = directly
- = immediately
**2** *adjective* **ちょくせつの**
- = immediate
- = direct

**ちょくせつてき・直接的**
**1** *adjective* **ちょくせつてき(な)** = direct
**2** *adverb* **ちょくせつてきに** = directly

**ちょくせん・直線** *noun* = straight line

**ちょくぜん・直前** *noun and suffix* = immediately before

**ちょくつう・直通** *prefix*
- = through (train)
- = direct (dial)

**ちょくめん(する)・直面 (する)**
*verb 3* 釒 **に**
- = to face

**ちょくやく・直訳** *noun* = literal translation

**ちょこ・猪口** *noun – a small cup used for drinking* **さけ**

**チョコレート** *noun* = chocolate

**ちょしゃ・著者** *noun* = author

**ちょっかく・直角** *noun* = right angle

**ちょっけい・直径** *noun* = diameter

**ちょっと** *adverb*
- = slightly
- = just a little
- = somewhat

**ちょっとまって ください** = please wait a moment

> **!** *often used to make expressions softer in tone and not always requiring translation. Another common use of the word is as a way of expressing hesitation, doubt or disapproval. Depending on the context the word itself can be a clear refusal of a request in the sense of 'I'm sorry but ..'*

**ちらかす・散らかす** *verb 1* 釒
- = to scatter
- = to make a mess

**ちらかる・散らかる** *verb 1* 釒
- = to be scattered
- = to be untidy

**ちらす・散らす** *verb 1* 釒 = to scatter

**ちり** *noun*
- = dust
- = dirt

**ちり・地理** *noun* = geography

**ちりがく・地理学** *noun* = geography (subject)

**ちりがみ・ちり紙** *noun* = tissue (paper)

**ちりとり・ちり取り** *noun* = dustpan

**ちりょう・治療**
**1** *noun* = medical treatment
**2** *verb 3* 釒 **ちりょうする** = to treat

**ちる・散る** *verb 1* 釒
- = to fall (leaves etc.)
- = to scatter

**ちんぎん・賃金** *noun* = wages

**ちんつうざい・鎮痛剤** *noun* = painkiller

**ちんぼつ・沈没**
**1** *noun* = sinking
**2** *verb 3* 釒 **ちんぼつする** = to sink

**ちんもく・沈黙** *noun* = silence

**ちんれつ・陳列**
**1** *noun* = display
**2** *verb 3* 釒 **ちんれつする** = to exhibit

ちチ

# つツ

つい *adverb*
- = just
- = carelessly
- = by mistake

ついか ・ 追加
**1** *noun* = supplement
**2** *verb 3* ⓦ ついかする = to add

ついたち ・ 一日 *noun* = the first
day of the month ▶ **174**

ついて ▶ つく ▶ **197**

〜について
- = about (concerning)
- = per

ついで ・ 序で
　ついでの とき = whenever it is
　convenient ▶ ついでに

ついで ・ 次いで *adverb* = next

ついでに ・ 序でに *adverb*
- = on the way
- = while (doing something else)

ついに ・ 終に ・ 遂に *adverb*
= at last

ついやす ・ 費やす *verb 1* ⓦ に
= to spend

ついらく ・ 墜落
**1** *noun* = (aeroplane) crash
**2** *verb 3* ⓚ ついらくする = to crash
　(aeroplane or helicopter)

つう ・ 通 *counter – used for letters
and documents* ▶ **181**

つうか(する) ・ 通過(する) *verb*
　*3* ⓚ = to pass through

つうか ・ 通貨 *noun* = currency

つうがく ・ 通学
**1** *noun* = travelling to school
**2** *verb 3* ⓚ つうがくする = to go to
　school

つうきん ・ 通勤
**1** *noun* = travelling to work
**2** *verb 3* ⓚ つうきんする = to
　commute

つうきんじかん ・ 通勤時間
　*noun* = commuting time

つうきんでんしゃ ・ 通勤電車
　*noun* = commuter train

つうこう ・ 通行
**1** *noun*
- = traffic
- = passage
**2** *verb 3* ⓚ つうこうする = to pass
　(along)

つうこうどめ ・ 通行止め *noun*
= no through road

つうこうにん ・ 通行人 *noun*
= passer-by

つうじて ・ 通じて – *a form of*
つうじる *used in certain
expressions with the sense of
'through' or 'by'* ▶ **197**

つうじる ・ 通じる *verb 2* ⓚ
- = to make (oneself) understood
- = to get through (on the telephone)
- = to be connected (by)
- = to be well informed (about)

つうしん ・ 通信
**1** *noun*
- = communication
- = correspondence
**2** *verb 3* ⓚ つうしんする = to
　communicate

つうしんきょういく ・ 通信教育
　*noun* = correspondence course

つうしんはんばい ・ 通信販売
　*noun* = mail order (selling)

つうち ・ 通知
**1** *noun* = notification
**2** *verb 3* ⓦ つうちする = to notify

つうちひょう ・ 通知表 *noun*
= (school) report card

つうちょう ・ 通帳 *noun*
- = bank book
- = pass book

つうやく ・ 通訳
**1** *noun*
- = interpreting
- = interpreter
**2** *verb 3* ⓦ つうやくする = to
　interpret

つうやくしゃ ・ 通訳者 *noun*
= interpreter

つうよう(する) ・ 通用(する)
　*verb 3* ⓚ = to be valid

つうろ・通路 *noun*
- = aisle
- = passage

つえ・杖 *noun* = walking stick

つかい・使い *noun* = errand

づかい *suffix – adds the meaning 'use'*

つかいかけ(の)・使い掛け(の) *adjective* = partly used

つかいかた・使い方 *noun* = way of using

つかいすて(の)・使い捨て(の) *adjective* = disposable

つかいます ▶つかう

つかいみち・使い道 *noun* = use

つかう・使う・遣う *verb 1* Ⓞ つかって・つかわない・つかいます
- = to use
- = to spend

つかって ▶つかう ▶197

つかまえる・捕まえる *verb 2* Ⓞ
- = to catch
- = to arrest

つかまる・捕まる *verb 1* Ⓜ
- = to be caught
- = to be arrested

つかむ・掴む *verb 1* Ⓞ
- = to grab
- = to take hold of
- = to grip

つかれ・疲れ *noun* = tiredness

つかれて ▶つかれる ▶197

つかれます ▶つかれる

つかれる・疲れる *verb 2* Ⓜ
- = to get tired
- = to be tired

つき・月 *noun*
- = month
- = moon

つき・付き *suffix* = with

つぎ・次 *noun* = next
つぎから つぎへ = one after another

つきあい・付き合い *noun* = acquaintance

つきあう・付き合う *verb 1* Ⓜ と = to associate with

! *often used in the form* つきあっている *to mean 'to be going out with', 'to have a relationship with'*

つきあたり・突き当たり *noun* = end

つきあたる・突き当たる *verb 1* Ⓜ = to run into

つぎつぎ・次々 *adverb* = one after another

つきひ・月日 *noun* = time

つきそい・付き添い *noun*
- = (being in) attendance
- = (being in) accompaniment

つきそう・付き添う *verb 1* Ⓜ に
- = to attend
- = to accompany

つきとめる・突き止める *verb 2* Ⓞ = to find out

つきます ▶つく

つく・着く *verb 1* Ⓜ
- = to arrive
- = to reach

つく・付く *verb 1* Ⓜ
- = to be stuck (to)
- = to be attached
- = to be included
- = to be with
- = to be stained (with/by)

つく・就く *verb 1* Ⓜ に = to take (a job)

つく・吐く *verb 1* Ⓞ = to tell (a lie)

つく・点く *verb 1* Ⓜ
- = to light
- = to catch fire
- = to come on

つく・突く *verb 1* Ⓞ = to poke

つぐ・注ぐ *verb 1* Ⓞ = to pour

つぐ・次ぐ *verb 1* Ⓞ に = to be next

つくえ・机 *noun* = desk

つくす・尽くす *verb 1* Ⓞ = to use up

つくって ▶つくる ▶197

つくり・造り・作り *noun* = construction

つくり・旁 *noun* – the right hand part of a かんじ character

ツツ

**つくる・作る** *verb 1* を **つくって・つくらない・つくります**
- = to make
- = to form
- = to grow

**つくる・造る** *verb 1* を
- = to build
- = to create

**っけ** *suffix – used to show an attempt to recall something and so translatable as 'wasn't it ...?', 'haven't we...?' or 'what was it again?'. Very commonly with the sense of '(what) did you say?' or '(where) did you say (it was)?' etc. Related to particle* か
▶ **205**

**つけて** ▶ つける ▶ **197**

**つけもの・漬物** *noun – traditional Japanese pickled vegetables served as a side dish with a main meal*

**つける・付ける** *verb 2* を **つけて・つけない・つけます**
- = to attach
- = to install
- = to spread (butter etc.)
  てんを つける = to mark (homework etc.)

**つける・着ける** *verb 2* を
- = to put on
- = to wear

**つける・点ける** *verb 2* を
- (*a light or machine*) = to turn on
- (*a fire*) = to light

**つごう・都合** *noun*
- = convenience
- = circumstances
  つごうが いい = convenient
  つごうが つく = to be convenient
  つごうを つける = to manage to

> ! *the phrase* つごうが わるい *is used to refuse requests and may be translatable as 'I'm very sorry but I am unable to ... at that time'*

**つじつま・辻褄**
  つじつまが あう = to be consistent
  つじつまが あわない = to be inconsistent

**つたえる・伝える** *verb 2* を
- = to tell
- = to transmit

**つたわる・伝わる** *verb 1* か = to be transmitted

**つち・土** *noun* = soil

**つつ** *suffix – attached to the pre* ～ます *form of a verb it adds the meaning 'while' or 'continuing to'*
▶ **191**

**つづき・続き** *noun* = continuation

**つづく・続く** *verb 1* か = to continue

> ! *added to the pre* ～ます *form of a verb as a suffix to mean 'continuing to ...'* ▶ **191**

**つづける・続ける** *verb 2* を = to continue

> ! *added to the pre* ～ます *form of a verb as a suffix to mean 'to continue to ...'* ▶ **191**

**つっこむ・突っ込む** *verb 1* を = to thrust (into)

**つつしむ・慎む** *verb 1* を = to be careful

> ! *has a range of uses which generally mean 'to exercise self-control'*

**つつみ・包み** ▶ こづつみ

**つつむ・包む** *verb 1* を = to wrap

**って** *suffix – an abbreviated from of* ～と いった *meaning '(somebody) said (that) ...'*

**つとめ・勤め** *noun*
- = work
- = duties

**つとめさき・勤め先** *noun* = place of work

**つとめる・勤める** *verb 2* を に = to work (for)

> ! *implies long term work*

**つとめる・努める** *verb 2* か に = to try hard to...

**つな・綱** *noun* = rope

**つながり・繋がり** *noun*
- = connection
- = context

つながる・繋がる *verb 1* Ⓜ = to be connected

つなぐ・繋ぐ *verb 1* Ⓦ
• = to connect
• = to join

つなげる・繋げる ▶ つなぐ

つなみ・津波 *noun* = tidal wave

つねに・常に *adverb* = always

つばさ・翼 *noun* = wing

つぶ・粒 *noun* = grain (of)

つぶす・潰す *verb 1* Ⓦ
• = to crush
　じかんを つぶす = to kill time

つぶる *verb 1* Ⓦ = to shut (eyes)

つぶれる・潰れる *verb 2* Ⓜ = to be crushed

つま・妻 *noun* = (one's own) wife
▶ 177

つまずく・躓く *verb 1* Ⓜ
• = to trip
• = to stumble

つまらない *adjective*
• = bored
• = boring
• = worthless

! *used in the set expression* つまらないものですが *when giving a gift and translatable as 'it's just a little something'*

つまり・詰まり *conjunction* = in other words

つまる・詰まる *verb 1* Ⓜ
• = to be blocked
• = to be stuffed full of

つみ・罪 *noun*
• = guilt
• = sin
• = offence

つむ・積む *verb 1* Ⓦ
• = to pile up
• = to load

つめ・爪 *noun*
• = nail
• = claw

つめたい・冷たい *adjective*
• = cool
• = cold

つめる・詰める *verb 2* Ⓦ = to pack (in)

つもり *noun* = intention

! *added to forms of the verb to make sentences with meanings like 'intend to ...' and 'plan to ...'.*

つもる・積もる *verb 1* Ⓜ = to be piled up

つや・艶 *noun*
• = shine
• = lustre

つゆ・露 *noun* = dew

つゆ・梅雨 *noun* – *the Japanese rainy season (June-July)*

つゆ *noun* – *sauce for dipping noodles or soup*

つよい・強い *adjective* = strong

つよき・強気
**1** *adjective* つよき(な) = brave
• = aggressive
**2** *adverb* つよきに
• = bravely
• = aggressively

つよまる・強まる *verb 1* Ⓜ = to become strong(er)

つよめる・強める *verb 2* Ⓦ = to strengthen

つらい・辛い *adjective*
• = hard
• = bitter

づらい・辛い *suffix* – *when added to the pre* 〜ます *form of a verb it adds the meaning 'hard to ...'*

つり・釣り *noun*
• = fishing
• = change ▶ おつり

つりあう・釣り合う *verb 1* Ⓜ
• = to be balanced
• = to be in proportion

つる・釣る *verb 1* Ⓦ = to catch (a fish)

つる・吊る *verb 1* Ⓦ = to hang

つる・鶴 *noun* = crane (bird)

つるす・吊るす *verb 1* Ⓦ = to hang

つれて *adverb*
〜につれて
• = as
• = in accordance with

つツ

つれ・連れ *noun* = companion

つれて・連れて ▶ つれる ▶ **197**

つれていく・連れて行く・
連れていく *verb 1* 圏 = to take
(a person)

つれてくる・連れてくる・
連れて来る *verb 3* 圏 = to bring
(a person)

つれる *verb 2* 圏 = to take/bring
(a person) ▶ つれていく ▶ つれて
くる

---

# て テ

---

て・手 *noun*
- = hand
- = way (of doing)
  てが かかる = to take time
  てが とどく = to reach
  ても あしも でない = to be
    helpless
  てを うつ = to take steps (to sort
    out)
  てを だす = to hold out the hand
    = to begin
  てを ぬく = to cut corners

て・手 *suffix – added to pre ～ます
form some verbs to indicate 'person
who does ...' i.e.* ききて = *listener*

～て *suffix – a form of the verb or
adjective allowing other words to be
added and supplementary meanings
created* ▶ **191,** ▶ **201**.

で *particle*
(*location of an action*) = at = in
- = on
- (*method or means*) = by
- = with
- (*cause or reason*) = because of
- = by
- (*describing materials used*) = from
- = with
- (*describing a limited time or space or
    group*) = in
- (*describing prices or quantities of
    things or people*) = for
- = by

> ❗ *particles show the grammatical
> functions of words and the context
> will determine an appropriate
> English translation which may vary
> considerably for the same particle in
> different uses. The above are a few
> of the more common possibilities.*
> ▶ **205**

で – *the ～て form of* です/だ *which is
used to join sentences together and
can be translated as 'and' or 'is ...
and' among other things.* ▶ **187**

であい・出会い *noun*
- = meeting
- = encounter

であう・出会う *verb 1* 圏 と
- = to meet
- = to encounter

てあて・手当て *noun* = allowance

てあらい・手洗い *noun* = toilet

である *a version of* です *used
in writing and formal speech
situations*

てい・低 *prefix* = low

ていあん・提案 *noun* = proposal

ていいん・定員 *noun* = (full)
capacity

ていか・低下
**1** *noun* = decline
**2** *verb 3* 圏 ていかする = to decline

ていか・定価 *noun* = (retail) price

ていき・定期 *noun*
- = fixed period of time
- = ▶ ていきけん

ていきけん・定期券 *noun*
= season ticket for bus or train

ていきゅうび・定休日 *noun –
the day or days which a shop or
restaurant is closed on a regular
basis and translatable as 'closed
on ...'*

ていきょう・提供
**1** *noun*

> ❗ *although translatable as 'offer' it is
> most commonly used to describe
> sponsors or advertisers and
> translatable as 'support' or
> 'sponsorship'*

**2** *verb 3* 㐀 ていきょうする = to provide

### ていこう・抵抗
**1** *noun* = resistance
**2** *verb 3* ⑩ ていこうする = to oppose

### ていし・停止
**1** *noun*
• = stop
• = suspension
**2** *verb 3* 㐀 ⑩ ていしする
• = to stop
• = to suspend

### ていしゃ(する)・停車(する)
*verb 3* ⑩ = to stop

### ていしゃえき・停車駅 *noun*
= (train) stop

### ていしゅつ・提出
**1** *noun* = submission (of)
**2** *verb 3* 㐀 ていしゅつする = to hand in

### ティシュ(ペーパー) *noun* = tissue (paper)

### ていしょく・定食 *noun* – a set menu in a restaurant

### ていでん・停電
**1** *noun* = power cut
**2** *verb 3* ⑩ ていでんする = to be cut off (electric power)

### ていど・程度 *noun*
• = extent
• = degree

### ていねい・丁寧
**1** *adjective* ていねい(な)
• = polite
• = careful
• = kind
**2** *adverb* ていねいに
• = politely
• = carefully
• = kindly

### ていねいご・丁寧語 *noun* – polite speech forms used in Japanese ▶ **187**

### ていねん・定年 *noun* = retirement age

### でいり・出入り *noun* = coming and going (in and out)

### でいりぐち・出入り口 *noun* = entrance and exit

### ていりゅうじょう・停留場 *noun* = bus stop

### ていれ・手入れ
**1** *noun* = care
**2** *verb 3* 㐀 ていれ(を)する
• = to care for
• = to repair

### データ *noun* = data

### データベース *noun* = database

### デート
**1** *noun* = a date
**2** *verb 3* ⑩ とデートする
• = to have a date
• = to go out with

### テープ *noun* = tape

### テーブル *noun* = table

### テープレコーダー *noun* = tape recorder

### テーマ *noun* = theme

### テーマパーク *noun* = theme park

### でかけて ▶ でかける ▶ **197**

### でかける・出かける・出掛ける
*verb 2* ⑩ でかけて・でかけない・でかけます = to go out

### でかけます ▶ でかける

### てがみ・手紙 *noun* = letter

### てがる・手軽
**1** *adjective* てがる(な) = easy
**2** *adverb* てがるに = easily

### てき・敵 *noun* = enemy

### てき・的 *suffix* – added to some nouns it produces an adjective or adverb (*depending on the particle used*) with the meaning 'being ...', 'of the character of' or '...like'. Similar to English endings -al and -ally in words like 'political|politically'.

### でき・出来 *noun*
• = workmanship
• = finish

### できあがり・出来上がり *noun* = completion

### できあがる・出来上がる *verb 1* ⑩ = to be completed

### てきかく・的確
**1** *adjective* てきかく(な) = accurate
**2** *adverb* てきかくに = precisely

### できごと・出来事 *noun*
• = event
• = happening

てテ

テキスト *noun* = textbook

テキストメッセージする *verb* =
to text message

てきする・適する *verb 3 ⑩* に
= to be suitable (for)

てきせつ・適切
**1** *adjective* てきせつ(な)
= appropriate
• = suitable
**2** *adverb* てきせつに = appropriately

できたて・出来立て *phrase*
= just made

できて ▶ できる

てきとう・適当
**1** *adjective* てきとう(な) = suitable
**2** *adverb* てきとうに = suitably

> ❗ *sometimes used in the sense of 'not making an effort' or 'taking it easy'*

できます ▶ できる

てきよう・適用
**1** *noun* = application
**2** *verb 3 ⑧* てきようする = to apply

できる・出来る *verb 2 ⑩* できて
・できない・できます
• = to be able to
• = to be possible
• = to be completed
• = to be made (of/from)
• = to appear
• = to be formed

> ❗ *can be used in the expression ～ことが できる after the dictionary form of a verb to mean 'can ...' which is an alternative to the potential form of the verb* ▶ **191**

できるだけ・出来るだけ *phrase*
• = as much as possible
• = as well as possible
• = as ... as possible

できれば・出来れば *phrase* = if
possible

でぐち・出口 *noun* = exit

てくび・手首 *noun* = wrist

てこ・梃子 *noun* = lever

てごたえ・手応え *noun*
• = response
• = effect

でこぼこ(な)・凸凹(な) *adjective*
• = uneven
• = bumpy

てごろ(な)・手ごろ(な) *adjective*
• = handy
• = reasonable (price)

デザート *noun* = dessert

デザイナー *noun* = designer

デザイナー ようひん・
デザイナー 用品 *noun* = designer
goods

デザイン *noun* = design

デジタル(の) *adjective* = digital

てじゅん・手順 *noun*
• = plan
• = order

でしょう *phrase – often translatable as 'I suppose' this is a polite form of* だろう *and can be used to get confirmation from the listener that what is being said is correct so also translatable as 'isn't it?', 'aren't they?', 'weren't you?', 'hasn't it?' etc.*
▶ **187**

です *– added to statements which do not have a verb or* い *adjective it means 'is', 'am' and 'are'. Also used after* い *adjectives to sound more polite. The plain form is* だ *and the negative is either* では ありません *or* じゃ ありません. *The plain negative form is* じゃ ない. *Past form is* でした *and plain form past is* だった. ▶ **187**

てすう・手数 *noun* = trouble
▶ おてすう

ですが *conjunction*
• = however
• = but

ですから *conjunction*
• = because
• = since

テスト *noun* = test

でたらめ
**1** *noun* = nonsense
**2** *adverb* でたらめに = haphazardly
**2** *adjective* でたらめ(な) = unreliable

てちょう・手帳 *noun* = notebook

> ❗ *can be used of personal organisers or diaries*

てつ・鉄 *noun* = iron

てつがく・哲学 *noun* = philosophy

**てっきょう・鉄橋** *noun* = bridge
(for railway)

**てつだい・手伝い** *noun*
• = help
• = helper

**てつだいます ▶ てつだう**

**てつだう・手伝う** *verb 1* 窗 てつ
だって・てつだわない・てつだ
います = to help ▶ **191**

**てつづき・手続き** *noun*
= procedures

> **!** *used of form filling and administrative work*

**てってい(する)・徹底 (する)**
*verb 3* 窗 = to be thorough

**てっていてき・徹底的**
**1** *adjective* てっていてき(な)
= thorough
**2** *adverb* てっていてきに
= thoroughly

**てつどう・鉄道** *noun* = railway

**てっぱん・鉄板** *noun* = metal plate

**てっぽう・鉄砲** *noun* = gun

**てつや・徹夜**
**1** *noun* = staying up all night
**2** *verb 3* 窗 てつやする = to stay up all
night

**でて ▶ でる ▶ 197**

**テニス** *noun* = tennis
　テニスする = to play tennis

**テニスコート** *noun* = tennis court

**てぬき・手抜き** *noun* = cutting
corners

**てぬぐい・手拭い** *noun* – *a towel
for wiping the hands*

**ては** – *a ～て form followed by
particle* は *. Also used to mark the
condition under which a following
statement holds and so meaning
'if ...is the case then ....' . Very
commonly the particles are being
used to highlight a topic and carry the
sense of 'as for ...' or 'in the case of ...'.
There is sometimes a comparison
(explicit or implicit) with something
else. When followed by* いけない *or*
だめ *it carries the meaning '... is
wrong' and is translatable as 'must
not ..' or 'should not ..'* ▶ **197, ▶ 205**

**では** – *a combination of particles used
to make the negative forms of* です
*and so part of a structure equivalent
to 'isn't', 'aren't' or 'am not' in the
present and 'wasn't' or 'weren't' in
the past. Also used to mark the
condition under which a following
statement holds and so meaning
'if ...is the case then ....' . Very
commonly the particles are being
used to highlight a topic and carry
a sense of 'as for ...' or 'in the case
of ...'. There is sometimes a
comparison (explicit or implicit) with
something else. This follows from a
word or phrase marked with particle
で being further marked as a topic
with particle* は *. Following some
nouns such as country names it could
be translated as 'in'. When followed
by* いけない *or* だめ *it carries the
meaning '... is wrong' and is
translatable as 'must not ..' or 'should
not ..'. Also used at the start of
sentences as a conjunction meaning
'well', 'next' etc.* ▶ **197, ▶ 205**

**デパート** *noun* = department store

**てぶくろ・手袋** *noun* = gloves

**てほん・手本** *noun* = example

**てま・手間** *noun*
• = time
• = trouble

**てまえ・手前** *noun*
• = (just in) front
• = (just) before

**でまえ・出前** *noun* = (restaurant
food) delivery service

**でます ▶ でる**

**でむかえ・出迎え** *noun* = meeting
(somebody)

**でむかえる・出迎える** *verb 2* 窗
= to meet (somebody at the station
etc.)

**ても** *suffix* – *representing the ～て
form of a verb and the particle* も
*and translatable as 'even if ...'.* ▶ **197,
▶ 205 ▶ も**

**でも**
　だれでも = anybody = everyone
　どこでも = anywhere = everywhere
　なんでも = anything = everything

いつでも = anytime

> **!** *as a suffix it is a form of* ても *above.* ▶**197,** ▶**205** *but more likely to be found as a combination of particles* で *and* も *translatable as 'even (in the case that ...)' . This usage is from a word or phrase marked with particle* で *being further marked as a topic with particle* も*. Also used with the meaning 'or something (else)' when making suggestions. When following words used to form questions such as 'who?', 'where?' and 'what?' it gives the meaning 'any...'.* ▶ で ▶ も

デモ *noun* = demonstration

デモンストレーション *noun* = demonstration

てら・寺 *noun* = (Buddhist) temple

てらす・照らす *verb 1* 他
- = to illuminate
- = to shine (a torch)

てる・照る *verb 1* 自 = to shine

でる・出る *verb 2* 自 でて・ でない・ でます
- = to leave
- = to go out (of)
- = to appear
- = to come out
- = to take part (in)
- = to protrude
- = to graduate (from)

テレビ *noun* = television

テレビばんぐみ・テレビ番組 *noun* = television programme

テレホンカード *noun* = telephone card

てれる・照れる *verb 2* 自 = to be shy

てん・点 *noun*
- = mark
- = point
  てんを つける = to mark (homework etc.)

てん・店 *suffix* = shop

てんいん・店員 *noun* – a member of the staff of a shop. Translatable as 'clerk' or 'sales assistant'.

でんか・殿下 *suffix* – title and form of address for the Japanese Imperial

family meaning 'your imperial|royal highness'

でんかせいひん・電化製品 *noun* = electrical goods

てんかぶつ・添加物 *noun* = additive

てんかい・展開
**1** *noun* = development
**2** *verb 3* 他 を てんかいする = to develop

てんき・天気 *noun* = weather

でんき・電気 *noun* = electricity

でんき・伝記 *noun* = biography

でんきスタンド・電気スタンド *noun* = desk light

でんきゅう・電球 *noun* = light bulb

てんきよほう・天気予報 *noun* = weather forecast

てんきん・転勤
**1** *noun* = transfer
**2** *verb 3* 他 てんきんする = to be transferred

> **!** *refers to the system operated by a company, school board or other organisation of moving staff around to different branches, departments and|or jobs*

てんけいてき・典型的
**1** *adjective* てんけいてき(な) = typical
**2** *adverb* てんけいてきに = typically

でんげん・電源 *noun*
- = power point
- = power (switch)

てんこう・天候 *noun* = weather

てんごく・天国 *noun* = heaven

でんごん・伝言 *noun* = message

てんさい・天才 *noun* = genius

でんし・電子 *prefix* = electronic

てんじ・点字 *noun* = Braille

でんしじしょ・電子辞書 *noun* = electronic dictionary

でんしてちょう・電子手帳 *noun* = electronic organiser

でんしメール・電子メール
*noun* = e-mail

でんしレンジ・電子レンジ
*noun* = microwave oven

でんしゃ・電車 *noun* = train

てんじょう・天井 *noun* = ceiling

てんすう・点数 *noun* = marks (in a test)

でんせん(する)・伝染 (する)
*verb 3 ㉝* = to be infectious

でんせんびょう・伝染病 *noun* = infectious disease

てんたいかんそく・天体観測
*noun* = astronomy

でんち・電池 *noun* = battery

てんちょう・店長 *noun* = manager (of a shop or bank)

てんてん(と)・転々(と) *adverb* = from place to place

てんてん・点々 – as an adverb in the form てんてんと it means 'here and there' but also describes the marks used to form voiced syllables in かな script, which are placed beside a kana character to transform the pronunciation from 'ka' か to 'ga' が etc. and known as だくおんふ ▶vii

テント *noun* = tent

でんとう・伝統 *noun* = tradition

でんとうてき(な)・伝統的(な)
*adjective* = traditional

てんねん・天然 *suffix* = natural

てんのう・天皇 *noun* = (Japanese) emperor

てんのうたんじょうび・
天皇誕生日 *noun* – The Emperor's Birthday (December 23) – a Japanese public holiday

てんのうへいか・天皇陛下
*noun* – a form of words equivalent to 'His Imperial Majesty, the Emperor (of Japan)'

てんぷ・添付 *noun* = attachment

てんぽ・店舗 *noun* = shops

テンポ *noun* = tempo

でんぽう・電報 *noun* = telegram

てんらんかい・展覧会 *noun* = exhibition

でんりょく・電力 *noun* = electric power

でんわ・電話 *noun* = telephone

でんわちょう・電話帳 *noun* = telephone directory

でんわばんごう・電話番号
*noun* = telephone number

---

# と ト

と *particle* – this particle has numerous uses. It can link two nouns and be translatable as '... and ...' or follow a noun referring to a person to mean 'with ...' . Sometimes used in expressions of comparison and so variously translatable as '(different) from', '(same) as' etc. It's use is compulsory with some verbs such as けっこん(する) 'to marry' and optional (but very common) with others such as はなす 'to speak' to express the meaning 'with'. Used in the verb 'to think' ～と おもう meaning '(I) think that ...' and with 'to say' in the idiom ～と いう meaning '... said that ...' or 'called ...' ▶ という ▶おもう▶いう The particle can also show that a preceding phrase is a quotation. Sometimes used with the verb なる in the sense of 'become' or with certain adverbs. Following the dictionary or ～ます form of a verb it makes a conditional.
▶ 191

と・戸 *noun* = door

ど・度 *suffix*
• = (number of ) times
• = degrees (of angle or temperature)

ドア *noun* = door

とい・問い *noun* = question

**といあわせ・問い合わせ**
**1** *noun* = enquiries
**2** *verb 3* ⓜ に といあわせ(を)する
= to enquire

**といあわせる・問い合わせる**
*verb 2* ⓦ に = to enquire

**ドイツ** *noun* = Germany

**という** *phrase – used following a noun or noun phrase to mean 'called ...' or 'something like ...' and in the expression* ということ *to mean 'apparently'*

**といって** *conjunction* = however

**というのは** *conjunction* = because ...

**トイレ** *noun* = toilet

**トイレットペーパー** *noun* = toilet paper

**といわんばかり** *phrase* = as if to say

**とう・塔** *noun* = tower

**とう・頭** *counter* = large animals
▶181

**とう・等** *suffix* = grade

**とう・島** *suffix* = island

**どう・銅** *noun* = copper

**どう** *adverb*
• = how
• = what
　どうですか = how are you? = how is it (going)?
　どうでしたか = how was it?
　どうしますか = what shall (I/we) do?
　どうしたんですか = what's the matter?
　どうおもいますか = what do you think (about ...)?
　どう なりますか = what will happen?

❗ *when followed by a* ～て *form and the particle* も *it means 'even if ....' or 'no matter how much one ...'*

**どういう** *phrase*
• = what kind of ..
• = how
• = why
　どういうふうに = in what way ...?
　どういう いみ ですか = what does it mean?

**どういたしまして** *phrase* = you're welcome

❗ *a polite response to expressions of thanks such as* どうも ありが とう ございます

**といつ・統一**
**1** *noun* = unity
**2** *verb 3* ⓦ とういつする = to make the same

**どうか** *adverb – can be used in the sense of 'please ...' and when following a phrase ending with the particle* か *it means 'whether or not ...'. It is also used idiomatically with a sense of something being not quite right.*

**とうかん(する)・投函(する)**
*verb 3* ⓦ = to post (a letter)

**とうき・陶器** *noun* = pottery

**どうき・動機** *noun* = motivation

**どうきゅう・同級** *noun* = same class/grade

**どうきゅうせい・同級生** *noun* = classmate

**どうぐ・道具** *noun*
• = tools
• = implements

**とうげ・峠** *noun* = (mountain) pass

**とうけい・統計** *noun* = statistics

**とうこう・登校**
**1** *noun* = going to school
**2** *verb 3* ⓜ とうこうする = to go to school

**どうさ・動作** *noun* = movements

**とうじ・当時** *noun* = at that time

**どうし・動詞** *noun* = verb

**どうし・同士** *suffix – shows that the people referred to are sharing a set of circumstances or are members of the same group with similar status such as* ともだちどうし *'(among) friends' or* なかまどうし *'colleagues'.*

**どうじ・同時**
**1** *noun* = at the same time
**2** *adverb* (～と)どうじに
= simultaneously

**どうしたんですか** ▶ どう

**とうじつ・当日** _noun_
- = that day
- = the day of the ...

**どうじつうやく・同時通訳**
_noun_ = simultaneous interpreting

**どうして** _adverb_
- = why
- = how

**どうしても** _adverb_
- = however
- = no matter what ...

> ! _also be used to give the meaning_
> _'(I) can't help ...' and to emphasise_
> _wanting something 'no matter what'._
> _Has a general sense of insistence_
> _and/or necessity._

**とうじょう・登場**
1 _noun_ = appearance
2 _verb 3_ ⑰ **とうじょうする** = to
　appear

**とうじょう・搭乗**
1 _noun_ = boarding (ship or plane)
2 _verb 3_ ⑧⑰ **とうじょうする** = to
　board (ship or plane)

**どうじょう・道場** _noun_ – _a place
for the practice of martial arts like_
**じゅうどう** _and_ **からて**

**とうじょうけん・搭乗券** _noun_
= boarding card (ticket)

**とうじょうじんぶつ・登場人物**
_noun_ = character (in a film or book etc.)

**どうせ** _adverb_
- = after all
- = anyhow
- = anyway

> ! _carries a negative or pessimistic
> nuance_

**どうせい・同棲**
1 _noun_ = living together
2 _verb 3_ ⑰ **どうせいする** = to live
　together

**どうせいあい・同性愛** _noun_
= homosexuality

**どうせいあいしゃ・同性愛者**
_noun_ = a homosexual

**とうぜん・当然**
1 _adjective_ **とうぜん(な)** = natural
- = reasonable
2 _adverb_ = naturally

**どうぞ** _adverb_
- = please
- = of course

**どうぞよろしく** _phrase – an
abbreviated form of_ **どうぞよろしく
おねがいします** _which is used to
express the speaker's hopes for a
future successful relationship of
some kind and carries a sense of
'thank you in advance for ...' or
'please think well of me'. Very difficult
to translate as there is no real English
equivalent._

**とうちゃく・到着**
1 _noun_ = arrival
2 _verb 3_ ⑰ **とうちゃくする** = to
　arrive

**とうてい・到底** _adverb_ = utterly

**とうとう** _adverb_
- = finally
- = after all

**どうとく・道徳** _noun_ = morality

> ! _Japanese schools teach 'moral
> education'_ **どうとくきょういく**
> _which is similar to social ethics_

**どうとくてき・道徳的**
1 _adjective_ **どうとくてき(な)**
　= moral
2 _adverb_ **どうとくてきに** = morally

**とうなん・盗難** _noun_ = theft

> ! _Japanese use covers a broad
> sense of 'theft' and can be
> translated with the most appropriate
> term from the English 'robbery',
> 'burglary' and 'theft'_

**どうにか** _adverb_ = somehow (or
other)
　**どうにか なる** = (it) will be ok
　**どうにか する** = do (it) somehow or
　other

**どうにゅう・導入**
1 _noun_ = introduction (of something)
2 _verb 3_ ⑧ **に どうにゅうする**
　= to introduce (something)

**とうばん・当番** _noun_ – _used in the
sense of 'turn' when there is a list of
duties to be performed_

**とうひょう・投票**
1 _noun_

• = vote
• = voting
**2** verb 3 ㋑ とうひょうする = to vote

**どうぶつ ・ 動物** noun = animal

**どうぶつえん ・ 動物園** noun
= zoo

**とうめい(な) ・ 透明(な)**
adjective = transparent

**どうも** adverb – the basic meaning
is 'somehow' but it is often used as
an abbreviation of polite phrases
where it acts something like 'very'.
This means that depending on the
context the word can mean 'hello'
and 'thank you' as well as 'sorry'.
When used with negative statements
and comments it is translatable
as 'apparently' or 'somehow or
other ...'
　**どうも ありがとう（ございます）**
　= thank you (very much)
　**どうも すみません（でした）**
　= I'm sorry to have troubled you

**どうやら** adverb
• = somehow
• = apparently

**とうゆ ・ 灯油** noun – kerosene or
paraffin oil used in many Japanese
homes for the mobile room heaters

**とうよう ・ 東洋** noun
• = Asia
• = Orient

**どうよう ・ 同様**
**1** adverb どうよう（に）= similarly
**2** adjective どうよう（な）= the same
　as

**どうりょう ・ 同僚** noun
= colleague

**どうろ ・ 道路** noun = road

**どうろこうじ ・ 道路工事** noun
= road-works

**とうろく ・ 登録**
**1** noun = registration
**2** verb 3 ㋼ に とうろくする = to
　register

**とうろん ・ 討論**
**1** noun = debate
**2** verb 3 ㋼ とうろんする = to
　debate

**どうわ ・ 童話** noun – Japanese
traditional stories for children.
Translatable as 'nursery stories' or
'fairy tales'

**とお ・ 十** noun = ten ▶ **181**

**とおい ・ 遠い** adjective
• = distant
• = far from

**とおか ・ 十日 ・ 10日** noun
• = the tenth (day of a month)
• = ten days ▶ **174**

**とおかかん ・ 十日間 ・ 10日間**
noun = ten days ▶ **174**

**とおく ・ 遠く** noun = a long way
away

**とおす ・ 通す** verb 1 ㋼
• = to let pass
• = through (someone or someone's
　connections)

**とおり ・ 通り** noun – used to mean
'road' especially in naming large and
famous roads. Used after other nouns
(sometimes connected with の and
sometimes not) and the past or
dictionary forms of verbs it signifies
'as' or 'like' or 'according to' or 'in the
manner of'. ▶ **191**
　**いつも の とおり** = as usual
　**せつめいの とおり** = following the
　explanation/instructions
　**そのとおり** = that's (you're) right!
　**わたしが するとおりにして くだ**
　**さい** = Please do (it) as I do

**どおり ▶ とおり**

**とおりかかる ・ 通りかかる** verb
1 ㋑ = to pass by

**とおりすぎる ・ 通り過ぎる** verb
2 ㋑ = to go past

**とおる ・ 通る** verb 1 ㋑
• = to pass
• = to go through

**とか** particles
• = and
• = etc.

　**!** as well as when giving examples
　it is sometimes used when trying to
　remember something and added
　to uncertain statements with the
　meaning 'or something like that'

とかい・都会 *noun* = large city
とかい の = urban

とかく *adverb* = tend to ...

とかす・溶かす *verb 1* を = to
dissolve (something)

どかす・退かす *verb 1* を = to
move (something out of the way)

とき・時 *noun* = time

> **!** *often used following another noun
> linked with の or following the plain
> forms of verbs or adjectives to mean
> 'when' or 'while'*

こどもの とき = when (I was) a child
さむい とき = when it is cold
はしるとき = while running
わからない とき = when you don't
understand

ときおり・時折 *adverb*
= occasionally

ときどき・時々 *adverb*
= occasionally

どきどき(する) *verb 3* か – the
basic meaning is to have the heart
beat faster with excitement or fear etc.
and so translatable as '(my) heart was
pounding' etc. or 'to be excited' , 'to
be anxious' etc. depending on the
context.

ときには・時には *adverb*
= sometimes

とく・得 *noun*
• = (a) benefit
• = profit

とく・溶く *verb 1* を = to dissolve

とく・解く *verb 1* を
• = to untie
• = to solve

とぐ・砥ぐ *verb 1* を – the basic
meaning is 'to sharpen' but it is also
used to describe washing rice grains
prior to cooking to remove the
powdery residue and ensure soft,
white cooked rice

どく・毒 *noun* = poison

どく・退く *verb 1* か = to get out of
the way

> **!** *used in the form* どいて(くださ
> い) *it is translatable as '(please) get
> out of the way'*

とくい・得意 *noun* – means
'something someone is good at' and
so is translatable as 'speciality' or
'strong point'

どくしゃ・読者 *noun* = reader

とくしゅ(な)・特殊(な)
*adjective* = TV or press special

どくしょ・読書
**1** *noun* = reading
**2** *verb 3* か どくしょする = to read
(as a hobby)

とくしょく・特色 *noun*
= characteristic

どくしん・独身 *noun* = single (not
married)

とくちょう・特徴 *noun*
= characteristic

とくちょう・特長 *noun*
= (someone's) strong point

とくてい(する)・特定(する)
*verb 3* を = to specify

とくてい(の)・特定(の)
*adjective* = specific

どくとく(な・の)・独特(な・の)
*adjective* = unique

とくに・特に *adverb*
• = especially
• = in particular

とくばい・特売
**1** *noun* = sale
**2** *verb 3* を とくばいする = to put on
sale

とくばいひん・特売品 *noun*
= sale item/s

とくべつ・特別
**1** *adjective* とくべつ(な) = special
**2** *adverb* とくべつに = especially

どくりつ・独立
**1** *noun* = independence
**2** *verb 3* か どくりつする = to become
independent

とけい・時計 *noun*
• = clock
• = watch

とけこむ・溶け込む *verb 1* か に
• = to dissolve
• = to fit in with

とくめい・匿名 *noun* = anonymity
とくめいで = anonymously

とト

とける・溶ける *verb 2* ㋑
- = to melt
- = to dissolve

とける・解ける *verb 2* ㋑
- = to come undone
- = to be solved

どける・退ける *verb 2* ㋜ = to move (something out of the way)

とこ・床 *noun*
　とこにつく = to go to bed

どこ *noun* = where

どこか
**1** *noun* = somewhere
**2** *adverb*
- = something
- = a little bit

どこで ▶ どこ

どこでも ▶ どこも

どこに
- = where?
- = where to?

どこへ = where (to)

どこまで
- = how far
- = to what extent

どこまでも *adverb* = endlessly

どこも *adverb*
- (*with positive*) = everywhere
- (*with negative*) = nowhere

とこのま・床の間 *noun* – the alcove in a traditional Japanese room where hanging scrolls, ornaments and flowers are often displayed

とこや・床屋 *noun* = barber

ところ・所 *noun*
- = place
- = point

> ! *added to the past tense of a verb and followed by* です・でした *it indicates point in time and is translatable as 'have/had just (done)' or 'when ...'. Added to a dictionary form of a verb and followed by* です・でした *it indicates that an action is just about to occur or has just started and is translatable as 'be just about to ...' See also* ところが *and* ところで
> ▶ **191**

ところが *conjunction*
- = however
- = well

> ! *when following a past tense it carries the meaning of 'however'*

どころか *particle*
- = on the contrary (to preceding statement) ...
- = not only ... but also ...

ところで *conjunction* = by the way

> ! *following a past tense it conveys a meaning of 'even if' or 'however much'. See also* ところでは

ところでは *phrase* – following a past tense means 'as far as (I know etc.)' or 'according to ...'.

ところどころ(に)・所々(に) *adverb* = here and there

とざん・登山
**1** *noun* = mountain climbing
**2** *verb 3* ㋑ とざんする = to go mountain climbing

とし・年 *noun*
- = year
- = age

とし・都市 *noun* = city

としうえ・年上 *noun* = (person) who is older

としたら *phrase* = supposing (that) ...

としつき・年月 *noun* = years

として *phrase*
- = as (a ...)
- = not even a ...

としては *phrase* = for (a ...)

としても *phrase* = even if

としとった・年取った *adjective* = old

どしゃぶり・どしゃ降り *noun* = heavy downpour

としょ・図書 *noun* = books

としょかん・図書館 *noun* = library

としより・年寄り *noun*
- = old person
- = old people

とじる・閉じる *verb 2* ㋜ = to close (the eyes)

**としん・都心** *noun* = the centre of a city

**とすると** *phrase* = assuming (that) ...

**とすれば** *phrase* = supposing (that) ...

**とそう・塗装** *noun* = paint

**どそく・土足** *noun* – refers to shoes that are worn outside (in contrast to slippers which can be worn inside a house or other building). Often seen in entrances and hallways in the phrase **どそくきんし** which can be translated as 'no shoes' or 'please remove your shoes'

**どそくきんし・土足禁止**
▶ どそく

**とだな・戸棚** *noun*
• = closet
• = cupboard

**とたん(に)・途端(に)** *suffix*
= just as ...

**とち・土地** *noun* = land

**とちゅう・途中** *noun*
• = in the middle of (doing)
• = on the way to

**どちら** *noun*
• = where
• = which
• = who

**どちらも** *phrase*
• = both
• = even

**とっきゅう・特急** *noun* = express (train)

**とつぜん・突然**
**1** *adjective* とつぜん(の・な)
    = sudden
**2** *adverb* = suddenly

**どっち** *noun*
• = where
• = which ▶ どちら

**どっちでも** *phrase*
• = both
• = even ▶ どちらでも

**どっちも** ▶ どちらも

**とって・取っ手** *noun* = handle

**とって** – used in the pattern 〜にとって to mean 'as for' or 'to' when giving an opinion or judgement
  にほんにとって = for Japan
  かいしゃにとって = to/for the company

**とって** ▶ とる ▶ **197**

**トップ** *noun* = top

**トップアップカード** *noun* = top-up card

**とても** *adverb*
• = very
• = extremely
• = completely

**とどく・届く** *verb 1* ㊍
• = to arrive (be delivered)
• = to reach

**とどける・届ける** *verb 2* ㊒
• = to deliver (something to ...)
• = to report

**ととのう・整う** *verb 1* ㊍ = to be ready

**ととのえる・整える** *verb 2* ㊒
= to get (something) ready

**どなた** *noun* = who
  どなたさま ですか = who is it (are you) please?

  ❗ *a more polite equivalent of* だれ

**となり・隣** *noun*
• = next to
• = neighbour(ing)

**となりさん・隣さん** *noun* = a neighbour ▶ おとなりさん

**どなる・怒鳴る** *verb 1* ㊍ = to shout

**となれば** ▶ とすれば

**とにかく** *adverb* = anyway

**どの** *attributive*
• = which
• = what
• = who

  ❗ *used in the pattern* どの... も *it means 'any ..' or 'every ...'*

**どの・殿** *suffix* – sometimes added to family names in the address or opening line of a letter (from an official organisation) and so translatable as 'Mr', 'Mrs', Miss or 'Ms'

とト

どのくらい *phrase*
- = how much
- = how many
- = how long

とばす・飛ばす *verb 1* 🖋
- = to (make) fly
- = to skip (omit)
- = to splash
- = to drive (at high speed)

とびこむ・飛び込む *verb 1* 🖋
- = to dive into
- = to jump into

とびだす・飛び出す *verb 1* 🖋
= to rush out

とびら・扉 *noun* = door

! *usually refers to a sliding or automatic door*

とぶ・飛ぶ *verb 1* 🖋 = to fly
とぶ・跳ぶ *verb 1* 🖋 = to jump

どぶ・溝 *noun*
- = ditch
- = drain

どぼく・土木 *suffix* = (civil) engineering

とぼしい・乏しい *adjective*
- = short of
- = lacking

トマト *noun* = tomato

とまって ▶ とまる

とまどう・戸惑う *verb 1* 🖋 = to be at a loss (to know what to do)

とまり・泊り *noun* = staying overnight

とまります ▶ とまる

とまる・止まる *verb 1* 🖋 とまって・とまらない・とまります
- = to stop
- = to be parked

とまる・泊まる *verb 1* 🖋 = to stay (overnight)

とめて ▶ とめる
とめます ▶ とめる

とめる・止める *verb 2* 🖋 とめて・とめない・とめます
- = to stop
- = to park

とめる・泊める *verb 2* 🖋
- = to put somebody up (overnight)

とめる・留める *verb 2* 🖋
- = to fasten
- = to fix

とも
- = all
- = both
- = at the (least/most/latest etc.)
- = of course

! *this is a combination of particles* と *and* も ▶ **205**

とも・友 *noun* = friend

ともかく *adverb*
- = anyway
- = regardless (of)

ともだち・友達 *noun* = friend

ともなう・伴う *verb 1* 🖋
- = to take
- = to bring
- = to be accompanied (by)

ともに・共に *adverb*
- = together with
- = as well as

! *usually in the form* ～と ともに

ともばたらき・共働き *noun* – *a couple who are both working*

どようび・土曜日 *noun* = Saturday

とら・虎 *noun* = tiger

ドライクリーニング *noun* = dry cleaning

ドライバー *noun*
- = screwdriver
- = driver

ドライブ
**1** *noun*
- = driving
- = (a) drive
**2** *verb 3* 🖋 ドライブする = to go for a drive

とらえる・捕らえる *verb 2* 🖋
- = to arrest
- = to catch

トラック *noun* = truck

トラブル *noun* = trouble

ドラマ *noun* = drama

ドラム _noun_ = drum/s

トランプ _noun_ = (playing) cards

とり・鳥 _noun_
- = bird
- = chicken

とりあえず _adverb_ = for the time being

とりあげる・取り上げる _verb 2_ ⓦ
- = to pick up
- = to adopt
- = to take away

とりあつかい・取り扱い _noun_
= treatment

とりあつかう・取り扱う _verb 1_ ⓦ
- = to handle
- = to deal with

とりあわせ・取り合わせ _noun_
- = combination
- = assortment

とりい・鳥居 _noun_ – the red gateway which marks the entrance to a Shinto shrine

とりいれる・取り入れる _verb 2_ ⓦ
- = to take in
- = to adopt

とりインフルエンザ・鳥インフルエンザ _noun_ = bird flu

とりかえ・取り替え _noun_
- = exchange
- = replacement

とりかえす・取り替えす _verb 1_ ⓦ = to get (something) back

とりかえる・取り替える _verb 2_ ⓦ
- = to exchange
- = to replace

とりくむ・取り組む _verb 1_ ⓝ に
= to get to grips with

とりけす・取り消す _verb 1_ ⓦ
= to cancel

とりしまり・取り締まり _noun_
= crackdown

とりしまりやく・取締役 _noun_
= company director

とりしまる・取り締まる _verb 1_ ⓦ = to crack down on

とりだす・取り出す _verb 1_ ⓦ
= to take (something) out (of)

とりつける・取り付ける _verb 2_ ⓦ = to install

とりにく・鳥肉 _noun_ = chicken (meat)

とりのぞく・取り除く _verb 1_ ⓦ
= to remove

とりひき・取り引き _noun_
= trading

とりもどす・取り戻す _verb 1_ ⓦ
= to get (something) back

どりょく・努力
**1** _noun_ = effort
**2** _verb 3_ ⓝ どりょくする = to make an effort

とる・取る _verb 1_ ⓦ とって・とらない・とります
- = to take
- = to get
- = to have

とる・採る _verb 1_ ⓦ
- = to pick
- = to employ

とる・撮る _verb 1_ ⓦ = to take (a picture)

とる・捕る _verb 1_ ⓦ = to catch

どれ _noun_ = which

> **!** when followed by も or でも it means 'whichever' or (with a negative) 'all'

トレーニング _noun_ = training

ドレス _noun_ = dress

どれでも
- = whichever
- = any ▶ どれ

どれも ▶ どれ

とれる・取れる _verb 2_ ⓝ = to come off

とれる・捕れる _verb 2_ ⓝ = to be caught

どろ・泥 _noun_ = mud

どろぼう・泥棒 _noun_
- = thief
- = burglar

とト

トン *noun* = metric tonne

とんでもない *adjective* = terrible

とんとん
とんとんです = to be (break) even

どんどん *adverb* = quickly

どんな *attributive*
• = what (kind of)

> ! *when followed by a noun and* も
> *or* でも *it means 'however', 'no*
> *matter what' or 'any', 'every'*

どんなに *adverb*
• = how
• = how much
• = no matter how
• = however

トンネル *noùn* = tunnel

どんぶり・丼 *noun* – a bowl for rice somewhat larger than the usual ちゃわん and by extension any meal served in such a bowl with rice under the meat, fish or vegetables

# なナ

な・名 *noun* = name

な *particle* – used after the dictionary form of a verb it acts as a strong negative imperative 'don't ...'. Sometimes used after a verb in the pre ～ます form as an abbreviation of なさい which produces an a polite imperative 'do ...' which is often used by teachers to students and parents to children ▶ 191

な *particle* – used by men when expressing emotion and also as an alternative to particle ね

なあ *particle* – an alternative form of particle な above

ない・無い – used in the formation of the plain negative of です which is ではない and variously translatable as 'am not', 'is not', 'are not'. Also for

the negative of ある to mean 'not existing' and translatable as 'don't have' or 'is|are' missing' in addition to the translations given above.

～ない *suffix* – indicates the negative form of a verb or an adjective ▶ 191, ▶ 201

ない・内 *suffix* = within

ないか・内科 *noun* = internal medicine

ないしょ・内緒 *noun* = secret

ないせん・内線 *noun* = (telephone) extension

> ! *often used in the sense of 'it's an internal call'*

ないせんばんごう・内線番号 *noun* = (telephone) extension number

ないで *suffix* – Used to form an expression similar to 'please do not ...'. In this use it is often followed by ください Also used to mean 'without doing ...'. In this usage it is usually followed by another verb ▶ 191

ナイフ *noun* = knife

ないぶ・内部 *noun* = interior

ないよう・内容 *noun* = contents

ナイロン *noun* = nylon

なお・尚 *adverb*
**1** *adverb*
(*in positive sentences*)
= still (more)
(*in negative sentences*)
= even (less)
**2** *conjunction* = furthermore

なおす・直す *verb 1* ⊛
• = to repair
• = to adjust
• = to correct
• = to translate (into)

> ! *as a suffix attached to the pre*
> *～ます form of other verbs it*
> *indicates that the action is done*
> *again so often equivalent to the 're'*
> *element of 'redone', 'reconsider' etc.*
> ▶ 191

なおす・治す *verb 1* ⊛
• = to cure
• = to heal

**なおる・直る** *verb 1* ㋕
- = to be repaired
- = to be corrected

**なおる・治る** *verb 1* ㋕
- = to get better (after illness or injury)

**なか・中** *noun*
- = inside
- = in
- = into
- = middle
- = among

**なか・仲** *noun* = relations
　なかが いい = to be friendly with ...
　なかが わるい = to be on bad terms
　with ...

**なが・長** *suffix* = long

**ながい・長い** *adjective* = long

**ながく(する)・長く(する)** *verb*
*3* ㋨ = to make something long(er)

**ながさ・長さ** *noun* = length

**ながし・流し** *noun* = (kitchen)
sink

**ながす・流す** *verb 1* ㋨
- = to run (water)
- = to flush (a toilet)
- = to empty (a bath)
- = to wash away

**なかなおり・仲直り**
**1** *noun* = reconciliation
**2** *verb 3* ㋕ と なかなおりする = to
make up

**なかなか** *adverb*
- (*with positives*) = quite = very
- (*with negatives*) = (not) easily

**なかば・半ば**
**1** *noun* = middle
**2** *adverb* = partly

**ながびく・長引く** *verb 1* ㋕ = to
drag on

**なかま・仲間** *noun* = friend (at
work)

**なかみ・中身** *noun*
- = contents
- = ingredients

**ながめ・眺め** *noun* = view

**ながめる・眺める** *verb 2* ㋨
- = to look
- = to watch

**なかよく・仲良く**
**1** *adverb* = happily
**2** *verb 3* ㋕ と なかよくする = to get
on well with (someone)

**なかよし・仲良し** *noun* = friend

**ながら** *suffix* – following the pre
～ます *form of a verb it adds*
*the meaning 'while ... ～ing' and*
*shows that two actions take place*
*simultaneously. Also used with*
*adjectives and nouns in the sense*
*of 'although ...' and in certain fixed*
*expressions.*

**ながれ・流れ** *noun* = flow

**ながれる・流れる** *verb 2* ㋕
- = to flow
- = to be washed away

**なく・泣く** *verb 1* ㋕ = to cry

**なく・鳴く** *verb 1* ㋕ = to call

> **!** *used for the noises made by birds*
> *and animals and so variously*
> *translatable as 'sing', 'roar',*
> *'screech' etc. depending on the*
> *animal concerned*

**なぐさめる・慰める** *verb 2* ㋨
= to console

**なくす・無くす** *verb 1* ㋨ = to
lose (something)

**なくす・亡くす** *verb 1* ㋨ = to lose
(a relative or friend by death)

**なくて** *suffix* – the ～て *form of*
**ない** *and the* ～ない *form of verbs*
*which is used in the expression*
*'don't have to ...'. In this use it is*
*followed by* もいい. *Also used as an*
*emphatic negative form of* ない
▶ **191**, ▶ **197** たべなくても いい
= you don't have to eat

**なくなる** *verb 1* ㋕
- = to run out
- = to disappear
- = to be missing

**なくなる・亡くなる** *verb 1* ㋕
= to die

**なぐる・殴る** *verb 1* ㋨ = to hit
(violently)

**なげる・投げる** *verb 2* ㋨ = to
throw

なナ

なければ *suffix and conjunction*
= if not (then ...)

なければいけない *suffix* = must

なければならない *suffix* = must

なさい *suffix – used after the pre*
~ます *form of a verb to form a polite imperative and translatable as 'do ... please' or 'please ...'* ▶ **191**

なさけない・情けない *adjective*
• = shameful
• = deplorable

なさる *verb 1* 🅰
▶ *honorific equivalent of* する ▶ **189**

なし・無し *noun* = nothing

> ! *used as a more emphatic form of* ない *in the sense of 'without...'.*

なし・梨 *noun* = Japanese pear

なしとげる・成し遂げる *verb 2* 🅰 = to accomplish

なじむ・馴染む *verb 1* 🅰 に = to get used to

なす・為す *verb 1* 🅰 = to do

なぜ *adverb* = why

なぜなら(ば) *conjunction* = the reason is ...

なぞ・謎 *noun* = mystery

なだらか(な) *adjective* = gentle

なだれ・雪崩 *noun* = avalanche

なつ・夏 *noun* = summer

なつかしい・懐かしい *adjective*
*– the meaning is similar to 'nostalgic' or 'longed for ...' so that it can be translated by '... reminds me of (something good)' but the specific memory is not stated and must be inferred. Sometimes translatable as 'I remember ... well' or 'I have a lot of (good) memories of ...'*

なって ▶ なる ▶ **197**

なっとく・納得
**1** *noun* = understanding
**2** *verb 3* 🅰 なっとくする = to be convinced
　なっとく させる = to persuade (someone)

なでる・撫でる *verb 2* 🅰 = to stroke

など・等 *particle*
• = such as
• = something like ...

なな・七 *noun* = seven ▶ **181**

ななつ・七つ *noun* = seven ▶ **181**

ななめ・斜め
**1** *adjective* ななめ(な)
• = slanted
• = diagonal
**2** *adverb* ななめに = diagonally

なに・何 *noun* = what

なにか・何か *interrogative*
• = something
• = anything

なにしろ *adverb* = at any rate

なになに・何々 *noun* = something or other

> ! *used by teachers to mean any word which could fill the blank in example sentences*

なにぶん・何分 *adverb* = anyway

なにも・何も *adverb* = (with negatives) nothing

なにより・何より *adverb* = better than (anything)

なのか・七日・7日 *noun*
• = seven days
• = the seventh (day of the month)
▶ **174**

なべ・鍋 *noun*
• = pot
• = pan

なま・生 *prefix and noun*
• = raw
• = live
• = draft/draught (beer)

なまいき・生意気
**1** *adjective* なまいき(な) = cheeky
**2** *adverb* なまいきに = cheekily

なまえ・名前 *noun* = name
▶ おなまえ

なまけもの・怠け者 *noun* = lazy person

なまける・怠ける *verb 2* 🅰 🅼
• = to be lazy
• = to neglect

**なまなましい・生々しい**
*adjective* = vivid

**なまぬるい・生ぬるい** *adjective*
= tepid

**なまほうそう・生放送** *noun*
= live (broadcast)

**なまり・鉛** *noun* = lead

**なまり・訛り** *noun* = accent

**なみ・波** *noun* = wave

**なみ・並** *noun and suffix*
• = ordinary
• = the same as

**なみだ・涙** *noun* = tear(s)

**なめらか・滑らか**
**1** *adjective* なめらか(な) = smooth
**2** *adverb* なめらかに = smoothly

**なやみ・悩み** *noun*
• = problem
• = (a) worry

**なやむ・悩む** *verb 1* 㐀
• = to worry (about)
• = to be troubled (by)

**なら** *suffix*
• = if
• = when it comes to ....
• = supposing ...

> **!** *a way of making conditional sentences.* ▶ **191**

**ならば** ▶ **なら**

**ならう・習う** *verb 1* 㐀 に
• = to learn
• = to study

**ならす・鳴らす** *verb 1* 㐀
• = to ring (a bell)
• = to sound (a horn)

**ならない** – *the negative form of* **なる** *and used in a number of idiomatic structures. When following a positive* ～て *form plus particle* は *it means 'must not ...' and when following a negative such as* **なければ** *or* **なくては** *it means 'must'. When following a* ～て *form it can mean 'can't help (doing) ...'*
▶ **197**

**ならぶ・並ぶ** *verb 1* 㐀 = to stand in a line

**ならべる・並べる** *verb 2* 㐀
• = to line (something) up
• = to display
• = to arrange

**なり** *particle* – *used after a verb it means 'as soon as ...' and used in the pattern* **A なり ... B なり** *it means 'either ... or ...'*

**なる・成る** *verb 1* 㐀 **なって ならない なります**
• = to become
• = to consist of

> **!** *following the dictionary or potential form of a verb in the form* **... ように なる** *it means 'to become able to ...'. Following the* **～く** *form of an adjective it means 'to get ...', 'to become ...'. Used to form honorific verb forms in the pattern* **お ...に なる.** ▶ **189**

**なる・鳴る** *verb 1* 㐀 = to ring

**なるべく** *adverb*
• = as ... as possible
• = if possible

**なるほど** *adverb*
• = I see
• = indeed

**なれる・慣れる** *verb 2* 㐀 に = to get used to

**なわ・縄** *noun* = rope

**なん・何** *noun and prefix*
• = what
• = how (many)
• = how (much)

> **!** *See the notes on counters for how to ask 'how many ...?' This is an alternative form of* **なに** ▶ **181**

**なんか** ▶ **なにか** ▶ **など** – *sometimes used to express doubt and hesitation*

**なんきょく・南極** *noun* = South Pole

**なんじ・何時** *phrase* = what time?
▶ **186**

**なんせい・南西** *noun* = south-west

**なんだか・何だか** *noun*
• = somehow
• = somewhat

**なんて** *adverb*
- = how
- = what

**なんて** *suffix*
- = like
- = such (as)

**なんで ・ 何で** *adverb* = why

**なんでも ・ 何でも** *adverb*
- = anything
- = everything
- = whatever

> ! *followed by a negative it means 'nothing'*

**なんと** *phrase*
- = what
- = how

**なんとう ・ 南東** *noun* = south-east

**なんとか** *adverb*
- = somehow
- = anyhow
- = somehow or other ► なんとか する ► なんとか なる

**なんとかして ► なんとか ► なんとか(する)**

**なんとか(する)** *verb 3* ㊙
- = to do ... somehow or other
- = to manage to do

**なんとか(なる)** *verb 3* ㊙
- = it will sort itself out
- = it will be ok in the end

**なんとなく** *adverb*
- = somehow (or other)
- = in some way (or other)
- = more or less

**なんにち ・ 何日** *phrase*
- = what is the date?
- = how many days?

**なんにん ・ 何人** *phrase* = how many people? ► 181

**なんぶ ・ 南部** *noun*
- = the south
- = the southern part

**なんべい ・ 南米** *noun* = South America

**なんみん ・ 難民** *noun* = refugee

**なんぼく ・ 南北** *noun* = North and South

# にニ

**に** *particle*
- = in
- = into
- = on
- = onto
- = to
- = toward
- = from
- = by
- = at
- = for
- = in order to
- = and

> ! *used in a variety of grammatical structures and idiomatically with certain verbs. Translations will depend on the words being used. Note that with verbs of giving and receiving it can be translated as either 'to' or 'from' depending on the verb.* ► **179**, ► **191**

**に ・ 二** *noun* = two ► **181**

**にあう ・ 似合う** *verb 1* ㊙ = to suit

**にいさん ・ 兄さん** ► **おにいさん**

**にえる ・ 煮える** *verb 2* ㊙ = to be cooked

**におい ・ 匂い** *noun* = smell
　〜の においが する = to smell of ...

**にがい ・ 苦い** *adjective* = bitter

**にかかわらず** *suffix* = regardless

**にがす ・ 逃がす** *verb 1* ㊞ = to let escape

**にがて ・ 苦手** *noun*
- = weak point
- = dislike

> ! *It is often translatable as 'not be very good at ...'*

**にぎやか ・ 賑やか**
**1** *adjective* にぎやか(な)
- = lively
- = noisy
- = busy
**2** *adverb* にぎやかに

• = noisily
• = cheerfully

**にぎる・握る** *verb 1* 🄰 = to grip

**にぎわう・賑わう** *verb 1* 🄰 = to be busy and noisy

**にく・肉** *noun and suffix* = meat

! *can also be used to refer to muscles or body fat*

**にくい・憎い** *adjective* = hateful

**にくい・難い** *suffix* = difficult to …

**にくたい・肉体** *noun* = (the) body

**にくたいろうどう・肉体労働** *noun* = physical labour

**にくむ・憎む** *verb 1* 🄰 = to hate

**にくらしい・憎らしい** *adjective* = hateful

**にくや・肉屋** *noun*
• = butcher
• = butcher's shop

**にげる・逃げる** *verb 2* 🄰
• = to run away
• = to escape

**にこにこ(する)** *verb 3* 🄰 = to smile

**にごり・濁り** *noun* – the basic meaning of the word is that a liquid is not 'clear' but it is also used to describe changes in sound such as those when the two marks " placed beside **かな** characters change the pronunciation from 'ka' **か** to 'ga' **が** etc. ▶ **vii**

**にごる・濁る** *verb 1* 🄰
• = to be cloudy (liquid) ▶ **にごり**

**にし・西** *noun* = west

**にじ・虹** *noun* = rainbow

**にせ(の)** *adjective* = fake

**にせい・二世** *noun* – meaning second generation it is especially used to describe people of Japanese ancestry who were born and now live in other countries. Can be translated as 'Japanese American', 'Japanese Canadian', 'Japanese Australian' etc.

**にせもの・偽物** *noun* = (a) fake item

**にち・日** *prefix* = Japan

**にち・日** *suffix* = day/s ▶ **174,** ▶ **181**

**にちえい・日英** *noun*
• = Japan and the UK
• = Japanese and English (languages)

**にちじ・日時** *noun* = date and time

**にちじょう・日常** *suffix* = everyday

**にちじょうかいわ・日常会話** *noun* = everyday conversation

**にちじょうせいかつ・日常生活** *noun* = everyday life

**にちべい・日米** *noun* = Japan and the USA

**にちようび・日曜日** *noun* = Sunday

**にちようひん・日用品** *noun* = daily necessities

**～について** *phrase*
• = about
• = regarding
　にほんについて はなす = talk about Japan

**にっか・日課** *noun* = daily task

**にっき・日記** *noun* = diary

**にづくり・荷造り**
**1** *noun* = packing
**2** *verb 3* 🄰 にづくり(を)する = to pack (for a holiday etc.)

**にっけい・日系** *noun and prefix* – used in front of words indicating nationality it means 'of Japanese origin' and so can be translated 'Japanese American', 'Japanese Brazilian' etc.

**にっこう・日光** *noun* = sunlight

**にっちゅう・日中** *noun* = Japan and China

**にってい・日程** *noun* = schedule

**にっぽん・日本** *noun and prefix* – an older and less common version of ▶ **にほん**

**には** ▶ **に**

**にぶい・鈍い** *adjective* = dull

**にほん・日本** *noun and prefix* = Japan ▶ **172**

にニ

**にほんご・日本語** *noun*
= Japanese (language)

**にほんじん・日本人** *noun*
= Japanese (person/people)

**にほんりょうり・日本料理**
*noun* = Japanese food

**にもかかわらず** *suffix*
- = in spite of ...
- = although

**にもつ・荷物** *noun*
- = baggage
- = luggage

**ニュアンス** *noun* = nuance

**にゅういん・入院**
**1** *noun* = going into hospital
**2** *verb 3* ㋕ **にゅういんする** = to go into hospital
にゅういん している = to be in hospital

**にゅうがく・入学**
**1** *noun* = entering school/college
**2** *verb 3* ㋕ **にゅうがくする** = to enter (school/college)

**にゅうがくしけん・入学試験**
*noun* = entrance examination (for a university or school)

**にゅうしゃ・入社**
**1** *noun* = entering a company
**2** *verb 3* ㋕ **にゅうしゃする** = to join a company

**にゅうじょう・入場**
**1** *noun* = admission
**2** *verb 3* ㋕ **にゅうじょうする** = to gain admission

**にゅうじょうけん・入場券**
*noun* = admission ticket

**にゅうじょうりょう・入場料**
*noun* = entrance fee

**ニュース** *noun* = news

**にょうぼう・女房** *noun* = (one's own) wife ▶ **177**

**～によって** *phrase* = by

**～による(と)** *phrase* = according to

**にらむ・睨む** *verb 1* ㋩ = to glare (at)

**にる・煮る** *verb 2* ㋩
- = to boil
- = to simmer

**にる・似る** *verb 2* ㋕ に
- = to resemble

**にわ・庭** *noun* = garden

**にわいじり・庭弄り** *noun*
= gardening

**にわし・庭師** *noun* = gardener

**にわかあめ・にわか雨** *noun*
= shower (of rain)

**にわかに・俄かに** *adverb*
= suddenly

**にわとり・鶏** *noun* = chicken

**にん・人** *counter* = people ▶ **181**

**にんき・人気** *noun* = popularity
にんきが ある = popular
にんきが ない = unpopular

**にんぎょう・人形** *noun*
- = doll
- = toy figurine

**にんげん・人間** *noun* = human

**にんしん・妊娠**
**1** *noun* = pregnancy
**2** *verb 3* ㋕ **にんしんする** = to get pregnant
にんしん している = to be pregnant

**にんじん・人参** *noun* = carrot

**にんずう・人数** *noun* = number (of people)

**にんにく** *noun* = garlic

# ぬ ヌ

**ぬいぐるみ** *noun* = child's soft toy

**ぬいで** ▶ぬぐ ▶ **197**

**ぬう・縫う** *verb 1* ㋩ = to sew

**ぬぎます** ▶ぬぐ

**ぬく・抜く** *verb 1* ㋩
- = to pull out
- = to outrun

**ぬぐ・脱ぐ** *verb 1* ㋩ ぬいで・ぬがない・ぬぎます = to take off (clothing or footwear)

**ぬける・抜ける** *verb 2* ㋕
- = to come out
- = to be missing

ぬすむ・盗む *verb 1* ㊅ = to steal

ぬの・布 *noun* = cloth

ぬま・沼 *noun* = marsh

ぬらす・濡らす *verb 1* ㊅ = to make wet

ぬる・塗る *verb 1* ㊅
• = to apply (paint etc.)
• = to spread (butter etc.)

ぬるい・温い *adjective* = lukewarm

ぬれる・濡れる *verb 2* ㊙ = to get wet

---

# ねネ

ね *particle* – *used at the end of phrases and sentences to seek confirmation or agreement and to add emphasis or express surprise. In the first instance it is somewhat similar to English tag questions such as 'isn't it?', 'don't you?', 'haven't they?' etc. and can sometimes be translated in that way.*

ね・根 *noun* = root

ね・値 *noun* = price

ねあがり・値上がり
**1** *noun* = price rise
**2** *verb 3* ㊙ ねあがりする = to increase in price

ねえ ▶ね

ねえさん ▶**noun** おねえさん

ネガ *noun* = (photographic) negatives

ねがい・願い *noun*
• = request
• = wish ▶ おねがい

ねがう・願う *verb 1* ㊅ = to wish for ...

ネクタイ *noun* = necktie

ねこ・猫 *noun* = cat

ねじ・ネジ *noun* = screw

ねじれる *verb 2* ㊙ = to be twisted

ねじる *verb 1* ㊅ = to twist

ねずみ *noun*
• = mouse
• = rat

ねだん・値段 *noun* = price

ねつ・熱 *noun*
• = fever
• = heat

ねつい・熱意 *noun* = eagerness

ネックレス *noun* = necklace

ねっしん・熱心
**1** *adjective* ねっしん(な) = eager
**2** *adverb* ねっしんに = eagerly

ねっする・熱する *verb 3* ㊅ = to heat

ねったい・熱帯 *prefix* = tropical

ねぼう・寝坊
**1** *noun* = oversleeping
**2** *verb 3* ㊙ ねぼうする = to sleep in

ねまき・寝間着・寝巻 *noun*
• = nightclothes
• = pyjamas

ねまわし・根回し *noun* – *the process in Japanese companies of consulting people widely prior to formal approaches being made in order to gain agreement or consensus and so translatable as 'laying the groundwork'. Also used as a verb in the form* ねまわし(を)する

ねむい・眠い *adjective* = sleepy

ねむれる・眠れる *verb 2* ㊙ = to be able to sleep

ねむる・眠る *verb 1* ㊙ = to sleep

ねらい・狙い *noun* = aim

ねらう・狙う *verb 1* ㊅ = to aim for/at

ねる・寝る *verb 2* ㊙
• = to sleep
• = to go to bed

ねん・年 *prefix and suffix* = year
▶ **174,** ▶ **181**

ねんがじょう・年賀状 *noun* – *a card sent for January 1st wishing people well in the new year*

ねんかん・年間 *counter* = year(s)
▶ **174**

ねんじゅう・年中 *noun* = throughout the year

ぬヌ

ねネ

**ねんせい・年生** *suffix* – following a number it indicates which year of a school a student is in

**ねんだい・年代** *noun* – the basic meaning is 'generation' although sometimes 'age' is a better translation. It is also added to numbers to express time 70 ねんだい *'the 70s'*

**ねんど・年度** *suffix* = year

**ねんりょう・燃料** *noun* = fuel

**ねんれい・年齢** *noun* = age

# の ノ

**の** *particle* – there are a number of uses of this particle. One of its most common uses is to connect nouns to show a relationship of some kind. In this use it can be thought of as similar to the apostrophe + s in the sense of 'belonging to' i.e. わたしの ほん *'my book'*. However the range of relationships expressed in Japanese is much wider and the meaning 'about' is also common i.e. くるまの ほん *'a book about cars'*. Used at the end of sentences, especially by women it can indicate a question.

**のう・脳** *noun* = (the) brain

**のうか・農家** *noun*
- = farmer
- = farmhouse

**のうぎょう・農業** *noun* = farming

**のうさんぶつ・農産物** *noun* = agricultural produce

**のうじょう・農場** *noun* = farm

**のうそん・農村** *noun* = farming village/community

**のうち・農地** *noun* = agricultural land

**のうど・濃度** *noun* = concentration (of)

**ノウハウ** *noun* = know how

**のうみそ・脳みそ** *noun* = brains

**のうみん・農民** *noun* = farmers

**のうやく・農薬** *noun* = agricultural chemicals

**のうりつ・能率** *noun* = efficiency

**のうりつてき・能率的**
**1** *adjective* のうりつてき(な) = efficient
**2** *adverb* のうりつてきに = efficiently

**のうりょく・能力** *noun* = ability

**ノート** *noun*
- = notebook
- = note

**のがれる・逃れる** *verb 2* ㊰ = to escape

**のがす・逃す** *verb 1* ㊀ = to lose (an opportunity etc.)

**のこす・残す** *verb 1* ㊀ = to leave

**のこり・残り** *noun* = remainder

**のこる・残る** *verb 1* ㊰ = to remain

**のせる・載せる** *verb 2* ㊀
- = to put on/in
- = to load

**のせる・乗せる** *verb 2* ㊀ = to give (someone) a lift

**のぞく・除く** *verb 1* ㊀
- = to remove
- = to exclude

**のぞく・覗く** *verb 1* ㊀ = to peep

**のぞましい・望ましい** *adjective* = desirable

**のぞみ・望み** *noun*
- = hope
- = chance (of)

**のぞむ・望む** *verb 1* ㊀
- = to hope for
- = to want

**のぞむ・臨む** *verb 1* ㊰ に
- = to face
- = to overlook

**のち・後** *noun* = after

**のちほど・後程** *adverb* = later

**ノック**
**1** *noun*
- = knock
- = knocking

**2** *verb 3* Ⓔ ノックする = to knock
(on the door)

のって ▶ のる ▶ **197**

ので *particle* = because

のです *– particle* の *and* です. *often
used at the end of a sentence for
slight emphasis in explanations
especially where personal sentiment
is involved. Also used to ask
questions in the form* のですか *and
contracted in casual speech to*
〜んです

のど・喉 *noun* = throat

のばす・伸ばす *verb 1* Ⓔ
• = to lengthen
• = to stretch
• = to let (hair) grow

のばす・延ばす *verb 1* Ⓔ
• = to extend
• = to postpone

のびる・伸びる *verb 2* Ⓚ
• = to grow
• = to lengthen
• = to improve

のびる・延びる *verb 2* Ⓚ
• = to be extended
• = to be postponed

のべる・述べる *verb 2* Ⓔ = to
state

のぼって ▶ のぼる ▶ **197**

のぼり・上り *noun* = ascent

> **!** *used in the form* のぼりでんしゃ
> *to describe trains travelling in the
> direction of a major city (especially
> Tokyo) which is the terminus*

のぼります ▶ のぼる

のぼる・上る・昇る *verb 1* Ⓚ
• = to go up
• = to rise

のぼる・登る *verb 1* Ⓚ に のぼっ
て のぼらない のぼります = to
climb

のみこむ・飲み込む *verb 1* Ⓔ
= to swallow

のみます ▶ のむ

のみもの・飲み物 *noun* = drink

のむ・飲む *verb 1* Ⓔ のんで・
のまない・のみます = to drink
• = to take (medicine)
• = to eat (soup)

のり *noun* = glue

のり・海苔 *noun – an edible
seaweed prepared in dry sheets and
often used to wrap rice balls and
sushi*

のりおくれる・乗り遅れる
*verb 2* Ⓚ = to miss (train, plane etc.)

のりかえ・乗り換え *noun*
= change (of train etc.)

のりかえる・乗り換える
*verb 2* Ⓚ = to change (train etc.)

のりこえる・乗り越える
*verb 2* Ⓔ
• = to climb over
• = to overcome

のりこす・乗り越す *verb 1* Ⓔ
= to miss (getting off at) the right
station

のりそこなう・乗り損なう
*verb 1* Ⓔ = to miss (train, plane etc.)

のりば・乗り場 *noun – a place to
get on and off transport such as
buses and taxis*

のります ▶ のる

のる・乗る *verb 1* Ⓚ に のって・
のらない・のります
• = to ride
• = to take (transport)
• = to get on (transport)

のる・載る *verb 1* Ⓚ に
• = to be on
• = to be in

のろい・鈍い *adjective* = slow

のろのろ
**1** *adverb* のろのろ(と) = slowly
**2** *verb 3* Ⓚ のろのろする = to be slow

のんき・呑気
**1** *adjective* のんき(な) = easy going
**2** *adverb* のんきに = care free

のんで ▶ のむ ▶ **197**

のんびり
**1** *adverb* のんびり(と) = relaxed
**2** *verb 3* Ⓚ のんびりする
• = to be care free
• = to relax

のノ

# はハ

は *particle* – *pronounced* わ *There are a number of uses of this particle. The most common is as a marker for the topic about which a comment is made. It marks the subject of a comment but NOT necessarily the grammatical subject* ▶ **205**

は・歯 *noun*
• = tooth
• = teeth

は・葉 *noun* = leaf

ば・場 *noun*
• = place
• = occasion

〜ば *suffix* – *indicates the conditional form of verbs and adjectives* ▶ **191**, ▶ **201**

バー *noun* = bar

ばあい・場合 *noun*
• = occasion
• = time
• = case

パーセント *noun*
• = percentage
• = percent

パーティー *noun* = party
　パーティーする = to have a party
　パーティーを ひらく = to hold a party

パート *noun* = part-time job

ハードウェア *noun* = (computer) hardware

バーベキュー *noun* = barbeque

はい *interjection* – *while the basic meaning is 'yes' it is also used to confirm a statement and can mean 'no' in response to negative questions etc. Also used as* あいづち *to indicate that someone is listening and not necessarily carrying any sense of agreement*

はい・灰 *noun* = ash

はい・肺 *noun* = lungs

はい・杯 *counter*
• = cups of
• = bowls of ▶ **181**

ばい・杯 ▶はい

ぱい・杯 ▶はい

ばい・倍 *noun and suffix* – *as a noun it means 'double' but as a suffix on a number it means '〜 times (that amount)'*

はいいろ・灰色 *noun* = grey

はいいろ(の)・灰色 (の) *adjective* = grey

ばいう・梅雨 *noun* = the rainy season

はいきガス・排気ガス *noun* = exhaust fumes

はいきょ・廃虚 *noun*
• = ruin
• = abandoned building

ばいきん・ばい菌 *noun*
• = germs
• = bacteria

ハイキング
1 *noun* = hiking
2 *verb 3* ㊥ ハイキングする = to go hiking

はいけい・拝啓 *phrase* – *used as the opening of a formal letter and equivalent to 'Dear Sir or Madam'*

はいけん(する)・拝見(する) *verb 3* ㊦ = to see

❗ *humble equivalent of* みる ▶ **189**

はいざら・灰皿 *noun* = ashtray

はいし(する)・廃止(する) *verb 3* ㊦ = to abolish

はいしゃ・歯医者 *noun* = dentist

ばいしょう・賠償 *noun* = compensation

ばいしょうきん・賠償金 ▶ばいしょう

はいたつ・配達
1 *noun* = delivery
2 *verb 3* ㊦ はいたつする = to deliver

はいって ▶はいる ▶ **197**

はいて ▶ はく ▶ **197**

ハイテク *noun* = high technology

> ❗ *can be used as an adjective with* な

**ばいてん・売店** *noun*
- = small shop
- = kiosk

バイト *noun* = part time job
バイト(を)する = to do a part-time/ short term job

バイバイ *phrase* = bye bye

**ばいばい・売買**
1 *noun* = buying and selling
2 *verb 3* ばいばいする = to buy and sell

ハイヒール *noun* = high heels

パイプ *noun* = pipe

> ❗ *sometimes used to describe 'connections' with people or companies*

**はいゆう・俳優** *noun* = actor

ハイライト *noun* = highlights

はいります ▶ はいる

**はいりょ・配慮**
1 *noun*
- = consideration
- = attention
2 *verb 3* ⓔ はいりょする
- = to consider
- = to give attention to

バイリンガル *noun* = bilingual

**はいる・入る** *verb 1* ⓘ に はいって・はいらない・はいります
- = to enter
- = to come in
- = to go in
- = to join
- = to be contained
- = to get in (bath)

パイロット *noun* = pilot

はう *verb 1* ⓘ = to crawl

ハウス *noun* = greenhouse

**はえ・蝿** *noun* = fly

**はえる・生える** *verb 2* ⓘ = to grow

**はか・墓** *noun* = grave

**ばか・馬鹿**
1 *noun* = an idiot
2 *adjective* ばか(な) = stupid
〜を ばかに する = to make fun of

> ❗ *this word carries more or less strength of feeling depending on the tone of voice. It can be used in teasing amongst friends but also be sufficiently offensive to cause a fight! It will thus vary greatly in translation!*

**はがき・葉書** *noun* = postcard

**はかせ・博士** *noun and suffix* = Doctor (PhD)

**ばかばかしい** *adjective* = stupid

**ばからしい・馬鹿らしい** *adjective* = stupid

**はかり・秤** *noun* = (kitchen or laboratory) scales

**ばかり** *suffix* – has a variety of meanings including 'just', 'only' and 'approximately'. It can also mean 'do nothing but ...', 'do ... continuously' and following the 〜た form it means 'have just ...'. ▶ **191**

**はかる・計る・測る** *verb 1* ⓘ = to measure

**はかる・図る** *verb 1* ⓘ = to attempt (to)

**はきけ・吐き気** *noun* = nausea

はきます ▶ はく

**はく・履く** *verb 1* ⓘ はいて・はかない・はきます
- = to wear
- = to put on

**はく・吐く** *verb 1* ⓘ
- = to vomit
- = to spit

**はく・掃く** *verb 1* ⓘ = to sweep

**はく・泊** *counter* = nights' stay ▶ **181**

ぱく・泊 ▶ はく

**はくし・博士** *suffix* = doctor of ... (PhD)

**はくしゅ・拍手**
1 *noun* = applause
2 *verb 3* ⓘ はくしゅする = to applaud

はハ

ばくぜん(と)・漠然(と) *adverb*
= vaguely

ばくだい(な)・莫大(な)
*adjective* = enormous

ばくだん・爆弾 *noun* = bomb

ばくはつ・爆発
1 *noun* = explosion
2 *verb 3* ⑩ ばくはつする = to
explode

はくぶつかん・博物館 *noun*
= museum

はぐるま・歯車 *noun* = gear

はげしい・激しい *adjective*
• = intense
• = violent

バケツ *noun* = bucket

はげます・励ます *verb 1* ⑧ = to
encourage

はこ・箱 *noun* = box

はこぶ・運ぶ *verb 1* ⑧
• = to carry
• = to transport
• = to go (well/badly)

はさまる・挟まる *verb 1* ⑩ = to
get something caught in (a door etc.)

はさみ *noun* = scissors

はさむ・挟む *verb 1* ⑧
• = to place (in/between)
• = to insert

はさん・破産
1 *noun* = bankruptcy
2 *verb 3* ⑩ はさんする = to go
bankrupt

はし・橋 *noun* = bridge

はし・箸 *noun* = chopsticks

はし・端 *noun*
• = edge
• = end
• = corner

はじ・恥 *noun*
• = shame
• = embarrassment
• = disgrace
　〜に恥をかかす = to embarrass

はしご *noun* = ladder

はしって ▶ はしる ▶ **197**

はじまって ▶ はじまる ▶ **197**

はじまり・始まり *noun*
= beginning

はじまります ▶ はじまる

はじまる・始まる *verb 1* ⑩ に
はじまって・はじまらない・
はじまります = to begin

はじめ・初め *noun* = beginning

はじめて・初めて
1 *noun* = (the) first time
2 *adverb* = first

はじめに・初めに *conjunction*
• = firstly
• = at the beginning

はじめは・始めは *phrase* = at first

はじめまして・始めまして
*phrase* = how do you do

はじめます ▶ はじめる

はじめる・始める *verb 2* ⑧ はじ
めて・はじめない・はじめます
= to start

> **!** *added to the pre* 〜ます *form of
> other verbs to express 'begin to ...'*
> ▶ **191**

パジャマ *noun*
• = pyjamas
• = nightdress

ばしょ・場所 *noun*
• = place
• = space (in a room)

はしら・柱 *noun* = pillar

はしります ▶ はしる

はしる・走る *verb 1* ⑩ はしって
・はしらない・はしります
• = to run
• = to travel (at high speed)

はず *noun* – *used after the plain forms
of verbs and adjectives the basic
meaning is 'expectation' and when
following positive statements it
conveys the idea of 'should ...', 'it is
expected that ...'. When following
negative statements it is translatable
as 'not expected' etc.*

バス *noun* = bus

パス
1 *noun* = pass
2 *verb 3* ⑧ ⑩ パスする = to pass

## はずかしい・恥ずかしい
*adjective*
- = embarrassing
- = embarrassed
- = shy
- = ashamed
- = shameful

## バスケットボール *noun*
= basketball

## はずす・外す *verb 1* を
- = to take off
- = to remove
- = to undo
- = to leave

## パスポート *noun* = passport

## はずれる・外れる *verb 2* が
- = to be loose
- = to be wrong
- = to be undone

## はた・旗 *noun* = flag

## はだ・肌 *noun* = skin

## バター *noun* = butter

## パターン *noun* = pattern

## はだか・裸 *noun and adjective*
- = nakedness
- = naked

## はたけ・畑 *noun* = (cultivated) field

## はだし(で)・裸足(で) *noun and adjective* = barefoot

## はたち・二十歳・20歳 *noun*
= twenty years old

**!** *In Japan this is the age at which young people become adults*

## はたらいて ▶はたらく ▶ 197

## はたらき・働き *noun and prefix*
= work

## はたらきます ▶はたらく

## はたらきもの・働き者 *noun*
= hard worker

## はたらく・働く *verb 1* が はたらいて・はたらかない・はたらきます = to work

## はち・八・8 *noun* = eight ▶ 171, ▶ 181, ▶ 186

## はち・蜂 *noun*
- = bee
- = wasp

## はち・鉢 *noun* = (flower) pot

## はちがつ・八月・8月 *noun*
= August ▶ 174

## はちみつ・蜂蜜 *noun* = honey

## パチンコ *noun* – a game related to pinball played by many Japanese

## はつ・初 *prefix* = (the) first

## はつ・発 *suffix* = departing at/from

## ばつ *noun* – has several meanings amongst which are 'incorrect answer', 'punishment' and a cross or X symbol.

## はつおん・発音
**1** *noun* = pronunciation
**2** *verb 3* を はつおんする = to pronounce

## はつか・二十日・20日 *noun*
- = the twentieth day of the month
- = twenty days ▶ 174, ▶ 181

## はっきり(と)
**1** *adverb* = clearly
**2** *verb 3* が はっきり(と)する = to be clear

## ばっきん・罰金 *noun* = (a) fine

## バック
**1** *noun* = background
**2** *verb 3* が バックする = to reverse

## バッグ *noun* = bag

## パックりょこう・パック旅行
*noun* = package holiday

## バックアップ
**1** *noun* = backup
**2** *verb 3* が を バックアップする = to back up

## はっけん・発見
**1** *noun* = discovery
**2** *verb 3* を はっけんする = to discover

## ばっさい・伐採
**1** *noun* = timber felling
**2** *verb 3* を ばっさいする = to fell

## はっしゃ・発車
**1** *noun* = departure
**2** *verb 3* が を はっしゃする = to depart

## ばっする・罰する *verb 3* を = to punish

はハ

はっせい・発生
1 *noun* = occurrence
2 *verb 3* ㋭ はっせいする = to occur

はっそう・発想 *noun* = way of
thinking

はったつ・発達
1 *noun* = development
2 *verb 3* ㋭ はったつする = to
develop

ばっちり *phrase* = just right!

バッテリー *noun* = (car) battery

はってん・発展
1 *noun* = development
2 *verb 3* ㋭ ㋾ はってんする = to
develop

はつでんしょ・発電所 *noun*
= (electricity) power station

バット *noun* = bat

ぱっと・パッと *adverb* = suddenly

はつばい・発売
1 *noun* = sale
2 *verb 3* ㋾ はつばいする = to put on
sale
　はつばいちゅう = now on sale!

はっぴょう・発表
1 *noun*
• = announcement
• = presentation
2 *verb 3* ㋾ はっぴょうする
• = to announce
• = to present

はつめい・発明
1 *noun* = invention
2 *verb 3* ㋾ はつめいする = to invent

はつもうで・初詣 *noun* – the first
visit to a shrine or temple of the year
(often just after midnight on January
1ˢᵗ and a major part of the new year
celebration for many Japanese
people)

はて・果て *noun* = (extreme) end

はで(な)・派手(な) *adjective*
• = brightly coloured
• = showy

パトカー *noun* = police car

バドミントン *noun* = badminton

はな・花 *noun* = flower

はな・鼻 *noun* = nose

はなし・話 *noun*
• = talk
• = subject (of/for a talk)

はなしあい・話し合い *noun*
= talks

はなしあう・話し合う *verb 1* ㋭
と = to discuss

はなしかける・話し掛ける
*verb 2* ㋾ に = to speak to

はなしちゅう・話し中 *phrase*
= (the telephone is) engaged

はなして ▶ はなす ▶ 197

はなします ▶ はなす

はなす・話す *verb 1* ㋭ に と
はなして・はなさない・はなし
ます
• = to talk
• = to speak

はなす・放す *verb 1* ㋾ = to release

はなす・離す *verb 1* ㋾ = to
separate

はなぢ・鼻血 *noun* = nosebleed

バナナ *noun* = banana

はなはだしい・甚だしい
*adjective* = serious

はなび・花火 *noun* = fireworks

はなみ・花見 *noun* – going to
see the blossoms of the plum tree
うめ and (especially) the cherry tree
さくら as an occasion for picnics
and partying.

はなやか(な)・華やか(な)
*adjective* = splendid

はなよめ(さん)・花嫁(さん)
*noun* = bride

はなれる・離れる *verb 2* ㋭ ㋾
= to be separated

はね・羽 *noun*
• = wing
• = feather

はねる・跳ねる *verb 2* ㋭
• = to jump up
• = to splash

はねる *verb 2* ㋾ = to run over
　くるまに はねられる = to be run
over by a car

はは・母 *noun* = (one's own) mother
▶ 177

はば・幅 *noun* = width

パパ *noun* = dad ▶ **177**

ははおや・母親 *noun* = mother
▶ **177**

はばひろい・幅広い *adjective*
= wide

はぶく・省く *verb 1* 를
• = to reduce
• = to leave out

バブル *noun* = bubble

> **!** *in the form* バブルけいざい・
> バブル経済 *it is used to describe
> an economic boom and subsequent
> collapse, and specifically that of
> the 1990s in Japan of which the
> good times are referred to as the*
> バブルじだい・バブル時代

はへん・破片 *noun* = fragment

はま・浜 *noun* = beach

はまべ・浜辺 *noun* = beach

はみがき・歯磨き *noun*
• = toothpaste
• = cleaning the teeth
  はみがきする = to clean the teeth

はみがきこ・歯磨き粉 *noun*
= toothpaste

はめる *verb 2* 를
• = to put on (a ring or gloves)
• = to wear (a ring or gloves)

ばめん・場面 *noun* = scene

はやい・早い・速い *adjective*
• = early
• = fast

はやおき・早起き
**1** *noun* = getting up early
**2** *verb 3* 를 はやおきする = to get up
early

はやさ・速さ *noun* = speed

はやし・林 *noun* = woods

はやる・流行る *verb 1* 를
• = to be prevalent
• = to be in fashion
  かぜが はやっている = a cold is
  going around

はら・原 *noun* = plain

はら・腹 *noun* = belly
  はらが たつ = to get angry

ばら・薔薇 *noun* = rose

はらいます ▶ はらう

はらいもどす・払い戻す *verb 1*
를 = to refund

はらう・払う *verb 1* 를 はらって・
はらわない・はらいます = to pay

はらって ▶ はらう ▶ **197**

ばらばら
**1** *noun* = scattered
**2** *verb 3* 를 ばらばら(に)なる = to be
scattered

バランス *noun* = balance

はり・針 *noun*
• = needle
• = hand (of a clock)

はりがね・針金 *noun* = wire

はりきる・張り切る *verb 1* 를
= to be full of energy

はる・春 *noun* = spring

はる・張る *verb 1* 를 를 = to stretch

はる・貼る *verb 1* 를 = to stick

はるか・遥か
**1** *adverb* = far away
**2** はるかに = by far

はれ・晴れ *noun* = clear skies

はれる・晴れる *verb 2* 를 = to be
fine (weather)

はん・班 *noun and suffix* = group

はん・半 *suffix*
• = half
• = half past ▶ **186**

はん・反 *prefix* = anti-

ばん・晩 *noun*
• = evening
• = night

ばん・番 *noun* = turn

> **!** *as a suffix it means 'number' and
> is used to make the ordinal numbers
> rather like the small letters attached
> to numbers in English* 1st, 2nd, 3rd, 4th,
> *etc.* ▶ **181**

バン *noun* = van

パン *noun* = bread

はんい・範囲 *noun* = scope

はんえい・反映
**1** *noun* = reflection
**2** *verb 3* 를 를 はんえいする = to be
reflected

はハ

**はんえい・繁栄**
1 *noun* = propsperity
2 *verb 3 ㋕* はんえいする = to prosper

**ハンガー** *noun* = (coat) hanger

**はんがく・半額** *noun* = half price

**ハンカチ** *noun* = handkerchief

**パンク**
1 *noun* = puncture
2 *verb 3 ㋕* パンクする = to be punctured

**ばんぐみ・番組** *noun* = (television or radio) programme

**はんけい・半径** *noun* = radius

**はんこ・判子** *noun* – a carved stamp with a person's surname which is often used in place of a signature on official documents

**はんこう・犯行** *noun* = crime

**はんこう・反抗**
1 *noun* = opposition
2 *verb 3 ㋕* に はんこうする = to resist

**ばんごう・番号** *noun* = number

**はんざい・犯罪** *noun* = crime

**ばんざい・万歳** *noun* – literally 'ten thousand years' it is used in the same way as English 'hip hip hooray' or 'three cheers'

**ハンサム(な)** *adjective* = handsome

**はんじ・判事** *noun* = judge

**ばんじ・万事** *noun* = everything

**はんせい・反省**
1 *noun* = thinking over
2 *verb 3 ㋕* はんせいする = to reflect (on)

**ばんせん・番線** *suffix* = platform number

**はんそで・半袖** *prefix* = short-sleeved

**はんたい・反対**
1 *noun* = opposition
2 *verb 3 ㋕* に はんたいする = to be against

**はんだくおん・半濁音** *noun* – the 'p' sound in Japanese which is represented by the small circle next to

かな *symbols to indicate a change in pronunciation i.e. from* ひ *'hi' to* ぴ *'pi'*

**はんだん・判断**
1 *noun* = judgement
2 *verb 3 ㋜* はんだんする
• = to judge
• = to decide

**ばんち・番地** *noun and suffix* – follows a number as a subdivision of a Japanese address which is similar to a 'block' in the USA or Canada

**パンチ**
1 *noun* = punch
2 *verb 3 ㋜* に パンチする = to punch

**パンツ** *noun*
• = underpants
• = knickers
• = shorts

**バント** *noun*
• = a bunt
• = a drudge

**バンド** *noun*
• = strap
• = bracelet
• = (pop) band

**はんとう・半島** *noun and suffix* = peninsula

**はんとし・半年** *noun* = a six month period

**ハンドバッグ** *noun* = handbag

**ハンドル** *noun* = steering wheel

**はんにん・犯人** *noun* = criminal

**はんのう・反応**
1 *noun* = reaction
2 *verb 3 ㋕* はんのうする = to react

**はんばい・販売**
1 *noun* = sales
2 *verb 3 ㋜* はんばいする = to sell

**はんばいき・販売機** *noun* = vending machine

**はんぱつ・反発**
1 *noun* = opposition
2 *verb 3 ㋕* に はんぱつする = to rebel

**はんぶん・半分** *noun* = half

**ばんめ・番め・番目** *suffix* – added to numbers to give position in a sequence like the ordinal numbers 1ˢᵗ, 2ⁿᵈ, 3ʳᵈ, 4ᵗʰ, etc. ▶ **181**

# ひヒ

**ひ・日** *noun*
- = day
- = the sun

**ひ・火** *noun* = fire
たばこに ひを つける = to light a cigarette

**ひ・灯** *noun* = the lights (of a town or building)

**ひ・非** *prefix* – a negative prefix similar to English 'un-' and 'non-'

**ひ・費** *suffix* = expenses

**ピアス** *noun* = earring

**ひあたり・日当たり** *noun*
= sunlight
ひあたりの いい へや = a sunny room

**ピアノ** *noun* = piano
ピアノを ひく = play the piano

**ヒーター** *noun* = heater

**ビール** *noun* = beer

**ひえる・冷える** *verb 2* ㊉
- = to get cold
- = to be chilled

**ひがい・被害** *noun* = damage

**ひがいしゃ・被害者** *noun*
= victim

**ひかえめ・控え目**
**1** *adjective* ひかえめ(な) = moderate
**2** *adverb* ひかえめに = moderately

**ひがえり・日帰り** *noun* = one day trip

**ひがえりりょこう・日帰り旅行**
▶ひがえり

**ひかく(する)・比較(する)** *verb 3* ㊉ と = to compare

**ひかくてき・比較的**
**1** *adjective* ひかくてき(な)
= comparative
**2** *adverb* ひかくてきに
= comparatively

**ひかげ・日陰** *noun* = shade

**ひがし・東** *noun* = east

**ぴかぴか(と)** *adverb* – the basic meaning is 'shining' or 'glittering' but it can be used to mean 'brand new' or 'clean', the latter especially in the form ぴかぴかに なる

**ひかり・光** *noun* = light

**ひかる・光る** *verb 1* ㊉ = to shine

**ひき・匹** *counter* = smaller animals and fish ▶181

**びき** ▶ ひき

**ぴき** ▶ ひき

**ひきいる・率いる** *verb 2* ㊎ = to lead (a group of people)

**ひきうける・引き受ける** *verb 2* ㊎ = to undertake

**ひきおこす・引き起こす** *verb 1* ㊎ = to cause

**ひきかえす・引き換えす** *verb 1* ㊉ = to turn around and go back

**ひきがね・引き金** *noun* = trigger

**ひきざん・引き算**
**1** *noun* = subtraction
**2** *verb 3* ㊎ ひきざんする = to subtract

**ひきだし・引き出し** *noun*
= drawer

**ひきだす・引き出す** *verb 1* ㊎
= to withdraw (money from a bank)

**ひきょう(な)・卑怯(な)**
*adjective*
- = cowardly
- = unfair

**ひきよせる・引き寄せる** *verb 2* ㊎ = to draw (something) closer

**ひきわけ・引き分け** *noun* = a draw

**ひきわたす・引き渡す** *verb 1* ㊎ = to hand over

**ひく・引く** *verb 1* ㊎ ひいて・ひかない・ひきます**
- = to pull
- = to attract
- = to draw
- = to catch (a cold)
- = to look up (in a dictionary)

**ひく・弾く** *verb 1* ㊎ ひいて・ひかない・ひきます = to play (an instrument with the fingers or plectrum) ▶180

ひヒ

ひく・轢く *verb 1* を = to run over (with a vehicle)

ひくい・低い *adjective*
• = low
　せが ひくい = short

ピクニック *noun* = picnic

ひげ・髭 *adjective*
• = moustache
• = beard

ひげき・悲劇 *noun* = tragedy

ひこう・飛行 *noun* = flight

ひこうき・飛行機 *noun* = aeroplane

ひこうじょう・飛行場 *noun* = airport

ひざ・膝 *noun*
• = knee
• = lap

ビザ *noun* = visa

ピザ *noun* = pizza

ひざし・日差し・陽射し *noun* = sunlight

ひさしぶり・久し振り *phrase*
• = it's been a long time (since we last had contact)
• = long time no see

ひさん(な)・悲惨(な) *adjective* = terrible

ひじ・肘 *noun* = elbow

ビジネス *noun* = business

ビジネスウーマン *noun* = businesswoman

ビジネスマン *noun* = businessman

びじゅつ・美術 *noun* = art

びじゅつかん・美術館 *noun* = art gallery

ひしょ・秘書 *noun* = secretary

ひじょう・非常 *noun* = emergency

ひじょうに・非常に *adverb* = extremely

ひじょうきん・非常勤 *prefix* = part-time

ひじょうぐち・非常口 *noun* = emergency exit

ひじょうしき・非常識 *noun* = lacking in common sense

ビスケット *noun* = biscuit

ピストル *noun* = pistol

びせいぶつ・微生物 *noun* = micro-organism

ひたい・額 *noun* = forehead

ひたすら *adverb* = whole-heartedly

ビタミン *noun* = vitamin

ひだり・左 *noun* = left

ひだりがわ・左側 *noun* = left hand side

ひだりきき・左利き *noun* = left handed (person)

ひだりて・左手 *noun* = left hand

ひっかかる・引っかかる *verb 1* が = to get caught

ひっかける・引っかける *verb 2* を = to catch

ひっきりなし *adverb* = constantly

びっくり(する) *verb 3* が
• = to be surprised
• = to be shocked

ひっくりかえす・引っくり返す *verb 1* を = to overturn

ひっくりかえる・引っくり返る *verb 1* が = to be overturned

ひづけ・日付 *noun* = date ▶ 174

ひっこし・引越し *noun* = moving house

ひっこす・引っ越す *verb 1* が = to move house

ひっし・必死
**1** *noun* = desperation
**2** *adverb* ひっしに = desperately

ひっし・必至 *noun* = inevitable

ひつじ・羊 *noun* = sheep

ひっしゃ・筆者 *noun* = author

ひっしゅうかもく・必修課目 *noun* = compulsory subject (of study)

ひつじゅひん・必需品 *noun* = necessities

ぴったり(に) *adverb* = exactly

ひっぱる・引っ張る *verb 1* を = to pull

ひつよう・必要
**1** *noun* = necessity
**2** *adjective* ひつよう(な) = necessary

**ひてい・否定**
**1** *noun*
• = denial
• = negative
**2** *verb 3* ㊞ **ひていする** = to deny

**ビデオ** *noun and prefix* = video

**ビデオプレーヤー** *noun* = video player

**ビデオレコーダー** *noun* = video recorder

**ひと・人** *noun*
• = person
• = people

**ひと・一** *prefix* = one

**ひどい・酷い** *adjective* = terrible

**ひとがら・人柄** *noun* = personality

**ひとこと・一言** *noun* = a few words

**ひとごみ・人込み** *noun* = a crowd

**ひとしい・等しい** *adjective* = equal

**ひとつ・一つ** *noun* = one ▶ **181**

**ひとつめ・一つ目** *noun* = (the) first ▶ **181**

**ひとで・人手** *noun* = (people to) help

**ひととおり・一通り**
**1** *adverb* = briefly
**2** *adjective* **ひととおりの** = general

**ひとどおり・人通り** *noun* = pedestrian traffic

**ひとびと・人々** *noun* = people

**ひとまず・一先ず** *adverb*
• = first
• = for a while

**ひとやすみ・一休み** *noun* = a break

**ひとり・一人・独り**
• = one person
• = on one's own ▶ **181**

**ひとりあたり・一人当たり** *noun* = per person

**ひとりぐらし・一人暮らし** *noun* = living alone
**ひとりぐらし(を)する** = to live alone

**ひとりっこ・一人っ子** *noun* = only child

**ひとりで・一人で** *phrase* = by oneself

> **!** *translations will vary with context i.e. 'by myself', 'by herself' etc.*

**ひとりでに・独りでに** *adverb* = automatically

**ひとりひとり(に)・一人一人(に)** *adverb*
• = one by one
• = one after another
• = in single file

**ひとりむすこ・一人息子** *noun* = only son

**ひとりむすめ・一人娘** *noun* = only daughter

**ひなた・日向** *noun* = sunny place
**ひなたぼっこを する** = to sunbathe

**ひなん・非難**
**1** *noun* = criticism
**2** *verb 3* ㊞ **ひなんする** = to criticise

**ひなん・避難**
**1** *noun* = shelter
**2** *verb 3* ㊞ **ひなんする** = to take refuge

**ビニールぶくろ・ビニール袋** *noun*
• = plastic bag
• = carrier bag

**ひにく・皮肉** *noun*
• = sarcasm
• = irony

**ひにち・日にち** *noun* = days

**ひにん・避妊** *noun* = contraception

**びねつ・微熱** *noun* = a slight temperature

**ひねる・捻る** *verb 1* ㊞ = to twist

**ひのいり・日の入り** *noun* = sunset

**ひので・火の手** *noun* = flames

**ひので・日の出** *noun* = sunrise

**ひのまる・日の丸** *noun* – the Japanese flag which shows a round red sun on a white background

**ひはん・批判**
**1** *noun* = criticism
**2** *verb 3* ㊞ **ひはんする** = to criticise

**ひび・日々** *noun* = days

**ひび** *noun*
- = crack
- = fracture

**ひびき・響き** *noun* = sound

**ひびく・響く** *verb 1* ⑰
- = to sound
- = to echo

**ひひょう・批評**
**1** *noun* = critical commentary
**2** *verb 3* ㉑ **ひひょうする** = to review

**ひふ・皮膚** *noun* = skin

**ひふか・皮膚科** *noun*
= dermatology

**ひま・暇** *noun*
- = free time
　**ひまですか** = are you free?

**ひみつ・秘密**
**1** *noun* = secret
**2** *adjective* **ひみつ(な)** = secret

**びみょう(な)・微妙(な)**
*adjective* = subtle

**ひめい・悲鳴** *noun* = scream
　**ひめいを あげる** = to scream

**ひも・紐** *noun* = string

**ひゃく・百** *noun* = hundred ▶ **181**

**びゃく・百** ▶ **ひゃく**

**ぴゃく・百** ▶ **ひゃく**

**ひやけ・日焼け**
**1** *noun*
- = suntan
- = sunburn
**2** *verb 3* ⑰ **ひやけする**
- = to get suntanned
- = to get sunburnt

**ひやす・冷やす** *verb 1* ㉑ = to chill

**ひゃっかじてん・百科事典・百科辞典** *noun* = encyclopaedia

**ひよう・費用** *noun* = expenses

**ひょう・表** *noun and suffix*
- = chart
- = table

**ひょう・票** *noun* = vote

**びょう・秒** *noun* = seconds ▶ **186**

**びょう・鋲** *noun* = tack

**びょう・病** *suffix* = illness

**びよういん・美容院** *noun*
= beauty salon

**びょういん・病院** *noun* = hospital

> ! *often translatable as 'doctor's surgery' or 'the doctor' as it describes the premises where a doctor has a consulting room as well as large hospitals*

**ひょうか・評価**
**1** *noun* = evaluation
**2** *verb 3* ㉑ **ひょうかする** = to evaluate

**びょうき・病気** *noun* = illness
　**びょうきに なる** = to become ill
　**びょうきが なおる** = to get well

**ひょうげん・表現**
**1** *noun* = expression
**2** *verb 3* ㉑ **ひょうげんする** = to express

**ひょうし・拍子** *noun* = rhythm

**ひょうしき・標識** *noun* = mark

**びようしつ・美容室** *noun*
= (women's) hairdresser

**びょうしゃ・描写**
**1** *noun* = description
**2** *verb 3* ㉑ **びょうしゃする** = to describe

**ひょうじゅん・標準** *noun*
- = criterion
- = standard

**ひょうじょう・表情** *noun*
= (facial) expression

**びょうどう・平等**
**1** *adjective* **びょうどう(な)** = equal
**2** *adverb* **びょうどうに** = fairly

**ひょうばん・評判** *noun*
= reputation

**ひょうめん・表面** *noun* = surface

**ひょうろん・評論** *noun*
= criticism

**ひらがな・平仮名** *noun* – one of the two **かな**, the syllabic scripts used in writing Japanese ▶ **vii**

**ひらく・開く** *verb 1* ㉑
- = to open
- = to hold (a party or meeting)

**ひりょう・肥料** *noun* = fertiliser

**ひる・昼** *noun*
- = (around) noon
- = daylight hours ▶ **おひる**

**ビル** *noun* = (a) building

**ひるごはん・昼ご飯** *noun*
= lunch

**ひるね・昼寝**
**1** *noun* = a nap
**2** *verb 3* ㋕ **ひるね(を)する** = to have
a nap

**ひるま・昼間** *noun* = daytime

**ひるめし** ▶ **ひるごはん**

**ひろい・広い** *adjective*
• = wide
• = spacious

**ひろう・拾う** *verb 1* ㋔ = to pick
up

**ひろがる・広がる** *verb 1* ㋕ = to
spread

**ひろげる・広げる** *verb 2* ㋔ = to
expand

**ひろさ・広さ** *noun*
• = width
• = extent

**ひろば・広場** *noun* = (town) square

**ひろまる・広まる** *verb 1* ㋕ = to
spread

**ひろめる・広める** *verb 2* ㋔ = to
spread

**ひん・品** *noun* = elegance

❗ *as a suffix it means 'item' or 'thing'*

**びん・便** *noun and suffix* = flight

**びん・瓶** *noun* = bottle

**ピン** *noun*
• = pin
• = focus

**びんかん(な)・敏感(な)**
*adjective* = sensitive

**ピンク** *noun* = pink

**ひんしつ・品質** *noun* = quality

**ひんしゅ・品種** *noun* = sort

**びんせん・便箋** *noun* = (letter)
writing paper

**ヒント** *noun*
• = hint
• = clue

**ひんぱんに・頻繁に** *adverb*
= frequently

**びんぼう・貧乏**
**1** *noun* = poverty
**2** *adjective* **びんぼう(な)** = poor

# ふフ

**ふ・不** *prefix* – negates the following
word or element in a way similar to
English prefixes such as 'un-' and 'in-'

**ぶ・分** *suffix* = per cent

**ぶ・部** *noun and suffix*
• = section
• = department

**ファイト** *noun* = fighting spirit

**ファクシミリ** *noun*
• = fax
• = fax machine

**ファスナー** *noun* = zipper

**ファックス** *noun* = fax

**ファックスき・ファックス機**
▶ **ファックスきかい**

**ふあん・不安**
**1** *noun* = anxiety
**2** *adjective* **ふあん(な)**
• = anxious
• = worried
　**ふあんが ある** = to feel anxious

**ファン** *noun* = fan

**ふあんてい(な)・不安定(な)**
*adjective* = unstable

**ふいに・不意に** *adverb*
= unexpectedly

**フィルム** *noun* = (photographic) film

**ふう・風** *suffix*
• = style
• = appearance

**ふうけい・風景** *noun* = scenery

**ふうせん・風船** *noun* = balloon

**ブーツ** *noun* = boots

**ふうとう・封筒** *noun* = envelope

**ふうふ・夫婦** *noun* = (married)
couple

**ブーム** *noun* = boom

**プール** *noun* = (swimming) pool

**ふうん・不運** *noun* = bad luck

**ふえ・笛** *noun*
• = whistle
• = flute

ふフ

ふえる・増える *verb 2* ㋑ = to increase

フォーク *noun* = fork

ぶか・部下 *noun* = staff (who work for/under someone)

ふかい・深い *noun* = deep

～ぶかい *suffix* – adds the meaning of very ...' or 'heavily involved in ...'

ふかさ・深さ *noun* = depth

ふかけつ・不可欠 *noun* = indispensable

ふかのう(な)・不可能(な) *adjective* = impossible

ふかまる・深まる *verb 1* ㋑ = to deepen

ぶき・武器 *noun* = weapon

ふきげん(な)・不機嫌(な) *adjective* = in a bad mood

ふきそく(な)・不規則(な) *adjective* = irregular

ふきゅう・普及
**1** *noun* = spread
**2** *verb 3* ㋑ ふきゅうする = to spread

ふきょう・不況 *noun* = economic recession

ふきん・付近 *noun* = neighbourhood

ふきん・布巾 *noun* = cloth

ふく・拭く *verb 1* ㋾ = to wipe

ふく・吹く *verb 1* ㋾ ㋑
• = to blow
• = to play (a wind instrument etc.)

ふく・服 *noun* = clothing

ふく・副 *prefix* = deputy

ふくざつ(な)・複雑(な) *adjective* = complicated

ふくし・福祉 *noun and suffix* = welfare

ふくしゅう・復習
**1** *noun* = revision
**2** *verb 3* ㋾ ふくしゅうする = to review

ふくすう・複数 *noun* = plural

ふくそう・服装 *noun* = clothing

ふくむ・含む *verb 1* ㋑ ㋾ = to be included

ふくめる・含める *verb 2* ㋾ = to include

ふくらむ・膨らむ *verb 1* ㋑ = to swell

ふくろ・袋 *noun* = bag

ふけいき・不景気 *noun* = poor economic conditions

ふけつ(な)・不潔(な) *adjective*
• = unclean
• = dirty

ふける・更ける *verb 2* ㋑ = to grow late

ふこう(な)・不幸(な) *adjective* = unhappy

ふごう・符号 *noun* = symbol

ふごうかく・不合格 *noun* = fail (in an exam or interview etc.)

ふこうへい(な)・不公平(な) *adjective* = unfair

ふごうり(な)・不合理(な) *adjective* = unreasonable

ふさい・夫妻 *suffix* = Mr and Mrs

ふざける *verb 2* ㋑ – the basic meaning is 'to play around', 'to mess about' but it can also mean 'to talk nonsense'. Often used in a form such as ふざけないで to mean 'stop messing around and behave yourself properly'

ふさわしい・相応しい *adjective* = appropriate

ふし・節 *noun* = tune

ぶじ・無事
**1** *adjective* ぶじ(な) = safe
**2** *adverb* ぶじに = safely
　ぶじに つく = to arrive safely

ふしぎ・不思議
**1** *adjective* ふしぎ(な) = mysterious
**2** *adverb* ふしぎに = mysteriously

ぶしゅ・部首 *noun* – the 'radical' of a かんじ character which can be used to look it up or to help explain the meaning

ふじゆう・不自由
**1** *adjective* ふじゆう(な) = inconvenient
**2** *verb 3* ㋑ ふじゆうする = to be short of

**!** *used as a euphemism for 'disabled' when describing people*

**ふじゅうぶん(な)・不十分(な)** *adjective*
- = insufficient
- = unsatisfactory

**ふしょう(する)・負傷(する)** *verb 3 ⓣ*
- = to be wounded
- = to be injured

**ふしょうしゃ・負傷者** *noun*
= injured person

**ぶじょく・侮辱**
**1** *noun* = insult
**1** *verb 3 ⓣ* **ぶじょくする** = to insult

**ふじん・婦人** *prefix* = women's

**ふじん・夫人** *suffix* – added to names with a meaning similar to 'Mrs' but merely a polite title and not related to marriage status

**ふすま・襖** *noun* – the paper covered sliding doors inside a Japanese house which divide the space into rooms

**ふせい・不正**
**1** *noun* = dishonesty
**2** *adjective* **ふせい(な)** = dishonest

**ふせぐ・防ぐ** *verb 1 ⓣ* = to prevent

**ふそく・不足**
**1** *noun* = shortage
**2** *verb 3 ⓣ* **ふそくする** = to be lacking

**!** *also appears as in the form ～ぶそく as a suffix meaning 'short of' or 'lacking in'*

**ふた・蓋** *noun*
- = lid
- = (bottle) top

**ぶた・豚** *noun* = pig

**ぶたい・舞台** *noun* = stage

**ふたご・双子** *noun* = twin/s

**ふたたび・再び** *adverb* = once again

**ふたつ・二つ** *noun* = two ▶ **181**

**ふたつめ・二つ目** *noun* = (the) second ▶ **181**

**ぶたにく・豚肉** *noun* = pork

**ふたり・二人** *noun* = two people ▶ **181**

**ふたん・負担** *noun*
- = burden
- = cost

**ふだん(の)・普段(の)** *noun and adjective* = everyday

**ふち・縁** *noun* = edge

**ふちゅうい・不注意**
**1** *noun* = carelessness
**2** *adjective* **ふちゅうい(な)** = careless

**ふちゅうい・不注意** *noun* = carelessness

**ぶつ** *verb 1 ⓣ* = to hit

**ぶつ・物** *suffix* = item

**ふつう・普通**
**1** *adjective* **ふつう(の)**
- = ordinary
- = usual
**2** *adverb* **ふつう(は)** = usually

**ふつか・二日・2日** *noun*
- = the second day of the month
- = two days ▶ **174**, ▶ **181**

**ぶっか・物価** *noun* = prices
**にほんは ぶっかが たかい** = Japan is expensive

**ぶつかる** *verb 1 ⓣ* **に**
- = to bang into
- = to clash with

**ぶっきょう・仏教** *noun* = Buddhism

**ぶつける** *verb 2 ⓣ*
- = to hit
- = to bump into

**ぶっしつ・物質** *noun* = substance

**ぶっそう(な)・物騒(な)** *adjective*
- = dangerous

**ふって** ▶ **ふる** ▶ **197**

**ぶつぶつ(いう)** *verb 1 ⓣ*
- = to grumble
- = to mumble

**ぶつりがく・物理学** *noun* = physics

**ふで・筆** *noun* – brush (used for Japanese calligraphy)

**ふと** *adverb* = unexpectedly

**ふとい・太い** *adjective* = thick

**ふどうさんや・不動産屋** *noun*
- = estate agent
- = realtor

**ふとる・太る** *verb 1 ㊃* = to put on weight

> ❗ *used in the form* ふとっている *it means 'fat'*

**ふとん・布団** *noun* = futon

> ❗ *a mattress and duvet for sleeping on the floor of a Japanese* たたみ *room. These have no wooden base, unlike the 'futons' sold in the west*

**ふなびん・船便** *noun* = sea mail

**ふね・船・舟** *noun*
- = ship
- = boat

**ぶひん・部品** *noun*
- = component
- = spare part

**ふぶき・吹雪** *noun* = blizzard

**ぶぶん・部分** *noun* = part

**ふへい・不平** *noun* = complaint

**ふべん(な)・不便(な)** *adjective* = inconvenient

**ふぼ・父母** *noun* = parents ▶ **177**

**ふほう・不法** *suffix* = illegal

**ふまん・不満** *noun* = dissatisfaction

**ふみきり・踏み切り** *noun* = level crossing

**ふむ・踏む** *verb 1 ㊂*
- = to tread on

**ふもと・麓** *noun* = foot (of a mountain)

**ぶもん・部門** *noun* = field (of expertise etc.)

**ふやす・増やす** *verb 1 ㊂* = to increase

**ふゆ・冬** *noun* = winter

**フライパン** *noun* = frying pan

**ブラウス** *noun* = blouse

**ぶらさげる・ぶら下げる** *verb 2 ㊂*
- = to swing
- = to carry
- = to wear

**ブラシ** *noun* = brush

**プラス** *noun* = plus

**プラスチック**
**1** *noun* = plastic
**2** *adjective* プラスチックの = plastic

**ブラック** *noun* = black

**ふり・不利** *noun*
- = disadvantage

**ふり(をする)・振り(をする)** *verb 3 ㊃* – *following the* 〜た *form of a verb or a noun and particle* の *it adds the meaning of 'pretending to ...' or 'faking ...' ...* ▶ **191**

**ぶり・振り** *suffix* – *Following time expressions it means 'for the first time since ...', 'for the first time in ...'. Following nouns and verb stems it means 'way of ...*

**フリー** *noun* = free

**ふりがな・振り仮名** *noun* – *the small* かな *characters used over or beside* かんじ *characters to indicate the pronunciation* ▶ **vii**

**ふります** ▶ ふる

**ふりむく・振り向く** *verb 1 ㊃* = to turn around

**ふりょう・不良**
**1** *adjective* ふりょう(の)
- = defective
- = bad
**2** *noun* = juvenile delinquent

**ふりょうひん・不良品** *noun* = defective item

**プリント** *noun* = print

**ブルー** *noun* = blue

**ふる・降る** *verb 1 ㊃* ふって・ふらない・ふります = to fall (rain or snow)

**ふる・振る** *verb 1 ㊂* = to swing

**ふる・古** *prefix* = old

**ふるい・古い** *adjective*
- = old
- = old fashioned

**ふるえる・震える** *verb 2 ㊃* = to tremble

**ふるさと・故郷・古里** *noun*
- = hometown
- = home

**ふるまい・振る舞い** *noun*
= behaviour

**ふるまう・振る舞う** *verb 1*
= to behave

**ブレーキ** *noun* = brakes

**プレゼント** *noun* = present

**ふれる・触れる** *verb 2*  に = to touch

**ふろ・風呂** *noun* = bath

**プロ** *noun and prefix* = professional

**ブローチ** *noun* = brooch

**ブロードバンド** *noun* = broadband

**プログラム** *noun* = programme

**ふろしき・風呂敷** *noun* – a *large cloth used for carrying things in*

**ふろば・風呂場** *noun* = bathroom

! *not in the sense of 'toilet'*

**フロント** *noun* = hotel reception desk

**ふわふわ（の）** *adjective* = soft and fluffy

**ふん・分** *noun and counter* = minute
▶ **186**

**ぶん・分** ▶ ふん

**ぶん・分** *noun*
• = part
• = share

**ぶん・文** *noun*
• = writing
• = sentence

**ぷん・分** ▶ ふん

**ふんいき・雰囲気** *noun*
= atmosphere

**ふんか・噴火**
**1** *noun* = (volcanic) eruption
**2** *verb 3*  ふんかする = to erupt

**ぶんか・文化** *noun* = culture

**ぶんかい(する)・分解(する)**
*verb 3*  = to take to pieces

**ぶんがく・文学** *noun* = literature

**ぶんかさい・文化祭** *noun* – a *festival or cultural event, especially at school or university*

**ぶんげい・文芸** *noun* = literature

**ぶんけん・文献** *noun* = literature

**ぶんしょ・文書** *noun*
• = writing
• = document

**ぶんしょう・文章** *noun*
• = writing
• = sentence

**ふんすい・噴水** *noun* = fountain

**ぶんせき・分析**
**1** *noun* = analysis
**2** *verb 3*  ぶんせきする = to analyse

**ふんそう・紛争** *noun* = conflict

**ぶんたい・文体** *noun* = style (of writing)

**ぶんぷ・分布**
**1** *noun* = distribution
**2** *verb 3*  に ぶんぷする = to be distributed

**ぶんぽう・文法** *noun* = grammar

**ぶんぼうぐ・文房具** *noun*
= stationery

**ふんまつ・粉末** *noun* = powder

**ぶんめい・文明** *noun* = civilisation

**ぶんや・分野** *noun* = field (of specialisation)

**ぶんりょう・分量** *noun* = quantity

**ぶんるい・分類**
**1** *noun* = classification
**2** *verb 3*  ぶんるいする = to classify

**ぶんれつ・分裂**
**1** *noun* = division
**2** *verb 3*  ぶんれつする = to split up

# へへ

**へい・塀** *noun*
• = fence
• = wall

**へいかい・閉会**
**1** *noun* = close of a meeting
**2** *verb 3*  に へいかいする = to close

**へいき・平気**
**1** *noun* = unconcern
**2** *adverb* へいきで = casually
わたしは なんでも へいき です
= anything's OK by me

**へいきん・平均** *noun* = average

## へいこう・平行
**1** *noun* = parallel
**2** *adverb* へいこうして = in parallel

## へいこうせん・平行線 *noun*
= parallel lines

## へいじつ・平日 *noun*
• = week day
• = working day

## へいせい・平成 *noun* – era name
for 1989 onwards and used for dates
during that period ▶ **174**

## へいたい・兵隊 *noun* = soldier

## へいほう・平方 *prefix* = used to
mean 'square' in measurements of
area especially へいほうメートル
'square metres'

## へいぼん(な)・平凡(な)
*adjective* = ordinary

## へいや・平野 *noun* = plain

## へいわ・平和
**1** *noun* = peace
**2** *adverb* へいわに = in peace
**3** *adjective* へいわ(な) = peaceful

## ページ *noun and counter* = page ▶ **181**

## へこむ・凹む *verb 1* ⑰ = to be
dented

## ベジタリアン *noun* = vegetarian

## ベスト *noun* = best

## ベストセラー *noun* = best seller

## へた(な)・下手(な) *adjective*
• = not very good at
• = unskilful

## へだてる・隔てる *verb 2* ⑥ = to
separate

## べつ・別
**1** *adjective* べつ(の・な)
• = another
• = different
**2** *phrase* 〜を べつにして = without
including ...
べつと して = apart from

> **!** as a suffix 〜べつ means
> 'classified by ...'.

▶ べつに

## べっそう・別荘 *noun* = a second
house in the country

## ペット *noun* = pet

## ベッド *noun* = bed

## ペットボトル *noun* = plastic bottle

## べつに・別に *adverb* = separately

> **!** sometimes used alone as an
> abbreviation of べつに + a negative
> verb meaning 'nothing special' or
> 'not particularly'

## べつべつ・別々
**1** *adjective* べつべつ(の・な)
= separate
**2** *adverb* べつべつに = separately

## ベテラン
**1** *noun* = an experienced person
**2** *adjective* ベテランの = experienced

## へび・蛇 *noun* = snake

## へや・部屋 *noun*
• = room
• = apartment

## へらす・減らす *verb 1* ⑥ = to
reduce
たいじゅうを へらす = to lose
weight

## ぺらぺら *adverb* = fluently

## ヘリコプター *noun* = helicopter

## へる・減る *verb 1* ⑰ = to decrease
おなかが へっている = to be
hungry

## へる・経る *verb 1* ⑥
• (*time*) = to pass
• (*place*) = to go via

## ベル *noun* = bell (bicycle or door)

## ベルト *noun* = belt

## ヘルメット *noun* = helmet

## へん(な)・変(な) *adjective*
• = strange
• = wrong

## へん・辺 *noun* = vicinity

## へん・偏 *noun* – the left hand
element of a かんじ character and
which can be used for describing and
looking it up in a dictionary

## べん・弁 *suffix* = dialect

## べん・便 *noun* = convenience (for
transport)

## ペン *noun* = pen

## へんか・変化
**1** *noun* = change
**2** *verb 3* ⑰ へんかする = to change

## へんかん・変換
**1** *noun* = conversion

**2** *verb 3* ㊾ に へんかんする = to convert

ペンキ *noun* = paint

べんきょう・勉強
**1** *noun* = studying
**2** *verb 3* ㊾ べんきょうする = to study

へんけん・偏見 *noun* = prejudice

べんごし・弁護士 *noun*
• = lawyer
• = solicitor
• = attorney

へんこう・変更
**1** *noun* = alteration
**2** *verb 3* ㊾ へんこうする = to alter

へんじ・返事
**1** *noun*
• = reply
**2** *verb 3* ㊿ に へんじ(を)する
• = to reply

べんじょ・便所 *noun* = toilet

ベンチ *noun* = bench

ペンチ *noun* = pliers

べんとう・弁当 *noun* – a packed lunch

べんり(な)・便利(な) *adjective*
• = convenient
• = useful

# ほ ホ

ほ・歩 *counter*
• = step
• = pace ▶ 181

～っぽい *suffix* – adds the meaning 'a little bit like ...', 'seems ...'. Similar to the English suffix '-ish' in 'childish' こどもっぽい

ほいくえん・保育園 *noun* = nursery

ほいくしょ・保育所 *noun* = nursery

ボイスメール *noun* = voicemail

ポイント *noun* = point

ほう・方 *noun*
• = direction
• = way
• = one (which is)

> **!** *used to make comparisons in the form ...のほうが translatable as 'which is', 'which are', 'which would be' etc. Used after a verb in the ～た form in the idiom ～た ほうが いい meaning 'should ...', 'it would be best to ...'.* ▶ 191

ぼう・棒 *noun* = stick

ぼう・防 *prefix* = anti-

ぼうえい・防衛 *noun* = defence

ぼうえき・貿易 *noun* = trade

ぼうえきがいしゃ・貿易会社 *noun* = trading company

ぼうえんきょう・望遠鏡 *noun* = telescope

ほうかい・崩壊
**1** *noun* = collapse
**2** *verb 3* ㊿ ほうかいする = to collapse

ぼうがい・妨害
**1** *noun* = obstruction
**2** *verb 3* ㊾ ぼうがいする = to obstruct

ほうがく・方角 *noun* = direction

ほうがく・法学 *noun* = law (as an academic subject)

ほうき・箒 *noun* = broom

ほうげん・方言 *noun* = dialect

ぼうけん・冒険 *noun* = adventure

ほうこう・方向 *noun* = direction

ぼうこう・膀胱 *noun* = bladder

ほうこく・報告
**1** *noun* = report
**2** *verb 3* ㊾ ほうこくする = to report

ぼうさん・坊さん *noun* = Buddhist priest

ぼうし・帽子 *noun*
• = hat
• = cap

ぼうし・防止
**1** *noun* = prevention
**2** *verb 3* ㊾ ぼうしする = to prevent

ほうしゃ・放射 *prefix* = radiation

ほうしん・方針 *noun* = policy

ほ ホ

ぼうず・坊主 *noun* – literally a (Buddhist) priest it can refer to closely cropped hair or a youth

ほうせき・宝石 *noun*
• = precious stone
• = jewel

ほうそう・放送
**1** *noun* = broadcast
**2** *verb 3* ㉟ ほうそうする = to broadcast

ほうそう・包装 *noun* = wrapping

ほうたい・包帯 *noun* = bandage

ほうだい・放題 *suffix* = as much as you like/want

ぼうだい(な)・膨大(な) *adjective* = enormous

ほうちょう・包丁 *noun*
• = large kitchen knife
• = cleaver

ほうてい・法廷 *noun* = court (of law)

ぼうどう・暴動 *noun* = riot

ぼうはん・防犯 *suffix* = crime prevention

ほうび・褒美 *noun* = reward

ほうふ・豊富
**1** *adjective* ほうふ(な)
• = plentiful
• = rich in
**2** *phrase* ほうふに あります = to have plenty of

ぼうふう・暴風 *noun* = gales

ほうほう・方法 *noun*
• = method
• = way

ほうぼう・方々 *adverb* = all over the place

ぼうめい きぼうしゃ・亡命希望者 *noun* = asylum-seeker

ほうめん・方面 *noun* = district

ほうもん・訪問
**1** *noun* = visit
**2** *verb 3* ㉟ ほうもんする = to visit

ぼうや・坊や *noun* = kid

ほうりこむ・放り込む *verb 1* ㉟ = to throw into

ほうりつ・法律 *noun* = law

ぼうりょく・暴力 *noun* = violence

ぼうりょくだん・暴力団 *noun* = organised crime

ほうる・放る *verb 1* ㉟ = to throw

ほえる・吠える *verb 2* ㋕
• = to bark
• = to howl

ほお・頬 *noun* = cheek

ボーイ *noun* = waiter

ボーイフレンド *noun* = boyfriend

ぼうっと *adverb* = absent mindedly
　ぼうっとする = to stare vacantly

ボート *noun* = boat

ボーナス *noun* – the bonus paid twice yearly as part of the salary package for many Japanese jobs

ホーム *noun* = platform

ボール *noun* = ball

ホームステイ *noun* = home-stay

ほか・他・外
**1** *noun*
• = other
• = another
**2** *adjective* ほかの = other

ほかに・外に・他に *adverb*
• = besides
• = as well as

ほがらか・朗らか
**1** *adjective* ほがらか(な) = cheerful
**2** *adverb* ほがらかに = cheerfully

ぼきん・募金
**1** *noun* = fund raising
**2** *verb 3* ㉟ ぼきんする = to raise money

ぼく・僕 *noun* = I

> ! *used by males*

ぼくし・牧師 *noun* = minister of religion

ぼくじょう・牧場 *noun*
• = ranch
• = pasture land

ぼくせい・北西 *noun* = north-west

ぼくちく・牧畜 *noun* = livestock farming

ぼくとう・北東 *noun* = north-east

ポケット *noun* = pocket

ほげい・捕鯨 *noun* = whaling

ほけん・保険 *noun* = insurance

ほけん・保健 *prefix* = health

ぼご・母語 *noun* = mother tongue

ほこうしゃ・歩行者 *noun*
= pedestrian

ぼこく・母国 *noun* = native country

ぼこくご・母国語 ▶ ぼご

ほこり・誇り *noun* = pride

ほこり・埃 *noun* = dust

ほし・星 *noun* = star

ほしい・欲しい *adjective*
• = want
• = would like

> ! *although an adjective in Japanese it is often best translated 'to want'. When following the ～て form of a verb it means 'want you to ...'. When following the ～ない form of a verb + で it means 'don't want you to ...'*
> ▶ 178, ▶ 191, ▶ 197

ぼしかてい・母子家庭 *noun*
= single parent family

> ! *literally a family consisting of a mother and child/children*

ほしがる・欲しがる *verb 1* 签 ⑰
= (seems) to want

> ! *an equivalent of* ほしい *used when talking about people other than oneself* ▶ 178

ぼしゅう・募集
**1** *noun* = recruitment
**2** *verb 3* 签 ぼしゅうする = to recruit

ほじょ・補助
**1** *noun* = help
**2** *verb 3* 签 ほじょする = to assist

ほしょう・保証 *noun* = guarantee

ほしょうにん・保証人 *noun*
• = guarantor
• = sponsor

ほす・干す *verb 1* 签 = to dry (in the sun)

ボス *noun* = boss

ポスター *noun* = poster

ホステス *noun* – *a female 'companion' employed by a bar or night club*

ポスト *noun*
• = letterbox
• = mailbox
• = post-box

ほそい・細い *adjective*
• = thin
• = fine

ほぞん・保存
**1** *noun* = preservation
**2** *verb 3* 签 ほぞんする = to preserve

ボタン *noun* = button

ほっきょく・北極 *noun* = North Pole

ぼっちゃん・坊ちゃん *noun* – *sometimes used by older people to mean 'boy'. Also used to mean 'spoiled' or 'naive'*

ほっておく *verb 1* 签 = to leave (someone) alone

ポット *noun* – *a jug for boiling water and keeping it hot for dispensing drinks*

ホテル *noun* = hotel

ほど・程 *noun* = extent

> ! *used after quantities it is translatable as 'about'. It can also be used to mean 'so ... that ...' and 'almost ...'. Following the plain form of a verb it means 'to the extent that ...'. Commonly used in association with negatives to mean 'not as ... as ...' and following a conditional ending and repeat of the verb or adjective to mean 'the more ... the better', 'the more you (do it) the more ...' etc.*

ほどう・歩道 *noun*
• = pavement
• = sidewalk

ほどうきょう・歩道橋 *noun*
= pedestrian bridge

ほどく・解く *verb 1* 签
• = to untie
• = to undo

ボトル *noun* = bottle

ほとんど *noun and adverb*
• = most
• = almost
• (*in positive structure*) = almost all
• (*in negative structure*) = almost none

ほね・骨 *noun* = bone
　ほねを おる = to break a bone

ほのお・炎 *noun* = flames

ほほ・頬 ▶ ほお

ほ ホ

ほぼ *adverb*
• = almost
• = approximately

ほほえむ・微笑む *verb 1* ㊙ = to smile

ほめる・褒める *verb 2* ㊙ = to praise

ほら *exclamation* = look!

ほり・掘り *noun*
• = moat

ポリ *prefix* = plastic

ほる・掘る *verb 1* ㊙ = to dig up/out

ほる・彫る *verb 1* ㊙ = to carve

ほん・本 *noun* = book

ほん・本 *prefix*
• = this
• = real
• = main

ほん・本 *counter – used to count long, thin or cylindrical things* ▶ **181**

ぼん・盆 *noun*
• = tray
• = Buddhist festival ▶ おぼん

ぼん・本 ▶ ほん

ぽん・本 ▶ ほん

ほんき・本気
**1** *adjective* ほんき（な）
• = serious
• = in earnest
**2** *adverb* ほんきに = seriously

ほんじつ・本日 *noun*
• = today
• = this day

ほんしゃ・本社 *noun* = head office

ぼんち・盆地 *noun* = basin

ほんど・本土 *noun* = mainland

ポンド *noun* = pound ▶ **181**

ほんとう・本当
**1** *noun* = truth
**2** *adjective* ほんとう（の）
• = true
• = real
**3** *adverb* ほんとうに = really

> ❗ also used as an exclamation to express surprise or disbelief and translatable as 'really?' or 'are you sure?'

ほんにん・本人 *noun – meaning 'the person in question' it is translatable as either 'he' or 'she'*

ほんね・本音 *noun – true feelings and intentions as opposed to* ▶ たてまえ

ほんの *phrase*
• = just a
• = merely

> ❗ often used with words indicating quantity like すこし and ちょっと to mean 'just a little'

ほんぶ・本部 *noun* = headquarters

ほんもの・本物 *noun* = (the) real thing

ほんや・本屋 *noun* = book shop

ほんやく・翻訳
**1** *noun* = translation
**2** *verb 3* ㊙ ほんやくする = to translate

ほんやくしゃ・翻訳者 *noun* = translator

ぼんやり（と） *adverb* = absent-mindedly

ほんらい・本来
**1** *adverb*
• = originally
• = essentially
**2** *adjective* ほんらいの = original

# まマ

ま・間 *noun*
• = interval
• = time
　まに あう = to be in time (for)
　まも なく = soon

まあ *exclamation* = well!

マウス *noun* = (computer) mouse

マーケティング *noun* = marketing

まあまあ *adverb*
• = so so
• = fairly
• = not bad

まい *suffix*

> **!** *a negative equivalent of* でしょう
> *and the volitional form* ▶ **191**
> *Translatable as 'probably won't',*
> *'shouldn't' 'don't expect that...' etc.*
> *depending on context.*

まい・毎 *prefix* = every

まい・枚 *counter*
▶ *used for flat things* ▶ **181**

マイカー *noun* = (private) car

マイク *noun* = microphone

まいご・迷子
　まいごになる = to get lost

まいしゅう・毎週 *noun* = every
week

まいすう・枚数 *noun* = number of
(pieces of paper) ▶ まい ▶ **181**

まいつき・毎月 *noun* = every month

まいった *phrase* – *used as an*
*exclamation to express feelings*
*of defeat and embarrassment.*
*Translatable as 'I am at a loss', 'I feel*
*overwhelmed' and a variety of other*
*things depending on the context.*

まいど・毎度 *noun* = every time

まいとし・毎年 *noun* = every year

マイナス *noun* = minus

まいにち・毎日 *noun* = every day

まいばん・毎晩 *noun* = every night

マイペース (で) *adverb* = at one's
own pace

マイホーム *noun* = private house

まいる・参る *verb 1* ⓰
• = to go
• = to come

> **!** *humble equivalent of* いく ▶ **189**

まえ・前
**1** *noun*
• = front
• = in front
**2** *prefix* = front

まかせる・任せる *verb 2* ⓔ
• = to leave (it) to (somebody) to do
• = to entrust

まがる・曲がる *verb 1* ⓰
• = to turn
• = to bend
• = to be crooked

まく・幕 *noun* = curtain

まく・巻く *verb 1* ⓔ
• = to wrap
• = to coil

まく・蒔く *verb 1* ⓔ
• = to sow (seeds)
• = to sprinkle (water)

まくら・枕 *noun* = pillow

まけ・負け *noun* = defeat

まける・負ける *verb 2* ⓰
• = to be beaten
• = to give a discount

まげる・曲げる *verb 2* ⓔ = to bend

まご・孫 *noun* = grandchild ▶ **177**

まことに・誠に *adverb* = sincerely
　まことにありがとうございます
　　= thank you most sincerely

まさか *adverb and exclamation*
• = surely not!
• = no way!

まさつ・摩擦
**1** *noun* = friction
**2** *verb 3* ⓰ ⓔ まさつする = to rub

まさに *adverb*
• = exactly
• = be just about to

まざる・混ざる・交ざる *verb 1*
⓰ = to be mixed

まして *adverb*
• (*with negatives*) = much less
• (*with positives*) = even more (so)

まじめ・真面目
**1** *adjective* まじめ(な)
• = serious
• = hard-working
**2** *adverb* まじめに = seriously

まじる・混じる・交じる *verb 1*
⓰ = to be mixed

ます・増す *verb 1* ⓰ = to increase

まず・先ず *adverb*
• = first of all
• = probably

まずい *adjective*
• = tastes awful
• = wrong

マスク *noun* – *a mask worn over the*
*nose and mouth to prevent the spread*
*of colds*

マスコミ *noun* = the media

まずしい・貧しい *adjective* = poor

マスター *noun* = proprietor of a bar or restaurant

ますます・益々 *adverb*
• (*with positives*) = more and more
• (*with negatives*) = less and less

まぜる・混ぜる・交ぜる *verb 2* 
⊛ = to mix

また・又 *adverb* = again
　または = or
　またね = see you soon

まだ・未だ *adverb*
• = still
• (*with a negative*) = (not) yet
　まだです = not yet

または・又は ▶ また

まち・町 *noun* = town

> ! also a subdivision of addresses in Japanese towns and cities
> ▶ ちょう

まち・街 *noun*
• = town centre
• = city centre

まちあいしつ・待合室 *noun*
= waiting room

まちあわせ・待ち合わせ *noun*
• = meeting
• = rendezvous

まちあわせる・待ち合わせる
*verb 2* ⊛ に = to meet

まちがい・間違い *noun* = mistake

まちがう・間違う *verb 1* ⑰ = to be mistaken

まちがえる・間違える *verb 2* ⊛
= to mistake

まちがって ▶ まちがう ▶ 197

まちかど・町角 *noun*
• = street corner
• = (in the) street

まちかねる・待ちかねる *verb 2* 
⑰ = to wait impatiently

まちます ▶ まつ

まちまち
**1** *adjective* まちまち(の) = various
**2** *adverb* まちまちに = variously

まつ・待つ *verb 1* ⑰ ⊛ まって・
またない・まちます
• = to wait
• = to wait for

まつ・松 *noun* = pine tree

まつげ・睫 *noun* = eyebrow

まっか(な)・真っ赤(な)
*adjective* = bright red

まっくら(な)・真っ暗(な)
*adjective* = very dark

まっくろ(な)・真っ黒(な)
*adjective* = pitch-black

マッサージ
**1** *noun* = massage
**2** *verb 3* ⊛ マッサージする = to massage

マッサージ *noun* = massage

まっさお(な)・真っ青(な)
*adjective* = deep blue
　かおが まっさおに なる = face turns white as a sheet

まっさきに・真っ先に *adverb*
= immediately

まっしろ(な)・真っ白(な)
*adjective* = brilliant white

まっすぐ・真っ直ぐ
**1** *adjective* まっすぐ(な) = straight
**2** *adverb* まっすぐ に = straight

まったく・全く *adverb* (*with negative expressions*) = utterly (not)

> ! also used as an exclamation to express annoyance

マッチ *noun* = match

まって ▶ まつ ▶ 197

まつり・祭り *noun* = festival

まで・迄 *particle* ▶ 205
• = as far as
• = until
• = to
• = even
　までも ない・なく = to be unnecessary to

までに・迄に *particle*
• = by
• = before

まど・窓 *noun* = window

まどぐち・窓口 *noun*
• = (ticket) window
• = enquiry point

まとまる *verb 1* か
• = to be gathered together
• = to be sorted out

まとめる *verb 2* を
• = to gather together
• = to put into shape

マナー *noun*
• = manners
• = behaviour

まなぶ・学ぶ *verb 1* を = to learn

まにあう・間に合う ▶ま

まねき・招き *noun* = invitation

まねく・招く *verb 1* を
• = to invite
• = to bring about

まねる・真似る *verb 2* を = to imitate

まぶしい・眩しい *adjective*
= dazzling

マフラー *noun* = (warm) scarf

ママ *noun*
• = mother

まま *noun* – the basic meaning is 'as it is', 'in an unchanged condition'. It can be used after the plain forms of verbs and adjectives and この・その・あの to mean 'without change' and 'as (you were told etc.)'.

ママさん *noun* – female proprietor of a bar

まめ・豆 *noun* = beans

まめ
**1** *adjective* まめ(な) = hardworking
**2** *adverb* まめに = carefully

まもなく・間も無く ▶ま

まもる・守る *verb 1* を
• = to protect
• = to defend

まやく・麻薬 *noun* = (illegal) drugs

まよう・迷う *verb 1* か
• = to be lost
• = to be at a loss to know what to do
　みちに まよう = to be lost

マラソン *noun*
• = marathon
• = long race

まる・丸
**1** *noun* = circle
**2** *prefix*

• = fully
• = whole

まるい・丸い *adjective* = round

まるで *adverb*
• = utterly (not)
• = as if

まれ・希
**1** *adjective* まれ(な) = rare
**2** *adverb* まれに = rarely

まわす・回す *verb 1* を
• = to turn
• = to forward (a letter)
• = to transfer (a phone call)

まわり・周り・回り *noun*
• = area around
• = circulation

まわりみち・回り道 *noun* = detour

まわる・回る *verb 1* か
• = to turn
• = to go around

まん・万 *counter* = ten thousand
▶**181**

まんいち・万一 *phrase* = in case (of emergency etc.)

まんがいち・万が一 → まんいち

まんいん・満員 *noun* = being full to capacity

まんいんでんしゃ・満員電車 *noun* = a crowded train

まんが・漫画・マンガ *noun*
• = cartoons
• = comic books
• = animations
• = manga

マンション *noun*
• = apartment
• = apartment block

まんせき・満席 *noun* = having all seats filled

まんぞく・満足
**1** *noun* = satisfaction
**2** *verb 3* か に まんぞくする = to be satisfied

満タン
　まんタンに する = to fill the car's tank up with petrol/gasoline

まんてん・満点 *noun* = full marks

まんなか・真ん中 *noun*
• = middle
• = centre

# み ミ

み・身 *noun* = body
みにつける = to wear = to acquire

み・実 *noun*
• = fruit
• = nut

み・未 *prefix* = incomplete

み・味 *suffix* = flavour

みあげる・見上げる *verb 2* 🅰
= to look up

みあい・見合い *noun* – an arranged meeting with a view to marriage ▶ おみあい

みえる・見える *verb 2* 🅰 に
• = to be visible
• = to seem

みおくり・見送り *noun* = (a) send off

みおくる・見送る *verb 1* 🅰
• = to see someone off

みおぼえ・見覚え *noun*
= recollection

みがく・磨く *verb 1* 🅰
• = to polish
• = to brush (the teeth)
うでを みがく = to practice

みかけ・見かけ *noun* = appearance

みかける・見かける *verb 2* 🅰
= to catch sight of

みかた・味方 *noun*
• = ally
• = supporter

みかた・見方 *noun* = point of view

みかん *noun* = mandarin orange

みぎ・右 *noun* = right

みぎがわ・右側 *noun* = the right hand side

みぎきき・右利き *noun* = right handed person

ミキサー *noun* = mixer

みぎて・右手 *noun* = right hand

みごと・見事
**1** *adjective* みごと(な) = wonderful
**2** *adverb* みごとに = skilfully

みこみ・見込み *noun*
• = prospect
• = expectation

みじかい・短い *adjective* = short

みじめ・惨め
**1** *adjective* みじめ(な) = miserable
**2** *adverb* みじめに = miserably

ミシン *noun* = sewing machine

ミス *noun* = error

みず・水 *noun* = (cold) water

みずうみ・湖 *noun* = lake

みずから・自ら *adverb*
• = on one's own initiative
• = in person

みずぎ・水着 *noun* = swimming costume

みずわり・水割り *noun* – whiskey|whisky or other spirit diluted with water or tea

みせ・店 *noun* = shop

みせいねん・未成年 *noun* – someone who is under the legal age of adulthood (which is twenty in Japan)

みせる・見せる *verb 2* 🅰 = to show

みそ・味噌 *noun* – a paste made from fermented soy beans and which forms the basis of miso soup

みぞ・溝 *noun* = ditch

みたい *suffix* – following the plain forms of verbs and adjectives it means 'looks like', 'is similar to' or '(it) seems (that)'. It can also be translated as 'such as ...'. ▶ **187**

みだし・見出し *noun* = headline

>みち・道 *noun*
• = street
• = road
• = way (to somewhere)

みぢか・身近
**1** *adjective*
• = close
• = familiar
**2** *adverb* みぢかに = close at hand

みちじゅん・道順 *noun* = route

みちる・満ちる *verb 2 ⑪* = to be full

みつに・密に *adverb* = densely

みっか・三日・3日 *noun*
- = the third day of the month
- = three days ▶ **174**

みつかる・見つかる *verb 1 ⑪* = to be found

みつける・見つける *verb 2 ⑫* = to find

みっつ・三つ・3つ *noun* = three ▶ **181**

みて ▶みる ▶ **197**

みっともない *adjective* = disgraceful

みつめる・見つめる *verb 2 ⑫* = to stare

みとおし・見通し *noun* = prospect

みとめる・認める *verb 2 ⑫*
- = to admit
- = to approve

みどり・緑 *noun*
- = green
- = greenery

みどりのひ・緑の日 *noun* – Greenery Day (April 29)

みな・皆 *noun*
- = everyone
- = everything

みなおす・見直す *verb 1 ⑫* = to look at again

みなさま・皆様 ▶みなさん

みなさん・皆さん *noun*
- = everyone
- = ladies and gentlemen

みなと・港 *noun*
- = harbour
- = port

みなみ・南 *noun* = south

みにくい・醜い *adjective* = ugly

みのる・実る *verb 1 ⑪* = to bear fruit

みぶん・身分 *noun*
- = position
- = status

みほん・見本 *noun* = sample

みまい・見舞い ▶おみまい

みまう・見舞う *verb 1 ⑫* = to visit (someone who is not well)

みます ▶みる

みまん・未満 *suffix*
- = less than
- = under

みみ・耳 *noun* = ear

みやげ(もの)・土産(物) ▶おみやげ

みやこ・都 *noun* = capital or large city

みょう・妙
**1** *adjective* みょう(な) = strange
**2** *adverb* みょうに = strangely

みょうじ・名字 *noun* = surname

みょうにち・明日 *noun* = tomorrow

みらい・未来 *noun* = future

ミリ *noun* = millimetres

みりょく・魅力 *noun* = attractiveness

みりょくてき(な)・魅力的(な) *adjective* = attractive

みる・見る *verb 2 ⑫* みて みない みます
- = to see
- = to watch
- = to look at

> **!** *following the 〜て form of a verb it adds the meaning 'try ... and see', 'have a go at (doing)'* ▶ **197**

ミルク *noun* = milk

みんかん・民間 *prefix* = civil

みんしゅ・民主 *prefix* = democratic

みんしゅく・民宿 *noun* = bed and breakfast

みんしゅしゅぎ・民主主義 *noun* = democracy

みんな ▶みな

みんぞく・民族 *noun and prefix*
- = people
- = tribe

みんよう・民謡 *noun* = folk songs

みミ

# むム

む・無 *prefix* – gives the meaning 'not' and similar to English prefix 'un-'

むいか・六日・6日 *noun*
• = the sixth day of the month
• = six days ▶ **174**

ムード *noun*
• = atmosphere
• = ambience

むかい・向かい *noun* = opposite side

むかう・向かう *verb 1* か
• = to face
• = to head for

むかえ・迎え ▶ むかえる
　むかえに いく = to go and meet

むかえる・迎える *verb 2* を
• = to meet
• = to welcome
• = to greet

むかし・昔 *noun* = long ago

むかしむかし・昔々 *noun* = once upon a time

むき・向き
**1** *noun* = direction
**2** *suffix* = aimed at

むく・向く *verb 1* か に
• = to turn
• = to face
• = to be suited to

むく・剥く *verb 1* を = to peel

むけ・向け *suffix* = for

むける・向ける *verb 2* を
• = to turn towards
• = to aim towards

むげん・無限 *noun* = without limits
　むげんの = endless

むこ・婿 *noun* = bridegroom

❗ can also mean 'son-in-law' where the husband joins the wife's family and changes his name to hers

むこう・向こう *noun*
• = the opposite side
• = over there

❗ often used to refer to a foreigner's country and translatable as 'your country'

むこうがわ・向こう側 *noun*
• = the other side
• = they

むし・虫 *noun* = insect

むし(する)・無視(する) *verb 3* を = to ignore

むじ(の)・無地(の) *adjective* = plain (without pattern)

むしあつい・蒸し暑い *adjective* = humid

むしば・虫歯 *noun*
• = a bad (decayed) tooth
• = a filling

むじゅん・矛盾 *noun* = contradiction

むしろ・寧ろ *adverb* = rather (than)

むす・蒸す *verb 1* を = to steam

むすう(の)・無数(の) *adjective* = countless

むずかしい・難しい *adjective* = difficult

むすこ・息子 *noun* = son ▶ **177**

むすぶ・結ぶ *verb 1* を
• = to tie
• = to connect

むすめ・娘 *noun* = daughter ▶ **177**

むだ・無駄
**1** *noun* = waste
**2** *adjective* むだ(な) = futile
**3** *adverb* むだに = uselessly

むだづかい・無駄遣い *noun* = (a) waste

むだん・無断 *noun and prefix* = without permission

むちゅう・夢中
**1** *noun* = being absorbed in (doing something)
**2** *adverb* むちゅうに = intently

むっつ・六つ・6つ *noun* = six ▶ **181**

むね・胸 *noun* = chest

むら・村 *noun* = village

むらさき・紫 *noun* = purple

**むり・無理**
1 *noun* = impossibility
2 *adjective* **むり(な)**
• = impossible
• = unreasonable
3 *verb 3* ㉛ **むり(を)する**
• = to overdo it
• = to work too hard

**むりょう・無料** *adjective* = free

**むれ・群れ** *noun* – *used to refer to a group of animals so the translation will be words like 'herd', 'pack' or 'swarm' etc. according to the type of creature*

# めメ

**め・目** *noun* = eye
　めにつく = to notice
　めにかかる = to see = to meet
　めをとおす = to look through
　めがさめる = to wake up

**め・芽** *noun*
• = bud
• = shoot

**め・目** *suffix*
• = number
• = place ▶ **181**

**めい・姪** *noun* = niece ▶ **177**

**めい・名**
1 *prefix* = famous
2 *counter* = people

**めいかく・明確**
1 *adjective* **めいかく(な)** = clear
• = accurate
2 *adverb* **めいかくに** = accurately

**めいさく・名作** *noun* = masterpiece

**めいし・名刺** *noun* = business card

**めいし・名詞** *noun* = noun

**めいじ・明治** *noun* – *era name for 1868–1912 and used for dates during that period* ▶ **174**

**めいしょ・名所** *noun*
• = (the) sights
• = famous places

**めいじる・命じる** *verb 1* ㉜ = to order

**めいしん・迷信** *noun*
= superstition

**めいじん・名人** *noun* = (an) expert

**めいずる・命ずる** ▶ めいじる

**めいはく(な)・明白(な)**
*adjective* = evident

**めいぶつ・名物** *noun* = speciality

**めいぼ・名簿** *noun* = register (of names)

**めいる・滅入る** *verb 1* ㉛ = to be depressed

**めいれい・命令** *noun* = order

**めいわく・迷惑** *noun*
• = nuisance
• = trouble
　めいわくをかける = to cause trouble

**めうえ・目上** *noun* = one's superior (at work)

**メーカー** *noun* = manufacturer

**メートル** *noun* = metre

> **!** *sometimes written with the Chinese character* 米

**メール** *noun* = email

**めがね・眼鏡・メガネ** *noun*
= glasses (for vision)

**めがねや・眼鏡屋** *noun* = optician

**めぐまれる・恵まれる** *verb 2* ㉜
　に = to be blessed (with)

**めくる** *verb 1* ㉛ = to turn (a page)

**めぐる・巡る** *verb 1* ㉛
• = to travel around
• = to come around

**めざす・目指す** *verb 1* ㉛
• = to aim for

**めざまし・目覚し** *noun*
= awakening

**めざましどけい・目覚し時計**
*noun* = alarm clock

**めざめる・目覚める** *verb 2* ㉜
= to wake up

**めし・飯** *noun*
• = (cooked) rice
• = meal

**めしあがる・召し上がる**
*verb 1* 㐂
- = to eat
- = to drink

! *an honorific equivalent of たべる and のむ* ▶ **189**

**めした・目下** *noun* = one's junior (at work)

**めじるし・目印** *noun*
- = sign
- = landmark

**めす・雌** *noun* = female

**めずらしい・珍しい** *adjective* = rare

**めだつ・目立つ** *verb 1* 㐰 = to stand out

**めちゃくちゃ（な）** *adjective* = disorganised

**メッセージ** *noun* = message

**めったに・滅多に** *adverb (with negative)* = rarely

**めでたい** *adjective* = fortunate

**めど・目処** *noun* = aim
めどが たたない = there is no prospect of ...

**メニュー** *noun* = menu

**めまい** *noun* = dizziness

**メモ** *noun* = memo

**メモ帳** *noun* = notebook

**めやす・目安** *noun*
- = standard
- = target

**メリット** *noun* = advantage

**めん・面** *noun*
- = aspect
- = surface
- = mask

**めん・綿** *noun* = cotton

**めん・麺** *noun* = noodles

**めんきょ・免許** *noun* = licence

**めんぜいてん・免税店** *noun* = duty free store

**めんせき・面積** *noun* = area

**めんせつ・面接** *noun* = interview

**めんどう（な）・面倒（な）**
*adjective* = troublesome
めんどうを みる = to look after (somebody)

**めんどうくさい・面倒くさい**
*adjective* = troublesome

**メンバー** *noun* = member

# もモ

**も** *particle*
- = also
- = even

! *used to emphasis negatives, quantities and examples. When in the pattern 〜も〜も it means 'both ... and ...', 'either ... or ...', neither ... nor ...'.* ▶ **205**

**もう** *adverb*
- = already
- = yet
- = any more
もう いちど = once more
もう すぐ = soon
もう いい です = that's OK = no thank you

**もうかる・儲かる** *verb 1* 㐰 = to be profitable

**もうける・儲ける** *verb 2* 㐂 = to make a profit

**もうける・設ける** *verb 2* 㐂 = to establish

**もうしあげる・申し上げる** *verb 2* 㐂 = to say

! *humble equivalent of いう* ▶ **189**

**もうしこみ・申込み・申込**
*noun* = application

**もうしこみしょ・申込書** *noun* = application form

**もうしこむ・申し込む** *verb 1* 㐂
に = to apply for

**もうしわけ・申し訳** *noun*
- = apology
- = excuse

もうしわけ ありません = (I am) extremely sorry

**もうしわけない・申し訳ない** ▶ もうしわけ

**もうす・申す** *verb 1* 🈫
• = to say
• = to be called

! *a humble form of* いう ▶ **189**

こいど と もうします = My name is Koido

**もうふ・毛布** *noun* = blanket

**もえないゴミ・燃えないゴミ** *noun* – rubbish|garbage which is not for incineration

**もえる・燃える** *verb 2* 🈔 = to burn

**もえるゴミ・燃えるゴミ** *noun* – rubbish|garbage which is for incineration

**モーター** *noun* = motor

**もくざい・木材** *noun*
• = wood
• = timber

**もくじ・目次** *noun* = (table of) contents

**もくてき・目的** *noun* = objective

**もくひょう・目標** *noun*
• = objective
• = target

**もくようび・木曜日** *noun* = Thursday

**もぐる・潜る** *verb 1* 🈔 = to dive

**もし・若し** *adverb* = if

**もじ・文字** *noun*
• = letter (of the alphabet)
• = script

**もしかして** ▶ もしかしたら

**もしかしたら** *adverb*
• = perhaps
• = possibly

**もしかすると** ▶ もしかしたら

**もしくは・若しくは** *conjunction* = or

**もじばけ・文字化け** *noun* – Japanese text which has been garbled by a computer programme into a series of unreadable symbols. Usually translated as 'gibberish'

**もしも** ▶ もし

**もしもし** *phrase*
• = (on telephone) hello
• = excuse me

**もたらす** *verb 1* 🈫 = to bring about

**もたれる** *verb 2* 🈔 に = to lean

**モダン(な)** *adjective* = modern

**もち・餅** *noun* – blocks or 'cakes' of pounded cooked rice

**もち・持ち** *suffix* = having

**もちあげる・持ち上げる** *verb 2* 🈫 = to lift up

**もちいる・用いる** *verb 2* 🈫 = to use

**もちかえり・持ち帰り** *noun and prefix* = take away (food etc.)

**もちかえる・持ち帰る** *verb 1* 🈫
• = to take home
• = to bring home

**もちぬし・持ち主** *noun* = owner

**もちます** ▶ もつ

**もちろん・勿論** *adverb* = of course

**もつ・持つ** *verb 1* 🈫 もって・もたない・もちます
• = to hold
• = to own
• = to have
• = to carry
• = to keep

**もったいない** *adjective*
• = wasteful
• = too good (for person, place or task)
　もったいない = what a waste!

**もって** ▶ もつ ▶ **197**

**もっていきます** ▶ もっていく

**もっていく・持っていく** *verb 1* 🈫 もっていって・もっていかない・もっていきます = to take

**もっていって** ▶ もっていく ▶ **197**

**もってきて** ▶ もってくる ▶ **197**

**もってきます** ▶ もってくる

**もってくる・持ってくる** *verb 3* 🈫 もってきて・もってこない・もってきます = to bring

**もっと** *adverb* = more

**もっとも・最も** *adverb* = most

もモ

**もっとも**
**1** *conjunction* = however
**2** *adjective* もっとも(な)
• = reasonable
• = natural

**もてなし** *noun* = hospitality

**もてなす** *verb 1* を = to treat
somebody (to food etc.)

**もてる** *verb 2* が に = to be popular
(especially with the opposite sex)

**モデム** *noun* = modem

**モデル** *noun* = model

**もと・元・基・素** *noun*
• = origin
• = cause
• = beginning

**もと・元** *prefix* = former

**もどす・戻す** *verb 1* を = to put
back

**もとづく・基づく** *verb 1* が に
= to be based on

**もとめる・求める** *verb 2* を
• = to ask for
• = to demand
• = to look for

**もともと・元々** *adverb*
• = from the beginning
• = by nature

**もどり・戻り** *noun* = return

**もどる・戻る** *verb 1* が
• = to return
• = to go back
• = to come back

**モニター** *noun* = monitor

**もの・物**
**1** *noun* = thing
**2** *suffix* = item

**もの・者** *noun* – a humble
equivalent of ひと meaning
'person'

**もの** *particle* – Used after past
tenses to mean 'used to ...' and
after non-past structures to mean
that something 'is only natural'
or to express obligation. In the
latter use it is translatable as
'should'.

**ものおき・物置** *noun*
• = closet
• = storeroom

**ものおと・物音** *noun* = sound

**ものがたり・物語** *noun*
• = story
• = tale

**ものがたる・物語る** *verb 1* を
= to tell

**ものごと・物事** *noun* = things

**ものさし・物差し** *noun* = ruler

**ものすごい・物凄い** *adjective*
= tremendous

**ものだ・物だ** ▶ もの

**ものです・物です** ▶ もの

**もみじ・紅葉** *noun*
• = maple tree
• = autumn change in the colour of
leaves

**もむ・揉む** *verb 1* を = to massage

**もめん・木綿** *noun* = cotton

**もやす・燃やす** *verb 1* を = to
burn

**もよう・模様** *noun* = pattern

**もよおし・催し** *noun*
• = meeting
• = function

**もよおす・催す** *verb 1* を = to
hold (a meeting etc.)

**もらいます** ▶ もらう

**もらう・貰う** *verb 1* を に もらっ
て・もらわない・もらいます
= to receive

> **!** *following the ～て form of another
verb it means to receive the favour
of someone doing something for
you or 'get (somebody) to (do
something)'. This usage is often not
reproduced in translation.* ▶ **179,**
▶ **197**

**もらって** ▶ もらう

**もり・森** *noun* = forest

**もりあがる・盛り上がる** *verb 1*
が = to grow lively

**もりあわせ・盛り合わせ** *noun*
= assortment

**もれ・漏れ** *noun* = leak

**もれる・漏れる** *verb 2 ⑩* = to leak

**もん・門** *noun* = gate

**もん・問** *suffix* = question

**もん** – *a reduced form of the particle* もの *and also used in speech (especially by women) as an emphatic particle at the end of sentences* ▶ もの

**もんく・文句** *noun* = complaint
もんくを いう = to complain

**もんだい・問題** *noun*
• = problem
• = issue
• = question

**もんどう・問答** *noun* = question and answer

**や** *particle* = and

> ❗ *joins a list of nouns which is not complete and although translatable as 'and' it carries the meaning of 'among other things'*

**や・屋** *suffix* = shop

> ❗ *also used to mean 'person who does ...'*

**や・夜** *suffix* = night

**〜やいなや** *phrase* = as soon as

**やおや・八百屋** *noun* = greengrocer

**やがて** *adverb* = after a while

**やかましい** *adjective*
• = noisy
• = fussy

**やかん・夜間** *noun* = night time

**やかん・薬缶** *noun* = non-electric kettle

**やき・焼き** *prefix* – cooked by grilling or roasting ▶ やく

**やきとり・焼き鳥** *noun* – kebabs of grilled chicken

**やきゅう・野球** *noun* = baseball

**やく・焼く** *verb 1* ⑯
• = to burn
• = to tan
• = to grill
• = to roast
• = to toast

**やく・約** *adverb*
• = about
• = approximately

**やく・役** *noun and suffix*
• = role
• = job
やくに たつ = to be useful

**やく・訳**
**1** *noun and suffix* = translation
**2** *verb 3* ⑯ やくする = to translate

**やくしゃ・役者** *noun*
• = actor
• = actress

**やくしょ・役所** *noun* – an office of local government ▶ やくば

**やくす・訳す** ▶ やくする

**やくする・訳する** *verb 1* ⑯ に = to translate

**やくそく・約束**
**1** *noun*
• = promise
• = arrangement
**2** *verb 3* ⑯ に やくそくする = to promise
やくそくを まもる = to keep a promise
やくそくを やぶる = to break a promise

**やくだつ・役立つ** *verb 1* ⑩ = to be useful

**やくにん・役人** *noun* = (an) official

**やくば・役場** *noun* = local government office

> ❗ *similar to 'town hall' or 'city hall'*

**やくひん・薬品** *noun*
• = medicines
• = chemicals

**やくぶつ・薬物** *noun* = chemicals

**やくめ・役目** *noun* = role

**やくわり・役割** *noun* = role

やや

**やけ**
やけに なる = to become desperate

**やけい・夜景** *noun* – the view by night over an area of a city with bright lights

**やけど・火傷**
**1** *noun* = burn
**2** *verb 3* ⑩ やけどする
• = to get burned
• = to get scalded

**やける・焼ける** *verb 1* ⑩
• = to be burned
• = to be tanned
• = to be grilled
• = to be roasted
• = to be toasted

**やこう・夜行** *prefix* = night time
**やさい・野菜** *noun* = vegetables
**やさしい・優しい** *adjective* = kind
**やさしい・易しい** *adjective* = easy
**やじるし・矢印** *noun* = arrows (indicating directions)
**やしん・野心** *noun* = ambition
**やすい・安い** *adjective* = cheap
**やすい・易い** *suffix* = easy to (do)
**やすっぽい・安っぽい** *adjective* = cheap-looking

**やすみ・休み** *noun*
• = holiday
• = rest
• = day off

**やすみます** ▶ やすむ
**やすむ・休む** *verb 1* ⑩ やすんで・やすまない・やすみます
• = to take time off work or school
• = to have a break
• = to have a rest

**やすんで** ▶ やすむ ▶ **197**
**やせる・痩せる** *verb 2* ⑩
• = to get thin
• = to lose weight

**やたらに** *adverb*
• = indiscriminately
• = irresponsibly

**やちん・家賃** *noun* = rent
**やつ・奴** *noun*
• = person
• = thing

! a rough term used when the proper name of the item has been momentarily forgotten or of someone with whom one is angry

**やっかい・厄介**
**1** *noun* = trouble
**2** *adjective* やっかい(な) = burdensome

**やっきょく・薬局** *noun*
• = pharmacy
• = chemist

**やっつ・八つ・8つ** *counter* = eight ▶ **181**

**やっつける** *verb 2* ⑧
• = to criticise
• = to beat up

**やっと** *adverb*
• = eventually
• = barely

**やっぱり** *adverb* – a more emphatic version of やはり

**やとう・雇う** *verb 1* ⑧ = to employ

**やぬし・家主** *noun* – meaning 'house owner' it could be translated as 'landlord' or 'landlady' according to the context

**やばい** *noun* – used to describe a state of danger or a feeling of risk especially as an exclamation when something important has been just remembered in time etc. As an exclamation it often means something like 'Oh no! (I've just realised|remembered that I have to ..)'

**やはり** *adverb*
• = as expected
• = nevertheless

**やぶる・破る** *verb 1* ⑧
• = to rip
• = to defeat
• = to break (a promise etc.)

**やぶれる・破れる** *verb 2* ⑩
• = to be ripped

**やぶれる・敗れる** *verb 2* ⑩ に = to be defeated

**やま・山** *noun*
• = mountain
• = a pile of ... ▶ **さん**

**やまあるき・山歩き** *noun*
= mountain/hill walking

**やまと・大和** *noun – an old word for Japan*

**やまとことば・大和言葉** *noun – words not derived from Chinese characters but of original Japanese stock*

**やまのて・山の手** *noun – the part of a town built on the hills (and as such a prosperous residential area) especially in Tokyo and often used to mean the rail network that circles Tokyo called the* **やまのてせん**

**やまのぼり・山登り** *noun*
= mountain climbing

**やむ・止む** *verb 1 ㊦* = to stop (raining)

**やむをえない・やむを得ない** *adjective* = unavoidable

**やめる・止める** *verb 2 ㊦*
• = to stop
• = to give up

**やめる・辞める** *verb 2 ㊦* = to resign

**やや** *adverb* = a little bit

**ややこしい** *adjective* = complicated and annoying

**やりとり・やり取り** *noun*
= exchange

**やりなおす・やり直す** *verb 1 ㊦*
= to redo

**やりにくい** *adjective* = difficult to do

**やりやすい** *adjective* = easy to do

**やる・遣る** *verb 1 ㊦*
• = to do
• = to give

> ❗ *A more informal version of* **する**. *In the meaning 'to give' it is used among friends or by older people to younger. When used after a verb in the* **～て** *form it means 'do for you (as a favour)' and carries strong overtones of social superiority or seniority*

**やるき・やる気** *noun*
• = will
• = drive

**やろう・野郎** *noun – used as a substitute for* **ひと** *meaning 'person' it is highly insulting and somewhat similar to the English 'bastard' as a term of abuse*

**やわらかい・柔らかい・軟らかい** *adjective*
• = soft

**ヤンキー** *noun – refers to youths with their hair dyed (usually blonde) which is seen as a sign of rebelliousness.*

# ゆユ

**ゆ・湯** *noun* = hot water

**ゆいいつ(の)・唯一(の)** *adjective*
• = one and only
• = sole

**ゆう** *verb 3 ㊦ – an alternative pronunciation of* **いう**

**ゆうえんち・遊園地** *noun*
= amusement park

**ゆうがた・夕方** *noun* = (early) evening

**ゆうき・勇気** *noun* = bravery

**ゆうこう・有効** *noun* = validity
**ゆうこうきげん** = valid until

**ゆうこう・友好** *noun* = friendship

**ゆうしゅう(な)・優秀(な)** *adjective* = excellent

**ゆうしょう・優勝**
**1** *noun* = victory
**2** *verb 3 ㊦* **ゆうしょうする** = to win

**ゆうじん・友人** *noun* = friend

**ゆうそう(する)・郵送(する)** *verb 3 ㊦* = to send by post

**ゆうそうりょう・郵送料** *noun*
= (cost of) postage

ゆうだち・夕立 *noun* = a brief shower (of rain)

ゆうのう(な)・有能(な) *adjective* = capable

ゆうはん・夕飯 *noun* = evening meal

ゆうびん・郵便 *noun and prefix* = mail

ゆうびんきょく・郵便局 *noun* = post office

ゆうびんぶつ・郵便物 *noun* = (items of) mail

ゆうべ・夕べ *noun*
• = evening
• = last night

ゆうめい・有名
1 *noun* = fame
2 *adjective* ゆうめい(な) = famous

ユーモア *noun* = humour

ゆうりょう・有料 *noun*
• = charge
• = requiring payment

ゆか・床 *noun* = floor

ゆかい(な)・愉快(な) *adjective* = pleasant

ゆかた・浴衣 *noun – a light, summer-weight* きもの *worn especially at festivals and hot spring resorts*

ゆき・雪 *noun* = snow

ゆき・行き *noun and suffix – an alternative form of* いき *attached to the names of train or flight destinations etc. to mean 'bound for ...'*

ゆく・行く *verb 1 ㊦ – an alternative form of* いく

ゆくえ・行方 *noun* = whereabouts

ゆくえふめい・行方不明 *noun*
• = missing
• = lost

ゆげ・湯気 *noun* = steam

ゆけつ・輸血 *noun* = blood transfusion

ゆしゅつ・輸出
1 *noun* = export
2 *verb 3 ㊦* ゆしゅつする = to export

ゆずる・譲る *verb 1 ㊦*
• = to hand over
• = to offer

ゆそう・輸送
1 *noun* = transportation
2 *verb 3 ㊦* ゆそうする = to transport

ゆたか(な)・豊か(な) *adjective*
• = abundant
• = affluent

ゆだん・油断
1 *noun* = carelessness
2 *verb 3 ㊦* ゆだんする = to be negligent

ゆっくり(と) *adverb* = slowly

ゆでる・茹でる *verb 2 ㊦* = to boil

ゆにゅう・輸入
1 *noun* = import
2 *verb 3 ㊦* ゆにゅうする = to import

ゆのみ・湯飲み *noun – a small Japanese style cup without handles*

ゆび・指 *noun* = finger

> ! *also used as* あしの ゆび *to mean 'toe'*

ゆびわ・指輪 *noun* = ring

ゆめ・夢 *noun* = dream
ゆめを みる = to have a dream

ゆるい・緩い *adjective* = loose

ゆるす・許す *verb 1 ㊦*
• = to forgive
• = to allow

ゆれる・揺れる *verb 2 ㊦* = to shake

# よ ヨ

よ・世 *noun* = world

よ・夜 *noun* = night

よ・四 *prefix* = four ▶ 181

よ *particle – a particle used at the end of sentences for emphasis and which expresses emotion, enthusiasm or rebuke etc.* ▶ 205

よあけ・夜明け *noun* = dawn

よい・良い *adjective* = good – *an alternative form of* いい *used in some*

parts of Japan, in formal speech and
which is the base of the negative and
past forms ▶ いい ▶**201**

**よう・用** *noun*
• = something to do

> ! *also used (especially as a suffix)
> with the meaning 'use' or 'for the use
> of'.*

**よう・様** *noun* – *the basic meaning
is 'appearance' and it is used in
expressions where it is often
translatable as 'look' or 'seem' or 'be
similar'. It can also mean 'something
like that'.* ▶ ように

**よう・洋** *prefix* – *the meaning is
'western' as opposed to Asian or
Japanese* ▶ わ

**よう・酔う** *verb 1 ㋕* に = to be
drunk

**ようい・用意**
**1** *noun* = preparation
**2** *verb 3 ㋕* よういする = to prepare

**ようい・容易**
**1** *adjective* ようい(な) = easy
**2** *adverb* よういに = easily

**ようか・八日・8日** *noun*
• = the eighth day of the month
• = eight days ▶**174**

**ようき・容器** *noun* = container

**ようき・陽気**
**1** *adjective* ようき(な) = cheerful
**2** *adverb* ようきに = cheerfully

**ようきゅう・要求**
**1** *noun* = demand
**2** *verb 3 ㋕* ようきゅうする = to
demand

**ようご・用語** *noun* = terminology

**ようこそ** *phrase*
= welcome (to ～)

**ようし・用紙** *noun and suffix* –
'paper' especially in compounds to
do with exam and answer papers or
referring to the squared paper used
for writing Japanese called げんこう
ようし

**ようし・養子** *noun*
• = adopted child
• = foster child

**ようじ・用事** *noun*
• = business
• = something to do

**ようじ・幼児** *noun* = infant

**ようしつ・洋室** *noun* – *a western
style room as opposed to a traditional
Japanese style one* ▶ わしつ

**ようじん・用心**
**1** *noun* = precautions
**2** *verb 3 ㋕* に ようじんする = to take
precautions

**ようす・様子** *noun*
• = appearance
• = condition

**ようするに・要するに** *adverb*
= essentially

**ようそ・要素** *noun* = element

**ようち(な)・幼稚(な)** *adjective*
= immature

**ようちえん・幼稚園** *noun*
= kindergarten ▶**185**

**ようてん・要点** *noun* = point

**ようと・用途** *noun* = use

**ように** *adverb*
• = so that
• = as
　**～ようになる**
• = reach the point when = to become
　able to …
　**～ようにする** = make a point of
　(doing something) ▶ よう

**ようび・曜日** *noun and suffix* = day
of the week

**ようふう・洋風** *noun* = Western
style (especially of cookery)

**ようふく・洋服** *noun* = clothing

> ! *sometimes meaning 'western style'
> clothing as opposed to わふく but
> also clothing in general*

**ようもう・羊毛** *noun* = wool

**ようやく・漸く** *adverb* = at last

**ようりょう・要領** *noun*
= essential point

**ヨーロッパ** *noun* = Europe

**よき・予期**
**1** *noun* = expectation
**2** *verb 3 ㋕* よきする = to expect

よヨ

よきん・預金 *noun* = savings

よく *adverb*
- = often
- = well
- = hard
- = kindly

よく・翌 *prefix* = the next

よくじつ・翌日 *noun* = the next day

よくばり(な)・欲張り(な) *adjective* = greedy

よけい・余計
**1** *adjective* よけい(な) = unnecessary
**2** *adverb* よけいに = all the more

よこ・横
**1** *noun*
- = width
- = side
**2** *adverb* よこに
- = sideways
- = across
  よこに なる = to lie down

よこぎる・横切る *verb 1* 図 = to cross

よこす・寄越す *verb 1* 図 = to come close

よごす・汚す *verb 1* 図 = to make dirty

よごれ・汚れ *noun* = dirt

よごれる・汚れる *verb 2* 図 = to be dirty

よさん・予算 *noun* = budget

よしゅう・予習 *noun* – studying in advance as preparation for a class and translatable as 'preparation', 'revision' or 'review' depending on the context

よす *verb 1* 図 = to stop

よせる・寄せる *verb 2* 図
- = to deliver
- = to hand over

よそ・余所 *noun*
- = somewhere else
- = another place
  よその ひと = stranger
  よそに する = to put on one side
- = ignoring

よそく・予測
**1** *noun* = estimate
**2** *verb 3* 図 よそくする = to predict

よち・余地 *noun*
- = room
- = space

よっか・四日・4日 *noun*
- = the fourth day of the month
- = four days ▶ 174

よつかど・四つ角 *noun*
- = crossroads

よっつ・四つ *noun* = four ▶ 181

よって ▶ によって ▶ よる

ヨット *noun* = yacht

よっぱらい・酔っ払い *noun* = a drunk

よっぱらう・酔っ払う *verb 1* 図 = to be drunk

よてい・予定 *noun*
- = plan
- = schedule

> ! *following the dictionary form of a verb +* です *it means that the action is planned* ▶ 191

よなか・夜中 *noun* = the middle of the night

よび(の)・予備(の) *adjective*
- = spare
- = extra

よびかける・呼びかける *verb 2* 図 に = to call out (to someone)

よびだす・呼び出す *verb 1* 図
- = to summon
- = to call

よぶ・呼ぶ *verb 1* 図
- = to call
- = to invite

よぶん・余分
**1** *adjective* よぶん(な)
- = additional
- = extra
**2** *adverb* よぶんに = additionally

よほう・予報 *noun* = forecast

よぼう・予防
**1** *noun* = prevention
**2** *verb 3* 図 よぼうする = to prevent

よぼうちゅうしゃ・予防注射 *noun* = vaccination

よみ・読み *noun* – the pronunciation or 'reading' of かんじ characters ▶ おんよみ ▶ くんよみ

よみあげる・読み上げる *verb 2* を = to read aloud

よみがえる・蘇る・甦る *verb 1* が = to revive

よみがな・読みがな *noun* another word for ふりがな

よみます ▶ よむ

よむ・読む *verb 1* を よんで・よまない・よみます = to read

よめ・嫁 *noun* = bride

! *can mean daughter-in-law*

よやく・予約
**1** *noun*
• = booking
• = reservation
**2** *verb 3* を よやくする
• = to book
• = to make a reservation

よゆう・余裕 *noun* = leeway

より *particle*
• = than
• = from
• = rather than
　アメリカは にほんより おおきい です = America is larger than Japan ▶ 205

よりかかる・寄りかかる *verb 1* が に = to lean on

よる・夜 *noun*
• = night
• = evening

よる・寄る *verb 1* が に
• = to come close
• = to drop in and visit (en route to somewhere else)

よる・因る *verb 1* が = to depend

! *in the form* 〜による *it means 'according to' or 'due to'*

よろこび・喜び *noun* = joy

よろこぶ・喜ぶ *verb 1* が = to be delighted

よろしい・宜しい *adjective* – a more formal version of いい meaning 'good' or 'ok'

よろしく・宜しく *adverb* – used alone or in phrases such as よろしく おねがい します and どうぞ よろしく おねがい いたします when asking for favourable treatment or consideration. It is difficult to translate as contexts will vary widely but the meaning ranges from 'please' to 'I humbly request that ...'. It is also used in phrases like 〜に よろしく おつたえ ください to mean 'please send my best wishes to ...'

よわい・弱い *adjective* = weak

よん・四 *noun* = four ▶ 181

よんで ▶ よむ ▶ よぶ ▶ 197

# らラ

ら・等 *suffix* – adds the meaning of 'more than one'

らい・来 *prefix* = next

らいげつ・来月 *noun* = next month

らいしゅう・来週 *noun* = next week

ライス *noun* = (cooked) rice

! *when served on a plate*

ライター *noun* = cigarette lighter

らいにち(する)・来日(する) *verb 3* が = to come to Japan

らいねん・来年 *noun* = next year

らく・楽
**1** *adjective* らく(な) = easy
**2** *adverb* らくに
• = easily
• = comfortably

ラケット *noun* = racket

らしい *suffix* – added to the end of phrases and sentences to express 'appropriate', 'as you would expect of a ...'. i.e. がくせいらしい・学生らしい = 'studentlike'.

ラジオ *noun* = radio

らラ

**らっかんてき・楽観的**
**1** *adjective* らっかんてき(な)
= optimistic
**2** *adverb* らっかんてきに
= optimistically

**ラッシュ** *noun* = rush hour

**ラッシュアワー** ▶ ラッシュ

**ラップトップ** *noun* = laptop

**ラボ** *noun* = (language) laboratory

**らん・欄** *noun* = column

**ランチ** *noun* = lunch

**ランニング** *noun* = running

**らんぼう・乱暴**
**1** *noun* = violence
**2** *adjective* らんぼう(な) = violent
**3** *adverb* らんぼうに = roughly
**4** *verb 3* ㉖ に らんぼうする = to use
violence against

**らんよう・乱用**
**1** *noun* = misuse
**2** *verb 3* ㉕ らんようする = to misuse

# りリ

**リアル(な)** *adjective* = realistic

**りえき・利益** *noun* = profit

**りか・理科** *noun* = science

**りかい・理解**
**1** *noun* = understanding
**2** *verb 3* ㉕ りかいする = to
understand

**りく・陸** *noun* = land

**りくぐん・陸軍** *noun* = army

**りくじょうきょうぎ・陸上競技**
*noun* = athletics

**りこう(な)・利口(な)** *adjective*
= clever

**りこん・離婚**
**1** *noun* = divorce
**2** *verb 3* ㉖ りこんする = to get
divorced

**りし・利子** *noun* = interest

**りじ・理事** *noun* = director

**りじかい・理事会** *noun* = board of
directors

**リストラ** *noun* = restructuring (of a
company)

**リズム** *noun* = rhythm

**りそう・理想** *noun* = (an) ideal

**りそうてき・理想的**
**1** *adjective* りそうてき(な)
= idealistic
**2** *adverb* りそうてきに
= idealistically

**りつ・率** *suffix* = rate

**リットル** *noun* = litre ▶ **181**

**りっぱ(な)・立派(な)** *adjective*
= splendid

**りっぽう・立方** *prefix* = cubic

**りてん・利点** *noun* = advantage

**りふじん(な)・理不尽(な)**
*adjective* = unreasonable

**りゃく・略** *noun* = abbreviation

**りゃくす・略す** *verb 1* ㉕ = to
abbreviate

**りゆう・理由** *noun* = reason

**りゅうがく・留学**
**1** *noun* = studying abroad
**2** *verb 3* ㉖ りゅうがくする = to
study overseas

**りゅうがくせい・留学生** *noun*
– a student studying overseas

**りゅうこう・流行**
**1** *noun* = trend
**2** *adjective* りゅうこう(の)
= fashionable

**りゅうちょう・流暢**
**1** *adjective* りゅうちょう(な)
= fluent
**2** *adverb* りゅうちょうに = fluently

**りよう・利用**
**1** *noun* = use
**2** *verb 3* ㉕ りようする = to use

**りょう・量** *noun* = amount

**りょう・寮** *noun*
• = dormitory
• = university residence

**りょう・両** *prefix* = both

**りょう・料** *suffix* = charge

**りょうがえ・両替**
**1** *noun* = money changing
**2** *verb 3* ㊙ りょうがえする = to change money

**りょうがえじょ・両替所** *noun*
• = money changer
• = bureau de change

**りょうがわ・両側** *noun* = both sides

**りょうきん・料金** *noun and suffix*
• = charge
• = fee

**りょうし・漁師** *noun* = fisherman

**りょうしゅうしょ・領収書** *noun* = receipt

**りょうしん・両親** *noun* = parents
▶ **177**

**りょうしん・良心** *noun* = conscience

**りょうて・両手** *noun* = both hands

**りょうほう・両方** *noun* = both

**りょうり・料理**
**1** *noun* = cooking
**2** *verb 3* ㊙ りょうりする = to cook

**りょうりや・料理屋** *noun* = restaurant

**りょかん・旅館** *noun* – a small hotel offering Japanese style accommodation

**りょけん・旅券** *noun* – the official term for a passport

**りょこう・旅行**
**1** *noun* = trip
**2** *verb 3* ㊙ りょこうする
• = to travel
• = to go on a trip

**りょこうあんないじょ・旅行案内所** *noun* = tourist information office

**りょこうしゃ・旅行者** *noun*
• = traveller
• = tourist

**りれきしょ・履歴書** *noun*
• = resume
• = CV

**りんご** *noun* = apple

**りんじ・臨時** *prefix* = extraordinary

# るル

**るい・類** *noun*
• = type
• = sort

**るいじ(する)・類似(する)** *verb 3* ㊙ に = to be similar

**ルーズ(な)** *adjective*
• = disorganised
• = careless

**ルール** *noun* = rules

**るす・留守** *noun* = absence

**るすでん・留守電** ▶ るすばんでんわ

**るすばん・留守番** *noun* – taking care of somewhere while the owner|s are absent (for either short and long periods)

**るすばんでんわ・留守番電話** *noun* = (telephone) answering machine

**ルビ** *noun* – another term for ふりがな

# れレ

**れい・例** *noun* = example

**れい・礼** *noun*
• = thanks
• = bow
• = reward
れいを する = to bow ▶ おれい

**れい・零** *noun* = zero ▶ **181**

**れいがい・例外** *noun* = exception

**れいぎ・礼儀** *noun* = politeness

**れいぎただしい・礼儀正しい** *adjective* = polite

**れいせい・冷静**
**1** *adjective* れいせい(な) = calm
**2** *adverb* れいせいに = calmly

**れいぞうこ・冷蔵庫** *noun* = refrigerator

りリ
るル
れレ

れいてん・零点 *noun* = zero marks

れいとう・冷凍
**1** *noun* = freezing
**2** *verb 3* ㋫ れいとうする = to freeze

れいとうこ・冷凍庫 *noun*
= freezer

れいとうしょくひん・冷凍食品
*noun* = frozen foods

れいはい・礼拝
**1** *noun* = worship
**2** *verb 3* ㋫ れいはいする = to worship

れいぶん・例文 *noun* = example sentence

れいぼう・冷房 *noun* = air-conditioning

レインコート *noun* = raincoat

れきし・歴史 *noun* = history

レクリエーション *noun*
= recreation

レジ *noun* = cash register

レジャー *noun* = leisure

レストラン *noun* = restaurant

れつ・列 *noun*
• = line
• = row
• = queue

れっしゃ・列車 *noun* = train

れっとう・列島 *noun and suffix*
= chain of islands

レベル *noun* = level

レポート *noun*
• = essay
• = (academic) paper

れんが・煉瓦 *noun* = bricks

れんきゅう・連休 *noun* – holidays occurring or taken in a row

れんごう・連合 *noun and suffix*
= alliance

レンジ *noun*
• = oven
• = microwave oven

れんしゅう・練習
**1** *noun*
• = practice
• = training
**2** *verb 3* ㋫ れんしゅうする
• = to practise
• = to train

レンズ *noun* = lens

れんそう(させる)・連想(させる) *verb 2* ㋰
= to be reminded of

れんぞく・連続
**1** *noun and prefix*
• = succession
• = in succession
**2** *verb 3* ㋫ れんぞくする = to occur in succession
　れんぞくドラマ = drama serial

レンタカー *noun* = car rental

れんだく・連濁 *noun* – the changes in sounds which occur when certain combinations of syllables are combined in words such as in the family name やまだ when the character usually pronounced た becomes pronounced as だ

レントゲン *noun* = X ray
　レントゲンしゃしんを とる = to have an X ray

れんらく・連絡
**1** *noun*
• = contact
• = connection
**2** *verb 3* ㋫ と れんらくする
• = to contact
• = to connect with

れんらくさき・連絡先 *noun*
= contact address

# ろ ロ

ろうか・廊下 *noun*
• = corridor

ろうじん・老人 *noun* = old person

ろうじんホーム・老人ホーム
*noun* = old people's home

ろうそく *noun* = candle

ろうどう・労働 *noun and suffix*
= labour

ろうどうしゃ・労働者 *noun*
= labourer

**ろうひ・浪費**
**1** *noun* = waste
**2** *verb 3* Ⓐ ろうひする = to waste

**ロープウエイ** *noun* = cable car

**ローマじ・ローマ字** *noun* – the roman (western) alphabet and especially Japanese words written in that script

**ろく・六** *noun* = six ▶ **181**

**ろくおん・録音**
**1** *noun* = (sound) recording
**2** *verb 3* Ⓐ ろくおんする = to tape (record sounds)

**ろくが・録画**
**1** *noun* = video recording
**2** *verb 3* Ⓐ ろくがする = to videotape

**ろくがつ・六月** *noun* = June ▶ **174**

**ろくじゅう・六十** *noun* = sixty
▶ **181**

**ロッカー** *noun* = locker

**ロビー** *noun* = hotel lobby

**ロマンチック(な)** *adjective*
= romantic

**ろん・論** *noun and suffix*
• = explanation
• = theory

**ろんじる・論じる** *verb 2* Ⓐ = to argue

**ろんそう・論争** *noun* = dispute

**ろんぶん・論文** *noun*
• = paper
• = thesis
• = dissertation

**ろんりてき・論理的**
**1** *adjective* ろんりてき(な) = logical
**2** *adverb* ろんりてきに = logically

---

# わワ

---

**WA** *particle*

！ *note that the topic particle is written with ひらがな character は 'ha' or (very occasionally) with the かたかな character ハ ▶ は ▶ vii*

**わ・輪** *noun* = ring

**わ・和** *noun* = harmony

！ *as a prefix or abbreviation it means 'Japanese' as opposed to western or 'Japanese (language)'*

**わ・羽** *counter* = birds ▶ **181**

**わ** *particle* – used at the end of sentences to give emphasis and a distinctive marker of women's speech although also used by men in some areas of Japan

**ワイシャツ** *noun* = shirt

**ワイン** *noun* = wine

**わえい・和英** *noun* = Japanese and English language ▶ **dictionary**

**わえいじてん・和英辞典** *noun*
= Japanese-English dictionary

**わが・我が・我** *prefix*
• = my
• = our

**わかい・若い** *adjective* = young

**わかす・沸かす** *verb 1* Ⓐ = to boil

**わがまま(な)** *adjective* = selfish

**わかります** ▶ わかる

**わかる・分かる** *verb 1* Ⓝ わかって・わからない・わかります
= to understand

！ *often used in situations where the most natural English would be 'to know'*

**わかれ・別れ** *noun* = parting

**わかれる・別れる** *verb 2* Ⓝ と
= to separate

**わかれる・分かれる** *verb 2* Ⓝ
= to divide

**わき・脇** *noun*
• = under the arm
• = side

**わきのした・脇の下** *noun*
= armpit

**わく・枠** *noun* = frame

**わく・沸く・湧く** *verb 1* Ⓝ = to boil

**わけ・訳** *noun*
• = reason
• = meaning

ろロ

わワ

・ = circumstances
〜わけでは ありません = it isn't that ... = it doesn't mean that ...
〜わけには いかない = cannot
〜わけはない = it can't be the case

! *the expression 〜わけには いかない is translatable as 'must' (following negatives) and 'must not' (following positives)*

わける・分ける *verb 2* 🈪
・ = to divide
・ = to distribute

わゴム・輪ゴム *noun* = elastic band

わざと *adverb* = deliberately

わしつ・和室 *noun* = Japanese style room

わしょく・和食 *noun* = Japanese food

わずか・僅か
**1** *adverb* = merely
**2** *adjective* わずか(な)
・ = slight
・ = a few

わすれて ▶ わすれる ▶ **197**

わすれます ▶ わすれる

わすれもの・忘れ物 *noun – things which are left behind or forgotten. Often used so that a translation along the lines of 'I've forgotten something!' or 'I'm afraid I left my ...' is most natural. Can be used as verb in the form* わすれもの をする *'to forget something'*

わすれる・忘れる *verb 2* 🈪 わすれて・わすれない・わすれます
= to forget

わた・綿 *noun* = cotton

わだい・話題 *noun* = topic (of conversation)

わたくし・私 *noun – a more formal version of* わたし

わたくしども・私ども *noun – a humble equivalent of* わたしたち

わたし・私 *noun* = I

わたしたち・私たち・私達 *noun*
・ = we
・ = us

わたしの *adjective* = my

わたしたちの *adjective* = our

わたす・渡す *verb 1* 🈪 = to hand over

わたる・渡る *verb 1* 🈫 🈪 = to cross over

わびる・詫びる *verb 2* 🈪 = to apologise

わふう・和風 *noun – Japanese style (as opposed to Western style)*

わふく・和服 *noun – traditional Japanese style clothing*

わらい・笑い *noun*
・ = a laugh
・ = laughter

わらう・笑う *verb 1* 🈫 わらって・わらわない・わらいます
・ = to laugh
・ = to smile

わり・割り *noun* = ratio

! *as a suffix with numbers it indicates multiples of 10% so* さんわり *is 30%*

わりあい・割合
**1** *noun* = rate
**2** *adverb* = comparatively

わりかん・割り勘 *noun – splitting a bill so that everyone pays for their own food and/or drinks*

わりざん・割り算 *noun* = division

わりに・割に *adverb*
・ = fairly
・ = in proportion to

わりびき・割引 *noun* = discount

わる・割る *verb 1* 🈪
・ = to split
・ = to smash
・ = to divide by (a number)

わるい・悪い *adjective* = bad

わるぐち・悪口 *noun* = speaking ill of people

われる・割れる *verb 2* 🈫
・ = to be broken
・ = to be divided

われわれ・我々 *noun* = we

わん・湾 *noun* = bay

わん・椀・碗 *noun* = bowl

ワンピース *noun* = dress

# ンン                                    をヲ

**ん** *an abbreviated form of* **の**
んだ ▶ のです
んです ▶ のです

**を** *particle*

> **!** *marks the direct object of a verb or the space through which an action moves. When used in telegrams etc.* **かたかな** *symbol* **ヲ** *is used to represent this particle. Pronounced as* **お** *but often represented in romanised text as 'wo' although 'o' is also used. Some Japanese do pronounce it as 'wo', usually in very formal situations.*
> ▶ **205**

# Age

To express age in Japanese, you use the number of years + the counter さい・才.

*How old are you?* = なんさいですか。・ 何才ですか。

(note that there is an alternative way of asking the same question = おいくつですか but the answers have no alternative style)

*How old is she?* = かのじょは なんさいですか。・ 彼女は 何才ですか。

The suffix さい・才 is never dropped.

*I am thirty-one (years old)* = さんじゅういっさいです。・ 三十一才です。

The only exception is 20 which is はたち・二十才

Note that you cannot use さい・才 for the age of things, only people.

*This car is two years old.* = この くるまを にねんまえに かいました。・ この 車を 二年前に 買いました。

                                       = *I bought this car two years ago.*

*This building is one hundred years old.* = この たてものは ひゃくねんまえに たてられました。・ この 建物は 百年前に 建てられました。

                                       = *This building was built 100 years ago.*

*A person in their fifties* = ごじゅうだいのひと・ 五十代の 人

*A person in their seventies* = ななじゅうだいの ひと・ 七十代の 人

*People over eighteen* = じゅうはっさいいじょうの ひと・ 十八才以上の 人

# Countries, Nationalities and Languages

Most countries have their names written in カタカナ, based on their pronunciation in English or in that country's language.

To talk about the people of a particular country, add the suffix じん・人 to the country name.

To talk about the language of a particular country, you can usually add the suffix ご・語 to the country name.

For example, Italy is イタリア, Italian people are イタリアじん・イタリア人 and the Italian language is イタリアご・イタリア語.

| | Country | People | Main Language |
|---|---|---|---|
| Argentina | アルゼンチン | アルゼンチンじん | スペインご |
| Australia | オーストラリア | オーストラリアじん | えいご・英語 |
| Austria | オーストリア | オーストリアじん | ドイツご |
| Belgium | ベルギー | ベルギーじん | フランスご |
| Brazil | ブラジル | ブラジルじん | ポルトガルご |
| Canada | カナダ | カナダじん | えいご・英語<br>フラソスご |
| Chile | チリ | チリじん | スペインご |
| China | ちゅうごく・<br>中国 | ちゅうごくじん・<br>中国人 | ちゅうごくご・<br>中国語 |
| Denmark | デンマーク | デンマークじん | デンマークご |
| Egypt | エジプト | エジプトじん | アラビアご |
| Finland | フィンランド | フィンランドじん | フィンランドご |
| France | フランス | フランスじん | フランスご |
| Germany | ドイツ | ドイツじん | ドイツご |
| Greece | ギリシャ | ギリシャじん | ギリシャご |
| Holland | オランダ | オランダじん | オランダご |
| Hungary | ハンガリー | ハンガリーじん | ハンガリーご |
| Iceland | アイスランド | アイスランドじん | アイスランドご |
| India | インド | インドじん | ヒンディーご |
| Iran | イラン | イランじん | ペルシャご |
| Iraq | イラク | イラクじん | アラビアご |
| Ireland | アイルランド | アイルランドじん | アイルランドご |
| Israel | イスラエル | イスラエルじん | ヘブライご |
| Jamaica | ジャマイカ | ジャマイカじん | えいご・英語 |
| Japan | にほん・日本 | にほんじん・日本人 | にほんご・日本語 |
| Malaysia | マレーシア | マレーシアじん | マレーシアご |
| Malta | マルタ | マルタじん | マルタご |
| Mexico | メキシコ | メキシコじん | スペインご |
| Morocco | モロッコ | モロッコじん | アラビアご |
| New Zealand | ニュージーランド | ニュージーランドじん | えいご・英語 |
| Norway | ノルウェー | ノルウェーじん | ノルウェーご |
| Pakistan | パキスタン | パキスタンじん | ウルドウご |
| Peru | ペルー | ペルーじん | スペインご |
| Philippines | フィリピン | フィリピンじん | フィリピンご |
| Poland | ポーランド | ポーランドじん | ポーランドご |

|              | Country | People | Main Language |
|--------------|---------|--------|---------------|
| Portugal | ポルトガル | ポルトガルじん | ポルトガルご |
| Russia | ロシア | ロシアじん | ロシアご |
| Scotland | スコットランド | スコットランドじん | えいご・英語 |
| Singapore | シンガポール | シンガポールじん | えいご・英語 |
| South Africa | みなみアフリカ・南アフリカ | みなみアフリカじん・南アフリカ人 | アフリカーンスご |
| South Korea | かんこく・韓国 | かんこくじん・韓国人 | かんこくご・韓国語 |
| Spain | スペイン | スペインじん | スペインご |
| Sweden | スウェーデン | スウェーデンじん | スウェーデンご |
| Switzerland | スイス | スイスじん | フランスご |
| Taiwan | たいわん・台湾 | たいわんじん・台湾人 | ちゅうごくご・中国語 |
| Thailand | タイ | タイじん | タイご |
| Turkey | トルコ | トルコじん | トルコご |
| UK | イギリス | イギリスじん | えいご・英語 |
| USA | アメリカ | アメリカじん | えいご・英語 |
| Vietnam | ベトナム | ベトナムじん | ベトナムご |
| Wales | ウェールズ | ウェールズじん | ウェールズご |

# Dates, days and months

(for counting periods of time see the note on numbers and counting)

## The days of the week:

|            |            |          | Abbreviation |
|------------|------------|----------|--------------|
| Monday     | げつようび  | 月曜日    | 月           |
| Tuesday    | かようび    | 火曜日    | 火           |
| Wednesday  | すいようび  | 水曜日    | 水           |
| Thursday   | もくようび  | 木曜日    | 木           |
| Friday     | きんようび  | 金曜日    | 金           |
| Saturday   | どようび    | 土曜日    | 土           |
| Sunday     | にちようび  | 日曜日    | 日           |

· In the notes below, **げつようび** stands for any day. They all work the same way.

| | |
|---|---|
| *On Monday* | = げつようびに ・ 月曜日に |
| *Every Monday* | = まいしゅう、げつようびに ・ 毎週、月曜日に |
| *Monday afternoon* | = げつようびの ごご ・ 月曜日の 午後 |
| *Last Monday* | = せんしゅうの げつようび ・ 先週の 月曜日 |
| *Next Monday* | = らいしゅうの げつようび ・ 来週の 月曜日 |
| *Last Monday night* | = せんしゅうの げつようびの ばん ・ 先週の 月曜日の 晩 |
| *From Monday on* | = げつようびから ・ 月曜日から |
| *From Monday to Friday* | = げつようびから きんようびまで ・ 月曜日から 金曜日まで |
| *What day is it?* | = なんようびですか。・ 何曜日ですか。 |

## The months of the year:

These can be made using the number of the month + **がつ ・ 月**

The numbers may also be written using Arabic numerals except when writing vertically.

| January   | いちがつ       | 一月    | July      | しちがつ       | 七月   |
|-----------|----------------|---------|-----------|----------------|--------|
| February  | にがつ         | 二月    | August    | はちがつ       | 八月   |
| March     | さんがつ       | 三月    | September | くがつ         | 九月   |
| April     | しがつ         | 四月    | October   | じゅうがつ     | 十月   |
| May       | ごがつ         | 五月    | November  | じゅういちがつ | 十一月 |
| June      | ろくがつ       | 六月    | December  | じゅうにがつ   | 十二月 |

In the notes below, April stands for any month. They all work the same way.

| | |
|---|---|
| *In April* | = しがつに ・ 四月に |
| *Every April* | = まいとししがつ ・ 毎年 四月 |
| *Next April* | = らいねんの しがつ ・ 来年の 四月 |
| *Last April* | = きょねんの しがつ ・ 去年の 四月 |
| *early April* | = しがつじょうじゅん ・ 四月上旬 |
| *mid-April* | = しがつちゅうじゅん ・ 四月中旬 |
| *Late April* | = しがつげじゅん ・ 四月下旬 |
| *What month is it?* | = なんがつですか。・ 何月ですか。 |

# Dates:

The days of the month are listed below. They are made from the number +
にち・日. Note that the readings are irregular for 1st-10th, 14th, 20th and 24th.

The numbers may also be written using Arabic numerals except when writing
vertically.

| | | | | | |
|---|---|---|---|---|---|
| 1st | ついたち | 一日 | 17th | じゅうしちにち | 十七日 |
| 2nd | ふつか | 二日 | 18th | じゅうはちにち | 十八日 |
| 3rd | みっか | 三日 | 19th | じゅうくにち | 十九日 |
| 4th | よっか | 四日 | 20th | はつか | 二十日 |
| 5th | いつか | 五日 | 21st | にじゅういちにち | 二十一日 |
| 6th | むいか | 六日 | 22nd | にじゅうににち | 二十二日 |
| 7th | なのか | 七日 | 23rd | にじゅうさんにち | 二十三日 |
| 8th | ようか | 八日 | 24th | にじゅうよっか | 二十四日 |
| 9th | ここのか | 九日 | 25th | にじゅうごにち | 二十五日 |
| 10th | とおか | 十日 | 26th | にじゅうろくにち | 二十六日 |
| 11th | じゅういちにち | 十一日 | 27th | にじゅうしちにち | 二十七日 |
| 12th | じゅうににち | 十二日 | 28th | にじゅうはちにち | 二十八日 |
| 13th | じゅうさんにち | 十三日 | 29th | にじゅうくにち | 二十九日 |
| 14th | じゅうよっか | 十四日 | 30th | さんじゅうにち | 三十日 |
| 15th | じゅうごにち | 十五日 | 31st | さんじゅういちにち | 三十一日 |
| 16th | じゅうろくにち | 十六日 | | | |

To say the date in Japanese, give the year, then the month and finally the date and day.

*Monday, 14th October 1968* = せんきゅうひゃく ろくじゅうねん じゅう
がつ じゅうよっか げつようび ・ 千九百六
十八年 十月 十四日 月曜日

*What's the date?* = なんにちですか。・ 何日ですか。
*In the year 2000* = にせんねんに ・ 二千年に
*In the twenty first century* = にじゅういっせいきに ・ 二十一世紀に

## Years and the Japanese Era system

Japan uses a system based on the ruling Emperor and official dates (such as date of
birth etc.) are usually referred to using these era names. The four most recent are
given below. Note that era names change part way through a year.

| | |
|---|---|
| めいじ・明治 | 1868 to 1912 |
| たいしょう・大正 | 1912 to 1926 |
| しょうわ・昭和 | 1926 to 1989 |
| へいせい・平成 | 1989 – |

*I was born in 1980* = **しょうわ ごじゅうごねんに うまれました・昭和五十五年に生まれました**
= *I was born in year 55 of Showa*

# Family Words

In Japanese, there are two sets of words for family members. The humble ones are used for your own family and the honorific ones for other people's families.

|  | humble (for your own family) | honorific (for other people's families) |
|---|---|---|
| Family | かぞく ・ 家族 | ごかぞく ・ ご家族 |
| Parents | りょうしん ・ 両親 | ごりょうしん ・ ご両親 |
| Mother | はは ・ 母 | おかあさん ・ お母さん |
| Father | ちち ・ 父 | おとうさん ・ お父さん |
| Older sister | あね ・ 姉 | おねえさん ・ お姉さん |
| Older brother | あに ・ 兄 | おにいさん ・ お兄さん |
| Younger sister | いもうと ・ 妹 | いもうとさん ・ 妹さん |
| Younger brother | おとうと ・ 弟 | おとうとさん ・ 弟さん |
| Siblings | きょうだい | ごきょうだい |
| Grandmother | そぼ ・ 祖母 | おばあさん |
| Grandfather | そふ ・ 祖父 | おじいさん |
| Grandchild | まご ・ 孫 | おまごさん ・ お孫さん |
| Child | こども ・ 子供 | おこさん ・ お子さん |
| Daughter | むすめ ・ 娘 | おじょうさん ・ お嬢さん |
| Son | むすこ ・ 息子 | むすこさん ・ 息子さん |
| Aunt | おば | おばさん |
| Uncle | おじ | おじさん |
| Cousin | いとこ | いとこさん |
| Wife (of speaker) | つま ・ 妻 | — |
| Wife (of someone else) | — | おくさん ・ 奥さん |
| Husband (of speaker) | しゅじん ・ 主人 | — |
| Husband (of someone else) | — | ごしゅじん ・ ご主人 |

Note that there are other terms used from time to time – these are all in the Japanese-English word list.

Note that the honorific terms are used when speaking face to face with or calling to your own family.

When you talk about the number of brothers and sisters you have, include yourself in the total.

*I have 2 brothers and sisters* = わたしは さんにん きょうだいです。・
私は ３人きょうだいです。
= *there are three children (including myself)*

*I am an only child.* = ひとりっこです。・ 一人っ子です。

In-laws are described using the structure ぎりの〜 ・ 義理の〜

*Father in law* = ぎりの ちち ・ 義理の父

Step-parents and siblings are not usually differentiated from 'blood' relatives

# Feelings

When describing certain feelings such as 'glad, 'sad' and 'lonely' etc. the　い
adjectives うれしい・嬉しい, かなしい・悲しい and さびしい・寂しい・
淋しい can only be used about oneself.

**I am glad**　　　　　　　　　　　　= うれしいです・嬉しいです

To talk about someone else's feelings using these adjectives the last　い is removed
and the ending がる is added. The adjective now behaves like a group 1 verb and is
often used in the present continuous i.e. ～がっている

**He is glad**　　　　　　　　　　　　= かれは うれしがっています・彼は 嬉しが
　　　　　　　　　　　　　　　　　っています。

Note that because it is now a verb it may take a direct object marked with　を

**I want a bicycle**　　　　　　　　　= じてんしゃが ほしいです・自転車が 欲し
　　　　　　　　　　　　　　　　　いです

**She wants a bicycle**　　　　　　　= かのじょは じてんしゃを ほしがっていま
　　　　　　　　　　　　　　　　　す。・彼女は 自転車を 欲しがっています。

You can also add a statement such as 'seems to be ...' or 'apparently is ...' to these
adjectives to allow them to refer to someone other than yourself

**She (seems to be) is lonely** = かのじょは さびしいみたいです。・彼女は
　　　　　　　　　　　　　　　　　寂しいみたいです。

The same issue affects the use of the verb よろこぶ・喜ぶ 'to be overjoyed' and
similar verbs

# Giving and Receiving

Verbs with meanings of giving and receiving are variable in Japanese depending on whether the direction of the giving is to you (or your family or 'in-group') or away from you and on the relationship between you and the other person or people involved.

## To Give

Simply put if the direction is away from the giver (but not to you) the verb is あげる and when the direction is to the speaker (i.e. you or a member of your family or 'in-group') the verb is くれる.

| | |
|---|---|
| My father gave me a book | = ちちが わたしに ほんを くれました。<br>・ 父が私に本をくれました。 |
| My father gave Mr Tanaka a book | = ちちが たなかさんに ほんを あげました。・ 父が田中さんに本をあげました。 |
| I gave my mother a book | = わたしは ははに ほんを あげました。<br>・ 私は母に本をあげました。 |

If someone with a high status (such as a teacher) gives something to someone with lower status (such as a student) then the verb can be くださる and if you give something to someone with high status the verb can be さしあげる but in everyday use あげる is sufficiently polite.

| | |
|---|---|
| The teacher gave me a book | = せんせいが わたしに ほんを くださいました。・ 先生が私に本をくださいました。 |
| I gave a book to the President | = だいとうりょうに ほんを さしあげました。・ 大統領に本を差し上げました。 |

## To Receive

The general verb is もらう and a more polite version is いただく

| | |
|---|---|
| I received a book from my mother | = ははに ほんを もらいました。・ 母に本をもらいました。 |
| I received a book from my teacher | = せんせいに ほんを いただきました。・ 先生に本をいただきました。 |

## Extended use of giving and receiving

Verbs with these meanings can be added to other verbs in the ～て form to indicate that a favour is being done.

| | |
|---|---|
| てつだってあげる・手伝ってあげる | = to do someone a favour by helping them |
| てつだってくれる・手伝ってくれる | = to receive the favour of someone helping you |

For further information see the notes to the relevant verb entries in the Japanese-English section and see 'give' and 'receive' etc. in the English-Japanese section and also the note on respect language.

# Musical instruments

Playing an instrument

The verb used depends on the way and instrument is played.

Use ふく ・ 吹く for instruments which you blow into.

*To play the flute* = フルートを ふく ・ フルートを 吹く

Use ひく ・ 弾く for instruments which you play using your fingers or a plectrum or a bow.

*To play the piano* = ピアノを ひく ・ ピアノを 弾く

Use うつ ・ 打つ for instruments which you strike.

*To play the drums* = ドラムを たたく ・ ドラムを 叩く

*To take guitar lessons* = ギターを ならう ・ ギターを 習う
　　　　　　　　　　　= to learn the guitar
*A piano teacher* = ピアノの せんせい ・ ピアノの 先生

# Numbers and counting

Japanese has two systems of numbers. The numbers in the following chart are not used for counting people, objects or time (see below). We have given characters for the numerals but note that the arabic numerals (1,2,3,4,etc.) are used for horizontal writing よこがき・横書き and character numerals (一、二、三、四 etc.) for vertical writing たてがき・縦書き.

| | | |
|---|---|---|
| 0 | ゼロ・れい | usually written as 0 |
| 1 | いち | 一 |
| 2 | に | 二 |
| 3 | さん | 三 |
| 4 | し・よん | 四 |
| 5 | ご | 五 |
| 6 | ろく | 六 |
| 7 | なな・しち | 七 |
| 8 | はち | 八 |
| 9 | きゅう・く | 九 |
| 10 | じゅう | 十 |
| 11 | じゅういち | 十一 |
| 12 | じゅうに | 十二 |
| 13 | じゅうさん | 十三 |
| 14 | じゅうよん・じゅうし | 十四 |
| 15 | じゅうご | 十五 |
| 16 | じゅうろく | 十六 |
| 17 | じゅうなな・じゅうしち | 十七 |
| 18 | じゅうはち | 十八 |
| 19 | じゅうきゅう・じゅうく | 十九 |
| 20 | にじゅう | 二十 |
| 21 | にじゅういち | 二十一 |
| 30 | さんじゅう | 三十 |
| 35 | さんじゅうご | 三十五 |
| 40 | よんじゅう | 四十 |
| 50 | ごじゅう | 五十 |
| 60 | ろくじゅう | 六十 |
| 70 | ななじゅう・しちじゅう | 七十 |
| 80 | はちじゅう | 八十 |
| 90 | きゅうじゅう | 九十 |
| 100 | ひゃく | 百 |
| 133 | ひゃくさんじゅうさん | 百三十三 |
| 200 | にひゃく | 二百 |
| 300 | さんびゃく | 三百 |
| 400 | よんひゃく | 四百 |
| 500 | ごひゃく | 五百 |
| 600 | ろっぴゃく | 六百 |
| 700 | ななひゃく | 七百 |
| 800 | はっぴゃく | 八百 |
| 900 | きゅうひゃく | 九百 |
| 1000 | せん | 千 |
| 3000 | さんぜん | 三千 |

| | | |
|---|---|---|
| 4000 | よんせん | 四千 |
| 10,000 | いちまん | 一万 |
| 14,000 | いちまんよんせん | 一万四千 |
| 50,000 | ごまん | 五万 |
| 1,000,000 | ひゃくまん | 百万 |
| 10,000,000 | いっせんまん | 一千万 |
| 100,000,000 | いちおく | 一億 |

The numbers in the next chart are used for counting objects (but not people).

Note that for numbers above 10 the appropriate counter (see below) is added to the number from the chart above

| | | |
|---|---|---|
| 1 | ひとつ | 一つ |
| 2 | ふたつ | 二つ |
| 3 | みっつ | 三つ |
| 4 | よっつ | 四つ |
| 5 | いつつ | 五つ |
| 6 | むっつ | 六つ |
| 7 | ななつ | 七つ |
| 8 | やっつ | 八つ |
| 9 | ここのつ | 九つ |
| 10 | とお | 十 |
| how many? | いくつ | |

## Counters

There is another way of counting things in Japanese that uses particular suffixes usually called 'counters' which are attached to the numbers given in the first chart. The counter used depends on the thing being counted. There are some changes in sound when certain numbers and counters are joined. The system for counting people is shown below as a separate chart because of a slight irregularity. Other common counters are given in the final table but they are representative and do not include all the sound changes. Note that the list is not exhaustive.

| | |
|---|---|
| 1 person | ひとり ・ 一人 |
| 2 people | ふたり ・ 二人 |
| 3 people | さんにん ・ 三人 |
| 4 people | よにん ・ 四人 |
| 5 people | ごにん ・ 五人 |
| 6 people | ろくにん ・ 六人 |
| 7 people | ななにん ・ しちにん ・ 七人 |
| 8 people | はちにん ・ 八人 |
| 9 people | きゅうにん ・ 九人 |
| 10 people | じゅうにん ・ 十人 |
| 11 people | じゅういちにん ・ 十一人 |
| 23 people | にじゅうさんにん ・ 二十三人 |
| how many people? | なんにん ・ 何人 |

| when counting | counter | example | how many ...? |
| --- | --- | --- | --- |
| small, round things | こ・個 | fruit | なんこ・何個 |
| long cylindrical things, | ほん・本 | bottles, cigarettes, | なんぼん・何本 |
| flat things | まい・枚 | stamps, pieces of paper | なんまい・何枚 |
| books and magazines | さつ・冊 | | なんさつ・何冊 |
| people | にん・人 | see separate chart above | なんにん・何人 |
| small animals | ひき・匹 | dogs, fish | なんびき・何匹 |
| machines and large objects | だい・台 | cars, machines, furniture | なんだい・何台 |
| number of times | かい・回 | | なんかい・何回 |
| floors | かい・階 | | なんがい・何階 |
| years of age | さい・才 note that 20 years old is はたち | | なんさい・何才 |
| bowl/cupful | はい・杯 | | なんはい・何杯 |
| minutes | ふん・分 | | なんぷん・何分 |
| hours | じかん・時間 | | なんじかん・何時間 |
| days | see the note on dates (the words are the same except for いちにち・一日 'one day' and にじゅうにち・二十日 'twenty days') | | |
| months | かげつ・ヶ月 note that the character resembles the katakana for 'ke' but is pronounced as 'ka' | | なんかげつ・何ヶ月 |
| years | ねんかん・年間 note that ねん is sometimes employed on its own | | なんねんかん・何年間 |

to say 'number' 1, 'number 2', 'number 3' etc. the counter ばん・番 is attached to the appropriate number.

いちばん・一番 = number 1
にばん・二番　= number 2

## Ordinal Numbers

to say 1st, 2nd, 3rd, etc. the counter ばんめ ・ 番目 is added to the number.

| | | |
|---|---|---|
| 1st | いちばんめ | 一番目 |
| 2nd | にばんめ | 二番目 |
| 3rd | さんばんめ | 三番目 |
| 21st | にじゅういちばんめ | 二十一番目 |
| 103rd | ひゃくさんばんめ | 百三番目 |

Sometimes the prefix だい ・ 第 is added with no real change in meaning

| | | |
|---|---|---|
| 1st | だいいちばん | 第一番 |
| 3rd | だいさんばん | 第三番 |

## Fractions

| | | |
|---|---|---|
| half | はんぶん | 半分 |
| a third | さんぶんのいち | 三分の一 |
| two thirds | さんぶんのに | 三分の二 |
| three quarters | よんぶんのさん | 四分の三 |

## Decimals

Numbers with a decimal point are pronounced as two numbers separated by the decimal point which is pronounced as てん

| | |
|---|---|
| 1.5 | いってんご |
| 3.6 | さんてんろく |
| 0.01 | れいてんれいいち |
| 25.8 | にじゅうごてうんはち |

Note that 0 can be pronounced as either れい or ゼロ

# Schools in Japan

The school system is Japan is similar to the American model.

Children may go to a ほいくえん・保育園 (nursery) from the age of four.

Children start compulsory schooling at the age of six.

*Elementary School* = しょうがっこう・小学校

They spend six years at Elementary School.

*At the age of twelve, they go to Junior High School* = ちゅうがっこう・中学校

They spend three years at Junior High School and compulsory education ends at the age of 15 in Japan when they そつぎょうする・卒業する (graduate) from this school.

However, almost all students continue their education to High School こうとうがっこう・高等学校 which is usually abbreviated to こうこう・高校. They attend this school from the age of 16–18.

Getting into a good High School is important in order to proceed to a good university and get a job in a good company. Competition to get into the best schools is intense and students often attend a じゅく・塾 ('cram schools') in order to pass the にゅうがくしけん・入学試験 (entrance examinations).

There are further cram schools to prepare students to pass the entrance examinations for だいがく・大学 (universities).

For students who do not go to university, they may attend a たんきだいがく・短期大学 (junior college) for just two years or a せんもんがっこう・専門学校 (a school where a practical trade is taught such as art, hairdressing or catering).

| | |
|---|---|
| *Which school year are you in?* = | なんねんせいですか。・何年生ですか。 |
| *I'm a first year (student)* = | いちねんせいです。・一年生です。 |
| *I'm a fourth year (student)* = | よねんせいです。・四年生です。 |
| *Teacher* = | せんせい・先生 |
| *Japanese Teacher* = | にほんごの せんせい・日本語の 先生 |
| *Head teacher\|Principal* = | こうちょうせんせい・校長先生 |
| *What is your favourite subject?* = | いちばんすきな かもくは なんですか。・ 一番好きな 科目は なんですか。 |
| *My favourite subject is maths.* = | いちばんすきな かもくは すうがくです。 ・一番好きな 科目は 数学です。 |
| *Private school* = | しりつがっこう・私立学校 |
| | ▶ *independent* |

# Time and the Clock

*What time is it now?* = いま なんじ ですか。・ 今 何時 ですか。

To tell the time in Japanese, say the number of the hour + じ・時

| | |
|---|---|
| *It is 1 o'clock* | = いちじ です。・ 一時 です。 |
| *It's 4 o'clock* | = よじ です。・ 四時 です。 |
| *It is 7 o'clock* | = しちじ です。・ 七時 です。 |

Note that:
4 o'clock is always pronounced よじ.
7 o'clock is always pronounced しちじ.
9 o'clock is always pronounced くじ.

To add a.m. or p.m. to the time, put ごぜん・午前 or ごご・午後 *before* the time.

| | |
|---|---|
| *2 a.m.* | = ごぜんにじ・午前二時 |
| *3 p.m.* | = ごごさんじ・午後三時 |

The twenty-four hour clock is not generally used in Japan except at airports and stations.

To give a time with minutes past the hour, say the hour first and then the number of minutes + 分 (this is pronounced ふん when following a number which ends in five (i.e. 15, 25, etc) and ぷん following a number which ends in zero (i.e 10, 20, etc).

| | |
|---|---|
| *Five past nine* | = くじごふん・九時五分 |
| *Twenty past three* | = さんじにじゅっぷん・三時二十分 |

Half past is expressed by giving the hour + はん・半 or さんじゅっぷん・三十分.

| | |
|---|---|
| *It's half past ten.* | = じゅうじはん です。・ 十時半 です。 |
| *For times such as five to ten, say 9:55* | = くじごじゅうごふん・九時五十五分 |
| *8 o'clock in the evening* | = よる はちじ・夜 八時 |
| *3 o'clock in the morning* | = あさ さんじ・朝 三時 |

Sometimes a time with minutes to the hour is used

| | |
|---|---|
| *five to ten* | = じゅうじごふんまえ・十時五分前 |

# Plain and Polite forms

Japanese as it is presented in most textbooks has two basic styles of speech. Polite and informal. In this dictionary we have used the terms polite form or (when referring to verbs) the 〜ます form and plain form. A chart of plain and polite equivalents is given below. See also the chart of adjectives elsewhere in the notes. Note that in the middle of sentences in the polite style there can some plain forms as it is at the end of a sentence that the polite markers tend to be employed. Most examples in this dictionary have been given in the polite form. In the chart below note that it is the *style* and not the meaning which is different.

The issue of speech levels in Japanese is beyond the scope of a learners' dictionary and what we are here calling plain styles and forms are everyday, informal spoken language called ふつうたい・普通体 or であるちょう・である調. What we are calling polite styles and forms are a part of the respect language system called けいご・敬語. Note that であるちょう is used in newspaper and formal writing whereas けいご is largely a spoken phenomenon. What we call the polite style is properly called ていねいご・丁寧語 and often called です・ます by teachers. Note that descriptions or translations of the Japanese terms into English have generated a wide range of terms and the use of them is not standardised. For more information see the note on respect language.

| element | polite form | plain form | example used |
|---|---|---|---|
| am,is,are | です | だ | |
| was, were | でした | だった | |
| am not, is not, are not | ではありません or じゃありません | じゃない | |
| was not, were not | ではありません でした or じゃありません でした | じゃなかった | |
| adjective (い) | おおきいです やすいです | おおきい やすい | big cheap |
| adjective (な) | きれいです しずかです | きれいだ しずかだ | clean, pretty quiet |
| group 1 verb non-past | とります | とる | take |
| group 1 verb past | とりました | とった | took |
| group 1 verb negative | とりません | とらない | don't take |
| group 1 verb past negative | とりませんでした | とらなかった | didn't take |
| group 2 verb non-past | たべます | たべる | eat |
| group 2 verb past | たべました | たべた | ate |
| group 2 verb negative | たべません | たべない | don't eat |
| group 2 verb past negative | 食べませんでした | たべなかった | did not eat |
| group 3 verb する non-past | します | する | see entry on する in the main dictionary |
| group 3 verb する past | しました | した | |

| element | polite form | plain form | example used |
|---|---|---|---|
| group 3 verb する negative | しません | しない | |
| group 3 verb する past negative | しませんでした | しなかった | |
| group 3 verb くる non-past | きます | くる | to come |
| group 3 verb くる past | きました | きた | |
| group 3 verb くる negative | きません | こない | |
| group 3 verb くる past negative | きませんでした | こなかった | |

# Respect Language

Japanese has a number of ways of showing politeness or respect. Two elements of this which can affect the use of the dictionary are briefly mentioned below. These are part of a much wider system whose full treatment is beyond the scope of this dictionary.

## Prefixes

Sometimes the prefixes お or ご are placed in front of nouns to make them more polite or to indicate that the nouns are related to someone to whom politeness or respect is being shown. For example

| | |
|---|---|
| せんせいの おにもつ ・ 先生のお荷物 | = the teacher's baggage |
| わたしの にもつ ・ 私の荷物 | = my baggage |
| せんせいの ごじゅうしょ ・ 先生のご住所 | = the teacher's address |
| ともだちの じゅうしょ ・ 友達の住所 | = a friend's address |

This dictionary gives words which are frequently used with these particles as separate entries under お or ご as well as under the basic unit word itself. For example 'water' is given under the headwords おみず ・ お水 and みず ・ 水.

## Verbs

Japanese has a choice of verb forms and sentence endings depending on the level of politeness (see the note on polite and plain forms). These special forms in Japanese and their use are called けいご ・ 敬語 and this is often translated as 'respect language'.

There are also alternative forms for some verbs depending on whether politeness/respect is shown with reference to someone else or humility with reference to the speaker/writer. This can extend to using polite forms about people and matters related to another person and humble forms about people and matters related to the speaker/writer. Forms of speech which are respectful are called そんけいご ・ 尊敬語 in Japanese. English translations vary widely and there is no standard usage. Forms of speech which are humble are called けんじょうご ・ 謙譲語 in Japanese. Again there is no consistently used English term.

Some of the most common alternatives are given in the table below.

| Form | dictionary form (plain style) | ～ます form (polite style) | honorific and polite alternative – used about others dictionary form | honorific and polite alternative – used about others ～ます form | humble and polite alternative – used about self and family dictionary form | humble and polite alternative – used about self and family ～ます form |
|---|---|---|---|---|---|---|
| Japanese name for this style of speech | ふつうたい・**普通体** Sometimes called で**あるちょう・である調** when used in writing | ですます たい・です・ます体 | (けいご・敬語) そんけいご・尊敬語 | (けいご・敬語) そんけいご・尊敬語 | (けいご・敬語) けんじょうご・謙譲語 | (けいご・敬語) けんじょうご・謙譲語 |
| to go | いく | いきます | いらっしゃる | いらっしゃいます | まいる | まいります |
| to come | くる | きます | いらっしゃる | いらっしゃいます | まいる | まいります |
| to be (people) | いる | います | いらっしゃる | いらっしゃいます | おる | おります |
| to be (non-living things) | ある | あります | | ございます | ございます | ございます |
| to see, to look | みる | みます | ごらんになる | ごらんになります | はいけんする | はいけんします |
| to eat | たべる | たべます | めしあがる | めしあがります | いただく | いただきます |
| to say | いう | いいます | おっしゃる | おっしゃいます | もうす | もうします |
| to know | しる | しります note that it is usually in the form しっています | | ごぞんじです | ぞんじる | ぞんじます |
| to ask | きく | ききます | | | うかがう | うかがいます |

# The Verb

The brief notes that follow are intended to help users of this dictionary understand and use the information that is provided in it.

## Verb Groups

NOTE that the forms in which Japanese verbs are usually presented in text books are part of the neutral polite style and will end in 〜ます, 〜ません or 〜ましょう etc. These endings are all formed on the pre 〜ます stem. The forms most commonly used to make other constructions and mentioned in the explanations in this dictionary are the so-called dictionary form, the 〜て, 〜ない, and pre 〜ます forms. The formation of these is shown by the tables below and the 〜て form is explained in some detail. Japanese verbs do not change their form for singular and plural or for person – which means that the verb 'go' in Japanese is the same for 'I go', 'they go' and 'she goes'. The personal pronouns 'I', 'you' and 'he' etc. are not required in Japanese and context is required to know which English pronoun to use for a translation.

This dictionary assigns each verb in the Japanese-English section to either group 1, 2 or 3. Examples of each group are fully conjugated below. In simple terms there are only two verbs in group 3, くる and する, group 2 is the vast majority of the verbs which end in '-iru' or '-eru' in the dictionary form and group 1 is everything else. For the convenience of beginners we have given examples of group 1 verbs are given for all the possible dictionary form endings. The verb いく does not follow the pattern of the example verb for its ending in that there is an irregularity in the the 〜て form and hence the 〜た form. いく・行く is conjugated separately below.

Japanese has a great many verbs that are made by adding する 'to do' to a noun such as べんきょう 'study'. These verbs can also often be used with なる 'to become' instead of する. We have listed many of these but note that there are other possible combinations.

NOTE that once a group 1 or 3 verb has acquired a form with an ending in '-eru' it is conjugated as a group 2 verb to form its negative etc.

There are several different 'conditional' forms but the discussion of their uses is beyond the scope of this dictionary.

# Group 1

A form appearing chart does not necessarily mean it is in common use

| Form | Group 1 verbs with a dictionary form ending in る | Group 1 verbs with a dictionary form ending in ぶ | Group 1 verbs with a dictionary form ending in む | Group 1 verbs with a dictionary form ending in す | Group 1 verbs with a dictionary form ending in う | Group 1 verbs with a dictionary form ending in つ | Group 1 verbs with a dictionary form ending in く | Group 1 verbs with a dictionary form ending in ぐ | Group 1 verbs with a dictionary form ending in ぬ |
|---|---|---|---|---|---|---|---|---|---|
| meaning | to take | to call | to read | to speak | to say | to wait | to write | to swim | to die |
| dictionary form plain non-past | とる | よぶ | よむ | はなす | いう | まつ | かく | およぐ | しぬ |
| ～ない form plain negative | とらない | よばない | よまない | はなさない | いわない | またない | かかない | およがない | しなない |
| ～て form conjunctive | とって | よんで | よんで | はなして | いって | まって | かいて | およいで | しんで |
| ～た form plain past | とった | よんだ | よんだ | はなした | いった | まった | かいた | およいだ | しんだ |

## Group 1 continued

| | とり | よび | よみ | はなし | いい | まち | かき | およぎ | しに |
|---|---|---|---|---|---|---|---|---|---|
| pre ～ます form | とり | よび | よみ | はなし | いい | まち | かき | およぎ | しに |
| potential form | とれる | よべる | よめる | はなせる | いえる | まてる | かける | およげる | しねる |
| passive form | とられる | よばれる | よまれる | はなされる | いわれる | またれる | かかれる | およがれる | しなれる |
| volitional form | とろう | よぼう | よもう | はなそう | いおう | まとう | かこう | およごう | しのう |
| causative form | とらせる | よばせる | よませる | はなさせる | いわせる | またせる | かかせる | およがせる | しなせる |
| causative passive form | とらせられる | よばせられる | よませられる | はなさせられる | いわせられる | またせられる | かかせられる | およがせられる | しなせられる |
| conditional form (if) | とれば | よべば | よめば | はなせば | いえば | まてば | かけば | およげば | しねば |
| conditional form (when) | とったら | よんだら | よんだら | はなしたら | いったら | まったら | かいたら | およいだら | しんだら |
| imperative form | とれ | よべ | よめ | はなせ | いえ | まて | かけ | およげ | しね |

## Group 1 continued

there is one slight irregularity in group 1, the verb いく・行く to go

| meaning | dictionary form plain non-past | ～ない form plain negative | ～て form conjunctive | ～た form plain past | pre ～ます | potential form | causative form | passive form | causative passive form | volitional form | imperative form | conditional form (if) | conditional form (when)2 |
|---|---|---|---|---|---|---|---|---|---|---|---|---|---|
| to go | いく | いかない | いって | いった | いき | いける | いかせる | いかれる | いかせられる | いこう | いけ | いけば | いったら |

## Group 2

Form

note that group 2 verbs are the vast majority of those with a dictionary form ending in 'eru' = ～える、～げる、～せる、～てる、～ねる、～へる、～める、～れる、～いる、～きる、～しる、～ちる、～にる、～びる、～みる、～りる。

note that when a group 1 verb is conjugated into a passive, causative or potential and then has a form ending in 'eru' = ～える、～げる、～せる、～てる、～ねる、～へる、～める、～れる it becomes treated as a group 2 verb for any subsequent transformations. See はなせる below

## Group 2 continued

| meaning of example verb | to eat | to go out, to leave to answer the phone | to wear | to borrow |
|---|---|---|---|---|
| dictionary form plain non-past | たべる | でる | きる | かりる |
| ~ない plain negative | たべない | でない | きない | かりない |
| ~て conjunctive | たべて | でて | きて | かりて |
| た plain past | たべた | でた | きた | かりた |
| pre ~ます | たべ | で | き | かり |
| potential | たべられる | でられる | きられる | かりられる |
| passive | たべられる | でられる | きられる | かりられる |
| volitional | たべよう | でよう | きよう | かりよう |
| causative | たべさせる | でさせる | きさせる | かりさせる |
| causative passive | たべさせられる | でさせられる | きさせられる | かりさせられる |
| conditional (if) | たべれば | でれば | きれば | かりれば |
| conditional (when) | たべたら | でたら | きたら | かりたら |
| imperative | たべろ | でろ | きろ | かりろ |

Common group 1 verbs that end in 'iru' or 'eru'. NOTE that some of these have the same dictionary form as a group 2 verb with a different meaning i.e. きる・切る 'to cut' (group 1) and きる・着る 'to wear' (group 2) but the negative and some other forms will be different. i.e. きらない・切らない = not cut, きない・着ない = not wear

| verb | meaning |
|---|---|
| きる・切る | to cut |
| ける・蹴る | to kick |
| しる・知る | to know |
| かえる・帰る | to return, to go home |
| はいる・入る | to enter |
| はしる・走る | to run |
| へる・減る | to reduce, to decline |
| しゃべる・喋る | to chat |

An example of a group 1 verb that has a dictionary form ending in 'iru' きる・切る = to cut

| meaning | dictionary form plain non-past | ~ない form plain negative | ~て form conjunctive | ~た form plain past | pre ~ます | potential form | causative form | passive form | causative passive form | volitional form | imperative form | conditional form (if) | conditional form (when) |
|---|---|---|---|---|---|---|---|---|---|---|---|---|---|
| to cut | きる・切る | きら ない | きって | きった | きり | きれる | きら せる | きら れる | きら せられる | きろう | きれ | きれば | きったら |

## Group 3

| meaning | dictionary form plain non-past | ~ない form plain form plain negative | ~て form conjunctive | ~た form plain form plain past | pre ~ます | potential form | causative form | passive form | causative passive form | volitional form | imperative form | conditional form (if) | conditional form (when) |
|---|---|---|---|---|---|---|---|---|---|---|---|---|---|
| to do (see entry under する) | する | しない | して | した | し | できる | させる | される | させられる | しよう | し | すれば | したら |
| to come | くる | こない | きて | きた | き | こられる | こさせる | こられる | こさせられる | こよう | こい | くれば | きたら |

## The ~て form

### Group 1 Verbs

The ~て form of group 1 verbs is formed by removing the last kana of the dictionary form and adding the endings according to the chart below

| meaning of the example | to take | to call | to read | to speak | to say | to wait | to write | to swim | to die |
|---|---|---|---|---|---|---|---|---|---|
| dictionary form | とる | よぶ | よむ | はなす | いう | まつ | かく | およぐ | しぬ |
| verbs ending in | ~る | ~ぶ | ~む | ~す | ~う | ~つ | ~く | ~ぐ | ~ぬ |
| ending | ~って | ~んで | ~んで | ~して | ~って | ~って | ~いて | ~いで | ~んで |
| て form | とって | よんで | よんで | はなして | いって | まって | かいて | およいで | しんで |

## Group 2 Verbs

The ~て form of group 2 verbs is formed by removing the final ~る of the dictionary form and replacing it with ~て

| dictionary form | たべる・食べる | みせる・見せる | みる・見る | おきる・起きる |
|---|---|---|---|---|
| meaning of the example | to eat | to show | to see, to look | to get up |
| ~て form | たべて | みせて | みて | おきて |

## Group 3 verbs

the ~て form of する is して
the ~て form of くる is きて

The principal use of the ~て form is to add other elements such as the verb いる (to form the continuous 'be ...ing' or perfective), and くださいto show requests and verbs of giving and receiving to show benefit and obligation. There are also other structures involving this form of the verb.

See also the notes on   plain and polite forms,
                 respect
                 transitive and intransitive verbs
                 giving and receiving

# Transitive and Intransitive Verbs

Verbs that take a direct object (usually marked with with the particle を) are called transitive verbs or たどうし・他動詞 in Japanese. In the sentence 'I open the door' the door is on the receiving end of the action and is the direct object. This direct object is marked with the particle を

I open the door = わたしは ドアを あけます

Those verbs that do not take a direct object are called intransitive verbs or じどうし・自動詞 in Japanese and take the particle が

The door opens = ドアが あきます

Sometimes there are different forms of a Japanese verb for the same English headword, for example 'stop'.

In the sentence I stopped the car = わたしは くるまを とめました。・ 私は 車を 止めました。 the direct object (the car) is marked with the particle を. In this case the transitive version of the verb 'to stop' とめる・止める is used.

In the sentence 'the car stopped' くるまが とまりました・車が 止まりました there is no direct object and the intransitive version of the verb 'to stop' とまる・止まる is used. The word for 'car' is marked with the particle が.

In the English to Japanese section we have tried to show the difference between transitive and intransitive verbs in the wording of our translations or by giving examples. In the Japanese-English section of this dictionary the verb group (1,2 or 3) is followed by ㊪ to mark transitive verbs and ㊙ to mark intransitive verbs. If both uses are possible we have given both symbols.

It may be that in a particular situation or construction a transitive verb does not use particle を or that an intransitive verb does not use particle が. The marks are intended for general guidance. Where there are other particles commonly associated with a verb we have given them after the circled transitivity marker. It should be noted that the particle を is used to indicate the space through which an action passes as well as to mark direct objects and that in conversational Japanese particles are often 'dropped'. This means that the presence or absence of the particle を is not a wholly reliable guide to the transitivity of a verb.

There are many pairs of transitive and intransitive verbs which have different forms. Some of the most common pairs are shown in the table below. It may be that there are different English translations for the intransitive and transitive versions (such as 'turn on' and 'be on')

| meaning | transitive | intransitive |
|---|---|---|
| to open | あける・開ける | あく・開く |
| to close | しめる・閉める | しまる・閉まる |
| to stop | とめる・止める | とまる・止まる |
| attach, turn on, be on | つける・付ける | つく・付く |
| be off, turn off | けす・消す | きえる・消える |
| to begin | はじめる・始める | はじまる・始まる |
| to put in | いれる・入れる | はいる・入る |
| to repair | なおす・直す | なおる・直る |
| to change | かえる・変える・代える・換える | かわる・代わる・変わる・換わる |
| to continue | つづける・続ける | つづく・続く |
| to break | こわす・壊す | こわれる・壊れる |
| to wake | おこす・起こす | おきる・起きる |
| to lock | かける | かかる |
| to drop, to fall | おとす・落とす | おちる・落ちる |
| to put out, to go out | だす・出す | でる・出る |

# Adjectives

The notes that follow are designed to help learners to use this dictionary and thus reflect the way in which adjectives are most commonly taught.

There are two main types of adjectives in Japanese. These are usually referred to as い adjectives (which end with the hiragana for that sound) such as むずかしい・難しい 'difficult'

これは むずかしい テストです。 = this is a difficult test
この テストは むずかしいです。 = this test is difficult

and な adjectives such as しんせつ・親切 'kind'.

あの せんせいは しんせつです。 = that teacher is kind
かのじょは しんせつな ひとです。 = she is a kind person

As can be seen from the example above it is not necessarily the case that the hiragana な will appear. The use of な is for when the adjective appears immediately before a noun as in しんせつな ひと・親切な人 'kind person'. Note also that there are a few common な adjectives that end with い such as きれい 'pretty/clean', しつれい・失礼 'rude' and ゆうめい・有名 'famous'.

Many Japanese nouns can function like adjectives by taking the particle の, for example アメリカの 'American'. Some of these are given in this form in the dictionary and called adjectives. There are also many adjectives in English that become verbs in the present continuous form when translated into Japanese such as 'broken' こわれている・壊れている or 'fat' ふとっている・太っている.

A conjugation chart of い and な adjectives is given below. Only the い adjectives change their form. The only irregular adjective is いい which is given in a separate chart below although there is only one consistent change in the stem for all inflected forms. As only the final い of the い adjective changes the remainder is the 'stem' and we have referred to adjective 'stems' in some of the main entries.

In the chart the plain and polite styles are shown for comparison but note that these charts are for guidance only and not exhaustive. As the use of です and related forms is restricted to sentence endings it is shown in brackets. For discussion of plain and polite forms see the note on plain and polite style.

| type of adjective | い | い | な | な |
|---|---|---|---|---|
| meaning | big | old | quiet | beautiful, clean |
| plain style non-past | おおきい | ふるい | しずか(だ) | きれい(だ) |
| polite style non-past | おおきい (です) | ふるい(です) | しずか(です) | きれい(です) |
| plain style negative | おおきくない | ふるくない | しずかではない・しずかじゃない | きれいではない きれいじゃない |
| polite style negative | おおきくない (です) | ふるくない (です) | しずかではありません・しずかじゃありません | きれいではありません・きれいじゃありません |
| plain style past | おおきかった | ふるかった | しずかだった | きれいだった |
| polite style past | おおきかった (です) | ふるかった (です) | しずか (でした) | きれい (でした) |
| plain style negative past | おおきくなかった | ふるくなかった | しずかではなかった・しずかじゃなかった | きれいではなかった・きれいじゃなかった |
| polite style negative past | おおきくありませんでした・おおきくなかった(です) | ふるくありませんでした・ふるくなかった(です) | しずかではありませんでした・しずかじゃありませんでした | きれいではありませんでした・きれいじゃありませんでした |
| ～て form conjunctive | おおきくて | ふるくて | しずかで | きれいで |
| negative conjunctive | おおきくなくて | ふるくなくて | しずかでなくて・しずかじゃなくて | きれいでなくて・きれいじゃなくて |
| adverbial form | おおきく | ふるく | しずかに | きれいに |
| conditional | おおきければ | ふるければ | しずかなら(ば) | きれいなら(ば) |
| negative conditional | おおきくなければ | ふるくなければ | しずかじゃなければ | きれいじゃなければ |
| ～たら conditional | おおきかったら | ふるかったら | しずかだったら | きれいだったら |
| negative ～たら conditional | おおきくなかったら | ふるくなかったら | しずかじゃなかったら | きれいじゃなかったら |

the only irregular adjective いい, good

| meaning | good |
|---|---|
| plain style non-past | いい |
| polite style non-past | いい(です) |
| plain style negative | よくない |
| polite style negative | よくない(です) |
| plain style past | よかった |
| polite style past | よかった(です) |
| plain style negative past | よくなかった |
| polite style negative past | よくなかった(です) |
| 〜て conjunctive | よくて |
| negative conjunctive | よくなくて |
| adverbial | よく |
| conditional | よければ |
| negative conditional | よくなければ |
| 〜たら conditional | よかったら |
| negative 〜たら conditional | よくなかったら |

# Coming and Going

Japanese use 'come' and 'go' from the viewpoint of the speaker. This means that sometimes translations between English and Japanese will use 'come' for 'go' and vice versa. Movement from the speaker's current position to another place will be described using いく・行く. Movement to the speaker's current position from another place will be described using くる・来る.

> I'll come (to your house) tomorrow = あした いきます。・明日行きます。
> I'll come (to your house) tomorrow = あした きます。・明日来ます。

In the first sentence the speaker is not in your house at the moment. In the second sentence the speaker is in your house.

Note that there are several possible words for 'come' and 'go' depending on the degree of politeness or relative status of individuals. These are listed in the note on respect language.

Verbs with the meaning 'come' and 'go' can be attached to the 〜て form of another verb to indicate the direction of an action or the subject of the action's movement.

| | |
|---|---|
| しんぶんを かってきます。・<br>新聞を買ってきます。 | = I will go and buy a newspaper<br>(and come back) |
| てがみを だして行きます。・<br>手紙を出していきます。 | = I will go and post the letter<br>(and then go somewhere else) |
| じんこうが ふえていきます。・<br>人口が増えていきます。 | = the population will increase<br>(over a period of time) |
| もうしこみが へってきました。・<br>申込が減ってきました。 | = applications have decreased<br>(over a period of time) |

Compare the following two sentences

| | |
|---|---|
| かえります・帰ります | = go home |
| かえってきます・帰ってきます | = return to the place where you are now |

# Particles

Japanese grammar features parts of speech called particles or postpositions in English and じょし・助詞 in Japanese.

These are placed after elements in a sentence to show the grammatical relationships and can be thought of as similar in function to English prepositions such as 'to', 'at', 'from' and 'by' etc.

There is also a group of particles which come at the end of sentences and which give an element of emphasis or emotional tone and distinguish male and female speech.

The functions of particles are such that it is not always possible to give a translation under the headword although we have tried to assist with possible equivalents.

Note that in conversation sometimes particles are left out and must be inferred.

Only the main uses of some of the most common particles are listed here.

| | |
|---|---|
| は | Indicates the topic of a sentence. Can sometimes be translated as "as for" |
| も | Indicates emphasis or addition. Can sometimes be translated by "too" or "also" |
| の | Indicates possession or a sense of belonging. Sometimes can be translated 'of', 'belonging to' or 'about' <br> Can make nouns into adjectives. |
| を | Indicates the direct object of a verb. |
| が | Indicates the grammatical subject of a sentence or clause. |
| に | Indicates the time or date of an action. <br> Indicates the person on the receiving end of an action. <br> Indicates the recipient with verbs meaning 'give' and giver with verbs meaning 'receive' <br> Indicates the location of someone or something. <br> Indicates the destination of a verb of motion. |
| へ | Indicates the direction or destination of travel. |
| で | Indicates the tool, language or mode of transport used to complete an action. <br> Indicates the location of an action. |
| と | Indicates the person with whom an action is completed. Often translated as "with". <br> Joins nouns in a finite list. |
| や | Joins nouns in a list which is incomplete. |
| から | Indicates the time or place where an action starts. Often translated as "from". |

| まで | Indicates the time or place where an action finishes. Often translated as "until". |
|------|------|
| までに | Indicates the time by which an action must be completed. Often translated as "by". |
| か | When added to the end of a statement it makes it into a question. |
| より | Indicates the starting point for a comparison. Often translated as "than". |
| ね | When added to the end of a statement it forms a tag question. |
| よ | Added to the end of a statement for emphasis. |

# Aa

**a, an** *determiner*

> ! *Not used in Japanese.*

**able** *adjective*
  to be able to... = use the potential
    form of the verb or the dictionary
    form of the verb + ことが できる
    ▶ 191
  to be able to swim = および げる・
    泳げる
  I am able to read hiragana = ひらが
    なを よむことが できます。・ ひ
    らがなを 読む ことが できます。

**about**

> ! *Often* about *occurs in
> combinations with verbs, for
> example:* bring about, run about *etc.
> To find the correct translations for
> this type of verb, look up the
> separate dictionary entries at* bring,
> run *etc.*

**1** *preposition* = ～について(の)
  it's a book about Japan = にほんに
    ついての ほんです。・ 日本に つ
    いての 本です。
  I want some information about this
    town = この まちに ついて、
    じょうほうが ほしいです。・
    この 町に ついて、 情報が ほし
    いです。
**2** *adverb*
  = ～ぐらい
  I have about 2000 yen left = にせんえ
    んぐらい のこっています。・
    二千円ぐらい 残っています。
  Kyoto is about 40km from here = きょ
    うとは、 ここから よんじゅっキ
    ロぐらいです。・ 京都は、 ここ
    から 四十キロぐらいです。
**3** *adverb*
  = ～ごろ
  (*approximate times*)
  We arrived at about 9 o'clock = くじ
    ごろ、 つきました。・ 九時頃、
    着きました。
**4** to be about to
  = ～ところ *use verb in dictionary
    form* + ところ ▶ 191

I was about to go out = でかける と
  ころでした。・ 出かける ところ
  でした。

**above**
**1** *preposition*
  = ～の うえ・ ～の 上
  their apartment is above the shop =
    かれらの アパートは みせの
    うえです。・ 彼らの アパートは
    店の 上です。
  there is a shelf above the door = ドア
    の うえに たなが あります。・
    ドアの 上に 棚が あります。
**2** above all = まず だいいちに・
  まず 第一に

**abroad** *adverb*
  = がいこく・ 外国
  *noun*
  to go abroad = がいこくに いく・
    外国に 行く

**absent** *adjective*
  = けっせき・ 欠席
  to be absent = けっせきする・ 欠席
    する

**accent** *noun*
  (*way of speaking*)
  = なまり
  (*stressed part*)
  = アクセント

**accept** *verb*
  (*a gift, invitation*)
  = うけとる・ 受け取る

**accident** *noun*
• (*causing injury or damage*)
  = じこ・ 事故
  car accident = こうつうじこ・ 交通
    事故
• (*by chance*) I heard about it by accident
  = ぐうぜん それを ききました。・
    偶然 それを 聞きました。

**accommodation** *noun*
  to look for accommodation = とまる
    ところを さがす・ 泊まる 所を
    探す

**accompany** *verb*
  to accompany someone = だれかと
    いっしょに いく・ 誰かと 一緒
    に 行く

**account** noun
- (in a bank or post office)
= こうざ・口座
there's money in my bank account =
ぎんこうこうざに おかねが
あります。・ 銀行口座にお金が
あります。

**accountant** noun
= かいけいし・会計士

**accuse** verb
(legal term)
= うったえる・訴える
to be accused of cheating = カンニン
グしたと いわれる・カンニン
グしたと 言われる

**across** preposition
- to go across the street = みちを わた
る・道を渡る
to go across a bridge = はしを わた
る・橋を渡る
a journey across the desert = さば
くを おうだんする たび・砂漠
を 横断する 旅
- (on the other side of) = 〜の むこうが
わに〜・〜の 向こう側に〜
he lives across the street = かれは
みちの むこうがわに すんでい
ます。・彼は 道の 向こう側に
住んでいます。

**act** verb
- (to do something) = こうどうする・
行動する
- (to play a role) = えんじる・演じる

**activity** noun
= かつどう・活動
sports activities = スポーツかつど
う・スポーツ活動

**actor** noun
= はいゆう・俳優

**actress** noun
= じょゆう・女優

**actually** adverb
actually, he's a very good tennis player
= じつは、かれは とてもじょう
ずな テニスプレーヤーです。・
実は、彼は とても 上手な テニ
スプレーヤーです。
what actually happened? = じっさ
い、なにが ありましたか。・
実際、何が ありましたか。

**adapt** verb
(to become used to) = なれる・慣れ
る

I have adapted to life in Japan = にほ
んの せいかつに なれました。・
日本の 生活に 慣れました。

**add** verb
- (to put in) = くわえる・加える
- (in arithmetic) = たす・足す

**address** noun
= じゅうしょ・住所

> ! Note that Japanese addresses do
> not usually include street names
> and are given in reverse order

**admit** verb
= みとめる・認める
I admitted that I'd stolen the money =
おかねを ぬすんだ ことを みと
めました。・お金を 盗んだ こと
を 認めました。
- to be admitted to (the) hospital = にゅ
ういんする・入院する

**adolescent** noun
= ティーンエージャー

**adopt** verb
(a child) = ようしに する・養子に
する

**adult** noun
= おとな・大人

> ! Irregular kanji reading

**advantage** noun
- (a positive point)
= りてん・利点
- to take advantage of a someone =
だれかを りようする・誰かを
利用する
to take advantage of an opportunity =
チャンスを つかむ

**adventure** noun
= ぼうけん・冒険

**advertisement** noun
= こうこく・広告
job advertisements = きゅうじん・
求人

**advertising** noun
= こうこくぎょう・広告業

**advice** noun
= アドバイス

**advise** verb to politely offer advice in
Japanese you can use the 〜た form
of the verb + ほうがいい ▶ 191

I've been advised not to go there =
あそこに いかない ほうが いい
と、いわれました。・ あそこに
行かない 方が いいと、言われ
ました。

**aerial** *noun*
= アンテナ

**aerobics** *noun*
= エアロビクス

**affect** *verb*
= えいきょうをあたえる・影響を
与える
the war will affect tourism = せんそう
は かんこうぎょうに えいきょ
うを あたえます。・ 戦争は 観光
業に 影響を 与えます。

**afford** *verb*
to be able to afford a car = くるまを
かう よゆうが ある・車を 買う
余裕が ある

**afraid** *adjective*
to be afraid = こわがる・怖がる
to be afraid of insects = むしを こわ
がる・虫を 怖がる
to be afraid to go out = そとに でる
ことを こわがる・外に 出る
ことを 怖がる

**Africa** *noun* ▶ **172**
= アフリカ

**after**
**1** *preposition*
= あと・後
we'll leave after breakfast = あさごは
んの あとに、しゅっぱつします。
・ 朝ご飯の 後に、出発します。
the day after tomorrow = あさって
**2** *conjunction*
after we had eaten, we went for a walk
= たべた あと、さんぽを しまし
た。・ 食べた 後、散歩を しまし
た。
I went in after the film had started =
えいがが はじまってから はい
りました。・ 映画が 始まってか
ら 入りました。
**3 after all** = さいごに・ 最後に

**afternoon** *noun* ▶ **186**
= ごご・午後

**afterwards, afterward**
(US English) *adverb*
• (*after*) = その あと・ その 後
• (*later*) = あとで・ 後で

**again** *adverb*
= また
are you going camping again this year?
= ことし、また キャンプを しま
すか。・ 今年、また キャンプを
しますか。

**against** *preposition*
= はんたい・反対
I'm against animal experimentation =
どうぶつじっけんに はんたいで
す。・ 動物実験に 反対です。

**age** *noun* ▶ **171**
= とし・年
he's my age = かれは わたしと おな
じ とします。・ 彼は 私と 同じ
年です。

**aged** *adjective*
= ～さい・～才
a boy aged 13 = じゅうさんさいの
おとこの こ・ 十三才の 男の子

**ago** *adverb*
= まえ・前
two weeks ago = にしゅうかん まえ
・ 二週間 前
long ago = むかし・昔

**agree** *verb*
• (*to have the same opinion*) = さんせい
する・賛成する
I don't agree with you = あなたに
さんせいしません。・ あなたに
賛成しません。
• (*to reach a decision*) = けつろんに
なる・結論に なる

**agriculture** *noun*
= のうぎょう・農業

**ahead** *adverb*
to go on ahead = さきに いく・先
に 行く

**Aids** *noun*
= エイズ

**aim**
**1** *noun*
= もくてき・目的
**2** *verb*
aimed at = むき・向き
a magazine aimed at young women =
わかい じょせい むきの ざっし
・ 若い 女性 向きの 雑誌

**air** *noun*
= くうき・空気
to let the air out of a rubber ring =
うきぶくろの くうきを ぬく・
浮袋の 空気を 抜く

**air force** *noun*
= くうぐん・空軍

**airmail** *noun*
= こうくうびん・航空便
to send a letter by airmail = こうくう
びんで てがみを おくる・航空
便で 手紙を 送る

**airport** *noun*
= くうこう・空港

**alarm clock** *noun*
= めざましどけい・目覚し時計

**alcohol** *noun*
= アルコール

**alive** *adjective*
= いきている・生きている

**all**
**1** *determiner*
(*for things*) = ぜんぶの・全部の
(*for people*) = みんな(の)・皆(の)
all the people have left = みんなが か
えりました。・皆が 帰りました。
I worked all day = いちにちじゅう
はたらきました。・一日中 働き
ました。
**2** *pronoun*
= ぜんぶ・全部
that's all = それで ぜんぶです。・
それで 全部です。
**3** *adverb*
all alone = ひとりぼっち・一人ぼ
っち

**allow** *verb*
smoking is not allowed here = ここは
きんえんです。・ここは 禁煙で
す。

**all right** *adjective*
• (*when giving your opinion*) = まあま
あ*
the film was all right = えいがは まあ
まあでした。・映画は まあまあ
でした。*
• (*when talking about health*)
are you all right? = だいじょうぶで
すか。・大丈夫ですか。
• (*when asking someone's permission*)
is it all right if I do it later? = あとで し
ても いいですか。・後でしても
いいですか。

come at about nine, all right? = くじ
ごろ きてくださいね。・九時頃
来てくださいね。
• (*when agreeing*) = いいです。

**almond** *noun*
= アーモンド

**almost** *adverb*
= ほとんど
almost everyone was Japanese =
ほとんどが にほんじんでした。
・ほとんどが 日本人でした。
I ate almost all the cake = ケーキを
ほとんど たべました。・ケーキ
を ほとんど 食べました。
There is almost no opportunity to speak
Japanese = にほんごを はなす
きかいがほとんど ありません。
・日本語を話す機会がほとんど
ありません。

**alone**
**1** *adjective*
= ひとり・一人、独り
I went alone = ひとりで いきました。
・一人で 行きました。
to be all alone = ひとりで いる・
一人で いる
leave me alone! = ほっておいてくれ
**2** *adverb*
to work alone = ひとりで はたらく
・一人で 働く
to live alone = ひとりで くらす・
一人で 暮らす
to travel alone = ひとりで りょこう
する・一人で 旅行する

**along** *preposition*
there are cherry trees blooming all
along the river = かわに そって、
さくらが さいています。・川に
沿って、桜が 咲いています。

**aloud** *adverb*
to read aloud = こえを だして よむ
・声を 出して 読む

**already** *adverb*
= もう
it's ten o'clock already = もう じゅう
じです。・もう 十時です。
have you finished already? = もう お
わりましたか。・もう 終わりま
したか。

**also** *adverb*
= Use particle も
I'm also studying Japanese = わたし
も にほんごを べんきょうして

---

います。・ 私も日本語を 勉強し
ています。▶205

**although** *conjunction*
= けれども
although Gillian's not Japanese, she
speaks Japanese very well = ジリ
アンさんは にほんじんではあり
ません。けれども にほんごが
よく はなせます。・ ジリアンさ
んは 日本人ではありません。け
れども 日本語が よく 話せます。

> ! Note word order is different to
> English. ▶ but

**always** *adverb*
= いつも
he always wears black clothes = かれ
は いつも くろい ふくを きてい
る。・ 彼は いつも 黒い 服を
着ている。

**amazed** *adjective*
= びっくりしている

**amazing** *adjective*
= すばらしい

**ambition** *noun*
= もくひょう・ 目標

**ambitious** *adjective*
= やしんてき(な)・ 野心的(な)

**ambulance** *noun*
= きゅうきゅうしゃ・ 救急車

**America** *noun* ▶ 172
= アメリカ

**American** ▶ 172
**1** *adjective*
= アメリカの
**2** *noun*
American person = アメリカじん・
アメリカ人

**amount**
**1** *noun*
(*quantity*)
= りょう・ 量
amount of water = みずの りょう。・
水の 量。
(*of money*)
how much is the total amount? = ごう
けいで いくらですか。・ 合計で
いくらですか。

**amusement arcade** *noun*
= ゲームセンター

**amusement park** *noun*
= ゆうえんち・ 遊園地

**an** ▶ **a**

**ancestor** *noun*
= そせん・ 祖先

**and** *conjunction*
• (*when connecting a finite list of nouns*)
= use particle と
there is a pen and a pencil on the desk
= つくえの うえに、えんぴつと
ペンが あります。・ 机の 上に、
鉛筆と ペンが あります。*
• (*when connecting an incomplete list
of nouns*) = use particle や
in the box there are photos and cards,
etc. = はこの なかに、しゃしん
や カードが あります。・ 箱の
中に、写真や カードが ありま
す。
• (*to join a series of actions*) = そして
I ate and then I watched TV = たべま
した。そして テレビを みまし
た。・ 食べました。そして テレ
ビを 見ました。▶ 205

**anger** *noun*
= いかり・ 怒り

**angry** *adjective*
to get angry = おこる・ 怒る
to be angry with someone = だれかに
おこっている・ 誰かに 怒って
いる

**animal** *noun*
= どうぶつ・ 動物

**ankle** *noun*
= あしくび・ 足首

**announcement** *noun*
= はっぴょう・ 発表

**annoy** *verb*
= いらいらさせる

**annoyed** *adjective*
to be annoyed with someone = だれ
かに おこっている・ 誰かに 怒
っている

**another**
**1** *determiner*
• another = もうひとつ・ もう一つ
another cup of coffee? = コーヒー、
もう いっぱい。・ コーヒー、
もう 一杯。
I'll buy another ticket = きっぷを
もう いちまいかいます。・ 切符
を もう 一枚 買います。
• (*different*) = ほかの・ 他の

there's another way of doing it = ほか
の やりかたが あります。・ 他の
やり方が あります。
another person
(one more) = もうひとり・もう一人
(different) = ちがうひと・違う人
**2** pronoun
would you like another? = もう ひと
つ どうですか。・ もう 一つ ど
うですか。

## answer

**1** noun
(to a question) = こたえ・答え、
かいとう・解答
what is the answer? = こたえは なん
ですか。・ 答えは 何ですか。
(to a letter) = へんじ・返事
there was no answer
(at the door) = だれも いませんでし
た。・ 誰も いませんでした。
(on the phone) = だれも でんわに で
ませんでした。・ 誰も 電話に 出
ませんでした。
**2** verb
to answer a question = しつもんに
こたえる・質問に 答える
to answer the phone = でんわに でる
・電話に 出る
answer back = くちごたえを する
・口答えを する

## answering machine noun
= るすばんでんわ・留守番電話

## ant noun
= あり

## antique noun
(Western) = アンティーク
(Japanese) = こっとうひん・骨董
品

## antique shop noun
(Western) = アンティークショップ
(Japanese) = こっとうや・骨董屋

## anxious adjective
= しんぱいしている・心配してい
る
then I started to get anxious = そして
しんぱいに なりました。・ そし
て 心配に なりました。

## any

**1** determiner
• (in questions)
is there any tea? = こうちゃが あり
ますか。・ 紅茶が ありますか。

is there any juice left? = ジュースは
のこっていますか。・ ジュース
は 残っていますか。
have you got any money? = おかねを
もっていますか。・ お金を 持っ
ていますか。
• (with the negative)
we don't have any bread = パンはあ
りません。
I didn't have any friends = ともだち
は いませんでした。・ 友達は い
ませんでした。
• (whatever)
choose any book you like = すきな
ほんを えらんでください。・
好きな 本を 選んでください。
**2** pronoun

> **!** Note that any is not translated in
> Japanese.

## anyone pronoun (also anybody)
• (in questions) = だれか・誰か
is there anyone there? = だれか いま
すか。・ 誰か いますか。
• (with the negative) = だれも・誰も
there isn't anyone in the house = うち
に だれも いません。・ 家に
誰も いません
• (everyone) = だれでも・誰でも
anyone could do it = だれでも でき
る。・ 誰でも できる。

## anything pronoun
• (in questions) = なにか・何か
do you need anything? = なにか いり
ますか。・ 何か いりますか。
• (with the negative) = なにも・何も
I didn't say anything = なにも いいま
せんでした。・ 何も 言いません
でした。
there isn't anything to do here = ここ
には、する ことが ありません。
• (everything) = なんでも・何でも
I like anything to do with sports = スポ
ーツなら なんでも すきです。・
スポーツなら 何でも 好きです。

## anyway adverb
it might be difficult but let's try anyway
= むずかしいかもしれませんが、
とにかく やって みましょう。・
難しいかもしれませんが、とに
かく やってみましょう。

## anywhere adverb
• (in questions) = どこか

did you go anywhere interesting in the summer holidays? = なつやすみ に、どこか おもしろい ところ へ いきましたか。・夏休みに、 どこか おもしろい 所へ 行きま したか。

• (with the negative) = どこも
I'm not going anywhere tomorrow = あした どこも いきません。・ 明日 どこも 行きません。

• (any place) = どこでも
we have time so we can go anywhere you like = じかんが あります から、すきな ところ どこでも いけますよ。・時間が あります から、好きな所 どこでも 行け ますよ。

**apart**
**1** adjective
= はなれている・離れている
I don't want to be apart from the children = こどもたちとはなれた くないです。・子供達と 離れた くないです。
**2 apart from** = ～の ほかに～・～の 外に～、～の 他に～

**apartment** noun
= アパート

**apartment block** noun
= アパート

**apologize** verb
= あやまる・謝る
I apologised to the teacher = せんせ いに あやまりました。・先生に 謝りました。

**appear** verb
• (to seem)
she appears to be happy = かのじょ は しあわせみたいです。・彼女 は 幸せみたいです。
• (to come into view) = あらわれる・ 現れる

**appetite** noun
= しょくよく・食欲
to have a good appetite = よく たべる ・よく 食べる

**apple** noun
= りんご

**apple juice** noun
= りんごジュース

**appliance** noun
electrical appliance(s) = でんきせい ひん・電気製品

**application** noun
application form(s) = もうしこみし ょ・申込書

**apply** verb
to apply for a job = しごとに おうぼ する・仕事に 応募する
to apply for a passport = パスポート を もうしこむ・パスポートを 申し込む

**appointment** noun
= よやく・予約
to make an appointment with the dentist = はいしゃに よやくを いれる・ 歯医者に 予約を 入れる

**appreciate** verb
I appreciate your help = てつだって くれて ありがとう。・手伝って くれて ありがとう。

**approach** verb
(a place or time) = ちかづく・近づく
(a person) = アプローチする

**approve** verb
= しょうにんする・承認する
The boss approved my plan = かちょ うが わたしの あんを しょうに んしました。・課長が 私の案を 承認しました。

**apricot** noun
= あんず

**April** noun ▶ 174
= しがつ・四月

**Aquarius** noun
= みずがめざ・水瓶座

**architect** noun
= けんちくか・建築家

**area** noun
(of a country) = ちほう・地方
(of a city) = ちく・地区
the area around here = このへん

**area code** noun (US English) = しが いきょくばん・市外局番

**argue** verb
• (to quarrel) = くちげんかを する・ 口げんかをする
to argue about money = おかねの こ とで、くちげんかを する・お 金の ことで、口げんかを する

- (*to discuss a subject*) = ぎろんする ・ 議論する
  to argue about politics = せいじの ことを ぎろんする ・ 政治の ことを 議論する

**argument** *noun*
(*quarrel*) = くちげんか ・ 口げんか
I had an argument with my mother = ははと くちげんかを しました。 ・ 母と 口げんかを しました。
(*debate*) = ぎろん ・ 議論

**Aries** *noun*
= おひつじざ ・ 牡羊座

**arm** *noun*
= うで ・ 腕
my arm hurts = うでが いたいです。 ・ 腕が 痛いです。

**armchair** *noun*
= ソファ

**armed** *adjective*
= ぶそうした ・ 武装した

**arms** *noun*
= ぶき ・ 武器

**army** *noun*
= りくぐん ・ 陸軍、ぐんたい ・ 軍隊
to join the army = りくぐんに にゅうたいする ・ 陸軍に 入隊する

**around**

> ! Often around *occurs in combinations with verbs, for example:* run around, turn around *etc. To find the correct translations for this type of verb, look up the separate dictionary entries at* run, turn *etc.*

**1** *preposition*
there are trees all around the garden = にわの まわりにきが あります。 ・ 庭の 周りに 木が あります。
at the party the people around me were speaking Japanese = パーティーで、まわりの ひとは にほんごを はなしていました。 ・ パーティーで、周りの 人は 日本語を 話していました。
to go around the world = せかいいっしゅうりょこうをする ・ 世界一周旅行をする

**2** *adverb*
it is around 2000 yen = にせんえんぐらいです。 ・ 二千円ぐらいです。

I'll arrive there at around one o'clock = いちじごろ、そこに つきます。 ・ 一時頃、そこに 着きます。

**arrange** *verb*
to arrange a trip to Kyoto = きょうと りょこうの じゅんびを する ・ 京都旅行の 準備を する
to arrange to have lunch together = いっしょに ひるごはんを たべる やくそくを する ・ 一緒に 昼ご飯を 食べる 約束を する

**arrest** *verb*
= たいほする ・ 逮捕する

**arrive** *verb*
= つく ・ 着く
I arrived at the station at noon = じゅうにじに えきに つきました。 ・ 十二時に 駅に 着きました。

**arrow** *noun*
- (*weapon*) = や ・ 矢
- (*symbol*) = やじるし ・ 矢印

**art** *noun*
- = びじゅつ ・ 美術

**art gallery** *noun*
= びじゅつかん ・ 美術館

**artificial** *adjective*
= じんこうの ・ 人工の

**artist** *noun*
= げいじゅつか ・ 芸術家

**arts and crafts** *noun*
arts and crafts = びじゅつと こうげい ・ 美術と 工芸

**as**
**1** *conjunction*
- = ～ように
  as you know, I used to live in Japan = しっている ように、にほんに すんでいました。 ・ 知っている ように、日本に 住んでいました。
- (*at the time when*) = ～とき
  the phone rang as I was getting out of the bath = おふろから あがっている ときに、でんわが なりました。 ・ お風呂から あがっている ときに、電話が 鳴りました。
  I used to live there as a child = こどもの とき、そこに すんでいました。 ・ 子供の とき、そこに 住んでいました。
- (*British English*)

(*because, since*) = から

as they were out, I left a message = るすでしたから、でんごんを のこして おきました。・ 留守でしたから、伝言を 残して おきました。

• (*when used with* the same)
mine is the same as yours = わたしの は あなたのと おなじです。・ 私のは あなたのと 同じです。

**2** *preposition*

I went to Japan as an English teacher = えいごの せんせいとして、にほんに いきました。・ 英語の 先生と して、日本に 行きました。

I was dressed as Santa = サンタの かっこうを しました。・ サンタの 格好を しました。

**3** *adverb*

as white as snow = ゆきの ようにしろい・ 雪の ように 白い

go there as fast as you can = できるだけ はやく いってください。・ できるだけ 速く 行ってください。

I have as much money as him = かれと おなじくらい おかねが あります。・ 彼と同じくらい お金が あります。

**4 as usual** = いつも どおりに・ いつも 通りに

**ashamed** *adjective*
= はずかしい・ 恥ずかしい

**ashes** *noun*
= はい・ 灰

**ashtray** *noun*
= はいざら・ 灰皿

**Asia** *noun* ▶ 172
= アジア

**Asian** *adjective* ▶ 172
= アジアの
**2** *noun*
Asian person = アジアじん・ アジア人

**ask** *verb*
• (*for information*) = きく・ 聞く
he asked me my name = かれは わたしの なまえを ききました。・ 彼は 私の 名前を 聞きました。
(*to ask someone a favour*) = たのむ・ 頼む

to ask someone to do the shopping = だれかに かいものを たのむ・ 誰かに 買い物を 頼む

I'll ask them if they are going to come = かれらが くるか どうか ききます。・ 彼らが 来るか どうか 聞きます。

I asked my parents for money = りょうしんに、おかねが ほしいと たのみました。・ 両親に、お金が 欲しいと 頼みました。

to ask to speak to someone = だれかに おねがいする・ 誰かに お願いする

to ask a question = しつもんを する・ 質問を する

• (*to invite to your own place*) = しょうたいする・ 招待する
(*somewhere else*) = さそう・ 誘う

to ask some friends to your party = ともだちを パーティーに しょうたいする・友達を パーティーに 招待する

he asked her out = かれは かのじょを デートにさそいました。・ 彼は 彼女をデートに 誘いました。

**asleep** *adjective*
to be asleep = ねむっている・ 眠っている
to fall asleep = ねむる・ 眠る

**assemble** *verb*
(*parts of a model, etc*) = くみたてる・ 組み立てる
(*people gathering*) = あつまる・ 集まる

**assignment** *noun*
school assignment = しゅくだい・ 宿題

**assistant** *noun*
= アシスタント

**asylum-seeker** *noun*
= ぼうめい きぼうしゃ・ 亡命 希望者

**at** *preposition*

> **!** *There are many verbs which involve the use of* at, *like* look at, laugh at, point at *etc. For translations, look up the entries at* look, laugh, point *etc.*

• (*when talking about a position or place of action*) = で

we met at a concert = コンサートで
あいました。・コンサートで 会
いました。

I saw her at the cinema = えいがかん
で かのじょを みました。・映画
館で 彼女を 見ました。

*(when talking about a position or place
of existence)* = に

she's at home = かのじょは いえに
います。・彼女は 家に います。

he's not at his desk = いま、かれは
せきを はずしております。・今、
彼は 席を 外しております。

- *(when talking about time)* = に

the film starts at nine o'clock = えいが
は くじに はじまります。・映画
は 九時に 始まります。

- *(when talking about age)* = 〜とき・
〜時

I was able to read at four (years old) =
よんさいの とき、ほんを よむ
ことが できました。・四才の
とき、本を 読む ことが できま
した。

**athlete** *noun*
= スポーツせんしゅ・スポーツ選
手

**athletics** *noun*
*(in Britain)* = りくじょうきょうぎ・
陸上競技
*(in the US)* = うんどうきょうぎ・
運動競技

**Atlantic** *noun*
the Atlantic Ocean = たいせいよう・
大西洋

**atmosphere** *noun*
- *(the air)*
= くうき・空気
- *(a mood, a feeling)*
= ふんいき・雰囲気

**attach** *verb*
= つける・付ける
to be attached to the wall = かべに
はって ある・壁に 貼って ある

**attachment** *noun*
= てんぷ・添付

**attack** *verb*
to attack a town = まちを こうげき
する・町を 攻撃する
to attack someone in the street = だれ
かに おそいかかる・誰かに
襲いかかる

**attempt**
**1** *verb*
= Use 〜て form of verb + みる
▶ **197**
**2** *noun*
= ちょうせん・挑戦

**attend** *verb*
to attend the village school = むらの
がっこうに かよう・村の 学校
に 通う
to attend a lecture = こうぎに しゅ
っせきする・講義に 出席する

**attention** *noun*
to pay attention to the teacher = せん
せいの いうことを きく・先生
の 言う ことを 聞く

**attic** *noun*
= やねうら・屋根裏

**attitude** *noun*
= たいど・態度
he has a bad attitude = かれは たい
どが わるいです。・彼は 態度が
悪いです。

**attract** *verb*
= ひきつける・引き付ける

**attractive** *adjective*
= すてき(な)・素敵(な)

**audience** *noun*
= かんきゃく・観客

**August** *noun* ▶ **174**
= はちがつ・八月

**aunt** *noun* ▶ **177**
*(one's own)*
= おば・叔母、伯母
*(someone else's)*
= おばさん

**au pair** *noun*
= オーペア

**Australia** *noun* ▶ **172** = オーストラ
リア

**Australian** ▶ **172**
**1** *adjective*
= オーストラリアの
**2** *noun*
Australian people = オーストラリア
じん・オーストラリア人

**author** *noun*
= さっか・作家

**automatic** *adjective*
= じどうの・自動の

**autumn** *noun*
= あき・秋
in (the) autumn = あきに・秋に

**available** *adjective*
- (*on sale*)
  tickets for the concert are still available
  = コンサートの チケットは まだ
  あります。
- (*free*) = あいている・空いている
  are you available on Thursday? = も
  くようびは あいていますか。・
  木曜日は 空いていますか。

**average** *adjective*
= へいきんの・平均の
the average teenager = ふつうの
ティーンエージャー・普通の
ティーンエージャー

**avoid** *verb*
- (*to prevent*)
  to avoid spending money = おかねを
  つかわない ようにする・お金を
  使わない ようにする
- (*to stay away from*) = さける・避ける

**awake** *adjective*
to be awake
(*having slept*) = めが さめている・
目が 覚めている
to stay awake = おきたままでいる・
起きたままでいる
the neighbours kept me awake = とな
りの ひとの せいで、ねむれま
せんでした。・隣の 人の せい
で、眠れませんでした。

**award** *noun*
= しょう・賞
she got the award for best actress =
かのじょは、さいゆうしゅうじ
ょゆうしょうを じゅしょうしま
した。・彼女は、最優秀女優賞
を 受賞しました。

**aware** *adjective*
to be aware of the danger = きけんだ
と わかっている・危険だと 分
かっている

**away** *adverb*
- (*absent*)
  to be away = けっせきする・欠席
  する
  she's away on business = かのじょ
  は しゅっちょうしています。・
  彼女は 出張しています。
- (*when talking about distances*)

to be far away = とおくに いる・
遠くに いる
Osaka is 40 km away = おおさかは
ここから よんじゅっキロです。
・大阪は ここから 四十キロで
す。

**awful** *adjective*
- (*no good*) = ひどい
  the film was awful = あの えいがは
  ひどかったです。・あの 映画は
  ひどかったです。
- (*causing shock*) = すさまじい
- I feel awful = きもちが わるいです。
  ・気持ちが 悪いです。

**awkward** *adjective*
(*describing a situation, a problem*) =
pre ます*form* + にくい ▶ 191
I feel awkward about telling him =
かれには いいにくいです。・
彼には 言いにくいです。

**axe, ax** (*US English*) *noun*
= おの

# **B**b

**baby** *noun*
= あかちゃん・赤ちゃん
**babysit** *verb*
= ベビーシッターを する
**back**

> ! Often back occurs in combinations
> with verbs, for example: come back,
> get back, give back etc. To find the
> correct translations for this type of
> verb, look up the separate
> dictionary entries at come, get, give
> etc.

**1** *noun*
- (*part of the body*)
  = せなか・背中
  my back hurts = こしが いたいです。
  ・腰が 痛いです。
- (*behind*)
  = うしろ・後ろ
  to sit in the back of the car = くるま
  の うしろに すわる・車の 後ろ
  に 座る

• (*rear of*) = うら・裏
at the back of the supermarket = スーパーの うら・スーパーの 裏

**2** *adverb*
• to be back = もどっている・戻っている
I'll be back tomorrow = あした もどります。・明日 戻ります。
• (*before in time*)
back in 1995 = せんきゅうひゃくきゅうじゅうごねんに・千九百九十五年に

**back door** *noun*
= うしろの ドア・後ろの ドア

**background** *noun*
• (*upbringing*)
= そだち・育ち
• (*career history*)
= けいれき・経歴
• (*of a picture*)
= はいけい・背景
in the background = はいけいに・背景に

**backpack** *noun*
= リュックサック

**back seat** *noun*
= こうぶざせき・後部座席

**back to front** *adverb*
= うしろまえに・後ろ前に
to put a sweater on back to front = セーターを うしろまえに きる・セーターを 後ろ前に 着る

**backwards, backward**
(*US English*) *adverb*
= うしろに・後ろに

**bacon** *noun*
= ベーコン

**bad** *adjective*

> ! Note that the Japanese prefer to refer to things as "not good" よくない rather than "bad"

= わるい・悪い
a bad person = わるい ひと・悪い人
a bad idea = まちがい・間違い
it was a bad idea to come here = ここに きたのは まちがいでした。・ここに 来たのは 間違いでした。
I have some bad news = あまり いい はなし じゃない ですが…。・あまりいい話 じゃないですが…。

I'm bad at maths = すうがくが にがてです。・数学が 苦手です。
'was the film good?'—'not bad' = 「えいがは よかったですか。」「まあまあ でした。」「映画は 良かったですか。」「まあまあ でした。」
smoking is bad for you = たばこは からだに よくないです。・煙草は 体に よくないです。
• (*serious*) = ひどい
a bad accident = ひどい じこ・ひどい 事故
• (*when talking about food*) = まずい
• (*not kind, not honest*) = わるい・悪い
to feel bad = きぶんが わるい・気分が 悪い
• (*severe*) = ひどい
I have a bad cold = ひどい かぜを ひきました。・ひどい 風邪を ひきました

**badger** *noun*
= あなぐま・穴熊

**badly** *adverb*
• (*not well*)
to think badly of someone = だれかを わるく おもう・誰かを 悪く 思う
she slept badly = かのじょは よく ねむれませんでした。・彼女は よく 眠れませんでした。
he did badly in the test = かれは テストの せいせきが わるかったです。・彼は 成績が 悪かったです。
• (*seriously*) = ひどく
I was badly injured = ひどい けがを しました。・酷い 怪我を しました。

**badminton** *noun*
= バドミントン

**bad-tempered** *adjective*
= おこりやすい・怒りやすい

**bag** *noun*
(*with fastener*) = かばん
plastic bag = ビニールぶくろ・ビニール袋
paper bag = かみぶくろ・紙袋

**baggage** *noun*
= にもつ・荷物

**bake** *verb*
= オーブンで やく・オーブンで 焼く

**baker** *noun*
= パンや・パン屋

**bakery** *noun*
= パンや・パン屋

**balance** *noun*
= バランス
to lose one's balance = バランスを
うしなう・バランスを 失う

**balcony** *noun*
= バルコニー

**bald** *adjective*
= はげている

**ball** *noun*
= ボール
to play ball = ボールあそびを する
・ボール遊びを する

**ballet** *noun*
= バレエ

**balloon** *noun*
= ふうせん・風船

**ban** *verb*
= きんしする・禁止する

**banana** *noun*
= バナナ

**band** *noun*
= バンド

**bandage** *noun*
= ほうたい・包帯

**bang**
**1** *noun*
• (*US English*)
(*a fringe*)
bangs = まえがみ・前髪
**2** *verb*
• (*to close with a bang*) = ばたんと
しめる・ばたんと 閉める
• (*to hurt*)
to bang one's head on the wall = かべ
に あたまを ぶつける・壁に 頭
を ぶつける

**bank** *noun*
= ぎんこう・銀行

**bank account** *noun*
= ぎんこうこうざ・銀行口座

**bank holiday** *noun* (*British English*)
= さいじつ・祭日

**bank manager** *noun*
my mother is a bank manager = はは
は ぎんこうの してんちょうで
す。・母は 銀行の 支店長です。

> ! *Note that the Japanese do not*
> *usually refer to their job title but just*
> *the name or type of company they*
> *work for*

**bar** *noun*
• (*a place*)
= バー
to go to a bar = バーに いく・バー
に 行く
• (*a piece of metal*)
= ぼう・棒
• (*on a cage or window*)
a bar = てつごうし・鉄格子
• (*other uses*)
a bar of soap = せっけん
a bar of chocolate = チョコレート
▶ 181

**barbecue** *noun*
= バーベキュー

**bargain** *noun*
= かいどく・買い得

**bark** *verb*
= ほえる・吠える

**barrel** *noun*
• (*of wine or beer*)
= たる・樽
• (*of oil*)
= バレル

**base** *verb*
based in London = ロンドンきょて
ん・ロンドン拠点
based on a true story = じじつに
もとづいた・事実に 基づいた

**baseball** *noun*
= やきゅう・野球

**basement** *noun*
= ちか・地下

**basically** *adverb*
= きほんてきに・基本的に

**basin** *noun*
= せんめんき・洗面器

**basket** *noun*
= かご

**basketball** *noun*
= バスケットボール

**bat** *noun*
• (*in cricket or baseball*)
= バット
• (*an animal*)
= こうもり

**bath** *noun*
- to have a bath = おふろに はいる・
  お風呂に 入る
  he's in the bath = かれは おふろに
  はいっています。・彼は お風呂
  に 入っています。
- *(a bathtub)*
  = ふろおけ・風呂おけ

**bathroom** *noun*
- = ふろば・風呂場
- *(US English)*
  *(the toilet)*
  to go to the bathroom = トイレに
  いく・トイレに 行く

**battery** *noun*
  *(for a torch etc.)* = でんち・電池
  *(for a car)* = バッテリー

**battle** *noun*
  = たたかい・戦い

**bay** *noun*
  = わん・湾

**be** *verb*

> ! There is no exact equivalent of this
> verb in Japanese.

- *(when describing)*

> ! Note that you can usually use
> adjective or noun + です。

  he is intelligent = かれは あたまが
  いいです。・彼は 頭が いいで
  す。
  I am tall = わたしは せが たかいで
  す。・私は 背が 高いです。
  it's a girl = おんなの こです。・女の
  子です。
  it's Monday = げつようびです。・
  月曜日です。
  it's late = おそいです。・遅いです。
  I am 18 years old = じゅうはっさい
  です。・十八歳です。
  my feet are cold = あしが つめたい
  です。・足が 冷たいです。
- *(when talking about location)*
  *(of people and animals)* = いる
  there are 3 pupils in the classroom =
  きょうしつに せいとが さんに
  ん います。・教室に 生徒が
  三人 います。
  *(of things)* = ある
  the dictionary is on the table = じしょ
  は テーブルの うえに あります。
  ・辞書は テーブルの 上に あり
  ます。

- *(when talking about jobs)* = job title +
  です。
  I am a lawyer = べんごしです。・
  弁護士です。
- *(when describing the weather)*
  it's not very warm = あまり あたたか
  くないです。・あまり 暖かくな
  いです。
  it's raining = あめが ふっています。
  ・雨が 降っています。
- *(when talking about experiences)*

> ! Use the ～た form of the verb +
> ことが ある to describe
> experiences

  ▶ 191
  I've never been to Tokyo = とうきょ
  うに いった ことが ありません。
  ・東京に 行った ことが ありま
  せん。
  have you ever been to Japan? = にほ
  んに いった ことが ありますか。
  ・日本に 行った ことが ありま
  すか。
- *(when talking about health)*
  how are you? = おげんきですか。・
  お元気ですか。▶ 187
  I'm well = げんきです。・元気です。
  how is your mother? = おかあさんは
  おげんきですか。・お母さんは
  お元気ですか。▶ 187
- *(in continuous tenses)* ▶

> ! Use the ～て form of the verb +
> いる ▶ 197

  I'm reading = よんでいます。・読ん
  でいます。
  it was snowing = ゆきが ふっていま
  した。・雪が 降っていました。
  he is playing = かれは あそんでいま
  す。・彼は 遊んでいます。
- *(in questions and short answers)* = use
  particle ね ▶ 205
  it's hot, isn't it? = あついですね。・
  暑いですね。
  *(become)* = なる
  he'll be famous = かれは ゆうめいに
  なります。・彼は 有名に なりま
  す。
  *(making a request)*
  please be quiet! = しずかに してく
  ださい。・静かに してくださ
  い。

**beach** *noun*
  = すなはま・砂浜

to go to the beach = かいがんに いく
・ 海岸に 行く

**beak** *noun*
=くちばし

**bean** *noun*
=まめ・豆

**bear**
**1** *noun*
=くま・熊
**2** *verb*
=がまんする・我慢する
I can't bear it = がまんできません。
・ 我慢できません。

**beard** *noun*
= ひげ

**beat** *verb*
(*to win against*) = 〜に かつ・〜に
勝つ
Scotland beat England two nil = スコッ
ットランドは イングランドに
に たい ゼロで かちました。・
スコットランドはイングランド
に 二対ゼロで 勝ちました。
beat up = なぐる・殴る
I was beaten up yesterday = きのう
なぐられました。・ 昨日 殴られ
ました。

**beautiful** *adjective*
= きれい(な)
beautiful girl = きれいな おんなの
こ・きれいな 女の子
beautiful place = きれいな ところ・
きれいな 所

**beauty** *noun*
= うつくしさ・美しさ

**because**
**1** *conjunction*
= から

> ! *Note that word order is different to
> English. Note that there are also
> other ways of expressing cause and
> effect in Japanese.*

I was late for school because I
overslept = ねぼうしましたから、
がっこうに ちこくしました。・
寝坊しましたから、学校に 遅刻
しました。
**2 because of** = 〜の ため
I didn't go because of the rain = あめ
の ため いきませんでした。・
雨の ため 行きませんでした。

**become** *verb*
= なる
to become an adult = おとなに なる
・ 大人に なる
to become cold = さ む く な る・
寒く なる

**bed** *noun*
= ベッド
to go to bed = ねる・寝る

**bed and breakfast** *noun*
(*Japanese-style*) = みんしゅく・民宿

**bedroom** *noun*
= しんしつ・寝室

> ! *Japanese people tend to say* わた
> しの へや *rather than* わたしの
> しんしつ

**bee** *noun*
= はち・蜂

**beef** *noun*
= ぎゅうにく・牛肉
roast beef = ローストビーフ

**beer** *noun*
• (*the product*)
= ビール
• (*a glass of beer*)
= ビールいっぱい・ビール一杯

**before**
**1** *preposition*
= まえ・前
before the holidays = やすみの まえ
・ 休みの 前
the day before yesterday = おととい
**2** *adjective*
= まえの・前の
the week before = まえの しゅう・
前の 週
the day before = まえのひ・前の 日
**3** *adverb*
= まえ・前
two months before = にかげつまえ・
二ケ月前
have you been to Paris before? = ま
えに パリに いった ことが あり
ますか。・前に パリに 行ったこ
とが ありますか。
**4** *conjunction*
I'd like to see him before I go = いく
まえに、かれに あいたいです。
・ 行く 前に、彼に 会いたいで
す。
I'd like to see him before he goes =
かれが いく まえに、あいたい

です。・彼が 行く 前に、会いた
いです。

**beg** *verb*
= ものごいを する・物乞いを
する

**beggar** *noun*
= こじき

**begin** *verb*
(*something starts*) = はじまる・始ま
る
(*to start something*) = はじめる・始
める
to begin working = はたらきはじめ
る・働き始める

**beginner** *noun*
= しょしんしゃ・初心者

**beginning** *noun*
(*relating to time*) = はじめ・初め
(*relating to an action*) = はじめ・始め
at the beginning of May = ごがつの
はじめに・五月の 初めに
the beginning of the race = きょうそ
うの はじめ・競争の 始め

**behave** *verb*
I behaved badly = わるい ことを
しました。・悪い ことをしまし
た。
behave yourself! = ちゃんとしなさ
い。

**behaviour** (*British English*),
**behavior** (*US English*) *noun*
= こうどう・行動

**behind** *preposition*
= うしろ・後ろ
I looked behind me = うしろをふり
かえりました。・後ろを 振り返
りました。

**Belgium** *noun* ▶ **172**
= ベルギー

**believe** *verb*
= しんじる・信じる

**bell** *noun*
• (*in a church*)
= かね・鐘
• (*on a door or bicycle*)
= ベル

**belong** *verb*
• (*to be the property of*)
that book belongs to me = あの ほん
は わたしの です。・あの 本は
私の です。

• (*to be a member of*)
to belong to a club = クラブに はい
っている・クラブに 入っている

**belongings** *noun*
= もちもの・持ち物

**below** *preposition*
= ～の した・～の 下
the kitchen is below my room = だい
どころは わたしの へやの した
です。・台所は 私の 部屋の
下です。

**belt** *noun*
= ベルト

**bench** *noun*
= ベンチ

**bend**
**1** *verb*
• (*to lean, to move, to make crooked*) =
まげる・曲げる
to bend one's knees = ひざを まげる
・ひざを 曲げる
**2** *noun* = カーブ
to bend down = かがむ

**beneath** *preposition*
= ～の した・～の 下

**beside** *preposition*
= ～の そば・～の 側
he is sitting beside me = かれは わた
しの そばに すわっています。・
彼は私の 側に 座っています。
to live beside the sea = うみの そば
に すむ・海の そばに 住む

**best**
**1** *noun*

! This isn't used as much in
Japanese as in English

= いちばん・一番
to do one's best = がんばる・頑張る
**2** *adjective*
= いちばん・一番
the best hotel in town = この まちの
いちばんいい ホテル・この
町の 一番いい ホテル
best friend = しんゆう・親友
the best thing to do would be to phone
him = かれに でんわした ほうが
いいです。・彼に 電話した 方が
いいです。
**3** *adverb*
I like tennis best = テニスが いちば
んすきです。・テニスが 一番 好
きです。

## better

**1** adjective

he is better at sports than me = かれは わたしより スポーツが じょうずです。・ 彼は 私より スポーツが 上手です。

the weather is going to get better = てんきは よくなります。・ 天気は 良くなります。

I was ill but now I'm better = びょうきでしたが げんきに なりました。・ 病気でしたが 元気に なりました。

**2** adverb

we'd better go = いった ほうが いいです。・ 行った 方が いいです。

## between

**1** preposition

= 〜の あいだ・ 〜の 間

between the post office and the flower shop there is a bank = ゆうびんきょくと はなやの あいだに ぎんこうが あります。・ 郵便局と 花屋の 間に 銀行が あります。

## beyond preposition

= 〜の むこう・ 〜の 向こう

beyond the village = むらの むこう・ 村の 向こう

## bicycle noun

= じてんしゃ・ 自転車

## big adjective

• (large) = おおきい・ 大きい

big party = おおきい パーティー・ 大きい パーティー

big car = おおきいくるま・ 大きい 車

big parcel = お お き い にもつ・ 大きい 荷物

(area) = ひろい・ 広い

big garden = ひろい にわ・ 広い 庭

big room = ひろい へや・ 広い 部屋

• (heavy, thick) = あつい・ 厚い

big book = あつい ほん・ 厚い 本

## bike noun

= じてんしゃ・ 自転車

(motorbike) = オートバイ

## bill noun

• (general household)

= せいきゅうしょ・ 請求書

gas bill = ガスだい・ ガス代

• (in a restaurant)

= かいけい・ 会計

could we have the bill please? = かいけいおねがいします。・ 会計お願いします。

• (in a hotel)

= せいさん・ 精算

• (US English)

(money)

= おさつ・ お札 ▶ 189

1000 yen bill = せんえんさつ・ 千円札

## billiards noun

= ビリヤード

## bin noun (British English)

= ごみばこ・ ごみ箱

## biology noun

= せいぶつがく・ 生物学

## bird noun

= とり・ 鳥

## bird flu noun

= とりインフルエンザ・ 鳥インフルエンザ

## biro® noun (British English)

= ボールペン

## birth noun

= しゅっさん・ 出産

date of birth = せいねんがっぴ・ 生年月日 ▶ 171

## birthday noun

= たんじょうび・ 誕生日

Happy birthday! = おたんじょうびおめでとうございます。・ お誕生日おめでとうございます。 ▶ 189

## biscuit noun (British English)

= ビスケット

## bit

**1** noun

(a small quantity of rice, bread, wood, string, etc) = すこし・ 少し

there's a bit of rice = ごはんが すこし あります。・ ご飯が 少し あります。

**2** a bit (British English)

= ちょっと

a bit odd = ちょっと へん・ ちょっと 変

## bite verb

= かむ

## bitter adjective

= にがい・ 苦い

## black adjective

= くろい・ 黒い

**blackboard** noun
= こくばん・黒板

**blade** noun
• (of a knife, a sword)
= は・刃

**blame**
1 verb = ～の せいに する
2 noun
to take the blame = せきにんを とる・責任を とる

> ! It is better to express this using "responsibility" or "fault"

**blank** adjective
(describing a page) = くうはく(の)・空白(の)
(describing a cassette) = から(の)・空(の)

**blanket** noun
= もうふ・毛布

**blaze** noun
= かじ・火事

**bleed** verb
= しゅっけつする・出血する
to have a nose bleed = はなぢが でている・鼻血が 出ている

**blind**
1 adjective
= めの みえない・目の 見えない
2 noun
a blind = ブラインド

**blister** noun
= みずぶくれ・水脹れ

**block**
1 noun
• (a building)
a block of apartments = アパート
• (a group of houses)

> ! Not used in Japan. Japanese abroad may use ブロック

• (a large piece)
a block = ブロック

**blond, blonde** adjective
= きんぱつ(の)・金髪(の)
I have blond hair = かみは きんぱつ です。・髪は 金髪です。
my older sister's blonde = あねは きんぱつです。・姉は 金髪です。

**blood** noun
= ち・血

blood test = けつえきけんさ・血液検査

**blood-type** noun
= けつえきがた・血液型

**blouse** noun
= ブラウス

**blow**
verb
• (if it's the wind) = ふく・吹く
the wind blows = かぜが ふきます。・風が 吹きます。
• (to blow one's nose) = はなを かむ・鼻を かむ
• (if it's a light bulb) = きれる・切れる

**blue** adjective
= あおい・青い

**blush** verb
= かおが あかく なる・顔が 赤く なる

**board**
1 noun
• (a piece of wood)
a board = いた・板
• (for games)
a board
= ボード
• (a blackboard)
= こくばん・黒板
2 verb
to board a ship = ふねにのる・船に 乗る
3 on board = のっている・乗っている

**boarding school** noun
= ぜんりょうせいの がっこう・全寮制の 学校

> ! Extremely unusual in Japan

**boast** verb
= じまんする・自慢する

**boat** noun
= ボート

**body** noun
= からだ・体
a dead body = したい・死体

**boil** verb
• (if it's a person boiling something)
to boil water = おゆを わかす・お湯を 沸かす
to boil an egg = たまごを ゆでる・卵を ゆでる

B

- (if it's water, milk) = わく・沸く
  the water is boiling = おゆが わいて
     います。・お湯が 沸いていま
     す。
  (if it's vegetables) = ゆでる

**boiled egg** noun
= ゆでたまご・ゆで卵

**boiler** noun
= ボイラー

**bomb**
**1** noun
= ばくだん・爆弾
**2** verb
- (from the air) = ばくだんを とうか
     する・爆弾を 投下する
- (to be blownup) = ばくは される・
     爆破 される

**bone** noun
= ほね・骨

**bonnet** noun (British English)
(in a car) = ボンネット

**book**
**1** noun
= ほん・本
**2** verb
= よやくする・予約する
to book a room = へやを よやくする
     ・部屋を 予約する
this flight is fully booked = この ひこ
     うきは まんせきです。・この 飛
     行機は 満席です。

**booking** noun
= よやく・予約

**bookshop, bookstore** noun
= ほんや・本屋

**boot** noun
- (worn on the feet)
  = ブーツ
- (British English)
  (of a car)
  = トランク

**border** noun
= さかい・境
to cross an international border = こっ
     きょうを こえる・国境を 越える

**bored** adjective
= つまらない

**boring** adjective
= つまらない

**born** adjective
to be born = うまれる・生まれる

I was born in February = にがつに う
     まれました。・二月に 生まれま
     した。
I was born in Italy = イタリアでうま
     れました。・イタリアで 生まれ
     ました。

**borrow** verb
= かりる・借りる
to borrow some money from someone
     = だれかに おかねを かりる・
     誰かに お金を 借りる

**boss** noun
= ボス

**both**
**1** determiner
both are blonde = りょうほうとも
     きんぱつです。・両方とも 金髪
     です。
both Anne and Brian came = アンも
     ブライアンも きました。・アン
     も ブライアンも 来ました。
**2** pronoun
= りょうほうとも・両方とも
you are both wrong, both of you are
     wrong = りょうほうとも まちが
     っています。・両方とも 間違っ
     ています。

**bother** verb
- (to take the trouble)
  don't go to any bother = おかまい
     なく
- (to worry, to upset) = しんぱいさせる
     ・心配させる
- (in polite apologies)
  I'm sorry to bother you, but... = すみ
     ませんが、...

**bottle** noun
= びん・瓶

**bottle-opener** noun
= せんぬき・栓抜き

**bottom**
**1** noun
- (the lowest part)
  the bottom of the mountain = やまの
     ふもと・山の ふもと
  the bottom of the page = ページの し
     た・ページの 下
  the bottom of the lake = みずうみの
     そこ・湖の 底
- (at the lowest level)
  bottom of the class = クラスで いち
     ばんした・クラスで 一番下

• (part of the body) ▶ **189**
= おしり
**2** adjective
the bottom drawer = いちばんしたの
ひきだし・一番下の 引き出し
**bound: to be bound to** verb
it's bound to create problems = かな
らず もんだいに なるでしょう。
・必ず 問題に なるでしょう。

**bow¹** noun
• (a knot)
= ちょうむすび・ちょう結び
• (a weapon)
= ゆみ・弓
**bow²** verb
= おじぎする
**bowl** noun
= ボール
(for rice) = ちゃわん・茶碗
**bowling** noun
= ボーリング
**box** noun
= はこ・箱
(cardboard box) = だんボール・段ボ
ール
**boxing** noun
= ボクシング
**boy** noun
= おとこの こ・男の 子
**boyfriend** noun
= ボーイフレンド
**bra** noun
= ブラ
**bracelet** noun
= ブレスレット
**braid** noun (US English)
= みつあみ・三つ編み
**brain** noun
= のう・脳
**brake** noun
= ブレーキ
**branch** noun
(of tree) = えだ・枝
(of company) = してん・支店
**brand-new** adjective
= しんぴん(の)・新品(の)
brand new computer = しんぴんの
コンピューター・新品の コン
ピューター
(new car) = しんしゃ・新車

**brandy** noun
= ブランデー
**brave** adjective
= ゆうきがある・勇気がある
**bread** noun
= パン
**break**
**1** verb
• (to be damaged) = こわれる・壊れる
the chair broke = いすが こわれまし
た。・椅子が 壊れました。
• (to crack or smash) = わる・割る
to break an egg = たまごを わる・
卵を 割る
• (bones) = おる・折る
to break one's leg = あしの ほねを
おる・足の 骨を 折る
I broke my arm = うでの ほねを おり
ました。・腕の 骨を 折りました。
• (to not keep) = やぶる・破る
to break a promise = やくそくを
やぶる・約束を 破る
to break the rules = ルールを やぶる
・ルールを 破る
**2** noun
• a break
(a short rest) = きゅうけい・休憩
(at school) = やすみじかん・休み
時間
to take a break = きゅうけいする・
休憩する
• (a holiday) = やすみ・休み
**break down**
• (if it's a machine) = こしょうする・
故障する
**break in**
• (to be broken into) = どろぼうに はい
られる・泥棒に 入られる
**break up**
• (a couple) = わかれる・別れる
to break up with someone = だれかと
わかれる・誰かと 別れる
**breakfast** noun
= あさごはん・朝ご飯
to have breakfast = あさごはんを た
べる・朝ご飯を 食べる A more
formal word which is often used in
hotels is ちょうしょく
**breast** noun
= むね・胸
**breath** noun
= いき・息
to be out of breath = いきが きれる・
息が 切れる

to hold one's breath = いきを とめる
・ 息を 止める

**breathe** *verb*
= いきを する・ 息を する
**to breathe in** = すいこむ・ 吸い込
む
**to breathe out** = いきを は く・
息を 吐く

**breeze** *noun*
= そよかぜ・ そよ風

**brick** *noun*
= れんが・ 煉瓦

**bride** *noun*
= はなよめ(さん)・ 花嫁(さん)

**bridegroom** *noun*
= はなむこ(さん)・ 花婿(さん)

**bridge** *noun*
= はし・ 橋

**brief** *adjective*
= みじかい・ 短い

**bright** *adjective*

> ! *Not usually used with colours*

• (*describing light*) = あかるい・ 明る
い
this room is not very bright = この へ
やは あまり あかるくないです。
・ この 部屋は あまり 明るくな
いです。
to get brighter = あかるく なる・
明るく なる
• (*intelligent*) = あたまが いい・ 頭が
いい

**brilliant** *adjective*
(*used for emphasis*) = すごい

**bring** *verb*
• to bring = もって くる・ 持って
来る
• (*to be accompanied by*) = つれてくる
・ 連れて 来る ▶ 204
I brought my younger sister to the party
= いもうとを パーティーに つれ
ていきました。・ 妹を パーティ
ーに 連れて 行きました。
bring back = もって かえる・ 持っ
て 帰る
I brought back some souvenirs = おみ
やげを もって かえりました。・
お土産を 持って 帰りました。
bring up = そだてる・ 育てる
to bring up a child = こどもを そだて
る・ 子供を 育てる

**Britain** *noun* ▶ 172
= イギリス
えいこく・ 英国 is also used

**British** ▶ 172
**1** *adjective*
= イギリスの
**2** *noun*
British person = イギリスじん・
イギリス人

**broad** *adjective*
= ひろい・ 広い

**broadband** *noun*
= ブロードバンド

**broadcast** *verb*
= ほうそうする・ 放送する
live broadcast = なま ほうそう・
生放送

**brochure** *noun*
= パンフレット

**broke** *adjective*
= おかねが ない・ お金が ない

**broken** *adjective*
= こわれている・ 壊れている

**bronze** *noun*
= ブロンズ

**brother**

> ! *Remember there are two sets of
> words for family members* ▶ 177

*noun*
(*your own older brother*) = あに・ 兄
(*your own younger brother*) = おとう
と・ 弟
(*someone else's older brother*) = おに
いさん・ お兄さん
(*someone else's younger brother*) =
おとうとさん・ 弟さん

**brother-in-law** *noun* ▶ 177
= ぎりの + word for brother
▶ **brother**

**brown** *adjective*
• (*in colour*) = ちゃいろい・ 茶色い

**brush**
**1** *noun*
• (*for hair, clothes or shoes*) = ブラシ
toothbrush = はブラシ・ 歯ブラシ
• (*for sweeping up*)
= ほうき
• (*for painting*)
(*for pictures*) = えふで・ 絵筆
(*for walls etc.*) = ブラシ

**2** *verb*

to brush one's hair = か みのけを とかす ・ 髪の毛を とかす

to brush one's teeth = はを みがく ・ 歯を 磨く

**bucket** *noun*
= バケツ

**build** *verb*
= たてる ・ 建てる

to build a house = いえを たてる ・ 家を 建てる

**building** *noun*
= たてもの ・ 建物

(*offices|apartments*) = ビル

**bully** *verb*
= いじめる

**bump** *verb*

to bump one's head = あたまを ぶつ ける ・ 頭を ぶつける

**bump into**
• (*to hit*) = ぶつかる
• (*to meet*) = ぐうぜんに あう ・ 偶然 に 会う

**bunch** *noun*

a bunch of flowers = はなたば ・ 花束

a bunch of grapes = ぶどう

a bunch of keys = かぎ ・ 鍵

**burger** *noun*
= ハンバーガー

**burglar** *noun*
= どろぼう ・ 泥棒

**burglar alarm** *noun*
= ぼうはんアラーム ・ 防犯アラー ム

**burglary** *noun*

we had a burglary = どろぼうにはい られました。・ 泥棒に 入られま した。

**burn**

**1** *verb*
• (*to destroy, to get rid of*) = もやす ・ 燃やす

to burn rubbish = ごみを もやす ・ ごみを 燃やす
• (*to injure*)

to burn oneself = やけどを する

to burn one's finger = ゆびを やけど する ・ 指を やけどする
• (*to be on fire*) = もえている ・ 燃えて いる
• (*when cooking*) = こげる ・ 焦げる

**2** *noun*

a burn = やけど

**burst** *verb*
• (*if it's a balloon or pipe*) = はれつする ・ 破裂する

**burst into**

to burst into tears = なきだす ・ 泣き 出す

**burst out**

to burst out laughing = わらいだす ・ 笑い出す

**bury** *verb*
= うめる ・ 埋める

**bus** *noun*
= バス

**bus driver** *noun*
= バスの うんてんしゅ ・ バスの 運転手

**business** *noun*
• (*commercial activities*)
= ビジネス

to go to Tokyo on business = とうき ょうに しゅっちょうする ・ 東 京に 出張する
• (*a company*)
= かいしゃ ・ 会社
• (*when protecting one's privacy*)

it's none of your business = あなたと は かんけい ありません。・ あな たとは 関係 ありません。

**bus station** *noun*
= バスのりば ・ バス乗り場

**bus stop** *noun*
= バスてい ・ バス停

**busy** *adjective*
= いそがしい ・ 忙しい

**but** *conjunction*
= が

that restaurant is good but expensive = あの レストランは おいしいで すが、 たかいです。・ あの レス トランは おいしいですが、 高い です。

> **!** *There are a number of other expressions similar in meaning.*
> ▶ **however**

**butcher** *noun*
= にくや ・ 肉屋

**butter** *noun*
= バター

**butterfly** *noun*
= ちょうちょう

**button** *noun*
= ボタン

**buy** *verb*
= かう・買う
to buy a present (for someone) = (だ
れかに)プレゼントを かって あ
げる・(誰かに)プレゼントを
買ってあげる

**by** *preposition*
• (*on one's own*)
by oneself = ひとりで・一人で
• (*using*)
= use particle で
to travel by bus = バスで いく・
バスで行く
we went there by bicycle = じてんし
ゃで いきました。・自転車で行
きました。
to pay by credit card = クレジットカ
ードで はらう・クレジットカ
ードで払う
to book by phone = でんわで よやく
する・電話で予約する
• (*as a result of*)
I passed the exam by studying hard

  **!** *Note word order*

= いっしょうけんめい べんきょう
した けっか、しけんに うかり
ました。・一生懸命 勉強した
結果、試験に受かりました。
• (*beside*) = そば・側
by the sea = うみの そば・海の側
• (*indicating the author or painter*) = use
particle の ▶ 205
a book by Soseki Natsume = なつめ
そうせきの ほん・夏目漱石の
本
a song by The Beatles = ビートルズ
のうた・ビートルズの歌
• (*when talking about time*)
= までに
by next Thursday = らいしゅうの も
くようび までに・来週の 木曜
日までに
• (*with passive verbs*) = に
I was bitten by a dog = いぬに かま
れました。・犬に 噛まれました。
(*other cases*)
by chance = ぐうぜん・偶然
by mistake = まちがって・間違って
one by one = ひとつずつ・一つずつ

# Cc

**cab** *noun*
= タクシー

**cabbage** *noun*
= キャベツ

**cable car** *noun*
= ケーブルカー

**café** *noun*
= きっさてん・喫茶店

**cake** *noun*
(*western style*) = ケーキ
(*Japanese style*) = おかし・お菓子
▶ 189

**cake shop** *noun*
(*Japanese style*) = わがしや・和菓
子屋
(*western style*) = ケーキや・ケー
キ屋

**calculator** *noun*
= でんたく・電卓

**calendar** *noun*
= カレンダー

**calf** *noun*
• (*the animal*)
= こうし・子牛
• (*part of the leg*)
= ふくらはぎ

**call** *verb*
• (*to name*) to say 'I'm called Michiko
Tanaka', you should say たなか
みちこです。 or to be more formal
you can say たなか みちこと
もうします。
her boyfriend is called Michael = かの
じょの ボーイフレンドは マイ
ケルと いいます。・彼女の ボー
イフレンドは マイケルと 言い
ます。
it's called hako in Japanese = にほん
ごで はこ いいます。・日本語
で 箱と 言います。
somebody called Tanaka telephoned
= たなかと いう ひとから でんわ
が ありました。・田中と いう
人から 電話が ありました。
• (*to call out (to)*) = よぶ・呼ぶ

the teacher is calling us = せんせい
は よんでいます。・先生は 呼ん
でいます。

- (to phone) = でんわする・電話する
who's calling? = どちら さまです
か。・どちら 様ですか。
- (to get to come) = よぶ・呼ぶ
to call the doctor = いしゃを よぶ・
医者を 呼ぶ
- (to wake) = おこす・起こす
- (to pay a visit) = たずねる・訪ねる
I called yesterday = きのうたずねま
した。・昨日 訪ねました。
call back
- (to come back) = また くる・また
来る
- (to phone back) = また でんわする・
また 電話する
call up (American English) = でんわ
する・電話する

**call centre** noun
= コールセンター

**calm**
**1** adjective
= しずか(な)・静か(な)
calm down = おちつく・落ち着く

**camcorder** noun
= ビデオカメラ

**camera** noun
(for taking photos) = カメラ
(in a studio, for videos) = えいがの
カメラ・映画の カメラ

**camp**
**1** noun
a summer camp = サマーキャンプ
**2** verb
to go camping = キャンプする

**campsite** noun
= キャンプじょう・キャンプ場

**can¹** verb
- (to have the possibility) = use the
potential form of the verb ▶ **191**
Note that there are a number of
other structures which also
express potential such as using
the dictionary form of the verb +
ことが できる.
can you come? = こられますか。・
来られますか。
where can I buy stamps? = きっては
どこで かえますか。・切手は ど
こで 買えますか。

he can't sleep when it's hot = かれは
あつい とき、ねむれません。・
彼は 暑い とき、眠れません。
- (to know how to) = use the potential
form of the verb ▶ **191** Note that
there are a number of other
structures which also express
potential such as using the
dictionary form of the verb +
ことが できる.
she can swim = かのじょは およげ
ます。・彼女は 泳げます。
he can't drive yet = かれは まだ うん
てんが できません。・彼は ま
だ 運転が できません。
can you speak French? = フランス
ごが はなせますか。・フランス
語が 話せますか。
I can read hiragana = ひらがなを
よむ ことが できます。・ひらが
なを 読む ことが できます。
- (seeing, hearing) See and hear have
two potential forms depending on
context. ▶ **191**
(when involuntary)
can see = みえる・見える
can hear = きこえる・聞こえる
I can see mountains from my room. =
へやから やまが みえます。・
部屋から 山が 見えます。
I can hear music = おんがくが きこ
えます。・音楽が 聞こえます。
- (when effort is required)
can see = みられる・見られる
can hear = きける・聴ける
you can see Kabuki theatre if you go
to Japan = にほんに いけば、
かぶきが みられます。・日本に
行けば、歌舞伎が 見られます。
I bought a radio so now I can hear the
news every night = ラジオを かい
ました から、いま まいばん ニ
ュースが きけます。・ラジオを
買いました から、今 毎晩 ニ
ュースが 聴けます。
- I can understand Japanese = にほん
ごが わかります。・日本語が
わかります。
- (when giving and receiving
permission, offering or suggesting)
= use the 〜て form of the verb + も
いい ▶ **197**
can we borrow your car? = くるまを
かりても いいですか。・車を
借りても いいですか。

can I smoke? = たばこを すっても
いいですか。・たばこを 吸って
も いいですか。

you can use a dictionary = じしょを
つかっても いいです。・辞書を
使っても いいです。

* (when refusing permission)
= use the 〜て form of the verb + は
いけない ▶ 197

you can't put san after your own name
= じぶんの なまえに さんを
つけては いけません。・自分の
名前に さんを つけては いけま
せん。

you can't use a dictionary = じしょを
つかっては いけません。・辞書
を 使っては いけません。

**can²** noun
= かん・缶

**Canada** noun ▶ 172
= カナダ

**Canadian** ▶ 172
**1** adjective
= カナダの
**2** noun
= カナダじん・カナダ人

**canal** noun
= うんが・運河

**cancel** verb
= キャンセルする

**cancer** noun
= がん・癌

**candle** noun
= ろうそく

**candy** noun (US English)
= あめ

**canoe** noun
= カヌー

**can-opener** noun
= かんきり・缶切り

**canteen** noun
= しょくどう・食堂

**cap** noun
= ぼうし・帽子
baseball cap = やきゅうぼう・野球
帽

**capital**
**1** noun
= しゅと・首都
Tokyo is the capital of Japan = とう
きょうは にほんの しゅとです。
・東京は 日本の 首都です。

**2** adjective
capital letter = おおもじ・大文字

**captain** noun
= キャプテン

**car** noun
= くるま・車

**caravan** noun (British English)
= キャンピングカー

**card** noun
* (for sending to someone)
= カード
* (for playing games) = トランプ
to play cards = トランプする
* (business card) = めいし・名刺

**care**
**1** noun
* (to take care) = きを つける・気を
つける
to take care when crossing the street
= みちを わたる とき、きを
つける・道を 渡る とき、気を
つける
* to take care of someone = だれかの
めんどうを みる・誰かの 面倒
を 見る

**2** verb
I don't care = かまいません。
to care about the environment = かん
きょうの ことを きに する・
環境の ことを 気に する

**career** noun
= キャリア

**careful** adjective
to be careful = きを つける・気を
つける
please be careful = きを つけてくだ
さい。・気を つけてください。

**careless** adjective
= ふちゅうい(な)・不注意(な)

**carer** noun
= ケアラ

**car ferry** noun
= カーフェリー

**carnival** noun
* (British English)
(a festival)
= まつり・祭り
* (US English)
(a fair)
= カーニバル

**car park** noun (British English)
= ちゅうしゃじょう・駐車場

**carpet** noun
= じゅうたん

**carrot** noun
= にんじん・人参

**carry** verb
• (to hold) = もつ・持つ
  I can't carry heavy things = おもい ものが もてません。・重い物が 持てません。
• (to move) = はこぶ・運ぶ
  to carry the baggage = にもつを はこぶ・荷物を運ぶ
  **carry on** = つづく・続く
  **carry (something) on** = (なにかを) つづける・(何かを)続ける

**cartoon** noun
= まんが・漫画
• (pictures) = まんが・漫画
• (animation) = アニメ

**case¹ in case** conjunction
= ねんの ため・念の ため
  I took my umbrella just in case = ねん の ため、かさを もって でかけ ました。・念の ため、傘を 持っ て 出かけました。

**case²** noun
= ケース

**cash**
**1** noun
= げんきん・現金
  I don't have any cash = げんきんが あ りません。・現金が ありません。
  to pay in cash = げんきんで はらう ・現金で 払う
**2** verb
= げんきんに する・現金に する

**cash dispenser** noun
= ATM

> ! This is pronounced エーティー エム

*Note that there are a number of terms in use, but this is perhaps the most general.*

**cassette** noun
= カセットテープ

**cassette player** noun
= カセットプレーヤー

**castle** noun
= おしろ・お城 ▶189

**cat** noun
= ねこ・猫

**catch** verb
• (to capture) = とる・採る
  to catch a fish = さかなを とる・ 魚を 採る
• (to take hold of) = つかむ・掴む
• (to pinch, to stick)
  I caught my finger in the door = ドア に ゆびが はさまりました。・ ドアに 指が 挟まりました。
  my shirt got caught on the thorns = シャツが とげに ひっかかりま した。・シャツが とげに 引っか かりました。
• (to get)
  = まにあう・間に合う
  I was running to catch the train = でん しゃに まにあう ように、はし っていました。・電車に 間に合 う ように、走っていました。
• (to take by surprise)
  = つかまえる・捕まえる
  to catch a pupil shoplifting = まんび きしている せいとを つかまえ る・万引きしている 生徒を 捕まえる
  to get caught = つかまえられる・ 捕まえられる
• (to become ill with)
  to catch flu = かぜを ひく・風邪を ひく
  to catch a cold = かぜを ひく・風邪 を ひく
• to catch fire = もえだす・燃え出す
  **catch up**
  to catch up (with someone) = (だれ かに) おいつく・(誰かに)追い つく

**caterpillar** noun
= けむし・毛虫

**cathedral** noun
= だいせいどう・大聖堂

**Catholic** adjective
= カトリックきょう(の)・カトリ ック教(の)

**cauliflower** noun
= カリフラワー

**cause** verb
= ひきおこす・引き起こす *The causative form of the verb can often be used* ▶191

it has caused us a lot of problems =
たくさん もんだいを ひきおこ
しました。・たくさん 問題を
引き起こしました。
it's going to cause delays = おくらせ
ます。・遅らせます。

**cautious** *adjective*
= ちゅういぶかい・注意深い

**cave** *noun*
= ほらあな・洞穴

**CD** *noun*
= CD *This is pronounced* シーディー

**CD player** *noun*
= CDプレーヤー *This is pronounced*
シーディープレーヤー

**ceiling** *noun*
= てんじょう・天井

**celebrate** *verb*
= いわう・祝う
to celebrate someone's birthday = だ
れかの たんじょうびを いわう
・だれかの 誕生日を 祝う

**celery** *noun*
= セロリ

**cell** *noun*
= さいぼう・細胞

**cellar** *noun*
= ちかしつ・地下室

**cello** *noun* ▶ 180
= チェロ

**cell phone, cellular phone**
(*US English*)
= けいたいでんわ・携帯電話

**cement** *noun*
= セメント

**cemetery** *noun*
= ぼち・墓地

**centigrade** *adjective*
thirty degrees centigrade = さんじゅ
うど・三十度 ▶ 181

**centimetre** (*British English*),
**centimeter** (*US English*) *noun*
= センチ ▶ 181

**central heating** *noun*
= セントラルヒーティング

**centre** (*British English*), **center**
(*US English*) *noun*
• (*a place for activities, meetings*)
= センター

a leisure centre = スポーツセンター
• (*the middle*)
= ちゅうしん・中心
the centre of Sapporo = さっぽろの
ちゅうしんち・札幌の 中心地

**century** *noun*
= せいき・世紀

**certain** *adjective*
(*definite*) – たしか(な)・確か(な)
(*particular*) = ある

**certainly** *adverb*
= もちろん

**chain** *noun*
= くさり・鎖

**chair** *noun*
= いす・椅子

**chalk** *noun*
= チョーク

**champagne** *noun*
= シャンペン

**champion** *noun*
= チャンピオン
tennis champion = テニスの チャン
ピオン

**chance** *noun*
• (*when talking about a possibility*) = か
のうせい・可能性
there is a chance that she'll get a job
in Osaka = かのじょは おおさか
で しごとが できる かのうせい
が あります。・彼女は 大阪で 仕
事が できる 可能性が あります。
• (*an opportunity*)
= きかい・機会
to have a chance to meet people =
ひとに あう きかいが ある・
人に 会う 機会が ある
• by chance = ぐうぜんに・偶然に

**change**
**1** *noun*
• = へんか・変化
• (*cash*)
small change = こぜに・小銭
• (*money returned*) = おつり・お釣
▶ 189
**2** *verb*
• (*to become different, to make different*)
= かわる・変わる
this town has changed a lot = この
まちは かなりかわりました。・
この 町は かなり変わりました。

C

I've changed my mind = きが かわり
ました。・ 気が 変わりました。
- (to replace, exchange) = とりかえる
・ 取り替える
to change a tyre = タイヤを とりか
える・ タイヤを 取り替える
to change a shirt for a different colour
= シャツを べつな いろに とり
かえる。・ シャツを 別な 色に
取り替える
- to change dollars into yen = ドルを
えんに かえる・ ドルを 円に
替える
- (to switch) = かえる・ 代える
to change places with someone = だ
れかと ばしょを かえる・ 誰か
と 場所を 代える
she keeps changing channels = かの
じょは いつも チャンネルを
かえています。・ 彼女は いつも
チャンネルを 代えています。
- (when talking about one's clothes)
to get changed = きがえる・ 着替
える
(when using transport) = のりかえる
・ 乗り換える

**changing room** noun
= こういしつ・ 更衣室

**channel** noun
= チャンネル

**Channel** noun
(English) Channel = イギリスかいき
ょう・ イギリス海峡

**chapter** noun
= しょう・ 章

**charge**
**1** verb
= せいきゅうする・ 請求する
to charge for the breakage = はそん
だいを せいきゅうする・ 破損
代を 請求する
**2** noun
- (a price, a fee)
= りょうきん・ 料金
there's no charge = むりょうです。
・ 無料です。
**3** in charge = たんとうしている・
担当している
to be in charge of the money = おかね
を たんとうしています。・ お金
を 担当しています。

**charming** adjective
= みりょくてき(な)・ 魅力的(な)

**chase** verb
= おいかける・ 追いかける

**chat**
**1** verb
- (face to face) = おしゃべりする
- (on the Internet) = チャットする
**2** noun
= おしゃべり ▶ 189
**chat up** (British English) = なんぱする

**cheap** adjective
- (not expensive) = やすい・ 安い
it's cheap = やすいです。・ 安い
です。
the bus is cheaper = バスの ほうが
やすいです。・ バスの 方が 安い
です。
- (of poor quality) = や すっぽい・
安っぽい

**cheat** verb
= カンニングする

**check**
**1** verb
- (to make sure) = かくにんする・
確認する
you should check whether it's true =
ほんとうか どうか、かくにんし
た ほうがいいです。・ 本当か ど
うか、確認した 方が いいです。
- (to inspect (tickets)) = (きっぷを)か
いさつする・ (切符を)改札する
our tickets weren't checked = きっぷ
は かいさつされませんでした。
・ 切符は 改札されませんでし
た。
**2** noun
- (US English)
(a bill)
= かんじょう・ 勘定
- (US English)
(a cheque)
= こぎって・ 小切手
to check in = チェックインする
to check out = チェックアウトする

**checkbook** noun (US English)
= こぎってちょう・ 小切手帳

**check-in** noun
= チェックイン

**checkout** noun
(in a shop) = レジ
(in a hotel) = チェックアウト
checkout time is 11:00 = チェックア
ウトじかんは じゅういちじで

す。・ チェックアウト時間は
十一時です。

**cheek** *noun*
= ほお

**cheeky** *adjective*
= なまいき(な)・ 生意気(な)

**cheerful** *adjective*
= きげんが いい・ 機嫌が いい

**cheese** *noun*
= チーズ

**chef** *noun*
= りょうりちょう・ 料理長

**chemist** *noun*
• (*in a shop*)
= やくざいし・ 薬剤師
• (*in a laboratory*)
= かがくしゃ・ 化学者
chemist's shop = くすりや・ 薬屋

**chemistry** *noun*
= かがく・ 化学

**cheque** *noun* (*British English*)
= こぎって・ 小切手
to write a cheque for £50 = ごじゅ
っポンドの こぎってを かく・
五十ポンドの 小切手を 書く

**cheque book** *noun* (*British English*)
= こぎってちょう・ 小切手帳

**cherry** *noun*
= さくらんぼ

**cherry tree** *noun*
= さくら・ 桜

**chess** *noun*
= チェス

**chest** *noun*
= むね・ 胸

**chestnut**
**1** *noun*
= くり・ 栗
**2** *adjective*
= くりいろ(の)・ 栗色(の)

**chew** *verb*
= かむ・ 噛む

**chewing gum** *noun*
= ガム

**chicken** *noun*
• (*the bird*)
= にわとり・ 鶏
• (*the meat*)
= とりにく・ 鳥肉
year of the chicken = とりどし・ 酉年

**child** *noun*
= こども・ 子供

**chilly** *adjective*
it's chilly = ちょっと さむいです。
・ ちょっと 寒いです。

**chimney** *noun*
= えんとつ・ 煙突

**chin** *noun*
= あご

**China** *noun* ▶ **172**
= ちゅうごく・ 中国

**chips** *noun*
• (*British English*)
(*French fries*)
= フライドポテト
• (*US English*)
(*crisps*)
= ポテトチップス

**chocolate** *noun*
= チョコレート

**choice** *noun*
= せんたく・ 選択
I had no choice = せんたくの よちが
ありませんでした。・ 選択の
余地が ありませんでした。

**choir** *noun*
• (*church*) = せいかたい・ 聖歌隊
• (*choral music*) = がっしょうだん・
合唱団

**choke** *verb*
I was choking with the smoke = けむ
りで むせていました。・ 煙で
咽ていました。
I choked on the rice cake = もちが の
どに つまりました。・ 餅が喉に
詰まりました。

**choose** *verb*
= えらぶ・ 選ぶ

**chopsticks** *noun*
= おはし ▶ **189**

**chore** *noun*
(*housework*) = かじ・ 家事
(*other work*) = ざつよう・ 雑用

**Christian** *adjective*
= キリストきょう(の)・ キリスト
教(の)

**Christian name** *noun*
= ファーストネーム

**Christmas** *noun*
= クリスマス

Merry Christmas!, Happy Christmas!
= メリークリスマス

**Christmas Eve** noun
= クリスマスイブ

**Christmas tree** noun
= クリスマスツリー

**church** noun
= きょうかい ・ 教会

**cider** noun
= りんごしゅ ・ りんご酒

**cigar** noun
= はまき ・ 葉巻

**cigarette** noun
= たばこ ・ 煙草

**cigarette lighter** noun
= ライター

**cinema** noun (British English)
= えいがかん ・ 映画館

**circle** noun
= えん ・ 円

**circus** noun
= サーカス

**citizen** noun
• (of a country)
= こくみん ・ 国民
• (of a city or town)
= しみん ・ 市民

**city** noun
= とし ・ 都市

**city centre** (British English), **city center** (US English) noun
= まちの ちゅうしん ・ 町の 中心

**civilized** adjective
= ぶんめいの すすんだ ・ 文明の 進んだ

**civil servant** noun
= こうむいん ・ 公務員

**clap** verb
= はくしゅする ・ 拍手する

**clarinet** noun ▶ 180
= クラリネット

**class** noun
• (a group of students)
= クラス
• (a lesson)
= じゅぎょう ・ 授業
history class = れきしの じゅぎょう ・ 歴史の 授業

• (a social group)
= かいきゅう ・ 階級

**classical music** noun
= クラシックおんがく ・ クラシック音楽

**classmate** noun
= クラスメート

**classroom** noun
= きょうしつ ・ 教室

**clean**
**1** adjective
• (not dirty) = きれい(な)
my hands are clean = ては きれいです。 ・ 手は きれいです。
to keep the house clean = うちを きれいに する ・ 家を きれいに する
• (not polluted) = きれい
**2** verb
(house) = そうじする ・ 掃除する
to clean a room = へやを そうじする ・ 部屋を 掃除する
(teeth, shoes) = みがく ・ 磨く
to have a jacket cleaned = ジャケットを クリーニングに だす ・ ジャケットを クリーニングに 出す

**clear**
**1** adjective
• (easy to understand, making sense) = わかりやすい ・ 分かりやすい
is that clear? = わかりますか。 ・ 分かりますか。
• (obvious) = あきらか ・ 明らか
it is clear that everyone is dissatisfied = みんなが ふまんなのは あきらかです。 ・ 皆が 不満なのは 明らかです。
• (easy to see or hear, distinct)
a clear voice = きれいな こえ ・ きれいな 声
clear writing = きれいな じ ・ きれいな 字
• (with no rain or cloud) = はれている ・ 晴れている
a clear day = はれている ひ ・ 晴れている 日
**2** verb
• (to empty, to remove from)
to clear the table = テーブルの うえを かたづける ・ テーブルの 上を 片づける

to clear the snow = じょせつする ・
除雪する
• (if it's rain) = あがる ・ 上がる

**clever** adjective
• (intelligent) = あたまが いい ・ 頭が
いい
clever at mathematics = すうがくが
とくい ・ 数学が 得意

**click** verb
(using a mouse) = クリック

**cliff** noun
= がけ ・ 崖

**climate** noun
= きこう ・ 気候

**climb** verb
• to climb (up) a tree = きに のぼる ・
木に 登る
to climb a mountain = やまに のぼる
・ 山に 登る
to climb over a wall = へいを のりこ
える ・ 塀を 乗り越える
• (to rise higher) = あがる ・ 上がる

**climbing** noun
= とざん ・ 登山

**clinic** noun
= しんりょうじょ ・ 診療所

**cloakroom** noun
(for coats) = クローク
(toilet) = トイレ A more polite word is
おてあらい

**clock** noun
= とけい ・ 時計

**close**¹
**1** adjective
• (near) = ちかい ・ 近い
the station is close = えきは ちかい
です。・ 駅は 近いです。
is the house close to the school? = い
えは がっこうに ちかいですか。
・ 家は 学校に 近いですか。
• (as a friend or relation) = したしい ・
親しい
**2** adverb
to be living close (by) = ちかくに す
んでいる ・ 近くに 住んでいる
to come closer = ちかづく ・ 近づく

**close**² verb
(to close something)
(eyes) = とじる ・ 閉じる
(doors, windows) = しめる ・ 閉める
(to be closed)

(buildings, doors, windows) = しまる
・ 閉まる
the shop closes at noon = みせは
じゅうにじに しまります。・
店は 十二時に 閉まります。
the door closed = ドアが しまりま
した。・ ドアが 閉まりました。
**close down** = しまう

**closed** adjective
(eyes) = とじている ・ 閉じている
(doors, windows) = しまっている ・
閉まっている
(buildings) = しまっている

**cloth** noun
• (material)
= ぬの ・ 布
• (for cleaning or dusting) = ふきん

**clothes** noun
= ふく ・ 服
to put on one's clothes = ふくを きる
・ 服を 着る
to take off one's clothes = ふくを
ぬぐ ・ 服を 脱ぐ

**cloud** noun
= くも ・ 雲

**clown** noun
= ピエロ

**club** noun
• = クラブ
a tennis club = テニスクラブ
to be in a club = クラブに はいって
いる ・ クラブに 入っている For
after school club activities, the suffix
ぶ can be added to the name of the
sport
• (a nightclub)
= ナイトクラブ

**clue** noun
• (in an investigation)
= てがかり ・ 手がかり
• (in a crossword)
= ヒント

**clumsy** adjective
= ぶきよう(な) ・ 不器用(な)

**coach**
**1** noun (British English)
• (a bus)
= バス
• (of a train)
= きゃくしゃ ・ 客車
**2** verb
= コーチする

**coach station** *noun*
= バスステーション
(*for long distance coaches*) = ちょう
きょりバスのりば・長距離バス
乗り場

**coal** *noun*
= せきたん・石炭

**coast** *noun*
= かいがん・海岸

**coat** *noun*
• = コート
• (*of an animal*)
= け・毛

**coat hanger** *noun*
= ハンガー

**cobweb** *noun*
= くもの す・くもの 巣

**cock** *noun*
= おんどり・雄鳥

**cocoa** *noun*
= ココア

**coconut** *noun*
= ココナッツ

**cod** *noun*
= たら

**coffee** *noun*
= コーヒー
would you like a coffee? = コーヒー
は いかがですか。

**coffee machine** *noun*
= コーヒーメーカー

**coin** *noun*
= コイン
ten yen coin = じゅうえんだま・十
円玉

**coincidence** *noun*
= ぐうぜん・偶然

**cold**
**1** *adjective*
• (*air temperature*) = さむい・寒い
it's very cold = とても さむいです。
・とても 寒いです。
it's cold in the classroom = きょうし
つは さむいです。・教室は 寒い
です。
it's going to get cold = さむく なりま
す。・寒く なります。
• (*food, drink*)
to go cold = さめる・冷める

the soup is getting cold = スープが
さめています。・スープが 冷め
ています。
**2** *noun*
• (*the lack of heat*)
= さむさ・寒さ
• (*common illness*)
= かぜ・風邪

**collapse** *verb*
(*if it's a building, a chair*) = くずれる
・崩れる
(*if it's a wall*) = たおれる・倒れる

**collar** *noun*
• (*on a shirt or jacket*)
= えり
• (*for a pet*)
= くびわ・首輪

**colleague** *noun*
= どうりょう・同僚

**collect** *verb*
• (*to gather or make a collection of*) =
あつめる・集める
to collect the exercise books = ノート
を あつめる・ノートを 集める
I collect stamps = きってを あつめ
ています。・切手を 集めていま
す。
• (*to take away*) = しゅうしゅうする
・収集する
to collect the rubbish = ごみを しゅ
うしゅうする・ごみを 収集
する

**collection** *noun*
• (*a set*)
= しゅうしゅう・収集
• (*money collected*)
= ぼきん・募金

**college** *noun*
= だいがく・大学
to go to college, to be at college = だ
いがくに かよっている・大学
に 通っている

**colour** (*British English*), **color**
(*US English*)
**1** *noun*
= いろ・色
what colour is the car? = くるまは
なにいろですか。車は 何色です
か。
**2** *verb*
to colour the drawings (in) = えに い
ろを ぬる・絵に 色を 塗る

**colourful** (*British English*)
  **colorful** (*US English*) *adjective*
  = はで(な) ・ 派手(な)

**comb**
**1** *noun*
  = くし
**2** *verb*
  to comb one's hair = かみを くしで
    とかす・髪を くしでとかす

**come** *verb* ▶ **204**
• to come = くる・来る
  she's coming today = かのじょは
    きょう きます。・彼女は今日来
    ます。
  please come to Paris with us = パリ
    に いっしょに いってください。
    ・パリに 一緒に 行ってくださ
    い。
  I came by bike = じてんしゃできま
    した。・自転車で 来ました。
  come and see! = みに きてくださ
    い。・見に 来てください。
  I'm coming! = いきます。・行きま
    す。
  is the bus coming? = バスは きて
    いますか。・バスは 来ています
    か。
  please be careful when you come
    down the stairs = かいだんを おり
    るとき、 きを つけてください。
    ・階段を 降りる とき、 気を
    付けてください。
  to come through the city centre =
    まちの ちゅうしんを とおる・
    町の 中心を 通る
• (*to call around*) = たずねる・訪ねる
• (*to reach*)
  turn left when you come to the traffic
    lights = しんごうを ひだりに
    まがってください。・信号を
    左に 曲がってください。
• (*to attend*) = さんかする・参加する
  will you be able to come to the meeting?
    = かいぎに さんか できますか。
    ・会議に 参加 できますか。
• (*to be a native or a product of*)
  I come from Britain = イギリスから
    きています。・イギリスから 来
    ています。*Note that you could also
    say* イギリスしゅっしんです。
  the strawberries all come from Spain
    = いちごは ぜんぶ スペインさん
    です。・いちごは 全部 スペイン
    産です。

• (*in a contest*)
  to come first = いちいに なる・一
    位に なる
  **come around** ▶ **come round**
  **come back** = もどる・戻る
  to come back home = かえる・帰る
  **come in**
• (*to enter*) = はいる ・ 入る
• (*if it's a plane, a train*) = つく・着く
• the tide's coming in = しおが みちる
  ・汐が 満ちる
  **come off**
  = とれる・取れる
  **come on**
• (*to start to work*) = つく・点く
• (*when encouraging someone*)
  come on! = がんばって・頑張って
  **come on to** (*US English*)
  to come on to someone = だれかをな
    んぱする・誰かを なんぱする*
  **come out**
• (*to leave a place*) = でる・出る
  I saw him as I came out of the shop =
    みせから でた ときに かれを
    みました。・店から 出たときに
    彼を 見ました。
• (*to become available*)
  (*if it's a film*) = じょうえいする・
    上映する
  (*if it's a book*) = しゅっぱんされる ・
    出版される
• (*if it's a photo*)
  the photo didn't come out = しゃしん
    は だめでした。・写真は だめで
    した。
• (*if it's smoke, fire*)
  there are flames coming out of the
    windows = ほのおが まどから で
    ています。・炎が 窓から 出てい
    ます。
  **come round**
• (*to visit*) = たずねる・訪ねる
• (*after fainting*) = いしきが もどる・
    意識が 戻る
  **come to**
  the bill came to 7500 yen = かんじょ
    うは ななせんごひゃくえんに
    なりました。・勘定は 七千五百
    円に なりました。
  how much does it come to? = いくら
    に なりますか。
  **come up**
• (*to be discussed*)

—————————————————————
***in informal situations**

to come up in conversation = はな
　しに でて くる ・ 話しに 出て
　来る
• (*if it's the sun*) = のぼる ・ 昇る

**comfortable** *adjective*
• (*if it's a chair*) = すわりごこちが
　いい ・ 座り心地が いい
　(*if it's a bed*) = ねごこちが いい ・
　寝心地が いい
　are you comfortable? = だいじょう
　ぶですか。・ 大丈夫ですか。
• (*relaxed*) = かんじの いい ・ 感じの
　いい
• (*having enough money*) = くらしに
　こまらない ・ 暮らしに 困らない

**comforter** *noun* (*US English*)
= もうふ ・ 毛布

**comic strip** *noun*
= まんが ・ 漫画

**commercial**
**1** *adjective*
= しょうぎょう(の) ・ 商業(の)
**2** *noun*
= こうこく ・ 広告

**commit** *verb*
to commit a crime = はんざいをおか
　す ・ 犯罪を 犯す
to commit suicide = じさつする ・
　自殺する

**common** *adjective*
= ふつうの ・ 普通の

**communicate** *verb*
= つたえる ・ 伝える

**community** *noun*
= しゃかい ・ 社会

**company** *noun*
• (*a business*)
= かいしゃ ・ 会社
• (*a group of actors*)
theatre company = げきだん ・ 劇団
• (*other people*)
to keep someone company = だれか
　の あいてをする ・ 誰かの 相手
　をする
to keep bad company = わるいつき
　あいを する ・ 悪い 付き合いを
　する

**company secretary** *noun*
= そうむぶちょう ・ 総務部長

**compare** *verb*
= くらべる ・ 比べる

to compare France with Italy = フラ
　ンスを イタリアと くらべる ・
　フランスを イタリアと 比べる
I am always compared to my older
　sister = いつも あねと くらべら
　れます。・ いつも 姉と 比べられ
　ます。

**compass** *noun*
= コンパス

**competition** *noun*
• = きょうそう ・ 競争
there's competition between the
　schools = がっこうと がっこうで
　きょうそうが あります。・ 学校
　と 学校で 競争が あります。
• (*a contest*)
= コンクール
a drawing competition = えの コンク
　ール ・ 絵の コンクール

**competitive** *adjective*
(*person*) = きょうそうしんが ある
　・ 競争心が ある
(*situation*) = きょうそうてき(な) ・
　競争的(な)

**complain** *verb*
= もんくを いう ・ 文句を 言う
to complain about the food = た べ
　ものに ついて もんくを いう ・
　食べ物に ついて文句を 言う

**complete**
**1** *adjective*
= かんぜん(な) ・ 完全(な)
it was a complete disaster = かんぜ
　んな しっぱいでした。・ 完全な
　失敗でした。
this is a complete waste of time = こ
　れは じかんの むだです。・ これ
　は 時間の 無駄です。
**2** *verb*
(*a form*) = きにゅうする ・ 記入する
(*a course*) = しゅうりょうする ・
　終了する
(*to finish something*) = おえる ・ 終え
　る

**completely** *adverb*
= かんぜんに ・ 完全に

**complicate** *verb*
= ふくざつにする ・ 複雑に する

**complicated** *adjective*
= ふくざつ(な) ・ 複雑(な)

**compliment**
**1** *noun*
= ほめことば ・ ほめ言葉

**2** *verb*

to compliment someone = だれかを
ほめる・誰かを ほめる

**comprehensive** *noun* (*British English*)

comprehensive school = そうごうち
ゅうとうがっこう・総合中等学
校

**!** *Note that the Japanese education
system does not follow this pattern.*
▶ **185**

**compulsory** *adjective*
= ぎむてき(な)・義務的(な)
compulsory education = ぎむきょう
いく・義務教育

**computer** *noun*
= コンピュータ

**computer game** *noun*
(*the game*) = コンピューターゲーム
(*the software*) = ゲームソフト

**computer programmer** *noun*
= プログラマー

**computer scientist** *noun*
= コンピュータかがくしゃ・コン
ピュータ科学者

**computer studies** *noun*
= コンピューター

**concentrate** *verb*
= しゅうちゅうする・集中する

**concert** *noun*
= コンサート

**concert hall** *noun*
= コンサートホール

**concrete** *noun*
= コンクリート

**condemn** *verb*
to condemn to death = しけいを
いいわたす・死刑を 言い渡す

**condition**

**1** *noun*
= じょうたい・状態
a terrible condition = じょうたいが
わるい・状態が 悪い
the engine is in good condition = エン
ジンの ちょうしが いいです。・
エンジンの 調子が いいです。
**2** on condition that = 〜というじょ
うけんで・〜と 言う 条件で

you can go on condition that you're
back by 10 o'clock = じゅうじまで
に かえると いう じょうけんで
いっても いいです。・十時まで
に 帰ると いう 条件で 行っても
いいです。

**condom** *noun*
= コンドーム

**conductor** *noun*
= しきしゃ・指揮者

**conference** *noun*
= かいぎ・会議

**confidence** *noun*
• = じしん・自信
• (*trust*)
to have confidence in someone =
だれかを しんようしている・
誰かを 信用している

**confident** *adjective*
= じしんの ある・自信の ある
she's a confident person = かのじ
ょは じしんの ある ひとです。
・彼女は 自信の ある 人です。

**confidential** *adjective*
= ひみつ(の)・秘密(の)

**confiscate** *verb*
= ぼっしゅうする・没収する

**conflict** *noun*
= ろんそう・論争

**confused** *adjective*
to get confused = とうわくする・
当惑する

**congratulate** *verb*
= おいわいを いう・お祝いを
言う ▶ **189**

**congratulations** *noun* (also
*exclamation*)
= おめでとうございます

**connection** *noun*
= かんけい・関係
it has no connection with the strike =
ストライキとは かんけい あり
ません。・ストライキとは 関係
ありません。

**conscientious** *adjective*
= りょうしんてき(な)・良心的(な)

**conscious** *adjective*
• (*aware*) = きが ついている・気が
付いている
• (*after an operation*) = めが さめて
いる・目が 覚めている

**construct** *verb*
= たてる・建てる

**consult** *verb*
= そうだんする・相談する

**contact**
**1** *noun*
to be in contact with someone = だれ かと れんらくを とりあっている ・ 誰かと 連絡を 取り合っている
to lose contact with someone = だれ かと れんらくを しなくなる・ 誰かと 連絡を しなくなる
**2** *verb*
= れんらくする・連絡する

**contact lens** *noun*
= コンタクトレンズ

**contain** *verb*
= はいっている・入っている
this contains sugar = さとうが はい っています。・砂糖が 入ってい ます。

**content** *adjective*
= まんぞくしている・満足して いる

**contents** *noun*
= ないよう・内容

**contest** *noun*
= コンクール

**continent** *noun*
• (*a large mass of land*)
= たいりく・大陸
• (*British English*)
(*Europe*)
= ヨーロッパたいりく・ヨーロッ パ大陸

**continental quilt** *noun* (*British English*)
= かけぶとん・掛け布団

**continue** *verb*
to continue = つづく・続く
to continue something = なにかを つづける・何かを 続ける
to continue to talk, to continue talking = はなしを つづける・話を続 ける

**continuous** *adjective*
= たえまない・絶え間ない
continuous effort = たえまない どり ょく・絶え間ない 努力

**contraception** *noun*
= ひにん・避妊

**contract** *noun*
= けいやく・契約
two-year contract = にねんけいやく ・二年契約

**contradict** *verb*
= むじゅんする・矛盾する
(*deny*) = ひていする・否定する

**contradiction** *noun*
= むじゅん・矛盾

**contrast** *noun*
= コントラスト

**contribute** *verb*
• (*to give money*) = きふする・寄付す る
• to contribute to a discussion = いけ んを いう・意見を 言う

**control**
**1** *noun*
(*of a situation*)
to be in control = しょうあくして いる・掌握している
**2** *verb*
(*country, organisation*) = しはいする ・支配する
(*to regulate*) = きせいする・規制す る

**convenient** *adjective*
• (*useful, practical*) = べんり(な)・ 便 利(な)
it's more convenient to take the bus = バスの ほうが べんりです。・ バスの 方が 便利です。
• (*suitable*) = いい
it's a convenient place to meet = まち あわせに いい ところです。・ 待ち合わせに いい 所です。
it's not convenient for me = わたし には ふべんです。・私には 不便 です。

**conversation** *noun*
= かいわ・会話
to have a conversation = かいわを する・会話を する

**convince** *verb*
= なっとくさせる・納得させる

**cook**
**1** *verb*
• (*to prepare food*) = りょうりする・ 料理する
to cook a meal = しょくじを つく る。・食事を 作る

to cook rice = ごはんを たく・ご飯
を 炊く
- (to be cooked in the oven) = オーブン
  で やく・オーブンで 焼く

**2** noun
= コック

**cooker** noun (British English)
= レンジ

**cookie** noun (US English)
= クッキー

**cooking** noun
= りょうりする こと・料理する
こと
to do the cooking = りょうりする・
料理する

**cool** adjective
- (air temperature) = すずしい・涼し
  い
  it's cool today = きょうは すずしい
  です。・今日は 涼しいです。
  (drinks) = つめたい・冷たい
  a cool drink = つめたい のみもの・
  冷たい 飲み物
- (calm) = おちついている・落ち着
  いている
- (fashionable) = すてき(な)・素敵
  (な)
- (relaxed) = へいき(な)・平気(な)
  **cool down**
- (to get colder) = さめる・冷める
- (to calm down) = おちつく・落ち
  着く

**cooperate** verb
= きょうりょくする・協力する

**cope** verb
- (to manage) = たいおうする・対応
  する
- I can't cope with this job = この しご
  とに たいおう できません。・
  この 仕事に 対応 できません。

**copper** noun
= どう・銅

**copy**
**1** noun
= コピー
**2** verb
= ふくしゃする・複写する
to copy in an exam = カンニング
する
**copy down, copy out** = うつす・
写す

**cork** noun
= コルク

**corkscrew** noun
= せんぬき・栓抜き

**corner** noun
- (of a street, a building)
  = かど・角
  the shop on the corner = かどの みせ
  ・角の 店
  to go around the corner = かどを
  まがる・角を 曲がる
- (in football)
  = コーナーキック

**correct**
**1** adjective
= ただしい・正しい
that is correct = それは ただしい
です。・それは 正しいです。
correct answer = せいかい・正解
**2** verb
= なおす・直す

**correction** noun
= しゅうせい・修正

**corridor** noun
= ろうか・廊下

**cost** verb
how much does it cost? = いくらで
すか。
it will cost a lot of money = おかねが
たくさん かかります。・お金が
たくさん 掛かります。
it cost a lot of money = たかかった
です。・高かったです。

**costume** noun
= いしょう・衣装

**cosy** adjective (British English)
cosy room = ここち よい へや・
心地良い 部屋

**cot** noun (British English)
= ベビーベッド

**cottage** noun
= コテージ

**cotton** noun
- (the material)
  = コットン
- (the thread)
  = ぬいいと・縫い糸

**cotton wool** noun (British English)
= だっしめん・脱脂綿

**couch** noun
= ソファー

**cough** verb
= せきを する

**could** *verb*

- (*had the ability*) = use the past potential form of the verb ▶ **191** Note that there are a number of other structures which also express potential such as using the dictionary form of the verb + ことが できる.

  I couldn't move = うごけませんでした。・ 動けませんでした。

  he couldn't sleep well for weeks = かれは なんしゅうかんも ねむれませんでした。・ 彼は 何週間 眠れませんでした。

- (*knew how to*) = use the past potential form of the verb ▶ **191** Note that there are a number of other structures which also express potential such as using the dictionary form of the verb + ことが できる.

  I couldn't speak Japanese = にほんごが はなせませんでした。・ 日本語が 話せませんでした。

  he couldn't type = かれは タイプが できませんでした。・ 彼は タイプが できませんでした。

  he couldn't read hiragana = ひらがなを よむ ことが できませんでした。・ ひらがなを 読むことが できませんでした。

- (*seeing, hearing*) See and hear have two potential forms depending on context. ▶ **191**

  (*when involuntary*)

  I could see = みえました。・ 見えました。

  I could hear = きこえました。・ 聞こえました。

  I could see mountains from my room. = へやから やまが みえました。・ 部屋から 山が 見えました。

  I couldn't hear the teacher's voice = せんせいの こえが きこえませんでした。・ 先生の 声が 聞こえませんでした。。

  (*when effort is required*)

  I could see = みられました。・ 見られました。

  I could hear = きけました。・ 聞けました。

- I could understand a little Japanese = にほんごが すこし わかります。・ 日本語が 少し 分かります。

- (*when implying that something did not happen*)

  she could have passed if she'd studied more = かのじょは もっと べんきょうすれば うかりました。・ 彼女は もっと 勉強すれば 受かりました。

- (*when indicating a possibility*)

  I could be wrong = まちがっているかもしれません。・ 間違っているかもしれません。

  a bike could be useful = じてんしゃは べんり かもしれません。・ 自転車は 便利 かもしれません。

- (*when asking, offering or suggesting*)

  could I speak to Nobumi? = のぶみさんは いらっしゃいますか。・ 暢美さんは いらっしゃいますか。

  could you take a message? = メッセージを おねがいします。・ メッセージを お願いします。

  we could ask John = ジョンさんに きいたら どうですか。・ ジョンさんに 聞いたら どうですか。

**count** *verb*

= かぞえる・数える

**count on**

to count on someone = だれか を しんらいする・誰かを 信頼する

**counter** *noun*

= カウンター

**country** *noun*

- (*a state*)

  = くに・国

- (*the countryside*)

  = いなか・田舎

  to live in the country = いなかで くらす・田舎で 暮らす

**countryside** *noun*

= いなか・田舎

**couple** *noun*

- a couple of days

  (*two days*) = ふつかかん・二日間

  (*a few days*) = に、さんにち・二、三日

- (*two people*)

  = カップル

  (*if married*) = ふうふ・夫婦

**courage** *noun*

= ゆうき・勇気

**courageous** *adjective*

= ゆうかん(な)・勇敢(な)

**course**

**1** *noun*
- (*a series of lessons or lectures*)
  = コース
  a Japanese course = にほんごの
  コース・日本語の コース
- (*part of a meal*)
  = コース
  main course = メイン
**2** of course = もちろん
  of course not = もちろん + negative

**court** *noun*
- (*of law*)
  = ほうてい・法廷
  to go to court = さいばんに いく・
  裁判に 行く
- (*for playing sports*)
  = コート

**court case** *noun*
  = さいばん・裁判

**cousin** *noun* ▶ 177
  (*one's own*) = いとこ
  (*someone else's*) = いとこさん

**cover**

**1** *verb*
- to cover = おおう・覆う
  the car is covered in mud = くるまは
  どろだらけです。・ 車は 泥だら
  けです。
**2** *noun*
- (*a lid*)
  = ふた
- (*for a cushion, a quilt*)
  = カバー
- (*a blanket*)
  = もうふ・毛布
- (*on a book, a magazine, an exercise book*)
  = ひょうし・表紙

**cow** *noun*
  = うし・牛

**coward** *noun*
  = おくびょうもの・臆病者

**cowboy** *noun*
  = カウボーイ

**cozy** *adjective* (*US English*)
  cozy room = ここちの よい へや・
  心地の 良い 部屋

**crab** *noun*
  = かに

**crack** *verb*
- (*to damage*) = わる・割る

- (*to get damaged*) = ひびが はいる・
  ひびが 入る
- (*to get broken*) = われる・割れる

**cradle** *noun*
  = ゆりかご・揺りかご

**cramp** *noun*
  = けいれん

**crash**

**1** *noun*
  = しょうとつ・衝突
  car crash = こうつうじこ・交通事故
**2** *verb*
  to crash into a tree = きに しょうと
  つする・木に 衝突する
  the plane crashed = ひこうきが つい
  らくしました。・ 飛行機が 墜落
  しました。

**crayon** *noun*
  = クレヨン

**crazy** *adjective*
  (*insane person*) = くるっている・
  狂っている
  (*idea*) = ばか(な)

**cream** *noun*
  = クリーム

**create** *verb*
  = つくる・作る
  to create employment = しごとを
  つくる・仕事を 作る

**credit** *noun*
  (*academic*) = たんい・単位

**credit card** *noun*
  = クレジットカード

**cricket** *noun*
  = クリケット

**crime** *noun*
  = はんざい・犯罪

**criminal**

**1** *noun*
  = はんざいしゃ・犯罪者
**2** *adjective*
  = いほう(の)・違法(の)

**crisis** *noun*
  = きき・危機

**crisps** *noun* (*British English*)
  = ポテトチップ

**critical** *adjective*
  (*person*) = ひはんてき(な)・批判
  的(な)
  (*illness*) = きとく(の)・危篤(の)

**criticize** *verb*
  = ひなんする・非難する

C

**crocodile** noun
= わに

**crooked** adjective
crooked line = まがった せん・
曲がった 線
the picture is crooked = えが まが
っています。・絵が 曲がってい
ます。

**cross**
**1** verb
• (to go across)
to cross the road = みちを おうだん
する・道を 横断する
to cross an international border =
こっきょうを こえる・国境を
越える
to cross a bridge = はしを わたる・
橋を 渡る
• (other uses)
to cross one's legs = あしを くむ・
足を 組む
our letters crossed = てがみは いき
ちがいに なりました。・手紙は
行き違いに なりました。
**2** noun
• (X mark) = ばつ
• (Christian symbol) = じゅうじか・
十字架
**3** adjective
= ふきげん(な)・不機嫌(な)
to get cross = おこる・起こる
cross out = せんを ひいて けす・
線を 引いて 消す

**crossroads** noun
= じゅうじろ・十字路

**crossword puzzle** noun
= クロスワードパズル

**crow** noun
= からす

**crowd** noun
• (a large number of people)
= ぐんしゅう・群集
crowds of people = ひとごみ・人込
み
• (watching a game)
= かんきゃく・観客

**crown** noun
= おうかん・王冠

**cruel** adjective
= ざんこく(な)・残酷(な)

**cruelty** noun
= ざんこくさ・残酷さ

**cruise** noun
= ふなたび・船旅

**crush** verb
= おしつぶす・押しつぶす

**crutch** noun
= まつばづえ・松葉づえ

**cry**
**1** verb
= なく・泣く
**2** noun
= なきごえ・泣き声

**cucumber** noun
= きゅうり

**cuddle** verb
= だきしめる・抱き締める

**culprit** noun
= はんざいにん・犯罪人

**cultural** adjective
= ぶんかぶんめいの・文化文明の

**culture** noun
= ぶんか・文化

**cunning** adjective
= こうかつ(な)

**cup** noun
• = カップ
a cup of coffee = コーヒー いっぱい
・コーヒー 一杯
• (in sport)
= カップ

**cupboard** noun
= とだな・戸棚

**curb** noun (US English)
= ほどう・歩道

**cure**
**1** verb
= なおす・治す
**2** noun
= ちりょうほう・治療法

**curious** adjective
= こうきしんが ある・好奇心が
ある

**curly** adjective
I have curly hair = まきげです。・
巻き毛です。

**currency** noun
= つうか・通貨
foreign currency = がいか・外貨

**curry** noun
= カレー

**curtain** noun
= カーテン
to draw the curtains = カーテンを
しめる・カーテンを 閉める

**cushion** noun
(on floor) = ざぶとん・座布団
(on sofa) = クッション

**custard** noun (British English)
= カスタード

**custom** noun
= しゅうかん・習慣

**customer** noun
= きゃく・客

**customs** noun
= ぜいかん・税関
to go through customs = ぜいかんを
とおる・税関を 通る

**customs officer** noun
= ぜいかんり・税関吏

**cut**
**1** verb
= きる・切る
to cut an apple in half = りんごを
はんぶんに きる・りんごを
半分に 切る
to cut one's fingers = ゆびを きる・
指を 切る
to have one's hair cut = かみを きる
・髪を 切る
**2** noun
(injury) = きりきず・切り傷
**cut down** = きりたおす・切り倒す
**cut out**
to cut a photo out of a magazine = ざ
っしから しゃしんを きりぬく・
雑誌から 写真を 切り抜く
**cut up** = きざむ・刻む

**cute** adjective
= かわいい

**CV** noun
= りれきしょ・履歴書

**cycle** verb
to cycle to school = がっこうに じて
んしゃで いく・学校に 自転車
で 行く
to go cycling = サイクリングする

**cycling** noun
= サイクリング

**cyclist** noun
= サイクリスト

**cynical** adjective
= ひにく(な)・皮肉(な)

# Dd

**dad, Dad** noun ▶ 177
(one's own) = ちち・父
(someone else's) = おとうさん・お
父さん

> ! Japanese children will address
> their father as おとうさん or パパ

**daffodil** noun
= すいせん・水仙

**daisy** noun
= ひなぎく・ひな菊

**damage**
**1** verb
• to damage = そんがいを あたえる・
損害を 与える
to be damaged = ひがいを うける・
被害を 受ける
the building was damaged by the fire
= たてものは かじでひがいをう
けました。・建物は 火事で被害
を 受けました。
• (to harm)
it can damage your health = けんこう
に わるいです。・健康に 悪いで
す。
**2** noun
= ひがい・被害

**damp** adjective
= しめっぽい・湿っぽい

**dance**
**1** verb
= おどる・踊る
**2** noun
= ダンス

**dancer** noun
= ダンサー

**dancing** noun
= ダンス

**danger** noun
= きけん・危険
she is in danger = かのじょは あぶ
ないです。・彼女は 危ないで
す。

**dangerous** adjective
= あぶない・危ない

**dare** *verb*
I didn't dare to say = こわくて いえ
ませんでした。・ 恐くて 言えま
せんでした。

**dark**
**1** *adjective*
• (*lacking light*) = くらい・ 暗い
it has got dark = くらく なりました。
・ 暗く なりました。
• (*describing a colour, clothes*)
I always wear dark coloured clothes =
いつも くらい いろの ふくを
きています。・ いつも 暗い色の
服を 着ています。
dark blue = こんいろ(の)・ 紺色(の)
• (*describing a person's character*) = せ
いかくが くらい・ 性格が 暗い
**2** *noun*
= くらやみ・ 暗闇

**darts** *noun*
= ダーツ

**date ▶ 174** *noun*
• (*in a calendar*)
= ひにち・ 日にち
what date is today? = きょうは なん
にちですか。・ 今日は 何日です
か。
• (*with a friend*)
= デート
to go out on a date with someone =
だれかと デートを する・ 誰か
と デートを する

**daughter** *noun* ▶ **177**
(*your own*) = むすめ・ 娘
(*someone else's*) = おじょうさん・
お嬢さん

**daughter-in-law** *noun* ▶ **177**
(*your own*) = よめ・ 嫁
(*someone else's*) = およめさん・ お
嫁さん

**dawn** *noun*
= よあけ・ 夜明け
at dawn = よあけに・ 夜明けに

**day** *noun*
one day = いちにち・ 一日
what day is it today? = きょうは なん
ようびですか。・ 今日は 何曜日
ですか。
daytime = ひるま・ 昼間
we had a very nice day = たのしい
いちにちでした。・ 楽しい 一日
でした。

the next day, the day after = つぎの
ひ・ 次の 日
the day before = まえのひ・ 前の 日

**daylight** *noun*
= にっちゅう・ 日中

**dazzling** *adjective*
= まぶしい・ 眩しい

**dead** *adjective*
= しんでいる・ 死んでいる
he is dead = かれは しんでいます。
・ 彼は 死んでいます。

**deaf** *adjective*
= みみの きこえない・ 耳の 聞こ
えない

**deal**
**1** *noun*
• (*in business*) = とりひき・ 取引
(*with a friend*) = やくそく・ 約束
• a great deal of money = たくさんの
おかね・ たくさんの お金
**2** *verb*
to deal the cards = トランプを くば
る・ トランプを 配る
deal with = しょりする・ 処理する
to deal with a problem = もんだいを
しょりする・ 問題を 処理する

**dear**
**1** *adjective*

> **!** *Not used in Japanese letters.*
> *Usually a general greeting such as*
> はいけい, *without the addressee's*
> *name, is used at the beginning of*
> *the letter and it is finished with*
> けいぐ

• (*expensive*) = たかい・ 高い
**2** *exclamation*
oh dear! = おやおや

**death** *noun*
= し・ 死

**death penalty** *noun*
= しけい・ 死刑

**debate** *noun*
= とうろん・ 討論

**debt** *noun*
= しゃっきん・ 借金
to be in debt = しゃっきんが ある・
借金が ある

**decade** *noun*
= じゅうねんかん・ 十年間

**decaffeinated** *adjective*
= カフェインの ない

**deceive** *verb*
= だます

**December** *noun* ▶ **174**
= じゅうにがつ・十二月

**decide** *verb*
= きめる・決める
I decided to go = いく ことに きめました。・行く ことに 決めました。

**decision** *noun*
= けってい・決定
to make a decision = けっていする・決定する

**deck** *noun*
= デッキ

**deckchair** *noun*
= デッキチェア

**decorate** *verb*
• (with ornaments) = かざる・飾る
• (with wallpaper or paint) = かいそうする・改装する

**decoration** *noun*
= かざりもの・飾り物

**deep** *adjective*
= ふかい・深い
how deep is the lake? = みずうみは どのくらい ふかいですか。・湖は どのくらい 深いですか。
the hole is three metres deep = あなは さんメートルの ふかさです。・穴は 三メートルの 深さです。

**deer** *noun*
= しか・鹿

**defeat**
**1** *verb*
to defeat an enemy = てきを やぶる・敵を 破る
the team was defeated = チームが まけました。・チームが 負けました。
**2** *noun*
= まけ・負け

**defence** (British English),
**defense** (US English) *noun*
(military) = ぼうえい・防衛
(sport) = ぼうぎょ・防御

**defend** *verb*
(military, sport) = まもる・守る
(legal) = べんごする・弁護する

**definite** *adjective*
• = かくじつ(な)・確実(な)

nothing is definite = なにも きまっていません。・何も 決っていません。
• (obvious, visible) = あきらか(な)・明らか(な)

**definitely** *adverb*
= ぜったい・絶対
they're definitely lying = かれらは ぜったい うそを ついています。・彼らは 絶対嘘を ついています。
I'm definitely coming = ぜったい いきます。・絶対 行きます。 ▶ **204**
'definitely!' = ぜったい・絶対

**degree** *noun*
• (from a university)
= がくい・学位
• (in measurements)
= ど・度

**delay**
**1** *verb*
= おくらせる・遅らせる
**2** *noun*
= おくれ・遅れ

**deliberate** *adjective*
= わざと

**deliberately** *adverb*
= わざと
He did it deliberately = わざと しました。

**delicious** *adjective*
= おいしい

**delighted** *adjective*
= うれしい
I was delighted to receive a present = プレゼントを もらって うれしかったです。 ▶ **178**

**deliver** *verb*
= とどける・届ける
to deliver newspapers = しんぶんを はいたつする・新聞を 配達する
to deliver mail = ゆうびんを とどける・郵便を 届ける
to be delivered = とどく・届く

**demand** *verb*
= ようきゅうする・要求する

**demolish** *verb*
= とりこわす・取り壊す

**demonstration** *noun*
= デモンストレーション

**denim** *adjective*
= デニム(の)

**dentist** *noun*
= はいしゃ・歯医者

**deny** *verb*
= ひていする・否定する

**department** *noun*
(*in a firm*) = ぶ・部
(*in a large store*) = うりば・売り場
shoe department = くつうりば・靴
売り場
(*in a school*) = か・課
(*in a university*) = がっか・学科

**department store** *noun*
= デパート

**depend** *verb*
to depend on someone = だれかに
たよる・誰かに 頼る
it depends on you = あなた しだいで
す。・あなた 次第です。

**depressed** *adjective*
= おちこんでいる・落ち込んでい
る

**depressing** *adjective*
= ゆううつ(な)・憂うつ(な)

**depth** *noun*
= ふかさ・深さ

**describe** *verb*
= びょうしゃする・描写する
please descibe what happened = な
にが おこったかをせつめい
して ください。・何が起こっ
たかを 説明して下さい。

**description** *noun*
= びょうしゃ・描写

**desert** *noun*
= さばく・砂漠

**deserve** *verb*
= あたいする・値する

**design**
**1** *verb*
• (*to plan*) = せっけいする・設計する
this house is designed for a hot climate
= この いえは あつい きこうに
あう ように せっけいされてい
ます。・この 家は 暑い 気候に
合う ように 設計されています。
• (*in fashion*)
to design clothes = ふくを デザイン
する・服を デザインする
**2** *noun*
• (*a subject of study*)
(fashion) design = デザイン

• (*a pattern*)
= もよう・模様

**desk** *noun*
= つくえ・机

**desperate** *adjective*
= ひっし(の)・必死(の)

**dessert** *noun*
= デザート

**destroy** *verb*
= はかいする・破壊する

**detail** *noun*
= しょうさい・詳細
to go into details = くわしく いう・
詳しく 言う

**detective** *noun*
= たんてい・探偵
private detective = しりつたんてい
・私立探偵

**detective story** *noun*
= すいりしょうせつ・推理小説

**determined** *adjective*
= いしのつよい・意思の強い
to be determined to become a doctor
= ぜったい いしゃに なると けっ
しんしている・絶対 医者に な
ると 決心している

**develop** *verb*
= はってんする・発展する

**development** *noun*
= はってん・発展

**diagram** *noun*
= ず・図

**dial** *verb*
= ダイヤルする

**dialling code** *noun* (*British English*)
= しがいきょくばん・市外局番

**dialling tone** (*British English*),
**dial tone** (*US English*) *noun*
= はっしんおん・発信音

**diamond** *noun*
= ダイヤモンド

**diary** *noun*
• (*for personal thoughts*)
= にっき・日記
• (*for appointments*)
= てちょう・手帳

**dice** *noun*
= さいころ

**dictionary** *noun*
= じしょ・辞書

**!** Note that an English-Japanese dictionary is called a **えいわじてん** and a Japanese-English dictionary is called a **わえいじてん**. As Chinese characters are used in Japanese, separate dictionaries for looking these up are necessary. A dictionary which translates Chinese characters into English is called a **かんえいじてん**

**die** verb
• = しぬ・死ぬ a more polite expression is なくなる
he died at the age of 65 = かれは ろくじゅうごさいでなくなりました。・ 彼は六十五歳で 亡くなりました。
to die of cancer = がんで しぬ・がんで 死ぬ
• (used for emphasis)
I'm dying to go on holiday = りょこうを ほんとうに たのしみに しています。・ 旅行を 本当に 楽しみにしています。
I'm dying to go to the toilet = トイレにいきたいです。・ トイレに 行きたいです。

**diet** noun
(way of eating) = しょくせいかつ・食生活
(to lose weight) = ダイエット
to go on a diet = ダイエットする

**difference** noun
= ちがい・違い
I can't tell the difference = ちがいがわかりません。・ 違いが わかりません。
it won't make any difference = どうやっても かわりません。・ どうやっても 変わりません。

**different** adjective
= ちがう・違う

**!** Note that ちがう is a verb

**difficult** adjective
= むずかしい・難しい
Japanese is not difficult = にほんごは むずかしくないです。・ 日本語は 難しくないです。
difficult to get along with = つきあいにくい・付き合いにくい

**difficulty** noun
= もんだい・問題

I have difficulty concentrating = しゅうちゅうしにくいです。・ 集中しにくいです。

**dig** verb
= ほる・掘る
**dig up**
• (to find what was buried)
= ほりだす・掘り出す

**digital** adjective
= デジタル

**dim** adjective
• (describing a light) = うすぐらい・薄暗い
• (describing a room) = くらい・暗い

**diner** noun (US English)
= レストラン

**dining room** noun
= しょくどう・食堂

**dinner** noun
(at home) = ばんごはん・晩ご飯 ゆうごはん・夕ご飯 is also used
(at a restaurant) = ゆうしょく・夕食
dinner's ready! = ゆうごはんですよ。・ 夕ご飯ですよ。

**dip** verb
(food) = つける

**direct**
**1** adjective
= ちょくせつ(な)・直接(な)
**2** verb
• (when talking about directions)
could you direct me to the station? = えきは どちらですか。・ 駅は どちらですか。
• (in cinema or theatre)
to direct a film = えいがを かんとくする・映画を 監督する
to direct a play = げきを えんしゅつする・劇を 演出する

**direction** noun
= ほうこう・方向
is this the right direction? = これは ただしい ほうこうですか。・ これは 正しい 方向ですか。
they were going in the other direction = かれらは はんたいのほうこうに いきました。・ 彼らは反対の 方向に 行きました。

**directions** noun
to give someone directions = だれかに みちを おしえる・ 誰かに 道を 教える

to ask someone for directions = だれ かに みちを きく・誰かに 道を 聞く

**director** *noun*
• (of a film or play)
= かんとく・監督
• (of a company)
= とりしまりやく・取締役

**dirt** *noun*
= よごれ・汚れ

**dirty**
**1** *adjective*
= きたない・汚い
to get dirty = きたなく なる・汚く なる
**2** *verb*
= よごす・汚す

**disabled** *adjective*
a disabled person = しんたいしょう がいしゃ・身体障害者

! When a person has a disability, it is more usual in Japanese to refer to it specifically rather than use the general word しょうがいしゃ which means a registered disabled person.

**disadvantage** *noun*
= ふりな てん・不利な 点

**disagree** *verb*
= いっちしない・一致しない
I disagree = わたしは はんたいで す。・私は 反対です。

**disappear** *verb*
= きえる・消える

**disappoint** *verb*
= がっかりさせる

**disappointed** *adjective*
= がっかりしている

**disappointing** *adjective*
= きたいはずれ(の)・期待はずれ (の)

**disappointment** *noun*
= きたいはずれ・期待はずれ

**disapprove** *verb*
= ～が わるいと おもう・～が 悪いと 思う
to disapprove of someone's behaviour = だれかの こうどうがわるいと おもう・誰かの 行動が 悪いと 思う

**disaster** *noun*
= さいがい・災害

**discipline** *noun*
= しつけ

**disco** *noun*
= ディスコ

**disconnect** *verb*
= きる・切る

**discouraged** *adjective*
(disheartened)
to be discouraged = やる きが なく なった・やる 気が なくなった

**discover** *verb*
= はっけんする・発見する

**discovery** *noun*
= はっけん・発見

**discrimination** *noun*
= さべつ・差別

**discuss** *verb*
(talk about) = はなしあう・話し合う
to talk about a trip = りょこうについ て はなしあう・旅行に ついて 話し合う
(discuss seriously) = とうろんする・ 討論する
to discuss politics = せいじに つい て とうろんする・政治に つい て 討論する

**discussion** *noun*
= とうろん・討論

**disease** *noun*
= びょうき・病気

**disguise**
**1** *noun*
= へんそう・変装
to wear a disguise = へんそうする・ 変装する
**2** *verb*
to disguise oneself as a police officer = けいさつかんに へんそうする ・警察官に 変装する

**disgusting** *adjective*
= いや(な)・嫌(な)
(food) = まずい

**dish** *noun*
• (food)
= りょうり・料理
• = しょっき・食器
to wash the dishes = しょっきを あ らう・食器を 洗う

**dishonest** *adjective*
= ふせい(な)・不正(な)

**dishwasher** noun
= しょっきあらいき・食器洗い機

**dislike** verb
= きらう・嫌う
I dislike him = かれが きらいです。・
彼が 嫌いです。

**dismiss** verb
(a worker) = かいこする・解雇する

**disobedient** adjective
= いう ことを きかない・言う
ことを 聞かない

**disobey** verb
to disobey the teacher = せんせいの
いう ことを きかない・先生の
言う ことを 聞かない

**display** noun
= てんじ・展示

**dispute** noun
= けんか

**disqualify** verb
= しかくを とりあげる・資格を
取り上げる

**disrupt** verb
= じゃまする・邪魔する

**dissatisfied** adjective
= ふまん(な)・不満(な)

**distance** noun
= きょり・距離
in the distance = ずっと むこうに・
ずっと 向こうに
to keep one's distance = はなれる・
離れる

**distinct** adjective
• (easy to see, to hear) = はっきりした
• (definite) = あきらか(な)・明らか
(な)

**distinguish** verb
= くべつする・区別する
to distinguish between truth and lies =
ほんとうか うそか くべつする・
本当か 嘘か 区別する

**distract** verb
= きをちらす・気を 散らす
to distract someone from working =
だれかの しごとの じゃまを す
る・誰かの 仕事の 邪魔を する

**distribute** verb
= くばる・配る

**disturb** verb
= じゃまする・邪魔する

**disturbing** adjective
= どうてんさせる・動転させる

**dive** verb
= とびこむ・飛び込む
to go diving = ダイビングする

**divide** verb
• (in arithmetic) = わる・割る
• (to share) = わける・分ける

**diving board** noun
= とびこみだい・飛び込み台

**divorce**
**1** noun
= りこん・離婚
**2** verb
= りこんする・離婚する

**DIY** noun (British English)
= にちようだいく・日曜大工

**dizzy** adjective
to feel dizzy = めまいが する

**do** verb

> ! Note that do or its related forms
> are not used when forming tenses
> as they are in English. ▶ 191

• = する
to do the cooking = りょうりする・
料理する
to do one's homework = しゅくだい
をする・宿題をする
what has she done to her hair? = かの
じょは かみを どう しましたか。
・彼女は 髪を どう しましたか。
please do as you're told = いわれた
ように してください。・言われ
た ように してください。

• (in questions, negatives) Questions
can be made in Japanese by
adding particle か to the end of
any statement. To make negative
statements, change the final verb to
a negative form. ▶ 191
do you like cats? = ねこが すきです
か。・猫が 好きですか。
I don't like cats = ねこが すきではあ
りません。・猫が 好きではあり
ません。
I didn't do anything = なにも しません
でした。・何も しませんでした。
please don't go = いかないでくださ
い。・行かないでください。

• (in short answers and tag questions)
The particle ね can be used as a
tag question.

he lives in London, doesn't he? = か
れは ロンドンに すんでいます
ね。・彼は ロンドンに住んでい
ますね。

Yuko didn't phone, did she? = ゆうこ
さんは でんわを しませんでし
たね。・祐子さんは 電話をしま
せんでしたね。

'do you like strawberries?'—'yes, I do'
=「いちごが すきですか。」「は
い、すきです。・「いちごが 好
きですか。」「はい、好きです。」

'I love chocolate'—'so do I!' =「チョ
コレートがだいすきです。」「わ
たしも。」・「チョコレートが 大
好きです。」「私も。」

'who wrote it?'—'I did' =「だれが か
きましたか。」「わたしが かきま
した。」・「誰が 書きましたか。」
「私が 書きました。」

'may I sit down?'—'yes, please do' =
「すわっても いいですか。」「は
い、どうぞ。」・「座っても いい
ですか。」「はい、どうぞ。」

• (to be enough) = たりる・足りる
ten pounds will do = じゅっポンド
で たります。・十ポンドで 足り
ます。

• (to perform)
he did well = かれは よく できまし
た。・彼は よく できました。
he did badly = かれは よく できませ
んでした。・彼は よく できませ
んでした。
**do up** (British English)
(buttons) = かける
(laces) = むすぶ・結ぶ
(dress) = しめる
(house) = かいそうする・改装する
**do with**
it's to do with computers = コンピュ
ーター かんけいです。・コンピ
ューター関係です。
it has nothing to do with him = かれと
かんけいが ありません。・彼と
関係が ありません。
**do without** = いらない・要らない
I can do without a television = テレビ
が いりません。・テレビが 要り
ません。

**dock** noun
= がんぺき・岸壁

**doctor** noun
(medical) = いしゃ・医者

(PhD) = はかせ・博士 Note that
せんせい is used to address a
doctor and can be added to family
names.
Doctor Takahashi = たかはしせんせ
い・高橋先生
**document** noun
= しょるい・書類
**documentary** noun
= ドキュメンタリー
**dog** noun
= いぬ・犬
year of the dog = いぬどし・戌年
**doll** noun
= にんぎょう・人形
**dollar** noun
= ドル
**dolphin** noun
= いるか
**dominoes** noun
= ドミノ
**donkey** noun
= ろば
**donut**
▶ doughnut
**door** noun
= ドア
(sliding door) = とびら・扉
**doorbell** noun
= よびりん・呼び鈴
**dormitory** noun
= きょうどうしんしつ・共同寝室
(in a university or school) = りょう・寮
**dose** noun
= いっかいりょう・一回量
**double**
**1** adjective
• (of an amount) = にばい(の)・二倍
(の)
• (when giving a number)
three double five (British English) = さ
ん ご ご・三五五
**2** verb
= にばいになる・二倍に なる
the population doubled = じんこうは
にばいに なりました。・人口は
二倍に なりました。
**double bass** noun ▶ 180
= コントラバス
**double bed** noun
= ダブルベッド

**double-decker** noun
= にかいだてバス・二階建てバス

**double room** noun
= ダブルベッドの ある へや・ダブルベッドの ある 部屋 Note that these are unusual in Japan.

**doubt**
**1** noun
there's no doubt that he is innocent = かれは むざいに ちがい ありません。・彼は 無罪に 違い ありません。
**2** verb
(to suspect) = うたがう・疑う
I doubt if she'll come = かのじょは こない かもしれません。・彼女は 来ない かもしれません。

**dough** noun
= きじ・生地

**doughnut, donut** (US English) noun
= ドーナツ

**down**

> ! Often down occurs in combinations with verbs, for example: calm down, let down, slow down etc. To find the correct translations for this type of verb, look up the separate dictionary entries at calm, let, slow etc.

**1** preposition
to walk down the street = みちを あるく・道を 歩く
he ran down the hill = かれは さかを はしって くだりました。・彼は 坂を 走って 下りました。
the office is down the stairs = じむしつは かいだんの したです。・事務室は 階段の 下です。
**2** adverb
she's down in the cellar = かのじょは ちかしつに います。・彼女は 地下室に います。
to go down
(prices) = さがる・下がる
(the sun) = しずむ・沈む
(to climb down) = おりる・下りる
(to descend a slope) = くだる・下る
to fall down
(people) = ころぶ・転ぶ
(things) = おちる・落ちる

**downstairs** adverb
= したの かい・下の 階

to go downstairs = したの かいに いく・下の 階に 行く
to take the boxes downstairs = したの かいに はこを もって いく・下の 階に 箱を 持って 行く

**dozen** noun
= いちダース・一ダース
a dozen bottles of beer = ビールいちダース・ビール 一ダース ▶ 181

**draft** noun (US English)
= すきまかぜ・隙間風

**drag** verb
= ひきずる・引きずる

**dragon** noun
year of the dragon = たつどし・辰年

**drain** verb
• (when cooking) = みずきりを する・水切りを する
• (if it's water)
to drain (away) = ながれる・流れる

**drama** noun
= げき・劇

**dramatic** adjective
= げきてき(な)・劇的(な)

**drapes** noun (US English)
= カーテン

**draught** noun (British English)
= すきまかぜ・隙間風

**draughts** noun (British English)
= チェッカー

**draw**
**1** verb
• (with a pen or pencil) = かく・描く
to draw a rabbit = うさぎを かく・うさぎを 描く
to draw a picture = えを かく・絵を 描く
to draw a line = せんを ひく・線を 引く
• (to pull)
to draw the curtains = カーテンを しめる・カーテンを 閉める
• (to take out)
to draw a knife = ナイフを とりだす・ナイフを 取り出す
• (in a lottery)
to draw a ticket = くじを ひく・くじを 引く
• (British English)
(in sport) = ひきわけに なる・引き分けに なる

**D**

- winter is drawing near = ふゆが ちか づいています。・冬が 近づいて います。

**2** noun
- (in sport)
  = ひきわけ・引き分け
- (in a lottery)
  = くじびき・くじ引き

  **draw back**
  to draw back the curtains = カーテン を あける・カーテンを 開ける

  **draw up**
  to draw up a list = リストを かく・ リストを 書く

**drawer** noun
= ひきだし・引き出し

**drawing** noun
= え・絵

**dread** verb
= おそれる・恐れる

**dreadful** adjective
= ひどい・酷い

**dream**
**1** noun
= ゆめ・夢
to have a dream = ゆめを みる・ 夢を 見る
**2** verb
= ゆめを みる・夢を 見る

**dress**
**1** noun
= ドレス
**2** verb
- (to put one's own clothes on) = ふくを きる・服を 着る
- (to put clothes on someone) = だれか に ふくを きせる・誰かに 服を 着せる

  **dress up**
- (in good clothes) = せいそうする・ 盛装する
- (in a disguise) = かそうする・仮装 する
  I dressed up as a clown = ピエロの かそうを しました。・ピエロの 仮装を しました。

**dressing gown** noun
= ガウン

**drill**
**1** noun
= ドリル
**2** verb

to drill a hole = ドリルで あなを あける・ドリルで 穴を 空ける

**drink**
**1** verb
= のむ・飲む
**2** noun
= のみもの・飲み物
a drink of water = みず・水

**drive**
**1** verb
- (in a car) = うんてんする・運転する
  to learn to drive = うんてんを ならう ・運転を 習う
  I drive to work = くるまで しごとに いきます。・車で 仕事に 行きま す。
  to drive someone home = だれかを くるまで いえに おくる・誰か を 車で 家に 送る
- (to make)
  to drive someone mad = だれかを い らいらさせる・誰かを いらい らさせる

**2** noun
= ドライブ
to go for a drive = ドライブする

  **drive away**
- (in a car) = くるまで さって いく・ 車で 去って 行く
- (to chase away) = おいはらう・追い 払う

**driver** noun
= うんてんしゅ・運転手

**driver's license** (US English),
  **driving licence** (British English)
  noun
= うんてんめんきょ・運転免許

**drizzle** noun
= きりさめ・霧雨

**drop**
**1** verb
- (to come down) = さがる・下がる
  the temperature has dropped = きお んが さがりました。・気温が 下がりました。
- (to let fall) = おとす・落とす
  she dropped her suitcase = かのじ ょは スーツケースを おとしま した。・彼女は スーツケースを 落としました。
- (to fall) = おちる・落ちる
**2** noun
- (a fall)

a drop in temperature = おんど が
さがる・温度 が 下がる
a drop in prices = ねだん が さがる・
値段 が 下がる
• (of liquid)
= しずく・滴
**drop in**
he dropped in to see me = かれは あ
そびに きました。・彼は 遊びに
来ました。
I'll drop in tomorrow = あした あそ
びに いきます。・明日 遊びに
行きます。
**drop off** = おろす・降ろす
please drop me off at the station? =
えきで おろしてください。・
駅で 降ろしてください。
**drop out**
to drop out of school = がっこうを ち
ゅうたいする・学校を 中退する
to drop out of a race = きょうそうか
ら だったいする・競争から 脱
退する

**drought** noun
= かんばつ・干ばつ

**drown** verb
= すいしする・水死する

**drug**
**1** noun
• (for illegal use)
= ドラッグ
to use drugs = ドラッグを らんよ
うする・ドラッグを 乱用する
• (for medical use)
= くすり・薬
to take drugs = くすりを のむ・薬
を 飲む
**2** verb
to drug someone = だれかを くす
りで ねむらせる・誰かを 薬で
眠らせる

**drug addict** noun
= まやくじょうしゅうしゃ・麻薬
常習者

**drum** noun ▶ 180
= ドラム
to play drums = ドラムを うつ・ド
ラムを 打つ

**drunk** adjective
= よっぱらった・酔っ払った

**dry**
**1** adjective
= かわいている・乾いている

the washing is dry = せんたくものが
かわいています。・洗濯物が
乾いています。
a dry day = あめの ふらない ひ・
雨の 降らない 日
**2** verb
(in air) = ほす・干す
to dry the washing = せんたくものを
ほす・洗濯物を 干す
(with a towel) = ふく・拭く
to dry oneself = からだを ふく・
体を 拭く
he dried his hands = かれは てを
ふきました。・彼は 手を 拭きま
した。
to dry the dishes = しょっきをふく
・食器を 拭く
(using heat) = かわかす・乾かす
I dried my hair = かみを かわかしま
した。・髪を 乾かしました。

**duck**
**1** noun
= あひる
**2** verb
= かがむ

**due**
**1** due to = 〜の ため
yesterday's game was cancelled due
to bad weather = あくてんこうの
ため、きのうの しあいは ちゅ
うしに なりました。・悪天候の
ため、昨日の 試合は 中止に な
りました。
**2** adjective
• (expected)
the train is due (in) at two o'clock = で
んしゃは にじに つく よていで
す。・電車は 二時に 着く 予定
です。

**dull** adjective
• (describing a person or book) = つま
らない
• (describing a colour) = にごった・
濁った
• (describing the weather) = うっとう
しい

**dumb** adjective
• (unable to speak) = はなせない・
話せない
• (stupid) = ばか(な)

**dump**
**1** verb
= すてる・捨てる

**2** *noun*
= ごみすてば・ごみ捨て場

**during** *preposition*
= 〜の あいだ(に)・〜の 間(に)
during the summer = なつの あいだ
(に)・夏の 間(に)

**dust**
**1** *noun*
= ほこり
**2** *verb*
= ほこりを ふく・ほこりを 拭く

**dustbin** *noun* (*British English*)
= ごみばこ・ごみ箱

**dustman** *noun* (*British English*)
= ごみしゅうしゅうにん・ごみ収
集人

**dustpan** *noun*
= ちりとり・ちり取り

**duty** *noun*
• (*a task, part of one's job*)
= しごと・仕事
• (*of a soldier, a nurse*)
to be on duty = とうばんで・当番で
• (*what one must do*)
= ぎむ・義務
it's my duty = わたしの ぎむです。・
私の 義務です。
• (*a tax*)
customs duties = ぜいきん・税金

**DVD** *noun*
= ＤＶＤ

**DVD player** *noun*
= ＤＶＤプレーヤ

**dye** *verb*
= そめる・染める
to dye one's hair = かみを そめる・
髪を 染める

# Ee

**each**
**1** *determiner*
each time = いつも
**2** *pronoun*
each of the students = それぞれの
がくせい・それぞれの 学生
each of them has a car, they each have
a car = かれらは それぞれ、くる

まを もっています。・彼らは そ
れぞれ、車を 持っています。

**each other** *pronoun*
= おたがい(に)・お互い(に)
they know each other = かれらは お
たがいに しっています。・彼ら
は お互いに 知っています。
we write to each other every year =
まいとし てがみを だしあって
います。・毎年 手紙を 出し合っ
ています。

**eager** *adjective*
= ねっしん(な)・熱心(な)

**eagle** *noun*
= わし

**ear** *noun*
= みみ・耳

**early**
**1** *adjective*
= はやい・早い
**2** *adverb*
= はやく・早く
to get up early = はやく おきる・
早く 起きる
early in the morning = あさ はやく・
朝 早く
to arrive early = はやく つく・早く
着く

**earn** *verb*
I earn a lot of money = きゅうりょう
は たかいです。・給料は 高いで
す。

**earring** *noun*
(*for pierced ears*) = ピアス
(*clip-on*) = イヤリング

**earth** *noun*
• (*the planet*)
= ちきゅう・地球
• (*soil*)
= つち・土

**easily** *adverb*
= かんたんに・簡単に

**east**
**1** *noun*
= ひがし・東
in the east of Japan = ひがしにほん
に・東日本に
**2** *adverb*
to go east = ひがしに いく・東に
行く
**3** *adjective*
= ひがし・東

to work in east London = ひがしロンドンで はたらく・東ロンドンで 働く

**Easter** *noun*
= ふっかつさい・復活祭

> ❗ *not generally celebrated in Japan (British English)*

Easter holiday = はるやすみ・春休み

**easy** *adjective*
= かんたん(な)・簡単(な)
it's easy to fix = なおすのは かんたんです。・直すのは 簡単です。
it's not easy to find work here = ここで しごとを みつけるのは かんたんではありません。・ここで 仕事を 見つけるのは 簡単ではありません。
easy to..... = verb in pre ます form + やすい ▶ 191

**eat** *verb*
= たべる・食べる
(soup) = のむ・飲む

> ❗ *There are various honorific and humble ways of expressing this verb* ▶ 189

eat out = がいしょくする・外食する

**EC** *noun* ▶ **EU**

**echo** *noun*
= こだま

**economic** *adjective*
= けいざいてき(な)・経済的(な)

**economics** *noun*
= けいざいがく・経済学

**economy** *noun*
= けいざい・経済

**edge** *noun*
• (of a road, table, an object)
= はし・端
the edge of the lake = こはん・湖畔
at the edge of the town = まちの はしに・町の 端に

**educate** *verb*
= きょういくする・教育する
I was educated in Paris = パリで きょういくを うけました。・パリで 教育を 受けました。

**education** *noun*
= きょういく・教育

to get a good education = いい きょういくを うける・良い 教育を 受ける

**effect** *noun*
= けっか・結果

**effective** *adjective*
= こうかてき(な)・効果的(な)

**efficient** *adjective*
= のうりつてき(な)・能率的(な)

**effort** *noun*
= どりょく・努力
to make an effort = どりょくする・努力する

**egg** *noun*
= たまご・卵

**eggcup** *noun*
= ゆでたまごおき・ゆで卵置き

**eight** *number* ▶ **171**, ▶ **181**, ▶ **186**
(on its own) = やっつ・八つ
(with a counter) = はち・八
eight books = ほん はっさつ・本八冊
I've got eight = やっつ あります。・八つ あります。

**eighteen** *number* ▶ **171**, ▶ **181**
= じゅうはち・十八

**eighteenth** *number*
• (in a series) = じゅうはちばん(め)・十八番(目)
• (in dates) ▶ **174**
the eighteenth of August = はちがつ じゅうはちにち・八月十八日

**eighth** *number*
• (in a series) = はちばん(め)・八番(目)
• (in dates) ▶ **174**
= ようか・八日
the eighth of August = はちがつようか・八月八日

**eighty** *number* ▶ **171**, ▶ **181**
= はちじゅう・八十

**either**
**1** *conjunction*
they're coming on either Tuesday or Wednesday = かれらは かようびか すいようびに きます。・彼らは 火曜日か 水曜日に 来ます。
I didn't contact either Helen or Paul = ヘレンさんにも ポールさんにも れんらくしませんでした。・ヘレンさんにも ポールさんにも 連絡しませんでした。

**2** *pronoun*
either one is OK = どちらでも いい です。
I don't know either = どちらも しりません。・ どちらも 知りません。
**3** *determiner*
I don't want to do either = どちらも したくないです。
**4** *adverb*
I can't do it either = わたしも できません。・ 私も できません。

**elbow** *noun*
= ひじ

**elder** *adjective*
= としうえ(の)・ 年上(の)

**elderly** *adjective*
= ねんぱい(の)・ 年配(の)

**eldest** *adjective*
= いちばんとしうえ(の)・ 一番年上(の)
eldest daughter = ちょうじょ・ 長女
eldest son = ちょうなん・ 長男

**elect** *verb*
= せんきょする・ 選挙する

**election** *noun*
= せんきょ・ 選挙

**electric** *adjective*
= でんき(の)・ 電気(の)

**electrician** *noun*
= でんきやさん・ 電気屋さん

**electricity** *noun*
= でんき・ 電気

**electronic** *adjective*
= でんし(の)・ 電子(の)
electronic organiser = でんしてちょう・ 電子手帳

**elegant** *adjective*
= じょうひん(な)・ 上品(な)

**elephant** *noun*
= ぞう・ 象

**elevator** *noun* (US English)
= エレベーター

**eleven** *number* ▶ 171, ▶ 181, ▶ 186
= じゅういち・ 十一

**eleventh** *number*
• (*in a series*) = じゅういちばん(め)・ 十一番(目)
• (*in dates*) ▶ 174
  = じゅういちにち・ 十一日

the eleventh of May = ごがつじゅういちにち・ 五月十一日

**else**
**1** *adverb*
someone else
(*additional person*) = もう ひとり・ もう 一人
(*different person*) = ちがう ひと・ 違う 人
there is nothing else = ほかに ありません。・ 外に ありません。
what else did he say? = かれは ほかに なんと いいましたか。・ 彼は 外に 何と 言いましたか。
something else
(*object*) = ほかの もの・ 外の 物
(*topic*) = ほかの こと・ 外の こと
everything else = ほかの ぜんぶ・ 外の 全部
**2 or else**
be quiet or else I'll get angry = しずかに しないと おこりますよ。・ 静かに しないと 怒りますよ。

**elsewhere** *adverb*
= べつの ばしょ・ 別の 場所

**email** *noun*
= メール

**embarrassed** *adjective*
= はずかしい・ 恥ずかしい

**embarrassing** *adjective*
= はずかしい・ 恥ずかしい

**embassy** *noun*
= たいしかん・ 大使館

**emergency** *noun*
= きゅうきゅう・ 救急
in an emergency = きゅうきゅうの ときに・ 救急の とき に

**emergency exit** *noun*
= ひじょうぐち・ 非常口

**emigrate** *verb*
= いじゅうする・ 移住する

**emotion** *noun*
= かんじょう・ 感情

**emotional** *adjective*
• (*describing a scene or moment*) = かんどうてき(な)・ 感動的(な)
• (*describing a person*) = かんじょうてき(な)・ 感情的(な)

**emperor** *noun*
= こうてい・ 皇帝
(*of Japan*) = てんのう・ 天皇

**employ** *verb*
 = やとう・雇う

**employed** *adjective*
 to be employed (taken on) = やとわ
 れる・雇われる
 I am working for Sony = ソニーに つ
 とめています。・ソニーに 勤め
 ています。

**employee** *noun*
 = しょくいん・職員

> **!** *There are various terms
> depending on the institution for
> which people work*

**employer** *noun*
 (*company*) = かいしゃ・会社
 (*individual*) = ボス *A more formal
 word for written Japanese is*
 こようしゃ

**employment** *noun*
 = しごと・仕事

**empty**
 **1** *adjective*
 (*container*) = から(の)・空(の)
 (*house*) = あき(の)・空き(の)
 the room is empty (no people) = へや
 に だれも いません。・部屋に
 誰も いません。
 **2** *verb*
 = からにする・空にする

**encourage** *verb*
 = はげます・励ます

**end**
 **1** *noun*
 • (*the final part*)
 = おわり・終わり
 at the end of the film = えいがの おわ
 りに・映画の 終わりに
 at the end of May = ごがつの おわ
 りに・五月の 終わりに
 in the end = おわりに・終わりに
 • (*the furthest part*)
 = おわり・終わり
 **2** *verb*
 • (*to come to an end*) = おわる・終わる
 • (*to put an end to*) = おえる・終える
 to end the war = せんそうを おえる
 ・戦争を 終える

**ending** *noun*
 (*story*) = けつまつ・結末

**enemy** *noun*
 = てき・敵

**energetic** *adjective*
 = げんき(な)・元気(な)

**energy** *noun*
 = エネルギー

**engaged** *adjective*
 • to get engaged = こんやくする・
 婚約する
 to be engaged = こんやくしている
 ・婚約している
 • (*British English*)
 (*describing a phone*) = はなしちゅう
 ・話し中
 (*describing a toilet*) = しようちゅう・
 使用中

**engine** *noun*
 = エンジン

**engineer** *noun*
 = ぎし・技師

**England** *noun* ▶ 172
 = イギリス

**English** ▶ 172
 **1** *adjective*
 = イギリスの
 **2** *noun*
 • (*the people*)
 = イギリスじん・イギリス人
 • (*the language*)
 = えいご・英語

**enjoy** *verb*
 • (*to like*) = たのしむ・楽しむ
 I enjoy fishing = つりを たのしみま
 す。・釣りを 楽しみます。
 did you enjoy your trip? = りょこう
 は どうでしたか。・旅行は どう
 でしたか。
 • (*to have a good time*)
 to enjoy oneself = たのしむ・楽しむ

**enjoyable** *adjective*
 = たのしい・楽しい

**enormous** *adjective*
 = きょだい(な)・巨大(な)

**enough**
 **1** *determiner*
 I don't have enough money = おかね
 が たりません。・お金が 足りま
 せん。
 I have enough time = じかんが たり
 ます。・時間が 足ります。
 there's enough room for everyone =
 みんなが はいれます。・皆 が 入
 れます。

**2** adverb

> ! enough is not usually translated

is it good enough? = いいですか。

he's not old enough (by law) = かれ は みせいねんしゃです。・ 彼は 未成年者です。

**3** pronoun

have you had enough? = たりました か。・ 足りましたか。

I've had enough = もう いいです。

**enquire** verb
= きく・ 聞く

I'll enquire about the price = ねだんを ききます。・ 値段を 聞きます。

**enquiry** noun
= といあわせ・ 問い合わせ

**enter** verb
- (to go into) = はいる・ 入る
- (to take part in) = さんかする・ 参加 する

to enter a competition = きょうぎに さんかする・ 競技に 参加する

**entertain** verb
(a client) = せったいする・ 接待する
(at home) = もてなす・ 持て成す

**entertaining** adjective
= おもしろい・ 面白い

**entertainment** noun
(organised) = ショー

**enthusiasm** noun
= ねっしん・ 熱心

**enthusiastic** adjective
= ねっしん(な)・ 熱心(な)

**entrance** noun
= いりぐち・ 入り口

the entrance to the museum = はくぶ つかんの いりぐち・ 博物館の 入り口

**envelope** noun
= ふうとう・ 封筒

**environment** noun
= かんきょう・ 環境

**envy**
**1** noun
= しっと
**2** verb
= うらやむ

**episode** noun
(of story)
episode 1 = だいいちわ・ 第一話

last week's episode of "Friends" = せ んしゅうの 「フレンズ」・ 先週 の 「フレンズ」

final episode = さいしゅうかい・ 最終回

(incident) = できごと・ 出来事

**equal**
**1** adjective
= びょうどう(な)・ 平等(な)

equal opportunities = きかいきんと う・ 機会均等

**2** verb

six plus four equals ten = ろく たす よんは じゅうです。・ 六足す 四 は 十です。

**equality** noun
= びょうどう・ 平等

gender equality = だんじょびょうど う・ 男女平等

**equator** noun
= せきどう・ 赤道

**equipment** noun
(in an office, a laboratory, a factory) = せつび・ 設備

(for an activity) = どうぐ・ 道具

**eraser** noun
= けしゴム・ 消しゴム

**escalator** noun
= エスカレーター

**escape** verb
- (to get away) = にげだす・ 逃げ出す

I escaped from prison = けいむしょ から にげだしました。・ 刑務所 から 逃げ出しました。

- (to avoid) = さける・ 避ける

to escape death = しを まぬがれる ・ 死を 免れる

**especially** adverb
= とくに・ 特に

**essay** noun
(by a pupil) = さくぶん・ 作文
(by a student) = レポート

**essential** adjective
= ひつよう(な)・ 必要(な)

**ethnic** adjective

ethnic minority = しょうすうみんぞ く・ 少数民族

**EU** ▶ European Union

**euro** noun
= ユーロ

**Europe** noun ▶ 172
= ヨーロッパ

**European** adjective ▶ 172
= ヨーロッパの

**European Union** noun
= おうしゅうれんごう・欧州連合

**evacuate** verb
= ひなんする・避難する

**even**¹
**1** adverb
• (when expressing surprise) = さえ
  I didn't even phone = でんわさえ し
  ませんでした。電話さえ しませ
  んでした。
  I even work at weekends = しゅうま
  つさえ はたらきます。・週末
  さえ 働きます。
• (in comparisons) = もっと
  it's even colder today = きょうは も
  っと さむいです。・今日は もっ
  と 寒いです。
**2 even though** = でも

  ! or use て form of verb + も ▶ 197

  he's bored even though he has lots of
  toys = かれは おもちゃが たくさ
  ん あっても たいくつしていま
  す。・彼はおもちゃがたくさん
  あっても 退屈しています。

**even**² adjective
• (flat, smooth) = たいら(な)・平ら
  (な)
• (when talking about numbers)
  even number = ぐうすう・偶数

**evening** noun ▶ 186
= よる・夜
  at eight o'clock in the evening = よる
  はちじに・夜 八時に
  to spend the evening at home = よる
  を いえで すごす・夜を 家で 過
  ごす
  this evening = こんばん・今晩

**event** noun
= イベント

**eventually** adverb
= けっきょく・結局

**ever** adverb
• (at any time)

  ! Not usually translated

  no-one will ever know = だれも しり
  ません。・誰も 知りません。

have you ever been to Japan = にほ
んに いった ことが ありますか。
・ 日本に 行った ことが ありま
すか。
I hardly ever go there = ほとんど
そこに いきません。・ほとんど
そこに 行きません。
• (always)
he's as lazy as ever = かれは あいか
わらず なまけものです。・彼は
相変わらず 怠け者です。

**every** determiner

  ! Often not translated. Sometimes
  まい + counter can be used. ▶ 181

  every day = まいにち・毎日
  every time I meet her = かのじょに
  あう たびに・彼女に 会う たび
  に
  every second day, every other day =
  いちにちおき・一日おき
  two out of every three people = さん
  にんに ふたり・三人に 二人

**everyone** pronoun (also
**everybody**)
= みんな・皆 Note that on more
formal occasions みな is used.
  everyone else = ほかの みんな・
  外の 皆

**everything** pronoun
= ぜんぶ・全部

**everywhere** adverb
= どこでも
  everywhere else = place + いがい =
  everywhere except that place

**evidence** noun
  piece of evidence = しょうこ・証拠
  to give evidence = しょうげんする
  ・証言する

**evil** adjective
= わるい・悪い

**exact** adjective
= せいかく(な)・正確(な)

**exactly** adverb
= せいかくに・正確に

**exaggerate** verb
= おおげさにいう・大げさに 言う

**exam** noun
= しけん・試験
  to pass an exam = しけんに ごうか
  くする・試験に 合格する
  to take an exam = しけんを うける
  ・試験を 受ける

**examine** *verb*
  (*a candidate*) = しけんする・試験する
  (*inspect*) = しらべる・調べる
  (*a patient*) = しんさつする・診察する

**example** *noun*
  = れい・例
  for example = たとえば・例えば

**excellent** *adjective*
  = すばらしい

**except** *preposition*
  = 〜いがい・〜以外
  all except apples = りんご いがい・りんご 以外

**exchange** *verb*
  = こうかんする・交換する
  to exchange money = おかねを かえる・お金を 替える

**exchange rate** *noun*
  = こうかんレート・交換レート

**excited** *adjective*
  = こうふんしている・興奮している

**exciting** *adjective*
  = どきどきさせる

**exclude** *verb*
  to be excluded from school = たいがくさせられる・退学させられる

**excuse**
**1** *noun*
  = いいわけ・言い訳
  to make excuses = いいわけを する・言い訳を する
**2** *verb*
  = ゆるす・許す
  excuse me! = すみません。

**exercise** *noun*
  • (*to keep fit*)
  = うんどう・運動
  to take exercise, to do exercise = うんどうを する・運動を する
  • (*a piece of work*)
  = れんしゅう・練習

**exercise book** *noun*
  = ノート

**exhausted** *adjective*
  = つかれている・疲れている

**exhibition** *noun*
  = てんらんかい・展覧会

**exit** *noun*
  = でぐち・出口

**expect** *verb*
  • (*to be prepared for something bad*) = かくごする・覚悟する
  I'm expecting bad news = わるい しらせを かくごしています。・悪い 知らせを 覚悟しています。
  (*general expectation*) = はず
  I expect to win = かつ はずです。・勝つ はずです。
  • (*to wait for*) = まつ・待つ
  I'm expecting visitors = おきゃくさんを まっています。・お客さんを 待っています。
  • (*to want*) = use verb in the 〜て form + ほしい for your own expectations and て form + ほしい という for reporting those of other people
  ▶ 197
  I expect you to arrive by five = ごじまでに ついて ほしいです。・五時までに 着いて ほしいです。
  my boss expects me to do overtime = ボスは ざんぎょうして ほしい といいました。・ボスは 残業して ほしいと 言いました。

**expenses** *noun*
  = けいひ・経費

**expensive** *adjective*
  = たかい・高い

**experience** *noun*
  = けいけん・経験

**experienced** *adjective*
  = けいけんの ある・経験の ある

**experiment**
**1** *noun*
  = じっけん・実験
**2** *verb*
  = じっけんする・実験する

**expert** *noun*
  = エキスパート
  computer expert = コンピューター・エキスパート

**explain** *verb*
  = せつめいする・説明する
  to explain a rule to someone = だれかに ルールを せつめいする・誰かに ルールを 説明する

**explanation** *noun*
  = せつめい・説明

**explode** *verb*
= ばくはつする・爆発する

**exploit** *verb*
= りようする・利用する

**explosion** *noun*
= ばくはつ・爆発

**export** *verb*
= ゆしゅつする・輸出する

**express**
**1** *verb*
= ひょうげんする・表現する
**2** *adverb*
to send a letter express = てがみを
そくたつで おくる・手紙を 速
達で 送る

**expression** *noun*
= ひょうげん・表現
facial expression = かおの ひょうじ
ょう・顔の 表情

**express train** *noun*
= とっきゅうれっしゃ・特急列車

**extinct** *adjective*
(*describing an animal*) = ぜつめつし
た・絶滅した
extinct volcano = しかざん・死火山

**extra**
**1** *adjective*
= よぶん(の)・余分(の)
an extra bed = よぶんの ベッド・
余分の ベッド
**2** *adverb*
to pay extra = よけいに はらう・余
計に 払う

**extraordinary** *adjective*
= いじょう(な)・異常(な)

**extreme** *adjective*
= ひじょう(な)・非常(な)

**extremely** *adverb*
= ひじょうに・非常に

**eye** *noun*
= め・目
my eyes are blue = めが あおいで
す。・目が 青いです。

**eyebrow** *noun*
= まゆげ・眉毛

**eyelash** *noun*
= まつげ・まつ毛

**eyelid** *noun*
= まぶた

**eye shadow** *noun*
= アイシャドー

**eyesight** *noun*
= しりょく・視力
to have good eyesight = めが いい・
目が いい

# Ff

**face**
**1** *noun*
= かお・顔
to make a face = かおを しかめる・
顔を しかめる
**2** *verb*
• (*to have to deal with*) = ～に むきあわ
なければ ならない・～に向き
合わなければ ならない
I can't face seeing them again = もう
かれらに あいたくないです。・
もう 彼らに 会いたくないです。
• (*to look toward(s*))
my room faces the sea = わたしの へ
やは うみに めんしています。・
私の 部屋は海に 面しています。

**fact**
**1** *noun*
= じじつ・事実
**2 in fact** = じつは・実は

**factory** *noun*
= こうじょう・工場

**fade** *verb*
(*if it's a colour*) = あせる

**fail** *verb*
= しっぱいする・失敗する
to fail an exam = しけんに おちる・
試験に 落ちる

**failure** *noun*
(*an event, an attempt*) = しっぱい・
失敗
(*a person*) = しっぱいしゃ・失敗者
(*in exam*) = ふごうかく・不合格

**faint** *verb*
= きぜつする・気絶する

**fair**
**1** *adjective*
• (*just*) = こうへい(な)・公平(な)

it's not fair = ふこうへいです。・
不公平です。
* (in colour)
  fair hair = きんぱつ・金髪
  fair skin = いろじろな はだ・色白
  な 肌
2 noun
* (British English)
  (a funfair)
  = いどうゆうえんち・移動遊園地
  rare in Japan
* (a display of goods)
  (trade) fair = (トレード)フェアー

**fairly** adverb
= まあまあ

**faith** noun
to have faith (in someone) = (だれか
を)しんらいする・(誰かを)信
頼する

**faithful** adjective
= ちゅうじつ(な)・忠実(な)

**fall**
1 verb
* (if it's a person) = たおれる・倒れる
* (to come down, to be reduced) = さが
  る・下がる
* (other uses)
  to fall asleep = ねむる・眠る
  to fall ill = びょうきに なる・病気
  に なる
  to fall in love with someone = だれか
  と こいに おちる・誰かと 恋に
  落ちる
2 noun
* = ていか・低下
* (US English)
  (autumn)
  = あき・秋
  **fall down**
* = たおれる・倒れる
  **fall off** = おちる・落ちる
  to fall off a chair = いすから おちる
  ・椅子から 落ちる
  **fall out**
* (from somewhere) = おちる・落ちる
  the letter fell out of my pocket = てが
  みが ポケットから おちました。
  ・手紙が ポケットから 落ちまし
  た。
* (to quarrel) = けんかする
  **fall over**
  (if it's a person) = ころぶ・転ぶ
  (if it's a thing) = たおれる・倒れる
  **fall through** = だめに なる

**false** adjective
(facts) = ただしくない・正しくな
い
true or false? = まるですか、ばつで
すか。・Oですか、Xですか。

**false teeth** noun
= いれば・入歯

**familiar** adjective
= しっている・知っている

**family** noun ▶ 177, ▶ 189
(your own) = かぞく・家族
(someone else's) = ごかぞく・ご家
族

**famous** adjective
= ゆうめい(な)・有名(な)

**fan** noun
* (of a pop star, an actor, a sport)
  = ファン
* (for cooling)
  (electrical) = せんぷうき・扇風機
  (hand-held) = うちわ

**fancy dress party** noun (British
English)
= かそうパーティー・仮装パーテ
ィー

**fantastic** adjective
= すばらしい・素晴らしい

**far**
1 adverb
* how far is it to London? = ロンドンま
  で、きょりは どのくらいですか。
  ・ロンドンまで、距離は どのく
  らいですか。
  how far is Tokyo from London? = と
  うきょうと ロンドンの きょり
  は どのくらいですか。・東京と
  ロンドンの 距離は どのくらい
  ですか。
  we went as far as the coast = かいが
  んまで いきました。・海岸まで
  行きました。
2 adjective
= とおい・遠い
at the far side of the room = へやの む
こうがわに・部屋の 向こう側
に
3 so far = いままで・今まで

**fare** noun
(on a bus, a train or the underground)
= うんちん・運賃
(on a plane) = りょうきん・料金

**farm** *noun*
= のうじょう・農場

**farmer** *noun*
= のうか・農家

**fascinating** *adjective*
= おもしろい・面白い

**fashion** *noun*
= ファッション
to be in fashion = はやっている・流行っている
to be out of fashion = はやっていない・流行っていない

**fashionable** *adjective*
= りゅうこう(の)・流行(の)

**fast**
**1** *adjective*
• (*describing movement*) = はやい・速い
• to be fast = すすんでいる・進んでいる
my watch is ten minutes fast = わたしの とけいは じゅっぷん すすんでいます。・私の時計は十分進んでいます。
**2** *adverb*
= はやく・速く

**fasten** *verb*
to fasten a seatbelt = シートベルトを しめる・シートベルトを締める

**fast-forward** *verb*
to fast-forward a cassette = カセットを さきおくりする・カセットを 先送りする

**fat** *adjective*
= ふとっている・太っている
to get fat = ふとる・太る

**fatal** *adjective*
= ちめいてき(な)・致命的(な)

**father** *noun* ▶ 177, ▶ 189
(*your own*) = ちち・父
(*someone else's*) = おとうさん・お父さん

**Father Christmas** *noun* (*British English*)
= サンタクロース

**father-in-law** *noun* ▶ 177
(*one's own*) = ぎりの ちち・義理の父

**faucet** *noun* (*US English*)
= じゃぐち・蛇口

**fault** *noun*
= せい
it's not my fault = わたしの せいではありません。・私の せいではありません。
whose fault was it? = だれの せいでしたか。・誰の せいでしたか。

**favour** (*British English*), **favor**
(*US English*)
**1** *noun*
= おねがい・お願い
I have a favour to ask = おねがいがあります。・お願いが あります。
to do someone a favour

> ! *no direct equivalent* ▶ 189

to ask someone a favour = だれかにたのむ・誰かに頼む
**2 in favour of**
to be in favour of that plan = その けいかくに さんせいしている・その 計画に 賛成している

**favourite** (*British English*),
**favorite** (*US English*) *adjective*
= いちばんすき(な)・一番好き(な)
this is my favourite film = これが わたしの いちばんすきな えいがです。・これが 私の 一番好きな映画です。

**fax** *noun*
= ファックス

**fear** *verb*
= しんぱいする・心配する

**feather** *noun*
= はね・羽根

**February** *noun* ▶ 174
= にがつ・二月

**fed up** *adjective*
= うんざりしている

**fee** *noun*
(*to attend an event, a show*) = にゅうじょうりょうきん・入場料金
(*to join a club, a union*) = にゅうかいきん・入会金

**feeble** *adjective*
= よわい・弱い

**feed** *verb*
(*people*) = ごはんを あげる・ご飯を あげる
(*animals*) = えさを あげる・餌をあげる

I must feed the dog = いぬに えさを あげなければ なりません。犬に 餌を あげなければ なりません。

**feel** *verb*
• = かんじる・感じる

> ! *Japanese is very different to English when describing feelings, it is often best to translate with an adjective + です when referring to yourself ▶ 178*

(*referring to an emotion, an impression or a physical feeling*)
I feel lonely = さびしいです。・寂しいです。
it feels cold = さむい です。
I feel tired = つかれました。・疲れました。
it feels nice = きもち いいです。・気持ち いいです。
• (*to touch*) = さわる・触る
• to feel like... = use the pre ます form of the verb + たい for yourself and the pre ます form of the verb + たがる for others ▶ 191
I feel like eating pizza = ピザが たべたいです。・ピザが 食べたいです。
I don't feel like it = したくないです。

**feeling** *noun*
• (*emotional*)
= きもち・気持ち
to hurt someone's feelings = だれかの きもちを きずつける・誰かの 気持ちを 傷付ける
• (*physical*)
= かんじ・感じ
• I have a feeling he's right = かれが ただしいと いう きが します。・彼が 正しいという 気がします。

**felt-tip pen** *noun*
= サインペン

**female** *adjective*
• (*in biology*) = めす(の)・雌(の)
• (*relating to women*) = おんな(の)・女(の)

**fence** *noun*
= フェンス

**fencing** *noun*
= フェンシング
(*Japanese traditional*) = けんどう・剣道

**festival** *noun*
= おまつり・お祭り ▶ 189

**fetch** *verb*
= もってくる・持ってくる
please fetch some water = みずを もって きてください。・水を 持って きてください。

**fever** *noun*
to have a fever = ねつが ある・熱が ある

**few** *adjective*
= に、さん + counter・二、三 + counter ▶ 181

> ! *Usage very different to English*

a few people = に、さんにん・二、三人
a few books = ほん に、さんさつ・本二、三冊
• (*not many*) = あまり + *negative*
few people came = あまり ひとが きませんでした。・あまり 人が 来ませんでした。
• (*several*)
= すう + counter・数 + counter
the first few weeks = はじめの すうしゅうかん・初めの 数週間

**field** *noun*
= のはら・野原
(*of crops*) = はたけ・畑

**fifteen** *number* ▶ 171, ▶ 181
= じゅうご・十五

**fifteenth** *number*
• (*in a series*) = じゅうごばん(め)・十五番(目)
• (*in dates*) ▶ 174
= じゅうごにち・十五日
the fifteenth of May = ごがつじゅうごにち・五月十五日

**fifth** *number* ▶ 181
• (*in a series*) = ごばん(め)・五番(目)
• (*in dates*) ▶ 174
= いつか・五日
the fifth of June = ろくがついつか・六月五日

**fifty** *number* ▶ 171, ▶ 181
= ごじゅう・五十

**fight**
**1** *verb*
(*in war*) = たたかう・戦う
to fight the enemy = てきと たたかう・敵と 戦う
• (*physically*) = けんかする
• (*to quarrel*) = くちげんかを する・口げんかを する

**2** *noun*
  (*physical*)
  = けんか

**figure** *noun*
- (*a number*)
  = すうじ・数字
- (*physical*) = すがた・姿

**file** *noun*
- = ファイル
- single file = ひとり ひとり・一人
  一人

**fill** *verb*
- (*to make full*) = いっぱいに する
- (*to become full*) = いっぱいに なる
  **fill in**
  (*form*) = きにゅうする・記入する

**film**
**1** *noun*
- (*in cinema or on TV*)
  = えいが・映画
- (*for a camera*)
  = フィルム
**2** *verb*
  = さつえいする・撮影する

**filthy** *adjective*
  = きたない・汚い

**final**
**1** *adjective*
  = さいご(の)・最後(の)
**2** *noun*
  = けっしょうせん・決勝戦

**finally** *adverb*
  = さいごに・最後に

**find** *verb*
  = みつける・見つける
  **find out**
  to find out the truth = しんじつを は
  っけんする・真実を 発見する

**fine**
**1** *adjective*
- (*weather*) = はれ(の)・晴れ(の)
  the weather will probably be fine =
  てんきは はれでしょう。・天気
  は 晴れでしょう。
- (*in good health*)
  I feel fine = げんきです。・元気です。
- (*expressing agreement*)
  (that's) fine = いいです。
**2** *noun*
  = ばっきん・罰金

**finger** *noun*
  = ゆび・指

**finish**
**1** *verb*
- (*to end*) = おえる・終える
  to finish writing a letter = てがみを か
  きおえる・手紙を 書き終える
- (*to come to an end*) = おわる・終わる
**2** *noun*
  (*in a race*) = ゴールライン

**fire**
**1** *noun*
  = かじ・火事
  (*open fire*) = だんろ・暖炉
  (*gas/electric*) = ストーブ
  (*causing damage*) = かじ・火事
  to catch fire = かじに なる・火事に
  なる
  to be on fire = もえている・燃えて
  いる
**2** *verb*
- (*to shoot*) = はっぽうする・発砲す
  る
- (*to dismiss*) = くびに する・首に す
  る

**fire alarm** *noun*
  = かさいけいほうき・火災警報機

**fire engine** *noun*
  = しょうぼうしゃ・消防車

**firefighter** *noun*
  = しょうぼうし・消防士

**fire station** *noun*
  = しょうぼうしょ・消防署

**fireworks** *noun*
  = はなび・花火

**firm**
**1** *noun*
  = かいしゃ・会社
**2** *adjective*
  = かたい・固い

**first**
**1** *adjective*
  = さいしょ(の)・最初(の)
  the first time = だいいっかい・第一
  回
  the first three weeks = さいしょのさ
  んしゅうかん・最初の 三週間
**2** *adverb*
- (*to begin with*) = さいしょに・最初に
  first of all = さいしょに・最初に
- (*for the first time*) = はじめて・初めて
- to arrive first = さいしょに つく・
  最初に 着く

**3** *noun*
- (*in a series or group*)
  the first = いちばんめ・一番目
- (*in dates*) ▶ **174**
  = ついたち・一日
  the first of June = ろくがつついたち
  ・六月一日
**4** at first = さいしょに・最初に

**first aid** *noun*
= おうきゅうてあて・応急手当

**first class** *adverb*
to travel first class = ファーストク
ラスで いく・ファーストクラ
スで 行く

**first floor** *noun*
the first floor
(*in Britain*) = にかい・二階
(*in the US*) = いっかい・一階

**first name** *noun*
= ファーストネーム *Note that
Japanese names are given in the
order of family name then given
name.*

**fish**
**1** *noun*
= さかな・魚
**2** *verb*
to go fishing = つりに いく・釣りに
行く

**fisherman** *noun*
= りょうし・漁師

**fishing** *noun*
= つり・釣り

**fishing rod** *noun*
= つりざお・釣り竿

**fist** *noun*
= こぶし

**fit**
**1** *verb*
these shoes don't fit me = この くつ
は あしに あいません。・この靴
は 足に 合いません。
this photo won't fit into the envelope =
この しゃしんは ふうとうに は
いりません。・この 写真は 封筒
に 入りません。
**2** *adjective*
(*healthy*)
= げんき(な)・元気(な)
**fit in**
- (*in a room or car*)
  = はいる・入る

- (*in a group or team*) = とけこむ・溶
  け込む

**fitness** *noun*
(*physical*) fitness = けんこう・健康

**five** *number* ▶ **171**, ▶ **181**, ▶ **186**
(*on its own*) = いつつ・五つ
(*with a counter*) = ご・五
five books = ほん ごさつ・本 五冊
I've got five = いつつ あります。・
五つ あります。

**fix** *verb*
- (*to decide on, to set*) = きめる・決め
  る
- (*to be decided on, to be set*) = きまる
  ・決まる
- (*to repair*) = なおす・直す
  to get a watch fixed = とけいを なお
  して もらう・時計を 直して も
  らう
- (*to prepare*) = つくる
  to fix dinner = ゆうごはんを つくる
  ・夕ご飯を 作る

**flag** *noun*
= はた・旗
(*national flag*) = こっき・国旗

**flame** *noun*
= ほのお・炎
to go up in flames = もえる・燃える

**flash**
**1** *noun*
(*for a camera*) = フラッシュ
**2** *verb*
to flash (on and off) = てんめつする
・点滅する

**flashlight** *noun*
= かいちゅうでんとう・懐中電灯

**flask** *noun*
(*water bottle*) = すいとう・水筒
(*vacuum flask*) = まほうびん・魔法
瓶

**flat**
**1** *noun* (*British English*)
= アパート
**2** *adjective*
= たいら(な)・平ら(な)
flat tyre = パンク

**flavour** (*British English*), **flavor**
(*US English*) *noun*
= あじ・味

**flea** *noun*
= のみ

**flight** *noun*
= フライト
(*flight number 147*) = ひゃくよんじゅうななびん・百四七便

**flight attendant** *noun*
= きゃくしつじょうむいん・客室乗務員

**float** *verb*
= うかぶ・浮かぶ

**flood** *noun*
= こうずい・洪水

**floor** *noun*
• (*a surface*)
= ゆか・床
to sit on the floor = ゆかに すわる・床に 座る
• (*a storey*)
= かい・階 ▶ 181

**florist** *noun*
= はなや・花屋

**flour** *noun*
= こむぎこ・小麦粉

**flow** *verb*
= ながれる・流れる

**flower**
**1** *noun*
= はな・花
**2** *verb*
= さく・咲く

**flu** *noun*
= かぜ・風邪

**fluent** *adjective*
her Japanese is fluent = かのじょの にほんごは ぺらぺらです。・彼女の 日本語は ぺらぺらです。

**flush** *verb*
to flush the toilet = トイレを ながす・トイレを 流す

**flute** *noun* ▶ 180
= フルート

**fly**
**1** *noun*
= はえ
**2** *verb*
• (*if it's a bird, a kite, a plane, an insect*)
= とぶ・飛ぶ
• (*if it's a passenger*) = ひこうきで いく・飛行機で 行く
to fly from London to Tokyo = ロンドンから とうきょうまで ひこうきで いく・ロンドンから 東京まで 飛行機で 行く
• to fly a plane・飛行機を 操縦する
うする・飛行機を 操縦する
• (*if it's a flag*) = かかげる・掲げる
**fly away** = とんで いく・飛んで 行く

**fog** *noun*
= きり・霧

**fold** *verb*
• to fold a shirt = シャツをおりたたむ・シャツを 折りたたむ
• to fold one's arms = うでを くむ・腕を 組む

**folder** *noun*
(*for work, school*) = ファイル
(*in computing*) = フォルダー

**follow** *verb*
• (*to go or come after*) = あとに ついて いく・後に ついて 行く
• (*to use, to look at*) = したがう・従う
I followed the instructions = せつめいどおりに しました。・説明通りに しました。

**following** *adjective*
= つぎ(の)・次(の)

**fond** *adjective*
I'm very fond of you = あなたが すきです。・あなたが 好きです。

**food** *noun*
= たべもの・食べ物

**fool** *verb*
= だます・騙す

**foot** *noun*
• (*part of the leg*)
= あし・足
on foot = あるいて・歩いて
I go to school on foot = がっこうに あるいていきます。・学校に 歩いて 行きます。
• (*in measurements*)
= フィート

! Note that a foot = 30.48 cm.

**football** *noun*
• (*soccer*) = サッカー
(*American football*) = アメリカンフットボール
• (*a ball*)
= サッカーボール

**footballer** (*British English*),
**football player** (*US English*)
*noun*
= サッカーせんしゅ・サッカー選手

**footprint** *noun*
= あしあと・足跡

**footstep** *noun*
= あしおと・足音

**for** *preposition*

> ! *not usually translated*

a letter has come for you = あなたにてがみが きました。・あなたに手紙が 来ました。
to work for a company = かいしゃにつとめる・会社に 勤める
he cooked dinner for me = かれは わたしに ゆうごはんを つくってくれました。・彼は 私に夕ご飯を 作って くれました。

> ! *doing favours for people is usually expressed using the 〜て form of the verb plus a verb of giving or receiving* ▶ **179,** ▶ **197**

• (*when talking about time*)

> ! *not usually translated*

I've been living here for two years = にねんかん ここに すんでいます。・二年間 ここに 住んでいます。
he's going to Paris for a year = かれはパリに いちねんかん いきます。・彼は パリに 一年間 行きます。

• (*when talking about distance*)

> ! *not translated*

I drove for 80 kilometres = はちじゅっキロ うんてんしました。・八十キロ 運転しました。

• (*when talking about money*)

I bought it for ¥500 = ごひゃくえんで かいました。・五百円で買いました。
a cheque for £20 = にじゅっポンドの こぎって・二十ポンドの小切手

• (*be in favour (of)*) = (〜に)さんせいする・(〜に)賛成する

• (*other uses*)

say hello to her for me = かのじょによろしく つたえてください。・彼女に よろしく 伝えてください。

T for Tom = トムの T
the Minister for Education = もんぶだいじん・文部大臣
what is the Japanese for 'book'? = 'book' はにほんごで なんですか。・ 'book' は 日本語で 何ですか。
I went for a swim = およぎに いきました。・泳ぎに 行きました。

> ! *use pre* ます *form* + に + *verb of motion* ▶ **191**

**forbid** *verb*
= きんしする・禁止する
smoking is forbidden here = ここは きんえんです。・ここは 禁煙です。
going out is forbidden = がいしゅつきんしです。・外出禁止です。

**force**
**1** *verb*
= きょうせいする・強制する
to force someone to work = だれかをはたらかせる・誰かを 働かせる

> ▶ *use causative form* ▶ **191**

**2** *noun*
force = ちから・力
by force = ちからで・力で

**forecast** *noun*
weather forecast = てんきよほう・天気予報

**forehead** *noun*
= ひたい・額

**foreign** *adjective*
= がいこく(の)・外国(の)

**foreigner** *noun*
= がいこくじん・外国人

> ! *usually refers to non-Japanese people*

**forest** *noun*
= もり・森

**forever, for ever** *adverb*
= いつまでも

**forget** *verb*
= わすれる・忘れる
to forget about someone = だれかのことを わすれる・誰かの ことを 忘れる
to forget to call = でんわするのを わすれる・電話するのを 忘れる

> ! *the pre* ます *form* + わすれる *can often be used*

**forgive** *verb*
to forgive someone = だれかを ゆる
す・誰かを 許す

**fork** *noun*
= フォーク

**form**
**1** *noun*
• (*a shape*)
= かたち・形
• (*a document*)
= ようし・用紙
• (*British English*)
(*a class*) ▶ 185
**2** *verb*
• (*to start (a band, business, group)*) =
つくる・作る

**formal** *adjective*
• (*describing language*) = せいしき(な)
・正式(な)
• formal clothes
= せいそう・正装
• (*official*) = こうしき(の)・公式(の)

**former** *adjective*
(*a former*) = まえの・前の
(*the former*) = もと・元

**fortnight** *noun* (*British English*)
= にしゅうかん・二週間

**fortunately** *adverb*
= うんよく・運良く

**fortune** *noun*
• (*money*) = たいきん・大金
to make a fortune = ざいさんを つく
る・財産を 作る
to tell fortunes = うらなう・占う

**forty** *number* ▶ 181, ▶ 186
= よんじゅう・四十

**forward**
**1** *adverb*
= まえへ・前へ
to take a step forward = まえに でる
・前に 出る
**2** *verb*
to forward a letter to someone = だれ
かに てがみを てんそうする・
誰かに 手紙を 転送する

**found** *verb*
= せつりつする・設立する

**fountain** *noun*
= ふんすい・噴水

**four** *number* ▶ 181, ▶ 186
(*on its own*) = よっつ・四つ

(*with a counter*) = よん、し・四
four books = ほん よんさつ・本
四冊
I've got four = よっつ あります。・
四つ あります。
it's four o'clock = よじです。・四時
です。

**fourteen** *number* ▶ 171, ▶ 181
= じゅうよん・十四

**fourteenth** *number*
• (*in a series*) = じゅうよんばん(め)・
十四番(目)
• (*in dates*) ▶ 174
= じゅうよっか・十四日
the fourteenth of July = しちがつじ
ゅうよっか・七月十四日

**fourth** *number*
• (*in a series*) = よんばん(め)・四番
(目)
• (*in dates*) ▶ 174
= よっか・四日
the fourth of July = しちがつよっか
・七月四日

**fox** *noun*
= きつね

**fragile** *adjective*
= こわれやすい・壊れやすい

**frame** *noun*
(*picture*) = わく・枠

**France** *noun* ▶ 172
= フランス

**frank** *adjective*
= そっちょく(な)・率直(な)

**freckle** *noun*
= そばかす

**free**
**1** *adjective*
• (*costing nothing*) = むりょう(の)・
無料(の)
▶ ただ *is often used in conversation*
• (*independent, able to come and go*) =
じゆう(な)・自由(な)
• (*not occupied, available*) = あいている
・空いている
▶ ひま *is often used between friends*
are you free on Monday? = げつよう
びは あいていますか。・月曜日
は 空いていますか。
is this seat free = この せきは あい
ていますか。・この 席は 空いて
いますか。

**2** *verb*
(*person*) = かいほうする・解放する
(*animal*) = にがす・逃がす

**3** *adverb*
= むりょうで・無料で

**freedom** *noun*
= じゆう・自由

**freeway** *noun* (*US English*)
= こうそくどうろ・高速道路

**freeze** *verb*
• (*in cold weather*) = こおる・凍る
   the river froze = かわが こおりました。・川が 凍りました。
   the ground was frozen = つちが こおっていました。・土が 凍っていました。
• (*in a freezer*) = れいとうする・冷凍する
• to freeze to death = とうしする・凍死する

**freezer** *noun*
= れいとうこ・冷凍庫

**freezing** *adjective*
it's freezing = さむいです。・寒いです。
this room is freezing = この へやは さむいです。・この 部屋は 寒いです。

**French** ▶ 172
**1** *adjective*
= フランスの
**2** *noun*
• (*the people*)
   = フランスじん・フランス人
• (*the language*)
   = フランスご・フランス語

**French fries** *noun*
= ポテトフライ

**fresh** *adjective*
= しんせん(な)・新鮮(な)

**Friday** *noun* ▶ 174
= きんようび・金曜日

**fridge** *noun*
= れいぞうこ・冷蔵庫

**fried** *adjective*
= いためた・炒めた
deep-fried = あげた・揚げた

**fried egg** *noun*
= めだまやき・目玉焼き

**friend** *noun*
= ともだち・友達

to make friends = ともだちに なる・友達に なる
to make friends with someone = だれかと ともだちに なる・誰かと 友達に なる

**friendly** *adjective*
(*people*) = あいそうが いい・愛想が いい
(*animals*) = ひとなつっこい・人なつっこい

**fright** *noun*
to get a fright = びっくりする
to give someone a fright = だれかを びっくりさせる・誰かを びっくりさせる

**frightened** *adjective*
to be frightened = こわがる・怖がる
I'm frightened = こわいです。・怖いです。

**fringe** *noun* (*British English*)
= まえがみ・前髪

**frog** *noun*
= かえる

**from** *preposition*

! *There are many verbs which involve the use of* from, *like* borrow from, escape from *etc. For translations, look up the entries at* borrow, escape *etc.*

• = から
I'm from Tokyo = とうきょうから きました。・東京から 来ました。

! *Japanese often say where they're from using place name +* しゅっしん *eg* ロンドンしゅっしんです。*I'm from London*

where is she from? = かのじょは どこからですか。・彼女は どこからですか。
to come back from the office = しごとから かえる・仕事から 帰る
to return from a holiday = りょこうから かえる・旅行から 帰る
there's a message from Paul = ポールからの メッセージが あります。
the train from Kyoto is late = きょうとからの でんしゃは おくれています。・京都からの 電車は 遅れています。
we live ten minutes from the city centre = まちの ちゅうしんから じゅっぷんの ところに すんでいます。

・町の 中心から 10分の 所に 住んでいます。
- (when talking about time) = から
  the shop is open from ten to six = みせは じゅうじから ろくじまで あいています。・ 店は 十時から 六時まで 開いています。
  from Monday to Saturday = げつようびから どようびまで・ 月曜日から 土曜日まで
  from April on = しがつから・ 四月から
  from then on = それから
  in fifty years from now = これから ごじゅうねんご・ これから 五十年後
- (British English)
  (in arithmetic)
  5 from 8 leaves 3 = はち ひくごは さんです。・ 八 引く 五は 三です。

## front
**1** noun
- in front of = ...のまえ・ ...の前
- (of a car, a train or queue)
  the front of the bus = バスの まえの ほう・ バスの 前の 方
  the front of the queue = れつの あたま・ 列 の 頭
**2 in front of** = まえに・ 前に

**front door** noun
= げんかん・ 玄関

**front page** noun
= だいいちめん・ 第一面

**front seat** noun
= ぜんぶざせき・ 前部座席

**frost** noun
= しも・ 霜

**frozen** adjective
= こおっている・ 凍っている
frozen food = れいとうしょくひん・ 冷凍食品

**fruit** noun
= くだもの・ 果物
▶ フルーツ is becoming increasingly common
a piece of fruit = くだもの・ 果物
I like fruit = くだものが すきです。・ 果物が 好きです。

**frustrated** adjective
= ふまんが ある・ 不満が ある

**fry** verb
= いためる・ 炒める

to fry onions = たまねぎを いためる・ 玉ねぎを 炒める
(to deep fry) = あげる・ 揚げる

**frying pan** noun (British English)
= フライパン

**full** adjective
- (not empty) = いっぱい
  the streets were full of people = みちは ひとで いっぱいでした。・ 道は 人で いっぱいでした。
- (describing a flight) = まんせき・ 満席
  (describing a hotel) = まんしつ・ 満室
  (describing a carpark) = まんしゃ・ 満車
  (maximum)
- to travel at full speed = ぜんそくりょくで いく・ 全速力で 行く
  to get full marks = まんてんを とる・ 満点を 取る

**full-time** adverb

> ! not usually expressed as all jobs are full-time unless otherwise stated

▶ **part-time**

**fumes** noun
= ガス
exhaust fumes = はいきガス・ 排気ガス

**fun** noun
it's fun = たのしいです。・ 楽しいです。
skiing is fun = スキーは たのしいです。・ スキーは 楽しいです。
to have fun = たのしむ・ 楽しむ
she's fun = かのじょは おもしろい ひとです。・ 彼女は 面白い人です。

**function** noun
(of a person) = やくわり・ 役割
(of a machine) = きのう・ 機能

**funeral** noun
= おそうしき・ お葬式 ▶ **189**

**funfair** noun (British English)
= いどうゆうえんち・ 移動遊園地

> ! rare in Japan

**funny** adjective
- (amusing) = おもしろい・ 面白い
- (odd) = へん(な)・ 変(な)

**fur** noun
(an animal's coat) = け・ 毛
(on a garment) = けがわ・ 毛皮

**furious** *adjective*
= ひじょうに おこっている ・ 非常
に 怒っている

**furniture** *noun*
= かぐ ・ 家具

**further** *adverb*
= もっと とおくに ・ もっと 遠くに
how much further is it? = あと どのく
らいですか。 ・ 後 どのくらいで
すか。

**fuss** *noun*
= おおさわぎ ・ 大騒ぎ to make a
fuss (complain) = もんくを いう ・
文句を 言う

**fussy** *adjective*
= うるさい
he's a fussy eater = かれは すききら
いが おおいです。 ・ 彼は 好き嫌
いが 多いです。

**future**
1 *noun*
(*general*) = みらい ・ 未来
(*person's*) = しょうらい ・ 将来
in the future = みらいに ・ 未来に
2 *adjective*
= しょうらいの ・ 将来の

# Gg

**gallery** *noun*
= ギャラリー ▶ びじゅつかん

**game** *noun*
= ゲーム、しあい ・ 試合
a game of football = サッカーの しあ
い ・ サッカーの 試合
a game of tennis = テニスの しあい
・ テニスの 試合

**games** *noun* (*British English*)
= たいいく ・ 体育

**game show** *noun*
= ゲームショー

**gang** *noun*
(*a group of friends, young people*) =
なかま ・ 仲間
(*of criminals*) = ギャング

**gap** *noun*
• (*in between things*) = すきま ・ 隙間

• (*a period of time*)
= くうはく ・ 空白

**garage** *noun*
(*place to keep car*) = しゃこ ・ 車庫
(*British English*) (*petrol station*) =
ガソリンスタンド
(*place for car repairs*) = じどうしゃ
しゅうりこうじょう ・ 自動車修
理工場

**garbage** *noun* (*US English*)
= ごみ

**garden**
1 *noun*
= にわ ・ 庭
2 *verb*
= にわしごとを する ・ 庭仕事をす
る

**gardener** *noun*
= にわし ・ 庭師

**gardening** *noun*
= にわいじり ・ 庭弄り

**garlic** *noun*
= にんにく

**gas** *noun*
• (*for cooking, heating*)
= ガス
• (*US English*)
(*gasoline*)
= ガソリン

**gas station** *noun* (*US English*)
= ガソリンスタンド

**gate** *noun*
= もん ・ 門
(*at an airport*) = ゲート

**gather** *verb*
• (*to come together*) = あつまる ・ 集
まる
• (*to collect*) = あつめる ・ 集める

**gay** *adjective*
= どうせいあい(の) ・ 同性愛(の)

**gear** *noun*
• (*in a car or bus, on a bike*)
= ギア
• (*equipment*)
= どうぐ ・ 道具
fishing gear = つりどうぐ ・ 釣り
道具
• (*clothes*)
football gear = サッカーの ユニフォ
ーム
swimming gear = みずぎ ・ 水着

**Gemini** noun
= ふたござ・双子座
**general**
**1** noun
= たいしょう・大将
**2** adjective
= いっぱん(の)・一般(の)
**3 in general** = ふつう・普通
**generation** noun
= せだい・世代
**generous** adjective
= かんだい(な)・寛大(な)
**genius** noun
= てんさい・天才
**gentle** adjective
= やさしい・優しい
**gentleman** noun
= しんし・紳士
**geography** noun
= ちり・地理
**germ** noun
= ばいきん・ばい菌
**German** ▶ 172
**1** adjective
= ドイツの
**2** noun
• (the people)
= ドイツじん・ドイツ人
• (the language)
= ドイツご・ドイツ語
**Germany** noun ▶ 172
= ドイツ

**get** verb
  **get away**
• (to escape) = にげる・逃げる
• he won't get away with it = かれは
  ただで すまないでしょう。・
  彼は ただで 済まないでしょう。
  **get back**
• (to arrive back) = かえる・帰る
• (to have something returned) = かえし
  て もらう・返して もらう
  (when something is returned) = かえ
  ってくる・返ってくる
  I got my bike back = じてんしゃを
  かえして もらいました。・自転
  車を 返して もらいました。
  the money will be returned = おかね
  は かえって きます。・お金は
  返って きます。
  **get down**
• (to come or go down) = おりる・下
  りる

• (to take down) = おろす・下ろす
  I got the box down from the shelf =
  はこを たなから 下ろしました。
  ・箱を 棚から 下ろしました。
  **get in**
  (car or taxi) = のる・乗る
  **get off**
• (to leave a bus or train) = おりる・降
  りる
  I'm getting off at the next stop = つぎ
  の バスていで おります。・次の
  バス停で 降ります。
• (to remove)
  to get a stain off = しみを とる・染
  みを 取る
  **get on**
• (to climb on board a bus or train) = のる
  ・乗る
  to get on the bus = バスに のる・
  バスに 乗る
• to get on well = きが あう・気が
  合う
  I get on well with her = かのじょと
  きが あいます。・彼女と 気が
  合います。
• (in polite enquiries)
  how did you get on? = どうでしたか。
  how are you getting on at school? =
  がっこうは どうですか。・学校
  は どうですか。
  **get out**
• (to leave) = でる・出る
  I got out of the building = ビルを
  でました。・ビルを 出ました。
• (to take out) = だす・出す
  to get the furniture out of the house =
  うちから かぐを だす・家から
  家具を 出す
  **get over**
  to get over an illness = びょうきが
  なおる・病気が 治る
  **get through to**
  to get through (to someone) = (だれ
  かに)れんらくする・(誰かに)
  連絡する
  **get together** = あう・会う
  **get up** = おきる・起きる

**ghost** noun
= おばけ・お化け
ghost story = かいだん・怪談

**gift** noun
• (a present)
= プレゼント
  (a present from a trip) = おみやげ・
  お土産

G

- (an ability)
  = さいのう ・ 才能
  he has a gift for languages = かれは
  ごがくが とくいです 。 ・ 彼は
  語学が 得意です 。

**ginger** adjective
  ginger hair (British English) = あかげ ・
  赤毛 noun
  = しょうが

**girl** noun
  = おんなの こ ・ 女の 子

**girlfriend** noun
  (in a couple) = ガールフレンド
  (a female friend) = おんなの ともだ
  ち ・ 女の 友達

**give** verb

> **!** For translations of expressions like
> to give someone a lift, to give
> someone an injection, to give
> someone a fright etc, look up the
> entries lift, injection, fright.

- (to someone else) = あげる
  (to you) = くれる
  to give a book (to someone) = (だれ
  かに)ほんを あげる ・ (誰かに)
  本を あげる
  he gave me the photos = かれは わた
  しに しゃしんを くれました。・
  彼は 私に 写真を くれました。
  give me the newspaper = しんぶんを
  ください。・ 新聞を ください。
  give that to me = それを ください。
  to give one's seat (to someone) = (だ
  れかに)せきを ゆずる ・ (誰か
  に)席を 譲る
- to give someone a message = でんご
  んを つたえる ・ 伝言を 伝える

> **!** Expressions of giving and
> receiving are dependant on the
> relationship between giver and
> receiver ▶ 179

  **give away**
- (to make a present of) = あげる
- to give away a secret = ひみつを
  いって しまう ・ 秘密を 言って
  しまう
  **give back** = かえす ・ 返す
  **give in** = あきらめる ・ 諦める
  **give off**
  to give off a smell = においが する ・
  臭いが する

  **give out** = くばる ・ 配る
  to give out paper = かみを くばる ・
  紙を 配る
  **give up**
- (to stop)
  = やめる
  to give up smoking = たばこを やめ
  る
  (to abandon) = あきらめる ・ 諦める
  to give up the idea of working abroad
  = がいこくではたらくことをあ
  きらめる ・ 外国で 働く ことを
  諦める
- to give oneself up to the police = けい
  さつに じしゅする ・ 警察に
  自首する

**glad** adjective
  = うれしい ▶ 178

**glass** noun
  (substance) = ガラス
  (for wine, spirits) = グラス
  (for water, soft drinks) = コップ

**glasses** noun
  = めがね

**glove** noun
  = てぶくろ ・ 手袋

**glue**
**1** noun
  (paper glue) = のり ・ 糊
  (strong glue) = せっちゃくざい ・
  接着剤
**2** verb
  = せっちゃくする ・ 接着する

**go** verb ▶ 204
  **go across** = わたる ・ 渡る
  **go ahead**
- (if it's an event) = おこなう ・ 行う
  the concert's going ahead = コンサ
  ートを おこないます。・ コンサ
  ートを 行います。
- (if it's a person)
  please go ahead = どうぞ
  **go around** = **go round**
  **go around with** = **go round with**
  **go away** = どこかに いく ・ どこか
  に 行く
  **go away!** = でて いけ。・ 出て 行け。

> **!** this should be used with extreme
> caution

  **go back**
  (home, hometown) = かえる ・ 帰る
  (somewhere else) = もどる ・ 戻る

to go back to work = しごとに もど
る・仕事に 戻る

to go back to sleep = ねなおす・
寝なおす

**go by**

(*people, cars*) = とおる・通る

(*time*) = たつ・経つ

**go down**

• (*quality, a price, a salary*) = さがる・
下がる

• (*person*) = おりる・下りる

I went down the stairs = かいだんを
おりました。・階段を 下りまし
た。

I went down the mountain = やまを く
だりました。・山を 下りました。

• (*the sun*) = しずむ・沈む

• (*a computer*) = うごかなくなる・
動かなくなる

**go in**

• (*to enter*) = はいる・入る

**go off**

• (*to explode*) = ばくはつする・爆発
する

• (*to ring*)
= なる・鳴る

• (*to rot*) = くさる・腐る

• (*lights*) = きえる・消える

**go on**

• (*to continue*) = つづく・続く

• (*to be switched on*)
= つく・点く

**go out**

• (*to leave the house*) = でかける・出
かける

are you going out this evening? =
こんばん でかけますか。・今晩
出かけますか。

• (*as a boyfriend, a girlfriend*)
(*single date*) = デートする
(*long term*) = つきあう・付き合う

• (*to be switched off, to stop burning*) =
きえる・消える

• the tide's going out = しおが ひきま
す。・潮が 引きます。

**go over**

• (*to check*) = チェックする

• (*to revise*) = ふくしゅうする・復習
する

**go round**

• (*British English*)
(*to call on*) = たずねる・訪ねる
to go round to see a friend = とも
だちの うちへ あそびに いく・
友達の 家へ 遊びに 行く

• (*to walk around, to visit*) = みて まわる
・見て 回る
to go round the museum = はくぶつ
かんを みて まわる・博物館を
見て 回る

• (*to be enough*) = たりる・足りる
is there enough bread to go round? =
パンが たりますか。・パンが
足りますか。

**go round with**

• (*British English*)
(*to spend time with*) = つきあう・付
き合う

**go through**

• (*to have, to live through*)
to go through a difficult time = たいへ
んな じきを のりこえる・大変
な 時期を 乗り越える

I don't want to go through that again =
にどと したくないです。・二度
と したくないです。

• (*to search*) = さがす・探す

• (*to check*) = チェックする

**go together** = あう・合う
the skirt and shoes go well together =
あの スカートと くつは よく あ
います。・あの スカートと 靴は
よく 合います。

**go up**

• (*if it's a person*)
I went up the stairs = かいだんを
あがりました。・階段を 上がり
ました。
to go up the mountain = やまを のぼ
る・山を 登る

• (*if it's a price, a salary*) = あがる・
上がる

**go well** = うまくいく・うまく 行く

**go with** = あう・合う
the trousers don't really go with the
jacket = あの ズボンは あの ジャ
ケットに あいません。・あの ズ
ボンは あの ジャケットに 合い
ません。

**goal** *noun*
(*sports*) = ゴール
(*aim*) = もくひょう・目標

**goalkeeper** *noun*
= ゴールキーパー

**goat** *noun*
= やぎ

**god** *noun*
= かみ・神
God = かみさま・神様

G

**goddaughter** noun
= なづけむすめ・名づけ娘

! this relationship is not common in Japan

**godfather** noun
= なづけおや・名付け親

! this relationship is not common in Japan. You could try to explain the situation with せんれいを うけた ときの だいふです。

(crime underworld) = おやぶん・親分

**godmother** noun
= なづけおや・名付け親

! this relationship is not common in Japan. You could try to explain the situation with せんれいを うけた ときの だいぼです。

**godson** noun
= なづけむすこ・名づけ息子

! this relationship is not common in Japan

**going: to be going to**
I'm going to go to Kobe = こうべに いきます。・神戸に 行きます。
I was going to phone you but I didn't have time = でんわを する つもり でしたが、じかんが ありません でした。・電話を する つもりで したが、時間が ありませんでし た。

! There is no specific future tense in Japanese. Use the non-past tense.

▶ 204

**gold**
**1** noun
= きん・金
**2** adjective
= きん(の)・金(の)
gold ring = きんの ゆびわ・金の 指輪

**goldfish** noun
= きんぎょ・金魚

**golf** noun
= ゴルフ

**golf course** noun
= ゴルフコース

**good**
**1** adjective
• = いい

! いい is the only irregular adjective in Japanese. To make past and negative forms the stem changes to よ

a good book = いい ほん・いい 本
we've got some good news = いい しらせが あります。・いい知ら せが あります。
good eyesight = めが いい・目が いい
good at maths = すうがくが とくい ・数学が 得意
it's a good time to visit Japan = に ほんに いくには いい じきです。 ・日本に 行くには いい 時期で す。
exercise is good for you = うんどう は からだに いいです。・運動は 体に いいです。
to look good
(healthy)
she looks good = かのじょはげんき そうです。・彼女は 元気そうで す。
I had a good time = たのしかったで す。・楽しかったです。
• (talking about food) = おいしい
• (obedient) = いい
good child = いい こ・いい 子
• (kind)
it's very good of you to let me know = おしらせ ありがとうございま す。・お知らせ ありがとうござ います。 ▶ 189
**2** noun
it's no good shouting = おおきい こえで いっても しょうが ありま せん。・大きい 声で 言っても しょうが ありません。
I am not good at French = フランス ごが とくいではありません。・ フランス語が 得意ではありませ ん。
**3** exclamation
• (when pleased or releived)
good = よかったですね。
• (when praising)
good! = よく できました。
**4** for good = ずっと

**good afternoon** *noun* (also *exclamation*)
(*when meeting*) = こんにちは・今日は

**goodbye** *noun* (also *exclamation*)
= さようなら

**good evening** *noun* (also *exclamation*)
= こんばんは・今晩は

**good-looking** *adjective*
= かっこういい・格好いい

**good morning** *noun* (also *exclamation*)
(*when meeting*) = おはようございます

**goodnight** *noun* (also *exclamation*)
= おやすみなさい・お休みなさい

**goods** *noun*
= しょうひん・商品

**goose** *noun*
= がちょう・鵞鳥

**gossip** *verb*
• (*to chat*) = しゃべる・喋る
• (*to talk in a harmful way*) = ゴシップをする

**got: to have got** *verb*
• (*to have*) ▶ have
  have you got any money? = おかねがありますか。・お金が ありますか。
  I've got a cold = かぜを ひいています。・風邪を ひいています。
  I've got a dog = いぬを かっています。・犬を 飼っています。
  I've got two children = こどもが ふたりいます。・子供が 二人います。
• (*to be obliged to*)
  **to have got to**

  ❗ Use the **ない** form of the verb minus the last **い** + **ければ なりません。** ▶ 181

  I've got to go = いかなければなりません。・行かなければ なりません。
  I've got to do my homework = しゅくだいを しなければ なりません。・宿題を しなければ なりません。

**government** *noun*
= せいふ・政府

**GP** *noun* (*British English*)

❗ The system is different and GPs do not exist in Japan. A general word for doctor is **いしゃ**

**grab** *verb*
  to grab (someone) by the arm = (だれかの)うでを つかむ・(誰かの)腕を 掴む
  he tried to grab my handbag = かれは わたしの ハンドバッグを ひったくろうと しました。・彼は 私の ハンドバッグを 引っ手繰ろうと しました。

**grade** *noun*
• (*a mark*)
  = せいせき・成績
• (*US English*)
  (*a class*)
  = ねんせい・年生
  I'm in the first grade = いちねんせいです。・一年生です。 ▶ 185

**grade school** *noun* (*US English*)
= しょうがっこう・小学校

**gradually** *adverb*
= すこしずつ・少しずつ

**graduate** *verb*
= そつぎょうする・卒業する

**gram(me)** *noun*
= グラム

**grammar** *noun*
= ぶんぽう・文法

**grandchild** *noun* ▶ 177
(*your own*) = まご・孫
(*someone else's*) = おまごさん・お孫さん

**granddaughter** *noun* ▶ 177

❗ Japanese prefer to use the word grandchild, **まご**

**grandfather** *noun* ▶ 177
(*your own*) = そふ・祖父
(*someone else's*) = おじいさん・お祖父さん

**grandmother** *noun* ▶ 177
(*your own*) = そぼ・祖母
(*someone else's*) = おばあさん・お祖母さん

**grandparents** *noun* ▶ 177
(*your own*) = そふぼ・祖父母

G

(*someone else's*) = おじいさんと お
ばあさん・お祖父さんと お祖
母さん

**grandson** noun ▶ 177

> ! *Japanese prefer to use the word*
> *grandchild,* まご

**grapefruit** noun
= グレープフルーツ

**grapes** noun
= ぶどう

**grass** noun
= くさ・草
(*in gardens*) = しばふ・芝生
to cut the grass = しばかりをする・
芝刈りをする

**grasshopper** noun
= ばった

**grateful** adjective
= ありがたい
I would be grateful if you could let me
know = おしえて くださって あ
りがたく おもいます。・教えて
くださって ありがたく 思いま
す。

**grave** noun ▶ 189
= おはか・お墓

**gray** (*US English*) ▶ grey

**greasy** adjective
= あぶらっぽい・油っぽい

**great** adjective
• (*stressing size, amount, importance*) =
たいへん・大変
a great improvement = たいへんな
じょうたつ・大変な 上達
to have great difficulty reading = よむ
のに たいへん くろうする・読
むのに 大変 苦労する
the guide book was a great help =
ガイドブックは たいへん やく
に たちました。・ガイドブック
は 大変 役に 立ちました。
• (*showing enthusiasm*)
that's great! = すごいですね。
I had a great time = たのしかったで
す。・楽しかったです。

**Great Britain** noun ▶ 172
= えいこく・英国
イギリス is also used

**great grandfather** noun ▶ 177
(*your own*) = そうそふ・そう祖父

(*someone else's*) = ひいおじいさん
・ひいお爺さん

**great grandmother** noun ▶ 177
(*your own*) = そうそぼ・そう祖母
(*someone else's*) = ひいおばあさん
・ひいお婆さん

**greedy** adjective
= どんよく(な)・貪欲(な)

**green** adjective
= みどり・緑

> ! *Note that the green of vegetation*
> *and traffic lights is usually*
> *expressed using* あおい

**greengrocer** noun
= やおや・八百屋

**greenhouse** noun
= おんしつ・温室

**grey** (*British English*), **gray**
(*US English*) adjective
= はいいろ(の)・灰色(の)
grey hair = しらが・白髪

**grill** verb
= やく・焼く

**grin** verb
= にやにや わらう・にやにや
笑う

**groceries** noun
= しょくりょうひん・食料品

**ground** noun
• = じめん・地面
• (*land used for sports*)
= グランド

**ground floor** noun (*British English*)
= いっかい・一階

**group** noun
• (*a number of people*)
= あつまり・集まり
a group of Japanese people = にほん
じんの あつまり・日本人の 集
まり
• (*a band*)
= グループ

**grow** verb
• (*to get big*) = おおきく なる・大き
く なる
• (*as a gardener, a farmer*) = そだてる
・育てる
to grow vegetables = やさいを そだ
てる・野菜を 育てる
• (*to get long (hair)*) = のびる・伸びる

I decided to let my hair grow = かみを のばす ことに しました。・ 髪を 伸ばす ことに しました。
- *(to let grow (a beard))*
  to grow a beard = ひげを はやす・ ひげを 生やす
- *(to become)* = なる
  to grow old = としを とる・年を とる
- *(to increase in size)* = ふえる・増える る
  the population will grow = じんこう が ふえます。・ 人口が 増えま す。
  grow up = おとなに なる・大人に なる
  when I grow up, I want to be a doctor = おとなに なったら、いしゃに なりたいです。・ 大人に なった ら、医者に なりたいです。

**grumble** *verb*
= もんくを いう・文句を 言う

**guard** *noun*
- *(at a bank)*
  = けいびいん・警備員
- *(in a prison)*
  = しゅえい・守衛
  to be on guard = けいかいする・ 警戒する

**guard dog** *noun*
= ばんけん・番犬

**guardian** *noun*
= ほごしゃ・保護者

**guess** *verb*
= すいていする・推定する
*(US English)*
I guess... = ～と おもいます。・ ～と 思います。

**guest** *noun*
- *(a person invited to stay)*
  = おきゃくさん・お客さん
- *(at a hotel)*
  = とまりきゃく・泊まり客

**guesthouse** *noun*
= みんしゅく・民宿

**guide**
**1** *noun*
- *(on a tour or holiday)*
  = ガイド
- *(a person showing the way)*
  = あんないにん・案内人
- *(British English)*
  *(Girl Guide)*
  = ガールスカウト

**2** *verb*
= あんないする・案内する

**guide book** *noun*
= ガイドブック

**guided tour** *noun*
= ガイドつきの ツアー・ガイド付 きの ツアー

**guilty** *adjective*
= ゆうざい(の)・有罪(の)
I feel guilty = りょうしんが いたい です。・ 良心が 痛いです。

**guinea pig** *noun*
= モルモット
*(figuratively in an experiment)* = じっ けんだい・実験台

**guitar** *noun* ▶ **180**
= ギター

**gum** *noun*
= はぐき・歯茎
chewing gum = ガム

**gun** *noun*
= じゅう・銃
*(handgun)* = けんじゅう・拳銃

**gym** *noun*
= たいいくかん・体育館

**gymnasium** *noun*
= たいいくかん・体育館

**gymnastics** *noun*
= たいそう・体操

**gypsy** *noun*
= ジプシー

# Hh

**habit** *noun*
= しゅうかん・習慣

**hail** *noun*
= あられ

**hair** *noun*
*(on the head)* = かみの け・髪の 毛

**hairbrush** *noun*
= くし

**hairdresser** *noun*
= とこや・床屋

**hairdryer** *noun*
= ヘアードライヤー

**hairstyle** *noun*
= かみがた・髪型

**half**
**1** *noun*
- = はんぶん・半分
  to cut a melon in half = メロンを は
  んぶんに きる・メロンを 半分
  に 切る
- (*in a game*)
  the first half = ぜんはん・前半
**2** *adjective*
  half a litre = ごひゃくＣＣ・五百Ｃ
  Ｃ *CC is pronounced* シーシー
**3** *pronoun*
- (*when talking about quantities,
  numbers*)
  to spend half of one's pocket money =
  こづかいを はんぶん つかう・
  小遣いを 半分 使う
  half the pupils speak French = せいと
  の はんすうは フランスごが は
  なせます。・生徒の 半数はフラ
  ンス語が 話せます。
- (*when talking about time, age*) ▶ **171**,
  ▶ **186**
  an hour and a half = いちじかんはん
  ・一時間半
  he's three and a half = かれは さん
  さいと ろっかげつです。・彼は
  三才と 六ヶ月です。 *Note that
  in Japanese age is only usually
  expressed in full years, even with
  small babies and children.*
  it's half (past) three (*British English*) =
  さんじはんです。・三時半です。
**4** *adverb*
  Toshihide's half Japanese half Chinese
  = としひでさんは にほんじんと
  ちゅうごくじんの ハーフです。
  ・俊英さんは 日本人と 中国人の
  ハーフです。

**half hour** *noun*
= さんじゅっぷん・三十分

**half term** *noun* (*British English*)
= ちゅうかんきゅうか・中間休暇

> ! *Note that there is no half-term
> holiday in Japanese schools.*

**hall** *noun*
- (*by the front door in a house or
  apartment*)
  = げんかん・玄関
- (*for public events*)
  = ホール

**ham** *noun*
= ハム

**hamburger** *noun*
= ハンバーガー

**hammer** *noun*
= かなづち・金づち

**hamster** *noun*
= ハムスター

**hand** *noun*
- (*the part of the body*)
  = て・手
  I had a pencil in my hand = えんぴつ
  を てに もっていました。・鉛筆
  を 手に 持っていました。
  to hold hands = てを つなぐ・手を
  つなぐ
- (*help*)
  please give me a hand = てつだって
  ください。・手伝ってください。
- (*on a clock or watch*)
  = とけいのはり・時計の針
- (*when judging a situation or subject*)
  on the other... = いっぽう・一方

**handbag** *noun*
= ハンドバッグ

**handball** *noun*
= ハンドボール

**handicapped** *adjective*
  a handicapped person = しょうがい
  しゃ・障害者

> ! *When a person has a disability, it
> is more usual in Japanese to refer to
> it specifically rather than use the
> general word* しょうがいしゃ
> *which means a registered disabled
> person.*

**handkerchief** *noun*
= ハンカチ

**handle** *noun*
= とって・取っ手

**handsome** *adjective*
= ハンサム(な)
  a handsome man = ハンサムな ひと
  ・ハンサムな 人

**handwritten** *noun*
= てがき(の)・手書き(の)

**handy** *adjective*
= べんり(な)・便利(な)

## hang *verb*

- (*on a hook, a coat hanger, a line*)
  to hang a picture (up) on the wall = かべに えを かける・壁に 絵を 掛ける
  to hang clothes (up) in a wardrobe = ふくを ようふくだんすに しまう・服を 洋服だんすに しまう
  to hang washing on a line = せんたくものを ほす・洗濯物を 干す
- (*to be attached*)
  the picture hangs over the piano = えは ピアノの うえの かべに かかっています。・絵は ピアノの 上の 壁に 掛かっています。
  to be hanging from the ceiling = てんじょうから つるしている・天井から 吊るしている
- (*to kill as capital punishment*) = こうしゅけいにする・絞首刑にする
  (*as suicide*) = くびつりじさつを する・首吊り自殺を する

### hang around

- (*to wait*) = まつ・待つ
- (*to waste time, to do nothing*) = ぶらぶらする

### hang on to = つかむ

she was hanging on to the rope = かのじょは ロープを つかんでいました。・彼女は ロープを つかんでいました。

### hang up

- (*on a hook, a coat hanger, a line*)
  to hang up one's coat = コートを かける・コートを 掛ける
  to hang washing up to dry outside = そとに せんたくものを ほす・外に 洗濯物を 干す
- (*when phoning*) = じゅわきを おく・受話器を 置く

## hang-gliding *noun*
= ハンググライダーを する こと

## happen *verb*

- (*to occur*) = おこる・起こる
  what happened? = なにが おこりましたか。・何が 起こりましたか。
  that accident happened last week = その じこは せんしゅう おきました。・その 事故は 先週 起きました。
  to happen again = また おこる・また 起こる
- (*to affect someone*)

what happened to you? = どうしましたか。
something odd happened yesterday = きのう ふしぎな ことが ありました。・昨日 不思議な ことが ありました。

## happy *adjective*

- (*content*) = しあわせ(な)・幸せ(な)
  to make happy = しあわせに する・幸せに する
  I'm happy with this language school = この ごがくがっこうに まんぞくしています。・この 語学学校に 満足しています。
- (*in greetings*)
  Happy birthday! = おたんじょうび おめでとう。・お誕生日 おめでとう。 ▶ 189
  Happy New Year! = あけまして おめでとうございます。・明けまして おめでとうございます。

## hard

**1** *adjective*

- (*firm, stiff*) = かたい
  the ground is hard = じめんが かたいです。・地面が かたいです。
- (*difficult*) = むずかしい・難しい
  a hard question = むずかしい しつもん・難しい 質問
  it's not hard to change a light bulb = でんきゅうを かえるのは むずかしくないです。・電球を 替えるのは 難しくないです。
  it's hard to understand = わかりにくいです。
  I find it hard to concentrate = しゅうちゅうしにくいです。・集中しにくいです。
- (*harsh, tough*)
  a hard winter = きびしい ふゆ・厳しい 冬
  I'm having a hard time at the moment = いま たいへんです。・今 大変です。
- (*severe*) = きびしい・厳しい

**2** *adverb*

to work hard = いっしょうけんめい はたらく・一生懸命 働く
he hit me hard = かれは つよく わたしをぶちました。・彼は 強く 私を ぶちました。
to try hard to concentrate = がんばって しゅうちゅうする・頑張って 集中する

**hardly** *adverb*
= ほとんど + negative
she hardly ate anything = かのじょ は ほとんど たべませんでした。 ・ 彼女は ほとんど 食べません でした。

**hardware** *noun*
(for computers) = ハードウェア

**hard-working** *adjective*
(at work) = しごとねっしん(な) ・ 仕事熱心(な)
(at school) = べんきょうねっしん (な) ・ 勉強熱心(な)

**harm** *verb*
to harm someone = だれかにきずを つける ・ 誰かに 傷を つける
to harm the environment = かんきょ うに わるい えいきょうを あた える ・ 環境に 悪い 影響を 与え る

**harmful** *adjective*
= ゆうがい(な) ・ 有害(な)

**harmless** *adjective*
= むがい(な) ・ 無害(な)

**harvest** *noun*
= しゅうかく ・ 収穫

**hat** *noun*
= ぼうし ・ 帽子

**hate** *verb*
• (to feel a strong dislike for)
I hate mice = ねずみが きらいです。 ・ ねずみが 嫌いです。
• (to feel hatred for) = にくむ ・ 憎む
to hate someone = だれかを にくむ ・ 誰かを 憎む

**hatred** *noun*
= けんお ・ 嫌悪

**have**
**1** *verb*
• (to eat, to drink)
to have a sandwich = サンドイッ チを たべる ・ サンドイッチを 食べる
to have a glass of wine = ワインを のむ ・ ワインを 飲む
to have dinner = ゆうごはんを たべ る ・ 夕ご飯を 食べる
• (to get)
I had a letter from Dennis yesterday = きのう、デニスさんから てがみ を もらいました。 ・ 昨日、デニ

スさんから 手紙を もらいまし た。
• (to hold or organize)
to have a party = パーティーをする
to have a competition = コンクール を する
• (to spend)
we had a nice day at the beach = すな はまで いい いちにちを すごし ました。 ・ 砂浜で いい 一日を 過 ごしました。
I had a good time in Kyoto = きょうと の たびは たのしかったです。 ・ 京都の 旅は 楽しかったです。
• (to suffer)
to have flu = かぜを ひく ・ 風邪を ひく
to have a headache = ずつうが する ・ 頭痛が する
I have toothache = はが いたいで す。 ・ 歯が 痛いです。
• (to get something done)
to have a pizza delivered = ピザを はいたつして もらう ・ ピザを 配達して もらう
she had her hair cut = かのじょはか みを きりました。 ・ 彼女は 髪を 切りました。
• to have a baby = こどもを うむ ・ 子供を 産む
**2** *auxiliary verb*
you've seen her, haven't you? = かの じょを みましたね。 ・ 彼女を 見 ましたね。
he hasn't called, has he? = かれは でんわしていませんね。 ・ 彼は 電話していませんね。
**3 to have to** = 〜ない form of the verb without the last い + ければ ならな い ▶ **181**
I have to study = べんきょうしなけ れば なりません。 ・ 勉強しなけ れば なりません。
I have to pay = はらわなければ なり ません。 ・ 払わなければ なりま せん。
I have to go home = かえらなければ なりません。 ・ 帰らなければ な りません。
you don't have to work on Saturday = どようびは はたらかなくても いいです。 ・ 土曜日は 働かなく ても いいです。

**hay** *noun*
= わら

**hazelnut** *noun*
= ヘーゼルナッツ

**he** *pronoun*
= かれ・彼 *Note that Japanese prefer to use a name rather than a pronoun*
he's coming next week = かれは らいしゅう きます。・彼は 来週 来ます。
there he is = かれは あそこです。・彼は あそこです。

**head**
**1** *noun*
- (*the part of the body*)
= あたま・頭
- (*the person in charge*)
= たんとうしゃ・担当者
**2** *verb*
- (*to be in charge of*) = ひきいる・率いる
- (*in soccer*)
to head the ball = ボールを ヘディングする
head for = むかう・向かう

**headache** *noun*
to have a headache = ずつうが する・頭痛が する
my headache's gone = ずつうが なおりました。・頭痛が 治りました。

**headlamp, headlight** *noun*
= ヘッドランプ

**headline** *noun*
= みだし・見出し
to hit the headlines = みだしに なる・見出しに なる
the news headlines = おもな ニュース・主な ニュース

**headquarters** *noun*
(*of a company, a business*) = ほんぶ・本部
(*of an army*) = しれいぶ・司令部

**headteacher** *noun*
= こうちょうせんせい・校長先生

**health** *noun*
= けんこう・健康

**healthy** *adjective*
- (*in good health*) = けんこうてき(な)・健康的(な)
- (*good for the health*) = けんこうに いい・健康に いい

**hear** *verb*
- to hear = きこえる・聞こえる

he can't hear anything = かれは なにも きこえません。・彼は 何も 聞こえません。
I heard someone's foorsteps = だれかの あしおとが きこえました。・誰かの 足音が 聞こえました。
you can hear him practising the piano = かれが ピアノの れんしゅうを しているのが きこえます。・彼が ピアノの 練習を しているのが 聞こえます。
- (*to learn, to discover*)
to hear the news = ニュースを きく・ニュースを 聞く
I heard about that school's reputation = あの がっこうの ひょうばんを ききました。・あの 学校の 評判を 聞きました。
we've heard a lot about you = いろいろ うかがっています。・色々 伺っています。 ▶ 189
- (*to listen to*) = きく・聞く
to listen to the radio = ラジオを きく・ラジオを 聞く
hear from = れんらくが ある・連絡が ある
have you heard from Joyce? = ジョイスさんから れんらくが きましたか。・ジョイスさんから 連絡が 来ましたか。
hear of = きく・聞く

**heart** *noun*
- (*part of the body*)
= しんぞう・心臓
- (*the centre*)
right in the heart of London = ロンドンの ちゅうしんに・ロンドンの 中心に
- to learn by heart = あんきする・暗記する

**heart attack** *noun*
= しんぞうほっさ・心臓発作

**heat**
**1** *verb*
(*to heat a room, part of body*) = あたためる・暖める
(*to heat food, liquid*) = あたためる・温める
**2** *noun*
- = あつさ・暑さ
I can't stand the heat = あつくて たえられません。・暑くて 耐えられません。

H

- (*on a cooker*)
  **at a low heat** = よわびで・弱火で
- (*in a sporting contest*)
  = よせん・予選
  **heat up**
- (*to cook*) = あたためる・温める
- (*to warm up again*) = あたためなおす・温め直す

**heater** *noun*
= だんぼうき・暖房機

**heating** *noun*
= だんぼう・暖房

**heatwave** *noun*
= ねっぱ・熱波

**heaven** *noun*
= てんごく・天国

**heavy** *adjective*
- (*in weight*) = おもい・重い
- (*in quantity, intensity*)
  **the traffic is very heavy** = くるまが おおいです。・車が 多いです。
  **heavy smoker** = ヘビースモーカー
  **to have a heavy cold** = ひどい かぜ を ひいている・ひどい 風邪を ひいている
- (*describing food*) = おもい・重い

**hedge** *noun*
= いけがき・生け垣

**hedgehog** *noun*
= はりねずみ

**heel** *noun*
= かかと

**height** *noun*
(*of a person*) = せ・背
(*of a building, a tree*) = たかさ・高さ
**fear of heights** = こうしょきょうふ しょう・高所恐怖症

**helicopter** *noun*
= ヘリコプター

**hell** *noun*
= じごく・地獄

**hello** *noun*
(*when greeting someone*) = こんに ちは・今日は *You can also use greetings appropriate to the time of day Not usually used between family members.*
(*on the phone*) = もしもし

**helmet** *noun*
= ヘルメット

**help**
**1** *verb The idea of helping someone is often expressed using the auxiliary verbs* あげる、くれる *and* もらう *after the* 〜て *form of the verb.* ▶ 179, ▶ 197
- = たすける・助ける
  **to help each other** = おたがいに た すけあう・お互いに 助け合う
  **to help with the housework** = かじを てつだう・家事を 手伝う
- (*at a meal*)
  **to help oneself** = じぶんで よそう・ 自分で よそう
  **please help yourselves!** = ごじゆう に おとり ください。・ご自由に お取り ください。
- **I can't help thinking about it** = どうし ても それを かんがえて しまい ます。・どうしても それを 考え て しまいます。
**2** *exclamation*
  **help!** = たすけて！・助けて！
**3** *noun*
  **help**
  (*a helping hand*) = てつだい・手伝 い
  (*urgent assistance*) = きゅうじょ・ 救助
  **to ask someone for help** = だれかに てつだいを たのむ・誰かに 手 伝いを 頼む
  **to shout for help** = たすけを もと める・助けを 求める
  **help out** = てを かす・手を 貸す

**helpful** *adjective*
(*useful*) = やくに たつ・役に 立つ

**helping** *noun*
**second helping** = おかわり・お代 わり ▶ 189

**helpless** *adjective*
- (*defenceless*) = むぼうび(の)・無 防備(の)
- (*because of weakness, ill health*) = む りょく(の)・無力(の)

**hen** *noun*
= めんどり・めん鳥

**her**
**1** *pronoun*
  = かのじょ・彼女 *Note that Japanese prefer to use a name rather than a pronoun*
  **I know her** = かのじょを しっていま す。・彼女を 知っています。

I don't know her = かのじょを しり
ません。・彼女を 知りません。
he's seen her = かれは かのじょを
みました。・彼は 彼女を 見ま
した。
please help her! = かのじょを たす
けてください。・彼女を 助けて
ください。
I gave the book to her = かのじょに
ほんを あげました。・彼女に
本を あげました。

**2** *determiner*
= かのじょの・彼女の
I hate her dog = かのじょの いぬが
きらいです。・彼女の 犬が 嫌い
です。
she broke her leg = かのじょは あし
をおりました。・彼女は 足を 折
りました。

**herd** *noun*
= むれ・群れ

**here** *adverb*
• (*when talking about location*) = ここ
is it far from here? = ここから とおい
ですか。・ここから 遠いですか。
I'm up here = うえに います。・上
に います。
• (*when drawing attention*)
here's the post office = ここは ゆう
びんきょくです。・ここは 郵便
局です。
here comes the train = でんしゃが
きました。・電車が 来ました。
• (*when offering something*)
here you are = どうぞ
• (*in general statements*)
please say I'm not here = いないと
いってください。・いないと 言
ってください。

**hers** *pronoun*
= かのじょの・彼女の

> **!** Note that Japanese prefer to use a
> name rather than a pronoun

the red pen is hers = あかい ペンは
かのじょのです。・赤い ペンは
彼女のです。
which bag is hers? = どの かばんが
かのじょのですか。・どの かば
んが 彼女のですか。
my jacket is red but hers is green =
わたしの ジャケットは あかい
ですが、かのじょのは みどりで
す。・私の ジャケットは 赤いで
すが、彼女のは 緑です。

**herself** *pronoun*
• *Not used as a reflexive pronoun in
Japanese*
she wants to enjoy herself = かのじ
ょは たのしみたいです。・彼女
は 楽しみたいです。
she's hurt herself = かのじょは けが
を しました。・彼女は 怪我をし
ました。
• (*when used for emphasis*)
she did it all by herself = かのじょ
は ぜんぶ じぶんで しました。・
彼女は 全部 自分で しました。

**hesitate** *verb*
= ためらう

**hi** *exclamation*
= こんにちは・今日は

**hiccups** *noun*
to have hiccups = しゃっくりする

**hidden** *adjective*
= かくれている・隠れている

**hide** *verb*
• (*to avoid showing*) = かくす・隠す
to hide the present = プレゼントを
かくす・プレゼントを 隠す
• (*to avoid being seen*) = かくれる・
隠れる

**hi-fi** *noun*
= ステレオ

**high**
**1** *adjective*
• (*having a great height, describing a
level, a price, a standard, grades, a
voice*) = たかい・高い
the mountains are high = やまは た
かいです。・山は 高いです。
prices are high = ねだんが たかいで
す。・値段が 高いです。
the standard is high = レベルが たか
いです。・レベルが 高いです。
to get high grades = いい せいせき
をとる・いい 成績を 取る
• (*describing a speed*)
high speed train = こうそく でんしゃ
・高速電車
**2** *adverb*
= たかく・高く
to climb higher = もっと たかく の
ぼる・もっと 高く 登る

**high rise block** *noun*
(*skyscraper*) = まてんろう・摩天楼
(*apartment block*) = 高層住宅

H

(offices) = こうそうオフィスビル・
高層オフィスビル

**high school** noun
(in the US) = こうとうがっこう・高
等学校 This is generally shortened
to こうこう ▶ **185**

**hijack** verb
= ハイジャックする

**hike** verb
to go hiking = ハイキングする

**hiking** noun
= ハイキング

**hill** noun
= おか・丘
(a rise in the road) = さか・坂

**him** pronoun
= かれ・彼 Note that Japanese
prefer to use a name rather than a
pronoun
I know him = かれを しっています。
・彼を 知っています。
I don't know him = かれを しりませ
ん。・彼を 知りません。
she's seen him = かのじょは かれ
を みました。・彼女は 彼を 見
ました。
please help him! = かれを たすけて
ください。・彼を 助けてくださ
い。
I gave the book to him = かれに ほ
んを あげました。・彼に 本を
あげました。

**himself** pronoun
• Not used as a reflexive pronoun in
Japanese
he wants to enjoy himself = かれは
たのしみたいです。・彼は 楽し
みたいです。
he's hurt himself = かれは けがを し
ました。・彼は 怪我を しました。
• (when used for emphasis)
he did it all by himself = かれは ぜん
ぶ じぶんで しました。・彼は
全部 自分で しました。

**hippopotamus, hippo** noun
= かば

**hire** verb
• (to employ) = やとう・雇う
• (British English)
(to rent) = かりる・借りる
to hire a car = くるまを かりる・車
を 借りる

(to lend for a fee) = かす・貸す
they hire (out) the skates = スケート
を かします。・スケートを 貸し
ます。

**his**
**1** determiner
= かれの・彼の Note that Japanese
prefer to use a name rather than a
pronoun
I hate his dog = かれの いぬが きら
いです。・彼の 犬が 嫌いです。
he broke his leg = かれは あしを お
りました。・彼は 足を 折りまし
た。
**2** pronoun
the red pen is his = あかい ペンは か
れの です。・赤い ペンは 彼の
です。
which house is his? = どの いえが
かれのですか。・どの 家が 彼の
ですか。
my shirt is white but his is yellow =
わたしの シャツは しろですが、
かれのは きいろです。・私の シ
ャツは 白ですが、彼のは 黄色
です。

**history** noun
= れきし・歴史

**hit**
**1** verb
• (to strike something) = うつ・打つ
(to strike a person) = ぶつ
• (to crash into)
to hit a wall = かべに ぶつかる・
壁に ぶつかる
to hit one's head on a chair = いすに
あたまを ぶつける・椅子に
頭を ぶつかる
to hit a pedestrian = ほこうしゃを
ひく・歩行者を ひく
**2** noun
(a song, film) = ヒット
hit back = なぐりかえす・殴り返
す
to hit someone back = だれかを なぐ
りかえす・誰かを 殴り返す

**hitchhike** verb
= ヒッチハイクを する

**hitchhiker** noun
= ヒッチハイクを する ひと・ヒ
ッチハイクを する 人

**hoarse** adjective
= しわがれた

**hobby** *noun*
= しゅみ・趣味

**hockey** *noun*
= ホッケー

**hold**
**1** *verb*
- = もつ・持つ
  I held some money in my right hand =
  みぎてに おかねを もちました。
  ・右手に お金を 持ちました。
- (*to arrange*)
  to hold a competition = コンクール
  を する
  the party will be held in the school =
  パーティーは がっこうで あり
  ます。・パーティーは 学校であ
  ります。
- (*to keep or hide*)
  to be held hostage = ひとじちに
  とられる・人質に 取られる
- (*to keep back*) = とって おく・取っ
  て おく
  to hold a seat for someone = だれか
  に せきを とって おく・誰かに
  席を 取って おく
- (*other uses*)
  to hold the world record = せかいき
  ろくを もっている・世界記録
  を 持っている
  please hold the line (telephone) = し
  ょうしょう おまち ください。・
  少々 お待ち ください。
**2** *noun*
- to get hold of someone
  (*to find*) = だれかを みつける・
  誰かを 見つける
  (*by phone*) = だれかに れんらくす
  る・誰かに 連絡する
  **hold on**
- (*to wait*) = まつ・待つ
- (*to grasp*) = つかむ・掴む please
  hold on tight! = しっかり つかんで
  ください。・しっかり 掴んでく
  ださい。
  **hold up**
- (*to raise*) = あげる・上げる
  to hold up one's hand = てを あげる
  ・手を 上げる
- (*to delay*)
  to hold someone up = だれかを おく
  らせる・誰かを 遅らせる
  to hold up the traffic = こうつうを
  おくらせる・交通を 遅らせる
- (*to rob*) = おそう・襲う

**hole** *noun*
= あな・穴

**holiday** *noun*
- (*British English*)
  (*a vacation*)
  = りょこう・旅行
  to go on holiday = りょこうする・
  旅行する
- (*a national or religious festival*)
  a (public) holiday = しゅくじつ・
  祝日
- (*British English*)
  (*time taken off work*)
  to take a day's holiday = いちにち ね
  んきゅうを とる・一日 年休を
  取る

**Holland** *noun* ▶ 172
= オランダ

**holly** *noun*
= ひいらぎ

**home**
**1** *noun*
- = いえ・家 うち *is also used in
  conversation*
  to leave home = いえを でる・家を
  出る
  to work from home = いえで しごと
  を する・家で 仕事をする
- (*for elderly, ill or disabled people*)
  a home for handicapped children =
  ようごしせつ・養護施設
  an old people's home = ろうじんホ
  ーム・老人ホーム
**2** *adverb*
  to go home
  = いえに かえる・家に 帰る
  on my way home = かえる とちゅう
  で・帰る 途中で
  to be home
  (*after school, work*) = かえっている・
  帰っている
  I will take you home = うちまで
  おくります。・家まで 送りま
  す。
**3** at home
- (*in one's house*)
  I'm working at home = うちでしごと
  を しています。・家で 仕事をし
  ています。
  I live at home = りょうしんと いっ
  しょに すんでいます。・両親と
  一緒に 住んでいます。
- to feel at home = リラックスする

H

please make yourselves at home =
どうぞ くつろいでください。・
どうぞ 寛いでください。
• (when talking about a sports team) =
じもと(の)・地元(の)

**homeless** adjective
=いえの ない・家の ない

**homesick** adjective
=ホームシック(の)
I am homesick =ホームシックに な
っています。

**homework** noun
=しゅくだい・宿題

**homosexual** noun
=どうせいあいしゃ・同性愛者

**honest** adjective
• =しょうじき(な)・正直(な)
to be honest, I'd rather go home =
しょうじきに いうと うちに か
えりたいです。・正直に 言うと
家に 帰りたいです。
• (frank, sincere) =そっちょく(な)・
率直(な)

**honestly** adverb
=しょうじきに・正直に

**honey** noun
=はちみつ・蜂蜜

**honeymoon** noun
=しんこんりょこう・新婚旅行

**hood** noun
• (to cover the head)
=フード
• (US English)
(of a car)
=ボンネット

**hoof** noun
=ひずめ

**hook** noun
• (for hanging clothes, pictures)
=フック
• (for fishing)
=つりばり・釣り針

**hooligan** noun
=ちんぴら

**hoover** verb (British English)
to hoover the carpet =じゅうたんに
そうじきを かける・絨毯に 掃
除機を 掛ける

**hope**
**1** verb
I hope you don't mind but I borrowed
your book =すみませんが、ほん
を かりました。・すみませんが、
本を 借りました。
we hope to meet lots of people =たく
さんの ひとに あいたいです。・
たくさんの 人に 会いたいです。
I hope it's sunny tomorrow =あした
は はれだと いいです。・明日は
晴れだと いいです。
I hope so =そうだと いいですね。
I'm hoping for a good result =いい
けっかを きたいしています。・
いい 結果を 期待しています。
**2** noun
=きぼう・希望

**hopeless** adjective
• (without hope of success) =ぜつぼう
てき(な)・絶望的(な)
• (without any ability) =へた(な)・下
手(な)
I am hopeless at cooking =りょうり
が へたです。・料理が 下手で
す。

**horn** noun
• (on a car, a bus)
=クラクション
to sound a horn =クラクションを
ならす・クラクションを 鳴ら
す
• (of an animal)
=つの・角
• (an instrument) ▶ 180
=ホルン

**horoscope** noun
=ほしうらない・星占い

**horrible** adjective
=ひどい・酷い
(of food) =まずい

**horror film** noun
=ホラーえいが・ホラー映画

**horse** noun
=うま・馬
he likes horses =かれは うまが す
きです。・彼は 馬が 好きです。
year of the horse =うまどし・午年

**horseracing** noun
=けいば・競馬

**horseriding** noun
=じょうば・乗馬

**hospital** *noun*
= びょういん・病院
he's still in (the) hospital = かれは
まだ にゅういんしています。・
彼は まだ 入院しています。
to be taken to (the) hospital = びょ
ういんに はこばれる・病院に
運ばれる

**host family** *noun*
= ホストファミリー

**hostage** *noun*
= ひとじち・人質

**hostel** *noun*
(*for homeless*) = しゅうようじょ・
収容所
youth hostel = ユースホステル

**hostess** *noun*
= ホステス

**hot** *adjective*
• (*very warm*)
(*air temperature*) = あつい・暑い
(*food, liquid, etc*) = あつい・熱い
It's hot today = きょうは あついで
す。・今日は 暑いです。
hot soup = あついスープ・熱い ス
ープ
it's too hot in this room = この へやは
あつすぎます。・この 部屋は
暑すぎます。
a hot meal = あたたかい しょくじ・
温かい 食事
• (*strong, with a lot of spices*) = からい
・辛い
this mustard is hot = この からしは
からいです。・このからしは
辛いです。
a hot curry = からい カレー・辛い
カレー

**hot air balloon** *noun*
= ききゅう・気球

**hot dog** *noun*
= ホットドッグ

**hotel** *noun*
= ホテル

**hour** *noun* ▶ 186
an hour = いちじかん・一時間
I earn four pounds an hour = じきゅ
うは よんポンドです。・時給は
四ポンドです。

**house** *noun*
= いえ・家 うち *is also used in
conversation*

to go to someone's house = だれかの
いえに いく・誰かの 家に行く
the bike is at my house = じてんしゃ
は うちにあります。・自転車は
家に あります。

**housewife** *noun*
= せんぎょうしゅふ・専業主婦

**housework** *noun*
= かじ・家事
to do the housework = かじをする・
家事を する

**housing estate** (*British English*),
**housing development**
(*US English*) *noun*
= じゅうたくだんち・住宅団地

**hovercraft** *noun*
= ホバークラフト

**how** *adverb*
• (*in what way*) = どうやって
how did you find us? = どうやって
みつけましたか。・どうやって
見つけましたか。
(*when talking about ability*) = use the
potential form of the verb ▶ 181
There are a number of other
structures which also express ability
such as using the dictionary form of
the verb + ことが できる.
I know how to swim = およげます。
泳げます。
I know how to ski = スキーが できま
す。
I know how to make a curry = カレー
が つくれます。・カレーが 作れ
ます。
• (*in polite questions*)
how are you? = おげんきですか。・
お元気ですか。
how is your father? = おとうさんは
おげんきですか。・お父さんは
お元気ですか。
how was your holiday? = りょこうは
どうでしたか。・旅行は どうで
したか。
• (*in questions requiring specific
information*)
how long will it take? = どのくらい
かかりますか。
how tall are you? = しんちょうは い
くつですか。・身長は いくつで
すか。
how old is he? = かれは なんさいで
すか。・彼は 何才ですか。

**H**

how much is this = これは いくらで
すか。
- (*when making a suggestion*)
how would you like to eat out? = がい
しょくするのは どうですか。・
外食するのは どうですか。
how about going to the cinema tonight?
= こんばん えいがを みに いく
のは どうですか。・今晩映画を
見に 行くのは どうですか。

**however** *adverb*
- (*nevertheless*) = しかし
- however hard I study, I can't pass the
exam = いくら べんきょうして
も、しけんに うかりません。・
いくら 勉強しても、試験に
受かりません。

**how many**
**1** *pronoun*
(*general*) = いくつ
(*with a counter*) = なん + counter ▶ 181
how many are there? = いくつですか。
how many people? = なんにんです
か。・何人ですか。
how many books? = ほんは なんさ
つですか。・本は 何冊ですか。
how many CDs did you buy? = CDは
なんまい かいましたか。・ CD
を 何枚 買いましたか。

**how much**
**1** *pronoun*
= いくら
how much does it come to? = ごう
けいは いくらですか。・合計は
いくらですか。
how much is that jacket? = その ジャ
ケットは いくらですか。
**2** *determiner*
how much money do you have left? =
おかねは どのくらい のこって
いますか。・お金は どのくらい
残っていますか。

**huge** *adjective*
= おおきい・大きい

**human being** *noun*
= にんげん・人間

**humour** (*British English*), **humor**
(*US English*) *noun*
= ユーモア
to have a sense of humour = ユーモ
アの センスが ある

**hundred** *number* ▶ 181
one hundred, a hundred = ひゃく・百

three hundred = さんびゃく・三百
eight hundred and fifty yen = はっぴ
ゃくごじゅうえん・八百五十円
about a hundred people = ひゃくに
んくらい・百人くらい

**hungry** *adjective*
= おなかが すいた・お腹が 空い
た ▶ 189
I'm very hungry = おなかが すいて
います。・お腹が 空いていま
す。

**hunt** *verb*
to go hunting = かりに いく・狩り
に 行く

**hurdles** *noun*
= ハードル

**hurrah, hurray** *noun* (also
*exclamation*)
= ばんざい・万歳

**hurry**
**1** *verb*
- = いそぐ・急ぐ
please hurry home! = いそいで かえ
ってください。・急いで 帰って
ください。
- to hurry someone = だれかを いそ
がせる・誰かを 急がせる
**2** *noun*
to be in a hurry = いそいでいる・
急いでいる
there's no hurry = いそいでいませ
ん。・急いでいません。
hurry up = いそいでください。・
急いで下さい。

**hurt** *verb*
- (*to injure*)
to hurt oneself = けがを する・怪我
を する
to hurt one's leg = あしを けがする
・足を 怪我する
- (*to be painful*)
my throat hurts = のどが いたいで
す。・喉が 痛いです。
that hurts = いたいです。・痛いで
す。
- (*to upset*) = きずを つける・傷を
つける
to hurt someone's feelings = だれか
をきずつける・誰かを傷つける

**husband** *noun*
(*one's own*) = おっと・夫
(*someone else's*) = ごしゅじん・ご
主人

# I i

**I** *pronoun*
= わたし・私 *When you are talking about yourself,* わたし *can often be left out if it is obvious.*
I've got to go = いかなければなりません。・行かなければ なりません。
I didn't do it = わたしが やりませんでした。・私が やりませんでした。
I'M the one who has to do it = わたしが しなければ なりません。・私が しなければ なりません。
she can drive but I can't = かのじょ はうんてんできますが、わたしはできません。・彼女は 運転できますが、私は できません。

**ice** *noun*
= こおり・氷

**ice cream** *noun*
= アイスクリーム

**ice hockey** *noun*
= アイスホッケー

**ice rink** *noun*
= スケートリンク

**ice-skate** *noun*
= アイススケート

**ice-skating** *noun*
= アイススケート

**icing** *noun*
= アイシング

**idea** *noun*
= かんがえ・考え
what a good idea! = いい かんがえですね。・いい 考え ですね。
I've no idea = そうぞうが つきません。・想像が つきません。

**identity card** *noun*
= みぶんしょうめいしょ・身分証明書

**idiot** *noun*
= ばか

**if** *conjunction*

! *There are several different ways of expressing the conditional in Japanese, a common one is to use the* 〜た *form of the verb* + ら *for the conditional clause.* ▶ **191**

if it rains, we won't go = あめが ふったら、いきません。・雨が 降ったら、行きません。
if I were rich, I would travel = おかね もちだったら、りょこうをします。・お金持ちだったら、旅行を します。
if I were you, I'd refuse = わたしだったら、ことわります。・私だったら、断ります。
I wonder if they'll come = かれらは きますかね。・彼らは 来ますかね。

**ignore** *verb*
= むしする・無視する

**ill** *adjective*
= びょうき(の)・病気(の)

**illegal** *adjective*
= ふほう(な)・不法(な)

**illness** *noun*
= びょうき・病気

**imagination** *noun*
= そうぞう・想像
to have imagination = そうぞうりょくが ある・想像力が ある

**imagine** *verb*
= そうぞうする・想像する

**imitate** *verb*
= まねを する

**immediately** *adverb*
= すぐに

**impatient** *adjective*
to be impatient = まちきれない・待ちきれない
impatient person = せっかちな ひと・せっかちな 人

**import** *verb*
= ゆにゅうする・輸入する

**important** *adjective*
= じゅうよう(な)・重要(な)
it is important to eat well = ちゃんと たべる ことは たいせつです。・ちゃんと 食べる ことは 大切です。

**impossible** *adjective*
= むり(な)・無理(な)

it's impossible to finish all that work today = きょう その しごとを ぜんぶする ことはむりです。・ 今日 その 仕事を 全部する ことは 無理です。

**impressed** adjective
= かんどうした・感動した
I was impressed by that film = その えいが は とても いいと おもいました。・ その 映画は とても いいと 思いました。

**impression** noun
= いんしょう・印象
to make a good impression = いい いんしょうを あたえる・いい 印象を 与える

**improve** verb
• (to make better) = よく する・良くする
to improve living conditions = せいかつを よくする・生活を 良くする
my Japanese has improved = にほんごが じょうたつしました。・ 日本語が 上達しました。
• (to get better) = よく なる・良くなる

**improvement** noun
= かいぜん・改善

**in**

> ! Often in occurs in combinations with verbs, for example: drop in, fit in, move in etc. To find the correct translations for this type of verb, look up the separate dictionary entries at drop, fit, move etc.

**1** preposition
• (inside) = use particle に
in the house = いえに・家に
there's a letter in the envelope = ふうとうに てがみが あります。・ 封筒に 手紙が あります。
there is a woman in the photograph = しゃしんに おんなの ひとが うつっています。・ 写真に 女の 人が 写っています。
• (at) = use particle で
I learned Japanese in school = がっこうで にほんごを ならいました。・ 学校で 日本語を 習いました。
in the countryside = いなかで さんぽする・田舎で 散歩する
• (when talking about countries or cities) = use particle に

to live in Japan = にほんに すむ・日本に 住む
my elder sister lives in New York = あねは ニューヨークに すんでいます。・ 姉は ニューヨークに 住んでいます。
• (dressed in)
she was in a skirt = かのじょは スカートを はいていました。・ 彼女は スカートを はいていました。
to be dressed in black = くろい ふくを きる・黒い 服を 着る
• (showing the way in which something is done) = Use particle で
written in Japanese = にほんごで かいて ある・日本語で 書いて ある
we paid in cash = げんきんで はらいました。・ 現金で 払いました。
in pencil = えんぴつで・ 鉛筆で
• (during)
in October = じゅうがつに・十月に
in the night = よなか(に)・夜中(に)
in the morning = ごぜんちゅう(に)・ 午前中(に)
• (within)
in ten minutes = じゅっぷんご・十分後
in three years = さんねんご・三年後
• (other uses)
she's in her twenties = かのじょは にじゅうだいです。・ 彼女は 二十代です。
one in ten = じゅうぶんの いち・十分の 一
to cut an apple in two = りんごを ふたつに きる・りんごを 二つに 切る
**2** adverb
• (at home, available) = いえに いる・家に いる

**inch** noun
= インチ

> ! Note that an inch = 2.54 cm.

**include** verb
= ふくむ・含む
breakfast is included = ちょうしょくは ふくまれています。・ 朝食は 含まれています。

**including** preposition
= ふくんで・含んで

including the children, there were eight people = こどもを ふくんで、はちにんでした。・ 子供を 含んで、八人でした。

**income** *noun*
= しゅうにゅう・ 収入

**income tax** *noun*
= しょとくぜい・ 所得税

**inconvenient** *adjective*
= ふべん(な)・ 不便(な)
it's an inconvenient time for me = つごうが わるいです。・ 都合が 悪いです。

**increase**
**1** *verb*
(*numbers*) = あがる・ 上がる
to increase in value = かちが あがる・ 価値が 上がる
(*volume*) = ふえる・ 増える
it increased by 20% = にじゅっパーセント ふえました。・ 二十パーセント 増えました。
**2** *noun*
= ぞうか・ 増加

**increasingly** *adverb*
= ますます・ 益々

**incredible** *adjective*
(*unbelievable*) = しんじられない・ 信じられない
(*astonishing*) = すごい

**independent** *adjective*
(*person*) = どくりつした・ 独立した
(*school*) = しりつ(の)・ 私立(の)

> **!** *In conversation, this is sometimes pronounced* わたくしりつ(の) *to avoid confusion with* しりつ(の)・ 市立 = *municipal*

**India** *noun* ▶ 172
= インド

**Indian** ▶ 172
**1** *adjective*
= インド(の)
**2** *noun*
• (*person from India*)
= インドじん・ インド人
• (*person from North America*)
= アメリカンインディアン

**indicate** *verb*
= しめす・ 示す

**indifferent** *adjective*
= むかんしん(な)・ 無関心(な)

**indigestion** *noun*
= しょうかふりょう・ 消化不良

**individual**
**1** *adjective*
= こせいてき(な)・ 個性的(な)
**2** *noun*
= こじん・ 個人

**indoor** *adjective*
= しつない(の)・ 室内(の)
an indoor swimming pool = しつないプール・ 室内プール

**indoors** *adverb*
= しつないで・ 室内で

**industrial** *adjective*
= こうぎょう(の)・ 工業(の)
Industrial Revolution = さんぎょうかくめい・ 産業革命

**industry** *noun*
= さんぎょう・ 産業

**inevitable** *adjective*
= さけられない・ 避けられない

**infant school** *noun* ▶ 185 (*British English*)
= しょうがっこう・ 小学校

**infection** *noun*
= かんせん・ 感染

**influence**
**1** *noun*
= えいきょう・ 影響
**2** *verb*
• (*to persuade*) = さゆうする・ 左右する
• (*to make a strong impression on*)
to influence (someone) = (だれかに) えいきょうを あたえる・ (誰かに)影響を 与える

**inform** *verb*
= しらせる・ 知らせる
to inform the police of an accident = けいさつに じこを しらせる・ 警察に 事故を 知らせる
to keep informed = しらせる・ 知らせる

**informal** *adjective*
• (*describing a person, a person's manner*) = カジュアル(な)
• (*describing a word, a language*) = くだけた・ 砕けた
• (*describing a discussion or an interview*) = ひこうしき(の)・ 非公式(の)

**information** *noun*
= じょうほう・ 情報

**information desk** *noun*
= あんないじょ ・ 案内所

**information technology** *noun*
= じょうほうこうがく ・ 情報工学

**ingredient** *noun*
= ざいりょう ・ 材料

**inhabitant** *noun*
= じゅうみん ・ 住民

**injection** *noun*
= ちゅうしゃ ・ 注射
to give (someone) an injection = (だ
れかに)ちゅうしゃを する ・ (誰
かに)注射を する

**injured** *adjective*
= けがを した ・ 怪我を した

**injury** *noun*
= けが ・ 怪我

**ink** *noun*
= インク

**innocent** *adjective*
(*not guilty of crime*) = むざい(の) ・
無罪(の)
(*without ill intent*) = むじゃき(な) ・
無邪気(な)

**inquiry** *noun*
= といあわせ ・ 問い合わせ

**insect** *noun*
= むし ・ 虫

**inside**
**1** *preposition*
= 〜の なか ・ 〜の 中
inside the house = うちの なか ・ 家
の 中
**2** *adverb*
= なか ・ 中
he's inside = かれは なかにいます。
・ 彼は 中に います。
let's play inside = なかで あそびま
しょう。・ 中で 遊びましょう。
I looked inside = なかを みました。
・ 中を 見ました。
let's bring the chairs inside = いすを
なかに いれましょう。・ 椅子を
中に 入れましょう。
**3** *noun*
= なか ・ 中
the inside of the palace = きゅうでん
の なか ・ 宮殿の 中
**4** *adjective*
= なか(の) ・ 中(の)

**5 inside out** = うらがえしに ・ 裏返
しに
to put one's shirt on inside out = シャ
ツを うらがえしに きる ・ シャ
ツを 裏返しに 着る

**inspect** *verb*
• (*if it's an official*) = しらべる ・ 調べる
• (*if it's a conductor*) = けんさつする ・
検札する

**inspector** *noun*
• (*of a school*) = けんさかん ・ 検査官
• (*on a bus, a train*) = しゃしょう ・ 車
掌
• (*in the police*) = けいぶ ・ 警部

**instantly** *adverb*
= あっというまに ・ あっという間
に

> **!** *Not usually used in very formal
> language. In this case* すぐ *is
> preferred.*

**instead**
**1 instead of**
= 〜の かわり(に) ・ 〜の 代わり
(に)
I hired a van instead of a car = くるま
の かわりに バンを かりました。
・ 車の 代わりに バンを 借りま
した。
use oil instead of butter = バターの
かわりに あぶらを つかう ・ バ
ターの 代わりに 油を 使う
his wife came instead of him = かれの
かわりに おくさんが きました。
・ 彼の 代わりに 奥さんが 来ま
した。

**instruction** *noun*
= せつめい ・ 説明
way of using = つかいかた ・ 使い方
instruction booklet = せつめいしょ ・
説明書

**instrument** *noun* ▶ **180**
= がっき ・ 楽器

**insult** *verb*
= ぶじょくする ・ 侮辱する

**insurance** *noun*
= ほけん ・ 保険

**insure** *verb*
= ほけんを かける ・ 保険を 掛ける
to insure a car = くるまに ほけんを
かける ・ 車に 保険を 掛ける

**intelligent** *adjective*
= あたまが いい・頭が いい

**intend** *verb*
= use a verb in dictionary form + つも
り ▶ **191**
I intend to study Japanese = にほん
ごを べんきょうする つもりで
す。・日本語を 勉強する つもり
です。

> ! *Note that there are several ways of expressing intention in Japanese*

**intense** *adjective*
= もうれつ(な)・猛烈(な)

> ! *not used in formal Japanese*

**intensive care unit** *noun*
= しゅうちゅうちりょうしつ・集
中治療室

**interest**
**1** *noun*
• (*enthusiasm*) = きょうみ・興味
to have an interest in music = おんが
くに きょうみが ある・音楽に
興味が ある
• (*financial*) = りそく・利息
**2** *verb*
= きょうみを そそる・興味を
そそる

**interested** *adjective*
to be interested in sports = スポーツ
に きょうみが ある・スポーツ
に 興味が ある
are you interested? = きょうみが あ
りますか。・興味が あります
か。

**interesting** *adjective*
= おもしろい

**interfere** *verb*
• (*to get involved in*) = かんしょうする
・干渉する
• (*to have a bad effect on*) = じゃまする
・邪魔する
it's going to interfere with my work =
しごとの じゃまに なります。・
仕事の 邪魔に なります。

**intermission** *noun*
= きゅうけいじかん・休憩時間

**international** *adjective*
= こくさいてき(な)・国際的(な)
international relations = こくさいか
んけい・国際関係

> ! こくさい is often used as a prefix element to form a new noun such as こくさいこうりゅう for international exchange

**internet** *noun*
= インターネット

**interpreter** *noun*
= つうやくしゃ・通訳者

**interrupt** *verb*
= じゃまを する・邪魔を する

**interval** *noun*
• (*in time or at a location*)
at intervals = ときどき・時々
• (*British English*)
(*during a play, a show*) = きゅうけい
じかん・休憩時間

**interview**
**1** *noun*
(*for a job*) = めんせつ・面接
(*with a journalist*) = インタビュー
**2** *verb*
(*if it's an employer*) = めんせつする・
面接する
(*if it's a journalist*) = インタビュー
する

**intimidate** *verb*
= おどす・脅す

**into** *preposition*
• (*when talking about a location*) = に
to go into the garden = にわに はい
る・庭に 入る
to get into a car = くるまに のる・
車に 乗る
to get into bed = ベッドに はいる・
ベッドに 入る
• (*indicating a change*) = に
to translate a letter into Japanese =
てがみを にほんごに ほんやく
する・手紙を 日本語に 翻訳す
る

**introduce** *verb*
• (*to bring in*) = どうにゅうする・導
入する
to introduce a new machine = あたら
しいきかいをどうにゅうする・
新しい 機械を 導入する
• (*when people meet*) = しょうかいす
る・紹介する
I introduced him to Ms Yamada =
かれに やまださんを しょうか
いしました。・彼に 山田さんを
紹介しました。

introduce oneself = じこしょうかい
する・自己紹介する
- (on radio or television) = しょうかい
する・紹介する
to introduce a programme = ばんぐ
みを しょうかいする・番組を
紹介する

**invade** verb
= しんりゃくする・侵略する

**invent** verb
= はつめいする・発明する

**invention** noun
= はつめい・発明

**investigate** verb
= とりしらべる・取り調べる

**investigation** noun
= とりしらべ・取り調べ

**invisible** adjective
= めに みえない・目に 見えない

**invitation** noun
= しょうたい・招待

**invite** verb
= しょうたいする・招待する
to invite (someone) to a party = パー
ティーに (だれかを)しょうたい
する・パーティーに (誰かを)招
待する

**involved** adjective
to be involved in an accident = じこに
まきこまれる・事故に 巻き込
まれる

**Ireland** noun ▶ 172
= アイルランド

**Irish** ▶ 172
**1** adjective
= アイルランドの
**2** noun
- (the people)
= アイルランドじん・アイルラン
ド人
- (the language)
= アイルランドご・アイルランド
語

**iron**
**1** noun
(metal) = てつ・鉄
(for clothes) = アイロン
**2** verb
= アイロンを かける

**island** noun
= しま・島

**it** pronoun

> ! Not used or translated in
> Japanese

where is it? = どこですか。
who is it? = だれですか・誰です
か。
it's me = わたしです。・私です。
it's a nice house = いい いえです。・
いい 家です。
it is difficult = むずかしいです。・難
しいです。
it's easy to make a mistake = まちが
いやすいです。・間違いやすい
です。
it's cold = さむいです。・寒いです。
I've heard about it = ききました。・
聞きました。
did you go to it? = いきましたか。・
行きましたか。

**itchy** adjective
= かゆい・痒い

**its** determiner

> ! Not used or translated in
> Japanese

its nose = はな・鼻
its tail = しっぽ・尻尾
its ear = みみ・耳
its eyes = め・目
my little sister has a rabbit, its ears are
long = いもうとは うさぎを かっ
ています。みみは ながいです。
・妹は うさぎを 飼っています。
耳は 長いです。

**itself** pronoun

> ! Not used as a pronoun in
> Japanese

- (when used as a reflexive pronoun)
the cat's going to hurt itself = ねこが
けがを します。・猫が 怪我を し
ます。
- (when used for emphasis)
the car itself was not damaged = くる
まじたいは ダメージを うけて
いません。・車自体は ダメージ
を 受けていません。
the heating comes on by itself = だん
ぼうは じどうてきに はいりま
す。・暖房は 自動的に はいりま
す。

# Jj

**jacket** *noun*
= ジャケット

**jail** *noun*
= けいむしょ・刑務所

**jam** *noun* (*British English*)
= ジャム

**Jamaica** *noun* ▶ 172
= ジャマイカ

**January** *noun* ▶ 174
= いちがつ・一月

**Japan** *noun* ▶ 172
= にほん・日本

> **!** *In formal speech or documents Japan is often called* にっぽん

**Japanese** ▶ 172
**1** *adjective*
= にほんの・日本の
**2** *noun*
• (*the people*)
= にほんじん・日本人
• (*the language*)
= にほんご・日本語

**jaw** *noun*
= あご

**jazz** *noun*
= ジャズ

**jealous** *adjective*
= うらやましい
I am jealous of her new shoes = かの
じょの あたらしい くつが うら
やましいです。・彼女の 新しい
靴が うらやましいです。

**jeans** *noun*
= ジーパン

**jeer** *verb*
to jeer = ばかに する

**jelly** *noun*
• (*US English*)
(*jam*) = ジャム
• (*British English*)
(*a dessert*)
= ゼリー

**Jesus** *noun*
(*Jesus Christ*) = イエス キリスト

**jet** *noun*
= ジェットき・ジェット機

**jewellery** (*British English*),
**jewelry** (*US English*) *noun*
= ほうせき・宝石

**Jewish** *adjective*
= ユダヤ(の)
(*Jewish person*) = ユダヤじん・ユ
ダヤ人

**jigsaw puzzle** *noun*
= ジグソーパズル

**job** *noun*
• (*work*)
= しごと・仕事
to look for a job = しごとを さがす・
仕事を 探す

**jogging** *noun*
= ジョギング

**join** *verb*
• (*meet up with*) = あう・会う
I'll join you at eight o'clock = はちじ
に いきます。・八時に 行きま
す。
• (*become a member of*) = はいる・
入る
to join a club = クラブに はいる・
クラブに 入る
to join a company = かいしゃにはい
る・会社に 入る
**join in**
= さんかする・参加する
to join in a game = ゲームに さんか
する・ゲームに 参加する

**joke**
**1** *noun*
= じょうだん・冗談
**2** *verb*
= じょうだんを いう・冗談を 言う

**journalist** *noun*
= きしゃ・記者

**journey** *noun*
= たび・旅
to go on a journey = たびを する・
旅を する
I hate my journey to work = かいしゃ
に かようのはいやです。・会社
に 通うのは いやです。

**joy** *noun*
= よろこび・喜び

**judge**
**1** *noun*
= さいばんかん・裁判官

**J**

**2** *verb*
= はんだんする・判断する

**judo** *noun*
= じゅうどう・柔道

**jug** *noun*
= みずさし・水差し

**juice** *noun*
= ジュース
fruit juice = フルーツジュース

**jujitsu** *noun*
= じゅうじゅつ・柔術

**July** *noun* ▶ 174
= しちがつ・七月

**jump** *verb*
• = とぶ・飛ぶ
the children were jumping on the bed
= こどもたちが ベッドのうえで
とびはねていました。・子供達
が ベッドの 上で 飛び跳ねてい
ました。
to jump across the river = かわを と
びこえる・川を 飛び越える
to jump out of the window = まどから
とびおりる・窓から 飛び降り
る
• to jump the queue (*British English*) =
れつに わりこむ・列に 割り込
む

**jumper** *noun* (*British English*)
= セーター

**June** *noun* ▶ 174
= ろくがつ・六月

**junior high school** *noun* ▶ 185
(*US English*)
= ちゅうがっこう・中学校

**junior school** *noun* ▶ 185 (*British English*)
= しょうがっこう・小学校

**jury** *noun*
= ばいしんいん・陪審員

**just¹** *adverb*
• (*very recently*) = use the 〜た form of
verb + ところ ▶ 191
I have just received the letter = いま、
てがみを もらった ところです。
・今、手紙を もらった ところで
す。
I had just turned on the TV = テレビ
を つけた ところでした。

• (*at this or that very moment*) = use the
dictionary form of verb + ところ
I was just about to phone you = でん
わする ところでした。・電話す
る ところでした。
I arrived just as he was leaving = かれ
が うちを でる ところに わた
しは つきました。・彼が 家を
出る ところに 私は 着きました。
• (*only*) = だけ
it was just 1000 yen = せんえん だけ
でした。・千円 だけでした。
there are only two left = ふたつ だけ
のこっています。・二つ だけ 残
っています。
• (*barely*)
I got there just in time = ちょうど ま
にあいました。・ちょうど 間に
合いました。
• (*when comparing*)
it takes just as long by train as by car
= でんしゃは くるまと おなじ
くらい じかんが かかります。・
電車は 車と 同じ くらい 時間が
かかります。
• (*immediately*)
just before = ちょくぜん・直前
just after = ちょくご・直後

**just²** *adjective*
= こうへい(な)・公平(な)

**justice** *noun*
= せいぎ
legal system of justice = しほう・
司法

# Kk

**kangaroo** *noun*
= カンガルー

**karate** *noun*
= からて・空手

**keen** *adjective*
= ねっしん(な)・熱心(な)
a keen student = ねっしんな がくせ
い・熱心な 学生
she is keen on dancing = かのじょは
ダンスが すきです。・彼女は ダ
ンスが 好きです。

**keep** *verb*
- we keep the wine in the cellar = ちか
  に ワインが おいて あります。・
  地下に ワインが 置いて あります。
  to keep (someone) waiting = (だれか
  を)またせる ・ (誰かを)待たせ
  る
- (*to delay*)
  what kept you? = どうして おくれま
  したか。・ どうして 遅れました
  か。
  I won't keep you long = ながく かか
  りません。・ 長く かかりませ
  ん。
- (*to put*)
  where do you keep the cups? = カッ
  プは どこに ありますか。
- (*not to break, not to reveal*)
  to keep a promise = やくそくを まも
  る ・ 約束を 守る
- (*to continue*) = pre ます form + つづけ
  る
  to keep walking = あるきつづける ・
  歩き続ける
- to keep calm = おちつく ・ 落ち着く
- (*if it's food*) = もつ ・ 持つ
  **keep away**
  keep away from the fire! = ひ から
  はなれなさい！・ 火から 離れな
  さい！
  **keep out**
  to keep out of the sun = にっこうを
  さける ・ 日光を 避ける
  **keep up** = ついて いく ・ ついて
  行く
  I can't keep up = ついて いけませ
  ん。・ ついて 行けません。

**kettle** *noun*
  = やかん

**key** *noun*
  = かぎ ・ 鍵

**keyhole** *noun*
  = かぎあな ・ 鍵穴

**kick** *verb*
  = ける
  I kicked the ball = ボールを けりま
  した。
  **kick off** = しあいを かいしする ・
  試合を 開始する
  **kick out** = おいだす ・ 追い出す

**kid** *noun*
- (*a child*) = こども ・ 子供

**kidnap** *noun*
  = ゆうかい ・ 誘拐

**kill** *verb*
  = ころす ・ 殺す
  to kill oneself = じさつする ・ 自殺
  する

**kilo** *noun*
  = キロ

**kilogram(me)** *noun*
  = キログラム

**kilometre** (*British English*),
  **kilometer** (*US English*) *noun*
  = キロメートル

**kind**
**1** *noun*
  it's a kind of... = ～の いっしゅです。
  ・ ～の 一種です。
  it's a kind of fish = さかなの いっし
  ゅです。・ 魚の 一種です。
  what kind = どんな
  what kind of film is it? = どんな えい
  がですか。・ どんな 映画です
  か。
  what kind of car is it? = どんな くる
  まですか。・ どんな 車ですか。
**2** *adjective*
  = しんせつ(な) ・ 親切(な)

**king** *noun*
  = こくおう ・ 国王

**kingdom** *noun*
  = おうこく ・ 王国

**kiss**
**1** *verb*
  = キスする
  to kiss (each other) = キスする
**2** *noun*
  = キス

**kitchen** *noun*
  = だいどころ ・ 台所

**kite** *noun*
  = たこ

**kitten** *noun*
  = こねこ ・ 子猫

**knee** *noun*
  = ひざ ・ 膝

**kneel down** *verb*
  = ひざまずく

**knife** *noun*
  = ナイフ

**knit** *verb*
  = あむ ・ 編む

**K**

## knock

**1** *verb*
= ノックする
to knock on the door = ドアを ノックする

**2** *noun*
to get a knock on the head = あたまを ぶつける・
**knock down**
- (*in a traffic accident*) = くるまにはねられる・車に 跳ねられる
- (*to demolish*) = とりこわす・取り壊す
**knock out**
- (*to make unconscious*) = ノックアウトする
**knock over**
(*in a traffic accident*) = はねる・跳ねる
(*a drink*) = こぼす

## knot *noun*
= むすびめ・結び目

## know *verb*
- (*understand*) = わかる・分かる
  I know why he phoned = かれが どうして でんわしたか わかります。・彼が どうして 電話したか 分かります。
- (*be informed about*) = しる・知る
  I don't know the Japanese word for it = にほんごで なんというか しりません。・日本語で 何というか 知りません。
  he knows everything = かれは なんでも しっています。・彼は 何でも 知っています。
  to know all about films = えいがの ことを なんでも しっている・映画の ことを 何でも 知っている
  to get to know (someone) = (だれかと) しりあいに なる・(誰かと) 知り合いに なる
  let me know = しらせてください・知らせてください。

> ! Note that when positive, しる is only used in the present or past progressive forms しっている and しっていた but when negative it becomes either しらない or しらなかった.

## knowledge *noun*
= ちしき・知識

# L1

## laboratory *noun*
(*institution*) = けんきゅうじょ・研究所
(*room*) = じっけんしつ・実験室
(*school laboratory*) = りかしつ・理科室

## lace *noun*
- (*the material*)
  = レース
- (*for shoes*)
  = ひも・紐
  to tie one's laces = ひもを むすぶ・紐を 結ぶ

## lack

**1** *noun*
lack of food = たべものが ない・食べ物が ない
lack of money = おかねが ない・お金が ない

**2** *verb*
= ない
he lacks confidence = かれは じしんが ありません。・彼は 自信が ありません。

## ladder *noun*
= はしご

## lady *noun*
= じょせい・女性

## lake *noun*
= みずうみ・湖

## lamb *noun*
(*animal*) = こひつじ・子羊
(*meat*) = ラム

## lamp *noun*
= ランプ
(*desk-lamp*) = スタンド

## lampshade *noun*
= ランプの かさ

## land

**1** *noun*
- (*as opposed to the sea*)
  = りく・陸
- (*property*)
  = とち・土地
  to own land = とちを もつ・土地を 持つ

**2** *verb*
- (*to fall*) = おちる・落ちる
- (*if it's a plane*) = ちゃくりくする・着陸する

**landscape** *noun*
= けしき・景色

**language** *noun*
- = げんご・言語
  foreign language = がいこくご・外国語
- bad language = げひんな ことば・下品な 言葉

**laptop** *noun*
= ラップトップ

**large** *adjective*
- (*big*) = おおきい・大きい
- (*large in area*) = ひろい・広い
  large garden = ひろい にわ・広い庭
  large room = ひろい へや・広い部屋

**last**
**1** *adjective*
= まえの・前の
my last place of work = まえの しょくば・前の 職場
last week = せんしゅう・先週
last month = せんげつ・先月
last year = きょねん・去年
**2** *adverb*
- (*most recently*) = この あいだ・この間 *not used in formal Japanese*
  when I last came here = この あいだ ここにきた とき・この 間 ここに 来た とき
- (*at the end*) = さいご(に)・最後(に)
  I'll do the dishes last (of all) = さいごに しょっきを あらいます。・最後に 食器を 洗います。
- (*in final position*)
  he came last in the race = かれは いちばん さいごでした。・彼は 一番 最後でした。
**3** *pronoun*
the last = さいご・最後
they were the last to arrive = かれらはさいごにつきました。・彼らは 最後に 着きました。
the night before last = おとといの よる・おとといの 夜
**4** *verb*
= つづく・続く

the film lasts two hours = えいがは にじかん つづきます。・映画は 二時間 続きます。

**late**
**1** *adverb*
- (*far into the day or night*) = おそい・遅い
  late in the afternoon = ゆうがた・夕方
  it's getting late = おそく なっています。・遅く なっています。
- (*not on time*)
  to arrive half an hour late = さんじゅっぷん おくれる・三十分 遅れる
**2** *adjective*
= おくれている・遅れている
to be late for work = しごとに おくれている・仕事に 遅れている
the train was two hours late = でんしゃは にじかん おくれました。・電車は 二時間 遅れました。
to make (someone) late = (だれかを) おくらせる・(誰かを)遅らせる

**later** *adverb*
= あとで・後で
I'll call back later = あとで また でんわします。・後で また 電話します。
see you later! = また あとで。・また 後で。

**latest**
**1** *adjective*
= さいきん(の)・最近(の)
the latest news = さいきんの ニュース・最近の ニュース
**2 at the latest** = おそくとも・遅くとも

**Latin** *noun*
= ラテンご・ラテン語

**laugh**
**1** *verb*
= わらう・笑う
to laugh at a joke = じょうだんに わらう・冗談に 笑う
to make (someone) laugh = (だれかを)わらわせる・(誰かを) 笑わせる
to laugh at (someone) = (だれかを) ばかに する・(誰かを)ばかに する

**laundry** *noun*
= せんたくもの・洗濯物

to do the laundry = せんたくする・
洗濯する

**law** noun
- (a set of rules in a country)
= ほうりつ・法律
to obey the law = ほうりつをまもる
・法律を 守る
it's against the law = ふほうです。・
不法です。
- (a rule)
the law of gravity = じゅうりょくの
ほうそく・重力の 法則
- (as a subject)
= ほうがく・法学

**lawn** noun
= しばふ・芝生

**lawnmower** noun
= しばかりき・芝刈機

**lawyer** noun
= べんごし・弁護士

**lay** verb
- (to put) = おく・置く
lay some newspapers on the floor =
しんぶんを ゆかに おく・新聞
を 床に 置く
- (to spread) = しく・敷く
to lay a carpet = じゅうたんを しく
・絨毯を 敷く
- to lay the table = テーブルに しょ
っきを ならべる・テーブルに
食器を 並べる
- (of a chicken)
to lay an egg = たまごをうむ・卵を
産む
lay down = おく・置く
I laid the tray down on the table =
おぼんを テーブルの うえに
おきました。・お盆を テーブル
の 上に 置きました。
lay off = かいこする・解雇する

**lazy** adjective
lazy person = なまけもの・怠け者

**lead¹** verb
- (to guide) = いく・行く
this road will lead you to the village =
この みちは むらに いきます。・
この 道は 村に 行きます。
- (in sport) = せんとうに たつ・先頭
に 立つ
- to lead a busy life = いそがしい せい
かつを おくる・忙しい 生活を
送る

- (to have as a result)
to lead to an accident = じこに なる
・事故に なる

**lead²** noun
(metal) = なまり・鉛
(in a pencil) = しん・芯

**leader** noun
= リーダー

**leaf** noun
individual leaf = は・葉
leaves = はっぱ・葉っぱ

**leak** verb
= もれる・漏れる
water is leaking from the pipe = パイ
プから みずが もれています。・
パイプから 水が 漏れています。

! in Japanese pipes don't leak, the
water leaks (from the pipe)

**lean**
**1** verb
- (to support oneself)
to lean against the wall = かべに より
かかる・壁に よりかかる
- (to put)
to lean a bicycle against the wall =
じてんしゃを かべに もたせか
ける・自転車を 壁に もたせか
ける
- to lean out of the window = まどから
のりだす・窓から 乗り出す
**2** adjective
(person) = やせた
(meat) = あかみ(の)・赤身(の)
lean back = うしろへ もたれる・
後ろへ もたれる
lean forward = まえに かがむ・前
に かがむ
lean on = よりかかる

**learn** verb
= ならう・習う
to learn how to drive = くるまの うん
てんを ならう・車の 運転を
習う

**leash** noun
= ひも・紐

**least**
**1** determiner
the least
= いちばんすくない・一番少ない
I have the least money = わたしの も
っている おかねが いちばんす

くないです。・私の 持っている
お金が 一番少ないです。

**2** *pronoun*

it was the least I could do! = たいした
おかまいも していません。・た
いした お構いも していません。

**3** *adverb*

the least = いちばん + opposite
adjective

the least expensive shop = いちばん
やすい みせ ・ 一番安い 店

the least difficult question = いちばん
かんたんな しつもん ・ 一番簡
単な 質問

**4 at least**

• (*at the minimum*) = すくなくとも ・
少なくとも

he's at least thirty = かれは すくな
くとも さんじゅっさいです。・
彼は 少なくとも 三十才です。

• (*when expressing some doubt*)

he's gone out—at least, I think so =
かれは でかけたと おもいます。
・ 彼は 出かけたと 思います。

**leather** *noun*

= かわ ・ 革

**leave** *verb*

• (*to go away*) = でる ・ 出る

to leave school (graduate) = そつぎ
ょうする ・ 卒業する

to leave school (go home) = がっこう
から かえる ・ 学校から 帰る

she left her husband = かのじょは
うちを でました。・ 彼女は 家を
出ました。

I left the next day = つぎの ひ、でま
した。・ 次の 日、出ました。

• (*to go out of*) = でる ・ 出る

I left the room = へやを でました。・
部屋を 出ました。

• (*to allow to remain*) = おいて おく ・
置いて おく

leave your coat here = ここに コー
トを おいて おいてください。・
ここに コートを 置いて おいて
ください。

I left the window open (deliberately) =
まどを あけて おきました。・
窓を 開けて おきました。

I left the window open (by accident) =
まどを あけっぱなしに しま
した。・ 窓を 開けっ放しに しま
した。

• (*to put, to give*) = のこす ・ 残す

I didn't leave a message = メッセー
ジを のこしませんでした。・ メ
ッセージを 残しませんでした。

I left him some money = かれに おか
ねを のこして あげました。・
彼に お金を 残して あげました。

• (*to put off*) = のばす ・ 延ばす

let's leave it until tomorrow = あした
まで のばしましょう。・ 明日ま
で 延ばしましょう。

• (*to remain*) = のこる ・ 残る

there's nothing left = なにも のこっ
ていません。・ 何も 残っていま
せん。

we've got ten minutes left = あと じ
ゅっぷん あります。・ 後 十分
あります。

• (*other uses*)

I left it up to them = かれらに まかせ
ました。・ 彼らに 任せました。

leave behind = おきわすれる ・ 置
き忘れる

I left my bag behind = かばんを おき
わすれました。・ かばんを 置き
忘れました。

leave out

• (*not to show or talk about*)

(*by accident*) = pre ます form + わす
れる

(*deliberately*) = 〜ない + ようにする

• (*to exclude (a person)*) = なかまはず
れに する ・ 仲間はずれに する

to feel left out = なかまはずれに な
っている ・ 仲間はずれに なっ
ている

leave over

there was not much left over = あまり
のこっていませんでした。・ あ
まり 残っていませんでした。

there is some food left over = たべも
のが のこっています ・ 食べ物
が 残っています。

**lecture** *noun*

(*to students*) = こうぎ ・ 講義

(*to the public*) = こうえん ・ 講演

**left**

**1** *noun*

= ひだり ・ 左

please take the first street on the left =
さいしょの みちを ひだりに は
いってください。・ 最初の 道を
左に 入ってください。

**2** *adjective*

= ひだり(の) ・ 左(の)

left hand = ひだりて・左手
left handed = ひだりきき・左利き

**3** *adverb*
= ひだりに・左に
to turn left = ひだりに まがる・左に 曲がる

**leg** *noun*
• (*of a person or animal*)
= あし・足
• (*of meat*) = もも

**legal** *adjective*
= ほうてき(な)・法的(な)

**leisure** *noun*
= レジャー

**leisure centre** (*British English*),
**leisure center** (*US English*)
*noun*
= レジャーセンター

**lemon** *noun*
= レモン

**lemonade** *noun*
= レモネード

**lend** *verb*
= かす・貸す
to lend (someone) money = (だれかに) おかねをかす・(誰かに)お金を 貸す

**length** *noun*
= ながさ・長さ

**leopard** *noun*
= ひょう・豹

**less**
**1** *determiner*
= もっと すくない・もっと 少ない
less money = もっと すくない おかね・もっと 少ない お金
I have less work than he does = かれより しごとが すくないです。・彼より 仕事が 少ないです。

**2** *pronoun*
it costs less = もっと やすいです。・もっと 安いです。
he reads less than she does = かのじょは かれより おおく よんでいます。・彼女は 彼より 多く 読んでいます。
my book is less useful than his book = わたしの ほんは かれの ほど やくに たちません。・私の本は 彼の ほど 役に 立ちません。

**3** *adverb*

we travel less in winter = ふゆは あまり りょこうしません。・冬は あまり 旅行しません。

**4** *preposition*
(*minus*) = ひく

**5** less and less = だんだん すくなく・だんだん 少なく
there is less and less time = だんだん じかんが すくなく なります。・だんだん 時間が 少なく なります。

**6** less than = 〜いか・〜以下
less than 1000 yen = せんえんいか・千円以下
in less than half an hour = さんじゅっぷんいない・三十分以内

**lesson** *noun*
= じゅぎょう・授業
Japanese lesson = にほんごの じゅぎょう・日本語の 授業

**let¹** *verb*
• (*when making suggestions*)
let's go home = かえりましょう。・帰りましょう。
let's go! = いきましょう。・行きましょう。
• (*to allow*) *Let often can be expressed using the causative form of the verb.*
▶ 191
my father let me go to and study abroad = ちちは りゅうがく させて くれました。・父は 留学させて くれました。
I let him do what he likes = かれを すきな ままに させています。・彼を 好きな ままに させています。
I'm letting my hair grow = かみのけを のばしっぱなしに しています。・髪の毛を 伸ばしっぱなしに しています。
**let down** = がっかりさせる
**let go**
• (*to stop holding*) = はなす・放す
please let go of me = はなしてください。・放してください。
• (*to release (animal)*) = かいほうする・解放する
(*to release (prisoner)*) = しゃくほうする・釈放する
**let in**
• (*to a room or house*) = いれる・入れる
he let me in = かれは わたしを いれて くれました。・彼は 私を 入れて くれました。

- the roof lets in the rain = やねが あま もりする・屋根が 雨漏りする

**let out**
- (to let the air out of a tyre) = タイヤの くうきを ぬく・タイヤの 空気 を 抜く

let me out! = だしてください。・出 してください。
- to let out a scream = ひめいを あげ る・悲鳴を あげる

**let through**
to let (someone) through = (だれか を)とおして あげる・(誰かを) 通して あげる

**let²** verb (British English)
= かす・貸す

**letter** noun
= てがみ・手紙
(of the alphabet) = もじ・文字

**letter box** noun (British English)
= ゆうびんうけ・郵便受け

**lettuce** noun
= レタス

**level**
**1** noun
= レベル
**2** adjective
= たいら(な)・平ら(な)

**liar** noun
= うそつき・嘘つき

**library** noun
= としょかん・図書館

**licence** (British English), **license**
(US English) noun
= めんきょ・免許
driving licence = うんてんめんきょ しょう・運転免許証

**license plate** noun (US English)
= ナンバープレート

**lick** verb
= なめる

**lid** noun
= ふた

**lie**
**1** verb
- (on the ground, on a bed) = よこに なる・横に なる
I lay down on the sofa = ソファーに よこに なりました。・ソファー に 横に なりました。

- (to be situated) = ある
- (not to tell the truth) = うそを つく・ 嘘を つく

**2** noun
= うそ・嘘
to tell a lie = うそをつく・嘘を つく

**lie around**
my children leave their toys lying around = うちのこどもは おもち ゃを めちこちに おきっぱなし に します。・家の 子供は おも ちゃを あちこちに 置きっぱな しに します。

lie down = よこに なる・横に なる

**life** noun
(human life in general) = じんせい・ 人生
(state of being alive) = いのち・命
(lifespan) = いっしょう・一生
(life expectancy) = じゅみょう・寿 命
(everyday life) = せいかつ・生活

**lifestyle** noun
= ライフスタイル

**lift**
**1** verb
= あげる・上げる
to lift one's arm = うでを あげる・ 腕を 上げる
to lift a lid = ふたを あげる・ ふたを 上げる
**2** noun
- (British English)
(an elevator)
= エレベーター
- (in a car)
to give (someone) a lift to the station = (だれかを) えきに おくって あげる・(誰かを) 駅に 送って あげる

lift up = もちあげる・ 持ち上げる

**light**
**1** noun
- (from the sun, moon)
= ひかり・光
- (in a room, on a machine)
= でんき・電気
to switch on a light = でんきを つけ る・電気を 点ける
- (for traffic)
the lights are green = しんごうは あおです。・信号は 青です。
- (in a street)

**L**

a light = あかり・明かり
• **have you got a light?** = ライターを おもちですか。・ライターを お 持ちですか。
**2** *adjective*
• (*not dark*) *not usually used to describe colours*
  **it's still light outside** = そとは まだ あかるいです。・外は まだ 明る いです。
• (*not heavy*) = かるい・軽い
**3** *verb*
  = ひを つける・火を 点ける
  **I lit a cigarette** = たばこに ひを つけ ました。・たばこに 火を 点けま した。
  **to light a fire** = ひを たく・火を たく

**light bulb** *noun*
  = でんきゅう・電球

**lighthouse** *noun*
  = とうだい・燈台

**lightning** *noun*
  = いなずま・稲妻

**like¹** *preposition*
  **people like us** = わたしたちの よう な ひと・私達の ような 人
  **what's it like?** = どうですか。

**like²** *verb*
• (*when expressing an interest*) = すき・ 好き *not a verb in Japanese*
  **I like dancing** = ダンスが すきです。 ・ダンスが 好きです。
  **I like it!** = すきです。・好きです。
  **how do you like America?** = アメリカ は どうですか。
• (*when expressing a wish*) = pre ます form of the verb + たい ▶ 191
  **I'd like to live here** = ここに すみた いです。・ここに 住みたいで す。
  (*when ordering food and drink*) = 〜を ください
  **I'd like coffee please** = コーヒーを ください。

**limit** *noun*
  = かぎり・限り

**line**
**1** *noun*
• = せん・線
  **straight line** = まっすぐの せん・真 っ直ぐの 線

• (*US English*)
  (*a queue*) = れつ・列
  **to stand in line** = れつに ならぶ・ 列に 並ぶ
• (*a row*)
  = れつ・列
• (*lines in play/film*)
  = せりふ
• (*line of writing*)
  = ぎょう・行
• (*telephone line*)
  = でんわせん・電話線 **the line is engaged** = はなしちゅうです。・ 話し中です。
**2** *verb*
  **to be lined with trees** = きが ならん でいる・木が 並んでいる

**link** *verb*
• (*by train*) = むすぶ・結ぶ
  **to link Paris to London** = パリと ロン ドンを むすぶ・パリと ロンド ンを 結ぶ
• (*to make a connection between*) = れ んけつする・連結する
  **the two murders are linked** = ふたつ の さつじんじけんは かんれん しています。・二つの 殺人事件 は 関連しています。

**lion** *noun*
  = ライオン

**lip** *noun*
  = くちびる・唇

**lipstick** *noun*
  = くちべに・口紅

**liquid**
**1** *noun*
  = えき・液
**2** *adjective*
  = えきたい(の)・液体(の)

**list** *noun*
  = リスト

**listen** *verb*
  = きく・聞く
  **to listen to someone** = だれかに きく ・誰かに 聞く

**litre** (*British English*), **liter** (*US English*) *noun*
  = リットル

**little¹**
**1** *determiner*
  = すこし(の)・少し(の)

little wine = すこしのワイン・少し
のワイン
there is very little time = じかんが あ
まり ありません。・ 時間が あま
りありません。
**2** *pronoun*
a little = すこし だけ・少し だけ
I only ate a little = すこし だけ たべ
ました。・ 少し, だけ 食べまし
た。
**3** *adverb*
= すこし・少し
**4 a little (bit)** = ちょっと
**5 little by little** = すこしずつ・少し
ずつ
**little²** *adjective*
= ちいさい・小さい

**live¹** *verb*
• (*to have one's home*) = すむ・住む
I live in London = ロンドンに すんで
います。・ ロンドンに 住んでい
ます。
• (*to be alive*) = いきる・生きる
(*to lead a life*) = くらす・暮らす
that's not enough to live on = せいか
つ できる ほどではありません。
・ 生活 できる ほどではありませ
ん。

**live²** *adjective*
• (*alive*) = いきている・生きている
• (*of a match, a show*) = なま(の)・生
(の)

**lively** *adjective*
(*person*) = げんき(な)・元気(な)
(*town, party*) = にぎやか(な)

**living room** *noun*
(*Japanese style*) = ちゃの ま・茶の
間
(*Western style*) = リビング

**load** *noun*
• (*on a truck, being carried*)
= かもつ・貨物
• loads of money = たくさんの おかね
・ たくさんの お金

**loaf** *noun*
= パン

**loan** *noun*
= ローン

**lobster** *noun*
= ロブスター

**local** *adjective*
= じもと(の)・地元(の)

a local newspaper = ちほうの しん
ぶん・地方の 新聞
the local people = じもとの ひと・
地元の 人

**lock**
**1** *verb*
= かぎを かける・鍵を かける
I locked the door = ドアの かぎを か
けました。・ ドアの 鍵をかけま
した。
**2** *noun*
= かぎ・鍵
a bicycle lock = じてんしゃの ロッ
ク・自転車の ロック
**lock in**
to lock (someone) in = (だれかを)と
じこめる・(誰かを)閉じ込める

**locker** *noun*
= ロッカー

**logical** *adjective*
= ろんりてき(な)・論理的(な)

**London** *noun*
= ロンドン

**lonely** *adjective*
= さびしい・寂しい

**long**
**1** *adjective*
= ながい・長い
a long letter = ながい てがみ・長い
手紙
long hair = ちょうはつ・長髪
the film is two hours long = えいがは
にじかんです。・ 映画は 二時間
です。
I haven't seen him for a long time =
かれに ながい あいだ あってい
ません。・ 彼に 長い 間 会って
いません。
**2** *adverb*
= ながく・長く
long ago = むかし・昔
please stay as long as you like = すき
な だけ とまってください。・
好きな だけ 泊まってください。
I won't be long = ながく かかりませ
ん。・ 長く かかりません。
**3 as long as** *Use a conditional form of
the verb.* ▶ 191
as long as the weather is nice = てん
きが よければ・天気が 良けれ
ば
as long as you ring me = でんわ さえ
すれば・電話 さえ すれば

L

## look

**1** *verb*
- = みる・見る
  to look at a picture = えを みる・絵を見る
  to look out of the window = まどから みる・窓から見る
- *(to appear)*
  to look tired = つかれている ように 見える・疲れている ように 見える
  to look well = げんきに みえる・元気に見える
  he looks young = かれは わかく みえます。・彼は 若く見えます。
  she looks like her mother = かのじょ は おかあさんに にています。・彼女は お母さんに 似ています。
  what does it look like? = どの ような ものですか。・どのような物で すか。
  **look after** = めんどうを みる・面倒を見る
  to look after a child = こどもの めんどうを みる・子供の面倒を見る
  **look down**
- *(to lower one's eyes)* = めを ふせる・目を伏せる
- to look down on someone = だれかを けいべつする・誰かを 軽蔑する
  **look for** = さがす・探す
  I am looking for a job = しごとを さがしています。・仕事を探して います。
  **look forward to**
  I am looking forward to meeting her = かのじょに あうのを たのしみ にしています。・彼女に 会うの を楽しみに しています。
  **look onto** = ながめる・眺める
  my room looks onto the garden = わたしの へやは にわに めん しています。・私の 部屋は 庭に 面しています。
  **look out** = ちゅういする・注意する
  **look up**
- to look up a word in a dictionary = じしょで ことばを しらべる・辞書で 言葉を 調べる
- *(to raise one's eyes)* = みあげる・見上げる

**loose** *adjective*
- *(describing clothes)* = ゆったりした
- *(describing a screw)* = ゆるい・緩い

**lorry** *noun* *(British English)*
= トラック

**lose** *verb*
= なくす

**lost** *adjective*
  to get lost = みちに まよう・道に 迷う
  lost property = おとしもの・落とし 物
  lost property office = いしつぶつと りあつかいじょ・遺失物取扱所

**lot** *pronoun*
  a lot = たくさん
  I eat a lot = たくさん たべます。・たくさん 食べます。
  a lot of money = たくさんの おかね・たくさんの お金
  there's not a lot left = たくさんは のこっていません。・たくさんは 残っていません。

**lottery** *noun*
= たからくじ・宝くじ

**loud** *adjective*
- *(too noisy)* = うるさい
  to talk in a loud voice = おおきい こ えで はなす・大きい 声で 話す

**loudspeaker** *noun*
= スピーカー

**lounge** *noun*
  *(Japanese style)* = いま・居間
  *(Western style)* = リビング
  *(in a hotel)* = ラウンジ

## love

**1** *verb*
- *(when talking about people)* = あいす る・愛する
  to love each other = おたがいに あい しあう・お互いに 愛し合う
- *(when talking about things, activities)* = だいすき・大好き
  I love reading = どくしょが だいす きです。・読書が 大好きです。
**2** *noun*
= あい・愛
  to be in love = あいしている・愛し ている
  to make love = セックスする

**lovely** *adjective*
- (*beautiful*) = きれい(な)
  a lovely apartment = きれいな アパート
  you've got lovely eyes = め が きれいです。・ 目 が きれいです。
- (*very nice, kind*) = すてき(な)・素敵(な)

**low**
**1** *adjective*
= ひくい・低い
to speak in a low voice = ひくい こえ で はなす・低い 声で 話す
**2** *adverb*
to turn the music down low = おんがくの おとを ちいさく する・音楽の 音を 小さく する

**lower** *verb*
= さげる・下げる

**loyal** *adjective*
= ちゅうじつ(な)・忠実(な)

**luck** *noun*
= うん・運
good luck! = がんばってください。・頑張ってください。
to bring someone (good) luck = だれ かに こううんを まねく・誰か に 幸運を 招く

**lucky** *adjective*
to be lucky = ラッキー(な)

**luggage** *noun*
= にもつ・荷物

**lunch** *noun*
= ひるごはん・昼ご飯

**lunchbreak** *noun*
= ひるやすみ・昼休み

**lung** *noun*
= はい・肺

**luxurious** *adjective*
= ぜいたく(な)・贅沢(な)

**luxury**
**1** *noun*
= ぜいたく・贅沢
**2** *adjective*
luxury hotel = ごうかな ホテル・豪華な ホテル

**lyric** *noun*
= かし・歌詞

# Mm

**machine** *noun*
= きかい・機械

**mad** *adjective*
- (*crazy*) = きちがい(の)・気違い(の)
- (*very angry*) = ひどく おこっている・ひどく 怒っている
- mad about (someone) = (だれかに) むちゅう・(誰かに)夢中

**magazine** *noun*
= ざっし・雑誌

**magic** *adjective*
= まほう(の)・魔法(の)

**maiden name** *noun*
= きゅうせい・旧姓

**M**

**mail**
**1** *noun*
- (*the postal system*)
= ゆうびん・郵便
- (*letters*)
= ゆうびんぶつ・郵便物
**2** *verb* (*US English*)
to mail a letter (to someone) = (だれ かに)てがみを だす・(誰かに) 手紙を 出す

**mailbox** *noun* (*US English*)
= ポスト

**mailman** *noun* (*US English*)
= ゆうびんや・郵便屋

**main** *adjective*
= おも(な)・主(な)

**main course** *noun*
(*western-style meal*) = メイン

**major**
**1** *adjective*
= じゅうよう(な)・重要(な)
a major event = じゅうような できごと・重要な 出来事
**2** *noun*
= しょうさ・少佐

**majority** *noun*
= かはんすう・過半数

## make *verb*

> ! Note that the word **make** can often be translated by つくる. This entry covers the most frequent uses of **make** but to find translations for other expressions like to make a mess, to make a mistake, to make sure *etc*, look up the entries at mess, mistake, sure *etc*.

- to make = つくる・作る
  to make a film = えいがを とる・映画を 撮る
  to make some coffee = コーヒーを いれる・コーヒーを 入れる
  to make a phone call = でんわを かける・電話を かける
  to make friends = ともだちが できる・友達が できる
  to make friends with someone = だれかと ともだちに なる・誰かと 友達に なる
  to make breakfast = あさ ごはんを つくる・朝ご飯を 作る
  to be made of gold = きんで できている・金で できている
  to be made in Japan = にほんせい・日本製
  to be made in Canada = カナダせい・カナダ製
- (*to cause a particular reaction*) Use the causative form of the verb. ▶ 191
  to make (someone) happy = (だれかを)よろこばせる・(誰かを)喜ばせる
  to make (someone) jealous = (だれかを)しっとさせる・(誰かを)嫉妬させる
  to make (someone) annoyed = (だれかを)いらいらさせる
  to make (someone) cry = (だれかを)なかせる・(誰かを)泣かせる
  to make (someone) eat = (だれかを)たべさせる・(誰かを)食べさせる
  to make (someone) laugh = (だれかを)わらわせる・(誰かを)笑わせる Note that often it is preferred in Japanese to use the expression to become... rather than to make...For example in English we might say "The medicine made him sleepy", in Japanese it would be preferable to say "He took some medicine and became sleepy"

- to make (someone) wait = (だれかを)またせる・(誰かを)待たせる
- (*to earn*)
  to make a lot of money = たくさん おかねを かせぐ・たくさん お金を 稼ぐ
  to make a profit = りえきを える・利益を 得る
  **make do** = まにあわせる・間に合わせる
  **make out**
  to make out a list = リストを つくる・リストを 作る
  **make up**
- (*to be friends again*) = なかなおりを する・仲直りを する
- to make up an excuse = いいわけを かんがえる・言い訳を 考える
- to make up a parcel = にづくりする・荷造りする

## make-up *noun*
= けしょうひん・化粧品
to wear make-up = けしょうする・化粧する

## male *adjective*
- (*in biology*) = おす(の)・雄(の)
- (*relating to men*) = おとこ(の)・男(の)

## man *noun*
- = おとこのひと・男の人
- (*as a species*) = じんるい・人類

## manage *verb*
- (*to run*) = けいえいする・経営する
- to manage to finish one's homework = なんとか しゅくだいを おわらせる・何とか 宿題を 終わらせる

## manager *noun*
(*of a project, a hotel*) = しはいにん・支配人
(*of a shop, a bank*) = てんちょう・店長
(*of a football team*) = マネージャー
(*senior manager in large company*) = ぶちょう・部長
(*line manager*) = かちょう・課長

## manners *noun*
= マナー
good manners = マナーが いい
bad manners = マナーが わるい・マナーが 悪い

## manufacture *verb*
= せいぞうする・製造する

## many

**1** *determiner*
- (*a lot of*) = たくさん

  were there many tourists? = たくさ
  ん かんこうきゃくが いました
  か。・ たくさん 観光客が いまし
  たか。

  not many = あまり + negative verb

  there weren't many people there =
  あまり ひとが いませんでした。
  ・ あまり 人が いませんでした。

- (*when used with* how, too, so, as)

  how many? = いくつ or なん +
  counter ▶ 181

  how many books have you got? =
  ほんが なんさつ ありますか。・
  本が 何冊 ありますか。

  too many = pre ます form of the verb
  + すぎる ▶ 191

  you eat too many chips = ポテトフラ
  イを たべすぎます。・ ポテトフ
  ライを 食べ過ぎます。

  there are so many things to do = たく
  さん する ことが あります。

  I got as many presents as you did =
  あなたと おなじぐらい プレ
  ゼントを もらいました。・ あな
  たと 同じぐらい プレゼントを
  もらいました。

**2** *pronoun*

  are there many left? = たくさん のこ
  っていますか。・ たくさん 残っ
  ていますか。

  I've got too many = ありすぎます。・
  あり過ぎます。

  take as many as you like = すきなだ
  け いくらでも とってください。
  ・ 好きなだけいくらでも 取って
  ください。

  many (of them) speak English = えい
  ごの はなせる ひとが おおいで
  す。・ 英語の 話せる 人が 多い
  です。

## map *noun*
= ちず・地図

## marble *noun*
= だいりせき・大理石

## marbles *noun*
= ビーだま・ビー玉

## march *verb*
- (*in the army*) = こうしんする・行進
  する
- (*in a demonstration*) = デモこうしん
  をする・デモ行進をする

## March *noun* ▶ 174
= さんがつ・三月

## margarine *noun*
= マーガリン

## mark

**1** *noun*
- (*on clothes*) = しみ・染み
  (*to indicate something*) = しるし・印
  (*damage to a surface*) = きず・傷

  to leave coffee cup marks on the table
  = テーブルに コーヒーカップの
  あとを つける・テーブルに コ
  ーヒーカップの 跡を つける

- (*British English*)
  (*a grade*) = せいせき・成績

  to get good marks = いい せいせき
  をとる・いい 成績をとる

**2** *verb*
- (*to stain*) = しみを つける・染みを
  付ける
- to mark the homework = しゅくだい
  を チェックする・宿題を チェ
  ックする

  to mark an exam = しけんを さいて
  んする・試験を 採点する

- (*to indicate*) = しめす・示す

## market *noun*
- (*the place*) = いちば・市場
  a flea market = のみの いち・蚤の
  市
- (*the system*) = しじょう・市場
  the stock market = かぶしきしじょ
  う・株式市場

## marketing *noun*
= マーケティング

## marmalade *noun*
= マーマレード

## marriage *noun*
= けっこん・結婚

## married *adjective*
= けっこんしている・結婚してい
る

  to be married (to someone) = (だれか
  と) けっこんしている・(誰か
  と)結婚している

## marry *verb*
  to marry (someone) = (だれかと) け
  っこんする・(誰かと) 結婚す
  る

## marsh *noun*
= ぬまち・沼地

**M**

**mashed potatoes** *noun*
= マッシュポテト

**mask** *noun*
= マスク

**mat** *noun*
= マット

**match**
**1** *noun*
* (*British English*)
  (*a game*) = しあい・試合
  a football match = サッカーの しあ
  い・サッカーの 試合
* (*a matchstick*) = マッチ
**2** *verb*
  the shoes match the belt = くつは
  ベルトに あいます。・靴はベル
  トに 合います。

**mate** *noun* (*British English*)
= なかま・仲間
workmate = しごとなかま・仕事仲
間

**material** *noun*
= きじ・生地

**math** (*US English*), **maths**
(*British English*) *noun*
= すうがく・数学

**mathematics** *noun*
(*school subject*) = すうがく・数学
(*calculations*) = さんすう・算数

**matter**
**1** *noun*
  what's the matter? = どうしました
  か。*A more emotive way to ask is*
  どうしたんですか。
  what's the matter with her? = かのじ
  ょは どうしましたか。・彼女は
  どうしましたか。
**2** *verb*
  it doesn't matter = たいした ことで
  はありません。・大した ことで
  はありません。

**maximum**
**1** *adjective*
  the maximum price = さいこうかか
  く・最高価格
  a maximum temperature of 30
  degrees (weather) = さいこうき
  おん さんじゅうど・最高気温
  三十度
**2** *noun*
= さいだいげん・最大限

**may** *verb*
* (*when talking about a possibility*) =
  plain form + かもしれない
  they may be able to come = かれらは
  こられる かもしれません。・彼
  らは 来られる かもしれません。
  she may not have seen him = かのじ
  ょは かれを みなかった かもし
  れません。・彼女は 彼を 見なか
  った かもしれません。
  it may rain = あめが ふる かもしれ
  ません。・雨が 降る かもしれま
  せん。
* (*when asking for or giving permission*)
  = 〜て form of the verb + も いい
  です(か)。 ▶ 197
  may I come in? = はいっても いいで
  すか。・入っても いいですか。
  you may sit down = すわっても いい
  です。・座っても いいです。

**May** *noun* ▶ 174
= ごがつ・五月

**maybe** *adverb*
= たぶん・多分

> ! *Note that* たぶん *often indicates a
> higher probability than 'maybe' does
> in English and is more similar to
> 'probably'*

**mayor** *noun*
(*of a city*) = しちょう・市長
(*of a town*) = ちょうちょう・町長
(*of a village*) = そんちょう・村長

**me** *pronoun*
* *Note that* わたし *can often be left out
  if it is obvious.*
  = わたし・私
  they asked me = かれらは わたしに
  ききました。・彼らは 私に 聞き
  ました。
  he hit me = かれは わたしを ぶちま
  した。・彼は 私を ぶちました。
* please help me! = たすけてくださ
  い。・助けてください。
  please don't bother me! = じゃまを
  しないでください。・邪魔を し
  ないでください。
* she gave the book to me = かのじょ
  は ほんを くれました。・彼女は
  本を くれました。
  please show it to me! = みせてくだ
  さい。・見せてください。
* in front of me = わたしの まえ・私
  の 前

**meal** *noun*
= しょくじ・食事

**mean**
**1** *verb*
- to mean = いみする・意味する
  what does that mean? = それは どう
  いう いみですか。・それは どう
  いう 意味ですか。
  what does じしょ mean? = じしょ
  は どう いう いみですか。・
  辞書は どう いう 意味ですか。
- (*to have as a result*)
  it means giving up my job = しごとを
  やめる ことに なります。・仕事
  を 辞める ことに なります。
- (*to intend*)
  I meant to order a pizza = ピザを ち
  ゅうもんする つもりでした。・
  ピザを 注文する つもりでした。
  I didn't mean to say that = そう いう
  つもりではありませんでした。
  ・そう 言うつもりではありませ
  んでした。
  I meant it as a joke = じょうだんの
  つもりでした。・冗談の つもり
  でした。
- (*to intend to say*)
  what do you mean? = どう いう こと
  ですか。
- her work means a lot to her = かのじ
  ょに とって しごとは たいせつ
  です。・彼女にとって 仕事は 大
  切です。
  money doesn't mean much to him =
  おかねは かれにとって たいせ
  つではありません。・お金は 彼
  に 大切ではありません。
**2** *adjective*
- (*British English*)
  (*not generous*) = けち(な)
- to be mean to someone = だれかを
  いじめる・誰かを いじめる

**meaning** *noun*
= いみ・意味

**means** *noun*
= ほうほう・方法
  a means of earning money = おか
  ねを かせぐ ほうほう・お金を
  稼ぐ 方法
  a means of transport = こうつうしゅ
  だん・交通手段

**meant to be meant to** *verb*
  I'm meant to be at my parents' house
  = ほんとうは りょうしんの うち

  に いる はずです。・本当は 両
  親の 家に いる はずです。
  it's meant to be difficult = むずかしい
  はずです。・難しい はずです。

**meanwhile** *adverb*
= その あいだに・その 間に

**measles** *noun*
= はしか

**measure** *verb*
= はかる・測る

**meat** *noun*
= にく・肉

**mechanic** *noun*
= じどうしゃせいびし・自動車整
  備士

**medal** *noun*
= メダル
  gold medal = きんメダル・金メダル

**media** *noun*
= マスメディア

**medical** *adjective*
= いがくてき(な)・医学的(な)
  to have medical treatment = ちりょ
  うを うける・治療を 受ける

**medicine** *noun*
= くすり・薬

**Mediterranean** *noun*
= ちちゅうかい・地中海

**medium** *adjective*
= ちゅうくらい(の)・中くらい
  (の)

**meet** *verb*
- (*by accident or appointment*) = あう・
  会う
  I'll meet him at the supermarket = かれに
  スーパーで あいました。・彼に
  スーパーで 会いました。
  can we meet (up) next week? = らい
  しゅう またあいませんか。・来
  週 また 会いませんか。
  to meet again = また あう・また 会
  う
- (*to be introduced to*) = しりあいに
  なる・知り合いに なる
  I met him at a wedding = かれと けっ
  こんしきで しりあいに なりま
  した。・彼と 結婚式で 知り合い
  に なりました。
- (*to fetch*) = むかえに いく・迎えに
  行く

M

I can meet you at the station = えきに むかえに いけます。・ 駅に 迎えに 行けます。

can you meet me at the station? = えきに むかえに こられますか。・ 駅に 迎えに 来られますか。

• (to have a meeting) = かいぎする ・ 会議する

**meeting** noun
= かいぎ ・ 会議

**melon** noun
= メロン

**melt** verb
• the snow is melting = ゆきが とけています。・ 雪が 溶けています。
• the salt will melt the ice = しおは こおりを とかします。・ 塩は 氷を 溶かします。

**member** noun
= かいいん ・ 会員
a member of staff
(in a school) = きょういん ・ 教員
(in a bank) = ぎんこういん ・ 銀行員
(in a company) = かいしゃいん ・ 会社員

**memory** noun
• = きおく ・ 記憶
good memory = きおくが いい ・ 記憶が いい
he's got a bad memory = かれは きおくが わるいです。・ 彼は 記憶が 悪いです。
• (of a person, a place or time) = おもいで ・ 思い出

**mend** verb
• (to fix) = しゅうりする ・ 修理する
• (by sewing) = つくろう ・ 繕う

**mental** adjective
= せいしんてき(な) ・ 精神的(な)
mental illness = せいしんびょう ・ 精神病

**menu** noun
= メニュー

**mess** noun
my room is in a mess = へやが ちらかっています。・ 部屋が 散らかっています。
to make a mess in the kitchen = だいどころを ちらかす ・ 台所を 散らかす

**message** noun
= メッセージ

**metal** noun
= きんぞく ・ 金属

**method** noun
= ほうほう ・ 方法

**metre** (British English), **meter** (US English) noun
= メートル

**Mexico** noun ▶ 172
= メキシコ

**microphone** noun
= マイク

**microwave oven** noun
= でんしレンジ ・ 電子レンジ

**midday** noun ▶ 186
= おひる ・ お昼 ▶ 189
at midday = おひるに ・ お昼に

**middle** noun
= まんなか ・ 真ん中
in the middle of the road = みちの まんなかに ・ 道の 真ん中に
I'm in the middle of cooking a meal = りょうりの とちゅうです。・ 料理の 途中です。
she's in the middle of writing a letter = かのじょは てがみを かいているところです。・ 彼女は 手紙を 書いている ところです。

**middle-aged** adjective
= ちゅうねん(の) ・ 中年(の)

**midnight** noun ▶ 186
= よる じゅうにじ ・ 夜 十二時
at midnight = よる じゅうにじに ・ 夜 十二時に

**might** verb
• (when talking about a possibility) = plain form + かもしれない
her answer might be right = かのじょの こたえが あっている かもしれません。・ 彼女の 答えが 合っている かもしれません。
they might have got lost = かれらは みちに まよった かもしれません。・ 彼らは 道に 迷った かもしれません。
'will you come?'—'I might' = 「きますか。」「いく かもしれません。」・「来ますか。」「行く かもしれません。」
we might miss the plane = ひこうきに まにあわない かもしれません。・ 飛行機に 間に合わない かもしれません。

he said he might not come = かれは
たぶん いけないと いいました。
・ 彼は 多分 行けないと 言いま
した。

• (when implying something didn't
happen)
you might have been killed! = しんだ
かもしれません。・ 死んだ かも
しれません。
you might have warned us = なにか
いって くれれば よかったのに。
・ 何か 言って くれれば 良かっ
たのに。

• (when making suggestions)
you might try leaving a message =
メッセージを のこすのは どう
ですか。・ メッセージを 残すの
は どうですか。
it might be better to wait = まつのは
どうですか。・ 待つのは どうで
すか。

**mild** adjective
= おだやか(な)・ 穏やか(な)
the weather's mild, it's mild = おだや
かな てんきです。・ 穏やかな 天
気です。

**mile** noun
= マイル

! Note that a mile = 1609 m.

**military** adjective
= ぐんたい(の)・ 軍隊(の)

**milk**
**1** noun
= ぎゅうにゅう・ 牛乳

**milkman** noun
= ぎゅうにゅうはいたつにん・
牛乳配達人

! note that milk delivery is rare in
Japan

**million** number
= ひゃくまん・ 百万
three million dollars = さんびゃくま
んドル・ 三百万ドル
a million inhabitants = ひゃくまんに
んの じんこう・ 百万人の 人口

**mind**
**1** noun
• = かんがえ・ 考え
I have a lot on my mind = かんがえる
ことが いっぱいです。考える
ことが いっぱいです。

• to make up one's mind = きめる・
決める
I changed my mind = きが かわりま
した。・ 気が 変わりました。

**2** verb
• (when expressing an opinion)
I don't mind = かまいません。
'where shall we go?'—'I don't mind' =
「どこに いきましょうか。」「ど
こでも いいです。」・「どこに 行
きましょうか。」「どこでもいい
です。」
I don't mind the heat = あつくても
かまいません。・ 暑くても かま
いません。

• (in polite questions or requests)
do you mind if I smoke? = たばこを
すっても いいですか。・ たばこ
を 吸っても いいですか。
would you mind closing the door? =
ドアを しめてください。・ ドア
を 閉めてください。

• (to be careful)
mind the steps! = だんさに ちゅう
いしてください。・ 段差に 注意
してください。
mind you don't break the glass = グラ
スを わらない ように きをつけ
てください。・ グラスを 割らな
い ように 気を つけてください。

• (to take care of) = めんどうをみる・
面倒を 見る

• never mind, I'll get the next train = し
んぱいしないでください。つぎ
の でんしゃにのります。・ 心配
しないでください。次の 電車に
乗ります。

**mine¹** pronoun
= わたしの・ 私の
the red pen is mine = あかい ペンは
わたしのです。・ 赤い ペンは 私
のです。

**mine²** noun
= こうざん・ 鉱山

**miner** noun
= こうざんろうどうしゃ・ 鉱山労
働者

**mineral water** noun
= ミネラルウォーター

**minimum**
**1** adjective
= さいてい・ 最低
the minimum temperature will be 15
degrees = さいてい きおんは じ

ゅうごどです。・最低 気温は
十五度です。

**2** noun
= さいてい・最低

**minister** noun
- (in government)
= だいじん・大臣
the minister for Education = もんぶだ
いじん・文部大臣
- (in religion)
= ぼくし・牧師

**minor** adjective
= じゅうようではない・重要では
ない
minor injury = けいしょう・軽症

**minority** noun
= しょうすう・少数
ethnic minority = しょうすうみんぞ
く・少数民族

**minus** preposition
four minus three is one = よん ひく
さんは いちです。・四 引く 三
は 一です。
it's minus four outside = そとは マイ
ナスよんどです。・外は マイナ
ス四度です。

**minute** noun ▶ 186
= ふん・分
they'll be here any minute now = かれ
らは もう すぐ つきます。・彼
らは もう すぐ 着きます。

**mirror** noun
(on a wall) = かがみ・鏡
(on a car) = ミラー

**miserable** adjective
= かなしい・悲しい
I feel miserable = かなしいです。・
悲しいです。

**miss** verb
- (to fail to hit) use the negative of あた
る・当たる to hit
to miss the target = まと に あたらな
い・的に 当たらない
- (to fail to see) = みそこなう・見損
なう
I missed the TV news = テレビニュ
ースを みそこないました。・
テレビニュースを 見損ないまし
た。
you can't miss it = すぐ わかります。
- (to fail to take)

to miss an opportunity = きかいを
のがす・機会を 逃す
- (to feel sad not to see)
I miss you = あなたが いなくて さ
びしいです。
I miss Japanese food = にほんの た
べものが こいしいです。・日本
の 食べ物が 恋しいです。
- (other uses)
don't miss this film = この えいがを
ぜったい みてください。・この
映画を 絶対 見てください。
I missed her plane = ひこうきに ま
にあいませんでした。・飛行機
に 間に合いませんでした。
to miss school
(due to illness) = がっこうを やすむ
・学校を 休む
(by skipping classes) = がっこうを
さぼる・学校を さぼる

**Miss** noun
= 〜さん

**missing** adjective
to be missing = みつからない・見
つからない
there's a book missing = ほんが みつ
かりません。・本が 見つかりま
せん。

**mist** noun
= きり・霧

**mistake** noun
= まちがい・間違い
a spelling mistake = つづりの まち
がい・つづりの 間違い
to make a mistake = まちがいを す
る・間違いを する

**mistletoe** noun
= やどりぎ・宿り木

**mix** verb
- (to put together) = まぜる・混ぜる
- (to go together) = まざる・混ざる
- to mix with the other students = ほか
の がくせいと まじわる・外の
学生と 交わる
mix up = まざる・混ざる
to get French and Japanese mixed up
= フランスごと にほんごが まざ
っている・フランス語と 日本
語が 混ざっている

**mobile phone** noun
= けいたいでんわ・携帯電話

**model** *noun*
- (*of a train, a car, a building*) = もけい ・ 模型
- (*fashion*) model = モデル

**modern** *adjective*
= げんだいてき(な) ・ 現代的(な)

**Mohammed** *noun*
= マホメット

**mole** *noun*
(*spot*) = ほくろ
(*animal*) = もぐら

**mom, Mom** *noun* (*US English*)
(*someone else's*) = おかあさん ・ お母さん
(*your own*) = はは ・ 母

> **!** *Japanese children will address their mother as* おかあさん *or* ママ

**moment** *noun*
= ちょっとのあいだ ・ ちょっとの間
at the moment = いま ・ 今
wait a moment = ちょっと まってください。・ ちょっと 待ってください。

**Monday** *noun* ▶ **174**
= げつようび ・ 月曜日

**money** *noun*
= おかね ・ お金 ▶ **189**

**monkey** *noun*
= さる ・ 猿
year of the monkey = さる どし ・ 申年

**month** *noun*
(*period of one month*) = いっかげつ ・ 一ヶ月
I'll be back in two months' time = にかげつご もどります。・ 二ヶ月後戻ります。

**monument** *noun*
= してききねんぶつ ・ 史的記念物

**mood** *noun*
I'm in a good mood = きぶんが いいです。・ 気分が いいです。
I'm in a bad mood = きぶんが わるいです。・ 気分が 悪いです。

**moon** *noun*
= つき ・ 月

**moped** *noun*
= スクーター

**moral** *adjective*
= モラル(の)

**more**
**1** *determiner*
I have more work than him = かれより しごとが あります。・ 彼より 仕事が あります。
there's no more bread = もう パンが ありません。・ もう パンが ありません。
there's more tea = コーヒーは まだ あります。
would you like more coffee? = コーヒーを もういっぱい どうですか。・ コーヒーを もう一杯どうですか。
he bought two more tickets = かれは きっぷを もう にまい かいました。・ 彼は 切符を もう 二枚 買いました。
**2** *pronoun*
= もっと
to cost more = もっと おかねが かかる ・ もっと お金が かかる
I got more than her = かのじょより もっと もらいました。・ 彼女より もっと もらいました。
I can't tell you any more = これ いじょういえません。・ これ 以上言えません。
we need more = もっと ひつようです。・ もっと 必要です。
**3** *adverb*
- (*when comparing*) = 〜より〜
it's more complicated than that = それより ふくざつです。・ それより 複雑です。
Kyoto is more beautiful than Tokyo = きょうとは とうきょうより きれいです。・ 京都は 東京より きれいです。
- (*when talking about time*)
he doesn't live there any more = かれは もう そこに すんでいません。・ 彼は もう そこに 住んでいません。
**4** more and more = もっともっと
more and more expensive = もっと もっと たかい ・ もっともっと 高い
**5** more or less = だいたい
**6** more than = 〜いじょう ・ 〜以上

**M**

there were more than 20 people there
= そこに にじゅうにんいじょう
いました。・ そこに 二十人以上
いました。

**morning** noun ▶ 186
= あさ・朝
at three o'clock in the morning = ごぜ
ん さんじに・午前三時に
(during) the morning = ごぜんちゅう
・午前中

**mosquito** noun
= か・蚊

**most**
**1** determiner
• (the majority of) = ほとんど(の)
most schools will be closed = ほとん
どの がっこうは しまります。・
ほとんどの 学校は 閉まります。
• (in superlatives)
the most = いちばん・一番
who has the most money? = だれが
いちばんおかねを もっています
か。・誰が 一番お金を 持ってい
ますか。
**2** pronoun
= ほとんど
most (of them) can speak Japanese =
ほとんどは にほんごが はなせ
ます。・ほとんどは 日本語が 話
せます。
**3** adverb
= いちばん・一番
the most expensive shop in Tokyo =
とうきょうの いちばんたかい
みせ・東京の 一番高い 店
the most beautiful town in Japan = に
ほんで いちばんきれいな まち・
日本で 一番きれいな 町
**4** at (the) most = せいぜい
**5** most of all = とくに・特に

**mostly** adverb
= ほとんど

**mother** noun ▶ 177
(someone else's) = おかあさん・お
母さん
(your own) = はは・母

> ! Japanese children will address
> their mother as おかあさん or
> ママ

**mother-in-law** noun ▶ 177
(someone else's) = ぎりの おかあさ
ん・義理の お母さん

(your own) = ぎりの はは・義理の
母

**motor** noun
= モーター

**motorbike** noun
= オートバイ

**motorcyclist** noun
= オートバイに のる ひと・オー
トバイに 乗る 人

**motorist** noun
= うんてんしゃ・運転者

**motor racing** noun
= カーレース

**motorway** noun (British English)
= こうそくどうろ・高速道路

**mountain** noun
= やま・山

**mountain bike** noun
= マウンテンバイク

**mountain climbing** noun
= とざん・登山

**mouse** noun
• (the animal) = ねずみ
• (for a computer) = マウス

**moustache, mustache**
(US English) noun
= くちひげ

**mouth** noun
• (of a person, animal)
= くち・口
• (of a river)
= かこう・河口

**move** verb
• (to make a movement) = うごく・動
く
please don't move! = うごかないで
ください。・動かないでくださ
い。
the train's started to move = でんし
ゃが うごきはじめました。・電
車が 動きはじめました。
• (to put elsewhere) = いどうする・
移動する
to move the car = くるまを いどう
する・車を 移動する
to move a chair (out of the way) =
いすを どかす・椅子を 退かす
• to move (house) = ひっこす・引っ
越す

to move to Gunma = ぐんまに ひっ こす・群馬に 引っ越す

**move away**
- (to live elsewhere) = ひっこす・引っ 越す
- (to make a movement away) = はなれ る・離れる
  to move away from the window = まど から はなれる・窓から 離れる
**move back** = もどる・戻る
**move forward** = すすむ・進む
**move into**
to move into university accomodation = だいがくの りょうに はいる・ 大学の寮に 入る
**move out** = でる・出る
**move over** = どく・退く
**move over please** = どいて くださ い。・退いてください。

**movement** noun
= うごき・動き

**movie** noun (US English)
= えいが・映画

**movies** noun (US English)
= えいが・映画

**movie theater** noun (US English)
= えいがかん・映画館

**moving** adjective
= うごいている・動いている

**mow** verb
to mow the lawn = しばかりを する ・芝刈りをする

**MP** noun (British English)
= こっかいぎいん・国会議員

**Mr** noun
= ～さん

**Mrs** noun
= ～さん

**Ms** noun
= ～さん

**much**
**1** adverb
- (a lot) = もっと
  this bag is much more expensive = この かばんは もっと たかい です。・この かばんは もっと 高いです。
- (not a lot) = あまり + negative
  he doesn't read much = かれは あま り よみません。・彼は あまり 読みません。

- (not often) = あまり + negative
  they don't eat out much = かれらは あまり がいしょくしません。・ 彼らは あまり 外食しません。
- (when used with very, too or so)
  I like it very much = だいすきです。・ 大好きです。
  I ate too much = たべすぎました。・ 食べ過ぎました。
  She drank too much = かのじょは の みすぎました。・彼女は 飲みす ぎました。
  I want to go so much = とても いき たいです。・とても 行きたいで す。
**2** pronoun
  (in questions) = たくさん
  is there much to be done? = する ことは たくさんありますか。
**3** determiner
- (not a lot of) = あまり + negative
  I haven't got much time = じかんが あまり ありません。・時間が あ まり ありません。
- (a lot of) = たくさん
  do you have much homework? = しゅ くだいが たくさん ありますか。 ・宿題が たくさん ありますか。
- (when used with how, very, too, so or as)
  how much money have you got? = お かねが どのくらい ありますか。 ・お金が どのくらい あります か。
  she doesn't eat very much meat = か のじょは にくを あまり たべま せん。・彼女は 肉を あまり 食 べません。
  I spent too much money = おかねを つかいすぎました。・お金を 使 い過ぎました。
  please don't put so much salt on = しおを そんなに かけないでく ださい。・塩を そんなにかけな いでください。
  she has as much work as me = かの じょは わたしと おなじ くらい しごとが あります。・彼女は 私 と 同じ くらい仕事が あります。

**mud** noun
= どろ・泥

**mug**
**1** noun
= マグカップ

**multiply** *verb*
(*increase*) = ふえる・増える
(*in maths*) = かける

**mum, Mum** *noun* (*British English*)
(*someone else's*) = おかあさん・お母さん
(*your own*) = はは・母

> ! Japanese children will address their mother as おかあさん or ママ

**mumps** *noun*
= おたふくかぜ・おたふく風邪

**murder**
**1** *noun*
= さつじん・殺人
**2** *verb*
= ころす・殺す

**murderer** *noun*
= ひとごろし・人殺し

**muscle** *noun*
= きんにく・筋肉

**museum** *noun*
= はくぶつかん・博物館

**mushroom** *noun*
= きのこ

**music** *noun*
= おんがく・音楽

**musical** *noun*
= ミュージカル

**musical instrument** *noun*
= がっき・楽器

**musician** *noun*
= ミュージシャン

**Muslim** *adjective*
= イスラムきょう(の)・イスラム教(の)

**mussel** *noun*
= ムールがい・ムール貝

**must** *verb*
- (*when stressing the importance of something*)
  you must go to hospital = びょういんに いかなければ なりません。・病院に 行かなければ なりません。
  we mustn't tell the teacher = せんせいに いっては いけません。・先生に 言っては いけません。

- (*when talking about a rule*)
  she must take the exam in June = かのじょは ろくがつに しけんを うけなければ なりません。・彼女は 六月に 試験を 受けなければ なりません。

- (*when assuming that something is true*)
  it must be nice to live there = あそこに すむのは いいでしょう。・あそこに 住むのは いいでしょう。
  you must be Mr Yamamoto's younger sister = やまもとさんの いもうとさんでしょう。・山本さんの 妹さんでしょう。
  it must have been boring = つまらなかったでしょう。

**mustard** *noun*
= からし

**mutton** *noun*
= マトン

**my** *determiner*
= わたしの・私の Not always used if the owner is obvious. うち can also mean my.
  they hate my dog = かれらは うちの いぬが きらいです。・彼らは 家の 犬が 嫌いです。
  what do you think of my car? = (わたしの)くるまは どうですか。・(私の)車は どうですか。
  I sold all my CDs = CDを ぜんぶ うりました。・CDを 全部 売りました。
  I broke my leg = あしの ほねを おりました。・足の 骨を 折りました。

**myself** *pronoun*
- Not used as a reflexive pronoun in Japanese
  I want to enjoy myself = たのしみたいです。・楽しみたいです。
  I didn't hurt myself = けがを しませんでした。・怪我を しませんでした。
- (*when used for emphasis*)
  I did it all by myself = ぜんぶ じぶんで しました。・全部 自分で しました。

**mystery** *noun*
= なぞ・謎

# Nn

**nail** noun
- (for use in attaching, repairing)
  = くぎ
- (on the fingers or toes)
  = つめ

**nail polish** noun
= マニキュア

**naked** adjective
= はだか(の)・裸(の)

**name** noun
- (of a person)
  = なまえ・名前
  what's your name? = おなまえは なんですか。・ お名前は何ですか。
  ▶ 189
  my name is Michiko = みちこです。・ 美智子です。
- (of a book, a play or film)
  = タイトル

**narrow** adjective
= せまい・狭い

**nasty** adjective
= いや(な)・嫌(な)

**national** adjective
= くにの・国の

**native** adjective
native language = ぼこくご・母国語
a native French speaker = フランスごが ぼこくごの ひと・フランス語が 母国語の 人

**natural** adjective
= しぜん(な)・自然(な)

**naturally** adverb
(of nature) = しぜんに・自然に
(of course) = とうぜん・当然

**nature** noun
= しぜん・自然

**naughty** adjective
= わんぱく(な)・腕白(な)

**navy** noun
= かいぐん・海軍

**navy blue** adjective
= こん(の)・紺(の)

**near**
**1** preposition
= ちかくに・近くに
he was sitting near us = かれは ちかくに すわっていました。・ 彼は 近くに 座っていました。
**2** adverb
they live near = かれらは ちかくに すんでいます。・ 彼らは 近くに 住んでいます。
**3** adjective
= ちかい・近い
the school is quite near = がっこうは けっこう ちかいです。・ 学校は 結構 近いです。
the nearest shops are several kilometres away = いちばんちかい みせは すうキロ はなれています。・ 一番近い 店は 数キロ 離れています。

**nearby** adverb
= ちかく・近く

**nearly** adverb
we're nearly there = あと もう すこしです。・ 後 もう 少しです。
nearly all (of them) = ほとんど
nearly 5% = ごパーセント ちかく・五パーセント 近く
I nearly forgot = わすれる ところでした。・ 忘れる ところでした。

**neat** adjective
(in how one looks) = きちんとした
(describing work, handwriting) = きれい(な)

**necessary** adjective
= ひつよう(な)・必要(な)

**neck** noun
= くび・首

**necklace** noun
= ネックレス

**need** verb
- ((to) have to)
  you don't need to get permission = きょかを えなくても いいです。・ 許可を 得なくても いいです。
  they'll need to come early = かれらは はやく こなければ なりません。・ 彼らは 早く 来なければ なりません。
- (to want) = いる・要る
  I need money = おかねが いります。・ お金が 要ります。

we need to know by Tuesday = かようびまでに しりたいです。・ 火曜日までに 知りたいです。

everything you need = ひつような もの ぜんぶ・ 必要な 物 全部

**needle** noun
= はり・ 針

**negative**
1 adjective
• = ひていてき(な)・ 否定的(な)
(pessimistic) = ひかんてき(な)・ 悲観的(な)
2 noun
= しゃしんの ネガ・ 写真の ネガ

**neighbour** (British English),
**neighbor** (US English) noun
(living next-door) = となりの ひと・ 隣の 人
(living close by) = きんじょの ひと・ 近所の 人

**neither**
1 conjunction
• (in neither... nor sentences)
she can speak neither French nor English = かのじょは フランスごも えいごも はなせません。・ 彼女は フランス語も 英語も 話せません。
• (nor)
'I can't sleep'—'neither can I' = 「ねむれません。」「わたしも。」・「眠れません。」「私も。」
2 determiner
= どちらも
neither answered = どちらも こたえませんでした。・ どちらも 答えませんでした。
3 pronoun
= どちらも
neither of them is coming = どちらも きません。・ どちらも 来ません。

**nephew** noun
= おい・ 甥

**nerves** noun
= しんけい・ 神経
to get on someone's nerves = だれかを いらいらさせる・ 誰かを いらいらさせる

**nervous** adjective
• (frightened) ▶ 178
= こわい・ 怖い

• (anxious) = ふあん(な)・ 不安(な)
nervous feeling = ふあんな きもち・ 不安な 気持ち
nervous disposition = しんけいしつ・ 神経質

**nest** noun
= す・ 巣

**net** noun
• (for fishing)
= あみ・ 網
• (in sport)
= ネット

**Netherlands** noun ▶ 172
= オランダ

**network** noun
= ネットワーク

**neutral** adjective
= ちゅうりつ(の)・ 中立(の)

**never** adverb
• (not ever)
they never come here = かれらは ぜんぜん ここに きません。・ 彼らは 全然 ここに 来ません。
she has never been to the opera = かのじょは オペラに いった ことがありません。・ 彼女は オペラに 行った ことがありません。
I'll never go back there again = にどと そこに いきません。・ 二度と そこに 行きません。
• (when used for emphasis)
she never even contacted us = かのじょは れんらく さえ しませんでした。・ 彼女は 連絡 さえ しませんでした。

**nevertheless** adverb
= それにもかかわらず

**new** adjective
= あたらしい・ 新しい
new bike = あたらしい じてんしゃ・ 新しい 自転車
new car = しんしゃ・ 新車
new computer = あたらしい コンピューター・ 新しい コンピューター
new clothes = あたらしいふく・ 新しい 服

**newborn baby** noun
= うまれた ばかりの あかちゃん・ 生まれた ばかりの 赤ちゃん

**news** noun
• a piece of news = じょうほう・ 情報

have you heard the news? = ききま
したか。・ 聞きましたか。

that's good news = よかったです
ね。・ 良かったですね。

have you any news of John? = ジョン
さんの こと、なにか ききまし
たか。・ ジョンさんの こと、 何
か 聞きましたか。

- (*on radio, TV*)
= ニュース

**newsagent's** *noun* (*British English*)

> ! No direct equivalent in Japan, but
> there are stands in stations and
> elsewhere where you can buy
> newspapers, magazines, cigarettes
> and sweets. These are called キオ
> スク

**newspaper** *noun*
= しんぶん・新聞

**New Year** *noun*
= しんねん・新年
Happy New Year! = あけまして おめ
でとうございます。

**New Year's Day, New Year's**
(*US English*) *noun*
= がんじつ・元日

**New Year's Eve** *noun*
= おおみそか・大晦日

**New Zealand** *noun* ▶ 172
= ニュージーランド

**next**
**1** *adjective*
(*when talking about what is still to*
*come*) = つぎ(の)・次(の)
I'll take the next train = つぎの でん
しゃに のります。・ 次の 電車に
乗ります。
the next day = つぎの ひ・次の 日
next week = らいしゅう・来週
the next week = つぎの しゅう・次
の 週
next month = らいげつ・来月
the next month = つぎの つき・次
の 月
next year = らいねん・来年
the next year = つぎの とし・次の
年
**2** *adverb*
- (*in the past*)
what did you do next? = つぎに なに
を しましたか。・ 次に 何を し
ましたか。

- (*now*)
what'll we do next? = つぎは なにを
しましょうか。・ 次は 何をしま
しょうか。
- (*in the future*)
when you next come to Niigata, please
give me a call = こんど にいがたに
きたら、 れんらくしてください。
・ 今度 新潟に 来たら、連絡して
ください。
**3 next to** = 〜の となり・ 〜の 隣

**next door** *adverb*
= となり・隣

**nice** *adjective*
- (*enjoyable*) = たのしい・楽しい
we had a nice time = たのしかった
です。・ 楽しかったです。
- (*kind, friendly*) = しんせつ(な)・親
切(な)
everyone was very nice to me = みん
なは わたしに とても しんせつ
でした。・ 皆は 私に とても 親
切でした。
- (*of weather, place*) = いい

**N**

**nickname** *noun*
= ニックネーム

**niece** *noun*
= めい・姪

**night** *noun*
- (*as opposed to day*)
= よる・夜
I didn't sleep last night = きのうの よ
る、 ねむれません でした。・ 昨
日の 夜、 眠れません でした。
he studied all night = かれは ひとば
んじゅう べんきょうしました。
・ 彼は 一晩中 勉強しました。
- (*evening*)
= ばん・晩
last night = きのうの ばん・昨日の
晩

**nightclub** *noun*
= ナイトクラブ

**nightdress** *noun*
= ねまき・寝巻き

**nightmare** *noun*
= あくむ・悪夢
to have a nightmare = あくむを みる
・ 悪夢を 見る

**nil** *noun*
= ゼロ

**nine** *number* ▶ **171**, ▶ **181**, ▶ **186**
  (*on its own*) = ここのつ・九つ
  (*with a counter*) = きゅう・九
  nine books = ほん きゅうさつ・本
  九冊
  I've got nine = ここのつ あります。
  ・九つ あります。
  nine o'clock = くじ・九時

**nineteen** *number* ▶ **181**
  = じゅうきゅう・十九

**nineteenth** *number*
• (*in a series*) = じゅうきゅうばん
  (め)・十九番(目)
• (*in dates*) ▶ **174**
  the nineteenth of July = しちがつじ
  ゅうくにち・七月十九日

**ninety** *number* ▶ **181**
  = きゅうじゅう・九十

**ninth** *number*
• (*in a series*) = きゅうばん(め)・九
  番(目)
• (*in dates*) ▶ **174**
  the ninth of December = じゅうにが
  つここのか・十二月九日

**no**
**1** *adverb*
• = いいえ *Note that when a question
  is asked in the negative and the
  answer would be "no" in English,
  it would be* はい *in Japanese
  to mean that that is correct e.g.*
  「それを しませんでしたか。」
  「はい、しませんでした。」
  no thanks = いいえ、けっこうです。
  ・いいえ、結構です。
• he no longer works here = かれは も
  う ここで はたらいていません。
  ・彼は もう ここで 働いていま
  せん。
**2** *determiner*
• (*not any*)
  we have no money = おかねが あり
  ません。・お金が ありません。
  there are no trains = でんしゃが
  ありません。・電車が ありませ
  ん。
• (*when refusing permission*)
  no smoking! = きんえん・禁煙
• (*when used for emphasis*)
  it's no problem = だいじょうぶです。
  ・大丈夫です。

**nobody** ▶ **no-one**

**noise** *noun*
  (*sound*) = おと・音
  (*disturbance*) = そうおん・騒音
  to make noise = さわぐ・騒ぐ

**noisy** *adjective*
  = うるさい

**none** *pronoun*
  none of them went to the class = だれ
  も クラスに いきませんでした。
  ・誰も クラスに 行きませんでし
  た。
  none of us can speak Chinese = だれ
  も ちゅうごくごが はなせませ
  ん。・誰も 中国語が 話せませ
  ん。
  none of the answers were right = こた
  えは ひとつも あっていません。
  ・答えは 一つも 合っていませ
  ん。
  there's none left = もう ありません。
  I've got none, I have none = ありませ
  ん。

**nonsense** *noun*
  that's nonsense! = ばかばかしいで
  す。

**noodle** *noun*
  = めん・麺

**noon** *noun* ▶ **186**
  = しょうご・正午
  at noon = しょうごに・正午に

**no-one** *pronoun* (*also* **nobody**)
  no-one = だれも + negative
  no-one tells me anything = だれも お
  しえて くれません。・誰も 教え
  て くれません。
  no-one saw him = だれも かれを み
  ませんでした。・誰も 彼を 見ま
  せんでした。
  there's no-one else in the office but me
  = わたし いがい、オフィスに
  だれも いません。・私 以外、
  オフィスに 誰も いません。

**nor** *conjunction*

  **!** *For translations of* **nor** *when used
  in combination with* **neither**, *look at
  the entry for* **neither** *in this
  dictionary.*

  'I don't like him'—'nor do I' = 「かれが
  すきじゃありません。」「わたし
  も。」・「彼が 好きじゃありませ
  ん。」「私も。」

**normal** *adjective*
= ふつう(の)・普通(の)

**normally** *adverb*
= ふつうに・普通に

**north**
**1** *noun*
= きた・北
in the north of Japan = にほんの きたに・日本の 北に
**2** *adverb*
to go north = きたに いく・北に 行く
**3** *adjective*
= きた(の)・北(の)
to work in north London = きたロンドンで はたらく・北ロンドンで 働く

**North America** *noun* ▶ 172
= ほくべい・北米

**northeast** *noun*
= ほくとう・北東

**Northern Ireland** *noun* ▶ 172
= きたアイルランド・北アイルランド

**northwest** *noun*
= ほくせい・北西

**nose** *noun*
= はな・鼻

**not**
**1** *adverb*

! Note that there is no translation in Japanese for not. The verb, adjective or noun in question must be made into a negative form.
▶ 191, ▶ 201

she's not at home = かのじょは うちに いません。・彼女は 家に いません。
hasn't he phoned you? = かれが でんわを しませんでしたか。・彼が 電話を しませんでしたか。
we're going to go out whether it rains or not = あめが ふっても でかけます。・雨が 降っても 出かけます。
not everyone likes football = みんな サッカーが すきだとは かぎりません。・皆サッカーが 好きだとは 限りません。
**2 not at all**

• (*in no way*)
he's not at all worried = かれは ぜんぜん しんぱいしていません。・彼は 全然 心配していません。
• 'thanks a lot'—'not at all' = 「どうも ありがとう。」「どういたしまして。」

**note**
**1** *noun*
• (*to remind oneself*)
= メモ
• (*a message*)
= メッセージ
I left you a note = メッセージを のこしました。・メッセージを 残しました。
• (*British English*)
(*money*)
= さつ・札
a 5000 yen note = ごせんえんさつ・五千円札
• (*in music*)
= おんぷ・音符
**2** *verb*
to note (down) = かいて おく・書いて おく

**notebook** *noun*
= ノート

**nothing** *pronoun*
= なにも + negative
nothing has changed = なにも かわっていません。・何も 変わっていません。
there's nothing left = なにも のこっていません。・何も 残っていません。
she said nothing = かのじょは なにも いいませんでした。・彼女は 何も 言いませんでした。
I knew nothing about it = それに ついては なにも しりませんでした。・それに ついては 何も 知りませんでした。
there's nothing we can do about it = なにも できません。・何も できません。
I had nothing to do with it! = わたしとは かんけいありません。・私とは 関係 ありません。
for nothing = ただで

**notice**
**1** *verb*
= きづく・気付く

**2** *noun*
- (*a written sign*)
= おしらせ・お知らせ ▶ 189
notice board = けいじばん・掲示板
- (*warning people*)
= よこく・予告
at short notice = きゅうに・急に
- don't take any notice, take no notice =
きに しないでください。・気に
しないでください。

**novel** *noun*
= しょうせつ・小説

**November** *noun* ▶ 174
= じゅういちがつ・十一月

**now**
**1** *adverb*
= いま・今
we have to do it now = いま しなけ
れば なりません。・今しなけれ
ば なりません。
I'm phoning her now = いま かのじ
ょに でんわを かけています。・
今 彼女に 電話を かけていま
す。
please do it right now = いま してく
ださい。・今 してください。
now is the time to contact them = いま
すぐ かれらに でんわしたほう
が いいです。・今すぐ 彼らに
電話した方が いいです。
I should have told you before now =
まえ いえばよかったです。・前
言えば よかったです。
it hasn't been a problem until now =
いままでは もんだいではありま
せんでした。・今までは 問題で
はありませんでした。
between now and next Monday = い
まから らいしゅうの げつよう
び までに・今から 来週の 月曜
日 までに
from now on = いまから・今から
**2** now and again, now and then =
ときどき・時々

**nowhere** *adverb*
= どこも + negative
I went nowhere yesterday = きのう
どこも いきませんでした。・
昨日 どこも 行きませんでし
た。
there's nowhere to sit = すわる とこ
ろが ありません。・座るところ
が ありません。

**nuclear** *adjective*
nuclear power = げんしりょく・原
子力
nuclear weapon = かくへいき・核
兵器

**nuisance** *noun*
to be a nuisance = じゃまを する・
邪魔を する
it's a nuisance paying in cash = げん
きんで はらうのは めんどうで
す。・現金で 払うのは 面倒で
す。

**numb** *adjective*
- to go numb = しびれる
my hands are numb = てが しびれま
した。・手が しびれました。

**number**
**1** *noun*
- (*a figure*) = すうじ・数字
(*of a house, a bus, a telephone, a
passport*) = ばんごう・番号
wrong number = まちがいでんわ・
間違い電話
- (*when talking about quantities*)
a number of = すう + counter ▶ 181
a number of people = すうにん・
数人
a number of times = すうかい・
数回
a small number of tourists = しょう
すうの りょこうしゃ・少数の
旅行者
**2** *verb*
= ばんごうを つける・番号を 付
ける

**numberplate** *noun* (*British English*)
= ナンバープレート

**nun** *noun*
= しゅうどうじょ・修道女

**nurse** *noun*
= かんごふ・看護婦

**nursery** *noun*
(*child care establishment*) = たくじし
ょ・託児所

**nursery school** *noun*
= ほいくえん・保育園

**nut** *noun*
= ナッツ
walnut = くるみ

**nylon** *noun*
= ナイロン

# Oo

**oar** *noun*
= オール

**obedient** *adjective*
= よく いう ことを きく・よく
言う ことを 聞く

**obey** *verb*
= したがう・従う
to obey someone = だれかに したが
う・誰かに 従う
to obey the law = ほうりつを まもる
・法律を 守る

**object**
**1** *noun*
= もの・物
**2** *verb*
= はんたいする・反対する

**objective** *adjective*
= きゃっかんてき(な)・客観的
(な)

**obligation** *noun*
= ぎり・義理

**oblige** *verb* to be obliged to leave a
job = しごとを やめざるを えない
・仕事を 辞めざるを 得ない

**obtain** *verb*
= てに いれる・手に 入れる

**obvious** *adjective*
= あきらか(な)・明らか(な)

**obviously** *adverb*
= あきらかに・明らかに

**occasion** *noun*
on special occasions = とくべつな
ときに・特別な ときに

**occasionally** *adverb*
= たまに

**occupy** *verb*
• (to take over) = せんりょうする・
占領する
• (to keep busy)
to keep oneself occupied = いそがし
くする・忙しくする

**occupied** *adjective*
(room, toilet) = しようちゅう・使用
中

**occupation** *noun*
= しょくぎょう・職業

**occur** *verb*
(happen) = おこる・起こる
(think)
a plan occurred to me = けいかくを
おもいつきました。・計画を 思
いつきました。

**ocean** *noun*
= うみ・海 ▶ Atlantic ▶ Pacific

**o'clock** *adverb* ▶ 186
it's five o'clock = ごじです。・五時
です。
at one o'clock = いちじに・一時に

**October** *noun* ▶ 174
= じゅうがつ・十月

**octopus** *noun*
= たこ

**odd** *adjective*
• (strange) = へん(な)・変(な)
• (one of a pair) = かたほう(の)・片
方(の)
• (when talking about numbers)
odd number = きすう(の)・奇数
(の)

**odour** (British English), **odor**
(US English) *noun*
= におい・臭い

**of** *preposition*
• = use particle の ▶ 205
the sound of an engine = エンジンの
おと・エンジンの 音
it's in the centre of Kobe = こうべの
ちゅうしんに あります。・神戸
の 中心に あります。
a photo of the dog = いぬの しゃし
ん・犬の 写真
half of the salad = サラダの はんぶ
ん・サラダの 半分
the names of the pupils = せいとの
なまえ・生徒の 名前
• (when talking about quantities) ▶ 181
a kilo of potatoes = じゃがいも いち
キロ・じゃがいも 一 キロ
a bottle of wine = ワイン いっぽん・
ワイン 一本
two bottles of cola = コーラ にほん・
コーラ 二本
have you heard of it? = きいた こと
が ありますか。・聞いた ことが
ありますか。

**o**

there are six of us in the family = かぞ
くは ろくにんです。・家族は
六人です。

## off

> ! Often off occurs in combinations
> with verbs, for example: get off, go
> off, take off etc. To find the correct
> translations for this type of verb,
> look up the separate dictionary
> entries at get, go, take etc.

**1** adverb
* (leaving)
  I'm off (British English) = いきます。・
  行きます。
  I'm off to Italy tomorrow = あした
  イタリアに いきます。・明日
  イタリアに 行きます。
* (away)
  the coast is a long way off = かいがん
  は とおいです。・海岸は 遠いで
  す。
  we could see them from a long way off
  = とおくから かれらが みえまし
  た。・遠くから 彼らが 見えまし
  た。
* (free)
  to take a day off = やすむ・休む
  today's my day off = きょうは やす
  みです。・今日は 休みです。
* (not working, switched off)
  the lights are all off = でんきは ぜん
  ぶ きえています。・電気は 全部
  消えています。
**2** adjective
  the milk is off = ぎゅうにゅうが わ
  るくなりました。・牛乳が 悪く
  なりました。

## offence (British English), offense
(US English) noun
* (a crime) = はんざい・犯罪
* to take offence = おこる・怒る

## offend verb
= おこらせる・怒らせる

## offer verb
to offer someone a job = だれかに
しごとを ていきょうする・誰
かに 仕事を 提供する
I offered to help Miyoko with her
homework = みよこさんに しゅく
だいを てつだって あげると い
いました。・美代子さんに 宿題
を 手伝って あげると 言いまし
た。When offering to do something

for someone, use the ～て form of
the verb + あげる. ▶ 179, ▶ 197
Miyoko offered to help me with my
homework = みよこさんは わたし
に しゅくだいを てつだって く
れると いいました。・美代子
さんは 私に 宿題を 手伝って くれ
ると 言いました。When someone
offers to do something for you, use
the ～て form of the verb + くれる.
▶ 179, ▶ 197

## office noun
= じむしょ・事務所
head office = ほんしゃ・本社
branch office = ししゃ・支社

## office block noun (British English)
= オフィスビル

## officer noun
(in the army or navy) = しょうこう・
将校
(in the police) = けいかん・警官

## office worker noun
= じむいん・事務員

> ! かいしゃいん can also be used

## official adjective
= こうしき(の)・公式(の)

## often adverb
= よく
I often go there = そこに よく いき
ます。・そこに よく 行きます。
not often = あまり + negative
I don't go there often = そこに あま
り いきません。・そこに あまり
行きません。

## oil noun
* (for energy)
  = せきゆ・石油
  oil company = せきゆがいしゃ・石
  油会社
* (for a car)
  = オイル
* (for cooking)
  = あぶら・油
* oil painting = あぶらえ・油絵

## okay, OK
**1** adjective
* (when asking or giving opinions)
  is it okay if I come back later? = あと
  で また きても いいですか。・
  後で また 来ても いいですか。

it's okay to invite them = かれらを しょうたいしても いいです。・ 彼らを 招待しても いいです。
- (when talking about health)
 I feel okay = げんきです。・ 元気で す。
 are you okay? (general greeting) = お げんきですか。・ お元気ですか。
 are you OK? (when concerned) = だ いじょうぶですか。・ 大丈夫で すか。

### old adjective
- (not new) = ふるい・古い
 an old chest of drawers = ふるい たんす・古い たんす
 old houses = ふるい いえ・古い 家
- (not young) = おとしより(の)・お 年寄り(の)
 an old woman = おばあさん・お婆 さん
 an old man = おじいさん・お爺さ ん
 old people = ろうじん・老人
 (when talking about a person's age)
 ▶ 171
 how old are you? = なんさいですか。・ 何歳ですか。
 a three-year old girl = さんさいの おんなのこ・三才の 女の 子
 a ten year old car = じゅうねんもの のくるま・十年物の 車
 I'm as old as he is = かれと おな いどしです。・ 彼と 同い年で す。
 she's eight years older than her brother = かのじょは おとうとさんより はっさい うえです。・ 彼女は 弟さんより 八才 上です。
 I am the oldest = いちばんとしうえ です。・ 一番年上です。
 I'm now old enough to drink = いま アルコールが のめるとしに な りました。・ 今 アルコールが 飲める歳に なりました。
- (previous) = まえ(の)・前(の)
 that's my old address = それは まえ の じゅうしょです。・ それは 前の 住所です。
 in the old days = むかし・昔

### old-fashioned adjective
(describing attitudes, ideas) = ふるく さい・古臭い
(describing people) = あたまが ふる い・頭が 古い

### olive
1 noun
= オリーブ
2 adjective
= オリーブいろ(の)・オリーブ色 (の)

### olive oil noun
= オリーブゆ・オリーブ油

### Olympics noun
= オリンピック

### omelette noun
= オムレツ

### on

> ! Often on occurs in combinations with verbs, for example: count on, get on, keep on etc. To find the correct translations for this type of verb, look up the separate dictionary entries for count, get, keep etc.

1 preposition
- on = use particle に ▶ 205
 you've got a spot on your nose = はな に にきびが あります。・ 鼻に にきびが あります。
 there's a stain on the jacket = ジャケ ットにしみがあります。・ ジャ ケットに 染みが あります。
 there is a poster on the wall = かべに ポスターが はって あります。・ 壁に ポスターが 貼って ありま す。
 to live on the third floor = さんがいに すむ・三階に 住む
- (on top of) = 〜の うえ・〜の 上
 it's on the table = テーブルの うえに あります。・ テーブルの 上に あ ります。
 it's on top of the drawers = たんすの うえに あります。・ たんすの 上に あります。
- (when talking about transport)
 to go on the bus = バスで いく・ バスで 行く
 I came on my bike today = きょうは じてんしゃで きました。・ 今日 は 自転車で 来ました。
 to get on the train = でんしゃに のる ・ 電車に 乗る
- (about) = 〜に ついて
 it's a book on Africa = アフリカに つ いての ほんです。・ アフリカに ついての 本です。

O

a programme on dinosaurs = きょう
りゅうに ついての ばんぐみ・
恐竜に ついての 番組

• (when talking about time)
I was born on the sixth of December =
じゅうにがつ むいかに うまれ
ました。・十二月 六日に 生まれ
ました。
I'll be there on Saturday = どようび
に いきます。・土曜日に 行きま
す。
we went there on my birthday = わた
しの たんじょうびに いきまし
た。・私の 誕生日に 行きまし
た。

• (when talking about the media)
on television = テレビで
I saw it on the news = ニュースで み
ました。・ニュースで 見ました。
is this film out on video? = この えい
がは もう ビデオに でています
か。・この 映画は もう ビデオ
に 出ていますか。

• (using)
to be on drugs = まやくを つかって
いる・麻薬を 使っている

2 adverb
• (when talking about what one wears)
to have a sweater on = セーターを
きている・セーターを 着ている
to have make-up on = けしょうして
いる・化粧している

• (working, switched on)
why are all the lights on? = なぜ でん
きが ぜんぶ ついていますか。・
なぜ 電気が 全部 点いています
か。
the radio was on all day = ラジオは
いち にちじゅう ついていまし
た。・ラジオは 一日中点いてい
ました。

• (showing)
what's on?
(on TV) = テレビで
(in the cinema) = えいがかんで・映
画館で

• (when talking about time)
from Tuesday on, I'll be here = かよう
びから ここにいます。・火曜日
から ここに います。
a little later on = あとで・後で

### once
1 adverb
• (one time) = いっかい・一回

once a day = いちにちいっかい・
一日一回
• (in the old days) = むかし・昔
2 conjunction
= いったん + conditional form of
verb ▶ 191
it'll be easier once we've found a
house = いったん いえを みつ
けたら あとは かんたんです。・
いったん 家を 見つけたら 後は
簡単です。
3 at once = いますぐ・今すぐ
4 once more = もういちど・もう一
度

### one
1 number ▶ 171, ▶ 181, ▶ 186
(on its own) = ひとつ・一つ
(with a counter) = いち・一
one book = ほん いっさつ・本
一冊
I've got one = ひとつ あります。・
一つ あります。
one child = こどもひとり・子供一
人
one of my colleagues = どうりょう
の ひとり・同僚の 一人
one hundred = ひゃく・百
2 determiner
• (the only)
Mauriceis the one person who can
help Zoe = ゾイさんを たすけ
られる ひとは モリスさんだ
けです。・ゾイさんを 助けら
れる 人は モリスさんだけで
す。
it's the one thing that annoys me =
それだけが いらいらさせます。
• (the same)
to take three exams in the one day =
いちにちに しけんを みっつも
うける・一日に 試験を 三つも
受ける
3 pronoun
• (when referring to something
generally)
I need an dictionary—have you got
one? = じしょが ひつようです。
ありますか。・辞書が 必要です。
あります。
• (when referring to a specific person or
thing)
I like the new one = あたらしいのが
すきです。・新しいのが 好きで
す。

the one who got sacked is Geoffrey = くびに なったのは ジェフリーさんです。・首に なったのは ジェフリーさんです。

which one? = どれですか。

this one = これです。

- (when used to mean 'you' or 'people') this pronoun is not used in Japanese

**4 one by one** = ひとつずつ・一つずつ

## one another *pronoun*

to love one another = おたがいに あいしあう・お互いに 愛し合う

we can't bear being apart from one another = いっしょに いないと たえられません。・一緒に いないと 耐えられません。

## oneself *pronoun*

= じぶん・自分

to enjoy oneself = たのしむ・楽しむ

by oneself = ひとりで・一人で

## onion *noun*

= たまねぎ・玉ねぎ

## online *adjective*

= オンライン

## only

**1** *adverb*

only = 〜だけ

it's only a game = ゲームだけです。

they've only met once = かれらは いっかいだけ あいました。・彼らは 一回だけ 会いました。

**2** *adjective*

she was the only one who couldn't speak Japanese = かのじょだけ は にほんごが はなせませんでした。・彼女だけは 日本語が 話せませんでした。

the only problem is that I can't drive = もんだいは、うんてんが できない ことです。・問題は 運転が できない ことです。

an only child = ひとりっこ・一人っ子

**3 only just**

= use the 〜た form of verb + ところ ▶ 191

I've only just arrived = いま ついた ところです。・今 着いた ところです。

I've only just moved house = ひっこした ところです。・引っ越した ところです。

## onto *preposition*

= use particle に ▶ 205

to get onto a train = でんしゃに のる・電車に 乗る

## open

**1** *verb*

> ! Note that there are two ways of expressing the action to open in Japanese depending on what is being opened

- (to open (something))

to open an umbrella = かさを ひらく・傘を 開く

to open a book = ほんを ひらく・本を 開く

to open a meeting = かいぎを ひらく・会議を 開く

to open a gate = もんを ひらく・門を 開く

to open an envelope = ふうとうを あける・封筒を 開ける

to open a package = こづつみを ひらく・小包を 開く

to open one's eyes = めを あける・目を 開ける

to open a shop = みせを あける・店を 開ける

to open a window = まどを あける・窓を 開ける

- (to become open)

what time do you open? = なんじに あきますか。・何時に 開きますか。

the shop opens at nine = みせは くじに あきます。・店は九時に 開きます。

the flowers opened = はなが ひらきました。・花が 開きました。

- (to start)

= はじまる・始まる

**2** *adjective*

- (not closed) = あいている・開いている

the pool isn't open = プールは あいていません。・プールは 開いていません。

leave the door open = ドアを あけて おいてください。・ドアを 開けて おいてください。

- (frank) = そっちょく(な)・率直(な)

**3** *noun*
out in the open = そとで・外で

**opener** *noun*
(*for bottles*) = せんぬき・栓抜き
(*for cans*) = かんきり・缶切り

**open-minded** *adjective*
= へんけんの ない・偏見の ない

**opera** *noun*
= オペラ

**operate** *verb*
• (*to make something work*) = そうさする・操作する
• (*to carry out an operation*) = しゅじゅつをする・手術を する
to operate on someone = だれかの しゅじゅつを する・誰かの 手術をする
to operate on Mr Kitamura's leg = きたむらさんの あしの しゅじゅつを する・喜多村さんの 足の 手術を する

**operation** *noun*
= しゅじゅつ・手術
to have an operation = しゅじゅつを うける・手術を 受ける

**operator** *noun*
= オペレーター

**opinion** *noun*
= いけん・意見
in my opinion, they're lying = かれらは うそを ついていると おもいます。・彼らは 嘘を ついていると 思います。

**opponent** *noun*
(*in sport*) = あいて・相手

**opportunity** *noun*
= きかい・機会
I took the opportunity to visit Nagasaki = きかいを りようしてながさきへ いきました。・機会を 利用して 長崎へ 行きました。

**oppose** *verb*
to oppose a plan = けいかくに はんたいする・計画に 反対する
to be opposed to nuclear weapons = かくへいきに はんたいする・核兵器に 反対する

**opposite**
**1** *preposition*
= むかいがわ・向かい側

she was sitting opposite me = かのじょは むかいがわに すわっていました。・彼女は 向かい側に 座っていました。
**2** *adjective*
the opposite sex = いせい・異性
he was walking in the opposite direction = かれは はんたいの ほうがくへ あるいていました。・彼は 反対の 方角へ 歩いていました。
opposite effect = ぎゃくこうか・逆効果
**3** *adverb*
= むかいがわに・向かい側に
**4** *noun*
= はんたい・反対
it's the exact opposite = せいはんたいです。・正反対です。

**optician** *noun*
= めがねや・眼鏡屋

**optimist** *noun*
= らくてんか・楽天家

**optimistic** *adjective*
= らっかんてき(な)・楽観的(な)

**or** *conjunction*

> ! There is no one word equivalent to 'or' in Japanese. See below for expressions in various contexts.

• (*when there's a choice between two or more things or options*) = AかBか
once or twice a week = しゅう いっかいか にかい・週 一回か 二回
is this Chinese or Japanese? = これは ちゅうごくごですか、にほんごですか。・これは 中国語ですか、日本語ですか。
do you have any brothers or sisters? = きょうだいが いますか。
(*in negative sentences with only one verb*) = 〜も〜も
I can't do it today or tomorrow = きょうも、あしたも、できません。・今日も、明日も、できません。
I don't like meat or fish = にくも、さかなも、すきではありません。・肉も、魚も、好きではありません。
• (*otherwise*) = そうで なければ
please be careful or the plates will get broken = きを つけてください。そうで なければ さらが われます。・気を つけてください。そうでなければ 皿が 割れます。

**oral** *adjective*
= こうとう(の)・口頭(の)

**orange**
**1** *noun*
= オレンジ
**2** *adjective*
= オレンジ(の)

**orange juice** *noun*
- オレンジジュース

**orchard** *noun*
= かじゅえん・果樹園

**orchestra** *noun*
= オーケストラ

**order**
**1** *verb*
- (*to tell*) = めいずる・命ずる
- (*to ask for*) = ちゅうもんする・注文する
  to order goods from a magazine = ざっしから しなものを ちゅうもんする・雑誌から 品物を 注文する
**2** *noun*
- (*an instruction*)
  = めいれい・命令
  to give orders = めいれいする・命令する
- the right order = ただしい じゅんばん・正しい 順番
  the list is in alphabetical order = リストは アルファベットじゅんです。・リストは アルファベット順です。
**3 in order to** = ～(の)ために
  I phoned in order to change the date = ひにちを かえる ために でんわをしました。・日にちを 変える ために 電話を しました。

**ordinary** *adjective*
- (*not unusual*) = ふつう(の)・普通(の)
  an ordinary family = ふつうの かぞく・普通の 家族
- (*average*) = へいぼん(な)・平凡(な)

**organ** *noun*
- (*the musical instrument*) ▶ **180**
  = オルガン
- (*a part of the body*)
  = ぞうき・臓器

**organic** *adjective*
  (*food*) = むのうやく(の)・無農薬(の)

**organization** *noun*
= そしき・組織

**organize** *verb*
= きかくする・企画する
to be organized = きちんとする

**original** *adjective*
- (*first*) = さいしょ(の)・最初(の)
- (*true, real*) = ほんもの(の)・本物(の)
- (*new, fresh*) = どくそうてき(な)・独創的(な)

**ornament** *noun*
= かざりもの・飾り物

**orphan** *noun*
= こじ・孤児

**ostrich** *noun*
= だちょう

**other**
**1** *adjective*

> ! *Note that other is not used in the same way as in English. If the other item has been previously mentioned, it will be referred to as "the previous one", "the one we saw before" etc rather than "the other one".*

not that dress, the other one we saw before = その ドレスではありません。さきに みた ほうです。・その ドレスではありません。先に 見た 方です。

they sold the other car = かれらは もう ひとつの くるまを うりました。・彼らは もう 一つの 車を 売りました。

to interrupt the other pupils = ほかの せいとの じゃまを する・外の 生徒の 邪魔を する

every other day = いちにちおき・一日おき

**2** *pronoun*

Haruki made the others laugh = はるきさんは ほかの ひとを わらわせました。・治樹さんは 外の 人を 笑わせました。

some students remember Japanese words easily, others have problems = いちぶの がくせいはにほんごの たんごをすぐ おぼえますが、そうじゃないがくせいも います。・一部の 学生は 日本語の 単語を すぐ 覚えますが、そうじゃない学生も います。

they came in one after the other = かれらは かわるがわる はいっ

て きました。・ 彼らは かわるが
わる 入って 来ました。

**otherwise** *conjunction*
= そうでなければ
it's safe, otherwise I wouldn't go =
あんぜんです。そうでなければ
わたしは いきません。・安全で
す。そうでなければ 私は 行き
ません。

**otter** *noun*
= かわうそ

**ought** *verb*
• (*when talking about what should be
done*) = use a plain form of the verb
+ べき ▶ **187**
you ought not to do that = それを
する べきではありません。
you ought do your homework before
watching TV = テレビを みるまえ
に しゅくだいをする べきです。
・テレビを 見る前に 宿題を
する べきです。
• (*when making a polite suggestion*) =
Use the 〜た form of the verb +
ほうが いい for positive
suggestions and the 〜ない form
of the verb + ほうが いい for
negative suggestions. ▶ **191**
you ought to go to bed = ねた ほうが
いいです。・寝た 方が いいで
す。
you ought not to smoke = たばこを
すわない ほうがいいです。・た
ばこを 吸わない 方が いいです。
• (*when saying something may happen*)
= Use plain form of the verb + はず
▶ **187**
they ought to arrive tomorrow = かれ
らは あした つく はずです。・
彼らは 明日 着く はずです。
it ought not to be finished before three
o'clock = さんじまえには おわ
らない はずです。・三時前には
終わらない はずです。
• (*when saying something didn't
happen*)
(*when expressing personal regret*) =
Use the 〜ば conditional form +
よかった ▶ **191**
I ought to have gone = いけば よかっ
たです。・行けば 良かったです。
(*when expressing obligation in the
past*) = Use plain form of verb +
べきだった ▶ **187**

I ought to have gone with them = わた
しが かれらと いっしょに いく
べきでした。・私が 彼らと 一緒
に 行く べきでした。

**our** *determiner* Not always used if the
owners are obvious. うちの *can also
mean our.* ▶ **177**
= わたしたちの・私達の
that's our dog = それは うちの いぬ
です。・それは 家の 犬です。
what do you think of our new house?
= あたらしい うちを どう おもい
ますか。・新しい 家を どう 思
いますか。
all our CDs have been stolen = わた
したちの CDは ぜんぶ ぬすま
れました。・私達の CDは 全部
盗まれました。

**ours** *pronoun* うちの *can also mean
ours.* ▶ **177**
= わたしたちの・私達の
the grey car is ours = はいいろの く
るまは わたしたちのです。・灰
色の 車は 私達のです。
which case is ours? = どの ケースが
わたしたちのですか。・どの ケ
ースが 私達のですか。
their car is bigger than ours = かれら
の くるまは わたしたちのより
おおきいです。・彼らの 車は 私
達のより 大きいです。

**ourselves** *pronoun*
• (*when used as a reflexive pronoun*)
not used as a pronoun in Japanese
we want to enjoy ourselves = たのし
みたいです。・楽しみたいです。
we didn't hurt ourselves = けがを し
ませんでした。・怪我を しませ
んでした。
• (*when used for emphasis*)
we did everything ourselves = じぶん
たちで ぜんぶ しました。・自分
達で 全部 しました。
we like to be by ourselves = ふたりき
りが すきです。・二人きりが 好
きです。

**out**

> ! *Often out occurs in combinations
> with verbs, for example: blow out,
> come out, find out, give out etc. To
> find the correct translations for this
> type of verb, look up the separate
> dictionary entries at* **blow**, **come**,
> **find**, **give** *etc.*

**1** *adverb*
• (*outside*)
she's out in the garden = かのじょは
にわに います。・彼女は 庭に い
ます。
I'm looking for the way out = でぐち
を さがしています。・出口を
探しています。
• (*absent*)
to be out = でかけている ・ 出かけ
ている
someone telephoned while you were
out = でかけた とき、だれかが
でんわを しました。・ 出かけた
とき、誰かが 電話を しました。
• (*not lighting, not on*)
to be out = きえている ・ 消えてい
る
all the lights were out = でんきが
ぜんぶ きえていました。・ 電気
が 全部 消えていました。

**2 out of**
to go out of the building = たてもの
を でる ・ 建物を 出る
to get out of the city = まちを でる ・
町を 出る
to take a pencil out of the drawer =
えんぴつを ひきだしから とり
だす ・ 鉛筆を 引き出しから
取り出す

**outdoor** *adjective*
= おくがい(の) ・ 屋外(の)
outdoor sport = おくがいスポーツ ・
屋外スポーツ

**outdoors** *adverb*
= そと(で) ・ 外(で)

**outer space** *noun*
= うちゅうくうかん ・ 宇宙空間

**outside**
**1** *preposition*
• (*in front of*) = ～の まえ ・ ～の 前
to wait outside the school = がっこう
の まえで まつ ・ 学校の 前で
待つ
• (*beyond*)
outside the city = しがい ・ 市外
**2** *adverb*
= そと ・ 外
let's go outside = そとに いきましょ
う。・ 外に 行きましょう。
let's play outside = そとで あそびま
しょう。・ 外で 遊びましょう。
please take the chairs outside = いす
を そとに もって いってくださ

い。・ 椅子を 外に 持って 行っ
てください。
**3** *noun*
= そと ・ 外
outside of the building = ビルの そと
・ ビルの 外
**4** *adjective*
= そとがわ(の) ・ 外側(の)

**oven** *noun*
= オーブン

**over**

! Often over occurs in combinations
with verbs, for example: get over,
move over etc. To find the correct
translations for this type of verb,
look up the separate dictionary
entries at get, move etc.

**1** *preposition*
• to climb over a wall = へいを のりこ
える ・ 塀を 乗り越える
to jump over a puddle = みずたま
りを とびこえる ・ 水溜まりを
飛び越える
• (*across*)
it's over there = むこうに あります。
・ 向こうに あります。
please come over here = ここに きて
ください。・ ここに 来てくださ
い。
• (*above*) = ～の うえ ・ ～の 上
the picture over the piano = ピアノの
うえの え ・ ピアノの 上の 絵
people over 18 = じゅうはっさいい
じょうの ひと ・ 十八歳以上の
人
• (*during*)
we saw them over the weekend = し
ゅうまつの あいだに かれらに
あいました。・ 週末の 間に 彼ら
に 会いました。
• (*everywhere*)
I've searched all over for my keys =
かぎを あっちこっち さがしま
した。・ 鍵を あっちこっち 探し
ました。
**2** *adverb*
• (*finished*) = おわっている ・ 終わっ
ている
the term is over = がっきが おわっ
ています。・ 学期が 終わってい
ます。
is the film over? = えいがは おわり
ましたか。・ 映画は 終わりまし
たか。

- (to one's home)
  to ask someone over = だれかを
  うちに しょうたいする・誰か
  を 家に 招待する
- to start (something) over again = (な
  にかを)やりなおす・(何かを)
  やり直す

**overtake** *verb*
= おいこす・追い越す

**overweight** *adjective*
= ふとりすぎ(の)・太りすぎ(の)

**owe** *verb*
I owe money to Ann = アンさんに
おかねを かりています。・アン
さんに お金を 借りています。

**owl** *noun*
= ふくろう

**own**
**1** *adjective*
= じぶんの・自分の
you should clean your own room =
じぶんの へやを そうじする べ
きです。・自分の 部屋を 掃除す
る べきです。
he'd like his own car = かれは じぶん
の くるまを ほしがっています。
・彼は 自分の 車を 欲しがって
います。
**2** *pronoun*
I didn't use his pencil—I used my own
= かれの えんぴつを つかいませ
んでした。 じぶんのを つかい
ました。・彼の 鉛筆を 使いませ
んでした。自分のを 使いまし
た。
they have a house of their own = かれ
らは じぶんたちの いえが あり
ます。・彼らは 自分達の 家があ
ります。
**3** *verb Note that in Japanese,
ownership is often expressed by
implication using 〜が ある. The
verb もつ can also be used in the
present progressive form.*
he owns a restaurant = かれは レス
トランを もっています。・彼は
レストランを 持っています。
I own three cars = わたしは くる
まが さんだいあります。・私は
車が 三台 あります。
Ms Sato owns her own business =
さとうさんは じぶんの かいし
ゃを もっています。・佐藤さん
は 自分の 会社を 持っています。

**4** on one's own = ひとりで・一人で
own up = じはくする・自白する

**owner** *noun*
= もちぬし・持ち主

**ox** *noun*
= おうし・牡牛
year of the ox = うしどし・丑年

**oxygen** *noun*
= さんそ・酸素

**oyster** *noun*
= かき

---

# Pp

**Pacific** *noun*
the Pacific Ocean = たいへいよう・
太平洋

**pack**
**1** *verb*
= にづくりする・荷造りする
I've got to pack my suitcase = にづく
りを しなければ なりません。・
荷造りを しなければ なりませ
ん。
**2** *noun*
a pack of cigarettes = たばこ ひとは
こ・たばこ 一箱
a pack of cards = トランプ
pack up = にもつを まとめる・
荷物を まとめる
to pack up one's belongings = もちも
のを まとめる・持ち物を まと
める

**package** *noun*
(large) = にもつ・荷物
(small) = こづみ・小包

**package holiday** *noun*
= パックりょこう・パック旅行

**packed** *adjective*
= こんでいる・混んでいる

**page** *noun*
= ページ
on page six = ろくページに・六ペ
ージに

**pain** *noun*
= いたみ・痛み

I've got a pain in my back = せなかが
いたいです。・ 背中が 痛いで
す。

**painful** adjective
= いたい・痛い

**paint**
**1** noun
= ペンキ
**2** verb
= ペンキを ぬる・ ペンキを 塗る
to paint a picture = えを かく・ 絵を
描く

**paintbrush** noun
= ブラシ

**painter** noun
(decorator) = ペンキや・ ペンキ屋
(artist) = がか・ 画家

**painting** noun
• (a picture)
= え・絵
• (the activity)
(decorating) = ペンキを ぬる こと・
ペンキを 塗る こと
(art) = かいが・ 絵画

**pair** noun the English expression 'a
pair of' is not usually expressed in
Japanese unless there is more than
one pair ▶ 181
two pairs of shoes = くつ にそく・
靴 二足

**pajamas** noun (US English)
= パジャマ

**Pakistan** noun ▶ 172
= パキスタン

**palace** noun
= きゅうでん・ 宮殿
Japanese Imperial Palace = こうきょ
・ 皇居

**pale** adjective
= しろっぽい・ 白っぽい
(face) = あおじろい・ 青白い
to go pale with fear = きょうふで あ
おざめる・ 恐怖で 青ざめる

**pancake** noun
= ホットケーキ

**panic** verb
= パニックじょうたいに なる・
パニック状態に なる

**pants** noun
• (British English)

(underwear)
women's underwear = パンティー
men's underwear = パンツ
• (US English)
(trousers)
= ズボン

**pantyhose** noun (US English)
= パンティーストッキング

**paper** noun
• (for writing or drawing on)
= かみ・ 紙
a piece of paper = かみ いちまい・
紙 一枚
• (a newspaper)
= しんぶん・ 新聞

**parachuting** noun
= パラシュート

**parade** noun
= パレード

**paralysed** (British English),
**paralyzed** (US English) adjective
= まひする・ 麻痺する

**parcel** noun
= にもつ・ 荷物

**parent** noun
(one's own) = おや・ 親
parent or guardian = ほごしゃ・ 保
護者

**parents** noun
(one's own) = りょうしん・ 両親
(someone else's) = ごりょうしん・
ご両親

**Paris** noun
= パリ

**park**
**1** noun
= こうえん・ 公園
**2** verb
to park a car = くるまを ちゅうしゃ
する・ 車を 駐車する
to park near the office = かいしゃの
ちかくに ちゅうしゃする・ 会
社の 近くに 駐車する
no parking = ちゅうしゃきんし・
駐車禁止

**parking lot** noun (US English)
= ちゅうしゃじょう・ 駐車場

**parking meter** noun
= パーキングメーター

**parliament** noun
= ぎかい・ 議会

P

**parrot** *noun*
= おうむ

**part**
• = いちぶ ・ 一部
part of the film = えいがの いちぶ ・ 映画の 一部
it's part of the job = しごとの いちぶ です。・ 仕事の 一部です。
this part of the country = この ちほう ・ この 地方
• (*a piece for a machine, a car*) = ぶひん ・ 部品
• (*in a series*)
part four = だいよんぶ ・ 第四部
• (*a role*)
= やく ・ 役
to play the part of Tommy = トミーの やくを えんじる ・ トミーの 役 を 演じる

**participate** *verb*
= さんかする ・ 参加する

**particular**
in particular = とくに ・ 特に

**partner** *noun*
• (*in a relationship*)
= あいて ・ 相手
• (*in dancing, sport*)
= パートナー

**part-time** *adverb*
= パートタイム(の)
to work part-time (on a permanent basis) = パートタイムで はたら く ・ パートタイムで 働く
to work part-time (on a temporary basis) = アルバイトする

**party** *noun*
• (*a social event*)
= パーティー
a birthday party = たんじょうびパー ティー ・ 誕生日パーティー
(formal) welcome party = かんげいか い ・ 歓迎会
(formal) farewell party = そうべつか い ・ 送別会
have a party = パーティーをひらく ・ パーティーを 開く
• a political party = せいとう ・ 政党

**pass** *verb*
• (*to go past*) = とおる ・ 通る
to let (someone) pass = (だれかを) とおす ・ (誰かを)通す
to pass the school = がっこうを と おる ・ 学校を 通る

to pass a car = くるまを おいこす ・ 車を 追い越す
to pass (someone) in the street = (だ れかと)みちで すれちがう ・ (誰 かと)道で すれ違う
• (*to give*) = わたす ・ 渡す
pass me the salt, please = しおを と ってください。・ 塩を 取ってく ださい。
to pass the ball (to someone) = (だれ かに)ボールを わたす ・ (誰か に)ボールを 渡す
• (*to spend*) = すごす ・ 過ごす
to pass the time listening to the radio = ラジオを きいて じかんを すご す ・ ラジオを 聞いて 時間を 過ごす
• (*to succeed in an exam*) = ごうかく する ・ 合格する
to pass an exam = しけんに ごうか くする ・ 試験に 合格する
**pass around**
to pass around the photos = しゃし んを まわす ・ 写真を 回す
**pass on** = つたえる ・ 伝える
to pass on a message (to someone) = (だれかに)メッセージを つた える ・ (誰かに)メッセージを 伝える

**passage** *noun*
(*indoors*) = ろうか ・ 廊下
(*outdoors*) = つうろ ・ 通路

**passenger** *noun*
= じょうきゃく ・ 乗客

**passport** *noun*
= パスポート

**past**
**1** *noun*
= かこ ・ 過去
in the past = かこに ・ 過去に
**2** *adjective*
= かこ(の) ・ 過去(の)
the past few days have been difficult = ここ に、さんにち たいへんで した。・ ここ二、三日 大変でし た。
**3** *preposition*
• (*when talking about time*) ▶ **186**
it's twenty past four = よじ にじゅっ ぷんです。・ 四時 二十分です。
it's past midnight = よなかの じゅう にじすぎです。・ 夜中の 十二時 過ぎです。

• (*beyond*) = むこう・向こう
  it's past the traffic lights = しんごう
  のむこうです。・信号の 向こう
  です。
**4** *adverb*
  to go past, to walk past = とおる・
  通る

**pasta** *noun*
  = パスタ

**pastry** *noun*
• (*for baking*)
  = パイきじ・パイ生地
  to make pastry = パイきじを つくる
  ・パイ生地を 作る
• (*a cake*)
  = ペストリー

**patch** *noun*
• (*on a garment*)
  = つぎ・継ぎ
• (*on a tyre*)
  = つぎはぎ・継ぎはぎ

**path** *noun*
  = こみち・小道

**patience** *noun*
  = にんたい・忍耐
  to lose patience = かんにんぶくろ
  の おが きれる・堪忍袋の 緒が
  切れる

**patient**
**1** *noun*
  = かんじゃ・患者
**2** *adjective*
  = にんたいづよい・忍耐強い

**patrol car** *noun*
  = パトカー

**pattern** *noun*
• (*a design*)
  = もよう・模様
• (*when making garments*)
  (*for knitting*) = あみものの パターン
  ・編み物の パターン
  (*for sewing*) = かたがみ・型紙

**pavement** *noun* (*British English*)
  = ほどう・歩道

**paw** *noun*
  = あし・足

**pay**
**1** *verb*
• to pay = はらう・払う
  to pay the bill = かんじょうを はら
  う・勘定を 払う

to pay for the shopping = かいものの
だいきんを はらう・買い物の
代金を 払う
Dennis paid for my meal = デニスさ
んは ごちそうして くれました。
• (*when talking about wages*)
  the work doesn't pay very well = ここ
  の しごとは きゅうりょうが よ
  くないです。・ここの 仕事は
  給料が 良くないです。
  I'm paid eight pounds an hour = じき
  ゅう はちポンドです。・時給
  八ポンドです。
• (*to give*)
  to pay attention to the teacher = せん
  せいの いう ことを よく きく・
  先生の 言う ことを よく 聞く
  to pay (someone) a visit = (だれかを)
  ほうもんする・(誰かを)訪問す
  る
  to pay (someone) a compliment = (だ
  れかを)ほめる・(誰かを)誉め
  る
**2** *noun*
  pay = きゅうりょう・給料
  the pay is good = きゅうりょうが
  いいです。・給料が いいです。
  pay back = かえす・返す

**PE** *noun*
  = たいいく・体育

**pea** *noun*
  = えんどうまめ・えんどう豆

**peace** *noun*
  = へいわ・平和

**peach** *noun*
  = もも・桃

**peacock** *noun*
  = くじゃく

**peanut** *noun*
  = ピーナツ

**pear** *noun*
  = せいようなし・西洋梨

**pearl** *noun*
  = パール

**pebble** *noun*
  = こいし・小石

**pedestrian** *noun*
  = ほこうしゃ・歩行者

**pedestrian crossing** *noun*
  = おうだんほどう・横断歩道

**peel** *verb*
= かわを むく・皮を むく

**pen** *noun*
= ペン

**penalty** *noun*
(for offence) = しょばつ・処罰
(in sport) = ペナルティー
penalty kick = ペナルティーキック

**pence** *noun*
= ペンス

**pencil** *noun*
= えんぴつ・鉛筆

**pencil case** *noun*
= ふでばこ・筆箱

**pencil sharpener** *noun*
= えんぴつけずり・鉛筆削り

**penfriend** (British English),
**penpal** *noun*
= ペンフレンド

**penguin** *noun*
= ペンギン

**penknife** *noun*
= ペンナイフ

**pensioner** *noun*
(someone living on a pension) = ねんきんぐらしの ひと・年金暮らしの人
(old person) = ろうじん・老人

**people** *noun*
(in general) = ひとびと・人々
▶ **person**
(if counting) = 〜にん・〜人 ▶ **181**
note that two people is ふたり
when counting. As Japanese has no
real plural forms, ひと can be used
for both person and people in most
cases.
we met very nice people = いい ひとたちに あいました。・いい人達に 会いました。
most people don't know what's going on = ほとんどの ひとは なにが おこっているか わかりません。・ほとんどの 人は 何が 起こっているか わかりません。
there were three people at the meeting = かいぎには さんにん いました。・会議には 三人 いました。
there are too many people here = ここは ひとが おおすぎます。・ここは 人が 多すぎます。

to help other people = ひとを てつだう・人を 手伝う

**pepper** *noun*
• (the spice)
= こしょう
• (the vegetable)
= ピーマン

**per** *preposition*
per person = ひとりに つき・一人に つき

**per cent, percent** (US English)
*noun*
= パーセント

**perfect** *adjective*
= かんぺき(な)・完璧(な)
to speak perfect Japanese = かんぺきな にほんごを はなす・完璧な 日本語を 話す
it's the perfect place for a picnic = ピクニックには ちょうど いい ばしょです。・ピクニック には ちょうど いい 場所です。

**perform** *verb*
• (to do)
= おこなう・行う
• (to act, to play) = じょうえんする・上演する

**perfume** *noun*
= こうすい・香水
to wear perfume = こうすいを つける・香水を つける

**perhaps** *adverb*
= たぶん・多分

**period** *noun*
• (in time)
= きかん・期間
a trial period = しようきかん・試用期間
• (in history)
= じだい・時代
• (for women)
= せいり・生理
to have one's period = せいりに なる・生理に なる
• (a school lesson)
= じげん・時限 This is often
shortened to げん
first period = いちじげん・一時限
I have 3 periods of maths a week = すうがくの じゅぎょうは しゅう さんかい あります。・数学の 授業は 週 三回 あります。

**permanent** *adjective*
= えいきゅうてき（な）・永久的
（な）

**permission** *noun*
= きょか・許可
to get permission to go to a party =
パーティーに いく きょかを も
らう・パーティーに 行く 許可
を もらう

**person** *noun*
= ひと・人
an old person = ろうじん・老人
kind person = しんせつな ひと・
親切な 人

**personal** *adjective*
= こじん（の）・個人（の）

**personality** *noun*
= せいかく・性格

**perspire** *verb*
= あせを かく・汗を かく

**persuade** *verb*
= せっとくする・説得する
to persuade (someone) to buy a car =
（だれかに）くるまを かうように
ときふせる・（誰かに）車を 買
う ように 説き伏せる

**pessimist** *noun*
= ひかんろんしゃ・悲観論者

**pessimistic** *adjective*
= ひかんてき（な）・悲観的（な）

**pet** *noun*
= ペット
do you have any pets? = ペットを
かっていますか。・ペットを
飼っていますか。

**petrol** *noun* (*British English*)
= ガソリン
to run out of petrol = ガソリンが な
く なる・ガソリンが なく なる

**petrol station** *noun* (*British
English*)
= ガソリンスタンド

**pet shop** *noun*
= ペットショップ

**phone**
**1** *noun*
= でんわ・電話
the phone's ringing = でんわが なっ
ています。・電話が 鳴っていま
す。

to answer the phone = でんわに でる
・電話に 出る
he's on the phone = かれは でんわち
ゅうです。・彼は 電話中です。
**2** *verb*
= でんわする・電話する
to phone someone = だれかに でん
わする・誰かに 電話する

**phone book** *noun*
= でんわちょう・電話帳

**phone booth** *noun*
= でんわボックス・電話ボックス

**phone call** *noun*
= でんわ・電話
to receive a phone call = でんわを
もらう・電話を もらう
to make a phone call = でんわを
かける・電話を かける

**phone card** *noun*
= テレホンカード

**phone number** *noun*
= でんわばんごう・電話番号

**photo** *noun*
= しゃしん・写真

**photocopier** *noun*
= コピーき・コピー機

**photocopy** *noun*
= コピー

**photograph** *noun*
= しゃしん・写真
to take a photograph = しゃしんを
とる・写真を 撮る

**photographer** *noun*
= カメラマン

**physics** *noun*
= ぶつり・物理
(*academic subject*) = ぶつりがく・
物理学

**piano** *noun* ▶ **180**
= ピアノ

**pick** *verb*
• (*to choose*) = えらぶ・選ぶ
to pick a number = ばんごうを えら
ぶ・番号を 選ぶ
• (*to collect*) = つむ・摘む
to pick apples = りんごを つむ・
りんごを 摘む
• (*to take*) = とる・取る
to pick a book off the shelf = たな
から ほんを とる・棚から 本を
取る

P

pick on = いじめる

he's always picking on me = かれは いつも わたしを いじめています。・ 彼は いつも 私を いじめています。

pick out = えらぶ・選ぶ

pick up
* (to lift)

to pick the clothes up off the floor = ゆかから ふくを ひろう・床から 服を 拾う

to pick a baby up = あかちゃんを だきあげる・赤ちゃんを 抱き上げる

to pick up the phone = でんわにでる・電話に 出る

* (to collect)

to pick up passengers = じょうきゃくを のせる・乗客を 乗せる

my father's coming to pick me up from school = ちちが がっこうにむかえに きます。・父が 学校に 迎えに 来ます。

* (to buy) = かう・買う

I stopped to pick up a newspaper = しんぶんを かう ために たちどまりました。・新聞を 買うために 立ち止まりました。

* (to learn) = おぼえる・覚える

**picnic** noun

= ピクニック

to go on a picnic = ピクニックに いく・ピクニックに 行く

**picture** noun
* = え・絵

to paint a picture of someone = だれかの えを かく・誰かの 絵を 描く

* (a photograph)
= しゃしん・写真

**piece** noun
* (a bit) not usually used in Japanese

a piece of cheese = チーズ

a piece of string = ひも・紐

* (a part of a machine)
= ぶひん・部品
* (a broken part)
= はへん・破片
* (a coin)

a 50 yen piece = ごじゅうえんだま・五十円玉

* (other uses) not usually used in Japanese

a piece of furniture = かぐ・家具

a piece of information = じょうほう・情報

a piece of advice = アドバイス

**pierce** verb
= あなを あける・穴を 開ける

**pig** noun
= ぶた

year of the pig = いのししどし・亥年

**pigeon** noun
= はと

**pile** noun
* = やま・山

a pile of rubbish = ごみの やま・ごみの 山

* (lots)

piles of toys = たくさんの おもちゃ

**pill** noun
* (a tablet)
= じょうざい・錠剤
* (a method of contraception)
= ピル

**pillow** noun
= まくら・枕

**pilot** noun
= パイロット

**pin**
1 noun
= ピン
2 verb
= ピンで とめる・ピンで 止める

**PIN** noun
= ＰＩＮナンバー

**pinball** noun
= スマートボール

**pinch** verb
= つねる

he pinched my arm, he pinched me on the arm = かれは わたしの うでを つねりました。・彼は 私の 腕を つねりました。

**pineapple** noun
= パイナップル

**pine tree** noun
= まつ・松

**pink** adjective
= ピンクいろ(の)・ピンク色(の)

**pint** *noun*
* (*the quantity*) = ごひゃく cc ・
五百 cc *Note that cc is
pronounced* シーシー *in Japanese*

> **!** *Note that a pint = 0.57 l in Britain
> and 0.47 l in the US.*

a pint of milk = ぎゅうにゅう ごひゃ
くcc・牛乳 五百ｃｃ
* (*British English*)
(*a drink*)
to go for a pint = いっぱい のみに
いく・一杯 飲みに 行く

**pipe** *noun*
* (*for gas, water*)
= かん・管
* (*for smoking*)
= パイプ

**pirate** *noun*
= かいぞく・海賊

**Pisces** *noun*
= うおざ・魚座

**pitch** *noun* (*British English*)
a football pitch = サッカーの グラ
ンド

**pity**
**1** *noun*
* = なさけ・情け
* (*when expressing regret*)
what a pity! = ざんねんです。・ 残念
です。
it's a pity you can't come = こられな
いのは ざんねんです。・ 来られ
ないのは 残念です。
**2** *verb*
= かわいそうにおもう・かわいそ
うに 思う

**pizza** *noun*
= ピザ

**place** *noun*
* = ところ・所
it's the best place to buy clothes =
ふくを かうには いちばんいい
ところです。・ 服を 買うには 一
番いい 所です。
Akita is a nice place = あきたは いい
ところです。・ 秋田は いい 所で
す。
they come from all over the place =
かれらは いろいろな ところか
らきています。・ 彼らは 色々な
所から 来ています。

this place is dirty = ここは きたない
です。・ ここは 汚いです。
* (*a home*)
at Alison's place = アリソンさんの
いえで・アリソンさんの 家で
I'd like a place of my own = じぶんの
うちが ほしいです。・ 自分の 家
が 欲しいです。
* (*on public transport, in a car park, at
table*)
is this place free? = この せきは あ
いていますか。・ この 席は 空い
ていますか。
to save a place for someone = だれ
かに せきを とって おく・誰か
に 席を 取って おく
to find a place to park = ちゅうしゃ
できる スペースを みつける・
駐車できる スペースを 見つけ
る
* (*on a team, a course*)
to get a place on a team = チームに
はいる・チームに 入る
to get a place on a course = コースに
はいる・コースに 入る
* (*in a contest*)
to win first place = だいいちいに
なる・第一位に なる

**plain**
**1** *adjective*
* (*simple*) = しっそ(な)・質素(な)
a plain dress = しっそな ドレス・
質素な ドレス
* (*not good-looking*) = ぶきりょう(な)
・不器量(な)
**2** *noun*
= へいげん・平原

**plait** *noun* (*British English*)
= みつあみ・三つ編

**plan**
**1** *noun*
* (*what one intends to do*)
= けいかく・計画
we need a plan = けいかくが ひつよ
うです。・ 計画が 必要です。
do you have any plans for the future?
= しょうらいはなにをしますか。
・ 将来は 何を しますか。
* (*what one has arranged to do*)
= よてい・予定
I don't have any plans for tonight =
こんばんは なんの よていも
ありません。・ 今晩は 何の 予定
も ありません。

**2** *verb*
- (*to prepare, to organize*)
  = けいかくを する・計画を する
  to plan a trip = りょこうの けいかく
  を する・旅行の 計画を する
  to plan a meeting = かいぎの けいか
  くを する・会議の 計画を する
- (*to intend*) = use verb in dictionary
  form + つもり ▶ **191**
  I'm planning to go to Scotland = スコ
  ットランドに いく つもりです。
  ・スコットランドに 行くつもり
  です。

**plane** *noun*
= ひこうき・飛行機

**planet** *noun*
= わくせい・惑星

**plant**
**1** *noun*
= しょくぶつ・植物
**2** *verb*
= うえる・植える

**plaster** *noun* (*British English*)
= ばんそうこう

**plastic**
**1** *noun*
= プラスチック
**2** *adjective*
= プラスチックせい(の)・プラス
チック製(の)

**plate** *noun*
= さら・皿

**platform** *noun*
= ホーム
on platform 4 = よんばんせんに・
四番線に

**play**
**1** *verb*
- (*to have fun*) = あそぶ・遊ぶ
  to play with friends = ともだちとあ
  そぶ・友達と遊ぶ
  to play a trick on someone = だれか
  に いたずらを しかける・誰か
  に いたずらを 仕掛ける
  to play cards = トランプを する
- (*when talking about sports*) = する
  to play football = サッカーを する
  France is playing (against) Ireland =
  フランスは アイルランドと た
  いせんしています。・フランス
  は アイルランドと 対戦してい
  ます。
- (*when talking about music*) ▶ **180**

(*piano, guitar, instruments played with
fingers*) = ひく・弾く
(*flute, trumpet, instruments played by
blowing*) = ふく・吹く
(*drums and percussion instruments*) =
たたく・叩く
- (*to put on*) = かける・掛ける
  to play a CD = CDを かける・
  CDを 掛ける *Note that CD is
  pronounced* シーディー
- (*when talking about theatre, cinema*) =
  えんじる・演じる
  to play the role of Romeo = ロミオの
  やくを えんじる・ロミオの 役
  を 演じる
  the film will be playing next week =
  えいがは らいしゅう じょうえ
  いします。・映画は 来週 上映し
  ます。
**2** *noun*
= げき・劇
play around = あそぶ・遊ぶ
play back
to play back a tape = テープを さい
せいする・テープを 再生する

**player** *noun*
= せんしゅ・選手
a tennis player = テニスの せんしゅ
・テニスの 選手

**playground** *noun*
= あそびば・遊び場
the school playground = こうてい・
校庭

**please** *adverb*
(*polite request*) = おねがいします。
・お願いします。
(*please do....*) = use the 〜て form of
the verb + ください ▶ **197**
please come in = どうぞ はいって
ください。・どうぞ 入ってくだ
さい。
please wait a moment = ちょっと ま
ってください。・ちょっと 待っ
てください。
(*please don't....*) = use the ない form
of the verb + でください ▶ **191**
please don't smoke = たばこを すわ
ないでください。・ たばこを
吸わないでください。
(*when accepting food and drink*) =
いただきます。
'more cake?'—'yes please' = 「ケー
キは いかがですか。」「いただき
ます。」

*(polite acceptance of a favour)* = おね
　がいします。・ お願いします。

**pleased** *adjective*
　= うれしい
　I was pleased to receive the letter =
　てがみを もらって うれしかっ
　たです。・ 手紙を もらって うれ
　しかったです。
　pleased to meet you = はじめまして。

**plenty** *pronoun*
　to have plenty of time = じかんが い
　っぱい ある・ 時間が いっぱい
　ある

**plot** *noun*
• *(a plan)*
　= けいかく・ 計画
• *(the story in a film, a novel, a play)*
　= プロット

**plug** *noun*
• *(on an appliance)*
　= コンセント
　to pull out the plug = コンセントを
　ひきぬく・ コンセントを 引き
　抜く
• *(in a sink or bath)*
　= せん・ 栓
　plug in = コンセントを さしこむ・
　コンセントを 差し込む

**plum** *noun*
　= うめ・ 梅

**plumber** *noun*
　= すいどうや・ 水道屋

**plus** *preposition*
　= プラス
　three plus three are six = さん たす
　さんは ろくです。・ 三 足す
　三は 六です。

**pocket** *noun*
　= ポケット

**pocketbook** *noun* *(US English)*
　= さいふ・ 財布

**pocket money** *noun*
　= こづかい・ 小遣い

**poem** *noun*
　= し・ 詩

**point**
**1** *noun*
• *(a statement in a discussion)*
　= しゅちょう・ 主張
• *(the most important idea)*
　= ようてん・ 要点

that's not the point = それは ちがい
　ます。・ それは 違います。
• *(use)*
　there's no point in shouting = どな
　っても しかたが ありません。・
　怒鳴っても 仕方が ありません。
• *(when talking about time)*
　to be on the point of..... = volitional
　form + と した ところ
　I am on the point of moving = ひっこ
　そうと したところです。・ 引っ
　越そうと した とこです。
　I was on the point of selling the house
　= いえをうろうとした ところで
　した。・ 家を 売ろうと した
　ところでした。
• *(the sharp end)*
　= とがった ところ・ 尖った 所
　the point of a pencil = えんぴつの
　さき・ 鉛筆の 先
• *(in a contest, a game)*
　= てん・ 点
**2** *verb*
• *(to indicate)*
　to point (one's finger) at someone =
　だれかを してきする・ 誰かを
　指摘する
• *(to aim)*
　to point a gun at someone = だれかに
　じゅうを むける・ 誰かに 銃を
　向ける
　point out = してきする・ 指摘する
　please point the mistakes out to me =
　まちがいを してきしてくださ
　い。・ 間違いを 指摘してくださ
　い。

**poison**
**1** *noun*
　= どく・ 毒
**2** *verb*
　= どくを のませる・ 毒を 飲ませる

**pole** *noun*
　= ぼう・ 棒
　North Pole = ほっきょく・ 北極
　South Pole = なんきょく・ 南極

**police** *noun*
　= けいさつ・ 警察

**policeman** *noun*
　= けいかん・ 警官

**police station** *noun*
　= けいさつしょ・ 警察署

**policewoman** *noun*
　= ふじんけいかん・ 婦人警官

**P**

**polish** *verb*
  to polish shoes = くつを みがく・
  靴を 磨く
  to polish the car = くるまを みがく
  ・車を 磨く

**polite** *adjective*
  = ていねい(な)・丁寧(な)

**political** *adjective*
  = せいじてき(な)・政治的(な)

**politician** *noun*
  = せいじか・政治家

**politics** *noun*
  = せいじ・政治

**pollute** *verb*
  = おせんする・汚染する

**pollution** *noun*
  = おせん・汚染
  environmental pollution = かんきょ
  うおせん・環境汚染

**pond** *noun*
  = いけ・池

**pony** *noun*
  = ポニー

**ponytail** *noun*
  = ポニーテール

**pool** *noun*
  • (*a swimming pool*)
  = プール
  • (*on the ground, the floor*)
  = みずたまり・水溜まり
  • (*the game*)
  = ビリヤード

**poor** *adjective*
  • (*not wealthy*) = びんぼう(な)・貧乏
  (な)
  • (*not satisfactory*) = へた(な)・下手
  (な)
  I am poor at sports = スポーツが へ
  たです。・スポーツが 下手で
  す。
  • (*expressing sympathy*) = かわいそう
  (な)

**popular** *adjective*
  a popular sport = りゅうこうのスポ
  ーツ・流行の スポーツ
  she's very popular = かのじょは に
  んきものです。・彼女は 人気者
  です。
  to be popular with the girls = おんな
  の こ に にんきが ある・女の
  子に 人気が ある

**population** *noun*
  = じんこう・人口

**pork** *noun*
  = ぶたにく・豚肉

**port** *noun*
  = みなと・港

**portrait** *noun*
  = ポートレート

**positive** *adjective*
  = せっきょくてき(な)・積極的
  (な)

**possibility** *noun*
  = かのうせい・可能性

**possible** *adjective*
  = かのう(な)・可能(な)
  they came as quickly as possible =
  かれらは できるだけ はやく
  きました。・彼らは できるだけ
  早く 来ました。
  I did as much as possible = できる
  だけ しました。

**post** (*British English*)
**1** *noun*
  the post
  (*the system*) = ゆうびん・郵便
  (*the letters*) = ゆうびんぶつ・郵便物
  has the post come yet? = ゆうびんは
  もう きましたか。・郵便は もう
  来ましたか。
**2** *verb*
  to post a letter = てがみを だす・
  手紙を 出す

**postbox** *noun* (*British English*)
  = ポスト

**postcard** *noun*
  = はがき・葉書

**postcode** *noun* (*British English*)
  = ゆうびんばんごう・郵便番号

**poster** *noun*
  = ポスター

**postman** *noun* (*British English*)
  = ゆうびんや・郵便屋

**post office** *noun*
  = ゆうびんきょく・郵便局

**postpone** *verb*
  to postpone a concert = コンサート
  を えんきする・コンサートを
  延期する
  let's postpone the party until next week
  = パーティーを らいしゅうま
  で えんきしましょう。・パーテ

ィーを 来週まで 延期しましょ
う。

**pot** *noun*
- (*a container*)
  = びん・瓶
  to make a pot of tea = こうちゃを
  いれる・紅茶を 入れる
- (*for plants*) = うえきばち・植木鉢
- (*a saucepan*)
  = なべ

**potato** *noun*
  = じゃがいも

**pottery** *noun*
  = とうき・陶器

**pound** *noun*
- (*the currency*)
  = ポンド
- (*the measurement*)
  = ポンド

  ❗ *Note that a* pound = *453.6 g.*

  two pounds of apples = りんご いち
  キロ・りんご 一キロ

**pour** *verb*
- (*from a container*) = つぐ
  to pour milk into a bowl = ミルクを
  ボールに つぐ
- (*to serve*) = ついであげる
  someone poured me some sake =
  だれかが おさけを ついで くれ
  ました。・誰かが お酒を ついで
  くれました。
- (*to flow*) = ながれる・流れる
- (*to escape*)
  smoke poured out of the window =
  まどから けむりが でて いきま
  した。・窓から 煙が 出て 行き
  ました。
- (*to rain*)
  it's pouring (with rain) = どしゃぶり
  です。・どしゃ降りです。
- (*to enter or leave in large numbers*)
  to pour into the city = まちに さっと
  うする・町に 殺到する
  people poured out of the stadium =
  ひとが スタジアムから どっと
  でて きました。・人が スタジア
  ムから どっと 出て 来ました。

**powder** *noun*
  = こな・粉

**power** *noun*
- (*control*)
  = けんりょく・権力

to be in power = けんりょくを にぎ
っている・権力を 握っている
- (*influence*)
  Joyce has great power = ジョイスさ
  んは えいきょうりょくが つよ
  いです。・ジョイスさんは 影響
  力が 強いです。
- (*electricity*)
  = でんりょく・電力
  power cut = ていでん・停電

**practical** *adjective*
  = じつようてき(な)・実用的(な)

**practise** (*British English*),
  **practice** (*US English*) *verb*
  = れんしゅうする・練習する
  to practise the violin = バイオリンを
  れんしゅうする・バイオリンを
  練習する

**praise** *verb*
  to praise someone
  = だれかを ほめる・誰かを 誉め
  る

**prawn** *noun* (*British English*)
  = えび・海老

**prayer** *noun*
  = いのり・祈り

**precaution** *noun*
  = ようじん・用心

**precious** *adjective*
  = きちょう(な)・貴重(な)

**precise** *adjective*
  = せいかく(な)・正確(な)

**prefer** *verb*
  = ～の ほうが すき・～の 方が
  好き
  I prefer chocolate to vanilla = バニラ
  より チョコレートが すきです。
  ・バニラより チョコレートが
  好きです。
  I'd prefer to phone = でんわした ほ
  うが いいです。・電話した 方が
  いいです。

**pregnant** *adjective*
  = にんしんしている・妊娠してい
  る

**prejudice** *noun*
  = へんけん・偏見

**prepare** *verb*
- (*to get ready*) = じゅんびする・準
  備する

to prepare for a trip = りょこうの じゅんびを する・旅行の 準備を する

the pupils are preparing for the exam = せいとは じゅけんべんきょうを しています。・生徒は 受験勉強を しています。

- (*to get something ready*) = よういする・用意する
to prepare the paperwork = しょるいを よういする・書類を 用意する

**prepared** *adjective*
- (*willing*)
I'm prepared to wait = まっても かまいません。・待っても かまいません。
- (*ready*)
to be prepared for an exam = しけんの じゅんびが できている・試験の 準備が できている

**prescription** *noun*
= しょほうせん・処方箋

**present**
**1** *noun*
- (*a gift*)
= プレゼント
to give (someone) a present = (だれかに)プレゼントを あげる・(誰かに)プレゼントを あげる
- (*now*)
= げんざい・現在
I'll be here for the present = しばらく ここに います。
**2** *verb*
- (*to give*)
to present a prize to someone = だれかに しょうを おくる・誰かに 賞を 贈る
- (*on radio or TV*)
to present a programme = ばんぐみを ていきょうする・番組を 提供する

**president** *noun*
= だいとうりょう・大統領

**press**
**1** *verb*
= おす・押す
to press the bell = ベルを おす・ベルを 押す
**2** *noun*
= ほうどうきかん・報道機関

**pressure** *noun*
= あつりょく・圧力

to put pressure on someone = だれかに あつりょくを かける・誰かに 圧力を かける

**pretend** *verb*
= 〜ふりをする
Mr Ueda's pretending to be annoyed = うえださんは おこっている ふりを しています。・上田さんは 怒っている ふりを しています。

**pretty**
**1** *adjective*
= かわいい
**2** *adverb*
= かなり
that's pretty good = それは かなり いいです。

**prevent** *verb*
= ふせぐ・防ぐ
to prevent a war = せんそうを ふせぐ・戦争を 防ぐ

**previous** *adjective*
= まえ(の)・前(の)

**price** *noun*
= ねだん・値段

**pride** *noun*
- = ほこり・誇り
- (*self-respect*)
= じそんしん・自尊心

**priest** *noun*
= しさい・司祭

**primary school** *noun*
= しょうがっこう・小学校

**primary school teacher** *noun*
= しょうがっこうの せんせい・小学校の 先生

**prime minister** *noun*
(*in Japan*) = そうりだいじん・総理大臣
(*in other countries*) = しゅしょう・首相

**prince** *noun*
= おうじ・王子

**princess** *noun*
= おうじょ・王女

**principal** *noun* (*US English*)
= こうちょう・校長

**print**
**1** *verb*
= いんさつする・印刷する
to print a book = ほんを いんさつする・本を 印刷する

**2** *noun*
- (*of a photo*)
= プリント
- (*of a finger*) = しもん・指紋
  (*of a foot*) = あしあと・足跡

**printer** *noun*
= プリンター

**priority** *noun*
= ゆうせん・優先

**prison** *noun*
= けいむしょ・刑務所

**prisoner** *noun*
= しゅうじん・囚人
  prisoner of war = ほりょ・捕虜

**private**
**1** *adjective*
- (*personal*) = こじん(の)・個人(の)
  my private life = しせいかつ・私生活
- (*not run by the state*) = しりつ(の)・
  私立(の)
  a private school = しりつ がっこう・
  私立 学校
**2 in private** = ひとの みえない とこ
  ろで・人の 見えない 所で

**prize** *noun*
= しょう・賞

**probably** *adverb*
= たぶん・多分

**problem** *noun*
= もんだい・問題
  to cause a problem = もんだいを
  おこす・問題を 起こす

**process** *noun*
= かてい・過程
  I am in the process of writing a letter =
  てがみを かいている とちゅう
  です。・手紙を 書いている 途中
  です。

**produce**
**1** *verb*
- (*to make*) = つくる・作る
- (*to create*)
  to produce a film = えいがを せいさ
  くする・映画を 制作する
  to produce a play = げきを えんしゅ
  つする・劇を 演出する
**2** *noun*
  agricultural produce = のうさんぶつ
  ・農産物

**product** *noun*
= さんぶつ・産物

**production** *noun*
= せいさん・生産

**profession** *noun*
= しょくぎょう・職業

**professional** *adjective*
= プロ(の)

**professor** *noun*
= きょうじゅ・教授

**profit** *noun*
= りえき・利益

**program**
**1** *noun*
- (*for a computer*)
= プログラム
- (*US English*) ▶ **programme**
**2** *verb*
= プログラミングする

**programme** (*British English*),
**program** (*US English*)
**1** *noun*
- (*on radio, TV*)
= ばんぐみ・番組
  a programme about China = ちゅう
  ごくに ついての ばんぐみ・
  中国に ついての 番組
- (*for a play, a concert*)
= プログラム

**progress** *noun*
= しんぽ・進歩
  to make progress = しんぽする・
  進歩する

**project** *noun*
(*at school*) = けんきゅうテーマ・
  研究テーマ

**promise**
**1** *verb*
= やくそくする・約束する
  we promised to finish by January =
  いちがつまでに おわると やく
  そくしました。・ 一月までに
  終わると 約束しました。
**2** *noun*
= やくそく・約束

**pronounce** *verb*
= はつおんする・発音する

**proof** *noun*
= しょうこ・証拠

**properly** *adverb*
= ちゃんと
  please do it properly = ちゃんと して
  ください。

**property** *noun*
= しょゆうぶつ・所有物

**protect** verb
= まもる ・ 守る
to protect oneself = じぶんを まもる ・ 自分を 守る

**protest** verb
• (to complain) = もんくを いう ・ 文句を 言う
• (to demonstrate) = こうぎする ・ 抗議する

**protester** noun
= こうぎしゃ ・ 抗議者

**proud** adjective
= ほこりに おもう ・ 誇りに 思う
she's proud of her work = かのじょは しごとを ほこりに おもっています。・ 彼女は 仕事を 誇りに 思っています。

**prove** verb
= りっしょうする ・ 立証する

**provided** conjunction
I'll lend you my car provided you pay for the petrol = ガソリンだいを はらうなら くるまを かして あげます。・ ガソリン代を 払うなら 車を 貸して あげます。

**psychiatrist** noun
= せいしんかい ・ 精神科医

**psychologist** noun
= しんりがくしゃ ・ 心理学者

**pub** noun (British English)
= パブ

**public**
**1** noun
= こうしゅう ・ 公衆
**2** adjective
a public park = こうえん ・ 公園
a public library = こうりつとしょかん ・ 公立図書館
**3** in public = ひとまえで ・ 人前で

**public holiday** noun
= きゅうじつ ・ 休日
(for celebration) = さいじつ ・ 祭日

**public transport** noun
= こうきょうゆそうきかん ・ 公共輸送機関

**pudding** noun (British English)
= デザート

**puddle** noun
= みずたまり ・ 水たまり

**pull** verb
• = ひく ・ 引く

to pull (on) a rope = ロープを ひく ・ ロープを 引く
to pull someone's hair = だれかの かみを ひっぱる ・ 誰かの 髪を 引っ張る
• (to move by dragging)
to pull the table into the kitchen = だいどころに テーブルを ひきずる ・ 台所に テーブルを 引きずる
• (to take out)
to pull a handkerchief out of one's pocket = ハンカチを ポケットから とりだす ・ ハンカチを ポケットから 取り出す
• to pull a face (British English) = へんな かおを する ・ 変な 顔を する
**pull down**
• (to knock down) = こわす ・ 壊す
• (to lower) = ひきさげる ・ 引き下げる
**pull out**
to pull a tooth out = はを ひきぬく ・ 歯を 引き抜く
**pull up**
• (to stop) = とまる ・ 止まる
• (to remove)
to pull up the weeds = くさを ねこそぎに する ・ 草を 根こそぎに する
• to pull up one's socks = くつしたを ひきあげる ・ 靴下を 引き上げる

**pullover** noun
= セーター

**pump** noun
= ポンプ
a bicycle pump = じてんしゃの くうきいれ ・ 自転車の 空気入れ
pump up = ポンプで ふくらます ・ ポンプで 膨らます

**pumpkin** noun
= かぼちゃ

**punch** noun
= パンチ

**puncture** noun
= パンク

**punish** verb
= ばっする ・ 罰する

**pupil** noun
= せいと ・ 生徒

**puppet** noun
= あやつりにんぎょう ・ 操り人形

puppet show = にんぎょうげき・
人形劇

**puppy** *noun*
= こいぬ・小犬

**pure** *adjective*
= じゅんすい(な)・純粋(な)

**purple** *adjective*
= むらさきいろ(の)・紫色(の)

**purpose**
**1** *noun*
= もくてき・目的
**2** on purpose = わざと
you did it on purpose, didn't you! =
わざと しましたね。

**purse** *noun*
• (*for money*)
= さいふ・財布
• (*US English*)
(*a handbag*)
= ハンドバッグ

**push** *verb*
• = おす・押す
to push a car = くるまを おす・
車を押す
to push the door open = ドアを おし
あける・ドアを 押し開ける
to push someone out of the way =
だれかを おしのける・誰かを
押しのける
• (*to sell*) = せんでんする・宣伝する
to push drugs = ドラッグを うる・
ドラッグを 売る

**pushchair** *noun* (*British English*)
= ベビーカー

**pusher** *noun*
= ばいにん・売人

**put** *verb*
= おく・置く
to put the cards on the table = カード
を テーブルの うえに おく・
カードを テーブルの 上に 置く
to put sugar in coffee = さとうを コ
ーヒーに いれる・砂糖を コー
ヒーに 入れる
to put someone in prison = だれかを
けいむしょに いれる・誰かを
刑務所に 入れる
to put someone in a bad mood = だれ
かを いやな きもちに させる・
誰かを 嫌な 気持ちに させる
**put away** = かたづける・片付ける

**put back**
• (*to return to its place*) = もどす・戻
す
to put a book back on a shelf = ほん
を たなに もどす・本を棚に 戻
す
• (*to change the time*)
to put the clocks back = とけいを
もどす・時計を 戻す
**put down**
• (*on a surface*) = おく・置く
please put your bag down here = ここ
に かばんを おいてください。・
ここに かばんを 置いてくださ
い。
• (*when phoning*)
to put the phone down = でんわを
きる・電話を 切る
• (*British English*)
(*to give an injection to*) = あんらくし
させる・安楽死させる
we had to put our dog down = いぬを
あんらくしさせなければ なりま
せんでした。・犬を 安楽死させ
なければ なりませんでした。
**put forward**
to put the clocks forward = とけいを
すすめる・時計を 進める
**put off**
• (*to delay*)
we have to put the party off until next
week = パーティーを らいしゅう
まで えんきしなければ なりま
せん。・パーティーを 来週まで
延期しなければ なりません。
• (*to switch off*) = けす・消す
**put on**
• (*when dressing*)
(*shirts, dresses*) = きる・着る
(*hats*) = かぶる
(*shoes, trousers, skirts, socks*) = はく
(*makeup*) = つける
(*spectacles*) = かける
• (*to switch on*)
to put the heating on = だんぼうを
つける・暖房を つける
to put the kettle on = おゆを わかす
・お湯を 沸かす
to put a CD on = CDを かける Note
that CD is pronounced シーディー
• to put on weight = ふとる・太る
• (*to organize, to produce*) = じょうえ
んする・上演する
to put on a play = げきを じょうえん
する・劇を 上演する

P

**put out**
- to put out a cigarette = たばこを けす ・ たばこを 消す
- (to take out)
  to put the bins out = ごみ ばこを だす ・ ごみ箱を 出す

  **put up**
- (to lift)
  to put one's hair up = かみを もちあ げる ・ 髪を 持ち上げる
  to put up one's hand
  (in class) ≈ = てを あげる ・ 手を 上げる
- (to attach)
  to put a poster up = ポスターを はる ・ ポスターを 貼る
- (when camping)
  to put up a tent = テントを はる ・ テントを 張る
- (British English)
  (to raise) = あげる ・ 上げる
  to put the rent up = やちんを あげる ・ 家賃を 上げる
- (to give someone a place to stay) = とめる ・ 泊める

  **put up with** = がまんする ・ 我慢する

**puzzle** noun
(mysterious thing) = なぞ ・ 謎
(game) = パズル

**pyjamas** noun (British English)
= パジャマ

# Qq

**qualified** adjective
- (having studied) = しかくが ある ・ 資格が ある
- (having experience, skills) = のうりょ くが ある ・ 能力が ある

**quality** noun
= ひんしつ ・ 品質

**quantity** noun
(amount) = りょう ・ 量
(number) = かず ・ 数

**quarrel**
**1** noun
= けんか

**2** verb
= くちげんかする ・ 口げんかする

**quarter**
**1** noun
= よんぶんの いち ・ 四分の 一
a quarter of an hour = じゅうごふん ・ 十五分
to cut the tomatoes in quarters = トマ トを よっつに きる ・ トマトを 四つに 切る
**2** pronoun
- (when talking about quantities, numbers)
a quarter of the population can't read = じんこうの よんぶんの いちは よめません。・ 人口の 四分の 一 は 読めません。
- (when talking about time) ▶ **186**
an hour and a quarter = いちじかん じゅうごふん ・ 一時間十五分
it's (a) quarter past five = ごじじゅう ごふんです。・ 五時十五分です。
it's (a) quarter to nine = はちじよん じゅうごふんです。・ 八時四十 五分です。

**quay** noun
= ふとう ・ 埠頭

**queen** noun
= じょおう ・ 女王

**question**
**1** noun
- (a request for information)
= しつもん ・ 質問
to ask someone a question = だれ かに しつもんを する ・ 誰かに 質問を する
- (a problem, a matter)
= もんだい ・ 問題
**2** verb
the police questioned the suspect = けいさつは ようぎしゃを とり しらべました。・ 警察は 容疑者 を 取り調べました。
(to suspect) = うたがう ・ 疑う

**questionnaire** noun
= アンケート

**queue** (British English)
**1** noun
= れつ ・ 列
to join the queue = れつに ならぶ ・ 列に 並ぶ
**2** verb
= れつを つくる ・ 列を 作る

**quick** *adjective*
= はやい・速い
a quick answer = すばやい こたえ・素早い 答え
it's quicker to go by train = でんしゃ で いった ほうが はやいです。・電車で 行った 方が 速いです。
quickest = いちばんはやい・一番 速い

**quickly** *adverb*
= はやく・速く
Chris's Japanese progressed quickly = クリスさんの にほんごは はやく じょうたつしました。・クリスさんの 日本語は 速く 上達しました。

**quiet**
**1** *adjective*
• (*silent*) = しずか(な)・静か(な)
to keep quiet = しずかに する・静かに する
to go quiet = しずかに なる・静かに なる
please be quiet! = しずかに してください。・静かに してください。
• (*not talkative*) = おとなしい
• (*calm*) = おだやか(な)・穏やか(な)
a quiet life = へいおんな せいかつ・平穏な 生活
**2** *noun*
= しずけさ・静けさ
to speak in a quiet voice = ちいさい こえで はなす・小さい 声で 話す

**quietly** *adverb*
= しずかに・静かに
to speak quietly = しずかに はなす・静かに 話す
to read quietly = しずかに よむ・静かに 読む

**quit** *verb*
• (*to resign*) = やめる・辞める
• (*US English*)
(*to give up*)
= やめる
to quit smoking = たばこを やめる

**quite** *adverb*
• (*rather*) = かなり
they go back to France quite often = かれらは かなり ひんぱんに フランスへ もどります。・彼らは

かなり 頻繁に フランスへ 戻ります。
I quite like Chinese food = ちゅうか りょうりが かなり すきです。・中華料理が かなり 好きです。
she earns quite a lot of money = かのじょは おかねを かなり かせぎます。・彼女は お金をかなり 稼ぎます。
• (*completely*)
= かんぜんに・完全に
it isn't quite ready yet = まだ かんぜんに できていません。・まだ 完全に できていません。
you're quite right = まったく あなたの いうとおりです。・全くあなたの 言うとおりです。
• (*exactly*)
I don't quite know what Mr Murakami does = むらかみさんが なにを しているか はっきりとは しりません。・村上さんが 何をしているか はっきりとは 知りません。

**quiz** *noun*
= クイズ

# Rr

**rabbit** *noun*
= うさぎ
year of the rabbit = うさぎどし・卯年

**race**
**1** *noun*
• (*ethnic group*) = じんしゅ・人種
• (*a contest*)
= きょうそう・競争
to have a race = きょうそうする・競争する
• (*for horse-racing*)
= けいば・競馬
**2** *verb*
• (*to compete with*)
to race (against) someone = だれか ときそう・誰かと 競う
let's race to the car = くるまの とこ ろまで きょうそうしましょう。・車の 所まで 競争しましょう。

**racehorse** *noun*
= きょうそうば・競走馬

**racetrack** *noun*
(*for horses*) = けいばじょう・競馬場
(*for cars*) = サーキット

**racism** *noun*
= じんしゅさべつ・人種差別

**racket, racquet** *noun*
= ラケット

**radiator** *noun*
= ヒーター

**radio** *noun*
= ラジオ
on the radio = ラジオで

**radio station** *noun*
= ラジオほうそうきょく・ラジオ放送局

**rage** *noun*
= げきど・激怒
to fly into a rage = いかりくるう・怒り狂う

**raid** *verb*
to raid a bank = ぎんこうを しゅうげきする・銀行を 襲撃する
the police raided the building = けいさつは ビルの ていれを しました。・警察は ビルの手入れをしました。

**rail** *noun*
• (*for holding on to*)
= てすり・手すり
• (*for trains*)
by rail = でんしゃで・電車で

**railway** (*British English*), **railroad** (*US English*) *noun*
• (*a track*)
= せんろ・線路
• (*the rail system*)
= てつどう・鉄道

**railway line** *noun* (*British English*)
= てつどう・鉄道

> ! *Note that Japanese railway lines have names with the suffix* せん *e.g. the* やまのてせん *in Tokyo*

**railway station** *noun* (*British English*)
= えき・駅

**rain**
**1** *noun*
= あめ・雨

**2** *verb*
= あめが ふる・雨が 降る
it's raining = あめが ふっている・雨が 降っている

**rainbow** *noun*
= にじ・虹

**raincoat** *noun*
= レインコート

**raise** *verb*
• (*to lift*) = もちあげる・持ち上げる
• (*to increase*) = あげる・上げる
to raise prices = ねだんを あげる・値段を 上げる
• (*in anger*)
to raise one's voice = こえを おおきく する・声を 大きく する
• (*to talk about*)
to raise a subject = ぎだいに とりあげる・議題に 取り上げる
• (*to bring up*)
to raise children = こどもを そだてる・子供を 育てる

**ram** *noun*
year of the ram = ひつじどし・未年

**range** *noun*
• (*a selection*)
there is a range of activities = いろいろな かつどうが あります。・色々な 活動が あります。
• (*of mountains*)
= さんみゃく・山脈
• (*US English*)
(*for cooking*)
= レンジ

**rare** *adjective*
• (*not common*) = まれ(な)
• (*very slightly cooked*) = レア(の)

**rarely** *adverb*
= めったに + negative
we rarely meet = めったに あいません。・めったに 会いません。

**raspberry** *noun*
= ラズベリー

**rat** *noun*
= ねずみ
year of the rat = ねずみどし・子年

**rather** *adverb*
• (*when saying what one would prefer*)
= むしろ + verb in 〜たい form ▶ **191**
I'd rather go home = むしろ かえりたいです。・むしろ 帰りたいです。

I'd rather be here = むしろ ここに い
たいです。

I'd rather read the paper = むしろ し
んぶんを よみたいです。・ むし
ろ 新聞を 読みたいです。

I'd rather you didn't do that = それを
しないでください。

• (quite) = かなり
I think it's rather valuable = これは か
なり ねうちが あるとおもいま
す。・ これはかなり 値打ちがあ
ると 思います。

**raw** adjective
= なま(の)・ 生(の)

**razor** noun
= かみそり

**razor blade** noun
= かみそりのは・ かみそりの 刃

**reach** verb
• (to arrive at) = つく・ 着く
we reached the town at midnight =
よる じゅうにじに まちに つき
ました。・ 夜 十二時に 町に 着
きました。

• (to be delivered to) = とどく・ 届く
the letter never reached him = てがみ
は かれに とどきませんでした。
・ 手紙は 彼に 届きませんでし
た。

• (by stretching)
to reach up = てを のばす・ 手を
伸ばす
I can't reach the shelf = たなに てが
とどきません。・ 棚に 手が 届き
ません。

• (to come to) = たっする・ 達する
to reach a decision = けつろんに
たっする・ 結論に 達する

• (to contact by phone)
I can be reached at this number =
この でんわばんごうに います。
・ この 電話番号に います。

**reach out** = てを のばす・ 手を
伸ばす

**react** verb
= はんのうする・ 反応する

**read** verb
= よむ・ 読む
difficult to read = よみにくい・ 読み
にくい
to read to someone = だれかに よみ
あげる・ 誰かに 読み上げる

**read out**
to read out the names = なまえを よ
みあげる・ 名前を 読み上げる

**read through**
= よみとおす・ 読み通す

**reading** noun
= どくしょ・ 読書

**ready** adjective
• (prepared) = よういが できている
・ 用意が できている
to get ready = じゅんびする・ 準備
する
to get a meal ready = りょうりする
・ 料理する

• (happy)
I'm ready to help at anytime = いつで
も よろこんで てつだいます。・
いつでも 喜んで 手伝います。

**real** adjective
• (not imagined) = ほんとう(の)・ 本
当(の)

• (not artificial) = ほんもの(の)・ 本物
(の)
are they real diamonds? = その ダイ
ヤは ほんものですか。・ その
ダイヤは 本物ですか。

• it's a real shame = ほんとうに ざん
ねんです。・ 本当に 残念です。

**reality** noun
= じじつ・ 事実

**realize** verb
= きが つく・ 気が 付く
I didn't realize (that) Mr Lindsay was
your boss = リンジーさんが あな
たの ボスとは しりませんで
した。・ リンジーさんが あな
たの ボスとは 知りませんでし
た。

**really** adverb
= とても
it's really easy to make = とても つく
りやすいです。・ とても 作りや
すいです。
what really happened? = じっさいは
どうしましたか。・ 実際は どう
しましたか。
really? = ほんとうですか。・ 本当
ですか。

**rear**
**1** noun
= うしろ・ 後ろ
**2** verb
= そだてる・ 育てる

**R**

**reason** noun
= りゆう・理由
tell me the reason why = どうしてか おしえてください。・どうしてか 教えてください。

**reassure** verb
= あんしんさせる・安心させる

**receipt** noun
= りょうしゅうしょ・領収書
a till receipt = レシート

**receive** verb
• (to get) = もらう
we received a letter from the teacher = せんせいから てがみを もらいました。・先生から 手紙を もらいました。
• (to meet) = むかえる・迎える
to be well received = かんげいを うける・歓迎を 受ける

**recent** adjective
= さいきん(の)・最近(の)

**recently** adverb
= さいきん・最近

**reception** noun
• (in a hotel, a hospital, a company)
= うけつけ・受付
ask at (the) reception = うけつけで きいてください。・受付で 聞いてください。
• (a formal event)
= かんげいかい・歓迎会

**receptionist** noun
= うけつけの ひと・受付の 人

**recipe** noun
= りょうりの つくりかた・料理の 作り方

**recognize** verb
= わかる・分かる

**recommend** verb
= すいせんする・推薦する

**record**
**1** noun
• (information)
(historical, public) = きろく・記録
(personal, career) = けいれき・経歴
medical records = カルテ
• (for playing music)
= レコード
• (in sport)
= きろく・記録

to break the world record = せかい きろくを やぶる・世界記録を 破る
**2** verb
(information) = きろくを とる・記録を とる
(audio) = ろくおんする・録音する
(video) = ろくがする・録画する

**recorder** noun ▶ 180
= リコーダー

**recover** verb
= かいふくする・回復する
to recover from an illness = びょうきが なおる・病気が 治る

**recycle** verb
= リサイクルする

**red** adjective
= あかい・赤い
to go red, to turn red = あかく なる・赤く なる
red hair = あかげ・赤毛

**red-haired** adjective
= あかげ(の)・赤毛(の)

**reduce** verb
to reduce prices = ねだんを さげる・値段を 下げる
to reduce the number of employees = しょくいんを へらす・職員を 減らす
to reduce speed = スピードを おとす・スピードを 落とす

**reduction** noun
(in prices) = ねさげ・値下げ
(in numbers) = げんしょう・減少

**redundant** adjective (British English)
to be made redundant = かいこされる・解雇される

**referee** noun
(in sports) = しんぱんいん・審判員
(when applying for a job) = すいせんしゃ・推薦者

**reflection** noun
= はんしゃ・反射

**refreshed** adjective
= すっきりした

**refrigerator** noun
= れいぞうこ・冷蔵庫

**refugee** noun
= なんみん・難民

**refuse¹** *verb*
= ことわる・断る
to refuse to do ..... = volitional form
of verb + と ▶ **191**
to refuse to listen = きこうと しない
・ 聞こうと しない
to refuse to stop = とまろうと しな
い・ 止まろうと しない
to refuse to pay = はらおうと しな
い・ 払おうと しない

**refuse²** *noun (British English)*
= ごみ

**regards** *noun*
please give Monica my regards = モ
ニカさんに よろしく つたえて
ください。・ モニカさんに よろ
しく 伝えてください。

**region** *noun*
= ちほう・ 地方

**regional** *adjective*
= ちほう(の)・ 地方(の)

**register** *noun*
= しゅっせきぼ・ 出席簿
to take the register = しゅっせきを
とる・ 出席を とる

**regret** *verb*
= こうかいする・ 後悔する
I regret changing my mind = きが か
わった ことを こうかいしてい
ます。・ 気が 変わった ことを
後悔しています。
I regret that I won't be able to take part
= ざんねんですが、さんか でき
ません。・ 残念ですが、参加 で
きません。

**regular** *adjective*
= きそくてき(な)・ 規則的(な)

**regularly** *adverb*
= きそくてきに・ 規則的に

**rehearsal** *noun*
= リハーサル

**rehearse** *verb*
= リハーサルを する

**reject** *verb*
= ことわる・ 断る
to reject advice = アドバイスを こと
わる・ アドバイスを 断る
to reject a candidate = りっこうほ し
ゃを みとめない・ 立候補者を
認めない

**relationship** *noun*
= かんけい・ 関係
to have a good relationship = いい
かんけいに ある・ いい 関係に
ある
she has a good relationship with her
parents = かのじょは ごりょうし
んと いいかんけいに あります。
・ 彼女は ご両親と いい 関係に
あります。

**relative** *noun*
= しんせき・ 親戚

**relax** *verb*
= くつろぐ

**relaxed** *adjective*
= くつろいだ

**relay race** *noun*
= リレー

**release** *verb*
(*person*) = じゆうに する・ 自由に
する
(*information*) = こうひょうする・ 公
表する

**reliable** *adjective*
a reliable person = しんらいできる
ひと・ 信頼できる 人
a reliable car = たよりに なる くる
ま・ 頼りに なる 車

**relieved** *adjective*
= あんしんした・ 安心した

**religion** *noun*
= しゅうきょう・ 宗教

**religious education, RE**
(*British English*) *noun*
= しゅうきょうの べんきょう・
宗教の 勉強

**rely** *verb*
• (*to depend on*) = たよる・ 頼る
• (*to count on*) = しんらいする・ 信頼
する
we can rely on him = かれは しんら
い できます。・ 彼は 信頼 でき
ます。

**remain** *verb*
= のこる・ 残る

**remark** *noun*
= はつげん・ 発言

**remarkable** *adjective*
= いちじるしい・ 著しい

**remember** *verb*
= おぼえる・ 覚える

**R**

do you remember her? = かのじょ を おぼえていますか。・ 彼女を 覚えていますか。

I remember writing down the address = じゅうしょを かいたのを おぼえています。・ 住所を 書いたの を 覚えています。

to remember to... = わすれずに...・ 忘れずに...

to remember to post the letter = わすれずに てがみを だす・ 忘れず に 手紙を 出す

to remember to turn off the lights = わすれずに でんきを けす・ 忘れずに 電気を 消す

**remind** verb

(to remind to do something) = わすれ ない ように いう・ 忘れない よ うに 言う

to remind someone to buy stamps = だれかに きってを かう ことを わすれない ように いう・ 誰か に 切手を 買う ことを 忘れない ように 言う

(to bring something from the past to mind) = おもいだす・ 思い出す

that reminds me of home = それは うちを おもいださせます。・ それ は 家を 思い出させます。

**remote control** noun
= リモコン

**remove** verb
(object) = とりのぞく・ 取り除く
(clothing) = ぬぐ・ 脱ぐ

**rent**
1 verb
= かりる・ 借りる
to rent an apartment = アパートを かりる・ アパートを 借りる
2 noun
= やちん・ 家賃
rent out = かす・ 貸す

**repair** verb
= なおす・ 直す
to have a bicycle repaired = じてんしゃを なおして もらう・ 自転車 を 直して もらう

**repeat** verb
• (to say again) = くりかえす・ 繰り 返す
• to repeat a year = りゅうねんする・ 留年する

**replace** verb
= かえる・ 代える・ 換える

**reply**
1 verb
= へんじする・ 返事する
2 noun
= へんじ・ 返事
to write a reply = へんじを かく・ 返 事を 書く

**report**
1 verb
• (to tell about) = ほうこくする・ 報 告する
(to police, emergency services) = つう ほうする・ 通報する
to report an accident = じこを つう ほうする・ 事故を 通報する
• (in the news)
to report on an event = できごとを ほうどうする・ 出来事を 報道 する
• (to complain about)
to report the noise = そうおんを う ったえる・ 騒音を 訴える
2 noun
• (in the news)
= ほうどう・ 報道
• (an official document)
= ほうこくしょ・ 報告書
• (British English)
(from school)
= つうちひょう・ 通知表

**report card** noun (US English)
= つうちひょう・ 通知表

**reporter** noun
= きしゃ・ 記者

**represent** verb
= だいひょうする・ 代表する

**representative** noun
= だいひょう・ 代表

**republic** noun
= きょうわこく・ 共和国

**request** noun
= おねがい・ お願い ▶ 189

**rescue** verb
(from danger) = すくう・ 救う

**resemble** verb
= にている・ 似ている
to resemble each other = おたがいに にている・ お互いに 似ている

**resentment** *noun*
= うらみ・恨み

**reservation** *noun*
= よやく・予約

**reserve** *verb*
= よやくする・予約する

**resign** *verb*
= じにんする・辞任する

**resist** *verb*
= ていこうする・抵抗する

**respect**
**1** *verb*
= そんけいする・尊敬する
**2** *noun*
= そんけい・尊敬

**responsibility** *noun*
= せきにん・責任

**responsible** *adjective*
• (*trustworthy*) = せきにんかんが ある・責任感が ある
• (*the cause of*)
  he is responsible for the accident = じこは かれの せいです。・事故は 彼の せいです。
• (*in charge*)
  I am responsible for the school timetable = がっこうの じかんわりを たんとうしています。・学校の 時間割を 担当しています。

**rest**
**1** *noun*
• (*what is left*)
  = のこり・残り
  we spent the rest of the time in the garden = のこりの じかんを にわ ですごしました。・残りの 時間 を 庭で 過ごしました。
• (*a break*)
  = きゅうけい・休憩
  to have a rest = きゅうけいする・休憩する
**2** *verb*
= やすむ・休む

**restaurant** *noun*
= レストラン

**result** *noun*
= けっか・結果
the exam results = しけんの けっか・試験の 結果
as a result of an accident = じ この ため・事故の ため

**résumé** *noun* (*US English*)
a résumé = りれきしょ・履歴書

**retire** *verb*
= たいしょくする・退職する

> **!** *Note that this can also refer to giving up ones job at any point even well before retirement age*

**return** *verb*
• (*to go|come back*) = もどる・戻る
• (*from abroad, to one's home*) = かえる・帰る
• (*to give|take back*) = かえす・返す
  can you return my book? = ほんを かえしてください。・本を 返し てください。
• (*to send back*) = おくりかえす・送り返す
  to return faulty goods (by post) = (ゆうびんで)ふりょうひんを おくりかえす・(郵便で)不良品を 送り返す
• (*to start again*)
  to return to work = しごとに もどる・仕事に 戻る
  to return to school (after a holiday) = (やすみの あと)がっこうが また はじまる・(休みの 後)学校が また 始まる

**return ticket** *noun*
= おうふく(きっぷ)・往復(切符)

**revenge** *noun*
= ふくしゅう・復讐
to get one's revenge = ふくしゅうする・復讐する

**revolution** *noun*
= かくめい・革命

**reward**
**1** *noun*
= ほうび・褒美
**2** *verb*
= ほうびを あたえる・褒美を 与える

**rewind** *verb*
= まきもどす・巻戻す

**rhinoceros, rhino** *noun*
= さい

**rhythm** *noun*
= リズム

**rib** *noun*
= ろっこつ・肋骨

R

**rice** *noun*
  (*uncooked*) = こめ・米
  (*cooked*) = ごはん・ご飯

> ! *Rice which is served on a plate is often referred to as* ライス

**rice field** *noun*
  = たんぼ・田んぼ

**rich** *adjective*
  = かねもち(の)・金持ち(の)
  to get rich = かねもちに なる・金持ちに なる

**rid: to get rid of** *verb*
  = とりのぞく・取り除く

**ride**
**1** *verb*
  to ride, to go riding = じょうばを する・乗馬を する
  to ride a horse = じょうばを する・乗馬を する
  to be riding a bike = じてんしゃに のっている・自転車に 乗っている
**2** *noun*
  to go for a ride
  (*in a car*) = ドライブに いく・ドライブに 行く
  (*on a bicycle*) = サイクリングに いく・サイクリングに 行く
  (*on a horse*) = じょうばに でかける・乗馬に でかける

**ridiculous** *adjective*
  = ばかげた

**rifle** *noun*
  = ライフル

**right**
**1** *adjective*
  • (*not left*) = みぎ(の)・右(の)
  right hand = みぎて・右手
  right handed = みぎきき・右利き
  • (*honest, good*) = いい
  it's not right to steal = ぬすみは よくないです。・盗みは 良くないです。
  to do the right thing = いい ことを する
  • (*correct*) = ただしい・正しい
  the right answer = ただしい こたえ・正しい 答え
  is this the right direction? = このほうこうは ただしいですか。・この方向は 正しいですか。

  she's right = かのじょの いう とおりです。・彼女の 言う とおりです。
  that's right = その とおりです。
**2** *noun*
  • (*the direction*)
  the right = みぎ・右
  please take the first street on the right = さいしょのみちをみぎに はいってください。・最初の 道を 右に 入ってください。
  • (*what one is entitled to*)
  a right = けんり・権利
  to have a right to be educated = きょういくをうけるけんりが ある・教育を 受ける権利が ある
  human rights = じんけん・人権
**3** *adverb*
  = みぎに・右に
  to turn right = みぎに まがる・右に 曲がる

**ring**
**1** *verb*
  • (*British English*)
  (*to phone*) = でんわする・電話する
  to ring for a taxi = でんわで タクシーを よぶ・電話で タクシーを 呼ぶ
  • (*to make a sound*) = ならす・鳴らす
  to ring the bell = ベルを ならす・ベルを 鳴らす
  the doorbell rang = ベルが なりました。・ベルが 鳴りました。
**2** *noun*
  • (*a piece of jewellery*)
  = ゆびわ・指輪
  wedding ring = けっこんゆびわ・結婚指輪
  engagement ring = こんやくゆびわ・婚約指輪
  • (*a circle*)
  = えん・円
  • (*in a circus*)
  = リング
  **ring up** (*British English*) = でんわする・電話する

**ringtone** *noun*
  = ちゃくメロ・着メロ

**rinse** *verb*
  = すすぐ

**ripe** *adjective*
  = じゅくした・熟した

**rise** *verb*
- (*if it's smoke, water, a price*) = あがる ・ 上がる
- (*if it's a plane*) = じょうしょうする ・ 上昇する
- (*if it's the sun*) = のぼる ・ 昇る

**risk**
**1** *noun*
(*danger*) = きけん ・ 危険
the business is at risk = かいしゃは きけんに さらされています。・ 会社は 危険に さらされています。

**river** *noun*
= かわ ・ 川
(*flowing into the sea*) = かこう ・ 河口

**riverbank** *noun*
= かわぎし ・ 川岸

**road** *noun*
= どうろ ・ 道路

**road sign** *noun*
= どうろひょうしき ・ 道路標識

**roadworks** *noun*
= どうろこうじ ・ 道路工事

**roar** *noun*
(*if it's a lion*) = ほえごえ ・ 吠え声
(*if it's a crowd*) = どよめき
(*if it's an engine*) = とどろき

**roast**
**1** *verb*
= オーブンで やく ・ オーブンで 焼く
**2** *adjective*
to eat roast beef = ローストビーフ を たべる ・ ローストビーフを 食べる

**rob** *verb*
= ぬすむ ・ 盗む

**robbery** *noun*
= ごうとう ・ 強盗

**robin** *noun*
= こまどり

**robot** *noun*
= ロボット

**rock** *noun*
- (*the material*)
  = がんせき ・ 岩石
- (*a large stone*)
  = いわ ・ 岩
- (*music*)
  = ロック

**rock climbing** *noun*
= ロッククライミング

**rocket** *noun*
= ロケット

**role** *noun*
= やく ・ 役

**roll**
**1** *verb*
= ころがる ・ 転がる
the ball rolled under a car = ボールは くるまの したに ころがりました。・ ボールは 車の 下に 転がりました。
**2** *noun*
- (*of paper, cloth, plastic*)
  = まき ・ 巻
  a roll of film = フィルム いっぽん ・ フィルム 一本
- (*bread*)
  = ロールパン
- (*US English*)
  (*at school*)
  to call the roll = しゅっせきを とる ・ 出席を 取る
**roll about, roll around**
(*if it's an object*) = ころがる ・ 転がる
**roll over**
she rolled over (in bed) = かのじょは (ベッドで)ねがえりをうちました。・ 彼女は(ベッドで)寝返りを うちました。
**roll up** = まく ・ 巻く
to roll up a newspaper = しんぶんを まく ・ 新聞を 巻く

**roller coaster** *noun*
= ジェットコースター

**roller-skate** *noun*
= ローラースケートの くつ ・ ローラースケートの 靴

**roller-skating** *noun*
= ローラースケート

**romantic** *adjective*
= ロマンチック(な)

**roof** *noun*
= やね ・ 屋根
(*if used for activity*) = おくじょう ・ 屋上

**room** *noun*
- = へや ・ 部屋
  (*for sleeping*) = しんしつ ・ 寝室

**R**

(*for teaching*) = きょうしつ・教室
(*for meetings*) = かいぎしつ・会議
室
• (*space*)
= ばしょ・場所
to make room = ばしょを あける・
場所を 空ける

**rooster** *noun*
year of the rooster = とりどし・酉
年

**root** *noun*
= ね・根

**rope** *noun*
= ロープ

**rose** *noun*
= ばら

**rotten** *adjective*
= くさった・腐った

**rough** *adjective*
• (*not smooth*) = あらい・粗い
• (*not gentle*) = あらっぽい・荒っぽ
い
• (*tough*) = ちあんの わるい・治安の
悪い
to live in a rough area = ちあんの
わるい ちいきに すむ・治安の
悪い 地域に 住む
• (*not exact, precise*)
a rough figure = おおまかな すうじ
・大まかな 数字
• (*difficult*) = たいへん (な)・大変
(な)
I had a rough time yesterday = きの
うは たいへんでした。・昨日は
大変でした。
• (*caused by bad weather*)
a rough sea = あれた うみ・荒れた
海

**round**

> ! Often round occurs in
> combinations with verbs. For more
> information, see the note at around.

**1** *preposition*
to be sitting round a table = テーブル
の まわりに すわっている・テ
ーブルの 周りに 座っている
to sail round the world = せかいいっ
しゅうの こうかいを する・世
界一周の 航海を する
to go round Oxford = オックスフォ
ードめぐりを する・オックス
フォード巡りを する

**2** *adverb*
to go round and round = ぐるぐる
まわる・ぐるぐる 回る
to go round to John's house = ジョン
さんの うちへ いく・ジョンさ
んの 家へ 行く
to invite someone round = だれかを
うちに よぶ・誰かを 家に 呼ぶ
**3** *noun*
(*in a quiz, sports*) = ラウンド
**4** *adjective*
= まるい・丸い

**roundabout** *noun*
• (*British English*)
(*in a fair*)
= メリーゴーラウンド
• (*for traffic*) Roundabouts are often
referred to as ロータリー or
ラウンドアバウト but there is
no real Japanese equivalent.

**route** *noun*
= ルート
a bus route = バスの ろせん・バス
の 路線

**routine** *noun*
daily routine = にっか・日課

**row¹**
**1** *noun*
• = れつ・列
the pupils were sitting in rows = せい
とは れつに なって すわってい
ました。・生徒は 列に なって
座っていました。
• (*when talking about frequency*)
to be absent five days in a row = つづ
けて いつか やすむ・続けて
五日 休む
**2** *verb*
= こぐ・漕ぐ
(*as a sport*) = ボートレースを する

**row²** *noun* (*British English*)
= けんか
to have a row (with someone) = (だれ
かと) けんかを する・(誰かと)
けんかを する

**rowing** *noun*
= ボートレース

**rowing boat** (*British English*),
**rowboat** (*US English*) *noun*
= ボート

**royal** *adjective*
(*of the Japanese royal family*) = こう
しつ(の)・皇室(の)

(*of other royal families*) = おうしつ
（の）・王室(の)

**rub** *verb*
to rub one's eyes = めを こする ・
目を こする
**rub out** (*British English*) = けす ・ 消す
to rub out a mistake = まちがいを
けす ・ 間違いを 消す

**rubber** *noun*
• (*the material*)
= ゴム
• (*British English*)
(*an eraser*)
= けしゴム ・ 消しゴム

**rubbish** *noun* (*British English*)
• (*refuse*)
= ごみ
• (*poor quality goods*)
= がらくた

**rubbish bin** *noun* (*British English*)
= ごみばこ ・ ごみ箱

**rucksack** *noun*
= リュックサック

**rude** *adjective*
• (*not polite*) = しつれい(な) ・ 失礼
(な)
she was rude to the teacher = かのじ
ょは せんせいに しつれいでし
た。・ 彼女は 先生に 失礼でし
た。
• (*vulgar*) = げひん(な) ・ 下品(な)
a rude word = げひんな ことば ・
下品な 言葉

**rug** *noun*
= じゅうたん

**rugby** *noun*
= ラグビー

**ruin**
**1** *verb*
• (*to spoil*) = だいなしに する ・ 台無
しに する
to ruin a meal = しょくじを だいな
しに する ・ 食事を 台無しに す
る
Geoffrey ruined the atmosphere = ジ
ェフリーさんの せいで ざが し
らけました。・ ジェフリーさん
の せいで 座が しらけました。
• (*to damage*) = だめに する
you'll ruin your shoes = くつを だめ
に します。・ 靴を だめに しま
す。

to be ruined = だめに なる
**2** *noun*
= はいきょ ・ 廃虚

**rule**
**1** *noun*
(*of a game*) = ルール
(*in a school, an organization*) = きそく
・ 規則
it's against the rules = きそくいはん
です。・ 規則違反です。
**2** *verb*
(*if it's a leader*) = しはいする ・ 支配
する
(*if it's a king, queen*) = くんりんする
・ 君臨する

**ruler** *noun*
= じょうぎ ・ 定規

**rumour** (*British English*), **rumor**
(*US English*) *noun*
= うわさ ・ 噂

**run**
**1** *verb*
• to run = はしる ・ 走る
to run after someone = だれかの あ
とを おいかける ・ 誰かの 後を
追いかける
to run across the street = みちを
はしって わたる ・ 道を 走って
渡る
to run in a race = きょうそうに さん
かする ・ 競争に 参加する
• (*from danger*) = にげる ・ 逃げる
• (*to manage*) = けいえいする ・ 経営
する
• (*to work, to operate*) = さどうする ・
作動する
the car runs on unleaded petrol = こ
の くるまは むえんガソリンで
はしります。・ この 車は 無鉛ガ
ソリンで 走ります。
the system is running well = システ
ムは うまく いっています。・
システムは うまく 行っていま
す。
• (*to organize*) = おこなう ・ 行う
to run a competition = コンクールを
おこなう ・ コンクールを 行う
• (*when talking about transport*) = うご
く ・ 動く
the buses don't run after midnight =
よる じゅうにじいこうは バス
が うごきません。・ 夜十二時以
降は バスが 動きません。

**R**

- (to flow) = ながれる・流れる
- (to fill with water)
  to run a bath = おふろに　おゆを　いれる・お風呂に　お湯を　入れる
- (to come off) = おちる・落ちる
- (in an election) = りっこうほする・立候補する
  to run for president = だいとうりょうせんに　しゅつばする・大統領選に　出馬する
- (other uses)
  to be running late = おくれている・遅れている
  to be running a temperature = ねつがある・熱が　ある

**2** noun
= ランニング
to go for a run = はしる・走る
**run about, run around** = はしゃぎまわる・はしゃぎ回る
**run away** = にげる・逃げる
**run off** = にげる・逃げる

**runner** noun
= ランナー

**rush**
**1** verb
- (to hurry) = いそぐ・急ぐ
  to rush to finish one's homework = しゅくだいを　いそいで　すます・宿題を　急いで　済ます
  to rush out of the house = いえから　ころがりでる・家から　転がり出る
  to be rushed to the hospital = びょういんに　いそいで　はこばれる・病院に　急いで　運ばれる
- (to put pressure on) = いそがせる・急がせる

**2** noun
to be in a rush = いそいでいる・急いでいる
to do one's homework in a rush = いそいで　しゅくだいを　する・急いで　宿題を　する

**rush hour** noun
= ラッシュアワー

**Russia** noun ▶ 172
= ロシア

**rusty** adjective
= さびた

# Ss

**sad** adjective
= かなしい・悲しい
she looks sad = かのじょは　かなしそうです。・彼女は　悲しそうです。▶ 178

**saddle** noun
(for horse) = くら
(for bicycle) = サドル

**safe**
**1** adjective
- (without risk) = あんぜん(な)・安全(な)
  a safe place = あんぜんな　ばしょ・安全な　場所
  it's not safe for children = こどもには　あぶないです。・子供には　危ないです。
  is it safe to go there? = あそこの　ちあんは　いいですか。・あそこの治安は　いいですか。
- (free from danger)
  to feel safe = あんしん　できる・安心　できる
  your car is safe here = くるまは　ここだと　あんぜんです。・車は　ここだと　安全です。
- (out of danger)
  I'm glad you're safe = ぶじで　よかったです。・無事で　良かったです。

**2** noun
= きんこ・金庫

**safety** noun
= あんぜん・安全

**Sagittarius** noun
= いてざ・射手座

**sail**
**1** noun
= ほ・帆
to set sail = こうかいする・航海する

**2** verb
to sail around the world = せかい　いっしゅうの　ふなたびに　でる・世界　一周の　船旅に　出る
to go sailing = ヨットあそびする・ヨット遊びする

**sailing** *noun*
= ヨットあそび・ヨット遊び

**sailing boat** (*British English*),
  **sailboat** (*US English*) *noun*
= ヨット

**sailor** *noun*
  (*general*) = ふなのり・船乗り
  (*naval*) = すいへい・水兵

**saint** *noun*
= せいじん・聖人

**salad** *noun*
= サラダ

**salary** *noun*
= きゅうりょう・給料

**sale** *noun*
• on sale
  (*available*) = はつばいちゅう・発
  売中
  (*special offer*) = やすうり・安売り
  for sale = うりもの・売り物
• the sales = セール

**sales assistant** *noun* (*British
  English*)
= てんいん・店員

**salmon** *noun*
= さけ・鮭

**salt** *noun*
= しお・塩

**same**
**1** *adjective*
= おなじ・同じ
  she's got the same coat as me = かの
   じょは わたしと おなじ コート
   をもっています。・彼女は 私と
   同じ コートを 持っています。
  they go to the same school = かれら
   は おなじ がっこうに かよって
   います。・彼らは 同じ 学校に
   通っています。
  it's the same as the car I had before =
   まえ もっていた くるまと おな
   じです。・前 持っていた 車と
   同じです。
  it's all the same to me = かまいませ
   ん。
  the houses all look the same = ぜんぶ
   の いえが おなじに みえます。・
   全部の 家が 同じに 見えます。
  people are the same everywhere =
   ひとは どこでも おなじです。・
   人は どこでも 同じです。

  it's the same as ever = いつもと お
   なじです。・いつもと 同じです。
**2** *pronoun*
  the same = おなじ・同じ
  I'll have the same = わたしも おなじ
   に します。・私も 同じに しま
   す。
  to do the same as the others = ほかの
   ひとと おなじに する・外の 人
   と 同じに する

**sand** *noun*
= すな・砂

**sandal** *noun*
= サンダル

**sandwich** *noun*
= サンドイッチ
  a ham sandwich = ハムサンド

**Santa (Claus)** *noun*
= サンタクロース *Children often
  call Santa* サンタさん

**sardine** *noun*
= いわし

**satellite TV** *noun*
= えいせいほうそう・衛星放送

**satisfactory** *adjective*
= いい

**satisfied** *adjective*
= まんぞくしている・満足してい
  る

**Saturday** *noun* ▶ **174**
= どようび・土曜日

**sauce** *noun*
= ソース

**saucepan** *noun*
= なべ

**saucer** *noun*
= うけざら・受け皿

**sausage** *noun*
= ソーセージ

**save** *verb*
• (*to rescue*) = すくう・救う
  I saved his life = かれの いのちを た
   すけました。・彼の 命を 助けま
   した。
• (*to avoid spending*)
  to save = せつやくする・節約する
  to save money = ちょきんする・貯
   金する
• (*to avoid wasting*)
  to save time = じかんを せつやくす
   る・時間を 節約する

**S**

• (to keep) = とっておく・取っておく

to save a piece of cake (for someone) = (だれかに)ケーキを とっておく・(誰かに)ケーキを 取っておく

to save a file = ファイルを セーブする

**savings** noun
= ちょきん・貯金

**saw** noun
= のこぎり

**saxophone** noun ▶ 180
= サキソホーン

**say** verb
= いう・言う

to say goodbye = さよならという・さよならと 言う

she says (that) she can't go out tonight = かのじょは こんばん でかけられないと いいました。・彼女は 今晩 出かけられないと 言いました。

he said to wait here = かれは ここに いてと いいました。・彼は ここに いてと 言いました。

they say she's very rich = かのじょは おかねもちだと いわれています。・彼女は お金持ちだと 言われています。

I can't say who did it = 誰が やったか いえません。・誰が やったか 言えません。

she wouldn't say = かのじょは いって くれませんでした。・彼女は 言って くれませんでした。▶ 179

what does the message say? = メッセージは なんですか。・メッセージは 何ですか。

it says here that smoking is not allowed = きんえんと ここに かいて あります。・禁煙と ここに 書いて あります。

I'd say she was forty = かのじょは よんじゅっさい くらいだと おもいます。・彼女は 四十才くらいだと 思います。

let's say there are twenty people come to the party = にじゅうにん くらい パーティーに くるとしてかんがえましょう。・二十人 くらい パーティーに 来ると して 考えましょう。

**scandal** noun
= スキャンダル

**scare** verb
= こわがらす・怖がらす

you scared me! = びっくりしました。

scare away = おどかして おいはらう・おどかして 追い払う

**scared** adjective
= こわい・恐い

**scarf** noun
(long, for warmth) = マフラー
(square, as fashion accessory) = スカーフ

**scenery** noun
= けしき・景色

**school**

> ! Note that the Japanese school system is different ▶ 185

**1** noun
= がっこう・学校
to be at school = がっこうに かよっている・学校に 通っている

**2** adjective
= がっこうの・学校の
a school bus = スクールバス

**schoolbag** noun
= かばん Japanese children at elementary school carry a regulation satchel called a ランドセル

**schoolboy** noun
= だんしせいと・男子生徒

**schoolgirl** noun
= じょしせいと・女子生徒

**schoolwork** noun
= がっこうのべんきょう・学校の勉強

**science** noun
(at university) = かがく・科学
to study science = かがくを べんきょうする・科学を 勉強する
(in school) = りか・理科

**scientist** noun
= かがくしゃ・科学者

**scissors** noun
= はさみ

**score** verb
to score a goal = とくてんする・得点する

**Scorpio** *noun*
= さそりざ・さそり座

**Scotland** *noun* ▶ **172**
= スコットランド

**scratch**
**1** *verb*
- (*when itchy*) = かく
  to scratch one's arm = うでを かく・
  腕を かく
- (*with nails*) = ひっかく・引っかく
  (*on a bush, thorns*) = ひっかかる・
  引っかかる
- (*to mark, to damage*) = きずつける・
  傷つける
**2** *noun*
= すりきず・擦り傷

**scream** *verb*
= ひめいを あげる・悲鳴を あげ
る

**screen** *noun*
(*at cinema*) = スクリーン
(*on TV, computer*) = がめん・画面

**screw** *noun*
= ねじ

**sea** *noun*
= うみ・海
beside the sea, by the sea = うみぞい
で・海沿いで

**seagull** *noun*
= かもめ

**seal** *noun*
= とど

**search** *verb*
- = さがす・探す
  to search for someone = だれかを
  さがす・誰かを 探す
- (*to examine a place*) = そうさくする
  ・捜索する
- (*Internet etc.*) = けんさく(する)・
  検索(する)

**seashell** *noun*
= かいがら・貝殻

**seasick** *adjective*
to be seasick, to get seasick = ふなよ
いに なる・船酔いに なる

**seaside** *noun*
at the seaside = かいがんで・海岸
で

to go to the seaside = うみに いく・
海に 行く

**season** *noun*
= きせつ・季節

**seat** *noun*
- (*a chair, a bench*)
  = いす・椅子
  to have a seat = すわる・座る
- (*on transport, in a theatre*)
  = せき・席

**seatbelt** *noun*
= シートベルト

**second**
**1** *adjective*
(*in a sequence*) = にばん(め)・二番
(め)
(*of a number of items*) = ふたつめ・
二つ目
(*of a number of times*) = にかいめ・
二回目
this is the second time I've called =
この でんわは にかいめです。・
この 電話は 二回目です。
the second Monday of each month =
まいつき だいに げつようび・
毎月 第二 月曜日
**2** *noun*
- (*in a series*)
  = にばんめ・二番目
- (*in time*)
  a second = いちびょう・一秒
  (*a very short time*) = しゅんかん・瞬
  間
- (*in dates*) = ふつか・二日 ▶ **174**
  the second of May = ごがつふつか・
  五月二日
**3** *adverb*
to come second = にいに なる・二
位に なる

**secondary school** *noun* (*British
English*)
= ちゅうとうこうとうがっこう・
中等高等学校 *The general word*
がっこう *is more often used
unless you have to be really
specific.* ▶ **185**

**second-hand** *adjective*
= ちゅうこ(の)・中古(の)
second hand car = ちゅうこしゃ・
中古車
second hand goods = ちゅうこひん
・中古品

**S**

## secret
**1** *adjective*
= ひみつ(の)・秘密(の)
**2** *noun*
= ひみつ・秘密
to tell someone a secret = だれかに ひみつを いう・誰かに 秘密を 言う
**3** in secret = ないしょで・内緒で

## secretary *noun*
= ひしょ・秘書

## see *verb*
• = みる・見る
what can you see? = なにが みえますか・何が 見えますか。
I can't see = みえません・見えません。
he saw the people running = かれは ひとびとが はしっているのを みました・彼は 人々が 走っているのを 見ました。
do they see each other often? = かれらは よく あいますか・彼らは よく 会いますか。
see you tomorrow! = また あした・また 明日。
I'll go and see = みに いきます・見に 行きます。
• (*to accompany*)
I'll see you home = うちまで おくります・家まで 送ります。

## seem *verb*
• (*to appear*)
she seems happy = かのじょは しあわせ みたいです・彼女は 幸せ みたいです。
Zoe seems annoyed = ゾイさんは いらいらしている みたいです。
he seems tired = かれは つかれている みたいです・彼は 疲れている みたいです。
they seem to be looking for someone = かれらは だれかを さがしている みたいです・彼らは 誰かを 捜している みたいです。
• (*when talking about one's impressions*)
= 〜と おもう・〜と 思う
it seems (that) there are a lot of problems = もんだいが たくさん あると おもいます・問題が たくさん あると 思います。
it seems strange (to me) = へんだと おもいます・変だと 思います。

> ! *Note that there are also several other ways to say 'seems' in Japanese.*

## seldom *adverb*
= めったに + negative
I seldom drive = めったに うんてん しません・めったに 運転しません。

## self-confident ▶ confident

## selfish *adjective*
= わがまま(な)

## sell *verb*
= うる・売る
to sell books to the students = がくせいに ほんを うる・学生に 本を 売る
he sold me his car = かれは わたしに くるまを うりました・彼は 私に 車を 売りました。
water is sold in bottles = みずは びんで うられています・水は 瓶で 売られています。
do you sell bread? = パンを うっていますか・パンを 売っていますか。

## send *verb*
= おくる・送る
to send a package to someone = だれかに こづつみを おくる・誰かに 小包を 送る
he sent her a letter = かれは かのじょに てがみを おくりました・彼は 彼女に 手紙を 送りました。
to send a pupil home from school = せいとを がっこうから うちに かえす・生徒を 学校から 家に 返す
send back = おくりかえす・送り返す
send for
to send for the doctor = おいしゃさんを よぶ・お医者さんを 呼ぶ ▶ 189
to send for some goods = しなものを たのむ・品物を 頼む
send on
to send on post = ゆうびんぶつを てんそうする・郵便物を 転送する

## senior high school (*US English*), senior school (*British English*)
*noun*
= こうとうがっこう・高等学校

! *Note that this is often abbreviated to* こうこう ▶ **185**

**sense** noun
- (common) sense = じょうしき・常識
- (allowing one to see, hear, smell etc) = かんかく・感覚
- (a meaning) = いみ・意味
  it doesn't make sense = わかりません。・分かりません。
  it makes sense to prepare properly = ちゃんと じゅんびした ほうが いいです。・ちゃんと 準備した 方が いいです。

**sensible** adjective
(describing a person) = しっかりした
(describing a decision, suggestion) = けんめい(な)・懸命(な)

**sensitive** adjective
(describing a person) = びんかん(な)・敏感(な)
(describing a situation) = きわどい・際どい

**sentence**
**1** noun
- (in grammar) = ぶん・文
- (for a crime)
  a (prison) sentence = せんこく・宣告
**2** verb
  to sentence to one year in prison = ちょうえき いちねんの はんけつを いいわたす・懲役一年の 判決を 言い渡す

**separate**
**1** adjective
  a separate room = べつの へや・別の 部屋
  that is a separate problem = それは べつの もんだいです。・それは 別の 問題です。
**2** verb
- to separate = わける・分ける
- (if it's a couple) = わかれる・別れる

**separated** adjective
= わかれている・別れている

**separately** adverb
= べつべつに・別々に

**September** noun ▶ **174**
= くがつ・九月

**serial** noun
  a TV serial = れんぞく ドラマ・連続ドラマ

**series** noun
= シリーズ

**serious** adjective
- (causing worry) = たいへん(な)・大変(な)
  a serious accident = だいじこ・大事故
  a serious illness = おもい びょうき・重い 病気
- (describing a personality) = しんけん(な)・真剣(な)
- to be serious about going to university = しんけんに だいがくに いくことを かんがえている・真剣に 大学に 行く ことを 考えている

**serve** verb
- (in a shop)
  are you being served? = いらっしゃいませ。
- (food) = だす・出す
- (in sport) = サーブする

**service** noun
- (in a shop, a restaurant) = サービス
- (in a church) = れいはい・礼拝

**service station** noun
= サービスエリア

**S**

**set**
**1** noun
- (a collection)
  a set of keys = かぎ・鍵
  a set of stamps = きっての セット・切手の セット
- (in tennis) = セット
**2** verb
- (to decide on) = きめる・決める
  to set a date = ひにちを きめる・日にちを 決める
- (for a particular time) = セットする
  to set an alarm clock = めざましどけいを セットする・目覚し時計を セットする
  to set a video (British English) = ビデオを セットする
- (in school)

to set homework = しゅくだいを だす・宿題を出す
to set an exam = しけんを つくる・試験を作る
* (to establish)
to set a record = きろくを つくる・記録を作る
* (when talking about a story, a film)
the film is set in Nagoya = なごやの えいがです。・名古屋の 映画です。
* (when talking about the sun) = しずむ・沈む
* (other uses)
to set the table = しょくたくの ようい をする・食卓の 用意をする
to set fire to a house = いえに ひを つける・家に 火を 付ける
to set someone free = だれかを じゆ うにする・誰かを 自由にする

**set off**
* (to leave) = しゅっぱつする・出発する
* (to cause to go off)
to set off fireworks = はなびを うち あげる・花火を 打ち上げる
to set off a bomb = ばくはつさせる・爆発させる
to set off a burglar alarm = ぼうはん アラームを ならす・防犯アラ ームを 鳴らす
**set up** = せつりつする・設立する
to set up a company = かいしゃをせ つりつする・会社を 設立する

**settle** verb
* (to decide on) = きめる・決める
nothing is settled yet = まだ なにも きめていません。・まだ 何も決 めていません。
* (to make one's home) = すみつく・住み着く
**settle down**
* (to calm down) = おちつく・落ち着く
* (to marry) = けっこんする・結婚する

**seven** number ▶ 171, ▶ 181, ▶ 186
(on its own) = ななつ・七つ
(with a counter) = なな・七 しち is also used
seven books = ほん ななさつ・本 七冊
I've got seven = ななつ あります。・七つ あります。

**seventeen** number ▶ 171, ▶ 181
= じゅうなな・十七
じゅうしち is also used

**seventeenth** number
* (in a series) = じゅうななばんめ(の)・十七番目(の)
* (in dates) ▶ 174 = じゅうしちにち・十七日
the seventeenth of May = ごがつじ ゅうしちにち・五月十七日

**seventh** number
* (in a series) = ななばんめ(の)・七番目(の)
* (in dates) ▶ 174 = なのか・七日
the seventh of July = しちがつなの か・七月七日

**seventy** number ▶ 171, ▶ 181
= ななじゅう・七十

**several** determiner
= いくつかの

**severe** adjective
* (serious) = はげしい・激しい
* (harsh) = きびしい・厳しい

**sew** verb
= ぬう・縫う

**sewing** noun
= さいほう・裁縫

**sewing machine** noun
= ミシン

**sex** noun
(gender) = せいべつ・性別
(love-making) = セックス
to have sex = セックスする

**shade** noun
* (out of the sun)
= ひかげ・日陰
to sit in the shade = ひかげに すわる・日陰に 座る
* (a colour)
a shade = いろあい・色合
* (for a lamp)
= ランプの かさ

**shadow** noun
= かげ・陰

**shake** verb
* (to tremble) = ゆれる・揺れる
the building shook with the earthquake = じしんで たてもの が ゆれました。・地震で 建物が 揺れました。
* (to shake something) = ふる・振る

*(to shake a bottle)* = びんを ふる ・ 瓶を 振る

**to shake hands with someone** = だれ かと あくしゅを する ・ 誰かと 握手を する

• *(when saying no)*
**to shake one's head** = あたまを ふる ・ 頭を 振る

• *(with cold, fear, shock)* = ふるえる ・ 震える

**his hands were shaking** = かれは てが ふるえていました。・ 彼は 手が 震えていました。

**shall** *verb*

• *Note that there is no true future tense in Japanese.* ▶ 191
*(when talking about the future)*
**I shall see you next Tuesday** = らいし ゅうの かようびに あいましょ う。・ 来週の 火曜日に 会いまし ょう。

• *(when making suggestions)*
**shall I help you?** = てつだいましょ うか。・ 手伝いましょうか。

**shall we eat out?** = がいしょくし ましょうか。・ 外食しましょう か。

**shame** *noun*

• = はじ ・ 恥

• *(when expressing regret)*
**that's a shame** = ざんねん です。・ 残念です。

**shampoo** *noun*
= シャンプー

**shape** *noun*

• *(a form)*
= かたち ・ 形

**a square shape** = しかくい かたち ・ 四角い 形

**in the shape of a square** = しかくの かたち ・ 四角の 形

• *(when talking about health)*
**he's in good shape** = かれは げんき です。・ 彼は 元気です。

**to get in shape** = うんどうする ・ 運動する

**share**

**1** *verb*
= きょうようする ・ 共用する

**to share a house** = いえを きょうよ うする ・ 家を 共用する

**2** *noun*
= わけまえ ・ 分け前

**to pay one's share** = じぶんの ぶん を はらう ・ 自分の 分を 払う

**share out** *(British English)*
*(amongst others)* = わける ・ 分ける

**shark** *noun*
= さめ

**sharp** *adjective*

• *(used for cutting)* = よく きれる ・ よ く 切れる

• *(with a point)* = するどい ・ 鋭い

• *(sudden)* = きゅう(な) ・ 急(な)
**a sharp bend** = きゅうな カーブ ・ 急な カーブ

• *(intelligent)* = ぬけめの ない ・ 抜け 目の ない

• *(in taste)* = したを さす よう(な) ・ 舌を 刺す よう(な)

**shave** *verb*
= そる

**she** *pronoun*
= かのじょ ・ 彼女 *Note that Japanese prefer to use a name rather than a pronoun*

**she'll be there too** = かのじょもいま す。・ 彼女も います。

**she's intelligent** = かのじょは あた まがいいです。・ 彼女は 頭がい いです。

**sheep** *noun*
= ひつじ ・ 羊

**sheet** *noun*

• *(for a bed)*
= シーツ

• *(a piece)*
*(of paper)* = かみ いちまい ・ 紙 一 枚 ▶ 181
*(of glass)* = ガラス いちまい ・ ガラ ス 一枚

**shelf** *noun*
= たな ・ 棚

**shell** *noun*
*(of an egg, a nut, a crab, a tortoise, a snail)* = から ・ 殻
*(on the beach)* = かいがら ・ 貝殻

**shelter**

**1** *noun*

• *(from rain)*
= あまやどり ・ 雨宿り

• *(for homeless people)*
= しゅうようじょ ・ 収容所

**2** *verb*

• *(to take shelter)* = ひなんする ・ 避難 する

**S**

**shin** *noun*
= むこうずね・向うずね

**shine** *verb*
- (*to give out light*) = ひかる・光る
  (*the sun*) = てる・照る
- (*to point*)
  to shine a torch at someone = だれか
  を かいちゅうでんとうで てら
  す・誰かを懐中電灯で 照らす
- (*to reflect light*) = かがやく・輝く

**ship** *noun*
= ふね・船
a passenger ship = きゃくせん・
客船

**shirt** *noun*
= シャツ

**shiver** *verb*
= ふるえる・震える

**shock**
**1** *noun*
- (*an upsetting experience*)
  = ショック
  to get a shock = ショックを うける
  ・ショックを 受ける
  to give someone a shock = だれかに
  ショックを あたえる・誰かに
  ショックを 与える
- (*the medical state*)
  = ショック
- (*from electricity*)
  = かんでん・感電
  to get a shock = かんでんする・
  感電する
**2** *verb*
- (*to upset*) = ショックを あたえる・
  ショックを 与える

**shoe** *noun*
(*for a person*) = くつ・靴
(*for a horse*) = ていてつ・てい鉄

**shoot** *verb*
- (*using a weapon*) = うつ・撃つ
  to shoot someone = だれかを うつ・
  誰かを 撃つ
  to shoot someone dead = だれかを
  うちころす・誰かを 撃ち殺す
- (*to make*)
  to shoot a film = さつえいする・
  撮影する

**shop**
**1** *noun*
= みせ・店
**2** *verb*

to go shopping = かいものに いく・
買い物に 行く

**shop assistant** *noun* (*British
English*)
= てんいん・店員

! *Often respectfully referred to as*
てんいんさん

**shopkeeper** *noun*
= てんしゅ・店主

**shopping** *noun*
= かいもの・買い物
to do the shopping = かいものする・
買い物する

**shopping cart** *noun* (*US English*)
= カート

**shopping centre** (*British English*),
**shopping mall** (*US English*)
*noun*
= ショッピングセンター

**shopping trolley** *noun* (*British
English*)
= カート

**shop window** *noun*
= ショーウインドー

**shore** *noun*
- (*the edge of the sea*)
  = きし・岸
- (*dry land*)
  = りく・陸

**short**
**1** *adjective*
- (*not long*) = みじかい・短い
  a short skirt = みじかい スカート・
  短い スカート
  I have short hair = かみが みじかい
  です。・髪が 短いです。
  the days are getting shorter = ひが
  みじかく なっています。・日が
  短く なっています。
- (*not tall*) = せが ひくい・背が 低い
- to be short of money = おかねが
  たりない・お金が 足りない
**2 in short** = ようするに・要するに

**short cut** *noun*
= ちかみち・近道

**shortly** *adverb*
- (*soon*) = まも なく・間もなく
- (*not long*)
  shortly before we left = でる ちょく
  ぜん・出る 直前

**shorts** *noun*
= はんズボン ・ 半ズボン

**shot** *noun*
• (*from a gun*)
= はっぽう ・ 発砲
• (*in sports*)
(*in football*) = シュート

**should** *verb*
• (*when talking about what is right, what one ought to do*) ▶ **must**
she should learn to drive = かのじょ はうんてんを ならう べきです。・ 彼女は 運転を 習う べきです。
shouldn't he be at school? = かれは がっこうに いる べきでしょう か。・ 彼は 学校に いる べきで しょうか。
• (*when saying something may happen*)
we should be there by midday = おひ るまでに そこに つく はずです。・ お昼までに そこに 着く はず です。
it shouldn't be too difficult = そんな に むずかしくない はずです。・ そんなに 難しくない はずで す。
• (*when implying that something, though likely, didn't happen*)
the letter should have arrived yesterday = てがみは きのう きた はずで す。・ 手紙は 昨日 来た はずで す。
• (*when asking for advice or permission*)
should I call the doctor? = いしゃを よんだ ほうが いいですか。・ 医者を 呼んだ 方が いいですか。

**shoulder** *noun*
= かた ・ 肩

**shout**
**1** *verb*
• (*general*) = おおごえで いう ・ 大声 で 言う
• (*in anger*) = どなる ・ 怒鳴る
**2** *noun*
= さけびごえ ・ 叫び声
**shout out** = さけぶ ・ 叫ぶ

**shovel** *noun*
= スコップ

**show**
**1** *verb*
• (*to let someone see*) = みせる ・ 見せ る

to show someone a photo = だれかに しゃしんを みせる ・ 誰かに 写 真を 見せる
I'll show you how to make it = つく りかたを みせます。・ 作り方を 見せます。
• (*to go with*)
I'll show you to your room = へやを あんないします。・ 部屋を 案内 します。
• (*to point to, to indicate*) = しめす ・ 示す
• (*to be on TV, at the cinema*)
where is that film showing? = その えいがは どこで じょうえいし ていますか。・ その 映画は どこ で 上映していますか。
to be shown (on TV) = (テレビ)で ほ うそうする ・ (テレビ)で 放送す る
**2** *noun*
• (*on a stage*) = ショー
(*on TV, radio*) = ばんぐみ ・ 番組
• (*an exhibition*)
= てんじかい ・ 展示会
**show off** = きどる ・ 気取る
**show round**
to show around the town = まちを あんないする ・ 町を 案内する
**show up** = あらわれる ・ 現れる

**shower** *noun*
• (*for washing*)
= シャワー
to have a shower = シャワーを あび る ・ シャワーを 浴びる
• (*rain*)
= にわかあめ ・ にわか雨

**shrimp** *noun*
= えび

**shrink** *verb*
to shrink = ちぢむ ・ 縮む
to shrink something = なにかを ちぢ める ・ 何かを 縮める

**shut**
**1** *adjective*
(*eyes*) = とじている ・ 閉じている
(*doors, windows*) = しまっている ・ 閉まっている
(*buildings*) = しまっている ・ 閉ま っている
my eyes were shut = めを とじていま した。・ 目を 閉じていました。
**2** *verb*
(*door, window*) = しめる ・ 閉める

S

to shut the windows = まどを しめる
・ 窓を 閉める

I can't shut the door properly = ドア
を ちゃんと しめられません。・
ドアを ちゃんと 閉められませ
ん。

(*eyes*) = とじる・閉じる

please close you eyes = めを とじて
ください。・ 目を 閉じてくださ
い。

(*shop*) = しまう

**shut down** = へいさする・閉鎖す
る

the factory shut down in May = こう
じょうは ごがつに へいさしま
した。・ 工場は 五月に 閉鎖しま
した。

**shut up**
• (*to be quiet*) = だまる・黙る

please shut up! = だまってくださ
い。・ 黙ってください。

**shy** *adjective*
= うちき(な)・内気(な)

**sick** *adjective*
• (*ill*) = びょうき(の)・病気(の)

to get sick = びょうきに なる・病
気に なる

to feel sick = むかつく

to be sick (*British English*)
(*to vomit*) = はく・吐く

• (*fed up*) = うんざりしている

I'm sick of it! = もう うんざりして
います。

**sickness** *noun* = びょうき・病気

**side** *noun*
• = がわ・側

on both sides = りょうがわに・両
側に

left hand side = ひだりがわ・左側

right hand side = みぎがわ・右側

the side of the river = かわぞい・川
沿い

• (*of a person's body*) = わきばら・
脇腹

on my right (side) = わたしの みぎが
わに・私の 右側に

• (*in a conflict, a contest*)
= がわ・側

• (*a team*)
= チーム

side with someone = だれかに み
かたする・誰かに 味方する

**sidewalk** *noun* (*US English*)
= ほどう・歩道

**sigh** *noun*
= ためいき・ため息

**sight** *noun*
= しかく・視覚

I have good sight = めが いいです。
・ 目が いいです。

out of sight = みえない ところに・
見えない 所に

**sightseeing**
go sightseeing = けんぶつ する・
見物 する

**sign**
**1** *noun*
• (*a symbol*)
= しるし・印

• (*for traffic, for advertising*)
= かんばん・看板

• (*a notice*)
= はりがみ・張り紙

**2** *verb*
= サインする

sign on (*British English*) = しつぎょ
うてあてを せいきゅうする・
失業手当を 請求する

**signal**
**1** *noun*
= しんごう・信号

**2** *verb*
• (*to make signs*) = あいずを する・
合図を する

to signal to someone to come = だれ
かに くる ように あいずを する
・ 誰かに 来る ように 合図を す
る

• (*when driving*)

to signal left = ひだりに ウインカ
ーを だす・左に ウインカーを
出す

**signature** *noun*
= サイン

**signpost** *noun*
= あんないひょうしき・案内標識

**silence** *noun*
(*of person*) = ちんもく・沈黙

(*of place*) = しずけさ・静けさ

**silent** *adjective*
• (*person*) = だまっている・黙って
いる

• (*place*) = しんとした

**silk** *noun*
= きぬ・絹

**silly** *adjective*
= ばか(な)

**silver**
**1** *noun*
= ぎん・銀
**2** *adjective*
= ぎん(の)・銀(の)
a silver ring = ぎんの ゆびわ・銀の
指輪

**SIM card** *noun*
= ＳＩＭカード

**simple** *adjective*
= かんたん(な)・簡単(な)

**since**
**1** *preposition*
= 〜いらい・〜以来
I haven't seen him since yesterday =
きのういらい かれを みていま
せん。・昨日以来 彼を 見ていま
せん。
she has been living in Japan since
April = かのじょは しがついらい
にほんに すんでいます。・彼女
は 四月以来 日本に 住んでいま
す。
**2** *conjunction*
• (*from the time when*) = 〜て form of
the verb + いらい ▶ 197
since she left = かのじょが でてい
らい・彼女が 出て以来
I've lived here since I was ten = じゅ
っさいの ときから ここに すん
でいます。・十才の ときから
ここに 住んでいます。
it's ten years since she died = かのじ
ょが なくなってから じゅうね
んです。・彼女が 亡くなってか
ら 十年です。
• (*because*) = から
since she was ill, she couldn't go =
かのじょは びょうき でしたか
ら いけませんでした。・彼女は
病気でしたから 行けませんでし
た。
**3** *adverb*
= それいらい・それ以来

**sincere** *adjective*
= せいじつ(な)・誠実(な)

**sincerely** *adverb*
= せいじつに・誠実に
**Yours sincerely**
**Sincerely yours** *Not used in Japanese*
*letters. Usually a general greeting*

けいぐ *is used at the end of the*
*letter.* ▶ **dear**

**sing** *verb*
= うたう・歌う

**singer** *noun*
= かしゅ・歌手

**singing** *noun*
= うたごえ・歌声

**single** *adjective*
• (*one*) = いち + counter counter
▶ 181
we did it three times in a single day =
いちにちに さんかいしました。
・一日に 三回しました。
• (*when used for emphasis*)
every single day = まいにち・毎日
I didn't see a single person = ひと
りも みませんでした。・一人も
見ませんでした。
• (*without a partner*) = どくしん・独
身

**single bed** *noun*
= シングルベッド

**single room** *noun*
= シングルべや・シングル部屋

**single ticket** *noun* (*British English*)
= かたみち(じょうしゃけん)・
片道(乗車券)

**sink**
**1** *noun*
= ながし・流し
**2** *verb*
= ちんぼつする・沈没する

**sister** *noun*

> **!** *Note that there are two sets of*
> *words for family members* ▶ 177

(*your own older sister*) = あね・姉
(*your own younger sister*) = いもうと
・妹
(*someone else's older sister*) = おねえ
さん・お姉さん
(*someone else's younger sister*) =
いもうとさん・妹さん

**sister-in-law** *noun* ▶ 177
= ぎり + word for sister

**sit** *verb*
• (*to take a seat*) = すわる・座る
to be sitting on the floor = ゆかに す
わっている・床に 座っている

**S**

- (*British English*)
  (*to take*)
  **to sit an exam** = しけんを うける・
  試験を 受ける
  **sit down** = すわる・座る
  **to be sitting down** = すわっている・
  座っている
  **sit up**
  **please sit up straight!** = きちんと す
  わってください。・ きちんと
  座ってください。

**sitting room** noun
  (*Japanese style*) = ちゃの ま・茶の
  間
  (*Western style*) = リビング

**situated** adjective
  **situated near the town centre** = まち
  の ちゅうしんの ちかくに ある
  ・ 町の 中心の 近くに ある

**situation** noun
  = じょうきょう・状況

**six** number ▶ 171, ▶ 181
  (*on its own*) = むっつ・六つ
  (*with a counter*) = ろく・六 ▶ 186
  **six books** = ほん ろくさつ・本 六冊
  **I've got six** = むっつ あります。・ 六
  つ あります。

**sixteen** number ▶ 171, ▶ 181
  = じゅうろく・十六

**sixteenth** number
- (*in a series*) = じゅうろくばんめ(の)
  ・ 十六番目(の)
- (*in dates*) ▶ 174
  = じゅうろくにち・十六日
  **the sixteenth of July** = しちがつじゅ
  うろくにち・ 七月十六日

**sixth** number
- (*in a series*) = ろく ばんめ (の)・
  六番目(の)
- (*in dates*) ▶ 174
  = むいか・六日
  **the sixth of February** = にがつむいか
  ・ 二月六日

**sixty** number ▶ 171, ▶ 181
  = ろくじゅう・六十

**size** noun
- (*when talking about clothes, shoes*)
  = サイズ
  **do you have this in a smaller size?** =
  もっと ちいさいのが あります
  か。・ もっと 小さいのがありま
  すか。

**what size do you take?**
  (*in clothes*) = サイズは いくつです
  か。
  (*in shoes*) = なんセンチですか。・
  何センチですか。
- (*when talking about how big
  something is*)
  = おおきさ・大きさ

**skateboard** noun
  = スケートボード

**skating** noun
  = スケート

**skating rink** noun
  = スケートリンク

**sketch** noun
- (*a drawing*)
  = スケッチ
- (*a funny scene*)
  = スキット

**ski**
**1** noun
  = スキー
**2** verb
  **to go skiing** = スキーに いく・ スキ
  ーに 行く

**skiing** noun
  = スキー

**skilful** (*British English*), **skillful**
  (*US English*) adjective
  = じょうず(な)・上手(な)

**skill** noun
  = ぎじゅつ・技術

**skin** noun
  = ひふ・皮膚

**skinny** adjective
  = やせた

**skip** verb
- (*to give little jumps*) = スキップする
- (*with a rope*) = なわとびする・ 縄跳
  びする
- **to skip classes** = じゅぎょうを さぼ
  る・ 授業を さぼる

**ski resort** noun
  = スキーじょう・スキー場

**skirt** noun
  = スカート

**sky** noun
  = そら・空
  **blue sky** = あおぞら・青空

**skydiving** noun
  = スカイダイビング

**slap** verb
to slap someone = だれかを ぴしゃ
りと うつ ・ 誰かを ぴしゃりと
打つ

**sled, sledge** (British English)
**1** noun
= そり

**sleep**
**1** noun
= すいみん ・ 睡眠
to go to sleep = ねむる ・ 眠る
to go back to sleep = ねなおす ・
寝直す
to put someone to sleep = だれかを
ねかす ・ 誰かを 寝かす
**2** verb
• (to be asleep) = ねむっている ・ 眠
っている
• to sleep with someone = だれかと
ねる ・ 誰かと 寝る
sleep in = ねぼうする ・ 寝坊する

**sleeping bag** noun
= ねぶくろ ・ 寝袋

**sleepy** adjective
= ねむい ・ 眠い

**sleet** noun
= みぞれ

**sleeve** noun
= そで ・ 袖
to roll up one's sleeves = そでを
めくる ・ 袖を めくる
short sleeves = はんそで ・ 半袖

**slice**
**1** noun
= スライス
**2** verb
to slice bread = パンを スライスす
る

**slide**
**1** verb
= すべる ・ 滑る
**2** noun
• (an image)
= スライド
• (in a playground)
= すべりだい ・ 滑り台

**slim**
**1** adjective
= スマート
**2** verb (British English)
= やせる ・ 痩せる

**slip** verb
• (to slide) = すべる ・ 滑る

**slipper** noun
= スリッパ

**slippery** adjective
= すべりやすい ・ 滑りやすい

**slot machine** noun
= スロットマシーン

**slow** adjective
• (journey, music) = ゆっくりした
(service, speed) = おそい ・ 遅い
• (not bright) = ものおぼえがわるい ・
物覚えが 悪い
• (describing a watch, a clock)
to be slow = おくれている ・ 遅れ
ている
that clock is 20 minutes slow = その
とけいは にじゅっぷん おくれ
ています。・ その 時計は二十分
遅れています。
slow down = スピードを おとす ・
スピードを 落とす

**slowly** adverb
= ゆっくり
to walk slowly = ゆっくり あるく ・
・ ゆっくり 歩く

**sly** adjective
= ずるい

**small** adjective
= ちいさい ・ 小さい
a small house = ちいさい いえ ・
小さい 家
a small quantity = すこしの りょう ・
少しの 量

**small ad** noun (British English)
= ぶんるいこうこく ・ 分類広告

**smart** adjective
• (British English)
(elegant) = おしゃれ(な)
• (intelligent) = あたまが いい ・ 頭が
いい
• (expensive) = こうきゅう(な) ・ 高
級(な)

**smash** verb
• (to break) = めちゃめちゃに こわす
・ めちゃめちゃに 壊す
• (to get broken) = めちゃめちゃに
こわれる ・ めちゃめちゃに
壊れる
smash up = めちゃめちゃに こわ
す ・ めちゃめちゃに 壊す

**S**

## smell
**1** *noun*
- (*an odour*)
= におい
- (*the sense*)
the sense of smell = きゅうかく・嗅覚
**2** *verb*
= におう
that smells nice = いい においです。
I can smell burning = こげた におい が します。・焦げたにおいがします。

## smile
**1** *verb*
= ほほえむ・微笑む
to smile at someone = だれかに ほほえむ・誰かに 微笑む
**2** *noun*
= ほほえみ・微笑み

## smoke
**1** *noun*
= けむり・煙
**2** *verb*
= たばこをすう・煙草を 吸う

**smooth** *adjective*
(*not rough*) = なめらか(な)・滑らか(な)

**smother** *verb*
= ちっそくさせる・窒息させる

**snack** *noun*
= けいしょく・軽食

**snail** *noun*
= かたつむり

**snake** *noun*
= へび
year of the snake = みどし・巳年

**snapshot** *noun*
= しゃしん・写真

**sneaker** *noun*
= スニーカー

**sneeze** *verb*
= くしゃみをする

**snobbish** *adjective*
(*about people*) = おうへい(な)・横柄(な)

**snooker** *noun*
= ビリヤード

**snore** *verb*
= いびきを かく

## snow
**1** *noun*
= ゆき・雪
**2** *verb*
= ゆきが ふる・雪が 降る
it's snowing = ゆきが ふっています。・雪が 降っています。

**snowball** *noun*
= ゆきだま・雪玉

**snowman** *noun*
= ゆきだるま・雪だるま

## so
**1** *adverb*
- = とても
I'm so happy = とても しあわせです。・とても 幸せです。
she's so smart = かのじょは とても あたまが いいです。・彼女は とても 頭が いいです。
I've so much work to do = しごとが たくさん あります。・仕事が たくさん あります。
she speaks so fast that I can't understand her = かのじょは わからない ほど はやくはなします。・彼女は 分からない ほど 速く 話します。
- (*also*)
I'm fifteen and so is he = わたしも かれも じゅうごさいです。・私も 彼も 十五才です。
if you go, so will I = あなたが いくなら、わたしも いきます。・あなたが 行くなら、私も 行きます。
- (*other uses*)
I think so = わたしも そう おもいます。・私も そう 思います。
I'm afraid so = そうです。
I told you so = わたしの いった とおりです。・私の 言った 通りです。
who says so? = だれが そう いいましたか。・誰が そう 言いましたか。
and so on = など
**2** so (that) = から
it's cold so please close the window = さむいですから、まどを しめて ください。・寒いですから、窓を 閉めてください。
**3** so as = 〜ように
we left home early so as not to miss the train = でんしゃに おくれない ように はやくうちを でまし

た。・電車に 遅れない ように 早
く 家を 出ました。 *Note that the
word order is different in Japanese in
this type of sentence.*

**soap** *noun*
• *(for washing)*
= せっけん・石けん
• *(on TV)*
= ドラマ

**soccer** *noun*
= サッカー

**social** *adjective*
*(history, background)* = しゃかい(の)
・社会(の)
*(life, event)* = しゃこうてき(な)・
社交的(な)

**social studies** *noun*
= しゃかいがく・社会学

**social worker** *noun*
= ソーシャルワーカー

**sock** *noun*
= くつした・靴下

**sofa** *noun*
= ソファー

**soft** *adjective*
• *(not hard or tough)* = やわらかい・
柔らかい
soft toy = ぬいぐるみ
• *(not harsh, strict or severe)* = やさし
い・優しい

**software** *noun*
= ソフト

**soldier** *noun*
= へいたい・兵隊

**sole** *noun*
• = あしの うら・足の 裏
• *(of a shoe)*
= くつの そこ・靴の 底

**solicitor** *noun (British English)*
= べんごし・弁護士

**solution** *noun*
= かいけつ・解決

**solve** *verb*
= かいけつする・解決する
to solve a problem = もんだいを か
いけつする・問題を 解決する

**some**
**1** *determiner*
• *(an amount or a number of)*

❗ *Not used in this way in Japanese.*

I have to buy some bread = パンを か
わなければ なりません。・パン
を 買わなければ なりません。
could I have some water? = みずを
ください。・水を ください。
she ate some strawberries = かのじ
ょは いちごをたべました。・彼
女は いちごを 食べました。
• *(certain)* = ある
there are some people who don't like
travelling by plane = ひこうきの
たびが きらいな ひとも います。
・飛行機の 旅が 嫌いな 人も い
ます。
**2** *pronoun*
• *(an amount or a number of)*

❗ *Not used in this way in Japanese.*

I made some yesterday = きのう つ
くりました。・昨日 作りました。
• *(certain people or things)*
some are quite expensive = たかいの
も あります。・高いのもありま
す。
some (of them) are Japanese-speakers
= にほんごが はなせる ひとも
います。・日本語が 話せる人も
います。

**someone** *pronoun (also*
**somebody***)*
= だれか・誰か
someone telephoned = だれかが で
んわしました。・誰かが 電話し
ました。

**something** *pronoun*
= なにか・何か
I'll show you something interesting =
なにか おもしろい ものを みせ
ます。・何か 面白いものを 見せ
ます。

**sometimes** *adverb*
= ときどき・時々

**somewhere** *adverb*
= どこか
they live somewhere in Ireland = かれ
らは アイルランドの どこかに
すんでいます。彼らは アイルラ
ンドの どこかに 住んでいます。
let's go somewhere else = どこか
ほかの ところに いきましょう。
・どこか 外の 所に 行きましょ
う。

**son** *noun*
　(*one's own*) = むすこ・息子
　(*someone else's*) = むすこさん・息
　子さん

**song** *noun*
　= うた・歌

**son-in-law** *noun*
　= ぎりのむすこ・義理の息子

**soon** *adverb*
• (*in a short time*) = もうすぐ
　see you soon! = またね。
• (*early*) = はやい・早い
　the sooner the better = はやければ
　はやいほどいいです。・早けれ
　ば早いほどいいです。
　as soon as possible = できるだけは
　やく・できるだけ早く
　come as soon as you can = できるだ
　けはやくきてください。・でき
　るだけ早く来てください。

**sore** *adjective*
　= いたい・痛い
　I have a sore throat = のどがいたい
　です。・喉が痛いです。
　I have a sore leg = あしがいたいで
　す。・足が痛いです。
　I have a sore back = せなかがいた
　いです。・背中が痛いです。
　it's very sore = とてもいたいです。
　・とても痛いです。

**sorry**
**1** *exclamation*
• (*when apologizing*)
　sorry! = すみません。
• (*when asking someone to repeat*)
　sorry? = はい?
**2** *adjective*
• (*when apologizing*) = すみません。
　I'm sorry I'm late = おそくなって
　すみません。・遅くなってすみ
　ません。 *Note that word order is*
　*different in Japanese*
　to say sorry = あやまる・謝る
• (*when expressing regret*) = ざんねん
　・残念
　I'm sorry he can't come = かれが
　こられなくてざんねんです。・
　彼が来られなくて残念です。
• (*to feel pity for*)
　to feel sorry for someone = だれかを
　かわいそうにおもう・誰かを
　かわいそうに思う

**sort**
**1** *noun*
　it's a sort of bird = とりのいっしゅ
　です。・鳥の一種です。
　it's a sort of computer = コンピュー
　ターのいっしゅです。・コンピ
　ューターの一種です。
　I don't like that sort of thing = そう
　いうことがすきではありませ
　ん。・そういうことが好きで
　はありません。
　he's not that sort of person = かれは
　そういうひとではありません。
　・彼はそういう人ではありませ
　ん。
**2** *verb*
　= ぶんるいする・分類する
　to sort the documents = しょるいを
　ぶんるいする・書類を分類す
　る
**sort out**
• (*to solve*) = かいけつする・解決す
　る
　to sort out a problem = もんだいを
　かいけつする・問題を解決する
• (*to deal with*) = する
　I'll sort it out = わたしがそれを
　します。・私がそれをします。
• (*to organize*) = よりわける・より分
　ける
　to sort out the washing = せんたく
　ものをよりわける・洗濯物を
　より分ける

**sound**
**1** *noun*
• = おと・音
　I like the sound of waves = なみの
　おとがすきです。・波の音が
　好きです。
• (*of a radio, a television*)
　= おんりょう・音量
　to turn the sound up = おんりょうを
　あげる・音量を上げる
**2** *verb*
　= Use い adjective minus last い + そう
　です
　　Use な adjective (or noun) + みたい
　です
　it sounds dangerous = あぶなそうで
　す。・危なそうです。
　it sounds interesting = おもしろそう
　です。
　it sounds like a piano = ピアノみた
　いです。

**soup** *noun*
(*Western style*) = スープ
(*Japanese style*) = しる・汁
miso soup = みそしる・みそ汁

**sour** *adjective*
= すっぱい・酸っぱい
to go sour = すっぱく なる・酸っ
ぱく なる

**south**
**1** *noun*
= みなみ・南
in the south of England = イギリスの
みなみに・イギリスの 南に
**2** *adverb*
to go south = みなみに いく・南に
行く
**3** *adjective*
= みなみ・南
to work in south London = みなみロ
ンドンで はたらく・南ロンド
ンで 働く

**South Africa** *noun* ▶ 172
= みなみアフリカ・南アフリカ

**South America** *noun* ▶ 172
= みなみアメリカ・南アメリカ

**southeast** *noun*
= なんとう・南東

**southwest** *noun*
= なんせい・南西

**souvenir** *noun*
= きねんひん・記念品

**space** *noun*
• (*room*)
= くうかん・空間
to take up space = ばしょを とる・
場所を 取る
• (*an area of land*)
an open space = ひらけた ばしょ・
開けた 場所
• (*outer space*)
= うちゅう・宇宙
• (*a gap*)
= すきま・隙間

**Spain** *noun* ▶ 172
= スペイン

**spare** *adjective*
• (*extra*) = よぶん(な)・余分(な)
• (*available*) = のこっている・残っ
ている
are there any spare seats? = のこっ
ている せきが ありますか。・残
っている 席が ありますか。

**spare room** *noun*
= おきゃくさんようの しんしつ・
お客さん用の 寝室

**spare time** *noun*
= ひまな とき・暇な とき

**speak** *verb*
= はなす・話す
to speak Japanese = にほんごを は
なす・日本語を 話す
who's speaking, please? = どちら さ
まですか。・どちら 様ですか。
generally speaking = いっぱんてき
に いうと・一般的に 言うと
speak up = おおきい こえで はな
す・大きい 声で 話す

**special** *adjective*
= とくべつ(な)・特別(な)
a special offer = とくばいひん・
特売品
Elena's a special friend = エレナさん
は とくべつな ともだちです。・
エレナさんは 特別な 友達です。

**speciality** (*British English*),
**specialty** (*US English*) *noun*
= めいぶつ・名物

**specially** *adverb*
= とくべつに・特別に

**spectator** *noun*
= かんきゃく・観客

**speech** *noun*
= スピーチ

**speed**
**1** *noun*
= スピード
**2** *verb*
• (*to drive too fast*) = スピードを だし
すぎる・スピードを 出しすぎ
る
speed up = スピードを あげる・
スピードを 上げる

**speed camera** *noun*
= スピードカメラ

**speed limit** *noun*
= そくどせいげん・速度制限

**spell** *verb*
(*when speaking*) = つづりを いう・
綴りを 言う
(*when writing*) = つづる・綴る
how do you spell it? = つづりは なん
ですか。・綴りは 何ですか。

S

**spelling** *noun*
= つづり・綴り

**spend** *verb*
- (*to pay money*) = つかう・使う
- (*to pass*) = すごす・過ごす
  to spend time reading = ほんを よん ですごす・本を 読んで 過ごす
  to spend time writing letters = てがみ を かいて すごす・手紙を 書い て 過ごす

**spider** *noun*
= くも

**spill** *verb*
- (*if it's a person*) = こぼす
  please don't spill the juice = ジュー スを こぼさないでください。
- (*if it's a liquid*) = こぼれる

**spinach** *noun*
= ほうれんそう

**spit** *verb*
= つばを はく・つばを 吐く

**spite: in spite of** *preposition*
= 〜(な)のに
  we went out in spite of the bad weather = てんきが わるいのに でまし た。・天気が 悪いのに 出まし た。

**spiteful** *adjective*
= いじわる(な)・意地悪(な)

**spoil** *verb*
- (*to damage*) = だいなしに する・ 台なしにする
- (*as a parent*) = あまやかす・甘やか す
  to spoil a child = こどもを あまやか す・子供を 甘やかす

**sponge** *noun*
= スポンジ

**spoon** *noun*
= スプーン

**sport** *noun*
= スポーツ
  I am good at sports = スポーツが とくいです。・スポーツが 得意 です。

**sports centre** (*British English*),
  **sports center** (*US English*) *noun*
= スポーツセンター

**sports club** *noun*
= スポーツクラブ

**spot**
**1** *noun*
- (*on an animal*)
  = はんてん・斑点
- (*British English*)
  (*on the face or body*)
  = にきび
- (*a place*)
  = ところ・所
  on the spot
  (*there and then*) = げんばに・現場 に
**2** *verb*
- (*to see*) = みる・見る
- (*to recognize*) = きが つく・気が 付 く

**sprain** *verb*
  to sprain one's wrist = てくびを ねん ざする・手首を ねんざする

**spring** *noun*
= はる・春
  in spring = はるに・春に

**spy** *noun*
= スパイ

**square**
**1** *noun*
- (*the shape*)
  = しかく・四角
- (*in a town*)
  = ひろば・広場
**2** *adjective*
= しかくい・四角い

**squash**
**1** *noun*
= スカッシュ
**2** *verb*
= つぶす・潰す

**squeak** *verb*
= きしむ

**squeeze** *verb*
  to squeeze a lemon = レモンを しぼ る・レモンを 搾る
  to squeeze someone's hand = だれか の てを にぎる・誰かの 手を 握 る

**squirrel** *noun*
= りす

**stable** *noun*
= うまごや・馬小屋

**stadium** *noun*
= スタジアム

**staff** *noun*
(*of a company*) = しゃいん ・ 社員
(*of a bank*) = ぎんこういん ・ 銀行員
(*of a school, a college*) = しょくいん
・ 職員

**stage** *noun*
= ステージ

**stain**
**1** *noun*
= しみ ・ 染み
**2** *verb*
= よごす ・ 汚す

**stairs** *noun*
= かいだん ・ 階段
to fall down the stairs = かいだんで
ころぶ ・ 階段で 転ぶ

**stamp** *noun*
• (*for an envelope*)
= きって ・ 切手
a hundred and ten yen stamp = ひゃ
くじゅうえん きって ・ 百十円
切手
• (*on a document, a passport*)
= スタンプ

**stamp-collecting** *noun*
= きってしゅうしゅう ・ 切手収集

**stand** *verb*
• to be standing = たっている ・ 立っ
ている
to be able to stand = たつ ことが
できる ・ 立つ ことが できる
you're standing in my way = じゃま
です。・ 邪魔です。
• (*to put*)
to stand a vase on a table = かびんを
テーブルの うえに おく ・ 花瓶
を テーブルの 上に 置く
• (*to step*)
to stand on a nail = くぎを ふむ ・
くぎを 踏む
• (*to bear*)
I can't stand the cold = さむさに た
えられません。・ 寒さに 耐えら
れません。
I can't stand his selfishness = かれの
わがままは がまん できません。
・ 彼の わがままは 我慢 できま
せん。
• (*other uses*)
to stand for election (*British English*) =
せんきょに りっこうほする ・
選挙に 立候補する

**stand back** = さがる ・ 下がる
**stand for**
• (*to represent*) = だいひょうする ・
代表する
• (*to mean*) = いみする ・ 意味する
**stand out** = めだつ ・ 目立つ
**stand up** = たちあがる ・ 立ち上が
る
**stand up for** = まもる ・ 守る
to stand up for oneself = じぶんを
まもる ・ 自分を 守る
**stand up to** = たちむかう ・ 立ち向
かう
to stand up to someone = だれかに
たちむかう ・ 誰かに 立ち向か
う

**star** *noun*
• (*in space*)
= ほし ・ 星
• (*a famous person*)
= スター

**stare** *verb*
to stare at someone = だれかを じ
ろじろ みる ・ 誰かを じろじろ
見る

**start**
**1** *verb*
• (*to begin*) = はじめる ・ 始める
*You can use the pre* ます *form of
the verb* ≠ はじめる *to indicate the
start of an action* ▶ **191**
to start working = はたらきはじめる
・ 働き始める
to start writing = かきはじめる ・
書き始める
to start running = はしりはじめる ・
走り始める
you should start by phoning them =
まず かれらに でんわした ほう
が いいです。・ まず 彼らに
電話した 方が いいです。
• (*to set up*) = せつりつする ・ 設立す
る
to start a company = かいしゃを せ
つりつする ・ 会社を 設立する
• (*to cause*) = ひきおこす ・ 引き起こ
す
to start a war = せんそうを ひきお
こす ・ 戦争を 引き起こす
• (*to begin working*) = うごきだす ・
動き出す
the engine won't start = エンジンが
かかりません。
• (*to put into action*)

S

to start a car engine = くるまの エンジンを かける・車の エンジンを かける

to start a machine = きかいの スイッチを いれる・機械の スイッチを 入れる

**2** *noun*

(*time*) = はじめ・初め

at the start of the week = しゅうの はじめに・週の 初めに

(*matter*) = はじまり・始まり

the start of married life = けっこんせいかつの はじまり・結婚生活の 始まり

**start off** = はじめる・始める

**start over** (*US English*) = やりなおす・やり直す

**starter** *noun* (*British English*)
= ぜんさい・前菜

**state** *noun*
• (*a country*)
= くに・国
• (*part of a country*)
= しゅう・州
• (*a government*)
= くに・国
• (*a condition*)
= じょうたい・状態

this house is in a bad state (of repair) = この うちは わるい じょうたいです。・この 家は 悪い 状態です。

she's in no state to work = かのじょは はたらける ような じょうたいではありません。・彼女は 働ける ような 状態ではありません。

**station** *noun*
• (*for trains*)
= えき・駅
• (*on TV*)
= テレビきょく・テレビ局
• (*for buses*)
= バス のりば・バス乗り場

**statue** *noun*
= ぞう・像

**stay**
**1** *verb*
• (*to remain*) = いる

we stayed there for a week = そこに いっしゅうかん いました。・そこに 一週間 いました。

• (*to have accommodation*) = とまる・泊まる

to stay at a friend's house = ともだちの うちに とまる・友達の 家に 泊まる

**2** *noun*
= たいざい・滞在

**stay away from**

to stay away from school = がっこうに いかない・学校に 行かない

**stay in** = いえに いる・家に いる

**stay up**

(*to go to bed late*) = おそく ねる・遅く 寝る

**steady** *adjective*
• (*continuous*)

to make steady progress = ちゃくじつな じょうたつを する・着実な 上達を する

• (*not likely to move*) = あんていしている・安定している

**steak** *noun*
= ステーキ

**steal** *verb*
= ぬすむ・盗む

to steal someone's money = だれかの おかねを ぬすむ・誰かの お金を 盗む

**steam** *noun*
= すいじょうき・水蒸気

**steel** *noun*
= こうてつ・鋼鉄

**steep** *adjective*
= けわしい・険しい

**steering wheel** *noun*
= ハンドル

**step**
**1** *noun*
• (*when walking*)
= いっぽ・一歩
to take a step = ふみだす・踏み出す
• (*in stairs, at a door*)
= だん・段
• (*a series of actions*)
to take steps = てを うつ・手を 打つ

**2** *verb*
to step on someone's foot = だれかの あしを ふむ・誰かの 足を 踏む
step aside = わきに よる・脇に 寄る

**stepbrother** *noun No distinction is usually made between step- and blood-relatives.* ▶ **brother** ▶ **177**

**stepfather** noun ▶ 177
(one's own) = ままちち ・ まま父
*No distinction is usually made
between step- and blood relatives.*
▶ **father**

**stepmother** noun ▶ 177
(one's own) = ままはは ・ まま母
*No distinction is usually made
between step- and blood relatives.*
▶ **mother**

**stepsister** noun *No distinction is
usually made between step- and
blood relatives.* ▶ **sister** ▶ 177

**stereo** noun
= ステレオ

**stick**
**1** verb
• (using glue or tape) = はる ・ 貼る
• (to become attached) = くっつく
• (to get blocked) = ひっかかる ・
　引っかかる
　the door is stuck = ドアが ひっかか
　っています。・ ドアが 引っかか
　っています。
**2** noun
• (a piece of wood)
　= ぼう ・ 棒
• (for walking)
　= つえ ・ 杖
　**stick at**
　to stick at something = なにかを
　さいごまで する ・ 何かを 最後
　までする
　**stick out** = でっぱる ・ 出っ張る
　there's a nail sticking out = くぎが で
　っぱっています。・ くぎが 出っ
　張っています。

**sticky tape** noun (British English)
= セロテープ

**stiff** adjective
• (not soft, not supple) = かたい
　(after sport, walking)
　to have stiff legs = あしが きんにく
　つうに なっている ・ 足が 筋肉
　痛に なっている
• (not easy to use)
　= かたい ・ 硬い

**still¹** adverb
• (when there has been no change) =
　まだ
　does she still learn the piano? = かの
　じょは まだ ピアノを ならって

いますか。・ 彼女は まだ ピアノ
を 習っていますか。
I still don't understand why he did that
= なんで かれが それを したか
まだ わかりません。・ 何で彼が
それを したか まだ 分かりませ
ん。
• (when referring to the future) = まだ
she still has a chance of winning =
かのじょには まだ かつ かのう
せいが あります。・ 彼女には
まだ 勝つ 可能性が あります。

**still²**
**1** adverb
　to sit still = じっと すわる ・ じっと
　座る
**2** adjective
　= うごかない ・ 動かない

**sting** verb
= さす ・ 刺す

**stir** verb
= かきまぜる ・ かき混ぜる

**stomach** noun
= い ・ 胃
I have a pain in my stomach = いが
いたいです。・ 胃が 痛いです。

**stone** noun
= いし ・ 石
(a pebble) = こいし ・ 小石

**stop**
**1** verb
• (to put an end to) = やめる
　to stop smoking = たばこを やめる
　・ 煙草を やめる
　to stop laughing = わらうのを やめ
　る ・ 笑うのを やめる
　to stop working = はたらくのを や
　める ・ 働くのを やめる
　please stop it! = やめてください。
• (to prevent)
　to stop someone from going = だれか
　が いくのを やめさせる ・ 誰か
　が 行くのを やめさせる
• (to come to a halt) = とまる ・ 止まる
　the bus didn't stop = バスが とまり
　ませんでした。・ バスが 止まり
　ませんでした。
• (when talking about machines, noise,
　weather) = やむ
　suddenly the noise stopped = きゅ
　うに おとがやみました。・ 急に
　音が やみました。

**S**

the rain stopped = あめが やみまし
た。・雨が やみました。

**2** noun

a (bus) stop = バスてい・バス停

to miss one's stop = のりこす・乗
り越す

**store** noun
= みせ・店

**storey** (British English), **story**
(US English) noun
= かい・階

**storm** noun
= あらし・嵐

**story** noun
• = ものがたり・物語

a true story = ほんとうの ものがた
り・本当の 物語

a ghost story = かいだん・怪談
• (in a newspaper)
= きじ・記事
• (a rumour)
= うわさ・噂
• (US English)
(of a house) ▶ storey

**stove** noun (US English)
= オーブン

**straight**

**1** adjective
• = まっすぐ(の)・真っ直ぐ(の)

a straight line = ちょくせん・直線

straight hair = まっすぐの かみ・真
っ直ぐの 髪
• (in the right position)

the picture isn't straight = えが まが
っています。・絵が 曲がってい
ます。
• (honest) = しょうじき(な)・正直
(な)

**2** adverb
• = まっすぐに・真っ直ぐに

to stand up straight = ちゃんと たつ
・ちゃんと 立つ

to go straight ahead = まっすぐ いく
・真っ直ぐ 行く
• (without delay) = すぐ

to go straight home = すぐ かえる・
すぐ 帰る

**strange** adjective
• (odd) = へん(な)・変(な)

it's strange that she doesn't come
here any more = かのじょが もう
ここに こないのは へんです。・

彼女が もう ここに 来ないのは
変です。
• (unknown) = みち(の)・未知(の)

**stranger** noun
(unknown person) = しらない ひと・
知らない 人
(outsider) = よその ひと・よその
人

**straw** noun
• (for feeding animals)
= わら
• (for drinking)
= ストロー

**strawberry** noun
= いちご

**stream** noun
= おがわ・小川

**street** noun
= みち・道

**streetlamp** noun
= がいとう・街灯

**strength** noun
= たいりょく・体力

**stressful** adjective
= ストレスが かかる

**stretch** verb
= のばす・伸ばす

to stretch one's arms = てを のばす
・手を 伸ばす

**strict** adjective
= きびしい・厳しい

**strike** noun
= ストライキ

to go on strike = ストライキに はい
る・ストライキに 入る

**string** noun
= ひも・紐

**striped** adjective
= しまもよう(の)・縞模様(の)

**stroke** verb
= なでる

**stroller** noun (US English)
= うばぐるま・乳母車

**strong** adjective
• (having physical, mental strength) =
つよい・強い

she's strong = かのじょは つよい
です。・彼女は 強いです。
• (not easily damaged) = じょうぶ(な)
・丈夫(な)

- (*having force, power*) = つよい・強
  い
  a strong wind = つよい かぜ・強い
  風
- (*tea, coffee*) = こい・濃い
  strong tea = こい こうちゃ・濃い
  紅茶
- (*obvious, noticeable*) = きょうれつ
  (な)・強烈(な)
  a strong smell ot garlic = きょうれ
  つな にんにくの におい・強烈
  な にんにくの 臭い
  a strong German accent = つよい
  ドイツごの なまり・強い ドイ
  ツ語の 訛り
- (*having military power*) = つよい・強
  い

**stubborn** *adjective*
= がんこ(な)・頑固(な)

**student** *noun*
(*at university*) = がくせい・学生
(*at school*) = せいと・生徒

**study**
**1** *verb*
= べんきょうする・勉強する
to study history = れきしを べんき
ょうする・歴史を 勉強する
to study to be a teacher = せんせいに
なるために べんきょうする・
先生に なるために 勉強する
to study for an exam = しけんべんき
ょうする・試験勉強する
**2** *noun*
- = べんきょう・勉強
- (*room*) = しょさい・書斎

**stuff**
**1** *noun*
(*things*) = もの・物
(*belongings*) = もちもの・持ち物
I have a lot of stuff to do = たくさん
する ことが あります。
**2** *verb*
= つめる・詰める
to stuff a suitcase with clothes = スー
ツケースを ふくで つめる・
スーツケースを 服で 詰める

**stuffing** *noun*
= つめもの・詰め物

**stupid** *adjective*
= ばか(な)

**style** *noun*
- (*a way of dressing, behaving*)
  = ゆうがさ・優雅さ

to have style = ゆうがさが ある・
優雅さが ある
- (*a design, a type*)
  (*of garment*) = スタイル
  (*of building*) = ようしき・様式
- (*a fashion*)
  = はやり

**stylish** *adjective*
= ゆうが(な)・優雅(な)

**subject** *noun*
- (*of a conversation*)
  = わだい・話題
  to change the subject = わだいを か
  える・話題を 変える
- (*being studied*)
  (*at school, college*) = がっか・学課
  (*for an essay, a report*) = テーマ

**suburb** *noun*
= こうがい・郊外

**subway** *noun*
- (*US English*)
  (*the underground*)
  = ちかてつ・地下鉄
- (*British English*)
  (*an underground passage*)
  = ちかどう・地下道

**succeed** *verb*
= せいこうする・成功する

**success** *noun*
= せいこう・成功
to be a success
(*if it's a party*) = せいこうする・
成功する
(*if it's a film, a book*) = だいヒットに
なる・大ヒットになる

**successful** *adjective*
to be successful
(*in an attempt*) = せいこうする・成
功する
(*describing a film, a book*) = だいヒッ
トになる・大ヒットに なる

**such**
**1** *determiner*
there's no such thing
(*when referring to a physical thing*) =
そう いう ことが ありません。
(*when referring to a concept*) = そう
いう ことが ありません。
**2** *adverb*
they have such a lot of money = かれ
らは おかねが たくさん ありま
す。・彼らは お金が たくさん
あります。

she's such a strange person = かのじょは とても へんな ひとです。・ 彼女は とても 変な 人です。

**suddenly** *adverb*
= とつぜん・突然

**suffer** *verb*
(*put up with*) = がまんする ・ 我慢する

**sugar** *noun*
= さとう・砂糖

**suggestion** *noun*
= ていあん・提案

**suicide** *noun*
to commit suicide = じさつする・自殺する

**suit**
**1** *noun*
(*a man's*) = せびろ・背広
(*a woman's*) = スーツ
**2** *verb*
• (*to be convenient*) = つごうが いい・都合が いい
that suits me = それは つごうが いいです。・ それは 都合が いいです。
does Friday suit you? = きんようびは つごうがいいですか。・ 金曜日は 都合が いいですか。
• (*to look well on*)
that hat suits you = その ぼうしは にあいます。・ その 帽子は 似合います。

**suitable** *adjective*
= てきとう(な)・適当(な)
a suitable present = てきとうな プレゼント・ 適当な プレゼント
it is unsuitable for children = こどもに ふさわしくないです。・ 子供に ふさわしくないです。
(*time*) = つごうが いい・都合が いい

**suitcase** *noun*
= スーツケース

**sum** *noun*
• (*amount of money*) = きんがく・金額
• (*total*) = ごうけい・合計
• = けいさん・計算
sum up = ようやくする・ 要約する

**summer** *noun*
= なつ・夏
in summer = なつに・夏に

**summer holiday** (*British English*), **summer vacation** (*US English*)
*noun*
(*a trip*) = なつの りょこう・夏の 旅行
(*from school*) = なつやすみ・夏休み

**sun** *noun*
= たいよう・太陽
to sit in the sun = ひなたに すわる・日向に 座る

**sunbathe** *verb*
= ひなたぼっこする・日向ぼっこする

**sunburn** *noun*
= ひやけ・日焼け

**sunburned** *adjective*
to get sunburned = ひに やける・日に 焼ける

**Sunday** *noun* ▶ 174
= にちようび・日曜日

**sunglasses** *noun*
= サングラス

**sunny** *adjective*
= はれた・晴れた
it's going to be sunny tomorrow = あした はれます。・ 明日 晴れます。

**sunrise** *noun*
= ひので・日の出

**sunset** *noun*
= にちぼつ・日没

**sunshade** *noun*
= パラソル

**sunshine** *noun*
= にっこう・日光

**suntan** *noun*
= ひやけ・日焼け
to get a suntan = ひやけする・日焼けする

**suntan oil** *noun*
= サンタンオイル

**supermarket** *noun*
= スーパー

**supper** *noun*
(*an evening meal*) = ゆうしょく・夕食

**support** *verb*
• (*to agree with, to help*) = しえんする・支援する

to support the strike = ストライキ
を しえんする・ストライキを
支援する
- *(to keep)* = やしなう・養う
to support a family = かぞくを やし
なう・家族を 養う
- *(to hold, to help physically)* = ささえ
る・支える

**supporter** *noun*
*(of a sports team)* = ファン
*(of a political party)* = しえんしゃ・
支援者

**suppose** *verb*
- *(to imagine)* = そうぞうする・想像
する
I don't suppose you know yet = まだ
しらないでしょう。・まだ 知ら
ないでしょう。
- *(to be meant to)*
to be supposed to = verb in dictionary
form + ことに なっている ▶ 191
I'm supposed to go to London = ロン
ドンへいく ことに なっていま
す。・ロンドンへ行く ことに な
っています。

**sure** *adjective*
- *(certain)* = たしか(な)・確か(な)
I'm sure he said nine o'clock = たしか
に かれは くじだと いいました。
・確かに 彼は 九時だと 言いま
した。
are you sure? = ほんとうですか。・
本当ですか。
I'm not sure if Emily's coming = エミ
リさんが くるか どうか わかり
ません。・エミリさんが 来るか
どうか わかりません。
to make sure = たしかめる・確か
める
- *(bound)*
he's sure to win = きっと かれは か
つでしょう。・きっと 彼は 勝つ
でしょう。
- sure of oneself = じしんが ある・
自信が ある

**surf** *verb*
to go surfing = サーフィンに いく・
サーフィンに 行く

**surface** *noun*
= ひょうめん・表面

**surface mail** *noun*
= ふなびん・船便

to send by surface mail = ふなびんで
おくる・船便で 送る

**surfboard** *noun*
= サーフボード

**surgeon** *noun*
= げかい・外科医

**surgery** *noun*
- to have surgery = しゅじゅつを う
ける・手術を 受ける
- *(British English)*
*(the place)*
= びょういん・病院

**surname** *noun*
= みょうじ・名字

**surprise**
**1** *noun*
- *(an event, a gift)*
= おもいがけない もの・思い掛け
ない 物
- *(being amazed)*
= おどろき・驚き
**2** *verb*
= おどろかす・驚かす
to surprise someone = だれかを お
どろかす・誰かを 驚かす

**surprised** *adjective*
= びっくりした
I'm not surprised = びっくりしてい
ません。

**surrender** *verb*
= こうふくする・降伏する

**surround** *verb*
= かこむ・囲む
to be surrounded by trees = きに
かこまれている・木に 囲まれ
ている

**surroundings** *noun*
= しゅうへん・周辺

**survey** *noun*
= アンケート

**survive** *verb*
= いきのこる・生き残る

**suspect**
**1** *verb*
= うたがう・疑う
she's suspected of having stolen
money = かのじょは おかねを ぬ
すんだ うたがいが あります。・
彼女は お金を 盗んだ 疑いが
あります。

S

**2** *noun*
= ようぎしゃ・容疑者

**suspicious** *adjective*
(*having suspicions*) = うたがわしい・疑わしい
(*causing suspicion*) = あやしい・怪しい
a suspicious person = あやしいじんぶつ・怪しい人物

**swan** *noun*
= はくちょう・白鳥

**swap** *verb*
= こうかんする・交換する

**sweat** *verb*
= あせをかく・汗をかく

**sweater** *noun*
= セーター

**sweatshirt** *noun*
= トレーナー

**Sweden** *noun* ▶ 172
= スウェーデン

**sweep** *verb*
= はく・掃く

**sweet**
**1** *adjective*
• = あまい・甘い
  I have a sweet tooth = あまいものがすきです。・甘い物が好きです。
• (*kind, gentle*) = しんせつ(な)・親切(な)
• (*cute*) = かわいい
**2** *noun* (*British English*)
  (*candy*) = あめ
  (*dessert*) = デザート

**swim**
**1** *verb*
= およぐ・泳ぐ
to swim in a lake = みずうみでおよぐ・湖で泳ぐ
**2** *noun*
to go for a swim = およぎにいく・泳ぎに行く

**swimming** *noun*
= すいえい・水泳

**swimming pool** *noun*
= プール

**swimsuit** *noun*
= みずぎ・水着

**swing**
**1** *verb*
• (*to move back and forth*) = ふる・振る

• (*to move something back and forth*) = ふる・振る
to swing one's legs = あしをふる・足を振る
**2** *noun*
= ぶらんこ

**switch**
**1** *noun*
= スイッチ
**2** *verb*
= とりかえる・取り替える
to switch seats = せきをとりかえる・席を取り替える
switch off = けす・消す
to switch off the light = でんきをけす・電気を消す
switch on = つける
to switch the radio on = ラジオをつける

**Switzerland** *noun* ▶ 172
= スイス

**sympathetic** *adjective*
(*showing pity*) = おもいやりのある・思いやりのある
(*showing understanding*) = どうじょうてき(な)・同情的(な)

**syringe** *noun*
= ちゅうしゃき・注射器

**system** *noun*
(*organisation*) = そしき・組織
(*method*) = やりかた・やり方

# Tt

**table** *noun*
= テーブル

**tablet** *noun*
= じょうざい・錠剤

**table tennis** *noun*
= たっきゅう・卓球

**tail** *noun*
= しっぽ・尻尾

**take** *verb*
• (*to take hold of*) = とる・取る
to take someone's hand = だれかのてをとる・誰かの手を取る

- (*to carry with one*) = もって いく・持って行く

  I took my umbrella = かさを もっていきました。・傘を 持って 行きました。

  I'll take the letters to Sharon = シャロンさんに てがみを もって いきます。・シャロンさんに 手紙を 持って 行きます。

- (*to accompany, to bring*) = つれて いく・連れて 行く

  to take the children for a walk = こどもたちを さんぽに つれて いく・子供たちを 散歩に 連れて 行く

  to take someone home = (だれかを) いえに おくる・(誰かを)家に 送る

- (*to remove*) = とる・取る

  to take a book off the shelf = ほんを たなから とる・本を 棚から 取る

- (*to steal*) = ぬすむ・盗む

- (*to cope with, to bear*) = がまんする・我慢する

  he can't take the pain = かれは いたみを がまんできません。・彼は 痛みを 我慢できません。

  I can't take any more = もう がまんできません。・もう 我慢できません。

- (*when talking about what is necessary*)

  it takes time = じかんが かかります。・時間が かかります。

  it takes two hours to get to Matsue = まつえまで にじかん かかります。・松江まで 二時間 かかります。

  to take time to do homework = しゅくだいに じかんが かかる・宿題に 時間が かかる

  it won't take long = ながく かかりません。・長く かかりません。

  it takes courage = ゆうきが いる・勇気が 要る

- (*to accept*) = うけとる・受け取る

- (*to use when travelling*) = いく・行く

  to take a taxi = タクシーで いく・タクシーで 行く

  take the first turn on the right = さいしょを みぎに まがってください。・最初を 右に 曲がってください。

- (*to do*)

  to take exams = しけんを うける・試験を 受ける

- (*to have*)

  to take a vacation = りょこうする・旅行する

  to take a shower = シャワーを あびる・シャワーを 浴びる

  to take driving lessons = くるまの レッスンを うける・車の レッスンを 受ける

  I don't take sugar = さとうを いれません。・砂糖を 入れません。

- (*to wear*)

  I take a size 10

  (*in clothes*) = ようふくの サイズは じゅうです。・洋服の サイズは 十です。

  I take a size 5

  (*in shoes*) = くつの サイズは ごです。・靴の サイズは 5です。

  **take apart** = ぶんかいする・分解する

  **take away**

  to take away the rubbish = ごみを もっていく・ごみを 持って 行く

  a pizza to take away = もちかえりの ピザ・持ち帰りの ピザ

  **take back** = かえす・返す

  I had to take the coat back = コートを かえさなければ なりませんでした。・コートを 返さなければ なりませんでした。

  **take down**

- (*to remove*)

  to take a box down off a shelf = たなから はこを おろす・棚から 箱を 降ろす

  to take a poster down = ポスターを はがす

  to take down a tent = テントを かいたいする・テントを 解体する

- (*to write down*) = かきとる・書き取る

  **take hold of** = つかむ・掴む

  **take off**

- (*from an airport*) = りりくする・離陸する

- (*to remove clothing*) = ぬぐ・脱ぐ

  I took off my shoes = くつを ぬぎました。・靴を 脱ぎました。

  to take off one's clothes = ふくを ぬぐ・服を 脱ぐ

  **take out**

- (*from a box, a pocket, a bag*) = とりだす・取り出す

  I took a pen out of my pocket = ポケットから ペンを とりだしまし

**T**

た。・ポケットから ペンを取り
出しました。
- (*from a bank account*) = ひきだす・
引き出す
to take money out = おかねを ひきだ
す・お金を 引き出す
**take part**
to take part in a game = ゲームに さ
んかする・ゲームに 参加する
**take place** = おこなう・行う
**take up**
- (*as a hobby*)
to take up golf = ゴルフを はじめる
・ゴルフを 始める
- (*to use up*)
to take up space = ばしょを とる・
場所を 取る
to take up time = じかんが かかる・
時間が かかる

**talented** *adjective*
= じょうず(な)・上手(な)

**talk**
**1** *verb*
- (*to speak*) = はなす・話す
to talk on the phone = でんわで はな
す・電話で 話す
to talk in Japanese = に ほんごで
はなす・日本語で 話す
to talk to someone = だれかと はな
す・誰かと 話す
I talked about the trip = りょこうに
ついて はなしました。・旅行に
ついて 話しました。
they were talking about you = かれら
は あなたの ことを はなしてい
ました。・彼らは あなたのこと
を 話していました。
to talk to oneself = ひとりごとを
いう・独り言を 言う
- (*to chat*) = しゃべる・喋る
**2** *noun*
- (*a conversation*)
= はなし・話
- (*about an academic subject*)
= はっぴょう・発表
give a talk = はっぴょうする・発表
する
- (*discussions*)
talks = かいだん・会談

**talkative** *adjective*
= おしゃべり(な)・お喋り(な)

**tall** *adjective*
(*describing a person*) = せが たかい
・背が 高い

(*describing a building, a tree*) = たか
い・高い
I am six feet tall = しんちょうは
ひゃくはちじゅうセンチです。・
身長は 百八十センチです。
to get tall = せがたかく なる・背が
高く なる

**tan** *noun*
= ひやけ・日焼け
to get a tan = ひに やける・日に 焼
ける

**tanned** *adjective*
= ひに やけた・日に 焼けた

**tap**
**1** *noun* (*British English*)
= じゃぐち・蛇口
to turn the tap on = みずを だす・
水を 出す
to turn the tap off = みずを とめる・
水を 止める
**2** *verb*
to tap on the door = ドアを かるく
たたく・ドアを 軽く たたく

**tape**
**1** *noun*
- = テープ
- (*for repairs, for sticking*)
= セロテープ
**2** *verb*
(*audio*) = ろくおんする・録音する
(*video*) = ろくがする・録画する

**tape recorder** *noun*
= テープレコーダー

**target**
**1** *noun*
(*for arrows*) = まと・的
(*aim*) = もくてき・目的
**2** *verb*
= もくひょうをたっせいする・目
標を達成する

**tart** *noun* (*British English*)
= タルト
apple tart = アップルパイ

**task** *noun*
= しごと・仕事

**taste**
**1** *noun*
- (*when eating, drinking*)
= あじ・味
- (*when talking about preferences*)
= このみ・好み

it's not to my taste = わたしの この
みではありません。・私の 好み
ではありません。
Yukiko has good taste = ゆきこは
しゅみが いいです。・幸子は 趣
味が いいです。
**2** *verb*
* (*when describing a flavour*)
  it tastes good = おいしいです。
  It tastes awful – まずいです。
  it tastes of cinnamon = シナモンの
  あじが します。・シナモンの 味
  が します。
* (*when eating, drinking*) = あじわう・
  味わう

**Taurus** *noun*
= おうしざ・牡牛座

**tax** *noun*
= ぜいきん・税金

**taxi** *noun*
= タクシー

**taxi rank** (*British English*), **taxi
stand** (*US English*) *noun*
= タクシーのりば・タクシー乗り
場

**tea** *noun*
* (*as drunk in the west*) = こうちゃ・
  紅茶
  (*as drunk in Japan*) = おちゃ・お茶
* (*British English*)
  (*a meal*) = ばんごはん・晩ご飯
  (ゆうしょく *is also used.*)

**tea ceremony** *noun*
= さどう・茶道

**teach** *verb*
= おしえる・教える
to teach Japanese = にほんごを お
しえる・日本語を 教える

**teacher** *noun*
= せんせい・先生

**team** *noun*
= チーム

**teapot** *noun*
(*for Japanese tea*) = きゅうす
(*for English tea*) = ティーポット

**tear¹** *verb*
* (*to cause damage to*) = やぶる・破る
  to tear pages out of a book = ほん
  の ページを やぶりとる・本の
  ページを 破り取る

* (*to get damaged*) = やぶれる・破れ
  る
  **tear off** = ひきさく・引き裂く
  **tear up** = ずたずたに やぶる・
  ずたずたに 破る

**tear²** *noun*
= なみだ・涙
to burst into tears = なきだす・泣き
出す

**tease** *verb*
= からかう

**teaspoon** *noun*
(*cutlery*) = ティースプーン
(*measurement*) = こさじ・小さじ

**technical** *adjective*
= ぎじゅつてき(な)・技術的(な)

**teenager** *noun*
= ティーンエージャー

**telephone** *noun*
= でんわ・電話

**telephone directory** *noun*
= でんわちょう・電話帳

**telescope** *noun*
= ぼうえんきょう・望遠鏡

**television** *noun*
= テレビ
I saw that film on television = あの
えいがを テレビで みました。・
あの 映画を テレビで 見ました。

**tell** *verb*
* (*to say to*) = いう・言う
  did you tell your parents? = ごりょう
  しんに いいましたか。・ご両親
  に 言いましたか。
  to tell someone about a problem =
  だれかに もんだいを うちあけ
  る・誰かに 問題を 打ち明ける
  to tell jokes = じょうだんを いう・
  冗談を 言う
* (*when giving information*) = おしえる
  ・教える
  to tell someone your address = だれ
  かに じゅうしょを おしえる・
  誰かに 住所を 教える
  to tell someone the way = だれかに
  みちを おしえる・誰かに 道を
  教える
* (*to work out, to know*)
  I can tell (that) she's disappointed =
  かのじょは がっかりした よう
  です。・彼女は がっかりした よ
  うです。

**T**

you can tell he's lying = かれは うそ を ついているのが わかるでし ょう。・ 彼は 嘘をついているの が 分かるでしょう。

* (when making distinctions)
  to tell the twins apart = ふた ご を みわける ・ 双子を 見分ける
  I can't tell which is which = みわけが つきません。・ 見分けが つきま せん。

* (to reveal) = いう ・ 言う
  please don't tell anyone = だれにも いわないでください。・ 誰にも 言わないでください。

**tell off**
  to tell someone off = だれかを しか る ・ 誰かを 叱る

**temper** noun
  to be in a temper = おこっている ・ 怒っている
  to lose one's temper = おこる ・ 怒る

**temperature** noun ▶ 181
  = おんど ・ 温度
  to have a temperature = ねつが ある ・ 熱が ある

**temporary** adjective
  = いちじてき(な) ・ 一時的(な)
  (describing a job) = りんじ(の) ・ 臨時(の)

**ten** number ▶ 171, ▶ 181, ▶ 186
  (on its own) = とお ・ 十
  (with a counter) = じゅう ・ 十
  ten books = ほん じゅっさつ ・ 本 十冊
  I've got ten = とお あります。・ 十 あります。

**tennis** noun
  = テニス

**tennis court** noun
  = テニスコート

**tense** adjective
  = きんちょうしている ・ 緊張して いる

**tent** noun
  = テント

**tenth** number
* (in a series) = じゅうばん(め) ・ 十 番(目)
* (in dates) ▶ 174
  the tenth of December = じゅうにが つとおか ・ 十二月十日

**term** noun
  = がっき ・ 学期

**terrible** adjective
* (expressing shock) = ひどい
* (used for emphasis) = すごい

**terrified** adjective
  = おそれを なした ・ 恐れを なし た

**terror** noun
  = きょうふ ・ 恐怖

**terrorist** noun
  = テロリスト

**test**
1 verb
* (to try out) = ためして みる ・ 試して みる
* (in exams) = テストする
2 noun
* = テスト
  (in school, college)
  = しけん ・ 試験
  a driving test = うんてんめんきょの しけん ・ 運転免許の 試験
* to have an eye test = しりょくけん さを うける ・ 視力検査を 受け る

**text**
1 noun
  (text message) = テキストメッセ ージ
2 verb
  = テキストメッセージ する

**than**
1 preposition
* Note that the word order is different to English in sentences expressing comparison.
  (in comparisons) = ～より～
  stronger than... = ～より つよい ・ ～より 強い
  more intelligent than... = ～より あた まが いい ・ ～より 頭が いい
  I've got more money than you = わた しは あなたより もっと おかね が あります。・ 私は あなたより もっと お金が あります。
* (when talking about quantities)
  more than = ～いじょう ・ ～以上
  more than £100 = ひゃくポンドいじ ょう ・ 百ポンド以上
  less than = ～いか ・ ～以下
  less than 2% = にパーセントいか ・ 二パーセント以下

**2** *conjunction*
= 〜より〜
he's older than I am = かれは わたし
より としうえです。・ 彼は 私よ
り 年上です。

**thank** *verb*
= かんしゃする・感謝する

**thanks**
**1** *adverb* = ありがとう。
**2 thanks to** = 〜の おかげで

**thank you** *adverb*
= ありがとうございます。
thank you for coming = きて くれて
ありがとうございます。・ 来て
くれて ありがとうございます。
(*when accepting food and drink*)
'more wine?'—'thank you' = 「ワイン
はいかがですか。」「いただきま
す。」

**that** *pronoun*
what's that? = それは なんですか。
・ それは 何ですか。
who's that? = その ひとは だれです
か。・ その 人は 誰ですか。
is that Lewis? = あの ひとは ルイス
さんですか。・ あの 人は ルイス
さんですか。
that's how jam is made = そうやって
ジャムが つくられます。・ そう
やって ジャムが 作られます。
that's not true = それは ほんとうで
はありません。・ それは 本当で
はありません。
that's the kitchen = そこは だいどこ
ろです。・ そこは 台所です。

**the** *determiner*

> ! *Not used in Japanese.*

**theatre** (*British English*), **theater**
(*US English*) *noun*
= げきじょう・劇場

**their** *determiner*
= かれらの・彼らの *Not used if*
*obvious. If you know their names,*
*it is better to use these rather than*
かれら
I don't like their house = かれらの い
えが すきではありません。・ 彼
らの 家が 好きではありません。

**theirs** *pronoun*
= かれらの・彼らの *If you know*
*their names, it is better to use these*
*rather than* かれら

that new house is theirs = あの あた
らしい いえは かれらのです。・
あの 新しい 家は 彼らのです。
which car is theirs? = かれらの くる
まは どれですか。・ 彼らの 車は
どれですか。

**theme park** *noun*
= テーマパーク

**themselves** *pronoun*
• *Not used as a reflexive pronoun in*
*Japanese.*
they want to enjoy themselves = かれ
らは たのしみたいです。・ 彼ら
は 楽しみたいです。
they didn't hurt themselves = かれ
らは けがを しませんでした。・
彼らは 怪我を しませんでし
た。
• (*when used for emphasis*)
they did it all by themselves = かれら
は じぶんたちで しました。・ 彼
らは 自分達で しました。

**then** *adverb*
• (*at that point in time*) = その とき
I was living in Paris then = その と
き、 パリに すんでいました。・
その とき、 パリに 住んでいま
した。
from then on = その ときから
• (*after, next*) = そして
I had breakfast and then I went to
work = あさごはんを たべまし
た。そして かいしゃに いきま
した。・ 朝ご飯を 食べました。
そして 会社に 行きました。
*The* 〜て *form of the verb can also*
*be used when describing a*
*chronological sequence of actions*
▶ 197
I watched a film, drank some beer,
then went home. = えいがを みて、
ビールをのんで、 かえりました。
・ 映画を 見て、 ビールを 飲ん
で、 帰りました。

**there**
**1** *pronoun*
there is a problem = もんだいが あ
ります・問題が あります。
there aren't any shops = みせが あり
ません。・ 店が ありません。
there was no room = よゆうが あり
ませんでした。余裕が ありませ
んでした。

T

there are a lot of people = ひとが た
くさん います。・ 人がたくさん
います。

**2** adverb

• (when talking about location)
the train wasn't there = でんしゃが
ありませんでした。・ 電車が
ありませんでした。

please go over there = あそこに
いってください。・ あそこに
行ってください。

when do we get there? = いつ つきま
すか。・ いつ 着きますか。

I don't go there very often = そこに
あまり いきません。・ そこに
あまり 行きません。

• (when drawing attention)
there's the sea = うみです。・ 海で
す。

(when offering something)
there you are, there you go = どうぞ。

**therefore** adverb
= ですから

**these**

**1** determiner
= この

these books aren't mine = この ほん
は わたしのではありません。・
この 本は 私のではありません。

**2** pronoun
= これ

what are these? = これは なんです
か。・ これは 何ですか。

these are my bags = これは わたし
の かばんです。・ これは 私の
かばんです。

I prefer these = これの ほうが いい
です。・ これの 方が いいです。

(when referring to people) = このひと
たち・ この 人達

these are my friends from Manchester
= このひとたちはマンチェスタ
ーからの ともだちです。・ この
人たちはマンチェスターからの
友達です。

**they** pronoun
= かれら・ 彼ら *Not used if obvious.*
*If you know their names, it is better*
*to use these rather than* かれら

they'll be there too = かれらも いま
す。・ 彼らも います。

they're intelligent = かれらは あた
まが いいです。・ 彼らは 頭が
いいです。

that's how they make tofu = それは
とうふの つくりかたです。・ そ
れは 豆腐の 作り方です。

**thick** adjective
= あつい・ 厚い

**thief** noun
= どろぼう・ 泥棒

**thigh** noun
= ふともも・ 太もも

**thin** adjective
(line) = ほそい・ 細い
(person, animal) = やせた・ 痩せた
to get thin = やせる・ 痩せる

**thing** noun

• (physical object) = もの・ 物
(abstract entity) = こと

please take the things off the chair =
いすから ものを どかしてくだ
さい。・ 椅子から 物を 退かして
ください。

I've got things to do = する ことが
あります。

that is a stupid thing to do = それは
ばかな ことです。

the best thing would be to call him =
かれに でんわした ほうが いい
です。・ 彼に 電話した 方が
いいです。

I can't hear a thing = なにも きこえ
ません。・ 何も 聞こえません。

• (belongings)
= もちもの・ 持ち物

**think** verb

• (when talking about opinions) = use a
plain form + と おもう

what do you think of it? = どう お
もいますか。・ どう 思いま
すか。

I think it's unfair = ふこうへいだと
おもいます。・ 不公平だと 思い
ます。

who do you think will win? = だれが
かつと おもいますか。・ 誰が
勝つと 思いますか。

• (to concentrate on an idea) = かんが
える・ 考える

please think hard before answering =
こたえるまえに よく かんがえ
てください。・ 答える前に よく
考えてください。

• (to remember) = おもいだす・ 思い
出す

I can't think of his name = かれの
なまえが おもいだせません。・
彼の 名前が 思い出せません。
- (to take into account, to have in mind)
  to think about someone = だれかの
  ことを かんがえる ・ 誰かの こ
  とを 考える
  I thought of you when I saw the dress
  = あの ドレスを みた とき、あな
  たの ことを おもいだしました。
  ・ あの ドレスを 見た とき、
  あなたの ことを 思い出しまし
  た。
- (to have vague plans to)
  to be thinking of going to America =
  アメリカに いく ことを かん
  がえている ・ アメリカに 行く
  ことを 考えている
- (to have an idea about)
  to think of a solution = かいけつほう
  を おもいつく ・ 解決法を 思い
  つく

## third
**1** adjective
= さんばん(め)・ 三番(目)
**2** noun
- (in a series)
  = さんばんめ(の)・ 三番目(の)
- (in dates) ▶ 174
  the third of June = ろくがつみっか・
  六月三日
- (when talking about quantities)
  = さんぶんの いち ・ 三分の 一
  a third of the population = じんこう
  の さんぶんの いち・人口の 三
  分の 一
**3** adverb
  to come third = さんいに なる ・ 三
  位に なる

## thirsty adjective
  to be thirsty = のどが かわいている
  ・ 喉が 渇いている

## thirteen number ▶ 171, ▶ 181
= じゅうさん ・ 十三

## thirteenth number
- (in a series) = じゅうさんばん(め)
  ・ 十三番(目)
- (in dates) ▶ 174
  Friday the thirteenth = じゅうさん
  にちの きんよう び ・ 十三日の
  金曜日

## thirty number ▶ 171, ▶ 181, ▶ 186
= さんじゅう ・ 三十

## this
**1** determiner
= この
I like this garden = この にわが すき
です。・ この 庭が 好きです。
do you know this place? = この ばし
ょを しっていますか。・ この 場
所を 知っていますか。
who is this woman? = この おんなの
ひとは だれですか。・ この 女の
人は 誰ですか。
I prefer this hotel = この ホテルの ほ
うが いいです。・ この ホテルの
方が いいです。
**2** pronoun
what's this? = これは なんですか。
・ これは 何ですか。
who's this? = この ひとは だれです
か。・ この 人は 誰ですか。
this is the kitchen = ここは だいどこ
ろです。・ ここは 台所です。
this is my older sister = こちらは
あねです。・ こちらは 姉です。
this isn't the right address = これは
ただしいじゅうしょではありま
せん。・ これは 正しい住所では
ありません。
how much is this? = これは いくら
ですか。

## thorn noun
= とげ

## those
**1** determiner
(referring to things near the listener) =
その
(referring to things not close to either
speaker or listener) = あの
those books are his = その ほんは
かれのです。・ その 本は 彼ので
す。
**2** pronoun
(referring to things near the listener) =
それ
(referring to things not close to either
speaker or listener) = あれ
what are those? = あれは なんです
か。・ あれは 何ですか。
those are my letters = それは わた
しの てがみです。・ それは 私の
手紙です。
I prefer those = あれの ほうが いい
です。・ あれの 方が いいです。
(when referring to people) = その ひと
たち ・ その 人達

T

those are my cousins = その ひとた
ちは いとこです。・ その人達は
いとこです。

**though** *conjunction*
= けれども
though it's expensive, I'll buy it = たか
い けれども かいます。・ 高いけ
れども 買います。

**thought** *noun*
(*idea*) = かんがえ・ 考え

**thousand** *number*
= せん・ 千 ▶181
three thousand pounds = さんぜんポ
ンド・ 三千ポンド
about a thousand people = せんにん
ぐらい・ 千人ぐらい

**thread** *noun*
= いと・ 糸

**threat** *noun*
= おどし・ 脅し

**threaten** · *verb*
= おどす・ 脅す

**three** *number* ▶171, ▶181, ▶186
(*on its own*) = みっつ・ 三つ
(*with a counter*) = さん・ 三
three books = ほん さんさつ・ 本
三冊
I've got three = みっつ あります。・
三つ あります。

**throat** *noun*
= のど・ 喉

**through**

> ! *Often* through *occurs in*
> *combinations with verbs, for*
> *example:* go through, let through,
> read through *etc. To find the correct*
> *translations for this type of verb,*
> *look up the separate dictionary*
> *entries at* go, let, read *etc.*

*preposition*
• (*from one side to the other*)
to drive through the desert = さばく
を とおりぬける・ 砂漠を 通り
抜ける
I ran through the park = こうえんを
はしりました。・ 公園を 走りま
した。
• (*via, by way of*)
to go through the town centre = まち
なかを とおって いく・ 町中を
通って 行く

to look through a window = まどから
みる・ 窓から 見る
• (*past*)
to go through a red light = あかしん
ごうを とおる・ 赤信号を 通る
to go through customs = ぜいかんを
とおる・ 税関を 通る
• (*when talking about time*)
right through the day = いちにちじ
ゅう・ 一日中
from Friday through to Sunday = きん
ようびから にちようびまで・
金曜日から 日曜日まで
it's open April through September (*US
English*) = しがつから くがつまで
あいています。・ 四月から 九月
まで 開いています。

**throw** *verb*
= なげる・ 投げる
to throw stones at someone = だれか
に いしを なげる・ 誰かに 石を
投げる
please throw me the ball = ボールを
わたしに なげてください。・ ボ
ールを 私に 投げてください。
throw away, throw out = すてる・
捨てる

**thumb** *noun*
= おやゆび・ 親指

**thunder** *noun*
= かみなり・ 雷

**thunderstorm** *noun*
= らいう・ 雷雨

**Thursday** *noun* ▶174
= もくようび・ 木曜日

**ticket** *noun*
= きっぷ・ 切符

**tickle** *verb*
= くすぐる

**tide** *noun*
= しお・ 潮
high tide = まんちょう・ 満潮
low tide = かんちょう・ 干潮

**tidy** *adjective*
(*describing a place, a desk*) = きちん
とした
(*describing a person*) = きれいずき
(な)・ きれい好き(な)
tidy up = かたづける・ 片づける

**tie**
**1** *verb*
= むすぶ・ 結ぶ

to tie a dog to a tree = いぬを きに つなぐ・犬を 木に つなぐ
to tie a parcel (up) with string = にもつを ひもで しばる・荷物を 紐で 縛る

**2** *noun*
• (*worn with a shirt*)
= ネクタイ
• (*in sport*)
= どうてん・同点

**tiger** *noun*
= とら・虎
year of the tiger = とらどし・寅年

**tight** *adjective*
(*too small*) = きつい
(*closely fitting*) = ぴったりした

**tights** *noun* (*British English*)
= タイツ

**till¹** ▶ until

**till²** *noun*
= レジ

**timber** *noun*
= もくざい・木材

**time** *noun*
• = じかん・時間
I don't have time to go there = そこに いく じかんが ありません。・そこに 行く 時間が ありません。
we haven't seen them for some time = しばらく かれらに あっていません。・しばらく 彼らに 会っていません。
a long time ago = むかし・昔
• (*when talking about a specific hour or period of time*)
the time when... = ～とき
what's the time?, what time is it? = なんじですか。・何時ですか。
what time does the film start? = えいがは なんじに はじまりますか。・映画は 何時に 始まりますか。
to arrive on time = じかんどおりに つく・時間通りに 着く
in five days' time = いつかごに・五日後に
in a week's time = いっしゅうかんごに・一週間後に
this time last year = きょねんの いまごろ・去年の 今ごろ
by this time next week = らいしゅうの いまごろまでに・来週の 今ごろまでに

it's time we left = そろそろ しつれいします。・そろそろ 失礼します。
• (*a moment*)
at times = ときどき・時々
this is no time to argue = けんかしている ばあいではありません。・けんかしている 場合ではありません。
any time now = もう すぐ
for the time being = いまの ところ・今の ところ
• (*a period in the past*)
= とき
we didn't know each other at the time = そのときは おたがいに しりませんでした。・その ときはお互いに 知りませんでした。
• (*an experience*)
to have a good time = たのしむ・楽しむ
to have a hard time = くろうする・苦労する
• (*an occasion*)
the first time we met = はじめて あった とき・初めて 会った とき
from time to time = ときどき・時々
• (*when comparing*)
three times more expensive = さんばい たかい・三倍 高い
ten times quicker = じゅうばい はやい・十倍 早い

**timetable** *noun*
• (*for trains, buses*)
= じこくひょう・時刻表
• (*in school, at work*)
= じかんわり・時間割

**tin** *noun*
• (*the metal*)
= すず
• (*British English*)
(*a can*)
= かん・缶
tinned tomatoes = かんづめの トマト・缶詰の トマト

**tin opener** *noun* (*British English*)
= かんきり・缶切り

**tiny** *adjective*
= ちいさ(な)・小さ(な)

**tip** *noun*
• (*the point, the end*)
= せんたん・先端
to stand on tiptoe = つまさきで たつ・爪先で 立つ

T

- (*given in a hotel, a restaurant*)
= チップ
- (*a piece of advice*)
= じょげん ・ 助言

**tire** *noun* (*US English*)
= タイヤ

**tired** *adjective*
- (*needing rest*) = つかれている ・ 疲れている
to get tired = つかれる ・ 疲れる
- (*needing a change*)
I'm tired of this job = この しごとに あきています。・ この 仕事に 飽きています。
I'm tired of computer games = コンピューターゲームに あきています。・ コンピューターゲームに 飽きています。

**tiring** *adjective*
= つかれさせる ・ 疲れさせる

**tissue** *noun*
= ティッシュ

**to** *preposition* ▶ xiv

> ! *There are many adjectives like* mean, nice, rude *etc and verbs like* belong, write *etc which involve the use of* to. *For translations, look up the adjective entries at* mean, nice, rude *or the verb entries at* belong, write.

**toast** *noun*
= トースト
a piece of toast = トースト いちまい ・ トースト 一枚

**toaster** *noun*
= トースター

**today** *adverb*
= きょう ・ 今日

**toe** *noun*
= あしの ゆび ・ 足の 指

**together** *adverb*
= いっしょに ・ 一緒に

**toilet** *noun*
= トイレ *A more polite word is* おてあらい ▶ 189

**toilet paper** *noun*
= トイレットペーパー

**tomato** *noun*
= トマト

**tomorrow** *adverb*
= あした ・ 明日

**tongue** *noun*
= した ・ 舌

**tonight** *adverb*
(*this evening*) = こんばん ・ 今晩
(*during the night*) = よなかに ・ 夜中に

**too** *adverb*
- (*also*) = use particle も ▶ 205
I'm going too = わたしも いきます。・ 私も 行きます。
- (*more than is necessary or desirable*)
= use い adjective without the final い + すぎる or the pre ます form of the verb + すぎる ▶ 191, ▶ 201
too big = おおきすぎる ・ 大きすぎる
too expensive = たかすぎる ・ 高すぎる
too far = とおすぎる ・ 遠すぎる
there were too many people = ひとが おおすぎました。・ 人が 多すぎました。
I ate too much = たべすぎました。・ 食べ過ぎました。

**tool** *noun*
= どうぐ ・ 道具

**tooth** *noun*
= は ・ 歯
false teeth = いれば ・ 入れ歯

**toothache** *noun*
I have toothache = はが いたいです。・ 歯が 痛いです。

**toothbrush** *noun*
= はブラシ ・ 歯ブラシ

**toothpaste** *noun*
= はみがきこ ・ 歯磨き粉

**top**
**1** *noun*
- (*the highest part*)
the top of the mountain = やまの ちょうじょう ・ 山の 頂上
the top of the stairs = かいだんの うえ ・ 階段の 上
top of the page = ページの あたま ・ ページの 頭
- (*a cover, a lid*)
(*on a bottle, pan*) = ふた
(*on a pen*) = キャップ
- (*the highest level*)
to be at the top of the class = クラスの なかで いちばん できる ・ クラスの 中で 一番 できる

**2** *adjective*
= いちばんうえ(の)・一番上(の)

**top-up card** *noun*
= トップアップカード

**torch** *noun* (*British English*)
= かいちゅうでんとう・懐中電灯

**torn** *adjective*
= やぶれている・破れている

**tortoise** *noun*
= かめ・亀

**total**
**1** *noun*
= ごうけい・合計
**2** *adjective*
= ぜんたい(の)・全体(の)

**touch**
**1** *verb*
• (*with one's hand*) = さわる・触る
• (*to interfere with*) = いじる
**2** *noun*
to get in touch = れんらくする・
連絡する

**tough** *adjective*
• (*not soft, not sensitive*) = かたい
• (*rough*)
this is a tough area = この へんは
ちあんが わるいです。・この
辺は 治安が 悪いです。
• (*difficult*) = むずかしい・難しい
• (*severe*)
a tough law = きびしい ほうりつ・
厳しい 法律

**tour**
**1** *noun*
= ツアー
to go on a tour of the castle = おしろ
の ツアーを する・お城の ツア
ーを する
**2** *verb*
to go touring = かんこうりょこうす
る・観光旅行する

**tourism** *noun*
= かんこうぎょう・観光業

**tourist** *noun*
= かんこうきゃく・観光客

**tourist information office**
*noun*
= かんこうあんないじょ・観光案
内所

**toward(s)** *preposition*
• (*when talking about place, time*) = use
particle へ ▶ 205

towards the east = ひがしへ・東へ
towards evening = ゆうがたごろ・
夕方ごろ
• (*when talking about attitudes*) = 〜に
たいして・〜に 対して
he has a bad attitude towards his work
= かれは しごとにたいしてたい
どが わるいです。・彼は 仕事に
対して 態度が 悪いです。

**towel** *noun*
= タオル

**tower** *noun*
= とう・塔

**tower block** *noun* (*British English*)
(*residential*) = こうそうじゅうたく
・高層住宅
(*commercial*) = こうそう ビル・高
層ビル

**town** *noun*
= まち・町
to go into town = まちへ いく・町へ
行く

**town hall** *noun*
= しやくしょ・市役所
(*for a small town*) = やくば・役場

**toy** *noun*
= おもちゃ

**track** *noun*
• (*a path*)
= みち・道
• (*for sports*)
= トラック
• (*the rails*)
= せんろ・線路
• (*left by a person, an animal, a car*)
= あと・跡

**tracksuit** *noun*
= トレーニングウエア

**trade** *noun*
• = ぼうえき・貿易
• (*skill*)
to learn a trade = ぎじゅつを ならう
・技術を 習う

**tradition** *noun*
= でんとう・伝統

**traditional** *adjective*
= でんとうてき(な)・伝統的(な)

**traffic** *noun*
= こうつう・交通

**traffic jam** *noun*
= こうつうじゅうたい・交通渋滞

**traffic lights** *noun*
= しんごう・信号

**train**
**1** *noun*
= でんしゃ・電車
the train to Hiroshima = ひろしまゆ きの でんしゃ・広島行きの 電車
**2** *verb*
- *(to teach, to prepare)*
to train employees = けんしゅうさ せる・研修させる
to train athletes = くんれんさせる・ 訓練させる
to train a dog = いぬを しつける・ 犬を 躾る
- *(to learn a job)*
to train as a doctor = いしゃの し かくを とる・医者の 資格を 取る
she trained as a teacher = かのじょ は きょういんめんきょを もっ ています。・彼女は 教員免許を 持っています。
- *(for a sporting event)* = トレーニング する

**trainer** *noun* *(British English)*
*(shoe)* = スニーカー
*(sports coach)* = コーチ

**training course** *noun*
= トレーニングコース

**tramp** *noun*
= ふろうしゃ・浮浪者

**translate** *verb*
= やくす・訳す

**translator** *noun*
= ほんやくしゃ・翻訳者

**transport, transportation**
*(US English)* *noun*
= ゆそう・輸送
a means of transport = ゆそうきかん ・輸送機関

**trap** *noun*
= わな
to set a trap for someone = だれかに わなを しかける・誰かに わな を 仕掛ける

**trash** *noun* *(US English)*
= ごみ

**trash can** *noun* *(US English)*
= ごみばこ・ごみ箱

**travel** *verb*
*(to travel to work or school)* = かよう ・通う
*(to take a holiday)* = りょこうする・ 旅行する
*(to travel on business)* = しゅっちょ うする・出張する
to travel abroad = がいこくりょこう する・外国旅行する

**travel agency** *noun*
= りょこうがいしゃ・旅行会社

**traveller** *(British English)*,
**traveler** *(US English)* *noun*
= りょこうしゃ・旅行者

**traveller's cheque** *(British
English)*, **traveler's check**
*(US English)* *noun*
= トラベラーズチェック

**tray** *noun*
= おぼん・お盆 ▶ **189**

**treat** *verb*
- *(to deal with, to behave with)* = あつか う・扱う
to treat someone badly = だれかを わるく あつかう・誰かを 悪く 扱う
- *(to pay for)* = おごる
to treat someone to a meal = だれ かに ごはんを おごる・誰かに ご飯を おごる

**treatment** *noun*
= ちりょう・治療
to receive treatment = ちりょうを うける・治療を 受ける

**tree** *noun*
= き・木

**tremble** *verb*
*(person)* = ふるえる・震える
*(ground)* = ゆれる・揺れる

**trendy** *adjective*
= トレンディ(な)

**trial** *noun*
*(test)* = テスト
*(in law)* = さいばん・裁判
to go on trial = さいばんに かけら れる・裁判に かけられる

**triangle** *noun*
= さんかく・三角
*(musical instrument)* = トライアング ル ▶ **180**

## trick

**1** *noun*
- *(a joke)*
= いたずら
to play a trick on someone = だれ かに いたずらを する・誰かに いたずらを する
- *(a clever way of doing something)*
= こつ
- *(to entertain)*
= てじな・手品

**2** *verb*
= だます

## trip

**1** *noun*
*(holiday)* = りょこう・旅行
*(a day out)* = ひがえりりょこう・ 日帰り旅行
*(business trip)* = しゅっちょう・出 張
*(school day trip)* = えんそく・遠足

**2** *verb*
to trip (up) = つまずく・躓く
to trip someone (up) = だれかを つま ずかせる・誰かを 躓かせる

## trouble *noun*
- *(difficulties)*
= こんなん・困難
to be in trouble = こまっている・困 っている
to get someone into trouble = だれ かを こまらせる・誰かを 困ら せる
to make trouble = もんだいを おこ す・問題を 起こす
- *(an effort)*
to go to a lot of trouble to... = わざわ ざ ～する

## trousers *noun*
= ズボン

## trout *noun*
= ます

## truck *noun*
= トラック

## truck driver *noun*
= トラックの うんてんしゅ・トラ ックの 運転手

## true *adjective*
= ほんとう(の)・本当(の)
is it true that he's coming? = かれが くるのは ほんとうですか。・彼 が 来るのは 本当ですか。

to come true = じつげんする・実現 する

## trumpet *noun* ▶ 180
= トランペット

## trunk *noun*
- *(of a tree)*
= みき・幹
- *(of an elephant)*
= はな・鼻
- *(US English)*
*(in a car)*
= トランク

## trunks *noun*
*(for swimming)* = みずぎ・水着

## trust *verb*
- *(to believe)* = しんようする・信用 する
to trust a friend = ともだちを しんよ うする・友達を 信用する
I don't trust them = かれらを しんよ うしません。・彼らを 信用しま せん。
- *(to rely on)* = しんらいする・信頼 する
I can't trust him = かれを しんらいで きません。・彼を 信頼できませ ん。

## truth *noun*
= しんじつ・真実

## try

**1** *verb*
- *(to try to do something)* = use the volitional form of the verb + とする ▶ 191
to try to go = いこうと する・行こ うと する
to try to forget = わすれようと する ・忘れようと する
*(to try it and see)* = use the ～て form of the verb + みる ▶ 197
please try phoning him = かれに でん わして みてください。・彼に 電話して みてください。
I tried writing my name in katakana = じぶんの なまえを カタカナで かいて みました。・自分の 名前 を カタカナで書いて みました。
- *(to test)* = use the ～て form of the verb + みる ▶ 197
to try (out) a new restaurant = あたら しい レストランに いって みる ・新しい レストランに 行ってみ る

**T**

to try (on) a pair of trousers = ズボン
を はいて みる
- *(to taste)* = あじわう ・ 味わう
- *(in court)* = さいばんに かける ・
裁判に かける
- to try hard = がんばる ・ 頑張る

**2** *noun*
*(in rugby)* = トライ

**T-shirt** *noun*
= Tシャツ

**tube** *noun*
- = くだ ・ 管
- *(British English)*
*(the underground)*
= ちかてつ ・ 地下鉄

**Tuesday** *noun* ▶ **174**
= かようび ・ 火曜日

**tuna** *noun*
*(fish)* = まぐろ
*(in can, sandwich)* = ツナ

**tunnel** *noun*
= トンネル

**turkey** *noun*
= しちめんちょう ・ 七面鳥

**turn**
**1** *verb*
- *(to move one's body)* = むける ・ 向
ける
to turn one's face toward(s) the sun =
たいように かおを むける ・ 太
陽に 顔を 向ける
- *(to change direction)*
to turn right = みぎに まがる ・ 右に
曲がる
to turn the corner = かどを まがる ・
角を 曲がる
- *(to twist)* = まわす ・ 回す
to turn the handle = ハンドルを まわ
す ・ ハンドルを 回す
- *(to change)*
to turn the bedroom into an office =
しんしつを オフィスに かえる ・
寝室を オフィスに 変える
to turn into a frog = かえるに なる ・
蛙に なる
- *(to become)* = なる
to turn into a butterfly = ちょうに な
る ・ 蝶に なる
to turn red = あかくなる ・ 赤く なる

**2** *noun*
- *(a bend)* = カーブ
- *(in games)* = ばん ・ 番

whose turn is it? = だれの ばんです
か。・ 誰の 番ですか。
**turn around, turn round**
- *(to face the opposite way)*
*(if it's a person)* = せなかを むける ・
背中を 向ける
*(if it's a car)* = むきを かえる ・ 向き
を 変える
to turn the table around = テーブルを
まわす ・ テーブルを 回す
- *(to go round and round)* = まわる ・
回る
to turn something round and round =
なにかを まわす ・ 何かを 回す
**turn back** = ひきかえす ・ 引き返す
**turn down**
- *(to lower)* = よわく する ・ 弱く する
to turn down the heater = ヒーターを
よわく する ・ ヒーターを 弱く
する
- *(to reject)* = ことわる ・ 断る
to turn someone down = だれかを
ことわる ・ 誰かを 断る
**turn off**
to turn the oven off = オーブンを
けす ・ オーブンを 消す
to turn off the light = でんきを けす
・ 電気を 消す
to turn the tap off = みずを とめる ・
水を 止める
**turn on** = つける
to turn on the TV = テレビを つける
to turn the tap on = みずを だす ・
水を 出す
**turn out**
it turned out to be easier than expected
= おもったより かんたんでし
た。・ 思ったより 簡単でした。
**turn over**
- *(to roll over)* = ねがえりを うつ ・ 寝
返りを 打つ
- to turn over the page = ページを
めくる
**turn up**
- *(to show up)* = あらわれる ・ 現れる
- *(to increase)*
to turn up the heater = ヒーターを
つよく する ・ ヒーターを 強く
する
to turn the music up = おんがくの
ボリュームを あげる ・ 音楽の
ボリュームを 上げる

**turtle** *noun*
= かめ ・ 亀

**TV** *noun* = テレビ

**twelfth** *number*
- (*in a series*) = じゅうにばんめ(の)・十二番目(の)
- (*in dates*) ▶ **174**
= じゅうににち・十二日
the twelfth of July = しちがつじゅうににち・七月十二日

**twelve** *number* ▶ **171**, ▶ **181**, ▶ **186**
= じゅうに・十二
twelve pupils = せいと じゅうににん・生徒 十二人
I've got twelve = じゅうに あります。・ 十二 あります。

**twenty** *number* ▶ **171**, ▶ **181**, ▶ **186**
= にじゅう・二十

**twice** *adverb*
= にばい(の)・二倍(の)
twice as many people = にばい の ひと・二倍の 人
twice as much time = にばいの じかん・二倍の 時間
(*two times*) = にかい・二回

**twin**
**1** *noun*
= ふたご・双子
**2** *adjective*
a twin brother ▶ **brother**
a twin sister ▶ **sister**

**twist** *verb*
- (*to bend out of shape*) = ひねる
- (*to injure*)
to twist one's ankle = あしくびを ねんざする・足首を ねんざする

**two** *number* ▶ **171**, ▶ **181**, ▶ **186**
(*on its own*) = ふたつ・二つ
(*with a counter*) = に・二
two books = ほん にさつ・本 二冊
I've got two = ふたつ あります。・ 二つ あります。

**type**
**1** *noun*
it's a type of fish = さかなの いっしゅです。・魚の 一種です。
this type of person = この ような ひと・この ような 人
that type of book = その ような ほん・その ような 本
he's not my type = かれは わたしの タイプではありません。・ 彼は 私の タイプではありません。

**2** *verb*
= タイプする

**typewriter** *noun*
= タイプライター

**typical** *adjective*
= てんけいてき(な)・典型的(な)

**typist** *noun*
= タイピスト

**tyre** *noun* (*British English*)
= タイヤ

# Uu

**ugly** *adjective*
= みにくい・醜い

**umbrella** *noun*
= かさ・傘

**unbelievable** *adjective*
= しんじられない・信じられない

**uncle** *noun*
(*one's own*) = おじ
(*someone else's*) = おじさん ▶ **177**

**uncomfortable** *adjective*
= ふゆかい(な)・不愉快(な)
(*describing shoes*) = きつい
(*describing a seat*) = すわりごこち が わるい・座り心地が 悪い

**unconscious** *adjective*
= いしきふめい(の)・意識不明(の)

**under** *preposition*
- = ～の した・～の 下
to hide under the bed = ベッドの したに かくれる・ベッドの 下に 隠れる
I found the newspaper under it = それの したで しんぶんを みつけました。・それの 下で 新聞を 見つけました。
- (*less than*) = ～いか・～以下
a wage of under three pounds an hour = さんポンドいかの じきゅう・三ポンド以下の 時給
children under five = ごさいいかの こども・五歳以下の 子供

U

**underground** noun (British English)
= ちかてつ ・ 地下鉄

**underline** verb
= かせんを ひく ・ 下線を 引く

**underneath**
**1** adverb
= した ・ 下
I want to see what's underneath = したに なにが あるか みたいです。・ 下に 何が あるか 見たいです。
**2** preposition
= 〜の したに ・ 〜の 下に
underneath the building = たてもの のしたに ・ 建物の 下に

**underpants** noun
= パンツ

**understand** verb
= わかる ・ 分かる
I can't understand what they're saying = かれらが なにを いっているか わかりません。・ 彼らが 何を 言っているか 分かりません。
to make oneself understood = つうじる ・ 通じる

**understanding** adjective
= おもいやりの ある ・ 思いやりの ある

**underwater** adverb
= すいちゅうで ・ 水中で

**underwear** noun
= したぎ ・ 下着

**undo** verb
= もとに もどす ・ 元に 戻す
(clothing) = はずす ・ 外す
to undo a button = ボタンを はずす ・ ボタンを 外す

**undress** verb
= ふくを ぬぐ ・ 服を 脱ぐ

**uneasy** adjective
= ふあん(な) ・ 不安(な)

**unemployed** adjective
unemployed person = しつぎょうしゃ ・ 失業者

**unemployment** noun
= しつぎょう ・ 失業
unemployment rate = しつぎょうりつ ・ 失業率
unemployment benefit = しつぎょうてあて ・ 失業手当

**unfair** adjective
= ふこうへい(な) ・ 不公平(な)

**unfortunately** adverb
= ざんねんながら ・ 残念ながら

**unfriendly** adjective
(describing a person) = ふしんせつ(な) ・ 不親切(な)
(describing a place) = ふんいきが わるい ・ 雰囲気が 悪い

**ungrateful** adjective
= おんしらず(の) ・ 恩知らず(の)

**unhappy** adjective
• (sad) = かなしい ・ 悲しい
• (not satisfied) = ふまんが ある ・ 不満が ある

**unhealthy** adjective
(describing a way of life, food, conditions) = けんこうに わるい ・ 健康に 悪い
(describing a person) = びょうじゃく(な) ・ 病弱(な).

**uniform** noun
= せいふく ・ 制服

**union** noun
trade union = くみあい ・ 組合

**unique** adjective
= どくとく(な) ・ 独特(な)

**United Kingdom** noun ▶ 172
= えいこく ・ 英国

❗ イギリス is also used for the UK

**United States (of America)**
noun ▶ 172
= アメリカがっしゅうこく ・ アメリカ合衆国

❗ アメリカ is more generally used.
べいこく ・ 米国 is often used in newspapers.

**universe** noun
= うちゅう ・ 宇宙

**university** noun
= だいがく ・ 大学

**unkind** adjective
= ふしんせつ(な) ・ 不親切(な)

**unknown** adjective
= しられていない ・ 知られていない

**unless** conjunction
I'm not going out unless it stops raining = あめが やまなければ、でかけません。・ 雨が やまなければ、出かけません。

she can't work unless she buys a car
= かのじょは くるまを かわなけ
れば、しごとが できません。・
彼女は 車を 買わなければ、
仕事が できません。

**unlock** *verb*
= かぎを あける ・ 鍵を 開ける

**unlucky** *adjective*
(*person*) = うんが わるい ・ 運が
悪い
you were unlucky = うんが わるか
ったです。・運が 悪かったで
す。
(*object, number*) = えんぎが わるい
・ 縁起が 悪い

**unpack** *verb*
= にもつを ほどく ・ 荷物を 解く

**unsuitable** *adjective*
(*clothes*) = ばちがい(の) ・ 場違い
(の)
(*person*) = ふてきとう(な) ・ 不適
当(な)

**untidy** *adjective*
(*room*) = ちらかった ・ 散らかった
(*in how one looks*) = だらしが ない
untidy handwriting = じが きたない
・ 字が きたない

**until**
**1** *preposition*
= use particle まで ▶ 205
I'm staying in a hotel until Thursday =
もくようびまで ホテルに とま
ります。・ 木曜日まで ホテルに
泊まります。
until now = いままで ・ 今まで
I'm going to wait until after Christmas
= クリスマスの あとまで まちま
す。・ クリスマスの 後まで 待ち
ます。
she won't get an answer until next
week = かのじょは らいしゅうま
で こたえを もらいません。・
彼女は 来週まで 答えを もらい
ません。
**2** *conjunction*
= verb in dictionary form + まで
I'll wait until I go home = うちに かえ
るまで まちます。・ 家に 帰るま
で 待ちます。
we'll be here until they come = かれ
らが くるまで ここに います。・
彼らが 来るまで ここに いま
す。

please don't look until it's ready = で
きあがるまで みないでくださ
い。・出来上がるまで 見ないで
ください。

**unusual** *adjective*
• (*rare*) = めずらしい ・ 珍しい
• (*different, out of the ordinary*) = かわっ
た ・ 変わった

**up**

> **!** *Often* up *occurs in combinations
> with verbs, for example:* blow up,
> give up, own up, *etc. To find the
> correct translations for this type of
> verb, look up the separate
> dictionary entries at* blow, give,
> own *etc.*

**1** *preposition* This is not used as a
preposition in Japanese.
she ran up the stairs = かのじょは
かいだんを はしって のぼりま
した。・彼女は 階段を 走って
登りました。
**2** *adverb* This is not used as an adverb
in Japanese.
up in the sky = そらに ・ 空に
up on (top of) the chest of drawers =
たんすの うえ ・ たんすの 上
to go up = あがる ・ 上がる
to go up to Scotland = スコットラン
ドに いく ・ スコットランドに
行く
**3** *adjective*
• (*out of bed*)
to be up = おきている ・ 起きてい
る
to be up all night = ひとばんじゅう
おきている ・ 一晩中起きている
• (*increase in amount*) = ふえる ・ 増え
る
to be up by 20% = にじゅっパーセ
ント ふえる ・ 二十パーセント
増える
(*increase in level*) = あがる ・ 上がる
**4 up to**
• (*well enough*)
I'm not up to it = できません。
• (*until*) = use particle まで ▶ 205
up to now = いままで ・ 今まで
up to 2010 = にせんじゅうねんまで
・ 二千十年まで

**upset**
**1** *adjective*
to be upset
(*annoyed*) = いらいらしている

(*crying*) = ないている・泣いている
to get upset
(*annoyed*) = いらいらする
(*cry*) = なく・泣く
**2** *verb*
- (*to make someone unhappy*)
to make someone cry = だれかを
なかせる・誰かを 泣かせる
- (*to annoy*) = いらいらさせる

**upside down** *adverb*
= さかさま・逆さま

**upstairs** *adverb*
= うえの かい・上の 階 *In a two
storey building or house use* にかい
to go upstairs = うえの かいに いく
・上の 階に 行く
to bring the boxes upstairs = うえの
かいに はこを もって いく・
上の 階に 箱を 持って 行く

**urgent** *adjective*
= きんきゅう(な)・緊急(な)

**us** *pronoun*
= わたしたち・私達 *This can often be
left out when it is obvious*
they know us = かれらは わたした
ちを しっています。・彼らは 私
達を 知っています。
he's seen us = かれは わたしたち
を みました。・彼は 私達を 見
ました。
please help us! = たすけてくださ
い。・助けてください。
please don't bother us! = じゃまを
しないでください。・邪魔を し
ないでください。
please don't show it to us! = みせない
でください。・見せないでくだ
さい。
he did it for us = かれは わたした
ちの ために しました。・彼は
私達の ために しました。

**USA** *noun* ▶ **172**
= アメリカがっしゅうこく・アメ
リカ合衆国

! アメリカ *is more generally used.*
べいこく・米国 *is often used in
newspapers.*

**use**
**1** *verb*
- (*to make use of*) = つかう・使う
I use the car to go to work = くるまを
つかって しごとに いきます。・
車を 使って 仕事に 行きます。

he uses this room as an office = かれ
は この へやを オフィスと して
つかっています。・彼は この
部屋を オフィスと して 使って
います。
what is it used for? = なにに つかい
ますか。・何に 使いますか。
to use a different word = ちがう こと
ばを つかう・違う 言葉を 使う
- (*to operate on*)
this car uses unleaded petrol = この
くるまは むえんガソリンで は
しります。・この 車は 無鉛ガソ
リンで 走ります。
- (*to take advantage of*)
to use someone = だれかを りよう
する・誰かを 利用する
**2** *noun*
- to make use of a room = へやを つか
う・部屋を 使う
to have the use of a car = くるまが
つかえる・車が 使える
- (*when talking about what is useful*)
to be of use = やくに たつ・役に
立つ
to be no use = やくに たたない・
役に 立たない
what's the use of complaining? = も
んくを いっても しかたが あり
ません。・文句を 言っても 仕方
が ありません。
**use up**
to use up all the money = おかねを
ぜんぶ つかって しまう・お金
を 全部 使って しまう ▶ **189**

**used**
**1** *verb*
I used to read books a lot = まえは
よく ほんを よんでいました。・
前は よく 本を 読んでいました。
you used not to smoke = まえはたば
こを すっていませんでした。・
前はたばこを 吸っていませんで
した。
there used to be a castle here = まえ
は ここに おしろが ありました。
・前は ここに お城が ありまし
た。 ▶ **189**
**2** *adjective*
= なれている・慣れている
I'm used to life in Japan = にほんの
せいかつに なれています。・
日本の 生活に 慣れています。
he's not used to living on his own =
かれは ひとりぐらしに なれて

いません。・彼は 一人暮らしに
慣れていません。
　to get used to a new job = あたら
　しい しごとに なれる ・ 新しい
　仕事に 慣れる

**useful** *adjective*
　= べんり(な) ・ 便利(な)

**useless** *adjective*
• (*not working, having no use*) = つかえ
　ない ・ 使えない
• (*having no point or purpose*) = むいみ
　(な) ・ 無意味(な)
　it's useless complaining = もんくを
　いうのは むいみです。・ 文句を
　言うのは 無意味です。
• (*not good at*) = にがて(な) ・ 苦手
　(な)
　I'm useless at chemistry = かがくが
　にがてです。・ 化学が 苦手です。

**usually** *adverb*
　= ふつうは ・ 普通は

# V

**vacant** *adjective*
　= あいている ・ 空いている

**vacation** *noun* (*US English*) = りょ
　こう ・ 旅行
　to take a vacation = りょこうに いく
　・ 旅行に 行く

**vacuum** *verb*
　to vacuum a room = へやに そうじ
　きを かける ・ 部屋に 掃除機を
　掛ける

**vacuum cleaner** *noun* = そうじき
　・ 掃除機

**vague** *adjective*
　= あいまい(な)

**vain** *adjective*
　= うぬぼれた

**valid** *adjective*
　= ゆうこう(な) ・ 有効(な)

**valley** *noun* = たに ・ 谷

**valuable** *adjective*
• (*very useful*) = きちょう(な) ・ 貴重
　(な)

• (*worth a lot of money*)
　= こうか(な) ・ 高価(な)

**van** *noun*
　= バン

**vandalize** *verb*
　= はかいする ・ 破壊する

**vanilla** *noun* = バニラ

**various** *adjective*
　= いろいろ(な) ・ 色々(な)
　there are various ways of saying this =
　いろいろな いいかたが ありま
　す。・ 色々な 言い方が ありま
　す。

**vary** *verb*
　it varies from town to town = まちに
　よって ちがいます。・ 町によっ
　て 違います。

**vase** *noun* = かびん ・ 花瓶

**vegetable** *noun* = やさい ・ 野菜

**vegetarian** *noun* = さいしょくし
　ゅぎしゃ ・ 菜食主義者

**vein** *noun* = じょうみゃく ・ 静脈

**velvet** *noun* = ベルベット

**versus** *preposition*
　= たい ・ 対

**very**
**1** *adverb* = とても
　(*with a negative*) = あまり + negative
　I don't know him very well = かれを
　あまり しりません。・ 彼をあま
　り 知りません。
　to eat very little = あまり たべない ・
　あまり 食べない
　you haven't said very much = あまり
　いっていません。・ あまり 言っ
　ていません。
　I like him very much = かれが とても
　すきです。・ 彼が とても 好きで
　す。
　for the very first time = はじめて ・
　初めて
　they called the very next day = かれら
　は つぎの ひ、でんわを しまし
　た。・ 彼らは 次の 日、電話を し
　ました。
**2** *adjective*
　at the very beginning = はじめに ・
　始めに
　to sit at the very front = いちばんまえ
　に すわる ・ 一番前に 座る

**V**

to stay to the very end = さいごまで
いる・最後まで いる

**vest** *noun*
- (*British English*)
  (*a piece of underwear*) = アンダーシ
  ャツ
- (*US English*)
  (*a waistcoat*) = チョッキ

**vet** *noun* = じゅうい・獣医

**via** *preposition*
= ～けいゆ・～経由
we came via Hong Kong = ホンコン
けいゆで きました。・ホンコン
経由で 来ました。

**vicious** *adjective*
- (*violent*) = もうれつ(な)・猛烈(な)
- (*nasty, meant to hurt*) = ざんこく(な)
  ・残酷(な)
- vicious dog = もうけん・猛犬

**victory** *noun*
= しょうり・勝利
to win a victory = しょうりする・勝
利する

**video**
**1** *noun*
- (*a recorded film, programme, event*) =
  ビデオ
- ▶ video cassette, video recorder
**2** *verb*
- (*to record*) = ろくがする・録画する
- (*to film*)
  to video a wedding = けっこんしき
  の ビデオを とる・結婚式の
  ビデオを 撮る

**video camera** *noun*
= ビデオカメラ

**video cassette** *noun*
= ビデオカセット

**video game** *noun*
= ビデオゲーム

**view** *noun*
- = けしき・景色
  you're blocking my view! = じゃまで
  す。・邪魔です。
- (*an opinion, an attitude*)
  = いけん・意見

**village** *noun*
= むら・村

**vinegar** *noun*
= す・酢

**vineyard** *noun*
= ぶどうえん・ぶどう園

**violent** *adjective*
= らんぼう(な)・乱暴(な)

**violin** *noun* ▶ 180
= バイオリン

**Virgo** *noun*
= おとめざ・乙女座

**visit**
**1** *verb*
  (*a place*) = いく・行く
  to visit someone
  (*to call on*) = たずねる・訪ねる
  (*to stay with*) = とまりに いく・泊
  りに 行く
**2** *noun*
  (*a call*) = ほうもん・訪問
  (*a stay*) = たいざい・滞在
  to pay someone a visit = だれかを
  たずねる・誰かを 訪ねる

**visitor** *noun*
- (*a guest*)
  = おきゃくさん・お客さん ▶ 189
  to have visitors = おきゃくさんが
  いる・お客さんが いる
- (*a tourist*)
  = かんこうきゃく・観光客

**vocabulary** *noun*
= ごい・語彙

**voice** *noun*
= こえ・声
to have a good voice = いい こえを
もつ・いい 声を 持つ
to speak in a low voice = ひくい こえ
で はなす・低い 声で 話す
in a loud voice = おおごえで・大声
で

**voicemail** *noun*
= ボイスメール

**volleyball** *noun*
= バレーボール

**vomit** *verb*
= はく・吐く

**vote** *verb*
= とうひょうする・投票する

# Ww

**wages** *noun*
＝きゅうりょう・給料

**waist** *noun*
＝ウエスト

**waistcoat** *noun* (*British English*)
＝チョッキ

**wait** *verb*
• ＝まつ・待つ
to wait for someone ＝だれかを まつ ・ 誰かを 待つ
I'm waiting to use the phone ＝でんわ を つかうのを まっています。・ 電話を 使うのを 待っています。
to wait for someone to go home ＝ だれかが かえるのを まつ・ 誰かが 帰るのを 待つ
let's have a beer while we're waiting for them ＝かれらを まっている あいだに ビールを のみましょ う。・ 彼らを 待っている 間に ビールを 飲みましょう。
I can't wait to meet them ＝かれらに あえるのを たのしみに してい ます。・ 彼らに 会えるのを 楽し みに しています。
**wait up**
to wait up for someone ＝だれかの かえりを まつ・ 誰かの 帰りを 待つ

**waiter** *noun*
＝ウェーター

**waiting room** *noun*
＝まちあいしつ・ 待合室

**waitress** *noun*
＝ウエートレス

**wake** *verb*
to wake someone ＝だれかを おこ す・ 誰かを 起こす
wake up ＝めが さめる・ 目が 覚 める

**Wales** *noun* ▶ 172
＝ウェールズ

**walk**
**1** *verb*
＝あるく・ 歩く

(*for pleasure*) ＝さんぽする・ 散歩 する
let's walk to the pool ＝プールまで あるきましょう。・ プールまで 歩きましょう。
to walk down the street ＝みちを あるく・ 道を 歩く
to walk the dog ＝いぬを さんぽに つれていく・ 犬を 散歩に 連れ て 行く
**2** *noun*
＝さんぽ・ 散歩
to go for a walk ＝さんぽする・ 散歩 する
it's five minutes' walk from here ＝ ここから あるいて ごふんです。 ・ ここから 歩いて 五分です。
**walk around** ＝あるきまわる・ 歩き回る
to walk around town ＝まちをあるき まわる・ 町を 歩き回る
to walk around the lake ＝みずうみの まわりを あるく・ 湖の 周りを 歩く
**walk back**
to walk back home ＝あるいて かえ る・ 歩いて 帰る
**walk round** ＝あるきまわる・ 歩き 回る
to walk round the park ＝こうえんを あるきまわる・ 公園を 歩き回 る

**walkman**® *noun*
＝ウォークマン

**wall** *noun*
＝かべ・ 壁

**wallet** *noun*
＝さいふ・ 財布

**wallpaper** *noun*
＝かべがみ・ 壁紙

**walnut** *noun*
＝くるみ

**wander** *verb*
＝ぶらぶら あるく・ぶらぶら 歩く
to wander around town ＝まちを ぶ らぶら あるく・ 町を ぶらぶら 歩く

**want** *verb*
• (*to want something*) ▶ 178
＝ほしい・ 欲しい *not a verb in Japanese*

**W**

I want a new camera = あたらしい
カメラが ほしいです。・新しい
カメラが 欲しいです。

I don't want it = ほしくないです。・
欲しくないです。

do you want some coffee? = コーヒ
ーは いかがですか。

(*to want to do...*) = Use the pre ます
form of the verb + たい ▶ 191

I want to go out = でかけたいです。
・出かけたいです。

I don't want to go home = かえりたく
ないです。・帰りたくないです。

I wanted to go to Japan = にほんに
いきたかったです。・日本に
行きたかったです。

I want to play = あそびたいです。・
遊びたいです。

the children want to eat it = こども
たちは たべたがっています。・
子供達は 食べたがっています。

(*to want someone else to do...*) =
use the 〜て form of the verb +
ほしい ▶ 197

I want you to read this = これを よん
で ほしいです。・これを 読んで
欲しいです。

do you want me to come with you? =
いっしょに いって ほしいです
か。・一緒に 行って 欲しいです
か。▶ 178

• (*to need*) = いる・要る

I don't want this anymore = これは
もう いりません。・これは もう
要りません。

**war** *noun*
= せんそう・戦争

**wardrobe** *noun*
= ようふくだんす・洋服だんす

**warm**
**1** *adjective*
= あたたかい・温かい
(*air temperature*) = あたたかい・暖
かい

I'm very warm = あたたかいです。・
暖かいです。

the classroom is warm = きょうし
つは あたたかいです。・教室は
暖かいです。

to get warm = あたたかく なる・
暖かく なる

**2** *verb*
to warm the plates = さらを あたた
める・皿を 温める

to warm the room = へやを あたため
る・部屋を 暖める

**warm up**
• (*to get warm*) = あたたかく なる・
暖かく なる
• (*for a sporting event*) = ウォーミング
アップする
• (*to make warm*) = あたためる・温め
る

**warn** *verb*
= けいこくする・警告する
to warn someone about the danger =
だれかに きけんを けいこく
する・誰かに 危険を 警告す
る
to warn someone to be careful = だれ
かに きを つける ように ちゅ
ういする・誰かに 気を 付ける
ように 注意する

**wash** *verb*
• (*to clean*) = あらう・洗う
to wash one's face = かおを あらう
・顔を 洗う
to wash one's clothes = せんたくす
る・洗濯する

**wash up**
• (*British English*) (*to do the dishes*) = し
ょっきを あらう・食器を 洗う
• (*US English*) (*to clean oneself*) = かお
を あらう・顔を 洗う

**washbasin** (*British English*),
**wash-hand basin** *noun*
= せんめんき・洗面器

**washing** *noun*
= せんたく・洗濯
to do the washing = せんたくする・
洗濯する

**washing machine** *noun*
= せんたくき・洗濯機

**washing-up** *noun* (*British English*)
= しょっきあらい・食器洗い
to do the washing-up = しょっきを
あらう・食器を 洗う

**wasp** *noun*
= すずめばち・雀蜂

**waste**
**1** *verb*
= むだに する・無駄に する
to waste one's time = じかんを むだ
に する・時間を 無駄に する
to waste electricity = でんきを むだ
に つかう・電気を 無駄に 使う

**2** *noun*
* = むだ・無駄
* that's a waste of money = それ は
  おかね の むだ です。・ それ は
  お金 の 無駄です。
  it's a waste of time = じかんの むだ
  です。・ 時間の 無駄です。
  it's a waste of time going there = あそ
  こに いくのは じかんの むだで
  す。・ あそこに 行くのは 時間の
  無駄です。

## watch

**1** *verb*
* (*to look at*) = みる・見る
  to watch television = テレビを みる
  ・テレビを 見る
  I feel I'm being watched = みられて
  いる ように かんじます。・ 見ら
  れている ように 感じます。
* (*to pay attention to*) = きを つける・
  気を つける
  please watch what you're doing = き
  をつけてください。・ 気を つけ
  てください。
  please watch you don't fall = ころば
  ない ように きを つけてくだ
  さい。・ 転ばない ように 気を
  つけてください。
**2** *noun*
  = とけい・時計
  **watch out** = きを つける・気を
  つける

## water

**1** *noun*
  (*cold*) = みず・水
  (*hot*) = おゆ・お湯 ▶ **189**
  drinking water = のみみず・飲み水
**2** *verb*
  = みずを やる・水を やる

## waterfall *noun*
  = たき・滝

## water-skiing *noun*
  = すいじょうスキー・水上スキー

## wave

**1** *verb*
  = てを ふる・手を 振る
**2** *noun*
  (*sea*) = なみ・波
  (*radio*) = でんぱ・電波

## way

**1** *noun*
* (*a means, a method*)
  = ほうほう・方法

it's a way of earning money = おかね
  を かせぐほうほうです。・ お金
  を 稼ぐ 方法です。
he does it the wrong way = かれの や
  りかたは まちがっています。・
  彼の やり方は 間違っています。
* (*how one does something*)
  = やりかた・やり方 *the suffix*
  〜かた *can also be added to the*
  *pre* ます *form of the verb in specific*
  *cases* ▶ **191**
  I prefer to do it my way = じぶんの
  やりかたが いいです。・ 自分の
  やり方が いいです。
  I like the way she speaks = かのじ
  ょの はなしかたが すきです。・
  彼女の 話し方が 好きです。
* (*a route, a road*)
  = みち・道
  I can't remember the way to the
  station = えきまでの みちを おぼ
  えていません。・ 駅までの 道を
  覚えていません。
  on the way = とちゅう・途中
  on the way to Hiroshima = ひろしま
  に いく とちゅうで・ 広島に
  行く 途中で
  where's the way out? = でぐちは ど
  こですか。・ 出口は どこですか。
  to lose one's way = みちに まよう・
  道に 迷う
* (*a direction*)
  which way are you going? = どちら
  に いきますか。・ どちらに 行き
  ますか。
  they went that way = かれらは あち
  らに いきました。・ 彼らはあち
  らに 行きました。
  please come this way = こちらへ き
  てください。・ こちらへ 来てく
  ださい。
* (*someone's route*)
  in the way = じゃま・邪魔
  to get out of the way = どく・退く
* (*when talking about distances*)
  it's a long way from here = ここからと
  おいです。・ ここから 遠いです。
  to go all the way to Japan = にほんま
  で いく・ 日本まで 行く
* if I had my way... = できれば。。。
**2 by the way** = ところで
  What's his name, by the way? = とこ
  ろで、 かれの なまえは なんで
  すか。・ ところで彼の 名前は 何
  ですか。

**W**

**we** *pronoun* Note that if the subject of the sentence is obvious, it can often be left out.
= わたしたち・私達
we saw her yesterday = きのう かのじょを みました。・昨日彼女を見ました。
we all make mistakes = だれ でも まちがえます。・誰でも 間違えます。

**weak** *adjective*
• = よわい・弱い
he has a weak heart = かれは しんぞうの ちょうしが わるいです。・彼は 心臓の 調子が 悪いです。
• (*not good or able*) = にがて・苦手
he is weak at languages = かれは ごがくが にがてです。・彼は 語学が 苦手です。
• (*easily damaged*) = こわれやすい・壊れやすい
• (*having very little power*) = ちからの ない・力の ない
• (*describing tea or coffee*) = うすい・薄い

**wealthy** *adjective*
= ゆうふく(な)・裕福(な)

**wear** *verb*
• (*shirts, dresses*) = きる・着る
(*hats*) = かぶる
(*shoes, trousers, skirts, socks*) = はく
(*makeup*) = つける
(*spectacles*) = かける
to be wearing a kimono = きものを きている・着物を 着ている
to wear boots = ブーツを はく
• (*to put on*) = きる・着る *other verbs may be used depending on which item of clothing is being worn. See above.*
what will you wear? = なにを きますか。・何を 着ますか。
I've got nothing to wear = なにも きる ものが ありません。・何も 着る 物が ありません。
• (*to damage*) = つかいふるす・使い古す

**wear out**
= つかいふるす・使い古す
to wear one's shoes out = くつを つかいふるす・靴を 使い古す
to wear someone out = だれ かを つかれさせる・誰かを 疲れさせる

**weather** *noun*
= てんき・天気
what's the weather like? = てんきは どうですか。・天気は どうですか。
the weather is bad = てんきが わるいです。・天気が 悪いです。
the weather is nice = てんきが いいです。・天気が いいです。
the weather is hot = あついです。・暑いです。

**weather forecast** *noun*
= てんきよほう・天気予報

**wedding** *noun*
= けっこんしき・結婚式

**Wednesday** *noun* ▶ 174
= すいようび・水曜日

**week** *noun*
one week = いっしゅうかん・一週間
in two weeks' time = にしゅうかん ご(に)・二週間後(に)

**weekend** *noun*
= しゅうまつ・週末

**weigh** *verb*
= おもさを はかる・重さを 計る
what do you weigh? = たいじゅうは なんキロですか。・体重は 何キロですか。
to weigh oneself = たいじゅうを はかる・体重を 計る

**weight** *noun*
(*body*) = たいじゅう・体重
(*object*) = おもさ・重さ
to lose weight = たいじゅうを へらす・体重を 減らす

**weird** *adjective*
= きみょう(な)・奇妙(な)

**welcome** *verb*
to welcome someone = だれかを かんげいする・誰かを 歓迎する
• (*when receiving people*)
(*to your house*) = いらっしゃい
(*in a formal situation*) = ようこそ
welcome to Japan = にほんへ ようこそ・日本へ ようこそ
• (*when acknowledging thanks*)
'thanks'—'you're welcome' = 「どうも ありがとう。」「どういたしまして。」
**3** *noun*
= かんげい・歓迎

# well

**1** *adverb*
- (*when talking about a skill*)
  = じょうずに・上手に
  he can speak English well = かれは えいごが じょうずに はなせます。・彼は 英語が 上手に 話せます。
  to go well = うまく いく
  the test went well = テストは うまく いきました。
  it is well paid = きゅうりょうが いいです。・給料が いいです。
  he's not eating well = かれは ちゃんと たべていません。・彼は ちゃんと 食べていません。

**2** *adjective*
  I feel well = げんきです。・元気です。
  to get well = げんきに なる・元気に なる

**3 as well** = use particle も ▶ 205
**4 as well as** = 〜の ほかに・〜の 外に

## well-known *adjective*
  = ゆうめい(な)・有名(な)

# west

**1** *noun*
  = にし・西
  in the west of Japan = にしにほんに・西日本に

**2** *adverb*
  to go west = にしに いく・西に 行く

**3** *adjective*
  = にし・西
  to work in west London = にしロンドンで はたらく・西ロンドンで 働く

## West Indies *noun* ▶ 172
  = にしインドしょとう・西インド諸島

# wet

**1** *adjective*
- (*damp*) = ぬれている・濡れている
  your hair is wet = かみが ぬれています。・髪が 濡れています。
  to get wet = ぬれる・濡れる
  she got her feet wet = かのじょは あしが ぬれました。・彼女は 足が 濡れました。
- (*when talking about weather*)
  in wet weather = あめが ふっている とき・雨が 降っている とき

  a wet day = あめの ひ・雨の 日

**2** *verb*
  = ぬらす・濡らす

# what

**1** *pronoun*
- (*used in questions*)
  = なん・何 *in some cases this is pronounced* なに
  what's that box? = あの はこは なんですか。・あの 箱は 何ですか。
  what's the Japanese for 'boring'? = にほんごで boring は なんですか。・日本語で boring は 何ですか。
  what is she like? = かのじょは どんな ひとですか。・彼女は どんな 人ですか。
  what's her phone number? = かのじょの でんわばんごうは なんばんですか。・彼女の 電話番号は 何番ですか。
  what time is it? = なんじですか。・何時ですか。
  what day of the week? = なんようび ですか。・何曜日ですか。
- (*used as a relative pronoun*)
  please do what you want = すきな ように してください。・好きな ように してください。

**2** *determiner*
  do you know what train to take? = どの でんしゃに のれば いいか わかりますか。・どの 電車に 乗れば いいか 分かりますか。
  what a great idea! = すばらしい アイディアですね。

**3** *exclamation*
  = へえ

**4 what if**
  what if I don't get there on time? = まに あわなければ どう しますか。・間に 合わなければ どう しますか。
  what if it rains? = あめが ふれば どう しますか。・雨が 降れば どう しますか。

## whatever *pronoun*
- (*when anything is possible*)
  please ask whatever you want = なんでも きいてください。・何でも 聞いてください。
- (*when it doesn't matter*) = use the 〜て form of the verb + も ▶ 197

W

whatever they do, it won't change anything = かれらが なにを して も かわりません。・彼らが 何を しても 変わりません。

**wheat** *noun*
=むぎ・麦

**wheel** *noun*
=ホイール

**wheelchair** *noun*
=くるまいす・車椅子

**when**

**1** *adverb*

(*generally*) = いつ

when did she go? = かのじょは いつ いきましたか。・彼女は いつ 行きましたか。

when is your birthday? = たんじょうびは いつですか。・誕生日は いつですか。

(*what time*) = なんじ・何時

I don't know when the film starts = えいがが なんじに はじまるか わかりません。・映画が 何時に 始まるか 分かりません。なん can be added to other time counters when referring to a day or date. ▶ なんにち ▶ なんようび ▶ なんがつ ▶ なんねん

**2** *conjunction*

=～とき

I was asleep when the phone rang = でんわが なった とき、ねていました。・電話が 鳴った とき、寝ていました。

when I was a student = がくせいの とき・学生の とき

when I'm 18 I can get married = じゅうはっさいに なったら けっこんが できます。・十八才になったら 結婚が できます。

**3** *pronoun* (*used as a relative pronoun*)
=～とき

in the days when there was no TV = テレビが なかった ときに

**where**

**1** *adverb*

=どこ

where are you going? = どこに いきますか。・どこに 行きますか。

where do they work? = かれらは どこで はたらいていますか。・彼らは どこで 働いていますか。

Do you know where he is? = かれが どこに いるか しっていますか。

・彼が どこに いるか 知っていますか。

Do you know where we're going? = どこに いくか わかりますか。・どこに 行くか わかりますか。

the village where we live = わたしたちが すんでいる むら・私達が 住んでいる 村

**2** *conjunction*

that's where the accident happened = じこが あったのは あそこです。・事故が あったのは あそこです。

I'll leave the key where you can see it = すぐ わかる ところに かぎを おいて おきます。・すぐ 分かる 所に カギを 置いて おきます。

**whether** *conjunction*
=～か どうか～

I don't know whether or not to go there = そこに いくか どうか わかりません。・そこに 行くか どうか わかりません。

**which**

**1** *pronoun*

the house which I saw yesterday = きのう みた いえ・昨日 見た 家

**2** *determiner*

which one? = どれですか。

which fruit do you like best? = どの くだものが いちばんすきですか。・どの 果物が 一番好きですか。

tell me which film you'd like to see = どの えいがを みたいか おしえてください。・どの 映画を 見たいか 教えてください。

**while** *conjunction*
=～あいだ・～間

I had a party while my parents were in Spain = りょうしんが スペインに いっている あいだ、パーティーを しました。・両親が スペインに 行っている 間、パーティーを しました。Note that ながら may also be added to the pre ます form of the verb to indicate that two action were taking place simultaneously. ▶ 191

she ate while watching TV = かのじょは テレビを みながら たべました。・彼女は テレビを 見ながら 食べました。

**whisper** *verb*
= ささやく

**whistle**
**1** *verb*
= くちぶえを ふく・口笛を 吹く
**2** *noun*
= ふえ・笛

**white** *adjective*
= しろい・白い

**who** *pronoun*
• (*used in questions*) = だれ・誰
who told you? = だれが いいました
か。・誰が 言いましたか。
who did you invite? = だれを しょう
たいしましたか。・誰を 招待し
ました。
who did he buy the book for? = かれ
は だれに ほんを かいましたか。
・彼は 誰に 本を 買いましたか。
• (*used as a relative pronoun*)
my friend who lives in Paris = パリに
すんでいる ともだち・パリに
住んでいる 友達
those who can't come by car = くるま
で こられない ひと・車で 来ら
れない 人
a friend who I see at school = がっこ
うの ともだち・学校の 友達

**whole**
**1** *noun*
= ぜんぶ・全部
the whole of Tokyo = とうきょうの
ぜんぶ・東京の 全部
the whole of the country = ぜんこく
・全国
**2** *adjective*
a whole day = まる いちにち・ま
る 一日
the whole day = いちにちじゅう・
一日中
three whole weeks = まる さんしゅ
うかん・まる 三週間

**whom** *pronoun*
• (*used in questions*) = だれに・誰に
whom did you meet? = だれに あい
ましたか。・誰に 会いましたか。
• (*used as a relative pronoun*)
the person to whom I spoke on the
phone = でんわで はなした ひと
・電話で 話した 人

**whose**
**1** *pronoun*

• (*used in questions*) = だれの・誰の
whose is the dog? = いぬは だれの
ですか。・犬は 誰のですか。
• (*used as a relative pronoun*)
the person whose bike was stolen =
じてんしゃを ぬすまれた ひと・
自転車を 盗まれた 人
**2** *determiner*
whose car is that? = それは だれの
くるま です か。・それは 誰の
車ですか。
whose pen did you borrow? = だれの
ペンを かりましたか。・誰の
ペンを 借りましたか。

**why**
**1** *adverb*
• (*used in questions*) = どうして
why did you do that? = どうして
それを しましたか。
why aren't they coming? = かれらは
どうして きませんか。・彼らは
どうして 来ませんか。
• (*when making suggestions*)
why don't we eat out tonight? = こん
ばん がいしょくしませんか。・
今晩 外食しませんか。
**2** *conjunction*
that's why I don't like him = だから
かれが すきではありません。・
だから 彼が 好きではありませ
ん。

**wide** *adjective*
• (*in size*) = ひろい・広い
a wide garden = ひろい にわ・広い
庭
the room is ten metres wide = この へ
やの はばは じゅうメートルで
す。この 部屋の 幅は 十メート
ルです。
• (*in range*)
there is a wide range = いろいろ あ
ります。・色々 あります。

**width** *noun*
= はば・幅

**wife** *noun* ▶ 177
(*one's own*) = つま・妻
(*someone else's*) = おくさん・奥さ
ん

**wild** *adjective* (*describing animals,
birds*) = やせい(の)・野生(の)

**wildlife** *noun*
= やせいどうぶつ・野生動物

W

## will *verb*

> ! *There is no specific future tense in Japanese. Use the non-past tense.* ▶ 191

- *(when talking about the future)*
  it will be sunny tomorrow = あしたは はれます。・ 明日は 晴れます。
  what will we do? = なにを しますか。・ 何を しますか。
- *(when talking about intentions)*
  I'll wait for you at the airport = くうこうで まちます。・ 空港で 待ちます。
  we won't be here long = ここに ながく いません。・ ここに 長く いません。
- *(in invitations and requests)*
  will you have some coffee? = コーヒーは いかがですか。
  will you close the door? = ドアを しめてください。・ ドアを 閉めてください。
- *(when making assumptions)*
  they won't understand = かれらは わからないでしょう。・ 彼らは 分からないでしょう。。
- *(in short questions and answers)* = Use particle ね ▶ 205
  you'll come again, won't you? = また きますね。・ また 来ますね。
  that will be cheaper, won't it? = それは もっと やすいですね。・ それは もっと 安いですね。

## win *verb*
= かつ・勝つ

## wind *noun* = かぜ・風

## window *noun*
= まど・窓

## windsurfing *noun* = ウィンドサーフィン

## windy *adjective*
it's windy = かぜが つよいです。・風が 強いです。

## wine *noun* = ワイン

## wing *noun*
(*of a bird*) = はね・羽
(*of an aeroplane*) = つばさ・翼

## winter *noun* = ふゆ・冬
in winter = ふゆに・冬に

## wipe *verb*
= ふく

to wipe one's feet = あしを ふく・足を 拭く
to wipe one's nose = はなを かむ・鼻を かむ

## wise *adjective*
= かしこい・賢い

## wish

**1** *noun*
- = きぼう・希望
  to make a wish = ねがいごとを する・願い事を する
- *(in greetings)*
  please give my best wishes to your family = ごかぞくに よろしく おつたえください。・ ご家族に よろしく お伝え ください。

> ! *Not used in Japanese letters. Usually a general greeting such as* はいけい *is used at the beginning of a formal letter and it is finished with* けいぐ

**2** *verb*
- *(expressing what one would like)*
  she wished she hadn't lied = かのじょは うそを つかなければ よかったと おもいました。・ 彼女は 嘘を つかなければ よかったと 思いました。
- *(in greetings)*
  to wish someone a happy birthday = 「おたんじょうび おめでとう」と いう・「お誕生日 おめでとう」と 言う ▶ 189

## with *preposition*
- = use particle と ▶ 205
  to go on holiday with friends = ともだちと りょこうする・友達と 旅行する
  I'm living with my parents = りょうしんと すんでいます。・ 両親と 住んでいます。
- *(when describing)*
  a girl with black hair = くろい かみの おんなの こ・黒い 髪の 女の 子
  the boy with the long legs = あしが ながい おとこのこ・足が 長い 男の 子
  my clothes were covered with mud = ふくは どろ だらけでした。・ 服は 泥 だらけでした。
  she's married with two children = かのじょは けっこんして こども

が ふたり います。・彼女は
結婚して 子供が 二人 います。

**without** preposition
= 〜なしで
I went out without my wallet = さいふ
なしで でかけました。・財布な
しで 出かけました。
(*without ...ing*) = use the verb in the
〜ない form + で ▶ **191**
we got in without paying = はらわな
いで はいれました。・払わない
で 入れました。
I went to school without eating
breakfast = あさごはんを たべな
いで がっこうに いきました。・
朝ご飯を 食べないで 学校に
行きました。

**wolf** noun = おおかみ

**woman** noun = おんなの ひと ・
女の 人
a single woman = どくしんの おん
なのひと ・ 独身の 女の 人

**wonder** verb
• (*to ask oneself*)
I was wondering why she's late =
かのじょが なぜ おくれている
のかなと おもっていました。・
彼女が なぜ 遅れているのかな
と 思っていました。
I wonder whether he's coming = かれ
がくるか どうか わかりません。
・ 彼が 来るか どうか 分かりま
せん。
• (*in polite requests*)
I wonder if you could help me? = ちょ
っと おねがい できますか。・
ちょっとお願い できますか。

**wonderful** adjective
= すばらしい

**wood** noun
• (*timber*) = き ・ 木
made of wood = きで つくられてい
る ・ 木で 作られている
• (*a small forest*) = はやし ・ 林

**wool** noun = ウール

**word** noun = ことば ・ 言葉
what's the Japanese word for
'breakfast'? = にほんごでbreakfast
は なんですか。・ 日本語で
breakfast は 何ですか。
in other words = いいかえると ・
言い換えると

**work**
**1** verb
• (*to have or do a job*) = はたらく ・ 働
く
to work at home = いえで はたらく
・ 家で 働く
to work as a doctor = いしゃとして
はたらく ・ 医者として 働く
• (*to operate properly*)
the TV isn't working properly – テ
レビの ちょうしが わるいで
す。・ テレビの 調子が 悪いで
す。
• (*to be successful*)
(*if it's an idea, a trick, a plan*) = うまく
いく
(*if it's a medicine, a treatment*) = きく
・ 効く
• (*to use, to operate*) = そうさする ・
操作する
do you know how to work the
computer? = コンピューターの
つかいかたが わかりますか。・
コンピューターの 使い方が
分かりますか。
**2** noun
• = しごと ・ 仕事
I've got work to do = しごとが あり
ます。・ 仕事が あります。
I am out of work = しつぎょうちゅう
です。・ 失業中です。
it's hard work learning Japanese =
にほんごを ならうのは たいへ
んです。・ 日本語を 習うのは
大変です。
• (*for building, for repairs*) = こうじ ・
工事
there are road works at the moment
= いま どうろは こうじちゅう
です。・ 今 道路は 工事中で
す。
• (*by an artist, a musician*) = さくひん ・
作品
**work out**
• (*to find*) = みつける ・ 見つける
to work out the answer = こたえを み
つける ・ 答えを 見つける
• (*to understand*) = わかる ・ 分かる
• (*with figures*) = けいさんする ・ 計算
する
• (*to go well*) = うまく いく
• (*to take exercise*) = うんどうする ・
運動する
**work up**
to get worked up = おこる ・ 怒る

**W**

**worker** noun (in a factory) = じゅう
ぎょういん・従業員
(in a bank) = ぎんこういん・銀行
員
(in a company) = かいしゃいん・会
社員
(for local government) = こうむいん・
公務員

**world** noun = せかい・世界
all over the world = せかいじゅう・
世界中
the biggest city in the world = せか
いで いちばん おおきい まち・
世界で 一番 大きい 町

**World Cup** noun = ワールドカップ

**worm** noun = みみず

**worried** adjective
= しんぱいしている・心配してい
る
to be worried about someone = だれ
かの ことをしんぱいしている・
誰かの ことを 心配している

**worry** verb
• (to be worried) = しんぱいしている
・心配している
there's nothing to worry about = しん
ぱいする ことは ありません。・
心配する ことは ありません。
• (to make someone worried) = しんぱ
いさせる・心配させる
that's worrying me = それが しんぱ
いです。・それが 心配です。

**worse** adjective
= もっと わるい・もっと 悪い
this book is worse than the others =
この ほんは ほかより わるい
です。・この 本は 他より 悪い
です。
she's worse than me at sports = スポ
ーツは かのじょの ほうが へた
です。・スポーツは 彼女の 方が
下手です。
the weather is going to get worse =
てんきが もっと わるく なりま
す。・天気が もっと 悪く なり
ます。
he's getting worse (in health) = かれ
の ぐあいが もっと わるく なっ
ています。・彼の 具合が もっと
悪く なっています。

**worst**
**1** noun = いちばんわるい・一番悪い

**2** adjective
= いちばんひどい・一番酷い
the worst hotel in town = この まちで
いちばんひどい ホテル・この
町で 一番酷い ホテル
the worst thing to do would be to tell
him = いちばんひどいのは かれ
に いう ことです。・一番酷いの
は 彼に 言う ことです。

**worth** adjective
it's worth £100 = ひゃく ポンドの
かちが あります。・百ポンドの
価値が あります。
it's not worth doing it = やる かちが
ありません。・やる 価値が あり
ません。

**would** verb
• (when talking about hypothetical
rather than real situations)
if I had more money, I would buy a car
= もっと おかねがあれば、くる
まを かいます。・もっと お金が
あれば、車を 買います。
we would have missed the train if we
hadn't go a taxi = タクシーに のら
なければ、でんしゃに まに
あいませんでした。・タクシー
に 乗らなければ、電車に 間に
合いませんでした。
• (in reported speech)
I thought you'd forget = わすれると
おもいました。・忘れると 思い
ました。
we were sure she would like it = きっ
と かのじょは すきだと おもい
ました。・きっと 彼女は 好きだ
と 思いました。
• (when making an assumption)
it would have been about midday =
たぶん じゅうにじ ごろでした。
・多分 十二時 ごろでした。
• (to be prepared to)
he wouldn't listen to me = かれ は
わたしの いう ことを きこうと
しませんでした。・彼は 私の
言う ことを 聞こうと しません
でした。
• (when talking about one's wishes)
I'd like a beer = ビールが ほしいで
す。・ビールが 欲しいです。
we would like to stay another night =
もう ひとばん とまりたいで
す。・もう 一晩 泊まりたい
です。

- *(when asking, offering or advising)*
  would you turn the TV off? = テレビ を けしてください。・ テレビを 消してください。
  would you excuse me for a moment? = ちょっと しつれいします。・ ちょっと 失礼します。
  would you like something to eat? = なにか たべませんか。・ 何か 食べませんか。
  you would do well to check = たしか めた ほうが いいです。・ 確かめ た 方が いいです。

**wrap** *verb*
  = つつむ・包む
  to wrap (up) a present = プレゼン トを つつむ・プレゼントを 包む

**wrestling** *noun* = レスリング

**wrist** *noun* = てくび・手首

**write** *verb*
  = かく・書く
  to write to someone, to write someone *(US English)* = だれかに てがみを かく・誰かに 手紙を 書く
  to write an essay = さくぶんを かく ・作文を 書く
  to write a cheque = こぎってを かく ・小切手を 書く
  to write a message = メッセージを かく・メッセージを 書く
  write back = へんじを かく・返事 を 書く
  write down = かきとめる・書き留 める

**writing** *noun* = じ・字
  your writing is good = じが じょうず です。・字が 上手です。

**wrong** *adjective*
- *(not as it should be)*
  there's something wrong = なにかが へんです。・何かが 変です。
  what's wrong? = どうしましたか。
- *(not proper or suitable)* = ちがう・ 違う
  I took the wrong key = ちがう かぎを とりました。・違う 鍵を 取りま した。
  to go the wrong way = ちがう みちを とおる・違う 道を 通る
- *(not correct)*
  that's wrong = ちがいます。・違い ます。

it was a wrong number = まちがい で んわでした。・間違い 電話でし た。
to be wrong *(if it's a person)* = まちが っている・間違っている
- *(not honest, not good)*
  it's wrong to steal things = ものを ぬ すむのは わるい ことです。・物 を 盗むのは 悪い ことです。
  she hasn't done anything wrong = か のじょは わるい ことを しませ んでした。・彼女は 悪いことを しませんでした。

# Xx

**X-ray**
**1** *noun*
  *(photo)* = レントゲンしゃしん・ レントゲン写真
**2** *verb*
  = レントゲンを とる・レントゲン を 撮る

# Yy

**yacht** *noun*
  = ヨット
**yard** *noun*
- *(when measuring)*
  = ヤード

  ❗ *Note that a* yard *= 0.9144 m.*

- *(US English)*
  *(a garden)*
  = にわ・庭
**yawn** *verb*
  = あくびする
**year** *noun*
- *(when talking about time)*
  = ねん・年
  last year = きょねん・去年
  two years ago = にねんまえ・二年 前

to work all year round = いちねんじ
ゅう はたらく・一年中 働く

he's lived there for five years = かれ
は そこに ごねんかん すんで
います。・彼は そこに 五年間
住んでいます。

that'll take years! = それは すうねん
かん かかります。・それは 数年
間 かかります。

- (when talking about age) ▶ 171
= ～さい・～才

I am 15 years old = じゅうごさいで
す。・十五才です。

a four-year old girl = よんさいの
おんなの こ・四才の 女の 子

- (in a school system) ▶ 185

first year, year one ≈ = いちねん・
一年

I am in the second year, I am in year
two = にねんせいです。・二年生
です。

a first year = いちねんせい・一年
生

## yell
**1** verb
= さけぶ・叫ぶ

to yell at someone = だれかに さけ
ぶ・誰かに 叫ぶ

**2** noun
= さけび・叫び

## yellow adjective
= きいろい・黄色い

to go yellow = きいろく なる・
黄色く なる

## yes adverb
= はい Note that when a question is
asked in the negative and the
answer would be "yes" in English, it
would be いいえ in Japanese to
mean "that is incorrect" e.g.

"Didn't you know that?" "Yes, I did" =
「それを しりませんでしたか。」
「いいえ、しっていました。」

'are you coming with us?'—'yes I am'
=「いっしょに いきますか。」
「はい、いきます。」・「一緒に
行きますか。」「はい、行きま
す。」

## yesterday adverb
= きのう・昨日

## yet
**1** adverb
(with negatives) = まだ

not yet = まだ

I haven't eaten yet = まだ たべてい
ません。・まだ 食べていませ
ん。

(with positives) = もう

have they eaten yet? = かれらは も
う たべましたか。・彼らは もう
食べましたか。

have you read this yet? = これを も
う よみましたか。・これを もう
読みましたか。

**2** conjunction
= しかし

## yogurt noun
= ヨーグルト

## you pronoun

> **!** There are various words for 'you'
> in Japanese, of which the most
> common is あなた however
> whenever possible the person's
> name should be used rather than
> this.

## young
**1** adjective
= わかい・若い

a young lady = わかい おんなの
ひと・若い 女の 人

young people = わかもの・若者

she is a year younger than me = か
のじょは わたしより いっさい
とししたです。・彼女は 私より
一才 年下です。

a younger brother ▶ **brother**

a younger sister ▶ **sister**

to look young = わかく みえる・
若く 見える

**2** noun
(of an animal) = こ・子

## your determiner

> **!** There are various words for 'your'
> in Japanese, of which the most
> common is あなたの however
> whenever possible the person's
> name + の should be used rather
> than this.

## yours pronoun

> **!** There are various words for
> 'yours' in Japanese, of which the
> most common is あなたの however
> whenever possible the person's
> name + の should be used rather
> than this.

**yourself** *pronoun*
- *Not used as a reflexive pronoun in Japanese.*
  you'll enjoy yourself
  = たのしみます。・ 楽しみます。
  did you hurt yourself?
  = けがを しましたか。・ 怪我を しましたか。
- *(when used for emphasis)*
  you did it yourself
  = じぶんで しました。・ 自分で しました。

**yourselves** *pronoun*
- *Not used as a reflexive pronoun in Japanese.*
  you'll enjoy yourselves = たのしみます。・ 楽しみます。
  did you hurt yourselves? = けがを しましたか。・ 怪我を しましたか。
- *(when used for emphasis)*
  are you going to do it yourselves? = じぶんたちで しますか。・ 自分達で しますか。

**youth** *noun*
- *(a young man)*
  = しょうねん・ 少年
- *(young people)*
  = わかもの・ 若者

**youth club** *noun*
  = せいしょうねんクラブ・ 青少年クラブ

**youth hostel** *noun*
  = ユースホステル

# Zz

**zap** *verb*
  *(to destroy)* = さくじょする・ 削除する

**zebra** *noun*
  = しまうま・ しま馬

**zebra crossing** *noun* *(British English)*
  = おうだんほどう・ 横断歩道

**zero** *number*
  = ゼロ *the alternative word* れい *is also used.*

**zip** *(British English)*, **zipper** *(US English) noun*
  = チャック
  to undo a zip = チャックを はずす・ チャックを 外す

**zip code** *noun* *(US English)*
  = ゆうびんばんごう・ 郵便番号

**zone** *noun*
  = ちたい・ 地帯

**zoo** *noun*
  = どうぶつえん・ 動物園

Z

# Learning and lifestyle kit

# Dictionary know-how

This section contains a number of short exercises which will help you to use your dictionary more effectively. You will find answers to all of these exercises at the end of the section on p. 435.

## 1 **Word order**

These words are all related to time, but what do they each mean? They are given here in time order, but can you rearrange them into the order in which they appear in the dictionary?

| Japanese word | English translation | Order in which words appear in dictionary |
|---|---|---|
| おととし | | |
| きょねん | | |
| せんしゅう | | |
| せんじつ | | |
| おととい | | |
| きのう | | |
| きょう | | |
| あした | | |
| あさって | | |
| らいげつ | | |
| さらいげつ | | |

## 2 **False friends**

Some words borrowed from other languages undergo a change of meaning when introduced into Japanese, while others appear to have a different meaning from the original by virtue of the way they are written in Japanese. The imports below all have meanings different from what it might seem. Use the dictionary to check if you are not sure of the meanings.

a) **ホーム** is not found at home – it's .................................................................................

b) **ワイシャツ** isn't white – it's.................................................................................

c) **スマート** isn't clever – it's .................................................................................

d) **ワンピース** isn't for wearing when swimming – it's.................................................

e) **マンション** isn't just for the rich – it's .................................................................

f) **リットル** isn't small – it's.................................................................................

g) **スーパー** isn't excellent – it's.................................................................................

h) **ミス** isn't a young woman – it's ................................................................................

i) **タレント** isn't particularly gifted – it's ................................................................

# 3 Practice with ～て forms

You can use this dictionary to find out more than just the meaning or spelling of a word. For example, entries for the most common verbs give not only the dictionary forms, but also the ～て form, ～ます form and ～ない form, and some are also listed by their ～て form. Use the dictionary to identify the ～て form verbs given below, and find out the plain forms and ～ます forms. The first one has been done for you.

| ～て form | plain form | ～ます form |
|---|---|---|
| Example: あいて | あく | あきます |
| a) かわって | | |
| b) がんばって | | |
| c) だして | | |
| d) たって | | |
| e) とって | | |
| f) のって | | |
| g) ふって | | |
| h) まって | | |
| i) しまって | | |
| j) すんで | | |
| k) たのしんで | | |

# 4 Categories

Look at the words below, and put them into the appropriate group based on their meaning.

きいろい、はな、わしつ、 しんぶん、はれ、ゆうびんきょく、
とこのま、ホテル、ふゆ、くび、きょうかしょ、みどり、くもり、
きせつ、しょうせつ、たたみ、げきじょう、はる、みみ、きり、しろい

a) ほん、ざっし、

b) あき、なつ、

c) あおい、むらさき、

d) ぎんこう、としょかん、

e) かお、あたま、

f) あめ、ゆき、

g) ふすま、しょうじ、

# 5 Beginnings and endings

Find out the meanings of these prefixes (the kanji are given in brackets where applicable), and match them to the endings. Check the dictionary if you are unsure of meanings.

| | |
|---|---|
| a) らい~ (来~) | i) ~いん、~こく、~ぜん、~たい |
| b) ぜん~ (全~) | ii) ~しつ、~しょく、~ふく |
| c) こ~ (小~) | iii) ~はん、~めんなさい、~ちそうさまでした |
| d) わ~ (和~) | iv) ~ちゃ、~とうさん、~かね |
| e) よう~ (洋~) | v) ~げつ、~しゅう、~ねん、~にち |
| f) こう~ (高~) | vi) ~あん、 ~うん、~しぎ、~じゅう |
| g) お~ | vii) ~こう、~か (な)、~ど |
| h) ご~ (御~) | viii) ~ゆび、~や、~がた、~づかい |
| i) ふ~ (不~) | ix) ~しつ、~しょく、~ふく |

# 6 Which meaning?

There are many homonyms (words which sound the same but have different meanings) in Japanese, though the differences in meaning often become clear in the written language because they have different kanji. We have given two definitions for Japanese words which sound the same – what are they? Check your dictionary to see the different kanji.

| Meaning 1 | Meaning 2 | Japanese |
|---|---|---|
| *Example: flower* | *nose* | はな |
| a) conference | stairs | |
| b) to change, switch | to go back, return | |
| c) musical instrument | term, semester | |
| d) money | bell | |
| e) river | leather | |
| f) bridge | chopsticks | |
| g) pride | dust | |
| h) to stick | spring (season) | |
| i) bee | eight | |
| j) tooth | leaf | |
| k) seat | a cough | |
| l) white | castle | |

## 7 Transitive or intransitive?

This dictionary shows which verbs are transitive and which intransitive by giving
the particle used with them. With transitive verbs (those which have a direct
object), the direct object is indicated by the particle を. With intransitive verbs
(those which do not have a direct object), the subject is usually indicated by the
particle が. This is neatly illustrated by the announcement often made at stations
in Japan when a train is preparing to leave a station:「ドアをしめます、
ドアが しまります」('We're going the close the doors; the doors are closing.').
Which particle is needed to complete the sentences below, and what do the
sentences mean?

| Japanese sentence | Particle | English translation |
|---|---|---|
| a) クラス___ はじまりました。 | | |
| b) しごと___ はじめました。 | | |
| c) コップ___ こわしました。 | | |
| d) さら___ こわれました。 | | |
| e) でんしゃ___ とまりました。 | | |
| f) くるま___ とめました。 | | |
| g) えいが___ みました。 | | |
| h) ふじさん___ みえました。 | | |
| i) ドア___ あきました。 | | |
| j) まど___ あけました。 | | |
| k) ゆび___ きりました。 | | |
| l) でんわ___ きれました。 | | |
| m) こども の こえ___ きこえました。 | | |
| n) ラジオ___ ききました。 | | |

## 8 Odd one out

Which word in each group below doesn't fit? Look up the meanings of the words to
check your answers.

   a) あに、おとうと、うま、あね、いとこ
   b) あおい、すずしい、あつい、あたたかい、むしあつい
   c) ときどき、たいてい、いつも、ぜんぜん、てんき
   d) いま、ふろば、げんかん、いぬ、だいどころ
   e) ねこ、うなぎ、ぶた、ひつじ、しか
   f) さけぶ、はなす、いう、ささやく、よぶ、くる
   g) きもの、くつした、ずぼん、ひざ、ぼうし

## 9 **Dictionary round-up**

The dictionary can help you to answer these questions.

a) What job does a **のうか** do? .....................................................................

b) Is a **むこ** male or female? ..........................................................................

c) Who would you find in a **こうばん**? ...........................................................

d) Who is likely to attend an **おみあい**? ........................................................

e) What's the opposite of **こうはい**? ..............................................................

f) What is full form of the abbreviated word **こうこう**? .................................

g) What is the humble form of **おっしゃる**? ...................................................

h) If a train carriage is **まんいん**, is it full or empty? ..................................

i) Look at the kanji character for **りょう** in the words **りょうがわ、りょうしん** and **りょうて**. What do you think it means? .....................................................

j) Is the word **ひろさ** a noun, adjective or adverb? ....................................

# Answers

**1**

あさって the day after tomorrow; あした tomorrow; おととい the day before yesterday; おととし the year before last; きのう yesterday; きょう today; きょねん last year; さらいげつ the month after next; せんしゅう last week; せんじつ the other day; らいげつ next month

**2**

a) station platform; b) shirt; c) slim; d) dress, e) apartment, apartment block; f) litre; g) supermarket; h) mistake, error; i) TV entertainer

**3**

a) かわる、かわります b) がんばる、がんばります c) だす、だします d) たつ、 たちます e) とる、とります f) のる、のります g) ふる、ふります h) まつ、 まちます i) しまる、しまります j) すむ、すみます k) とのしむ、たのしみます

**4**

a) (publications) しんぶん、きょうかしょ、しょうせつ、b) (seasons) ふゆ、きせつ、 はる、c) (colours) きいろい、みどり、しろい d) (buildings) ゆうびんきょく、ホテル、 げきじょう、e) (parts of the body) はな、くび、みみ、f) (weather) はれ、くもり、 きり、g) (Japanese house) わしつ、とこのま、たたみ

**5**

a) v b) i c) viii d) ii or ix e) ii or ix f) vii g) iv h) iii i) vii

**6**

a) かいだん b) かえる c) がっき d) かね e) かわ f) はし g) ほこり h) はる i) はち j) は k) せき l) しろ

**7**

a) が The class began. b) を I started work. c) を I broke the glass. d) が The plate broke. e) が The train stopped. f) を I stopped the car. g) を We saw a movie. h) が Mt Fuji could be seen. i) が The door opened. j) を I opened the window. k) を I cut my finger. l) が We were cut off. (lit: the phone was cut) m) が Children's voices could be heard. n) を I heard the radio.

**8**

a) うま b) あおい c) てんき d) いぬ e) うなぎ f) くる g) ひざ

**9**

a) farming b) male ('bridegroom') c) policemen d) those who want to get married e) せんぱい f) こうとう がっこう g) いう h) full i) both j) noun

# Hiragana Chart

Note that Japanese words in this and other dictionaries are arranged according to this chart from left to right and top to bottom. The Japanese equivalent of 'from A to Z' is 'from あ to ん'. In dictionary order the K and G and S and Z etc. will not be separated i.e. the next word after かい (floor) is がい (damage).

| 'a' line | | 'i' line | | 'u' line | | 'e' line | | 'o' line | |
|---|---|---|---|---|---|---|---|---|---|
| あ | a | い | i | う | u | え | e | お | o |
| か | ka | き | ki | く | ku | け | ke | こ | ko |
| が | ga | ぎ | gi | ぐ | gu | げ | ge | ご | go |
| さ | sa | し | shi | す | su | せ | se | そ | so |
| ざ | za | じ | ji | ず | zu | ぜ | ze | ぞ | zo |
| た | ta | ち | chi | つ | tsu | て | te | と | to |
| だ | da | ぢ | ji | づ | zu | で | de | ど | do |
| な | na | に | ni | ぬ | nu | ね | ne | の | no |
| は | ha | ひ | hi | ふ | fu | へ | he | ほ | ho |
| ば | ba | び | bi | ぶ | bu | べ | be | ぼ | bo |
| ぱ | pa | ぴ | pi | ぷ | pu | ぺ | pe | ぽ | po |
| ま | ma | み | mi | む | mu | め | me | も | mo |
| や | ya | | | ゆ | yu | | | よ | yo |
| ら | ra | り | ri | る | ru | れ | re | ろ | ro |
| わ | wa | | | | | | | を | o/wo |
| ん | n | | | | | | | | |

Hiragana symbol plus small や、ゆ or よ

| きゃ | kya | きゅ | kyu | きょ | kyo |
|---|---|---|---|---|---|
| ぎゃ | gya | ぎゅ | gyu | ぎょ | gyo |
| しゃ | sha | しゅ | shu | しょ | sho |
| じゃ | ja | じゅ | ju | じょ | jo |

| ちゃ | cha | ちゅ | chu | ちょ | cho |
|------|-----|------|-----|------|-----|
| にゃ | nya | にゅ | nyu | にょ | nyo |
| ひゃ | hya | ひゅ | hyu | ひょ | hyo |
| びゃ | bya | びゅ | byu | びょ | byo |
| ぴゃ | pya | ぴゅ | pyu | ぴょ | pyo |
| りゃ | rya | りゅ | ryu | りょ | ryo |

## Pronunciation Guide

Vowels:                    Long vowels:

'a' as in cat
'i' as in sheep
'u' as in boot
'e' as in bed              えい is pronounced as a long え
'o' as in dog              おう is pronounced as a long お

Small つ

A small つ has an effect similar to doubling the following consonant. For example in the word ちょっと, the と following the small つ is pronounced in a similar manner to the double t in 'hot toddy'.

Note that は is read 'ha' when it is part of a word, but when used as the topic particle it is pronounced 'wa'.

Similarly, へ is pronounced 'he' when it is part of a word but 'e' when it is used as a particle showing the direction of travel.

## Katakana chart

| 'a' line | | 'i' line | | 'u' line | | 'e' line | | 'o' line | |
|------|-----|------|-----|------|-----|------|-----|------|-----|
| ア | a | イ | i | ウ | u | エ | e | オ | o |
| カ | ka | キ | ki | ク | ku | ケ | ke | コ | ko |
| ガ | ga | ギ | gi | グ | gu | ゲ | ge | ゴ | go |
| サ | sa | シ | shi | ス | su | セ | se | ソ | so |
| ザ | za | ジ | ji | ズ | zu | ゼ | ze | ゾ | zo |
| タ | ta | チ | chi | ツ | tsu | テ | te | ト | to |
| ダ | da | ヂ | ji | ヅ | zu | デ | de | ド | do |
| ナ | na | ニ | ni | ヌ | nu | ネ | ne | ノ | no |
| ハ | ha | ヒ | hi | フ | fu | ヘ | he | ホ | ho |
| バ | ba | ビ | bi | ブ | bu | ベ | be | ボ | bo |

| パ | pa | ピ | pi | プ | pu | ペ | pe | ポ | po |
|---|---|---|---|---|---|---|---|---|---|
| マ | ma | ミ | mi | ム | mu | メ | me | モ | mo |
| ヤ | ya | | | ユ | yu | | | ヨ | yo |
| ラ | ra | リ | ri | ル | ru | レ | re | ロ | ro |
| ワ | wa | | | | | | | ヲ | o/wo |
| ン | n | | | | | | | | |

Katakana symbol plus small ヤ、ユ or ヨ

| キャ | kya | キュ | kyu | キョ | kyo |
|---|---|---|---|---|---|
| ギャ | gya | ギュ | gyu | ギョ | gyo |
| シャ | sha | シュ | shu | ショ | sho |
| ジャ | ja | ジュ | ju | ジョ | jo |
| チャ | cha | チュ | chu | チョ | cho |
| ニャ | nya | ニュ | nyu | ニョ | nyo |
| ヒャ | hya | ヒュ | hyu | ヒョ | hyo |
| ビャ | bya | ビュ | byu | ビョ | byo |
| ピャ | pya | ピュ | pyu | ピョ | pyo |
| リャ | rya | リュ | ryu | リョ | ryo |

Note that in katakana, long vowels are usually written by putting a ー after the sound as in the case of コーヒー (coffee) or ヒーター (heater). As katakana is used to indicate the pronunciation of foreign words there are other possible combinations not included in the chart.

# The Japanese words you must know

あア
あいだ
アイスクリーム
あう、あいます
あおい
あかい
あかちゃん
あかるい
あがる、あがります
あき
あく、あきます
あける、あけます
あげる、あげます
あさ
あさごはん
あさって
あし
あじ
あした
あそこ
あそぶ、あそびます
あたたかい
あたま
あたらしい
あつい
あと
あなた
あに
あね
アパート
あぶない
あまい
あまり
あめ
あらう、あらいます
ある、あります
アルバイト
あるく、あるきます
あれ
あんぜん

いイ
いい
いいえ
いえ
いう、いいます
いかが
イギリス
いく、いきます
いくら
いす

いそがしい
いそぐ、いそぎます
いたい
いただく、いただきます
いち
いちばん
いつ
いつか
いっしょ（に）
いっしょうけんめい
いっぱい
いつも
いなか
いぬ
いま
いみ
いもうと、いもうとさん
いや（な）
いらっしゃる、いらっしゃ
います
いりぐち
いる、います
いれる、いれます
いろ
いろいろ（な）

うウ
ウイスキー
うえ
うしろ
うた
うたう、うたいます
うつくしい
うで
うどん
うま
うまれる、うまれます
うみ
うる、うります
うるさい
うれしい
うんてんしゅ
うんどう

えエ
え
えいが
えいがかん
えいご
えいこく
ええ

えき
エスカレーター
えらぶ、えらびます
エレベーター
えん
えんぴつ

おオ
おいしい
おうふく
おおい
おおきい
オートバイ
おかあさん
おかしい
おかね
おきる、おきます
おくさん
おくる、おくります
おくれる、おくれます
おこる、おこります
おしえる、おしえます
おじ、おじさん
おじいさん
おそい
おちゃ
おとうさん
おとうと、おとうとさん
おとこ
おととい
おとな
おなか
おなじ
おにいさん
おねえさん
おば、おばさん
おばあさん
おぼえる、おぼえます
おまわりさん
おみやげ
おめでとう
おもい
おもしろい
おもう、おもいます
おりる、おります
オレンジ
およぐ、およぎます
おわる、おわります
おんがく
おんせん
おんな

かカ
～かい
かいぎ
がいこく
がいこくじん
かいしゃ
かいもの
かいわ
かう、かいます
かえる、かえります
かお
かかる、かかります
かく、かきます
かいしゃ
かさ
かす、かします
かぜ
かぞく
かど
かない
かねもち
かばん
かべ
かみ
カメラ
かようび
からい
かりる、かります
かるい
カレーライス
かわ
かわいい
かわる、かわります
かんがえる、かんがえます
かんじ
かんじる、かんじます
かんたん
がんばる、がんばります

きキ
き
き を つける、き を つけます
きいろい
きく、ききます
きた
きたない
きっさてん
きって
きっぷ
きのう
きめる、きめます
きもち
きもの
きゃく
きゅう、く

きゅうりょう
きょう
きょうしつ
きょうだい
きょうみ
きょねん
きらい（な）
きる、きます
きれい（な）
キロ、キログラム
キロ、キロメートル
ぎんこう
きんようび

くク
くうこう
くださる、くださいます
くすり
くだもの
くち
くつ
くつした
くに
くび
くも
くらい
ぐらい
クラス
くらべる、くらべます
くる、きます
くるま
くれる、くれます
くろい

けケ
けいさつ
ケーキ
けいたい でんわ
けさ
けっこう（な）
けっこん する、します
げつようび
げんかん
げんき（な）

こコ
ご
こうえん
こうこう
こうじょう
こうばん
こえ
こおり
こくさい
ここ

ごご
こころ
ごぜん
こたえる、こたえます
ごちそう する、します
こちら
こつづみ
コップ
こと
ことし
ことば
こども
ごはん
こまる、こまります
ごみ
こめ
これ
ころ
こわい
こんげつ
コンサート
こんしゅう
こんばん
コンピューター

さサ
～さい
さいきん
さいふ
さかな
さく、さきます
さくら
さけ
さしみ
サッカー
さとう
さびしい
さむい
さら
サラリーマン
さん
～さん、～さま
ざんねん

しシ
～じ
しお
じかん
しけん
じこ
しごと
じしょ
じしん
しずか（な）
した

しち、なな
しつもん
しつれい（な）
じてんしゃ
じどうしゃ
じぶん
しぬ、しにます
しま
しまる、しまります
じむしょ
しめる、しめます
しゃしん
しゃちょう
じゃま
シャワー（を あびる、あび
ます）
じゅう
じゅうしょ
ジュース
じゅうぶん
しゅくだい
しゅじん
しゅふ
しゅみ
しょうがつ
しょうがっこう
じょうず（な）
しょうせつ
しょうゆ
しょくじ
しょくどう
しらべる、しらべます
しる、しります
しろい
しんごう
じんじゃ
しんじる、しんじます
しんせつ（な）
しんぱいする、します
しんぶん

すス
すいか
すいようび
スーパー
すき（な）
スキー
すぐ
すくない
すごい
すこし
すずしい
ずっと
すてき（な）
すてる、すてます

ストーブ
すばらしい
ズボン
スリッパ
する、します
すわる、すわります

せセ
せいじ
せいと
せいふ
セーター
せかい
せつめい
ぜひ
せまい
せんげつ
せんしゅう
せんせい
ぜんぜん
せんたく
センチ
せん
ぜんぶ

そン
そうじ する、します
そこ
そして
そつぎょう
そと
そば
そら
それ

たタ
だいがく
だいがくせい
だいじょうぶ
たいせつ（な）
だいたい
たいてい
だいどころ
たいふう
たいへん
たかい
だから
たくさん
タクシー
だけ
だす、だします
たすける、たすけます
ただしい
たつ、たちます
たてもの

たとえば
たに
たのしい
たのむ、たのみます
たばこ
たべもの
たべる、たべます
たまご
だめ（な）
だれ
たんじょうび
だんだん

ちチ
ちいさい
ちかい
ちがう、ちがいます
ちかく
ちかてつ
ちず
ちち
ちゃいろ
～ちゃん
ちゅうがっこう
ちゅうがくせい
ちゅうごく
ちゅうもん
ちょうど
ちょっと

つッ
つかう、つかいます
つかれる、つかれます
つき
つぎ
つく、つきます
つくえ
つくる、つくります
つける、つけます
つまらない
つめたい
つもり
つよい

てテ
て
てあらい
ていねい（な）
テーブル
でかける、でかけます
てがみ
でぐち
できる、できます
デザート
てつだう、てつだいます

デパート
てら
でる、でます
テレビ
てんき
でんき
でんしゃ
でんわ

とト
ドア
どうぞ
どうぶつ
どうも
とおい
とおる、とおります
とき
ときどき
どくしん
とくべつ（な）
とけい
どこ
ところ
とし
としょかん
とだな
とても
どなた
となり
とまる、とまります
とめる、とめます
ともだち
とり
とりにく
とる、とります
どんな

なナ
ナイフ
なおす、なおします
なか
ながい
なく、なきます
なぜ
なつ
なに
なべ
なまえ
ならう、ならいます
なる、なります

にニ
に
におい
にぎやか（な）

にく
にし
にちようび
にもつ
ニュース
にわ
～にん
にんぎょう
にんじん

ぬヌ
ぬぐ、ぬぎます

ねネ
ネクタイ
ねこ
ねだん
ねむい
ねる、ねます

のノ
ノート
のど
のぼる、のぼります
のみもの
のむ、のみます
のる、のります

はハ
は
はい
はいる、はいります
はがき
はくぶつかん
はこ
はさみ
はし
はじまる、はじまります
はじめる、はじめます
はしる、はしります
バス
はずかしい
パスポート
はたけ
はたらく、はたらきます
はち
はな
はなす、はなします
はは
はやい
はやし
はらう、はらいます
はる
ばん
パン

ばんぐみ
ばんごう
はんたい
はんぶん

ひヒ
ひ
ビール
ひがし
ひく、ひきます
ひくい
ひこうき
ひざ
ビザ
びじゅつかん
ひだり
びっくり する、します
ビデオ
ひと
ひま（な）
ひゃく
びょういん
びょうき
ひる
ビル
ひろい
ピンク

ふフ
ふうとう
プール
フォーク
ふすま
ぶたにく
ふつう
ふとん
ふね
ふべん（な）
ふゆ
ふる、ふります
ふるい
プロ
ふろ
ふろば
ふん、ぶん
ぶんか

へヘ
ページ
へた（な）
ベッド
へや
へん（な）
べんとう
べんり（な）

ほ ホ
ボーナス
ホーム
ほか
ぼく
ほしい
ポスト
ホテル
ほん
ほんとう

ま マ
まいにち
まえ
まご
まじめ（な）
まず
まずい
また
まち
まちがえる、まちがえます
まつ、まちます
まっすぐ
まつり
まど
まるい
まん
まんが

み ミ
みえる、みえます
みかん
みぎ
みじかい
みず
みせ
みせる、みせます
みそしる
みち
みつける、みつけます
みどり
みな、みなさん
みなと
みなみ
みみ

みょうじ
みる、みます
みんしゅく

め メ
め
めいし
メートル
めがね
めずらしい
メニュー
メンバー

も そ
もくようび
もしもし
もちろん
もつ、もちます
もって いく、いきます
もって くる、きます
もっと
もの
もらう、もらいます
もり
もんだい

や ヤ
やおや
やきゅう
やく、やきます
やくそく
やさい
やさしい
やすい
やすむ、やすみます
やせる、やせます
やま
やめる、やめます

ゆ ユ
ゆ
ゆうびんきょく
ゆうめい（な）
ゆかた
ゆき
ゆっくり

よ ヨ
ようこそ
ヨーロッパ
よく
よてい
よぶ、よびます
よむ、よみます
よやく
よる
よろこぶ、よろこびます
よわい
よん、し

ら ラ
らいげつ
らいねん
らいしゅう
ラジオ
ラッシュアワー

り リ
りょうしん
りょうり
りょかん
りょこう
りんご

れ し
れきし
レストラン
れんしゅう
れんらく

ろ ロ
ろく
ローマじ

わ ワ
わかい
わかる、わかります
わしょく
わすれる、わすれます
わたし
わらう、わらいます
わるい

# Phrasefinder

## Contents

| Useful phrases | べんりな ひょうげん |
|---|---|
| yes, please | はい、おねがいします |
| no, thank you | いいえ、けっこう です |
| sorry / excuse me | すみません |
| you're welcome | どう いたしまして |
| I'm sorry, I don't understand | すみませんが、わかりません |
| where is the (toilet)? | （トイレ）は どこ ですか |
| do you speak English (*Japanese)? | えいご（＊にほんご）を はなしますか |

| **Greetings** | **あいさつ** |
|---|---|
| good morning | おはよう ございます |
| hello *(daytime)* | こんにちは |
| good evening | こんばんは |
| goodbye | さようなら |
| how are you? | おげんき ですか |
| goodnight *(in the sense 'sleep well')* | おやすみ なさい |

| **Meeting people** | **あいさつ** |
|---|---|
| how do you do? | はじめまして |
| pleased to meet you | どうぞ よろしく |
| my name is (John) | わたし は （ジョン）です |
| what's your name? | おなまえ は なん ですか |
| I'm English (*American) | イギリスじん（＊アメリカじん）です |
| where are you from? | どちら から ですか |
| I'm not very good at Japanese | にほんご は よく できません |
| I'm here on holiday (*business) | ホリデー（＊しごと）です |
| I live near (London) | （ロンドン）の ちかく に すんでいます |
| would you like (a coffee)? | （コーヒー）は いかが ですか |

| **Emergencies** | **こまった とき** |
|---|---|
| can you help me, please? | たすけて ください |
| I'm lost | みち に まよいました |
| I'm ill | びょうき です |
| call an ambulance (*the police) | きゅうきゅうしゃ（＊けいさつ）を よんで ください |
| where is the police box? | こうばん は どこですか |
| watch out! | き を つけて |

## ❶ Going places

# りょこう を する ❶

### At the train station

where can I buy a ticket?

what time is the next train to Tokyo?

do I have to change?

which platform for the train to Kyoto?

there's a train to Hiroshima at 10:00

a single (*return) to Kyoto, please

I'd like to reserve a seat

do you mind if (I sit here)?

### えき で

きっぷは どこ で かえますか

つぎの とうきょう ゆき は なんじ ですか

のりかえは ありますか

きょうと ゆき は なんばんせん から ですか

１０：００（＝じゅうじ）に ひろしま ゆき が
あります

きょうとまで、かたみち（＊おうふく）ください

していせきを ください

（ここ に すわって）も いいですか

### By taxi

can you call me a taxi, please?

I'll take a taxi

to (Tokyu Hotel), please

to this place, please (*showing address or map*)

take the first turning right

turn left (*right) here

here is fine

please stop here

could I have a receipt, please?

### タクシー に のる

タクシーを よんで ください

タクシーで いきます

（とうきゅう ホテル）まで おねがいします

ここまで おねがい します

さいしょの かど を みぎ に まがって ください

ここで ひだり（＊みぎ）に まがって ください

ここで けっこう です

ここで とめて ください

レシートを ください

### Getting there

could you tell me the way to (Tokyo station)?

how long will it take to get there?

is it far from here?

which bus do I take for (Shibuya)?

can you tell me where to get off?

how much is the fare to (the airport)?

what time is the last bus?

how do I get to (the airport)?

is there an underground (subway) station near here?

### いきかた を きく

（とうきょう えき）へ の いきかた を おしえて
ください

じかんは どれ ぐらい かかりますか

ここ から とおい ですか

（しぶや）ゆき の バス は どれ ですか

どこ で おりる か おしえて ください

（くうこう）まで いくら ですか

さいしゅの バス は なんじ ですか

（くうこう）まで、どういう ふうに いきますか

この ちかく に ちかてつ の えき が ありますか

## ❷ Keeping in touch　　　　れんらく を とりあう ❷

### On the phone

でんわ で

| | |
|---|---|
| where can I buy a phone card? | テレホンカード は どこ で かえますか |
| may I use your phone? | でんわ を かして ください |
| do you have a mobile? | けいたい を もって いますか |
| I want to make a phone call | でんわ を かけたい ん です |
| the line's busy | はなしちゅう です |
| there's no answer | だれ も でません |
| hello? this is (John) | もしもし、（ジョン）です |
| is (Keiko) there please? | （けいこ）さん は いらっしゃいますか |
| who's calling? | どちらさま ですか |
| sorry, wrong number | すみません、まちがい でんわ です |
| just a moment, please | ちょっと まって ください |
| would you like to hold? | まちますか |
| please tell him / her I called | でんわ が あった と おつたえ ください |
| I'd like to leave a message for him/her | でんごん を おねがい します |
| I'll try again later | あと で もう いちど でんわ します |
| please tell him/her that John called | ジョン から でんわ が あった と おつたえ ください |
| please ask him/her to call me back | でんわ を ください と おつたえ ください |
| my home number is ... | うち の でんわ ばんごう は ... |
| my business number is ... | かいしゃ の でんわ ばんごう は ... |
| my fax number is ... | ファックス ばんごう は ... |
| we were cut off | でんわ が きれました |

### Writing

てがみ

| | |
|---|---|
| what's the address? | じゅうしょ は なん ですか |
| here's my business card | どうぞ、わたし の めいし です |
| where is the post office? | ゆうびんきょく は どこ ですか |
| could I have a stamp for the UK (USA), please? | イギリス（＊アメリカ）への きって を ください |
| how much is it to send a postcard to the UK? | イギリス まで えはがき は いくら ですか |
| I'd like to send this parcel | この こづつみ を おくりたい ん ですが |

### On line

インターネットで

| | |
|---|---|
| are you on the internet? | インターネット を りよう しますか |
| what's your email address? | メール アドレス を おしえて ください |
| we could send it by email | メール で おくれます |
| I'll email it to you (on Thursday) | （もくようびに）メール します |
| I looked it up on the internet | インタネット で しらべました |
| the information is on their website | ウェブサイト に じょうほう が あります |

### Meeting up

まちあわせ

| | |
|---|---|
| what would you like to do this evening? | こんばん なに が したい ですか |
| where shall we meet? | どこ で まちあわせましょうか |
| I'll see you outside the restaurant at 6:00 | レストランの まえ で ６：００（＝ろくじ）にあいましょう |
| see you later | また あと で |
| sorry, but I'm busy today | すみません が、きょう は ちょっと いそがしい です |

# ❸ Food and drink

# がいしょく する ❸

---

**Booking a restaurant**

can you recommend a good restaurant?

I'd like to reserve a table for four

a reservation for 8:00 tomorrow evening please

I booked a table for two

## レストラン の よやく

いい レストラン を しって いますか

よんめい、 よやく して ください

あした の ばん 8:00 （＝はちじ）の よや
く おねがいします

ふたり、 よやく しました

---

**Ordering**

could we see the menu, please

I'd like this, please

the (sushi) set meal, please

do you have a vegetarian menu?

what would you recommend?

could I have another beer, please

could we have some more bread?

I'd like a coffee

... an espressso

... a decaffeinated coffee

could I have the bill (check)?

## ちゅうもん

メニュー を みせて ください

これ を ください

（すし）ていしょくを ください

ベジタリアン メニュー は ありますか

なに を すすめますか

ビール もう いっぽん、 ください

パン を もう すこし ください

コーヒー を ください

エスプレッソ...

デカフェ...

おかんじょう を おねがいします

---

**You will hear ...**

welcome!

a table for how many?

are you ready to order?

what would you like?

and to drink?

would you like (a starter)?

what will you have for the main course?

I can recommend ...

would you like a dessert?

who ordered the (ice cream)?

anything else?

enjoy your meal!

here is some green tea

here you are

## ...を きく

いらっしゃいませ

なんめい さま ですか

おきまり でしょうか

なに に なさいますか

おのみもの は？

（スターター）は いかが ですか

メーンコース は なに に しますか

...を おすすめ します

デザート は いかが ですか

（アイスクリーム）の おきゃくさま は？

ほか に なにか

ごゆっくり、 どうぞ

おちゃ を どうぞ

どうぞ

---

**Etiquette**

bon appétit; let's start

that was a lovely meal; thank you for the meal

that was delicious

cheers!

I've had enough, thank you

## エチケット

いただきます

ごちそうさま でした

おいしかった

かんぱい

もう けっこう です

| The menu | メニュー |
|---|---|
| **fish** | さかな |
| sushi rolls | まきずし |
| pieces of fish on vinegared rice balls | にぎりずし |
| raw fish without rice | さしみ |
| abalone | あわび |
| bonito | かつお |
| clam | はまぐり |
| crab | かに |
| eel | うなぎ |
| herring | にしん |
| horse mackerel | あじ |
| mackerel | さば |
| octopus | たこ |
| oyster | かき |
| salmon | さけ |
| salmon roe | いくら |
| scallop | ほたてがい |
| sea bream | たい |
| sea urchin | うに |
| shrimp | えび |
| squid | いか |
| trout | ます |
| tuna | まぐろ |
| **meat** | にく |
| bacon | ベーコン |
| beef | ぎゅうにく |
| breaded pork cutlet | とんかつ |
| chicken | とりにく |
| grilled chicken on a stick | やきとり |
| ham | ハム |
| hamburger | ハンバーガー |
| liver | レーバー |
| pork | ぶたにく |
| sausage | ソーセージ |
| steak | ステーキ |
| **vegetables** | やさい |
| aubergine (eggplant) | なす |
| bamboo shoot | たけのこ |
| bean | まめ |
| bean sprout | もやし |
| broccoli | ブロッコリ |
| cabbage | キャベツ |
| carrot | にんじん |
| Chinese cabbage | はくさい |
| cucumber | きゅうり |
| garlic | にんにく |
| green pepper | ピーマン |
| leek | ながねぎ |
| lettuce | レタス |

| メニュー | The menu |
|---|---|
| さかな | **fish** |
| さしみ | raw fish without rice |
| にぎりずし | pieces of fish on vinegared rice balls |
| まきずし | sushi rolls |
| あじ | horse mackerel |
| あわび | abalone |
| いか | squid |
| いくら | salmon roe |
| うなぎ | eel |
| うに | sea urchin |
| えび | shrimp |
| かき | oyster |
| かつお | bonito |
| かに | crab |
| さけ | salmon |
| さば | mackerel |
| たい | sea bream |
| たこ | octopus |
| にしん | herring |
| はまぐり | clam |
| ほたてがい | scallop |
| まぐろ | tuna |
| ます | trout |
| にく | **meat** |
| ぎゅうにく | beef |
| ステーキ | steak |
| ソーセージ | sausage |
| とりにく | chicken |
| とんかつ | breaded pork cutlet |
| ハム | ham |
| ハンバーガー | hamburger |
| ベーコン | bacon |
| ぶたにく | pork |
| やきとり | grilled chicken on a stick |
| レーバー | liver |
| やさい | **vegetables** |
| かぼちゃ | pumpkin |
| キャベツ | cabbage |
| きゅうり | cucumber |
| さつまいも | sweet potato |
| サラダ | salad |
| たけのこ | bamboo shoot |
| たまねぎ | onion |
| だいこん | radish (Japanese) |
| トマト | tomato |
| ながねぎ | leek |
| なす | aubergine (eggplant) |
| にんじん | carrot |
| にんにく | garlic |

| mushroom | マッシュルーム、きのこ | はくさい | Chinese cabbage |
| onion | たまねぎ | ピーマン | green pepper |
| potato | ポテト、じゃがいも | ブロッコリ | broccoli |
| | | ほうれんそう | spinach |
| pumpkin | かぼちゃ | ポテト、じゃがいも | potato |
| salad | サラダ | マッシュル ム、きのこ | mushroom |
| spinach | ほうれんそう | | |
| sweet potato | さつまいも | まめ | bean |
| tomato | トマト | もやし | bean sprout |
| radish (Japanese) | だいこん | レタス | lettuce |
| **fruit** | **くだもの** | **くだもの** | **fruit** |
| apple | りんご | いちご | strawberry |
| banana | バナナ | オレンジ | orange |
| cherry | さくらんぼ | かき | persimmon |
| chestnut | くり | くり | chestnut |
| grape | ぶどう | さくらんぼ | cherry |
| lemon | レモン | すいか | watermelon |
| mandarin orange | みかん | なし | pear (Japanese) |
| melon | メロン | バナナ | banana |
| orange | オレンジ | ぶどう | grape |
| peach | もも | みかん | mandarin orange |
| pear (Japanese) | なし | メロン | melon |
| persimmon | かき | もも | peach |
| strawberry | いちご | りんご | apple |
| watermelon | すいか | レモン | lemon |
| **how it's prepared** | **りょうりのしゅるい** | **りょうりのしゅるい** | **how it's prepared** |
| Japanese food | にほん りょうり | あげもの | deep fried food |
| Chinese food | ちゅうかりょうり | おこのみやき | Spanish-style omelette |
| fish, meat or vegetables deep fried in a light batter | てんぷら | おでん | one-pot meal with fish cake, vegetables, seaweed |
| chicken and vegetables cooked on an open grill | やきとり | おべんとう | boxed lunch |
| | | さしみ | raw fish |
| raw fish on vinegared rice | すし | しゃぶしゃぶ | very thin slices of beef cooked in broth |
| raw fish | さしみ | | |
| pickled vegetables | つけもの | すきやき | beef and vegetables cooked in sake and soy sauce |
| deep fried food | あげもの | | |
| beef and veg cooked in sake and soy sauce | すきやき | すし | raw fish on vinegared rice |
| very thin slices of beef cooked in broth | しゃぶしゃぶ | ちゅうか りょうり | Chinese food |
| | | つけもの | pickled vegetables |
| Spanish-style omelette | おこのみやき | ていしょく | set meal |
| meat and veg cooked on a central griddle | てっぱんやき | てっぱんやき | meat and veg cooked on a central griddle |
| boxed lunch | おべんとう | てんぷら | fish, meat or vegetables deep fried in a light batter |
| set meal | ていしょく | なべ | hot-pot meal with meat and vegetables |
| hot-pot meal with meat and vegetables | なべ | にほん りょうり | Japanese food |
| one-pot meal with fish cake, vegetables, seaweed | おでん | やきとり | chicken and vegetables cooked on an open grill |

## types of noodles / めんるい

|  |  |
|---|---|
| **types of noodles** | **めんるい** |
| buckwheat noodles | そば |
| thick noodles made with wheat flour | うどん |
| thin Chinese-style noodles in a broth | ラーメン |

|  |  |
|---|---|
| **めんるい** | **types of noodles** |
| うどん | thick noodles made with wheat flour |
| そば | buckwheat noodles |
| ラーメン | thin Chinese-style noodles in a broth |

## accompaniments / その た

|  |  |
|---|---|
| **accompaniments** | **その た** |
| bread | パン |
| chopsticks | はし |
| green tea | おちゃ |
| Japanese horseradish | わさび |
| ketchup | ケチャップ |
| mayonnaise | マヨネーズ |
| miso soup | みそ しる |
| mustard | からし |
| pickled plum | うめぼし |
| rice served with Japanese food | ごはん |
| rice served with western food | ライス |
| salt | しお |
| seaweed | のり |
| soy sauce | しょうゆ |
| Worcestershire sauce | ソース |
| tofu | とうふ |
| vinegar | す |

|  |  |
|---|---|
| **その た** | **accompaniments** |
| うめぼし | pickled plum |
| おちゃ | green tea |
| からし | mustard |
| ケチャップ | ketchup |
| ごはん | rice served with Japanese food |
| しお | salt |
| しょうゆ | soy sauce |
| す | vinegar |
| ソース | Worcestershire sauce |
| とうふ | tofu |
| のり | seaweed |
| はし | chopsticks |
| パン | bread |
| マヨネーズ | mayonnaise |
| みそしる | miso soup |
| ライス | rice served with western food |
| わさび | Japanese horseradish |

## alcoholic drinks / アルコール

|  |  |
|---|---|
| **alcoholic drinks** | **アルコール** |
| beer | ビール |
| draught beer | なまビール |
| sake | おさけ、にほんしゅ |
| warm sake | あつかん |
| cold sake | ひやざけ |
| whisky with water | みずわり |
| whisky with ice ('on the rocks') | オンザロック |
| gin and tonic | ジントニック |
| red wine | あかワイン |
| white wine | しろワイン |
| traditional distilled spirit | しょうちゅう |

|  |  |
|---|---|
| **アルコール** | **alcoholic drinks** |
| あかワイン | red wine |
| あつかん | warm sake |
| おさけ、にほんしゅ | sake |
| オンザロック | whisky with ice ('on the rocks') |
| しょうちゅう | traditional distilled spirit |
| しろワイン | white wine |
| ジントニック | gin and tonic |
| なまビール | draught beer |
| ひやざけ | cold sake |
| ビール | beer |
| みずわり | whisky with water |

## in the coffee shop / きっさてん で

|  |  |
|---|---|
| **in the coffee shop** | **きっさてん で** |
| (cheese) sandwich | （チーズ）サンド |
| apple pie | アップルパイ |
| (chocolate) cake | （チョコレート）ケーキ |
| cocoa | ココア |
| coffee | ホット（コーヒー） |
| cola | コーラ |
| ice cream | アイスクリーム |
| iced coffee | アイス（コーヒー） |
| latte | ラッテ |
| lemon tea | レモンティー |
| milk | ミルク |
| orange juice | オレンジジュース |
| salad | サラダ |
| tea with milk | ミルクティー |
| tea | こうちゃ |
| toast | トースト |
| water | みず |

|  |  |
|---|---|
| **きっさてん で** | **in the coffee shop** |
| アイス（コーヒー） | iced coffee |
| アイスクリーム | ice cream |
| アップルパイ | apple pie |
| オレンジジュース | orange juice |
| こうちゃ | tea |
| コーラ | cola |
| ココア | cocoa |
| サラダ | salad |
| チーズサンド | cheese sandwich |
| チョコレートケーキ | chocolate cake |
| トースト | toast |
| ホット（コーヒー） | coffee |
| みず | water |
| ミルク | milk |
| ミルクティー | tea with milk |
| ラッテ | latte |
| レモンティー | lemon tea |

# ❹ **Places to stay**                    しゅくはく ❹

☆☆☆

| Types of accommodation | ホテル の しゅるい |
| --- | --- |
| hotel | ホテル |
| business hotel | ビジネス ホテル |
| Japanese inn | りょかん |
| Japanese-style bed and breakfast | みんしゅく |
| youth hostel | ユース ホステル |
| Japanese-style tatami room | わしつ |
| Western-style room | ようしつ |
| room | へや |
| with bath | ふろつき |

| At the hotel | ホテル で |
| --- | --- |
| I'd like a double (*single) room | ダブル （＊シングル） おねがい します |
| with bath | ふろつき |
| I have a reservation in the name of (Morris) | （モリス） と いう なまえ で よやく しました |
| we'll be staying three nights | さんぱく です |
| how much does the room cost? | へや は いくら ですか |
| I'd like to see the room, please | へや を みせて ください |
| what time is breakfast? | ちょうしょく は なんじ からですか |
| we'd like to stay another night | もう いっぱく おねがい します |
| please call me at 7:30 | ７。３０ （＝しちじはん）に ウエックアップコール おねがいします |
| are there any messages for me? | でんごん は ありましたか |
| what time does the hostel close? | ユースホステル は なんじに しまりますか |

## ❺ Shopping and money  かいもの と りょうがえ ❺

---

| **At the bank** | **ぎんこう で** |
| I'd like to change some money | りょうがえ を おねがい します |
| I want to change some yen into pounds | えん を ポンド に りょうがえ して ください |
| do you take Eurocheques? | ユーロチェック で いい ですか |
| what's the exchange rate today? | きょうの レート は いくら ですか |
| I prefer traveller's cheques to cash | トラベラズチェック の ほう が いい です |
| I'll get some money from the cash machine | ＡＴＭで おかね を ひきだします |

---

| **Finding the right shop** | **みやをさがす** |
| where's the main shopping district? | ショッピングセンター は どこ ですか |
| where's a good place to buy (souvenirs)? | （おみやげ）を かう の は、どこ が いい ですか |
| where can I buy (batteries)? | （でんち）は どこ で うって いますか |
| where the nearest (bookshop)? | このちかく に （ほんや）は ありますか |
| what time do the shops open (*close)? | みせ は なんじ から （*まで）あいて いますか |
| where did you get those? | それは、どこ で かいましたか |
| I want to buy some presents for my family | かぞく に プレゼント を かいたい です |
| I love shopping | かいもの が だいすき です |

---

| **Are you being served?** | **みせ の なか で** |
| do you have (any postcards)? | （えはがき）は ありますか |
| can I have this, please? | これ を ください |
| how much does that cost? | それは いくら ですか |
| can I try it on? | しちゃくして も いい ですか |
| can I pay by credit card? | クレジットカード で はらえますか |
| do you have this in another colour? | ほかの いろ は ありますか |
| do you have a bigger (*smaller) size? | もっとおおきい （*ちいさい）サイズ が ありますか |
| I take a small (*medium, large) size | わたしの サイズ は Ｓ （*Ｍ，Ｌ）です |
| it doesn't suit me | わたし に は にあいません |
| that's all, thank you | これで いい です |
| I'll take it | これ を かいます |
| I won't take it | これ を かいません |

## ⑥ Weights and measures　　　　どりょうこう ⑥

### Length/ ながさ

| inches | 1.30 | 13 | 26 | 39 | 52 | 65 | 130 |
|---|---|---|---|---|---|---|---|
| cm | 3.33 | 33.3 | 66.7 | 100 | 133.3 | 166.7 | 333.3 |

### Distance/ きょり

| miles | 0.31 | 3.1 | 6.2 | 9.3 | 12.4 | 15.5 | 31 |
|---|---|---|---|---|---|---|---|
| km | 0.5 | 5 | 10 | 15 | 20 | 25 | 50 |

### Weight/ じゅうりょう

| pounds | 1.1 | 11 | 22 | 33 | 44 | 55 | 110 |
|---|---|---|---|---|---|---|---|
| kg | 0.5 | 5 | 10 | 15 | 20 | 25 | 50 |

### Capacity/ ようりょう

| gallons | 0.22 | 2.2 | 4.4 | 6.6 | 8.8 | 11 | 22 |
|---|---|---|---|---|---|---|---|
| litres | 1 | 10 | 20 | 30 | 40 | 50 | 100 |

### Temperature/ おんど

| °C | 0 | 5 | 10 | 15 | 20 | 25 | 30 | 37 | 38 | 40 |
|---|---|---|---|---|---|---|---|---|---|---|
| °F | 32 | 41 | 50 | 59 | 68 | 77 | 86 | 98.4 | 100 | 104 |

### Women's clothing sizes

| UK | 10 | 12 | 14 | 16 | 18 |
|---|---|---|---|---|---|
| US | 8 | 10 | 12 | 14 | 16 |
| Europe | 38 | 40 | 42 | 44 | |
| Japan | 7 | 9 | 11 | 13 | |

### Men's waist sizes

| UK/US | 24 | 26 | 28 | 30 | 32 | 34 | 36 | 38 |
|---|---|---|---|---|---|---|---|---|
| Europe/Japan | 61 | 66 | 71 | 76 | 80 | 87 | 91 | 97 |

### Shoe sizes

| UK | 4 | 4$^1/_2$ | 5 | 5$^1/_2$ | 6 | 6$^1/_2$ | 7 | 7$^1/_2$ | 8 | 8$^1/_2$ | 9 | 9$^1/_2$ | 10 |
|---|---|---|---|---|---|---|---|---|---|---|---|---|---|
| US (women) | 6.5 | 7 | 7.5 | 8 | 8.5 | 9 | 9.5 | 10 | 10.5 | | | | |
| US (men) | 5.5 | 6 | 6.5 | 7 | 7.5 | 8 | 8.5 | 9 | 9.5 | 10 | | 10.5 | |
| Europe | 37 | 37.5 | 38 | 39 | 39.5 | 40 | 40.5 | 41 | 42 | 42.5 | 43 | 44 | 44.5 |
| Japan | 23 | 23.5 | 24 | 24 | 24.5 | 25 | 25.5 | 26 | 26.5 | 27 | 27.5 | 28 | 28.5 |

# ❼ Street signs and information notices

| | |
|---|---|
| shrine | 神社（じんじゃ） |
| temple | 寺（てら） |
| underground, subway (train) | 地下鉄（ちかてつ） |
| train station | 駅（えき） |

| | |
|---|---|
| entrance | 入り口（いりぐち） |
| exit | 出口（でぐち） |
| north exit | 北口（きたぐち） |
| south exit | 南口（みなみぐち） |
| east exit | 東口（ひがしぐち） |
| west exit | 西口（にしぐち） |
| toilet | お手洗い（おてあらい） |
| men | 男（おとこ） |
| women | 女（おんな） |
| bathroom | 風呂場（ふろば） |

| | |
|---|---|
| stop | 止まれ（とまれ） |
| danger | 危険（きけん） |
| no entry | 立入禁止（たちいり きんし） |
| under construction | 工事中（こうじちゅう） |
| one way street | 一方通行（いっぽうつうこう） |

| | |
|---|---|
| open for business | 営業中（えいぎょうちゅう） |
| closed for business | 休業中（きゅうぎょうちゅう） |
| no smoking | 禁煙（きんえん） |
| Tokyo | 東京（とうきょう） |
| *ryokan*, Japanese inn | 旅館（りょかん） |

455

# Dates for your diary

## January
(1)  8  15  22  29
2  9  16  23  30
3  10  17  24  31
4  11  18  25
5  12  19  26
6  13  20  27
7  14  21  28

## February
1  8  15  22
2  9  16  23
3  10  17  24
4  (11)  18  25
5  12  19  26
6  13  20  27
7  (14)  21  28

## March
1  8  15  22  29
2  9  16  23  30
(3)  10  17  24  31
4  11  18  25
5  12  19  26
6  13  20  27
7  14  21  28

## April
1  8  15  22  (29)
2  9  16  23  30
3  10  17  24
4  11  18  25
5  12  19  26
6  13  20  27
7  14  21  28

## May
1  8  15  22  29
2  9  16  23  30
(3)  10  17  24  31
(4)  11  18  25
(5)  12  19  26
6  13  20  27
7  14  21  28

## June
1  8  15  22  29
2  9  16  23  30
3  10  17  24
4  11  18  25
5  12  19  26
6  13  20  27
7  14  21  28

## July
1  8  15  22  29
2  9  16  23  30
3  10  17  24  31
4  11  18  25
5  12  19  26
6  13  20  27
(7)  14  21  28

## August
1  8  (15)  22  29
2  9  16  23  30
3  10  17  24  31
4  11  18  25
5  12  19  26
6  (13)  20  27
7  (14)  21  28

## September
1  8  15  22  29
2  9  16  23  30
3  10  17  24
4  11  18  25
5  12  19  26
6  13  20  27
7  14  21  28

## October
1  8  15  22  29
2  9  16  23  30
3  10  17  24  31
4  11  18  25
5  12  19  26
6  13  20  27
7  14  21  28

## November
1  8  (15)  22  29
2  9  16  (23)  30
(3)  10  17  24
4  11  18  25
5  12  19  26
6  13  20  27
7  14  21  28

## December
1  8  15  22  29
2  9  16  (23)  30
3  10  17  (24)  31
4  11  18  (25)
5  12  19  26
6  13  20  27
7  14  21  28

○ Celebrated in Japan

## 1 January

がんじつ (New Year's Day)

The first day of the new year festival period, which is known as *shōgatsu*, しょうがつ, is a national holiday. This is a time for families to spend time together, and to make the first visit of the year to a shrine or temple. Children receive presents of money in special envelopes. New year cards posted well in advance are kept back at the post office so they can be delivered all together on January 1. Businesses are usually closed for three days.

## 2nd Monday in January

せいじん の ひ (Coming of Age Day)

This a national holiday to celebrate all those who turn 20 years old during the year, which is the age at which people can legally smoke, drink and vote. Towns and cities hold gatherings and ceremonies in the city hall, and many 20-year-olds wear traditional kimono on this day.

## 3 or 4 February

せつぶん (beginning of spring)

On this last day of winter it is traditional to hold a ritual at temples and shrines to get rid of evil spirits, in preparation for the beginning of spring. Beans (usually dried soy beans) are thrown, accompanied by shouts of *Oni wa soto! Fuku wa uchi!* おに は そと、ふく は うち ('Devils out, happiness in!'). Another custom is to eat the number of beans which corresponds to your age.

## 11 February

けんこく きんねんび (National Foundation Day)

This national holiday is in celebration of the day when it is believed that the first emperor acceded to the throne in 660BC.

## 14 February

バレンタインデー (Valentine's Day)

In Japan, only women give presents on Valentine's Day, usually chocolate. But confectioners do not lose out on any business as men are supposed to reciprocate with presents on White Day, a month later on March 14. White Day is believed to have been invented by a marshmallow manufacturer.

## 3 March

ひな まつり (Girls' Festival or Doll Festival)

Families celebrate *hina matsuri* to wish their daughters happiness. Special shelving is erected in the home to display a set of traditional dolls dressed in the costume of the imperial court, and girls dress up in formal wear. Peach blossom is a symbol commonly displayed on this day.

## 20 or 21 March

しゅんぶん の ひ (Spring Equinox)

It is traditional on this national holiday to visit family graves to tidy and clean them.

## 29 April–5 May

ゴールデンウィーク (Golden Week)

Golden Week is so named because four national holidays fall within a period of seven days, so many people take the intervening days off work to gain a long holiday. This is one of Japan's busiest holiday periods, with millions of people thronging the stations and airports. The four national holidays of Golden Week are given below.

## 29 April

みどり の ひ (Greenery Day)

This was originally a national holiday to mark the birthday of the previous emperor, Hirohito (now known as Emperor Showa), who died in 1989. It was kept as a holiday after his death and renamed Greenery Day to celebrate nature and plants, both great loves of the emperor. From 2007 this will be renamed Showa Day, and Greenery Day will move to May 4th, currently a national holiday by default as it lies between two other national holidays.

## 3 May

けんぽう きんねんび (Constitution Day)

This national holiday celebrates the new post-war constitution which came into effect on 3 May 1947.

## 4 May

こくみん の きゅうじつ (national holiday)

This day has been designated a national holiday by virtue of the fact that it falls between two other national holidays. From 2007 it will be renamed Greenery Day.

## 5 May

こども の ひ (Children's Day)

On this national holiday dedicated to children, especially boys, large streamers in the shape of carp can be seen flying from tall posts, symbolising strength and power. In the home, special shelves are set up to display stylised dolls clothed in traditional armour. Parents dress their children in kimono or formal western-syle clothing and take them out and about, often to a shrine or temple.

## 7 July
たなばた (Star Festival)

Colourful *tanabata* festivals take part in many areas of Japan around this time to celebrate the day on which, according to legend, the two stars Vega and Altair can meet across the Milky Way. Everyone hopes for a clear night so the stars can see each other. At this time children write wishes on pieces of paper and attach them to bamboo to make the wishes come true. In some areas of Japan this festival takes place in August.

## 3rd Monday in July
うみ の ひ (Marine Day)

This is a national holiday to celebrate the ocean.

## 13–15 August
おぼん (O-Bon Festival, Festival of the Dead)

This is a family time during which people honour the souls and memories of their ancestors, and the souls and spirits of the ancestors are thought to return to visit their families. Lanterns are hung outside to guide the spirits back to the family home, and later lanterns are floated down rivers to guide them back to their own world. Most neighbourhoods hold festivals with *bon odori* dances. This is one of the main holiday periods in Japan as people take time off work to visit family and to go on trips. In some parts of Japan, O-Bon is celebrated in July.

## 3rd Monday in September
けいろう の ひ (Respect for the Aged Day)

On this national holiday the elderly are honoured for their contributions to the nation.

## 23 or 24 September
しゅうぶん の ひ (Autumn Equinox)

On this national holiday it is traditional to visit the family grave to leave flowers and incense, as at the Spring Equinox.

## 2nd Monday in October
たいいく の ひ (Sports Day)

Sporting events take place across Japan on this national holiday which celebrates the day in 1964 when the Tokyo Olympics were opened.

## 3 November
ぶんか の ひ (Culture Day)

This national holiday is held to promote cultural activity. Schools traditionally hold various cultural events for the public on this day, and the government makes awards to those who have contributed to the cultural life of the country. This was originally a holiday to mark the birthday of Emperor Meiji, the current emperor's great-grandfather.

## 15 November
しちごさん (Seven Five Three Festival)

This festival is held for boys of five years old, and girls of three and seven years old, praying for their good health. Parents dress up their children in formal wear and visit shrines and temples. On this day children receive presents of candy canes decorated with turtles and cranes, all of which symbolise long life.

## 23 November
きんろう かんしゃ の ひ (Labour Thanksgiving Day)

This national holiday gives thanks for people's labour and for the harvest.

## 23 December
てんのう たんじょうび (Emperor's birthday)

This national holiday celebrates the birthday of the present emperor, Akihito.

## 24–25 December
クリスマス (Christmas)

Christmas is not a holiday period in Japan, but it is increasingly celebrated, especially in department stores and shopping malls, with Christmas music and decorations, and the appearance of Santa Claus. It is customary to eat Christmas cake, a sponge covered in cream and strawberries, on Christmas Eve.

# Quick reference guide to life and culture

## Ainu アイヌ

The Ainu are the indigenous people of northern Japan, and are physically quite distinct, with their thick wavy hair, and facial features closer to Caucasian than Asian. The men have heavy facial hair. The Ainu were oppressed and discriminated against for centuries, and today there are only around 24,000 left, most living in northern Japan. Of these, perhaps only 200 or so have pure Ainu blood. Their culture and language are now protected. The Ainu traditionally live by hunting, fishing and farming, and today they also make a living through selling crafts to tourists.

## Bathing

The Japanese bath is small and deep, a place to sit up to your neck in hot water, soaking away the tensions of the day, relaxing, and getting warmed through. The bath is not for washing, which is done outside the bath. Only when you have washed and rinsed your hair and body several times and you are squeaky clean do you submerge yourself in the extremely hot water. As the water is very hot and stays clean, it is usually shared by the whole family, one after the other. A cover is placed over the top of the bath when not in use to retain the heat until the next person is washed and ready to get in.

## Bentō べんとう

These are the boxed meals that can be bought at stations, airports, street stalls, and department stores. There are many local specialities, and it is possible, for example, to buy different kinds of *bentō* from the trolley on the SHINKANSEN (Bullet train) at different stages of its journey through Japan. A traditional *bentō* consists of fish or meat, pickled or cooked vegetables, and rice. Soy sauce and disposable chopsticks are also included. While everyday *bentō* bought at station kiosks may be packed in throwaway containers, it is also possible to buy them in the most beautiful lacquer boxes.

## Blood types

Everyone in Japan knows his or her blood type, which is considered to be an indicator of personality type. It is not at all unusual in general conversation to be asked for your blood group, in much the same way that Zodiac signs might be discussed in the west. Type A people are considered to be calm, composed and reliable. They are shy and prefer harmony, and are the most artistic of the blood groups. Type B people are practical,

interested in everything, and goal-oriented. They are individualists, and are full of energy and enthusiasm. Type O people are outgoing, sociable and carefree, which means they do not always finish what they start. They like to be the centre of attention, are creative and popular. Type AB people are trustworthy and dependable, and enjoy helping others, but do not deal well with a lot of responsibility. They are sociable but need personal space.

## Bonsai ぼんさい

Bonsai is the art of cultivating dwarf trees in ceramic pots in forms that are both natural and elegantly pleasing to the eye. Some bonsai live for decades and even centuries, and may be bought and sold for huge amounts of money. Great skill and patience are needed to restrain the growth, and techniques include trimming the roots, regulating the amount of water provided, and pruning the branches, all the time maintaining the shape and health of the tree.

## Cherry blossom

The advent of the cherry blossom season between late March and early April is eagerly awaited throughout Japan, and is celebrated with lively blossom viewing picnics, or *hanami* はなみ. The blossoms only last for seven or eight days, depending on the weather, so it is important to know the time when they are looking their best in order to plan the picnics. The television weather reports at this time include maps showing the 'cherry blossom front' as it gradually moves north, indicating where the blossoms are fully out, and where they can be expected to be in bloom in the next few days. The most popular parks become extremely crowded, and by evening the *hanami* picnics often turn into raucous affairs as copious amounts of beer and SAKE are drunk to accompany the food.

## Comic books

Comic books, or *manga* まんが, are big business in Japan, and on the whole it is not small children who read them. It is not at all uncommon to see businessmen on commuter trains whiling away the journey with their heads stuck into thick comic books, and doing so quite openly without any sense of embarrassment. Most manga are aimed at men, and many depict quite graphic sex and violence, but there are others aimed at young women which have stories of love and romance and sport. The comic books are cheap considering their thickness, but the turnover is huge, with around five million copies being sold each week.

## Earthquakes

The earth's crust beneath the Japanese archipelago is very unstable, being at a meeting place of several continental and oceanic plates, and this is the cause of the frequent earthquakes that shake Japan every year, as well as the abundance of volcanoes and hot springs. Minor tremors occur all the time, with those of magnitude four or five on the Richter scale quite common. However, most tend to be so mild that they are hardly noticeable. The Japanese scale for measuring earthquakes, *shindō* しんどう, tends to be used more than the Richter scale. *Shindō* 1 is a minor earthquake which can only be felt by people who are completely still. Up to *shindō* 4, there is unlikely to be damage. At *shindō* 5 objects fall. *Shindō* 7, the highest rating, is for a major earthquake.

The most recent major earthquake was in January 1995 in the city of Kobe, when 4,500 people were killed. The worst earthquake in recent history was in 1923 when the Great Kanto Earthquake hit the Tokyo area, and the resulting devastation and fires killed over 100,000 people.

## Era names

It is still common in Japan to count years with the era system, which uses the number of years the current emperor has been on the throne. The modern version of the system began with the Meiji era (1868–1912), followed by the Taisho era (1912–1926). In 1926 Emperor Hirohito ascended the throne, and chose the name Showa for his reign. 1926 was therefore known as Showa 1. He died at the beginning of 1989, so the first few weeks of the year were known as Showa 64, while the rest of the year was the first year of Heisei, the era name chosen for the new emperor, Akihito, son of Hirohito. In business, the western calendar tends to be used, but government offices usually require the era name for official papers. After the death of an emperor, he is generally referred to by the name of the era rather than by his own name. The late Emperor Hirohito is now known to the Japanese as Emperor Showa.

## Emperor Akihito

Emperor Akihito became the 125th emperor of Japan in 1989 on the death of his father, Hirohito. The post-war constitution of 1946 stated that the emperor would no longer be considered as a god, but would have only a symbolic function, and so Emperor Akihito has no political power. He is married to Empress Michiko, the first empress who did not come from the nobility. Their eldest son is Crown Prince Naruhito. The imperial family live in the Imperial Palace in central Tokyo.

## Face masks

It is not uncommon in Japan to see people walking around wearing white cotton masks covering their mouth and nose, the kind of mask that has loops to hook over the ears and that is normally seen in the west only on dentists. This is a sure sign that the wearer has a cold: the mask is worn both to protect others from the cold germs and to protect the nose and mouth area of the wearer. Although to the western visitor the sight of a smartly dressed businessman or a woman in formal kimono sporting a face mask might seem incongruous, to the Japanese it simply indicates a courtesy to others.

## Geisha げいしゃ

The word *geisha* means 'artist'. A *geisha* is essentially a professional entertainer skilled in various performing arts such as classical dance and song, as well as being able to play several musical instruments and keep guests amused with conversation and games. Sex is rarely part of the entertainment, and the western notion of a *geisha* as a prostitute is very far from the truth. The intense training to become a *geisha* begins at a young age in order to study the various arts and other skills such as flower arrangement, tea ceremony, calligraphy and the correct way of wearing the elaborate kimono, wig and make-up typical of a *geisha*. The *geisha* must also learn to be graceful, charming and refined. All this means that *geisha* houses can charge extremely high fees for their services. The number of *geisha* is declining, with perhaps no more than a thousand remaining throughout Japan. Most *geisha* houses today can be found in the Gion area of Kyoto.

## Hiroshima

On August 6, 1945, an atomic bomb was dropped on Hiroshima from a B-29 bomber named Enola Gay, and exploded 600 metres above the city. Everything below was destroyed over a wide area except the building directly below the explosion, the new Promotion of Industry Building, which now stands in the Peace Memorial Park. Around 200,000 people died in the aftermath of the bomb, but many of the survivors continued to suffer, and are still dying at the rate of thousands each year from causes related directly to the bomb. On August 9th a second atomic bomb was dropped on the city of Nagasaki, killing around 140,000 people. Japan formally surrendered on September 2, 1945.

## Hot springs

Japan has an abundance of natural hot springs, or *onsen* おんせん, and many of these have been turned into resorts where families, couples and groups go to enjoy relaxing in the hot water. They tend to be in mountainous areas, and it is considered particularly pleasant to sit outside in a pool of steaming hot water while surrounded by snow and views of the mountains, and perhaps chatting and sipping SAKE. Mixed-sex bathing is the norm and continues at some rural *onsen*, though recently more resorts have introduced women-only baths. Although bathing is done nude, it is etiquette to look away while someone is getting into or out of the bath. Cotton kimono, or *yukata*, are provided by the hotel for guests to slip in and out of as they use the *onsen*.

## Kimono きもの

In urban areas kimono are usually seen only on special occasions such as graduation ceremonies, weddings, and on festival days. For women, the many layers, tight sashes and restriction on taking any but tiny steps mean they are not suited to the busy lifestyle of most city dwellers. Men's formal kimono are more comfortable, with a *haori* はおり half-coat on the top half and *hakama* はかま on the bottom half, similar to a long divided skirt. There is some variation in colour, design and style of kimono for married and unmarried women, the most obvious difference being the very long sleeves that adorn the kimono of unmarried women. Wearing a kimono is a skill in itself, and it is not unusual for young women to attend classes to learn how to get dressed and tie the complicated bows needed on the *obi* おび or sash. When wearing a kimono attention also has to be paid to the appropriate hairstyle, shoes, *tabi* たび socks, handbag and underwear.

## Mt. Fuji

Mt. Fuji, one of Japan's most famous sights, is the highest volcano in Japan, rising to a height of 12,387 feet (3,776 metres) from the surrounding plain. It is considered to be dormant, rather than extinct, the last eruption being at the end of 1707. Mt. Fuji is about 100km south of Tokyo and can be seen from there on a clear day. The official climbing season is during July and August, and there are a number of routes to the top which can be clearly seen at peak times by the snake of people climbing on the bare mountain. It is divided vertically into ten 'stations', but many people begin climbing from the fifth station, which can be reached by bus. The mountain can be climbed in a day, and it is not technically difficult – children and elderly people climb it regularly – but it is arduous. It is somewhat of a disappointment to some that it is possible to buy souvenirs, food and drinks at the top. The mountain is known as *Fuji-san* ふじさん in Japanese, the suffix –*san* meaning 'mountain'.

## Name stamps

Name stamps, or *hanko* はんこ or *inkan* いんかん, are used instead of a signature in Japan. These are thin blocks of wood or stone with an imprint on one end showing a circular image with the Chinese characters of the person's family name inside. In situations such as opening a bank account or completing business at the post office, you will be expected to put the imprint of the name stamp on the document. Most people have two stamps, an everyday one and an official registered one. The everyday *hanko* is carried in a small plastic case, often with a tiny inkpad with red ink. Mass-produced ones, usually plastic, are available cheaply in stationery shops and even convenience stores, while custom-made ones may be carved of stone or wood, or even jade. The registered stamp is necessary for important legal documents such as formalising a will, buying land, or arranging a bank loan. These must be registered at the local government office, and must be unique. They are very important and so tend to be kept in a safe or at the bank.

## National flag

The national flag shows a red circle on a white ground, representing the rising sun, and is known as the *hi no maru* ひのまる. However, it was not officially adopted as the national flag until 1999. The flag with a sun in the middle and rays emanating from it was historically the military flag, and in particular was adopted as the naval ensign. As such it was used in World War II, but it was not a war flag, and has never been the national flag.

## Noh のう (or Nō) theatre

Noh is one of the traditional forms of Japanese theatre, characterised by a sparse stage set, but magnificently ornate costumes, and highly stylised, minimalist movements. The main actors wear masks, and all action takes place very slowly. Noh has been popular since around the 14th century, and was originally for the enjoyment of the samurai class.

## Pachinko パチンコ

*Pachinko* parlours can be easily recognised by their bright, flashing lights outside, the rows of people sitting inside staring at the upright pinball machine in front of them, and the raucous sound of millions of small steel balls speeding around inside the machines. Although *pachinko* is a passive and mindless game, or perhaps because of it, many people find it very relaxing to spend some time in front of a machine. Most of the balls disappear through slots in the face of the machine, but if they fall into the right combination of slots, the player is rewarded with a boxful of new balls. The aim is simply to accumulate as many of the steel balls as possible. It is illegal for *pachinko* parlours to pay out cash, but the balls can be exchanged for goods such as chocolate and cigarettes. It is not unusual to flout the law against gambling by choosing tokens, which can then be converted into cash at a hole in the wall outside the parlour. The tokens are then sold back to the *pachinko* parlour.

## Police boxes

Japan is one of the safest countries in the world, and many people put this down at least in part to the abundance of small one-room police boxes, or *kōban* こうばん, that can be found in most neighbourhoods, near stations, and in entertainment areas. These are always open, and one of the main ways of helping the public is by being available to give directions (see STREET NAMES) – the *kōban* always has a large map of the local area showing all the addresses. The police in the *kōban* are also commonly called upon to deal with lost children in shopping areas and those who are raucous or drunk in the entertainment areas. At quiet times, neighbourhood policemen also take it upon themselves to shut up the *kōban* for a while and go around visiting people in the local area to make themselves known. The *kōban* usually has a red light above the door.

## Rice

In Japan there are hot summers and abundant rainfall, and this makes it an ideal environment for growing rice. It is the most important staple of the diet, and perhaps the main part of almost every meal. Rice is taken very seriously, and every home has a rice cooker. The taste of the rice may differ depending on the grade, the time of harvesting, and the location where it was grown. There are many words for rice in Japanese, depending on the situation. *Kome* こめ refers to rice in general, as a plant or as an uncooked foodstuff. When it is cooked and served in a bowl, it is referred to as *gohan* ごはん, a word which can also mean 'meal'. A more informal version of this is *meshi* めし. However, when rice is served as part of a non-Japanese meal, such as curry, it is simply called *raisu* ライス, even though it is prepared in exactly the same way as *kome*.

## Sake さけ

*Sake* is brewed from rice, and at around 17% alcohol it is as well to treat it with respect. There are many different brands, and lovers of *sake* delight in sampling the local brew when they travel to different parts of Japan. In addition to variations according to locality, *sake* also comes in different grades, and in sweet, medium and dry. *Sake* can be drunk warm, or *atsukan* あつかん, when it is served in a flask known as a *tokkuri* とっくり along with tiny cups called *choko* ちょこ. It can also be served cold, when it is called *hiyazake* ひやざけ, and there are even brands which can be drunk iced, which are popular in the summer.

## School uniforms

Almost all schools in Japan have a school uniform, and most are still based on the traditional uniform first introduced in the late 19th century, which was modelled on the lines of western naval dress. It is common to see crowds of youngsters on the streets in their military-style uniforms, even at weekends. The girls wear navy blue sailor-style dresses with short white socks, while the boys wear tunic-style jackets with brass buttons and high stand-up collars.

## Shinkansen (Bullet train) しんかんせん

The first Shinkansen line, which began running in 1964, connected Tokyo with Osaka, and ran at speeds of around 200 kilometres per hour. Today there is a network of Shinkansen lines all over Japan and the trains reach speeds of over 300 kilometres per hour. The efficiency of the system is extraordinary. In the forty years or so of their existence, Shinkansen trains have carried over 6 billion passengers without one serious accident. At least six trains an hour run during the daytime between Tokyo and Osaka. Statistics from 2003 for punctuality show that for 160,000 train journeys, most covering hundreds of kilometres, the average delay was 6 seconds. To maintain this record of efficiency, the trains stop only for a prescribed number of seconds at each station, so it is better to be ready to alight when the train pulls into the station.

## Street names

One aspect of Japanese towns and cities hard for the visitor to get to grips with is that, apart from main roads, Japanese streets do not have names. Instead, towns are divided into named areas, and the areas into smaller and smaller numbered blocks. The blocks and the buildings are numbered not in geographical sequence, but in the order they were built, and this makes it virtually impossible to find a location or give directions simply from the address. Business cards often have a map on the reverse side, and these can be used to give to taxi drivers to indicate where you want to go, as even taxi drivers cannot be expected to find a place based only on the address. Japanese addresses start with the postal code and work from the general to the specific, ending with the name of the recipient, although when written in English for foreigners this order tends to be reversed.

A typical Tokyo address in English might be: Mr Ichiro Tanaka, 8-26-28 Kamiuma, Setagaya ku, Tokyo 157. Working backwards, 157 is the postcode, and Setagaya is one of the 23 wards (*ku*) of Tokyo. Kamiuma is an area within Setagaya, and Kamiuma 8 is a district of Kamiuma. Within the district of Kamiuma 8, 26 shows the block, and 28 is the house number within the block.

## Sumō すもう

*Sumō* is the national sport of Japan, and six *sumō* tournaments are held every year, three in Tokyo and one each in Osaka, Nagoya and Fukuoka. Each tournament lasts fifteen days, and each wrestler fights once every day. They go up or down in rank depending on how many fights they win or lose at these tournaments. Those in the lower ranks have their bouts earlier in the day, while the higher-ranked *ōzeki* おおぜき or *yokozuna* よこずな fight towards the end. The basic rule is simply that the first person to step outside the ring or allow any part of his body to touch the ground is the loser. Although the bouts may last only a few seconds, the preliminaries of tossing salt into the ring, stamping the feet, drinking water and repositioning the feet as the wrestlers ready themselves all add to the tension and excitement. The person with the greatest number of wins over losses at the end of the tournament is the winner, and receives the Emperor's Cup.

## Tatami たたみ

*Tatami* is the straw matting used in traditional Japanese homes. It is not matting in the western sense of flexible fabric covering the floor, but instead consists of solid blocks fitting tightly together to form the floor itself. The fixed size of the mats is approximately two metres by one metre, although in recent years a new smaller size has evolved for use in apartment blocks. This regular sizing means that rooms are generally built to standard sizes whose area can be measured in the number of mats: the Japanese talk in terms of a four-and-a-half mat room, or a six-mat room, for example, rather than the number of square metres. Even western style rooms covered in carpet tend to be measured like this. Although *tatami* is sturdy, it is not as durable as carpet or wooden flooring, which is one reason why even slippers are not worn in *tatami* rooms.

## Tattoos

The Japanese full traditional *irezumi* いれずみ tattoo covers almost all the body, stopping only at the neck, wrists and ankles. At the beginning of the Meiji period in the middle of the 19th century, tattooing was made illegal, but was legalised again after the end of the Second World War by the occupation forces in 1945. Getting a full body *irezumi* tattoo is a long, painful and expensive process, and can take several years of weekly visits to complete. Tattoos have long been associated with the *yakuza* やくざ, or Japanese mafia, and so tend to have negative connotations. Today small western-style tattoos are beginning to be popular among the younger generation, but in the minds of many people tattoos still retain their association with crime. For this reason, many swimming pools, hot spring resorts and public baths still ban people with tattoos.

## Woodblock prints

Japanese woodblock prints, or *ukiyo-e* うきよえ, became popular in the 17th century, originally for use in posters and advertising for theatres and other entertainment venues, and later developing into a highly regarded art form. The prints are easily recognisable by their curving outlines and flat areas of colour. Each area of colour required a different block to be carved, so a print with 15 colours would require 15 blocks skilfully carved so the coloured areas matched exactly when printed. Woodblock prints were closely associated with the world of entertainment, *geisha*, teahouses and theatres, and the word *ukiyo-e* translates as 'pictures of the floating world', the world of fleeting pleasures. The prints often depicted contemporary images such as actors, celebrities, and beautiful women, as well as travel scenes. Some of the most famous *ukiyo-e* artists from the 19th century – Utamaro, Sharaku, Hiroshige, and Hokusai, with his scenes of Mt. Fuji – became well known in Europe and had an influence on Impressionists such as Degas and Toulouse-Lautrec.

## Yakuza やくざ

The *yakuza* are Japan's organized criminals, similar to the mafia, with perhaps around 100,000 members, divided into 2,500 'families'. The image of a typical *yakuza* member is someone with a shiny suit, greased hair, a flashy car, elaborate full-body tattoos, and a little finger missing its tip if he has had to make retribution to a boss for some misdemeanour in the past. Although not all *yakuza* look like this, they certainly do not make any attempt to hide, and their existence is accepted by the police and Japanese society. Like organized criminals in many other countries, they are involved in extortion, prostitution, and drugs, and have close links with the construction industry.